Known to the Police: The Criminal Justice System in Victorian Norfolk

Gregory J. Durston

Published 2023 by Abramis academic publishing

www.abramis.co.uk

ISBN 978 1 84549 820 7

Abramis is an imprint of arima publishing

arima publishing

ASK House, Northgate Avenue

Bury St Edmunds, Suffolk IP32 6BB

t: (+44) 01284 717884

www.arimapublishing.com

Acknowledgments

I would like to thank the Norfolk Record Office, the National Archives, the Norfolk Police Historians, the British Library, the British Library of Political and Economic Science, and the libraries of Kingston University and Lincoln's Inn for their assistance. I would also like to thank Rhoda Koenig, Peter Pilgram, Victor Temple KC, and His Honour Nicholas Philpot for their help in preparing the manuscript.

Readers should note that only the most frequently employed or important sources are set out in the Select Bibliography. All other works referred to are cited in full in the footnotes. The cover illustration is a cast of the post-execution death mask of the murderer James Rush, who was hanged at Norwich in 1848.

Gregory Durston

Northeastern University,
London,
Michaelmas, 2023

Contents

Chapter 1: Setting the Scene

Introduction

William Blake speculated on the possibility of seeing the world in a grain of sand. This book attempts the rather less ambitious task of considering the Victorian criminal-justice system in the context of a single English county. This is done by scrutinizing all its aspects, from the commission of a crime, via the detection and arrest of suspects, to their investigation, prosecution, trial, and conviction, up to their final penal disposal.

Inevitably, several caveats must be entered about the wider value of such a study. For example, at the start of the period the very notion of a criminal-justice "system" is slightly debatable. It has been termed a useful shorthand for a series of institutions and organizations that had emerged at different times, for different reasons, over previous centuries, and which did not always readily mesh together, albeit that this became steadily less true as the era advanced.[1] More importantly, extrapolating from the particular to the general (county to country) is fraught with dangers, not least because it requires that any localised study reflect a wider national pattern, something that is rarely entirely the case, even in the modern era.

In this regard, it is important to note that the county selected, Norfolk, differed from many other parts of the country because it was not: in the immediate environs of the Metropolis (unlike counties such as Essex); in an area of heavy urbanisation and industrialisation (unlike parts of Lancashire and Yorkshire); on the Celtic fringe (unlike Cornwall or the Welsh counties); or geographically remote (unlike Westmorland and Cumberland). Scotland, with a legal system separate from that found in England and Wales, does not bear direct comparison, although it saw many of the same general developments found south of the border. By contrast, Norfolk shows more similarities with counties such as Lincolnshire, Suffolk, Devonshire, Sussex, Dorset, Hampshire, Wiltshire, Herefordshire, Shropshire, and Gloucestershire, which shared many of its general characteristics.

As a result, this study will consider the experiences of people who made up a very substantial part, but no longer a majority, of English (let alone British) society in 1837, and who declined further, as a proportion of that society, over the remainder of the nineteenth century, albeit retaining an important presence in 1901. Nevertheless, despite this continuing significance, nineteenth-century criminal justice in counties like Norfolk has often been neglected. One reason for this is that during the 1800s England moved from being a predominantly rural and agricultural society to one that was primarily urban and industrialized. Thus the 1851 census revealed that, for the first time, more Britons were living and working in towns than in the countryside, and the divergence increased swiftly thereafter. Consequently, most contemporary and many modern studies were/are oriented towards the phenomenon that was London

1 David Taylor, *Hooligans, Harlots and Hangmen: Crime and Punishment in Victorian Britain* (Santa Barbara: Praeger, 2010), pp. 2-3.

or the country's Midland and northern manufacturing and mining areas, with their burgeoning cities, pits, and factories. When Victorians such as Charles Dickens and Henry Mayhew wrote about the country's crime problem, they were usually thinking of these places, with their (apparently) teeming slums and (allegedly) almost feral "criminal class." They were not thinking about the villages and small towns of East Anglia or even a relatively modest city (in national terms) such as Norwich.

Despite this reservation, much of what occurred in Norfolk is still highly relevant to more urban and industrialized areas of the country, or those which were near to, or distant from, London, especially in the latter part of the Victorian era, when the English criminal-justice system had become standardized to an unprecedented extent. As a result, it still serves as a valuable introduction to the national situation, if proper allowances are made for local conditions.

The Period

In June 1837 King William IV died, and his niece, the 18-year-old Victoria, was crowned Queen. She would rule for the next 64 years, until January 1901, and become the longest-reigning monarch in British history until Queen Elizabeth II. This period, essentially the final two thirds of the nineteenth century, sets the chronological parameters for this book, although some mention will be made of the years immediately before and after these dates (the "long" Victorian period).

The new Queen gave her name to an era and a set of values. Whether this is entirely warranted is a matter of much academic debate. As has often been noted, she was not born a Victorian, and no single pattern can be imposed on her lengthy reign. To many, the very notion of such an era is inherently flawed, not least because the years between the late 1830s and early 1900s saw tremendous change in virtually all fields – politics, demographics, economics, society, culture, science, and technology.

Even so, some observers have identified patterns and continuities during this period that warrant special consideration and justify the notion of a Victorian Age. Most important for this book, the era saw a quite unprecedented expansion in the role of the state which was to be particularly manifest when it came to dealing with crime and disorder.[2] As a result, it occupies a crucial space in the history of the English criminal-justice system, witnessing numerous changes that herald the present one.[3]

The County

Norfolk, an integral part of the East Anglian region of England, is bordered by the sea to the north and east, Lincolnshire to the northwest, Cambridgeshire to the west and southwest, and Suffolk to the south (the last two counties make up the rest of

---

2 Martin Hewitt, "Why the Notion of Victorian Britain Does Make Sense," *Victorian Studies*, vol. 48, no. 3 (2006), pp. 395-438.

3 David C. Churchill, "Rethinking the State Monopolisation Thesis: The Historiography of Policing and Criminal Justice in Nineteenth-Century England," *Crime, History & Societies*, vol. 18, no. 1 (2014), pp. 131-152, p. 131.

East Anglia). It was the fourth-largest county in England, and one of its most rural shires, with an area of just under 2,100 square miles. Although much of Norfolk is flat and low lying, there are a few areas of small hills and a variety of soil types, encouraging some diversity in agriculture, albeit primarily arable. Unsurprisingly, given its extensive coast, fishing played a significant role in its economy. Its traditional (and only major) industry was cloth manufacture, although this had long been in decline by 1837.

Victorian Norfolk had four incorporated boroughs: Norwich (which was also a city and urban county), King's Lynn, Great Yarmouth, and Thetford. (Lynn and Yarmouth were also significant coastal ports). All had been "reformed" by the Municipal Corporations Act 1835 (5 & 6 Wm. IV, c. 76), which established a uniform system of English municipal boroughs governed by ratepayer-elected town councils. It also had many much smaller towns, such as Walsingham and Diss, as well as hundreds of villages and hamlets.

Population and Migration

Britain saw very high population growth during the Victorian era, increasing from about 25 million inhabitants in 1837 to 41 million at Queen Victoria's death in 1901.[4] Towns and cities were at the forefront of this process, not least because farmworkers made redundant by technology and changes in agriculture migrated to urban areas to find work. Even at the start of the period, many people lived in relatively large towns and cities. In 1831 a quarter of the population of England and Wales lived in urban areas of more than 20,000 inhabitants, with 16.3 percent of them living in the Metropolis or a town of over 100,000 people. By the census of 1891, the figure was 53.6 percent and 31.8 percent respectively.[5] More specifically, Manchester and Sheffield quadrupled in size between 1801 and 1851, while Bradford grew eightfold. The population of London was about 1 million inhabitants in 1801 but had reached 4 million in 1889.

Nevertheless, in the East Anglian counties, with their lack of major urban areas, population increase was below the national average.[6] In 1801 Norfolk had 286,092 people.[7] Like other mainly rural counties, it then grew, but at a slower rate than more urbanised parts of the country, during the ensuing century and, in one decade, 1851 to 1861, its population even fell, from 433,716 to 427,466 inhabitants.[8] According

4 Hewitt, "Victorian Britain," pp. 395-438.

5 E. Hennock, "Finance and Politics in Urban Local Government in England, 1835–1900," *The Historical Journal*, vol. 6, no. 2 (1963), p. 212.

6 D. C. Coleman, "Growth and decay during the industrial revolution: The case of East Anglia," *Scandinavian Economic History Review*, vol. 10, no. 2 (1962), p. 118.

7 E. A. Wrigley, "English County Populations in the Later Eighteenth Century," *Economic History Review*, vol. 60, no. 1 (2007), p. 35.

8 Roger Woods, *Mid-Nineteenth Century Migration from Norfolk to London: Migratory patterns, migrants' social mobility and the impact of the railway,* Institute of Historical Research MA dissertation, 2014, p. 14.

to the census, the county had reached 476,553 people by 1901, an increase of about 60 percent over the previous 100 years (but much less for the Victorian era). By contrast, to consider a more urbanised county, the population of Kent increased from 733,887 to 977,706 between 1860 and 1880 alone.[9]

In Norfolk population growth was largely a result of natural increase, as net migration from the county, whether assisted or independent, was an ongoing feature of the Victorian period, especially in difficult decades, such as the 1850s, or the years after the agricultural depression of the 1870s set in. The latter, combined with changes in agriculture, resulted in rural depopulation in some parts of the county. Norfolk supplied migrants to London, to the textile districts of the northwest, and to other countries. The USA and Canada were especially popular in the 1830s, particularly after the introduction of the New Poor Law in 1834, and again in the 1850s.[10] Australia and New Zealand gradually joined them as chosen destinations over the course of the nineteenth century. Sometimes there was official support and organization to encourage and assist the poorest elements in the county to go abroad.

Norfolk's "county town" (technically a city), Norwich, by far its largest urban settlement, shared in the relatively slow growth seen by the wider county, its expansion being dwarfed by that of London and the new industrial cities. In 1831 the census revealed that it had 60,998 inhabitants.[11] By 1851 the figure was 68,706, of whom 31,213 were males and 37,493 females.[12] A decade later, Norwich had 74,414 inhabitants (33,717 men and 40,697 women).[13] Twenty years further on again, the total had reached 87,841, with a similar gender imbalance.[14]

Social and Economic Conditions

Many of the inhabitants of Victorian Norfolk were poor. The county was of increasingly marginal significance to the wider British economy. It was not favoured by the Industrial Revolution, lacking deposits of coal and iron ore, as well as adequate waterpower to drive machines; it was remote from the centres of technological change that transformed the country after 1800, and its roads were poor. By the start of the Victorian era, there had been a protracted and terminal decay in its cloth manufacture, one that would continue throughout the 1840s, concluding with the failure of its silk industry. In 1840 a census of hand-loom silk and worsted weavers in Norwich and its surroundings showed that, while 4,054 were employed, 1,021 (a fifth) were out of work. Furthermore, wages had fallen by about a fifth in 1829 and

---

9 Carolyn A. Conley, *The Unwritten Law: Criminal Justice in Victorian Kent* (Oxford: OUP, 1991), p. 11.

10 Coleman, "Growth and decay," pp. 115-127.

11 *The Norfolk Chronicle*, 11 June, 1831.

12 12 *Ibid.*, 3 May, 1851.

13 13 *Ibid.*, 18 May, 1861.

14 *Ibid.*, 7 May, 1880.

failed to recover thereafter, while the growth in irregular employment meant that even this could not be guaranteed.[15]

Although the most common occupation in the county was agriculture, farm wages were also low, and work was sometimes scarce, something that contributed to the Captain Swing disturbances in the county in 1831. In 1861 it was claimed that the average income of farm labourers in Norfolk was just 8s 6d a week. Admittedly, this was better than Suffolk, where it (apparently) stood at 7s, but it was markedly less than the 10s seen in Lincolnshire and, even more so, the 13s achieved in Cumberland. The low wages in East Anglia were attributed to the large amount of labour available for what was often a limited amount of agricultural work, key seasons such as harvest apart, this situation being exacerbated by growing mechanization. As a result, rural labourers' diets were frequently inadequate, often consisting of small amounts of bread, puddings, and potatoes, perhaps supplemented by occasional pieces of bacon and other meat, especially in the first half of the Victorian era. Squalid, overcrowded homes with little segregation produced a high incidence of bastardy. On one estimate, from 1867, Norfolk (like Suffolk) had one of the worst records for illegitimacy in the country.[16] Together these factors also encouraged significant levels of emigration.

For many people, throughout England, the 1840s were particularly bleak and hungry; the country experienced acute economic and social strife and felt itself to be in danger of revolution, with Corn Law agitation and Chartist activity. Norfolk was no exception to the national pattern. At the start of 1849, when an outbreak of cholera was recorded at Rudham, with at least 24 deaths occurring, it was noted that "extreme poverty and dirt had much to do with this awful visitation."[17] Norfolk, like its fellow East Anglian counties had some of the highest rates of poor relief per head in the country. Although the physical environment was free of much of the smoke and soot of the fast-growing industrial towns in other parts of England, it is arguable that the monetary position of its inhabitants was often worse.[18]

Nevertheless, after the crisis of the early Victorian period was weathered, conditions gradually and very unevenly improved, in Norfolk as elsewhere in the country, while the latter years of the era saw a marked growth in disposable income, something that was assisted by the end of the corn laws in 1854 and the arrival of cheap imported food, including frozen and tinned meat towards the end of the century. By 1898 average agricultural weekly earnings (including the value of allowances) in Norfolk had reached 14s 9d, despite periodic depressions in agriculture.[19] Various social improvements, such as the advent of free universal elementary education in

[15] D. C. Coleman, *Myth, History and the Industrial Revolution* (London: Hambledon Continuum, 1992), p. 103.

[16] *The Ipswich Journal*, November 2, 1867.

[17] *The Norfolk Chronicle*, 17 February, 1849.

[18] Coleman, "Growth and decay," pp. 115-127.

[19] *The Bury and Norwich Post*, September 4, 1900.

1870, as well as technical developments, also had a major impact on society, as did an expansion of the male franchise as part of what might be termed a wider process of political incorporation. England in 1901 was a much less "stressed" society than it had been in 1837 and had enjoyed a period of relative peace and prosperity.[20] This applied to Norfolk as much as to any other county.

Travel and Communication

England was transformed during the Victorian era by improvements in transportation and communication. The first railway, the Stockton and Darlington line, had been opened in 1825, and the initially slow introduction of such lines accelerated swiftly after the late 1830s. By 1852 there were 6,600 miles of railway in England and Scotland, and they would soon quickly expand very much further. By then train speeds could reach 60 miles per hour, while even their average speed of 21 miles was about twice the pace of a fast stagecoach. The speed, ease, and reduced cost of travel led to the purchase of 73 million tickets in Britain in 1850 and 507 million by 1875.[21]

In Norfolk the presence of a relatively flat landscape meant that laying railroads was usually straightforward. As the Lynn and Bury St. Edmunds Direct Railway Company noted in 1845, its new track was "very easy of construction, no engineering difficulties present themselves, and every circumstance is favourable for an early and economic completion, no tunnels nor any embankments of consequence being necessary on the line."[22] As a result, the county saw a rash of new railways in the 1840s and 1850s. Thus, in July 1847 the railroad from Reedham to Lowestoft was inaugurated, and in October it was followed by the line from King's Lynn to Ely.[23]

Other forms of communication also became easier. The Penny Post came into operation in January 1840, allowing a letter weighing up to half an ounce to be sent between all parts of the United Kingdom for one penny (if paid when posted). It was quickly claimed that it had trebled the number of letters sent in and around Norwich, although printed circulars (Victorian "junk mail") apparently formed a significant part of this increase.[24] The electric telegraph followed (on a commercial basis) over the ensuing decade. By the end of the century the telephone had joined them. Although credit for its invention during the 1870s is often disputed, as early as the winter of 1878 experiments with a telephone were being conducted in Norfolk under the direction of the superintendent of the Great Eastern Railway telegraph department. People in London and Norwich were able to converse with each other, their words being clearly understood, although there was limited confidence in

---

20 C.H.S. Fifoot, *Judge and Jurist in the Reign of Victoria* (London: Stevens, 1959), p. 1.

21 Robin J. Barrow, "Rape on the Railway: Women, Safety, and Moral Panic in Victorian Newspapers," *Journal of Victorian Culture*, vol. 20, no. 3 (2015), pp. 341-356.

22 *The Norfolk Chronicle*, 30 October, 1845.

23 *Ibid.*, 1 July and 25 October, 1847.

24 *Ibid.*, 10 and 18 January, 1840.

its potential. Nevertheless, in December 1880 there were two advertisements in the *Eastern Daily Press*, one from the Postmaster General, setting out the rates for subscribing to the new telephone service.[25]

The changes effected by enhanced communication had an enormous impact on society, especially government. They meant that central initiatives were more likely to be acted on and followed through ; they had a particular influence on the criminal-justice system. On a very practical level, in 1853, the MP Edward Rice noted in Parliament, "It was true that railroads afforded prisoners great facilities for escape; but it was equally true that the message by the electric telegraph, by which their escape might be arrested, travelled immeasurably faster." Thus, after a murder in 1885, the deputy chief constable for Norfolk immediately sent telegraphs to all major locations to keep a "sharp watch" on the roads.[26] More generally, the new means of communication greatly increased homogeneity and consistency in the justice system of the country as knowledge, experience, and "best practice" were shared.

The 'Spirit of the Age'

The Enlightenment of the seventeenth and eighteenth centuries had been committed to replacing allegedly outmoded or irrational ways of thinking in a way that reflected the advance of scientific knowledge and method. As such it spawned what might be termed modernity and its hallmark, an unprecedented faith in the capacity of human reason to make sense of the world. This reached a peak during the Victorian period, which had far less time for obscurantism and tradition than previous eras. Instead, it preferred to embrace what it perceived to be rational utilitarianism based on (what was thought to be) empirical evidence, often produced by parliamentary committees of enquiry. In February 1828 an indication of what the future held was provided by a major speech made to the House of Commons by the future Lord Chancellor, Henry Brougham (1778-1868), in which he called for major legal reform. The constitutional authority Albert Venn Dicey (1835-1922) was later to claim that it ushered in an era of utilitarianism and individualism, not least because it coincided with a major shift in public opinion.[27]

No matter how long a practice or institution had existed, that was no longer a sufficient justification for its survival. As a clerical JP from the West Country observed in 1841, "We live in times of a very restless and uneasy character: ... inroads have been made, year after year, upon almost all our institutions, both civil

---

[25] Eric Clayton, *The First 100 Years of Telephones Viewed from Norwich* (London: British Telecom, 1980), pp. 1-30.

[26] *The Bury and Norwich Post*, 8 December, 1885.

[27] David J.A. Cairns, *Advocacy and the Making of the Adversarial Criminal Trial, 1800-1865* (Oxford: Clarendon Press, 1998), pp. 1-2.

and ecclesiastical."[28] There was a new willingness to question the continuance of long-established practices, in the criminal-justice arena as elsewhere. Typically, the historian Frederic Maitland lamented (prematurely, as it transpired) that although the rural magistrate, the JP, had many strengths, this would not be enough to ensure his survival: "He is capable, but he is doomed, he is to be sacrificed to a theory on the altar of the spirit of the age."[29]

Such changes did not go unchallenged. They might be resisted by appealing to traditional liberties, so that the jurist James Fitzjames Stephen (1829-1894) could complain that reform was sometimes limited by the "passion of the English people for personal freedom, and in their intolerance of personal restraint or interference for any purpose whatever." An acute reluctance to incur expense (often an inherent aspect of change), whether local or national, might also dampen proposals for reform. Together these factors frequently delayed, but rarely prevented, change. The trend was irreversible.

A minor, local to Norfolk, but highly illustrative example of the clash between tradition and innovation and the latter's usual triumph over the former, can be seen at King's Lynn in 1864. In November that year it was noted that an ancient but (allegedly) "absurd" system of inspection for weights and measures, conducted by a jury of local parish constables, who went round the town in a posse, was about to come to an end. Several businesses would not admit the constables to their premises, and some of those who did refused to pay the fines later imposed on them. As their authority was based on ancient charters of doubtful legal force, and it was no longer being respected, the jurors themselves had refused to be appointed again by the local court leet. As a result, it was claimed that "very shortly a proper and efficient officer will be appointed under the provisions of the Weights and Measures Act."[30]

Many arcane legal survivals of the past were gradually extinguished in the years immediately before and during the Victorian period. To take an extreme example, until 1823 suicides (unless insane) were supposed to be buried at a crossroads, at twilight, with a stake driven through their bodies. In 1813, Mary Turrel from Harleston was suspected of having drowned her new-born daughter and then taken poison to kill herself. She was "buried in the highroad with a stake driven through her body." The parish constable fixed the stake, using a heavy mallet to drive it home, in front of a large crowd. The final case in Norfolk, albeit without the stake, appears to have occurred in April 1821, after Stephen Cutting, a septuagenarian labourer, drowned

---

[28] Reverend Harry Farr Yeatman, *A Letter to the Right Honourable the Earl of Devon on the Proposed Plan of the Summary Trial of Offenders at Special Petty Sessions* (Sherborne: T.H. Toll, 1841), p. 6.

[29] H.A.L. Fisher, *Frederick William Maitland, Downing Professor of the Laws of England* (Cambridge: CUP, 1910), p. 50.

[30] *The Norfolk Chronicle,* 12 November, 1864.

himself and was "buried in the crossway."[31] Such behaviour appeared utterly bizarre by the end of the nineteenth century.

Similarly, public whipping for men was rarely used after the early 1830s and was abolished in 1861. Any form of whipping of women had been abolished in 1820. Drawing and quartering of traitors was formally abolished in 1870, although it had not been employed since 1820. The Deodand Abolition Act of 1846 did away with the forfeiture to the Crown of the weapon or other instrument by which a murder or manslaughter was committed, whether it was a knife or a carriage. (This change was partly promoted by railway magnates, who disliked seeing their trains confiscated by inquest jurors after grossly negligent fatal accidents.)[32] Imprisonment for civil debt was finally abolished by s.4 of the Debtors Act 1869, although its use had been in steady decline for many years. This avoided situations like that of the nonagenarian William Cole, formerly an attorney at Loddon, who died in the Norwich Castle prison in 1846, having been committed there for debt in 1830.[33]

The Decline in Discretion

One of the most remarkable, albeit never universally held, nineteenth-century notions was that, ideally, the commission of every crime would be followed by detection, prosecution, and punishment, and that it was the duty of the state to effect this by identifying offences, apprehending offenders, and ensuring that they were convicted and punished, irrespective of the inclinations of their victims.[34] Not everyone agreed with such an approach. In 1845, a barrister giving evidence to the Royal Commission on Criminal Law argued that only a selection of prosecutions was necessary, feeling that: "The punishment of every crime that is committed is clearly unattainable. ... The only attainable object is example". Nevertheless, many influential Victorian Englishmen were unwilling to accept their predecessors' apparent lack of concern about crime as a social problem and their tolerance of the arbitrary mechanisms previously employed to deal with it, especially the importance placed on self-help measures.[35]

The criminal-justice system at the start of the nineteenth century had been subject to very high levels of attrition. The journey from the commission of an offence to conviction and punishment could fail at numerous hurdles along the way, some of them extra-legal, the crime being diverted out of the justice system according

---

31 Robert Halliday, "The Roadside Burial of Suicides: An East Anglian Study," *Folklore*, vol. 121, no. 1 (2010), pp. 81-93. *The Bury and Norwich Post*, 18 April, 1821.

32 Elisabeth Cawthon, "New Life for the Deodand: Coroners' Inquests and Occupational Deaths in England, 1830-46," *American Journal of Legal History*, vol. 33, no. 2 (1989), pp. 137-47.

33 *The Norfolk Chronicle,* 26 August, 1846.

34 Carolyn A. Conley, "Rape and Justice in Victorian England," *Victorian Studies*, vol. 29, no. 4 (1986), pp. 519-536.

35 V.A.C. Gatrell, *The Hanging Tree: Execution and the English People 1770-1868* (Oxford: OUP, 1996), p. 245.

to the whims of a variety of people, in what has been termed a "golden age" for discretionary justice.[36] Of course, this did not disappear altogether. Almost all legal systems contain an element of discretion, and this was certainly true of Victorian England. Nevertheless, although criminal prosecution was still an interactive social process, the role of discretion was far more muted, and much less blatant, than had been the case in earlier centuries.

Arguably, the Victorian "achievement" was to reduce the number of escape routes between the commission of a crime and its penal disposal, something that was necessary in a system that quickly came to be premised (in theory) on relatively mild (by earlier standards) but uniformly enforced punishments, rather than selective but draconian example. Thus in 1836 Lord Wharncliffe, the former Lord Privy Seal, who was also a JP and chairman of quarter sessions, thought that it was axiomatic, indeed "an admitted fact that the uncertainty of convictions led to an increase of crime."[37] Such a change was also encouraged by other social trends during the early nineteenth century, such as the emergence of a society with burgeoning, socially stratified urban areas and increased population mobility, in which the stable and personalised social relationships in which discretion could flourish were often attenuated or absent.[38] As a result, it has been argued that the repeal of the "bloody code" in the 1820s and 1830s marked the point of transition from an essentially personal and discretionary system of justice to one based on uniformity, certainty, and proportionality.[39]

Being processed through the justice system became more mechanistic and bureaucratic, and subject to increasingly consistent and uniformly applied criteria. Those suspected of offending in Victorian England were much more likely to come to official notice, fall into the criminal-justice "net" if they did, and then be prosecuted to conviction and punishment. This required and reflected an unprecedented growth in the state's responsibility for, and involvement in, crime control, this usually being at the expense of the involvement of private citizens and local bodies. The power to provide responses to offending was increasingly transferred from the public to government agencies. New forms of police emerged that relieved ordinary citizens of much of their role in law enforcement.[40] Perhaps indicative of this general change, the criminal section of the Home Office was upgraded from a branch to a department in 1870, this being its most important division by the early 1900s.

---

36 Peter King, *Crime, Justice and Discretion in England, 1740–1820* (Oxford: OUP, 2000), p. 355.

37 Hansard HL Deb 14 July 1836, vol. 35, cols. 171-86.

38 Martin J. Wiener, *Reconstructing the Criminal: Culture, Law, and Policy in England, 1830–1914* (Cambridge: CUP, 2008), p. 60.

39 Phil Handler, "The Law of Felonious Assault in England, 1803–61," *The Journal of Legal History*, vol. 28, no. 2 (2007), pp. 183-206.

40 Churchill, "Rethinking the state," pp. 131-152.

The Growth of the Interventionist State

The eighteenth-century state had been reluctant to intervene in the lives of its subjects. Its Victorian successor, influenced by what has been termed the "incessant promptings of Benthamite reformers," shed this reluctance, and was consciously seen by many as an active vehicle of progress.[41] As a result, England experienced a revolution in government during the middle 50 years of the nineteenth century, as a combination of unprecedented social change and new expectations of order forced the government to increase its involvement in, and control over, the lives of its subjects.[42] Such intervention was characterized by being publicly funded, rationally planned, bureaucratically administered, and (often) centrally directed. As a vital part of this process, the state gradually assumed control over the national response to crime and disorder.[43]

Linked to this process, social mores changed during the Victorian era, whether spontaneously or as the result of government and private campaigns and initiatives. Most important, people became more squeamish about previously accepted levels of brutality. The casual Hogarthian violence and cruelty of the eighteenth century were no longer deemed acceptable by growing parts of society. Such a change in outlook could even extend to military men. For example, in October 1840 a meeting at the Assembly Rooms in Norwich formed the Animals' Friend Society. Its aim was the prevention of cruelty to beasts.[44]

However, this change did not happen at an equal speed across society. It took root in the upper and (even more so) the middle classes at a much faster rate than it did amongst some elements of the poor, so that what had previously been widely held attitudes and popular recreations were increasingly confined to the lowest social strata. Contemporary observers were aware of this, even as it occurred. As an old man in 1904, the judge Henry Hawkins recalled his youthful fondness for watching prizefighting, something that was, apparently, shared by some magistrates and even clergymen of the time. However, and indicative of change, in 1840, when a Norfolk prize-fight was not as well attended as had previously been the case, especially by the well-to-do, and (necessarily) kept fairly secret, it was claimed, "But that these brutal attacks are fast declining in the estimation of the middle classes may be fairly presumed by the paucity in number and the circuitous route taken by many of them to the battlefield."[45]

Similarly, and whether rightly or wrongly, journalists, judges, juries, and social commentators increasingly associated domestic abuse with the working classes.

41 Clive Emsley and Robert D. Storch, "Prosecution and the Police in England Since 1700," *IAHCCJ Bulletin*, no. 18 (1993), pp. 45-57.

42 John A. Stack, "The Juvenile Delinquent and England's "Revolution in Government, 1825-1875," *The Historian*, vol. 42, no. 1 (1979), pp. 42-57.

43 Churchill, "Rethinking the state," pp. 131-152.

44 *The Norfolk Chronicle,* 6 October 1840.

45 *Ibid.*, 7 January, 1840.

In 1878 the social reformer Frances Power Cobbe claimed, albeit with some exaggeration, that, while the better sort of Englishmen were "exceptionally humane and considerate to women, the men of the lower class of the same nation are proverbial for their unparalleled brutality, till wife-beating, wife-torture, and wife-murder have become the opprobrium of the land."[46]

However, members of the "political nation" were not content to confine their newfound refinement to themselves, or to limit their new powers and social apparatus to enforcing existing limits on behaviour. Instead, they sought to extend them down the social hierarchy. As a result, and as the chief constable of Staffordshire observed in 1895, the Victorian era had witnessed a "constantly-growing intolerance of disorder."[47] Modern sociologists have developed the notion of "civilizing offensives," attempts by powerful social groups to change aspects of traditional behaviour that they consider to be immoral or disorderly, and to replace them with temperance and control. This might be done by, for example, monitoring and punishing previously accepted (or ignored) conduct. This certainly occurred in England, where the nineteenth-century civilizing process has even been described as a middle-class moral crusade, one that was supported by bourgeois mentalities, which sought to educate and, where necessary, coerce the populace into better standards of conduct and respectability.[48] Typically, in 1896 Frederick Pollock, Professor of Jurisprudence at Oxford, noted in his textbook that the law could have an effective role not merely in preserving but also in "elevating the standard of current morality." Journalists sometimes lamented that the police, although originally created to maintain order, had become "censors of morality."[49] Newspapers were to complain of the prevailing compulsion to "dragoon us all into virtue."[50]

Indicative of this process, bull-baiting, cock-fighting, and prize-fighting, three long-standing aspects of popular culture, went from being tolerated to being prohibited, as did other, more localized "rough" pastimes, while various hitherto violent ball games became sanitized and regulated as association and rugby football.[51] Similarly, excessive consumption of alcohol was targeted by a justice system that increasingly valued sobriety.[52] This happened at different speeds, in different parts of the country; for example, cockfighting lasted into the twentieth century in Cumberland

46 Jade Shepherd, "'I am not very well I feel nearly mad when I think of you': Male Jealousy, Murder and Broadmoor in Late-Victorian Britain", *Social History of Medicine*, vol. 30, no. 2 (2017), p. 281.

47 G.A. Hanson, *The Fluctuations of Crime* (Stafford,1895), pp. 3-4.

48 Wiener, *Reconstructing*, p. 56.

49 S. Petrow, "The Legal Enforcement of Morality in Late-Victorian and Edwardian England," *University of Tasmania Law Review*, vol. 11, no. 1 (1992), pp. 59-74.

50 Gatrell, *Hanging Tree,* p. 259.

51 Guy Woolnough, "Blood Sports in Victorian Cumbria: Policing Cultural Change," *Journal of Victorian Culture*, vol. 19, no. 3 (2014), pp. 278-294.

52 John Carter Wood, "Drinking, Fighting and Working-Class Sociability in Nineteenth-Century Britain," in *Drink in the Eighteenth and Nineteenth Centuries: Perspectives in Economic and Social History*, ed. Susanne Schmid and Barbara Schmidt-Haberkamp (London: Pickering and Chatto, 2014), pp. 1-10.

and Westmorland, whereas prize-fighting was eliminated much earlier in the same counties. The greater local popularity of the former delayed various police attempts to curb it.[53]

More generally, it has been argued that much legal reform was actively aimed at encouraging a national character type that was more controlled and willing to defer immediate gratification.[54] In 1879 Joseph Kidd, a journalist and temperance activist, captured the sought-after ideal when he observed that promoting "self-restraint and moderation in all things is one of the chief delights and aspirations to the moral nature of a true man."[55] Victorian criminal courts increasingly promulgated a coherent view as to how, ideally, Englishmen (if not foreigners) were expected to behave.[56]

As a result, the first half of the nineteenth century saw a steady increase in the reach of the criminal law, as new offences and police forces were introduced and summary forums grew in power. More offenders were brought into the reach of the law, often for less serious crimes, not a few of which were entirely novel.[57] This process was recognised at the time. Some complained that the legislature had "gone on continually and foolishly turning innocent actions into offences, and modern magistrates embrace in their better constructed nets a number of small matters that escaped their predecessors."[58] Luke Owen Pike, a Victorian crime-historian, thought it clear that the number of criminals in the country could be made to appear formidable by including in it people who were guilty "of offences which our hard-drinking great-grandfathers would have regarded as merits rather than as faults."[59] At a meeting of the Royal Statistical Society in 1894, it was noted that a large proportion of the well over half a million convictions returned in England and Wales each year, such as begging and obstructing highways, did not involve "moral depravity" and were crimes only in the most technical sense.[60]

Such change was aided by the growing surveillance powers of the 'modern' state. For example, in 1888 Hannah Dorling was prosecuted at Thetford petty sessions for assaulting her 11-year-old stepdaughter, Lucy. Hannah had moved to the town with her blacksmith husband a few years earlier, and regularly been heard beating

53 Woolnough, "Blood Sports," pp. 278-294.

54 Wiener, *Reconstructing*, p. 56.

55 Manuel Eisner, "From Swords to Words: Does Macro-Level Change in Self-Control Predict Long-Term Variation in Levels of Homicide?" *Crime and Justice*, vol. 43, no. 1 (2014), pp. 65-134.

56 Martin J. Wiener, "Homicide and 'Englishness': Criminal Justice and National Identity in Victorian England," *National Identities*, vol. 6, no. 3 (2004), pp. 203-213.

57 Wiener, *Reconstructing*, pp. 49-51.

58 John Clay, "On the Effect of Good or Bad Times on Committals to Prison," *Journal of the Statistical Society of London*, vol. 20, no. 4 (1857), pp. 378-388.

59 John Carter Wood, *Violence and Crime in Nineteenth-Century England: The Shadow of Our Refinement* (Abingdon: Routledge, 2004), p. 147.

60 *The Times*, 16 December, 1896, p. 10.

the child, who was also severely malnourished. Her spouse appears to have done nothing to intervene. The matter came to light when a school attendance inspector called to discover why Lucy was not going to the local elementary school (free and compulsory since 1870). After seeing the child's general condition and injuries he reported the matter to the police. The magistrates found Hannah guilty and declared her a "disgrace to her sex." She was sentenced to four months' imprisonment with hard labour. (Some 400 local people were at the local railway station to see her set off to prison, hooting, spitting, and shouting abuse).[61]

---

61 *The Ipswich Journal*, 14 February, 1888.

Chapter 2: The New Police

Introduction

Until shortly before the new Queen's reign, policing in Norfolk, like most other counties, had been dominated by the "traditional" English system, which had roots going back hundreds of years. Radical policing reform in Norfolk started in the middle of the 1830s with the creation of the county's four borough forces and was advanced by the establishment of a rural force for the rest of the county at the beginning of 1840. The five new police forces that emerged, and their style of policing, were a major departure from the traditional system, although there were some initial continuities, especially in urban areas. Their impact on law enforcement eventually transformed the entire criminal-justice process in Norfolk, as it did everywhere else in the country, not least because they came to dominate prosecution. As a result, their advent forms a major part of what has been termed the "state monopolization thesis," by which much of the responsibility for the control of crime was gradually transferred from ordinary people to government agents during the nineteenth century.[62]

However, unlike the situation found in the capital following the advent of the Metropolitan Police in 1829, the traditional policing system survived in rural parts of the county for decades after 1840, coexisting with the new police forces.

Traditional Policing in Norfolk

In the early decades of the nineteenth century, the historic system of provincial policing, inherited from the late medieval period, was manifest in Norfolk by three main types of law-enforcement officer: high constables, petty or "parish" constables, and watchmen (who supplemented parish constables in urban areas). All three positions were usually held by part-time, unsalaried (though not necessarily unpaid), amateurs, recruited locally and based in their own homes. By then England's fragmented policing system was relatively unusual by Continental standards, and foreign commentators were sometimes critical of the country's failure to establish a state-run, professional police force.[63]

Perhaps the most important of the three types of traditional officer was the parish constable, one or two of whom were chosen annually by leets or (much more commonly) vestries for (in theory) a year or (less commonly) two years of local service. Such men were chosen from householders and usually selected by rota, with exemptions being granted for reasons of age, health, or occupation. However, many of those selected were reluctant to undertake what was often an onerous task and preferred to pay a fine of £10 for failing to do so, or to pay another man to take their place (this usually being slightly cheaper than the fine). For this

---

62 Churchill, "Rethinking the state," p. 132.

63 David Philips, "A 'Weak' State? The English State, the Magistracy and the Reform of Policing in the 1830s," *The English Historical Review*, vol. 119, no. 483 (2004), p. 875.

reason, by the early 1800s, some men were serving as parish constables for very much longer than a year. They served for payment in place of others who had been selected, for the fees and perquisites of the office (remuneration for specific tasks, etc.), the annual retainers (often several pounds) offered by some parishes to those who held the position, the modest power and prestige that the office bestowed, or a combination of the four. Some constables were in office for lengthy periods, sometimes more than four years, under successive annual appointments, although almost none matched the tenure of Charles Kerrison.[64] When Kerrison died in 1889, after a long battle with gout, it was noted that, slightly earlier in life, he had "held the position of parish constable for East Harling for upwards of fifty years."[65]

High or chief constables were traditionally very minor gentlemen or (more commonly) substantial yeomen who headed up the parish constables in a particular hundred, usually serving for relatively long periods. The only remuneration they received in the early Victorian period was the (recently introduced) sum of £1 a parish for assisting with the collection of the county rate, which cost Norfolk a total of £690 a year. This seems to have been removed by statute in 1844. By then the position was petering out, although high constables still presented jury lists to quarter sessions and were involved with highway maintenance. After the early Victorian period such officers were often not replaced in Norfolk and many other counties when they left their positions, and only a few remained actively involved in policing.[66] For example, the last high constable in Essex was appointed for the Witham Division of the county in January 1865. The High Constables Act 1869 (which came into force in January 1870) formally abolished the office altogether.[67]

Watchmen were found in urban areas; they secured the nocturnal streets by patrolling. By the early nineteenth century, this office was always conducted by regular volunteers for payment, rather than being carried out by residents as a civic duty, as had often been the case in the early seventeenth century. Many watchmen in Norwich and other Norfolk boroughs also had diurnal employment, which hindered their efficiency, and led to allegations of sleeping on duty. Throughout the country, regular watchmen were sometimes incorporated into the new borough forces in the years after 1836, and this was the case with Norwich (see below).

Significant numbers of men became involved in traditional policing. In December 1831 the Essex authorities were asked by Lord Melbourne to survey all peace officers in their county, excluding special constables, who were sworn in on an *ad hoc* and temporary basis. (Watchmen would also not come into this category.) A total of 810 officers were identified, many of the 402 communities involved (some of them

---

64 J.B. Freeland, *State of the police in the rural districts, with some suggestions for its improvement* (London: Ridgway, 1839), p. 5.

65 *The Bury and Norwich Post*, 10 September, 1889.

66 *The Ipswich Journal*, 16 January, 1847.

67 Maureen Scollan, *Parish Constable Versus Police Constables: Policing Early-Nineteenth Century Essex*, Open University PhD thesis, 2007, p. 250.

just hamlets) having two constables. Of these, some 95 percent were described as "active." The youngest were a pair of seventeen-year-olds, and the oldest was a 77-year-old constable serving at Bradwell-juxta-Coggeshall, the next most senior men in the county being 71 and 70. The average age for officers in Essex was about 41 years.[68]

The Reverend Charles Brereton (1790-1868), a philanthropic parson and the rector of Little Massingham, who published several reports and papers aimed at ameliorating the plight of the rural poor, thought that these substantial numbers were matched, if not exceeded in Norfolk during the 1830s. He claimed that almost 1,000 parish officers were resident in villages and hamlets there, their ubiquity allegedly allowing them to be reached within five minutes by most of the county's inhabitants. He saw the sheer number of men involved as one of the strengths of the traditional system. Nobody was very far from a parish constable.[69] For illustrative example, in 1838, James Hazel, a farmer from Stoke Ferry, was the victim of a grain theft and, having a suspect in mind, urgently sought assistance, "about 15 minutes elapsed from the time of my going for [a] constable to my returning." He was accompanied by the parish officer.[70]

Ability of Parish Constables

It is difficult to evaluate the quality of parish constables in Norfolk, or any other part of England, in the years prior to the advent of the new urban and rural police forces. Many observers, both local and national, reiterated already longstanding criticism in holding that they were often elderly, physically feeble, untrained, unwillingly appointed, easily intimidated, indolent, and even corrupt. In 1821 John Hopkins Warden, a Bedfordshire parish constable, noted that an inexperienced and temporary officer was inevitably ignorant of criminals' tactics but aware that his own trade or business must be maintained. Such a man might become passive, wink at crime, and not give his position the "attention his office and the Country require."[71]

The same analysis can be found in Norfolk. In early 1836, after a carefully planned burglary had been committed at Stoke Ferry, a local observer claimed that such crimes were evidence of the need for an effective rural police, as "parish constables (most commonly the little tradesmen of the place), even if they have the power, have not always the inclination to ferret out the perpetrators of crime from among their own neighbours, of whom they have an aversion to become the enemies whether open, or secret. Then again, a feeling of compassion (a most mistaken one to be sure), operates in some cases to screen the delinquents." He thought

68 *Ibid.*

69 Charles David Brereton, *A Letter to the Lord Lieutenant and Magistrates of the County of Norfolk* (Swaffham: Hatchard, 1839), pp. 1-4.

70 *The Norfolk Chronicle,* 12 January, 1839.

71 Bedfordshire Archives QSR/25/1821/711.

that a professional police officer, who was a total stranger to the place in which he worked, would be far better than numerous men "playing" at being constables.[72] In early 1842 Isaac Jermy, the recorder of Norwich, claimed that no-one could say a word in favour of Norfolk's traditional parish officers, who were generally "aged and infirm persons, who, by being constables along with some other occupation, contrived to eke out a scanty subsistence."[73]

Such views were also reiterated at more elevated levels. The parliamentary committee that produced a report on rural policing in 1839 heard evidence from JPs about the general "incompetency and inefficiency" of traditional constables. Again, it was claimed that they dreaded making themselves unpopular and that their private occupations as small tradesmen took up all their time, so that a parish constable often had "an interest in keeping out of the way when his services are called for."[74] It was apparently still common for quite elderly or illiterate men to be appointed.[75] Prisoner escapes from their custody were a regular phenomenon. Typically, in January 1821, after Robert Starks escaped from the parish constable of Mattishall, a £5 reward was offered to anyone who apprehended him and returned him to the officer.[76]

Nevertheless, not everyone shared such negative opinions of parish constables. In the late 1830s Brereton was adamant that such criticism, at least insofar as it related to Norfolk, was greatly exaggerated, while the existing parish constables were, he claimed, largely satisfied with their positions and not desirous of change. Certainly, several were killed in the line of duty, suggesting some commitment to their office. For example, in December 1830 James Weston, a young constable from Downham Market, was shot and killed by a gang of poachers. In June the following year, two arsonists waylaid and shot dead another Norfolk parish constable who had thwarted one of their fire-raising ventures.[77] Others made important arrests: in November 1832 two men suspected of a highway robbery near Aylsham were apprehended by a single constable.[78]

Most parish constables were probably moderately diligent, albeit severely hampered by local pressures, personal limitations, lack of experience, and the need to look elsewhere for most of their income. This also meant that they were necessarily reactive rather than proactive when it came to dealing with crime. However, there

---

72 *The Bury and Norwich Post*, 15 February, 1836.

73 *The Times*, 11 January, 1842.

74 David Cox, "The Habitual Eccentricities of the Solons of Staffordshire: An Investigation of the Circumstances Surrounding the Parliamentary Enquiry into the Ill-treatment of Mrs Eliza Price of Brierley Hill, 1845," *Plymouth Law and Criminal Justice Review*, vol. 3 (2010), pp. 114-115.

75 Freeland, *State*, p. 7.

76 *The Norfolk Chronicle*, 6 January, 1821.

77 *Bell's Life in London and Sporting Chronicle*, 12 June, 1831.

78 *The Bury and Norwich Post*, 21 November, 1832.

were always a few men who were both highly competent and extremely energetic, while there were others who lived up to the very worst stereotypes.[79]

Desire for Reform

Provincial police reform had been regularly mooted, at numerous levels, in all parts of the country, from early in the nineteenth century. For example, the Bedford parish constable cited above wrote to quarter sessions in 1821 suggesting the introduction of an "active" police force of salaried full-time constables, with professional knowledge of the local criminals and ready to go anywhere in the county to deal with offenders.[80] This idea was slightly ahead of its time, but by the early 1830s many others were arguing that the traditional provincial policing model had become outmoded in the light of population increase, growing mobility, industrialization, and new expectations for public order, the last having been fanned by the advent of the Metropolitan Police and (to a much smaller extent) ventures such as the new Cheshire constabulary (both of which were established in 1829) and earlier experiments in Ireland and Glasgow. This view was encapsulated in a journal leader in 1842, which opined that a new "Rural Police has on account of the increased population of this country become indispensable. The days of constables of hundreds and tithing-men are past: the divisions of territory for which they were originally appointed have become obsolete."[81]

More locally, by the 1830s, there was clear evidence of a desire for an enhanced form of policing in several parts of Norfolk, one that was stronger than in many other English counties. This was not confined to its major towns (often a focus for change). Indicative of this, several rural or small municipal vestries, such as those in the parishes of Hingham and Wymondham, quickly took advantage of the powers contained in the 1833 Lighting and Watching Act to appoint an inspector who could select paid watchmen.[82] Various other local bodies passed resolutions encouraging reform or took steps to enhance their own policing by establishing local subscription forces. For example, in October 1839, shortly before it was overtaken by events in the form of the new rural police, the Walsham division for Norfolk had mooted establishing its own police force, consisting of a superintendent on £90 a year and three constables earning £45.[83] Correspondence between the East Anglian counties and the Home Office after 1816, especially in the 1830s, reveals a growing

---

79 David Taylor, "'No remedy for the inefficiency of Parochial Constables': Superintending constables and the transition to 'new' policing in the West Riding of Yorkshire in the third quarter of the nineteenth century," *Crime, History & Societies*, vol. 19, no. 1, 2015, pp. 67-88.

80 Bedfordshire Archives QSR 1821/711.

81 *The Spectator*, 26 March, 1842, p. 11.

82 David Taylor, *The New Police in Nineteenth-Century England: Crime, Conflict and Control* (Manchester: MUP, 1997), p. 25.

83 *The Times*, 28 October, 1839, p. 3.

awareness of the potential value of a professional body of police who were actively engaged in patrolling, even if this meant increased expense.[84]

There were several reasons for this enhanced local desire for police reform, some of which went beyond longstanding concerns about the abilities of parish constables. The Swing Riots at the start of the 1830s, which were particularly acute in Norfolk, had encouraged a questioning of the existing system. In 1878 the obituary of the Reverend Henry Lombe, who had died at the age of 86, noted that, before the days of the new post-1840 rural police, he had organized a voluntary system of constabulary in the very disturbed parish of Lyng, in central Norfolk, where he was rector. In company with farmers from the area, he had patrolled it for an entire winter, visiting every farmstead and, it was claimed, preserved the village from ruin.[85] Similarly, when John Dawson died at Bergh Apton in 1853, it was noted that, earlier in his life, prior to the establishment of the new rural force, he had been what was termed a "running constable," these officers being appointed in some petty sessional divisions in Norfolk, at a time when the "requisite tact and intelligence" to deal with crime effectively was not (apparently) found in all parish constables. Such a man was considered the "detective-officer" for the district and Dawson had excelled at this task (and presumably been remunerated for it).[86]

During the late 1830s, Chartism reinforced public concern about policing amongst the well-to-do, in Norfolk as elsewhere in the country. In February 1839 it was reported that a group of Norwich Chartists had armed themselves by purchasing 68 miniature "pikes." These 18-inch weapons had a knife-edged hook at their end, that seemed to be for the purpose of cutting reins and which suggested that they anticipated confronting the military.[87] In August that year, weapons were taken from alleged members of the movement by the Norwich borough police. When the Chartists demonstrated on Mousehold Heath, special constables were sworn in, and elements of the West Norfolk Militia held in readiness to deal with possible disturbances. Chartism continued to flourish over the next decade. In the early summer of 1847, Feargus O'Connor, a leader of the movement, addressed a large meeting at St. Andrew's Hall in Norwich.[88]

The New Borough Police Forces

The Municipal Corporations Act of 1835 allowed the surviving borough councils to organise police forces for their towns and cities that would operate under the immediate supervision of a locally established watch committee, this normally being headed by the mayor of the corporation. By 1837 93 out of the 171 boroughs in

84 D.J.V. Jones, "The New Police, Crime and People in England and Wales, 1829-1888," *Transactions of the Royal Historical Society*, vol. 33 (1983), pp. 151–68.

85 *The Norfolk Chronicle*, 10 October, 1878.

86 *The Norfolk Chronicle* , 30 April, 1853.

87 *The Ipswich Journal*, 16 February, 1839.

88 *The Norfolk Chronicle*, 5 July, 1847.

the country had created such forces. In 1840, the figure had reached 108. However, as late as 1856, there were still at least half a dozen boroughs that had not done so. Perhaps significantly, all four of the post-1835 Norfolk municipal boroughs – Norwich, Great Yarmouth, King's Lynn, and Thetford – took this step at the very earliest opportunity.

Borough forces made up most of the 300 or so police forces in Britain in the 1850s. Some more urbanized counties had more than Norfolk, but population size and history also affected their numbers. For example, 14 towns in Kent had their own police forces, including Sandwich, which had just one officer in 1860 (making it the smallest in the country), Tenterden and Hythe, which had four men each. Similarly, Lancashire had 13 borough forces. Other counties had fewer borough forces than Norfolk. Herefordshire and Hertfordshire each had just two, in addition to their county forces (once introduced).[89] It should be noted that borough officers had legal authority over a seven-mile radius from their towns.

The 1835 Act set no maximum or minimum to the number of police that could be appointed, unlike the maximum of one police officer for each 1,000 inhabitants provided for by the County Police Act of 1839 (see below), although an acute civic reluctance to incur cost placed firm limits on the numbers recruited, the big cities apart. For example, in 1860 there was one officer for every 384 people in Liverpool, and one in 636 in Birmingham.[90] However, in most municipal corporations it was very much lower. Although it is difficult to make a precise estimate, a national average of one officer for each 1,000 people in the boroughs during the early 1840s seems plausible, this ratio improving slightly in the 1850s. As a result, it seems that, in the period from 1836 to 1856, those municipal corporations which maintained separate police forces normally had about half as many policemen in proportion to their population as, for example, the Metropolitan area.[91]

More specifically to Norfolk, although, in 1844, the six or seven officers in Thetford provided it with a ratio of one man for each 557 inhabitants, at least some of these constables were part time.[92] In 1858 Great Yarmouth, then a town of 31,000 inhabitants, had 31 policemen, putting it close to the national average.[93] Nevertheless, between 1861 and 1891, regular police officers nationally increased by more than 30 percent, from 102 to 135 per 100,000 people, a process that was

---

89 *Return of Judicial Statistics of England and Wales, 1860* (London: HMSO, 1861), p. 3. Conley, *Unwritten Law*, p. 17.

90 *Return of Judicial Statistics, 1860*, p. vi.

91 Jenifer Hart, "Reform of the Borough Police, 1835-1856," The English Historical Review, vol. 70, no. 276 (1955), pp. 411-427.

92 Taylor, *The New Police*, p. 35.

93 *The Norfolk Chronicle*, M 22March, 1858.

aided by increasing levels of government financial assistance.[94] This improved ratios in Norfolk, as elsewhere.

The Norwich City Police

In January 1836 the then newly elected Norwich City Council agreed on the appointment of a new city police force pursuant to the 1835 Act. The Norwich force, the largest and arguably most professional borough police force in Norfolk, went on duty for the first time in March 1836, under the (short-lived) superintendence of William Wright.[95] It was based in the town hall, in a station house that was open at all hours of the day and night and continuously manned. The force was made up of 18 policemen (rising to 24 in 1839), with six supernumeraries to provide increased cover for special occasions and stand in for officers on sick leave. These extra officers also provided a source of full-time recruits when an officer left service (they were quite widely found amongst English borough forces). Initially the city's nocturnal force of 32 watchmen (with seven supernumeraries) continued to operate from 11 pm to 6 am (or sunrise), encouraging the new force to focus on diurnal operations within the city walls, and nocturnal operations in its extra-mural suburbs.[96] This general pattern was typical of first-generation urban police forces. In Exeter, for example, reform after the 1835 Act meant that a watch committee established a police force of 30 men in January 1836, including ten supernumerary policemen, but initially, as in Norwich, the watchmen continued to serve.[97]

At first, coordination between the two Norwich policing bodies was not very good, with both forces keen to receive the small rewards available for detaining offenders, while it was argued that watchmen were often not supervised properly and (as previously) continued with their diurnal employments, reducing their efficiency.[98] However, watchmen were swiftly incorporated into the new police, on a *de facto* basis, and formal amalgamation took place in 1852. As a result, in 1853 Norwich had 61 constables and 12 higher-ranking officers, placing it very slightly below the national per capita average, given its population.[99] By 1860 the force had some 90 officers.[100] There followed something of a plateau, as in 1879 it was apparently

---

94 See generally, J. Martin and G. Wilson, *The Police: A Study in Police Manpower* (London: Heinemann, 1989).

95 *The Norfolk Chronicle,* 1 March, 1836.

96 *The Bury and Norwich Post*, 17 February 1836. Norwich Watch Committee, *Report of the Watch Committee Made to the Council of the Body Corporate of Norwich, on the 9th of February, 1837,* Norwich, 1837, p. 1.

97 Roger Swift, "Urban Policing in Early Victorian England, 1835-86: A Reappraisal," *History*, vol. 73, no. 238 (1988), pp. 211–37.

98 *The Bury and Norwich Post*, 13 July 1853.

99 Maurice Morson, *A Force Remembered: The Illustrated History of the Norwich City Police 1836-1967* (Derby: Breedon Books, 2000), pp. 10-11, p. 13.

100 *Judicial Statistics 1860,* p. 2.

only 87 men strong.[101] The survival of watchmen from the pre-1836 policing regime meant that there were, at least, continuities between old and new forms of policing in Norwich and the other Norfolk boroughs, more so than was the case with the new county force after 1840.

Recruits to the Norwich force had to be healthy men, at least 5 feet, 6 inches tall and (initially) between the ages of 25 and 50, although relatively few men were taken on in their late forties. At the outset their pay was just under 15 shillings a week for constables, while in 1837 the force's three sergeants received an extra 2s 6d a week. The initial superintendent, William Wright, earned £40 per annum when he first went on duty, but this was increased significantly a few years later. By the end of the era, it was a very well-remunerated position. In 1897 Edwin Winch, the chief constable of Truro, was appointed chief constable of Norwich at a salary of £350 per annum.[102] There could be extra, specific payments for officers carrying out certain duties, such as attending court to give evidence or searching for stolen property, 5 shillings often being granted for such tasks. There were also rewards for arresting felons – 5 shillings if the case was committed for trial, 3s 6d if it was not – supplementing the basic stipend and encouraging extra diligence, but also occasioning concern that they might promote officiousness.[103]

At first, like most of the new post-1829 police forces, the Norwich constabulary was plagued with disciplinary problems, with drunkenness on duty being a particular problem (the city had numerous public houses) and a significant turnover of officers. Many of the officers' failings would be matched by those of the post-1840 county force (discussed in more detail in the following chapter). As in the county force and all other forces in England and Wales, this problem lessened as the Victorian era advanced.

The new Norwich force was attired in chimney-pot hats, a dark-blue uniform with long-tailed coat, and "waterproof capes similar to those worn by the police in London."[104] Initially each man had to provide his own trousers, in an appropriate colour. They were also issued with truncheons, rattles (replaced by whistles in 1860), lanterns, and handcuffs; notebooks were added later.[105] An allowance was given for purchasing boots. The use of the Metropolitan Police model uniform is unsurprising: it was widespread amongst the new borough (and later county) police forces of the era.[106] However, in 1855 the Norwich Police varied their uniform, the principal alteration being the substitution of a frock coat for the "unsightly long-

---

101 *Return of Judicial Statistics of England and Wales, 1879* (London: HMSO, 1880), p. 2.

102 *The Norfolk Chronicle,* 13 April, 1897.

103 Morson, *A Force Remembered,* pp. 10-11. *Report of the Watch Committee*, pp. 1-2.

104 *The Norfolk Chronicle,* 1 March, 1836.

105 Morson, *A Force Remembered,* pp. 10-11.

106 Swift, "Urban Policing."

tailed coat."[107] This in turn was replaced by a short coat in 1879; the tall hat had been replaced by the classic "Roman" helmet, which was less likely to be displaced during disturbances, in 1871. (Other British forces did likewise at about this time). There were periodic complaints from officers about the low quality of the uniforms.

Great Yarmouth Borough Police

The Great Yarmouth Police, the second-largest municipal force in the county, were also established in 1836 (and like the Norwich force survived until 1967). In 1857 it consisted of a superintendent, four sergeants, and 23 constables. It had reached 31 officers of all ranks by the following year, 32 in 1860, 43 in 1879, and 57 in 1901.[108] As with many of the new forces, initial public expectations of their effectiveness were often exaggerated. Shortly after they went on duty there were complaints that a man named Cullingford had "cut down the doorstalls of Mr. Wm. Sayer's house in which he was engaged nearly two hours without being detected by any of the new police."[109] Even so, the force had a surprising reach. One of the first international arrests involving telegraphy was made by Great Yarmouth Borough Police in 1882, when officers travelled to Cape Town, South Africa, to collect John Robert Durrant, a local fish merchant, who was wanted for fraudulently concealing and removing his property when adjudged a bankrupt in the town.[110] (The considerable expense entailed in such actions was often a major deterrent to pursuing them.)

King's Lynn Borough Police

The King's Lynn Borough Police Force was established in January 1836, and survived until 1947. Initially the force had 14 men of all ranks and descriptions. They included Daniel Rolin, the mayor's beadle; four men who constituted the day police; William Catchpole, the keeper of the police office; William Andrews, the superintendent of the night police (and their commander); and six other men who made up the nocturnal force.[111] They appear to have been arranged around the three wards that had recently been created, with two men on duty in each ward at night, and one by day. The constables were initially paid the modest sum of 10s a week, with the Superintendent receiving just 16 shillings. They also received the standard (for police officers) greatcoat, cape, lantern, rattle, and staff.[112] By 1860 the King's Lynn borough force had increased to 20 men; it reached 25 officers in 1879.[113]

---

107 *The Norfolk Chronicle,* 9 March, 1855; *Figaro in London*, 13 August, 1836.

108 *The Norfolk Chronicle,* 22 March, 1858; *Judicial Statistics, 1860*, p. 2; *Judicial Statistics, 1879*, p. 2.

109 Frederick Danby Palmer, *Yarmouth Notes: 1830–1872* (Great Yarmouth, Buckle, 1889), p. 74.

110 *The Bury and Norwich Post, and Suffolk Herald*, 9 May, 1882.

111 *Municipal Corporations Act 1835, the Borough of King's Lynn in the County of Norfolk.*

112 Brian Butcher, *"A Movable Rambling Police": An Official History of Policing in Norfolk* (King's Lynn: Norfolk Constabulary, 1989), pp. 9-10.

113 *Judicial Statistics, 1860*, p. 2. *Judicial Statistics 1879*, p. 2.

Thetford Borough Police

The Thetford Police was the smallest of the borough forces when established in 1836 and remained so throughout its short history. It had just six constables who went on duty as and when required, and one salaried chief constable (also responsible for the borough's prison), Philip Penn Wilson, who was quickly followed by John Nixon. They were based in an office in the town hall. Another salaried man (albeit on just £9 a year) was added in 1837, recruited from one of the six redundant parish constables. During the 1840s Thetford continued to be reliant on volunteer officers to supplement its two full-time professional men. However, two more paid constables were added in early 1857, shortly before amalgamation with the county force, bringing it up to four salaried men plus supernumeraries.

The Thetford Corporation opposed the creation of the new Norfolk County Constabulary in 1840 and preserved their miniature force (one of the smallest in the country) for reasons of civic pride and, perhaps, because it initially appeared a cheaper option than joining the county scheme. In practice, it was more expensive, because there were no economies of scale. There was also a history of internecine discord among the few paid men in the force and between them and their local watch committee. Nevertheless, it had a few successes. For example, in 1853, Superintendent John Tyler arrested a horse thief after he attempted to sell two valuable mares at less than half their worth.[114]

In 1853 the force survived a voluntary move towards consolidation with the rural (county) police. However, running a separate but efficient force became too much for the small borough, especially after the County and Borough Police Act of 1856 provided for a Home Office grant of 25 percent of approved expenditure (pay and clothing), to forces certified to the Secretary of State as efficient, but withheld this for smaller (under 5,000 inhabitants) or inefficient forces.[115] The Act also created an Inspectorate, Her Majesty's Inspectors of Constabulary, who were required to certify annually that a police force warranted such a grant, something that small forces often found difficult. For example, those belonging to the smallest towns in Kent, such as Hythe, Tenterden, and Sandwich, regularly failed inspections and were recommended for incorporation into their surrounding county force.[116] Faced by the financial advantages, Thetford joined the Norfolk County Constabulary system in 1857.[117] In any event, its force could not have lasted to the end of the Victorian era. After 1888 most boroughs with fewer than 10,000 inhabitants were legally required to join their surrounding county force.[118] (The following year, the number of police forces nationally fell from 231 to 183 as a result).

---

[114] *The Bury and Norwich Post, and Suffolk Herald*, August 31, 1853.

[115] Butcher, *A Movable Rambling Police; an Official History of Policing in Norfolk*, 1989, pp. 19-21.

[116] Conley, *Unwritten Law*, p. 30.

[117] *The Bury and Norwich Post, and Suffolk Herald*, 14 April, 1857.

[118] David Bentley, *English Criminal Justice in the Nineteenth Century* (London: Hambledon Press, 1998), p. 6.

Operation of the Borough Police

When first formed, provincial police in England, both county and borough, often drew on the Metropolitan Police (established in 1829) for their officer cadres, organizational patterns, and operational behaviour. (Some also looked to Ireland.)[119] In the late 1830s the Norwich Police used a system of three seven-to-nine-hour shifts, shorter than those employed by some other Borough forces at this time. The night shift (conducted in the suburbs until the watchmen were absorbed) involved constables patrolling in pairs from 11 pm to 7 am. There were two day shifts outside these hours, in most of which officers patrolled alone.[120] Ensuing years saw several variations in force distribution, and total shifts of 12 or more hours were often employed.

Like the Metropolitan force, the work of the borough police forces was largely based on patrolling or "perambulating" set beats, walked at a steady pace of about two-and-a-half miles an hour. In 1880 there were some 40 numbered nocturnal and a dozen (slightly longer) diurnal beats in Norwich. For example, daytime beat no. 1 started and finished at the Guildhall and went via St. Giles Gates, Dove Street, and Bank Plain, taking an hour and a quarter to cover. Two experienced officers were also usually detailed to assist in the running of the Justice Room or Public Police Office, executing warrants, serving summonses, and assisting the magistrates.

Occasionally routine patrolling had some direct successes. In 1841 at Pockthorpe, a rough suburb west of Norwich, one young officer, PC Ames, captured two housebreakers red-handed. The residents of the house had gone out to an evening service at a local chapel, leaving the premises empty. A passing woman overheard the intruders in the house, and Ames (her nearest beat officer), who then showed great courage in confronting and arresting the two men after "some resistance." They had rifled the house, amassing a pile of silver items, and were carrying a crowbar and picklock when detained.[121] Nevertheless, and as is the case today, it was rare for patrolling officers to encounter significant crimes being committed. More commonly they dealt with low-level street disorder and incivilities. For example, in Salford, in the late 1840s, more than a third of arrests were for alcohol-related offences.[122] In Norwich the proportion was also substantial.

Relations with other borough forces and with the surrounding county police force were broadly amicable, after the latter was introduced in 1840, though there was some initial tension, which occasionally resurfaced in later years. There were some differences in style between the four Norfolk urban forces and their more traditional rural counterpart. In 1841 one Colonel Molyneux complained to the Norwich mayor and magistrates that the city policemen, unlike the Norfolk County (and

119 Clive Emsley, "A typology of nineteenth-century police," *Crime, History & Societies*, vol. 3, no. 1 (1999), pp. 29-44.

120 Taylor, *The New Police,* p. 52.

121 *The Bury and Norwich Post*, 13 January, 1841.

122 Wood, "Drinking, Fighting," pp. 1-10.

the Metropolitan) police, were not saluting uniformed military officers when they passed them in the street. He threatened to report the matter to the horse guards. In response, the mayor pointed out that the force was regulated by the Municipal Corporations Act, and controlled by the city watch committee, who did not feel that saluting army officers was a formal requirement of the position, although stressing that their men should "behave respectfully to all classes."[123]

In emergencies, or even in slightly unusual situations, the delineation between the different Norfolk police forces was not rigidly observed, and assistance might be tendered between them. For example, when James Rush was executed for murder in Norwich in 1848, in front of tens of thousands of spectators, "about sixty constables of the rural force were stationed thirty yards apart in the garden walk of the castle."[124] This was, of course, in the Norwich police area. Similarly, in December 1851, the Norwich watch committee agreed to lend one of the city police officers to assist a group of men from the new rural police who were sent to confront nocturnal poaching gangs in nearby Letton. The constable chosen, PC Noller, was selected because he was a "strong, powerful man."[125] In June 1871, after Henry Stebbings, a 30-year-old drover, raped his sweetheart's nine-year-old sister in East Winch, near King's Lynn, then cut her throat, he abandoned her in a wood and fled. Some passersby heard her cries and saved her life. A county-wide search for the fugitive was then organised by the rural and King's Lynn borough police working together.[126]

It should be noted that the creation in 1856 of the Inspectorate of Constabulary (whose certificates of efficiency secured Treasury grants) as well as the emergence of police experts within the Home Office encouraged the dissemination of perceived best practice and an increased degree of uniformity among all of England's police forces. They also promoted central influence during the latter decades of the Victorian era.[127]

The New Rural Police

As the Metropolitan and borough forces developed it was inevitable that attention would focus on more rural parts. Some saw these areas as weak links in the emerging chain of policing. In late 1836 one observer claimed that nationally "the inefficiency of the Country Constabulary force is notorious. A country constable is laughed at everywhere."[128] In the same year, another critic complained, as others had done for centuries, that they were often recruited from physically worn-out

---

123 *John Bull*, January 9, 1841.

124 Anon., 1849, *The Stanfield Hall Assassinations!*, Cleave, London, pp. 1-10

125 *The Morning Post*, 15 December 1851.

126 *The Bury and Norwich Post*, 27 June 1871.

127 Emsley, "A typology," pp. 29-44.

128 *The Spectator*, 19 November, 1836, p. 13.

men who, to make some profit from the office, would commit petty fraud when claiming allowances. He then reiterated all the other longstanding criticisms of such constables.[129]

As a result, three constabulary commissioners were appointed by Royal Commission in 1836 to review the policing needs of rural parts. One was Sir Charles Rowan, one of the two founding commissioners of the Metropolitan Police. Another was Edwin Chadwick, a keen social reformer. The third was the Whig politician Charles Shaw-Lefevre. Perhaps unsurprisingly, when it reported, in March 1839, the committee was keen to see the establishment of a rural constabulary nationwide and painted a graphic picture of lawlessness in rural areas, something that was allegedly encouraged by poor-quality parish constables.[130]

However, to many observers the whole notion of a full-time preventative and patrolling force, rather than reactive officers who went on duty only to deal with a specific assignment, appeared wrong. They were afraid of the potential impact of a new rural force on traditional civil liberties and concerned about its impact on local autonomy. As one observer noted in 1836, objections to the establishment of a rural police usually focused on a fear that it would produce French-style centralization, depriving country gentlemen of their authority over the police, and vesting it in the Home Office in London, as was the case with the Metropolitan force.[131] To a certain type of person, rural police, wherever they were introduced, appeared "oppressive, unconstitutional, inquisitorial, un-English—everything that is bad." [132] There was also concern that any form of new police, unlike the traditional parish constables, might not accommodate the informal resolution of disputes and the traditional enforcement of social norms often found in rural areas, without recourse to legal proceedings.[133] Furthermore, there was very considerable anxiety about the potential cost of any new force.

In late 1839 the Reverend Charles Brereton hurriedly produced a lengthy critique of the new force that was proposed for rural Norfolk, reiterating many longstanding criticisms and adding others. Brereton thought that, unlike the traditional system of parish constables, the relatively small number of new-type officers would be a "movable rambling police, which no one will ever know where to find." He also thought that the new officers would be salaried for "lounging and loitering" about their villages and would conduct prosecutions purely for career advancement. The cleric claimed that the traditional system was time-honoured, allowing the blending

---

129 Edward Mullins, *A Treatise on the Magistracy of England and the Origin and Expenditure of County Rates* (London: Richards & Co., 1836), pp. 39-40.

130 *The Royal Commission on Constabulary Forces,* March 1839.

131 *The Spectator*, 19 November, 1836, p. 13.

132 *The Spectator*, 26 March, 1842, p. 11

133 J. Carter Wood, "Self-Policing and the Policing of the Self: Violence, Protection and the Civilising Bargain in Britain," *Crime, History & Societies,* vol. 7, no. 1 (2003), pp. 109-128.

of monarchical and democratic principles; the Crown chose the magistrates, but the parishes appointed the constables.[134]

The County Police Act

In 1839, the County Police Act (also known as the Rural Police Act) was passed into law. However, it did not follow the recommendations of the police commissioners, who had suggested that a rural police force be introduced throughout the country. Instead, the 1839 Act was a permissive statute, one that could be adopted in any county, or part of a county, where the justices at quarter sessions decided that they should levy a rate and set up a police force. It was rushed through Parliament in the face of considerable concern about public disorder occasioned by Chartism.

On 22 November 1839, a special meeting was held for Norfolk magistrates to allow them to decide whether to establish such a force in their county. (Brereton complained that this had been inadequately publicised.)[135] One of the JPs present, the Reverend Robert Wilson, argued that the existing police arrangements in Norfolk were inefficient and (very speculatively) that the combined effects of vagrancy and theft cost the county some £120,000 each year, whereas the new police force would cost between £3,000 and £10,000 (a significant underestimate as it turned out). Another JP, Lord Wodehouse, claimed that any new force would not see a diminution in magistrates' power (a frequent objection), not least because they would control the police, unlike the model used in the Metropolis (where the police were answerable to the Home Secretary). However, a small minority of the JPs present vigorously but unavailingly advanced traditional concerns, such as that any new type of salaried police would be a platform for government intervention. They lost a vote on introducing a rural force by 84 to 13.[136] This was a large margin compared to, for example, Hertfordshire, where the vote for introduction was 38 to 34, and indicative of a much stronger than average desire for change in Norfolk compared to many other counties.[137]

At the same November meeting, the JPs decided to appoint a chief constable at £500 per annum, 12 superintendents with a salary of £100 a year (quickly increased to £150), and 120 constables on £1 each per week, so forming the Norfolk constabulary.[138] As a result, Norfolk joined the first (and relatively small) wave of counties (or parts of counties) that implemented the 1839 Act. In other areas of the country, resistance was much stronger and, at least initially, successful. County JPs in Yorkshire were bombarded with petitions from many townships, arguing that proposals for a rural police force were unnecessary and uncalled for,

---

134 Brereton, *Letter*, p. 9, p. 11, p. 22, and p. 27.

135 *Ibid.*, p. ii.

136 *The Morning Chronicle,* 3 December, 1839.

137 *John Bull*, vol. xxl, no. 1,049, 16 January 1841, p. 28.

138 *John Bull*, vol. xx, no. 1,044, 12 December 1840, p. 597.

defeating initial proposals to have recourse to the statute.[139] In 1840 the Whig politician Thomas Law Hodges observed in Parliament that the 1839 Act had been adopted by only 13 counties in England and Wales, even in part (as was the case in Suffolk), and far fewer to the full extent. He thought that the main reason was the attendant expense. Certainly, in Devonshire complaints from ratepayers led local JPs to abandon their initial plans to introduce such a force. Similarly in Derbyshire, resistance from ratepayers was the decisive factor in overriding the initial desire of local JPs to introduce a county police. The potential expense also prevented West Suffolk from joining the eastern part of the same county when such a proposal was made to its JPs.[140]

Well over a decade later, many counties had still failed to introduce a police force. In 1853 the MP Edward Rice noted that the Rural Police Act had been fully adopted in 25 counties, partially adopted in five, and not adopted at all in 22. The establishment of such a force was eventually made mandatory by the County and Borough Police Act of 1856, which required that JPs in any county without a constabulary meet at the first quarter sessions held after 1 December 1856, to remedy the defect and establish a police force.

By contrast, in Norfolk Colonel Richard Montague Oakes, late of the First Life Guards, was appointed as the first chief constable of the force on January 3, 1840.[141] Lieutenant Hatton, an unsuccessful fellow candidate for the office, eventually secured the equivalent position for the three hundreds in Suffolk that introduced a police force at the same time.[142] James Adams, who had also been considered for the position of chief constable, and came well recommended from the Metropolitan Police, of which he had been a founder member, was offered and accepted a position as superintendent in the Norfolk force, though he was quickly mired in scandal.[143]

The new "rural police" (as it was often termed until the 1850s) went on duty shortly afterwards. Although an eventual body of about 300 constables had been mooted on foundation, a newspaper correspondent noted that in 1844 there were still only the initial 120 constables plus higher-ranking officers, although he thought that, to make it efficient, at least twice that number were required.[144] Nevertheless, the force gradually and unevenly expanded over subsequent years. For example, at the county quarter sessions in July 1855, and following the request of the chief constable, the Police Committee recommended an increase of 15 constables, to be

139 M. Koyama, "The law & economics of private prosecutions in industrial revolution England," *Public Choice*, vol. 159, no. 1/2 (2014), pp. 277–298.

140 Taylor, *Hooligans*, p. 128. *John Bull*, vol. xxiv, no. 1,215 (25 March, 1844), p. 192.

141 *The Bury and Norwich Post*, 23 December, 1862.

142 *John Bull*, vol. xx, no. 1,005, 15 March, 1840, p. 129.

143 *The Ipswich Journal*, 17 April, 1841.

144 *The Bury and Norwich Post*, 31 January 1844.

paid at 19 shillings a week each, to ensure that an "efficient system of patrol" could be preserved.

Small though the county force was, it was an expensive venture, as many had feared, costing £12,000 a year in the early 1840s and helping to increase the levied county rate to £36,000 per annum.[145] Expense was to be a constant concern over ensuing years, slowing the growth of the force. Indeed, at the Norfolk quarter sessions in the autumn of 1850, it was decided that there should be an attempt to reduce the wages paid out to the Norfolk constabulary by an annual total of £225 to save one-eighth of a penny in the pound on the county rates.

The County Policing Model

Everywhere in England, the new rural forces faced problems when it came to developing an appropriate policing model. Most important, and as the Earl of Orford noted in early 1842, the beat system, on which the Metropolitan model, and that of many boroughs (such as Norwich), was based, was not obviously viable in a large and sparsely populated rural environment of the type found in much of Norfolk: distances were too great and officers too few.146 As a West Suffolk tenant farmer observed in 1844, when discussing the new Norfolk Police (he had numerous relatives across the border), rural policing was totally different from that of heavily built-up and highly populated areas such as the Metropolis: "Supposing all the men employed to be active and expert at their business (which I by no means admit) all they can do is walk over a certain beat, too large to enable them to do much good."[146] He deplored attempts to add a rural force to his own part of Suffolk, and asked what assistance the occasional "straggling" constable, wandering around the countryside, could provide against the then prevalent crime of arson. (He suggested that villages might invest in bloodhounds instead).[147]

More specifically to Norfolk, Brereton also thought that the small number of "rambling" officers available would achieve little. According to the Earl of Chichester, even Colonel Rowan was sympathetic to such views, feeling that the beat-based London preventive model he had developed was not suitable in the countryside, so that the role of a "rural police was rather to prevent crime by detecting offenders rather than to prevent it by their actual presence in every village."[148]

Nevertheless, despite such reservations, most rural constables *were* given, and duly walked, a lengthy beat, as well as responding to specific requests for assistance. For example, in Bedfordshire police officers served ten-to-twelve-hour shifts in the middle of the nineteenth century and might walk 20 miles during this time. Norfolk was broadly similar. This could take a toll on officers. In October 1853 it was

---

145 *Ibid.*

146 *Ibid.*

147 *Ibid.*, 14 February 1844.

148 Clive Emsley, *Crime and Society in England: 1750–1900*, p. 247.

noted that PC John Piper, an "exemplary" constable who had diligently covered a 35-square-mile area near Thetford for the previous seven years, had been so worn out by his exertions in the line of duty that he was no longer fit for further service. (The chief constable arranged a payment of seven months' wages to be made to him from the force's superannuation fund.)[149] As with urban forces, absence from the beat was a regular ground for dismissal from the county force, especially early in the era. For example, PC Robert Moller was dismissed in 1857 for being "absent from his duty and found in bed."[150]

Of course, although the area involved was very large, major roads were comparatively few, and fields of visibility in a relatively flat landscape like Norfolk often quite extensive, slightly ameliorating this situation. Officers on routine patrol did sometimes interrupt crimes while they were in progress or, more commonly, intercept criminals who were fleeing after committing them. Other patrolling officers identified offences or discovered valuable evidence while on their beats. Indeed, in 1854 Captain Black (he was later promoted to Colonel in the Volunteers), the then chief constable, felt that the number of criminals caught red-handed by officers' coming upon them during their nightly rounds made manifest the efficacy of a "system of uncertain and ever changing patrol." Certainly, the new rural police provided an unprecedented degree of nocturnal surveillance. Charging the grand jury at the Norfolk quarter sessions in October 1844, Henry Dover, the chairman of the bench, was struck by the general absence of cases of animal theft, compared to earlier years, in what were otherwise very busy sessions. He attributed this, in part, to the impact of the new police, and to the "regularity of their watching at night."[151]

Some energetic rural officers achieved considerable success while patrolling. For example, PC Hambling, based in Trowse, was a model of the better sort of Norfolk policeman in the early years of the new force. Returning from night duty in 1843, he encountered James Fisk, a notorious, if relatively minor, local criminal on the road, with two ducks, which turned out to have been stolen. Hambling arrested him after a considerable fight. On being searched, Fisk had several picklock (skeleton) keys on his person, providing yet "another instance of the advantage of an active rural police."[152]

More than three decades later, in December 1877, a PC Butcher, stationed at Croxton, was on evening duty near Bridgham when he heard two shots being fired from a neighbouring field. He then heard men talking and, when he investigated, was confronted by Moses Webb, a notorious character from nearby Thetford. A vicious struggle ensued, in which Webb struck Butcher in the face with the muzzle of his gun. However, with the assistance of a local man, Webb was eventually

149 *The Bury and Norwich Post*, 26 October, 1853.

150 *Norfolk Constabulary Force, Appointments from 1854-1861*, Book 1, original document at NC, p. 108.

151 *The Bury and Norwich Post*, 23 October, 1844.

152 *The Bury and Norwich Post,* 19 April, 1843.

arrested and marched to Thetford gaol.[153] (In rural areas, what were reported as "chance" encounters while patrolling may sometimes have involved the deliberate surveillance of suspects.)

Of course, not all nocturnal operations were so successful, especially in the early days of the force. For example, in January 1841 Constable William Dye was walking a beat near Mundford, at about 11 pm when, according to his account, he came across John Neal (whom he recognised) and another "man" in a turnip field, carrying pieces of timber near a woodshed. Dye attempted to arrest Neal on suspicion of theft while the other person ran off. Neal fought back, belabouring Dye with his fists. Although the latter managed to get his handcuffs around one of Neal's wrists, and struck him with his staff, Neal wrestled Dye's truncheon from him, struck him with it, and eventually broke it over his head, cutting his scalp to the bone. Even so, Dye ultimately prevailed, although he would later spend two days in bed recovering from his injuries, and a further fortnight off duty. At trial the defendant claimed that he had been having an assignation with a woman (the person who ran off), not stealing, and footprints seemed to confirm that his companion had been female. After a six-hour hearing, he was acquitted.[154]

The powers of patrolling officers were considerably enhanced by s.2 of the Poaching Prevention Act of 1862, under which constables could search anyone whom they had good cause to suspect had come from land where they had been unlawfully pursuing game. This provided rural police with a potent, if bitterly resented, weapon, as it gave them power to stop and search large numbers of people on suspicion. In these circumstances, officers frequently found evidence of minor larcenies, unconnected to poaching, such as the theft of vegetables or timber, and arrests and prosecutions often ensued.

A major consequence of the advent of the new police, in both borough and county, was that numerous minor and victimless offences were pursued in a way that had not been done previously, the expanding petty sessions providing a ready forum in which such prosecutions could be brought. This greatly advanced the reach and impact of the criminal law, actively encouraging a more regulated society. By the start of 1842 the chief constable for the rural police could claim that the number of vagrants committed to Norwich prison from various parts of the county had increased by 150 percent since the advent of the new force less than two years earlier.[155] In the same year, the Earl of Orford complained that, as a result of the new Norfolk rural force, "the expenses of the county were much increased by the costs arising from the prosecution of persons apprehended by the police for offences of a very trivial nature."[156]

---

153 *The Bury and Norwich Post*, 4 December, 1877.

154 *Ibid.*, 14 April, 1841. *The Ipswich Journal*, 10 April, 1841.

155 *The Bury and Norwich Post*, 12 January, 1842.

156 *The Norfolk Chronicle,* 7 January, 1842.

The new rural police also had considerable powers of coordination and collaboration, allowing them to attempt tasks that had not usually been open to traditional parish officers, at least not without laborious recourse to high constables. They proved invaluable when, as increasingly occurred, the authorities sought to crack down on rough, largely (but not entirely) working-class entertainments such as cockfighting, bear-baiting, and prize-fighting, which were thought to coarsen the public moral sensibility and to encourage idleness.[157]

For example, ungloved but regulated fist-fighting for reward was a popular spectator sport in the 1830s, the bouts attracting large crowds. However, it was a breeding ground for disorderly, often drunken behaviour, and often had associations with crime, unsurprisingly given that prominent bouts attracted heavy gambling. Prize-fights were not illegal per se until quite late in the period (the ruling in *R* v. *Coney* in 1882) but were often viewed as unlawful assemblies by both participants and spectators. JPs had sometimes tried to suppress them as breaches of the peace, even early in the century.[158] Even so, such a meeting was not something that a local parish constable of the old type would ever feel able to break up on his own, even if he had had the inclination.

By contrast, and indicative of the new, more interventionist, approach to maintaining order, in January 1840 it was noted that the then new rural police had intervened in a prizefight on Pulham North Green. One of the fighters was taken into custody, conveyed to Harleston, and bound over to keep the peace for twelve months.[159] Similarly, a quarter of a century later, when a prizefight took place on Grimston Common, between Pooley Mace and a man named Rackaby, the police arrived to stop proceedings after just five rounds had been fought.[160] Larger numbers of officers could also readily be assembled for specific operations. Thus, in late 1851, near East Dereham, a police patrol led by a superintendent confronted and attempted to arrest a gang of nine poachers who had attacked a local gamekeeper's house. The poachers opened fire, wounding two officers, but seven were captured during the ensuing affray.[161]

Other Policing Agencies in Norfolk

Even after their advent, Norfolk's policing agencies, broadly construed, were not confined to the county's five professional forces. For example, in a very minor instance, the Home Secretary in 1892 sanctioned the use of extra officers from a division of the Metropolitan Police force to secure the Prince of Wales's residence at

157 Randall McGowen, "Civilizing Punishment: The End of the Public Execution in England," *Journal of British Studies*, vol. 33, no. 3 (1994), pp. 257-282.

158 Carole King, *The leisure activities of the rural working classes with special reference to Norfolk 1840-1940*, University of East Anglia PhD thesis, 2015, pp. 35-37.

159 *The Norfolk Chronicle,* 7 January, 1840.

160 *The Norfolk Chronicle,* 8 September, 1865.

161 *Bell's Life in London and Sporting Chronicle*, 21 December, 1851.

Sandringham.[162] Much more important were the surviving elements of the traditional system, the new railway police, special constables, military aid to the civil power, public assistance to the police, and the public's capacity to self-police.

Survival of Parish Constables

In January 1840 Henry Dover, the chairman of the Norfolk quarter sessions, made it clear that, unlike the situation in the boroughs and London, the advent of the new rural police should not affect the existing system and powers of traditional parish constables (the "old constabulary"), who would continue to be appointed and whose duties, in both criminal and civil matters, would remain the same.[163] The parish vestry would still make a list of residents who were suitable to serve as constables, and this list would then be delivered to local magistrates, who would select constables to appoint.[164] Those chosen would then be sworn in before JPs at petty sessions. For example, at the petty sessions for the Earsham Hundred in April 1842, three parish constables were sworn in for the following year, Joseph Abbott for Langmere (which traditionally appointed only one officer) along with two other men for Redenhall.[165]

In numerous parts of Norfolk, parish constables survived for many years after the new rural police force came into existence. In theory, the amended County Police Act of 1840 (3 & 4 Vict. c. 88) even allowed chief constables to appoint men to these positions. However, after 1842 they could no longer be chosen by courts leet in the few parishes where such forums survived.[166] Parish constables continued to serve on similar terms to those present before 1840. Thus in 1841 it was noted that those in Norfolk still received a shilling a mile for conveying men to prison on a magistrate's warrant.[167] Similarly, in 1848 the county justices ordered that the overseers of the poor at Reedham make payments to their parish constable for a variety of tasks, as had always been the case.[168] More than 20 years later, in 1869, they were still making the same orders with regard to his successor.[169]

Sections five to seven of the 1842 Parish Constables Act (5 & 6 Vict.) required that parish constables be selected from able-bodied men aged between 25 and 55, resident in the appointing parish, assessed at £4 or more for the poor or county

162 *The Leicester Chronicle*, 24 September, 1892, p. 2.

163 *The Ipswich Journal*, 25 January, 1840.

164 George Black, *The police of England: as it was, as it is, and as it should be* (London: J. Ridgway, 1856), p. 21.

165 Minutes of the Business transacted at the Petty Sessions for the Hundred of Earsham Commencing April 1st 1842, NRO PS 21/7/6.

166 Black, *The Police*, pp. 1-52.

167 *The Ipswich Journal*, 30 October, 1841.

168 NRO PD 290/51.

169 NRO PD 653/90.

rate, and not otherwise exempt (gaolers, lawyers, ministers of religion, military officers etc.) or disqualified (those licensed to sell liquor, gamekeepers, or men convicted of "infamous crimes"). As before, section 12 of the same Act allowed the appointment of substitutes, approved by the JPs, to be provided by those selected, in lieu of personal service. Under s.13 of the statute, those who were chosen but refused to serve or appoint a substitute without reasonable excuse, could be fined up to £10.

Parish constables continued to be sworn in in large numbers by local JPs. For example, in March 1845 James Cook, Benjamin Webb, Richard Newton, and Richard Eglington were formally appointed as constables for the parishes of Horsham St Faith and Newton St Faith by JPs sitting at special petty sessions held for the Hundred of Taverham.[170] There continued to be considerable continuity of service among those appointed. During the 1850s parish constables for the 16 villages and hamlets in the Hundred of Earsham were sworn in at special petty sessions held in late March at the Corn Hall in Mundham. Most of these parishes appointed two men, but three appointed a single officer, so that 29 or so men might be sworn before the JPs at any one time. A scrutiny of names for 1854/5/6 shows many of the same men serving from year to year. Thus, at Thorpe Abbotts, George Smith served two and George Catchpole all three years from 1854. Similarly, at Billingford, George King and James Balls served two and three years respectively.[171]

Obviously, on an individual basis, parish constables had much less impact on law enforcement than the new regular police officers. The Select Committee on Police of 1852/3, considering the hybrid superintending constable system introduced in some English counties by the Parish Constables Acts of 1842 and 1850, heard evidence from David Smith, a superintending constable from Oxfordshire, who had observed parish constables in his own county and new rural policemen appointed under the 1839 Act in Essex. Smith thought that 60 or 70 of the former were the equivalent of half a dozen of the latter.[172] Nevertheless, even if such an estimate were correct, and a ratio of 10 to one in effectiveness were accepted, the sheer number of parish constables meant that they would still play a fairly important role in county policing.

Norfolk was certainly not unusual in retaining its parish constables; the same pattern can be seen in other counties, including its neighbours Suffolk and Cambridgeshire and, further south, Essex.[173] This continuation is unsurprising, as the initial Norfolk rural police force (like many others) was tiny and very thinly spread around the county, as Brereton had presciently warned would be the case. It required bolstering. The traditional constables had the same power as their new counterparts, albeit that, as previously, its exercise was (normally) legally confined to their own parishes, unlike

[170] NRO MS 12858/37, 31F2.

[171] NRO PS 21/7/6 Minutes of the Business.

[172] Taylor, "'No remedy'," pp. 67-88.

[173] Maureen Janet Scollan, *Parish constables versus police constables: policing early nineteenth-century Essex*, Open University PhD thesis, 2007, p. 81.

that of the post-1840 officers, who had countywide jurisdiction.[174] Significantly, after 1840, they were, in theory, subject to the authority and control of the chief constables of the new rural forces, these men effectively replacing high constables in this role.[175] (In practice, they were more often subject to the orders of their parish vestry and area magistrates.)[176]

Parish constables might still be punished by local JPs for their failings in office. For example, at the start of 1851, magistrates sitting at Reepham inquired into a series of disturbances and assaults at Lenwade, in which stones had been thrown at preachers leaving a chapel, something that had been prompted by a schism in the local Wesleyan congregation. They fined two parish constables, Samuel Fairman and John Elliott, 10 shillings each for refusing to carry out their duty to suppress the disturbances when requested to do so by the Reverend Charles Povah.[177]

It has sometimes been suggested that there was often barely disguised rivalry and mutual suspicion between the parish constables and the new police officers.[178] This may have been the case in some counties but was not necessarily the situation in Victorian Norfolk. In practice, it seems that the new police usually worked closely with traditional constables, often taking a coordinating and supervisory approach to the latter's work. For example, in January 1841 PC William Dye, who had lost his hat and truncheon during a fracas, while patrolling at night near Mundford, subsequently liaised with the parish constable in the village to arrange for their recovery.[179] At the Norfolk assizes in 1842, John Hastings, the Mundesley parish constable, noted that he had worked with an officer from the new force after hearing of a burglary, and "immediately went to North Walsham with Towncley, a [new] policeman." There they conducted a joint search of the suspect's premises, and both officers gave evidence at trial.[180]

A random selection of cases gives an indication of the continuing importance of parish constables to rural policing in Norfolk during the first half of the Victorian era. In 1842 Thomas Loveless, who was both the blacksmith and parish constable for Pulham St Mary in South Norfolk, took what transpired to be a legally inadmissible (at trial) confession from a juvenile murder suspect.[181] In 1847 William Bloomfield, a parish constable in Tibenham, gave evidence to an inquest about the local discovery

---

174 Cox, "Habitual Eccentricities," pp. 114-115.

175 Black, *The Police,* p. 29.

176 Cox, "Habitual Eccentricities," pp. 114-115.

177 *The Norfolk Chronicle*, 20 January, 1851. *The Leicester Chronicle,* 11 January, 1851. *The Morning Post,* 31 January, 1851.

178 Cox, "Habitual Eccentricities," pp. 114-115.

179 *The Bury and Norwich Post*, 14 April, 1841. *The Ipswich Journal*, 10 April, 1841.

180 *Ibid.*, 9 April, 1842.

181 *The Standard*, 13 November, 1841.

of a bottle that was allegedly used to hold arsenic.[182] A few years later, in 1853, when William Thompson was arrested for murder and robbery on the highway, two local parish constables were heavily involved in the initial investigation. At first there were few clues to go on, but late at night a local man visited one of the men, John Hook, and told him that he thought that he had recognised Thompson near the scene of the crime. Hook then alerted the other parish constable, and the two of them went to Thompson's house and woke him up. They then searched the house, examined his clothes (they found bloodstains), and asked him where his hatchet was (the murder weapon had been abandoned at the crime scene). He was then arrested, held overnight in a public house, and produced before two magistrates. Indicative of the intimacy of parochial life, Thompson had earlier used some of the money he secured from the robbery to pay off a debt he owed to one of the same parish constables.[183]

Less seriously, but probably more typically, at the Diss petty sessions in November 1864, a labourer named Robert Fulcher was charged by Robert Drivers, the parish constable of Winfarthing, with being drunk and disorderly in the same village and fined five shillings.[184] Similarly, in April 1872, when a group of German musicians became drunk and obstreperous in a public house in Diss, they were arrested with the assistance of a man named Olley, who was "one of the parish constables, who lived nearby and [who] had been sent for." Two of the musicians escaped but were later arrested by a member of the professional, post-1836 city force in Norwich.[185]

Decline in Parish Constables

The debate on the value of old-style rural parish constables continued after 1840. They remained popular with the public, not least because they were local and so both accountable and easily reached, while also being comparatively cheap. In 1853 the MP for Bath, George Scobell, still believed that, for a rural population, parochial constables were "far preferable to a rural police."[186] However, their critics continued to reiterate the traditional objections to such officers. In 1853 Henry Dover, chairman of the Norfolk quarter sessions, still thought that the individual selected to be a local constable might be the "most unfit man in the parish."[187] The chief constable for Norfolk was still complaining in 1856 that they were often reluctant to leave their work to search for thieves, would not go anywhere without a guarantee that their expenses would be covered, and were swayed by local pressure.[188] More generally, the MP for Dover, Edward Rice, claimed that the evidence clearly showed that they

182 *The Times*, 1 May, 1847, p. 7.

183 *The Ipswich Journal*, 26 November, 1853. *The Morning Chronicle*, 21 November, 1853.

184 *The Bury and Norwich Post*, 29 November, 1864.

185 *The Ipswich Journal*, 27 April, 1872.

186 Hansard HC Deb 26 April, 1853 vol. 126 cols. 545-52.

187 *The Morning Chronicle*, 26 July, 1853

188 Black, *The Police*, pp. 1-52.

remained "unfit for the duties of police, and in consequence of their local connexions they were particularly unqualified to control public-houses and beer-shops."[189]

It seems that by the 1860s an improvement in the number and professional ability of the new rural police had encouraged a gradual fall in both the use and appointment of traditional constables. Even so, men were regularly selected for the position until the Parish Constables Act 1872 (35 and 36 Viet., c. 92) declared that, because such officers were often no longer needed, they were not to be appointed to a particular parish unless the local county quarter sessions had first determined by resolution that they were necessary. Where there was an appropriate quarter-sessions resolution, the vestry's role in appointing such officers was transferred to the parish council. However, the 1872 Act still required parish overseers to list potential constables and that anyone chosen to act in this capacity would still be bound to do so, or to submit another suitable person to the justices to be appointed in his stead.[190]

In practice, quarter-sessions resolutions seeking the appointment of parish constables were quite rare. Even so, they appear to have been appointed or present in some parts of Norfolk until the end of the Victorian era, even if, by then, their duties were often very modest. For example, in March 1895 it was reported that three men (a slightly unusual number), William Mullinger, Henry Yovell, and William Palmer, had been appointed as parish constables at Pulham St Mary in the south of the county.[191] Mullenger is recorded as living in the village in the 1891 census, having been born there in 1851, making his age about 44 when he was selected. He was a married man with three children. Norfolk was certainly not unique in this. The simultaneous appointment of a dozen parish constables in 11 East Cambridgeshire villages, including Soham and Fordham, along with other parish officers, was formally announced in the press in April 1887.[192] Of course, some late Victorian constables may have been long-serving, pre-1872 appointments who had survived in office, while it is at least possible that others had been appointed in a less formally recognised manner than by a quarter-sessions resolution.

Parish constables continued to play a very limited and declining role in policing after 1872. Occasionally, they made the news. For example, Thomas Bett Gell, a one-eyed 53-year-old wheelwright and parish constable for Hemingby in Lincolnshire, was killed late one evening in October 1876 by William Drant, the local blacksmith, when he intervened to protect the latter's mother from assault.[193] In Norfolk their residual role was less dramatic. Late one night in February 1873, two men attempted to steal dozens of chickens from a farmer's shed, breaking the birds' necks as they put them in a sack. The farmer confronted them, but his gun failed to go off. The three men

---

189 Hansard,Hansard, HC Deb 26 April, 1853 vol. 126 col. 545.

190 *Ibid.*, HC Deb 01 March 1895 vol 31 cols. 154-5.

191 *The Ipswich Journal*, 30 March, 1895.

192 *The Bury and Norwich Post*, 12 April, 1887.

193 *The Daily Gazette For Middlesbrough*, 29 November, 1876.

then grappled fiercely. One intruder ran off, but the farmer got the better of the other, his yardman and his wife helping him tie up the suspect. The farmer "sent for the parish constable, who sent word that he would come in the morning."[194] Perhaps his rather lackadaisical attitude reflected the reduced importance of the office.

In September 1875, after Henry Webster stabbed and killed his wife, Sarah, following a heated argument, he walked to Southburgh in the Breckland area of the county, and gave himself up to the parish constable, saying that he "wanted to keep with him until he could fetch a policeman" (a county police force officer in this context). He also took the opportunity to pay off a small debt that he owed the same officer, the two men being socially acquainted.[195] Less seriously, in early 1890, Mr Yallop, the parish constable of Bramerton, discovered a very confused local clergyman, who had had been missing for several days, in a plantation. Yallop had him conveyed to hospital in Norwich.[196] In July 1895 Arthur Whitehead, a (possibly elderly and long-serving) parish constable was called to give rather inconsequential evidence at petty sessions about an election disturbance and assault involving Lord Wodehouse at Ludham, near the Broads.[197]

Railway Police in Norfolk

The rapidly expanding Victorian rail network, with large quantities of valuable but unattended merchandise being moved around the country, provided ready opportunities for offending. The various railway companies quickly established their own police forces, if only to reduce claims for compensation. When four rail companies united in August 1862 to form the Great Eastern Railway (GER), two of them already had their own police forces. These joined to form the GER Police, which protected the railways in Norfolk and other Eastern counties. In 1902 the force had 226 men, led by a superintendent based at Liverpool Street Station in London. It was quickly called into action after establishment.

For example, in 1866 a conspiracy between all three members of a GER train crew (a driver, fireman, and guard) was found to be behind a series of thefts of large amounts of valuable goods on their way to Norwich. Each man had covered and provided alibis for the other two, making detection difficult. The ring was eventually broken up by the labours of Mr Russell, the police superintendent responsible for the GER goods' department, assisted by the Norwich police. A publican from the city, who had fenced some of the goods, was also arrested, with stolen boots found hidden on his premises. James Clarke, the fireman, was caught red-handed in Wymondham

---

194 *The Bury and Norwich Post*, 25 February, 1873.

195 *The Leicester Chronicle*, 25 September ,1875.

196 *The Bury and Norwich Post*, 18 March, 1890.

197 *The Standard*, 31 July, 1895.

while purloining bundles of cloth and putting them into a horse-drawn truck that was on its way to Norwich.[198]

Special Constables

Special constables were ad hoc, temporary police officers who were appointed and sworn in to assist the authorities in towns or rural areas in preserving the public peace during emergencies. They were first formally recognised by statute in 1662, although their roots were even older. Acts from the reign of William IV (1 and 2 Wm. IV., c. 41, and 5 and 6 Wm. IV, c. 43) regulated their appointment. In 1831 a statute authorized magistrates to appoint as many special constables as they deemed necessary if local disorder were threatened. Such men were normally drawn from householders and possessed of modest levels of property. In the countryside they might be small farmers and gamekeepers, while in the towns they would often be shopkeepers, merchants, and skilled craftsmen, such as gold- and silversmiths. Their period of service was determined by the magistrates, and, if appropriate men refused to be sworn in, they could be fined £5. The normal maximum service was three months.[199] In 1837 the Norfolk magistrates were reminded by the Attorney General that such officers could be appointed only temporarily and should be reappointed if needed later. Expenses and modest remuneration for their trouble, loss of time, and any attendant disbursements occasioned by embodied service could be approved by county JPs.[200]

Special constables were granted all the "powers, authorities, advantages and immunities" accorded to ordinary constables. In 1835 statute authorized them to act outside their own parishes and townships, unlike parish constables. They were normally issued with staves, which they had to hand in within a week of their appointment's being terminated. Firearms could be issued by the Board of Ordnance, with permission from the Home Secretary, but this was not usually done, although, in 1839, Lord John Russell directed JPs in particularly troubled districts to provide cutlasses and pistols if necessary. In August 1842 Robert Peel's government rescinded this directive, advising JPs to call for military assistance instead.[201]

Special constables were regularly appointed during the first half of the nineteenth century, including the early Victorian period, especially in periods of strife. In Norfolk many were recruited during the 1830s to deal with the Swing Riots and (subsequently) clusters of Chartist activity. It was not always a popular duty; in December 1830 residents of Holt who faced being recruited argued that it was likely to inflame the local situation and should not be done until there was a disturbance

---

198 *The Ipswich Journal*, 31 March, 1866.

199 Black, *The Police of England,* p. 30.

200 *The Bury and Norwich Post*, 15 March, 1837.

201 R.E. Swift, "Policing Chartism, 1839-1848: The Role of the 'Specials' Reconsidered," *The English Historical Review*, vol. 122, no. 497 (2007), pp. 669-699.

in the town.[202] More officers were appointed to deal with, inter alia, disturbances in 1842 and 1851. In Norfolk the growing efficiency of the police meant that the use of special constables waned after the mid-century, although in other parts of the country large numbers were appointed to deal with emergencies. For example, 4,000 were sworn in at Liverpool in 1911 to deal with industrial unrest.

Military Aid to the Civil Power

The military, whether regular or part-time volunteer soldiers, provided the next level of state power above the police. JPs could request help from troops or embodied yeomanry (volunteer cavalry) if they felt that the threat to law and order required it.[203] Eighteenth and early nineteenth-century Norfolk, like other parts of England, saw regular recourse to the army both to deal with major public disturbances and for more quotidian forms of policing, such as prisoner escort or securing scaffolds. In 1835, for instance, men in Great Bircham and Bircham Tofts rioted over fears that labourers were being imported from neighbouring villages, attacking the houses of two local farmers. Two troops of yeomanry, based in Melton and Rainham, were called out to quell the disturbance.[204]

However, employing the military for policing was increasingly seen to be against the spirit of the age. At the start of the Victorian period the part-time yeoman cavalry still suffered from the stain of their involvement in the Peterloo Massacre of 1819. In 1839 Sir Charles Napier, the military commander of the troubled northern district of England, held that it was not "decent" to have the law upheld by soldiers on a regular basis. He thought that disorder should, where possible, be contained by police and special constables, without recourse to the army. His views reflected wider sentiment. In 1853 the MP Joseph Hume claimed that one of the great evils of maintaining a large military establishment was that it tempted magistrates to call out soldiers to repress disturbances. He, too, thought that an effective police system in every county was the only way to avoid this.[205] Similarly, George Black, the chief constable of Norfolk, noted in 1856 that if armed troops were thought to be unfitting instruments for the suppression of tumults and the support of civil authority, the police necessarily became "an indispensable engine for ensuring the safety of life and property and for preserving internal peace and social order." [206]

Using the army was not ideal for practical as well as political reasons. Soldiers themselves could be responsible for local disorder. For example, in 1861 a serious disturbance took place between troops based in Yarmouth. Men of the Royal Artillery and the East Norfolk Militia clashed, belts and stones being freely used

202 *The Bury and Norwich Post*, 1 December,1830.

203 Philips, "A 'Weak' State?" pp. 873-891.

204 *The Norfolk Chronicle*, 29 June, 1835.

205 Hansard HC Deb 26 April 1853 vol 126 cols. 545-52.

206 Black, *The police*, p. 2.

to inflict injury. Escalation was only narrowly avoided, with strong pickets being stationed to keep the units apart.[207]

Nevertheless, it was not always possible to avoid recourse to the military in the early decades of the Victorian era. In March 1842 there were disturbances at King's Lynn following a reduction in the wages given to local coal porters and sailors. The new rural police were summoned (the borough force presumably being seen as inadequate), and special constables sworn in, but it was still felt necessary to send for a troop of cavalry from the 13th Light Dragoons, who were based in Norwich. Several of the ringleaders of the disturbance were arrested and sent to prison.[208]

More seriously, in early 1851, a riot occurred at Yarmouth following serious unrest amongst local sailors about wages and conditions. Although special constables were sworn in, the full-time embodied members of the East Norfolk Militia and elements of the Coast Guard were also called out to keep the rioters in check, and special trains from Norwich conveyed two troops of the 11th Hussars to assist in quelling the disturbance. On arrival, the cavalry rode through the town, and quickly cleared the streets: "The rioters, frightened by the mere appearance of the troops, flew in every direction up the narrow rows of the town, and in a few hours tranquillity was restored." It was thought that any delay in the deployment of the soldiers would have been disastrous. Several of the rioters were subsequently tried at quarter sessions on 6 March, when, to the surprise of the court, but with numerous historical precedents in similar situations, a verdict of "not guilty" was returned by the jury.[209]

Nevertheless, routine military aid to the civil power became much less common in the country as the century advanced, largely disappearing in mainly rural areas in the 1850s and 1860s, although there was some service involvement in security during the Fenian troubles of the 1870s.[210] (As Norfolk contained relatively few Irishmen, this was not a major issue in the county.) Nationally, troops were still used for occasional major emergencies in cities or industrial areas, such as the disturbances at Featherstone Colliery in Yorkshire in 1893, when (very unusually) two men were shot and killed, and others wounded; this type of incident did not normally trouble Norfolk.[211]

---

207 *The Norfolk Chronicle,* 20 May, 1861.

208 *Ibid.,* 23 March, 1842.

209 *The Ipswich Journal*, 1 March, 1851.

210 John Briggs et al., *Crime and Punishment in England* (Abingdon: Routledge, 2016), p. 145.

211 Fred Corbett, "The Military Estate in the North of England 1790 to 1914–Shaped by Changing Military Priorities," *Northern History*, vol. 59, no. 1 (2022), pp. 71-97.

Public Assistance to the Police

Traditionally, such basic aspects of law enforcement as crime detection and pursuit and arrest of the criminal were left to members of the public. When these tasks were taken over by the police, the public were still obliged at common law to assist them in the execution of their duty when requested (as is the case today). However, in practice, this was a less frequent occurrence than had been the case with the old parish constables. The new police acquired a dominance of law enforcement that sometimes marginalised public participation in the pursuit of offenders.[212] Indeed, by the end of the 1850s, there were fears that their presence was encouraging people to abdicate personal responsibility for dealing with crime, as had formerly been the case, and leaving it to the constabulary. For example, after a respectable tradesman was murdered near Andover, in Wiltshire, it was noted that five local people had ignored his cries of "Murder!"[213]

When made, police requests for assistance were not always complied with, not least because of the dangers that might be involved. In November 1855, at the East Dereham petty sessions, James Guyton, a local publican, was summonsed by one PC Oakley for refusing to help when requested to do so, earlier in the month. The constable did not pursue the charge and stated that he had summsoned him as a warning to others, and to make him understand that he was compelled to assist a police officer when called upon. Guyton was merely ordered to pay prosecution expenses of 7 shillings.[214]

Nevertheless, members of the public often did still fulfil this duty, assisting police constables with searches and restraining suspects when requested, just as they had helped parish constables in the previous century, and far more commonly than is the case today. For example, in 1867, after Benjamin Black was murdered in a plantation at Barton Bendish, the police organized a search involving 200 local people that turned up important evidence.[215]

Personal Law Enforcement

Before the Victorian era, if traditional parish constables were not up to the task, citizens would often pitch in. For example, in 1825 a gang of six men broke into cottages near Reepham while their occupants were away, stealing anything of value they came across. On being discovered, they were pursued by farm workers, overpowered after a fierce fight, and conveyed to Norwich Castle prison.[216] In 1832 Susan Gayton, a 23-year-old married woman, was convicted at the Norfolk quarter sessions of stealing meat from a butcher's shop in Downham Market and sentenced

---

212 Churchill, "Rethinking the state," p. 132.

213 *The Spectator*, 1 January, 1859, p. 21.

214 *The Norwich Mercury,* 14 November, 1855.

215 *The Bury and Norwich Post*, 21 May, 1867.

216 *The Morning Post*, 7 September, 1825.

to a year's imprisonment (she had a previous conviction). The butcher had noticed that meat had gone missing when she had been in his shop on earlier occasions and resolved to watch her closely. He eventually caught her in the act.[217] The offer of private rewards was also commonplace. Typically, in April 1825 George Gulyer offered a guinea as a reward for the recovery of a horse that had been stolen from his stable in Mattishall. A detailed description of the animal was provided.[218]

Such private initiatives continued long after the advent of the new police, if at a declining level. For example, in early 1841 John Hunter of Barwick noticed the loss of numerous sheep fleeces from the granary where they were stored. Eventually, his yardman strewed the granary's floor with barley meal and marked the building's lock. When they next missed some wool, the men followed the tracks of two people in the meal out of the granary and over adjacent fields, locating tufts of wool as they went, these producing a trail that led almost to a suspect's door in the neighbouring village of Stanhoe. They then searched his cottage and found and identified the missing fleeces and, in another building, discovered a picklock.[219] Five years later, after William Clarke's silver watch was stolen in Thetford, he had its loss "cried in the town by the Town Crier." (It subsequently turned up at a pawnbroker's shop in Bury St Edmunds).[220] In 1858 William Tyrell became suspicious that someone was stealing oats and corn from his farm in Diss. He set his brother to keep watch, and the latter secreted himself in the stable where the grain was stored. He had been there only a short while when two men came in and helped themselves to the contents of a corn bin. Both were convicted at the Norfolk quarter sessions.[221]

Fragmentation and Liaison

Perhaps unsurprisingly, it was regularly suggested, both in official reports and informally, that the high degree of fragmentation in English provincial policing was counterproductive. It was often argued that the police forces in smaller (or even all) boroughs should be incorporated into their surrounding county forces, while larger borough forces should be made accountable in the same way as those for the counties.[222] According to Captain Dunne, head of the Norwich force in the early 1850s, most of the inhabitants of Norwich would not have been concerned had an amalgamation between the rural and city police forces taken place, but the latter's watch committee would not countenance such a measure.[223]

---

217 *The Bury and Norwich Post*, 18 January, 1832.

218 *The Norwich Mercury*, 9 April, 1825.

219 *The Bury and Norwich Post*, 7 April, 1841.

220 *The Ipswich Journal*, 17 January, 1846.

221 *The Bury and Norwich Post*, 30 March, 1875.

222 *Ibid.*, 27 July, 1853.

223 *Ibid.*, 13 July, 1853.

Nevertheless, from their foundation, Norfolk's various police forces seem to have been able to operate outside their bounds, even if this meant crossing county lines, while liaison with other national police forces, let alone those found within Norfolk itself, seems to have been quite good. For example, in 1837, after Henry Downing stole a watch, four sovereigns, and some clothes in Thetford, "the prisoner was traced to Bury [Suffolk] by the Thetford officer, and taken with the property on him."[224] Similarly, in 1846, PC Tyler, another Thetford policeman, followed a barmaid to Bury after she stole a watch in the Green Dragon. There, he arrested her and found and identified the timepiece in a local pawnbroker's shop.[225]

In 1867 Jane Garron, from South Shields, who found that she was pregnant by a lover shortly after becoming engaged to marry another man, who was unaware of her condition, went to Peterborough, where she had the baby, and then on to Great Yarmouth, where she suffocated and abandoned him. She then returned to her hometown and married her fiancé. Inspector Berry of the Yarmouth Police tracked her there, with an arrest warrant, which he enforced while accompanied by a superintendent from the local borough police. She was then taken back to the coastal town.[226]

In another example of the forces' cooperation, in October 1840 Edward Websdale was indicted at the Old Bailey in London for stealing a pewter pot valued at just 1 shilling from John Howard, who ran the Swan public house in Hungerford Market. At his trial, Henry Mount, a superintendent in the new Norfolk County Police, based at Brinton, gave evidence that he had searched a bundle that had been left by the defendant at Melton Constable, finding seven pots, one of which he identified as coming from the Swan. Howard confirmed that it was from his establishment. Clearly, Mount had contacted his Metropolitan counterparts about his discovery, as well as travelling to the capital to testify against the suspect.[227]

In September 1888 a more sophisticated piece of policing secured the arrest of a railway thief. At 1:30 am Sergeant Lovick was on duty in Cromer (by then a popular resort) when he encountered Edward Dodd, who appeared suspicious but claimed to have missed the last train back to Ipswich. The sergeant searched him and found a small amount of change but nothing untoward. He directed Dodd to the train station. The next day it was reported that there had been a break-in at the station, and that a desk in the clerk's office had been forced and money taken. The sergeant immediately suspected the man he had met the previous night and searched the town's public houses for him. After informing his superintendent at North Walsham, he went to Norwich and told officers in the city force and in the railway police about the man he was seeking. Not picking up his suspect's trail, he went on to Ipswich in Suffolk, and spoke to the chief constable there, who gave him the assistance of a

224 *Ibid.*, 18 October, 1837.

225 *The Ipswich Journal*, 17 January, 1846.

226 *The Liverpool Mercury*, 10 October, 1867.

227 OBSP Edward Websdale, 19 October, 1840, t18401019-2571.

detective sergeant from the local force. They searched the town and eventually saw a man who resembled the suspect but who, after a short pursuit, gave them the slip. Nothing daunted, Lovick moved on to Colchester in Essex and was given the assistance of another local constable. Eventually they identified the suspect walking down a street and arrested him after a brief struggle. He was found in possession of a stolen medal and boots. On the journey back to Cromer, Dodd told Lovick that he would plead guilty, and that had he had a knife when detained he would have got away.[228]

---

228 *The Ipswich Journal*, 7 September, 1888.

Chapter 3: Aspects of Policing

Introduction

This chapter will consider aspects of the new professional police forces that came on stream in Norfolk in 1836 and 1840, including recruitment to, and turnover in, the county force, popular attitudes towards the police, the dangers inherent in policing, the accountability of the police, as well as their senior command, day-to-day operation, and detective work.

County Police Recruits

Police recruits throughout provincial England had similar backgrounds. Given that the provinces supplied many Metropolitan Police officers, that force valuing agricultural workers for their strength, stoicism, perceived honesty, and social deference, they were often not dissimilar to many of their counterparts in the capital. Norfolk appears to have been a particularly popular source of recruits for the two London forces. Indeed, in one Norfolk parish it was noted that "thirty-one sons of the soil have been enrolled as London policemen in thirty years–the very pick of the parish."[229]

Considering the county's neighbour, in East Suffolk, between 1840 and 1900, 48 percent of rural police recruits were labourers, while 38 percent of those in the separate Ipswich borough force had a similar background.[230] Others were drawn from a variety of trades, such as baking and blacksmithing, or specialist agricultural work. Recruits to the Norfolk Rural, Norwich, Thetford, King's Lynn, and Great Yarmouth forces were from broadly similar social backgrounds, though they manifest slightly less bias towards agricultural occupations.

Men joining the Norfolk County Police Force in the 1850s tended to be in their twenties. None was younger, although a few were in their early thirties. They were fit and healthy, with a significant number over six feet in height and most being more than five foot, nine inches tall, which was significantly above average by the standards of the time, even in non-urban areas (albeit typical for rural policemen throughout the country). All could read and write, which was a requirement of enlistment, as it was elsewhere in England. Most were drawn from unskilled or modestly skilled manual occupations, although a few were qualified craftsmen. For example, William Dye, an early recruit, was a former Norwich weaver, escaping a local trade that was in terminal decline. The vast majority were Norfolk born, with a few being military veterans and a small number having been in other police forces or having served as traditional parish constables in the county. (It can be noted that the urban forces in the county were quite similar in recruit-profile, although the age limits were more relaxed.)

---

229 Neil Phillip, *Victorian Village Life* (Idbury: The Albion Press, 1993), p. 112.

230 Taylor, *The New Police*, p. 48.

Turnover

Initially there was a very high turnover of men in all the Norfolk forces, a pattern that was found almost everywhere in England when the new police were introduced. There were several reasons for this. Discipline was strict, with infractions being punished harshly. Many officers were dismissed for, inter alia, being drunk on duty, absent from their beats, or disobeying orders. Although they were normally ordinary workingmen in origin – indeed, often drawn from the same class as the poachers they confronted – officers were expected to eschew many aspects of working-class culture, such as frequenting public houses and attending popular entertainments such as prize-fights. They were supposed to be "respectable" in their lifestyles and relationships. Many found this isolating and difficult. As George Sturt observed of a rural village in Victorian Surrey, "There is probably no lonelier man in the parish than the constable."[231]

Furthermore, their lives were physically hard and the rewards comparatively modest. The work, with its emphasis on patrolling, was often arduous, and leisure-time scarce. The pocketbook of one Norfolk constable reveals that between February 1845 and August 1846 he took just two days off work, and these were to attend his mother's funeral.[232] The position carried some physical dangers and attracted a degree of active hostility (see below). The remuneration provided was relatively modest, often matching the very best rates found on farms, although allowance should be made for housing benefits and, later in the period, the possibility of a pension. Prospects for promotion beyond constable were extremely small, even for those who made a career of policing, although the introduction of differing grades of police constable eventually allowed modest intra-rank promotion. Nevertheless, it seems that nationally, only about 10 percent of English police officers rose above constable. Thus, in 1879 the Norfolk rural force had 236 officers of all ranks, of whom 201 were constables, 11 were sergeants, nine inspectors, and 14 superintendents, along with the single chief constable.[233]

The demands of being a rural constable, in particular the need for physical fitness and a degree of self-reliance and judgment, required men of some quality, who could often command decent wages in other lines of work. This was important, as most new police recruits in the 1830s and 1840s were seeking employment, and a regular wage when it was otherwise scarce, rather than following a vocation. When the economy picked up, the number coming forward fell. As a result, in October 1853 the chief constable for Norfolk noted that the then high pay commanded by skilled men, and even some unskilled agricultural workers, had created recruiting problems for his force. Some officers had left, and it had become harder to recruit suitable replacements. This meant that a quarter of his constables had been appointed in the previous year. Even worse, manning pressures meant that they were being

[231] Phillip, *Victorian Village Life*, p. 112.

[232] Taylor, *The New Police*, p. 52.

[233] *Judicial Statistics, 1879*, p. 2.

sent out to their duties on rural beats without first serving a period of supervised probation, and with almost no preliminary instruction.[234] This problem also affected the borough forces. At one point, Robert Hitchman, the chief constable of Norwich from 1859 to 1897, suggested that if a constable were offered a shilling a week more than his police wage of 22 shillings for agricultural work, he would usually accept it and leave his force.[235]

As a result of these two factors, many new officers served for short periods of time before either being dismissed or resigning from their positions. For example, Charles Hawkins was quite young (21) and tall (6 feet, 4 inches) when he joined the county force in 1856. He was a single man, and his previous employment had been as a labourer at Claxton, although he was born in Norwich. He was recruited in January 1856 and dismissed from the force for being drunk at Downham Fair in November 1857.[236] Francis Meek was age 27 and 6 foot, 2 inches tall, when recruited. He was a married labourer who had been born in Loddon, had seen service in the East Norfolk Militia, was a former railway employee, and had even served for three months in the Metropolitan Police. He was recruited in August 1856 and voluntarily resigned in June 1860. Robert Moller was 22 years old, 5 foot, 9 inches tall, a carrier by trade, single, and originally from Dereham. He was recruited in December 1856 and dismissed in May 1857 for being absent from his duties.[237]

Inevitably, more serious offences than simple drunkenness were also committed by officers, although they could not always be proved. Shortly after its establishment, Robert Rust was discharged as a constable from the Norwich force and committed to prison for ten days for low-level electoral corruption, despite having a previously good record.[238] Less than a year after its inception, one of the first county superintendents, James Adams, who was resident at East Dereham, allegedly started living beyond his means of £150 a year, and was thought to have been pocketing his constables' wages to do so, while forging their signatures on a form that attested to their receiving the money. He fled to Herefordshire, but was arrested, returned to Norfolk, and taken before the magistrates who committed him to Norwich gaol, to await trial for forgery at the assizes.[239] Nevertheless, in April 1841, aided by two barristers and a sympathetic judge, he was speedily acquitted of all charges. It appears to have been accepted by the jury that this was a case of an irregularity in filling in forms, which may have been contrary to police regulations, but not a felony.[240] He was not the only man of this rank to come before the courts, a phenomenon which was

---

234 *The Bury and Norwich Post*, 26 October, 1853.

235 Taylor, *The New Police*, p. 49.

236 *Norfolk Constabulary Force*, p. 64.

237 *Ibid.*, p. 93, p. 108.

238 *The Bury & Norwich Post, & East Anglian*, 30 August, 1837.

239 *John Bull*, 12 December, 1840, p. 597.

240 *The Ipswich Journal*, 17 April, 1841.

certainly not confined to East Anglia and could involve much worse allegations. One early Victorian superintendent in Herefordshire was accused of raping a 17-year-old girl, albeit eventually acquitted.[241]

In the latter years of the century, the turnover of men slowed down considerably; the boroughs, where the typical recruit had been somewhat older than in the counties, also started to attract younger men, who, more significantly, served for longer before leaving. This was helped by a significant increase in police wages during the late Victorian period, at a time when prices for some commodities, especially foodstuffs, were falling. A core of career officers slowly emerged, who would spend most of their working lives in service, provide a force with its sergeants and higher officers (although most did not progress so far), and eventually retire on a pension. Initially, these were a matter of discretion for the relevant county. Thus, at the Norfolk quarter sessions in January 1857, and with the agreement of the assembled JPs, a police superintendent and a constable from the county force were retired on a pension of 16 shillings and 7 shillings a week respectively.[242] However, pensions eventually became standard for long-serving officers, being received by about a fifth of departing officers at the end of the century.

The process of professionalization was probably encouraged in the Norfolk forces, both borough and county, by the recruitment of several very long-serving chief constables. For example, when Robert Hitchman, who had been chief constable of Norwich, died at the age of 72 in 1898, it was noted that he had been appointed in March 1859 and retired in April 1897, after giving some 38 years of service to the city.[243] (The Norwich City Council had granted him a retiring pension of £273 6s. 8d the previous year as a token of appreciation.)[244]

Although it took time for the new police forces established during the nineteenth century to develop an *esprit de corps*, whether in the capital or the provinces, there were signs that this was being achieved by the later decades of the Victorian era, in Norfolk as elsewhere in the country. Perhaps indicative of this, police sporting societies sprang up. In 1878, a four-oared boat race took place between a crew of the 21st Hussars and one drawn from the Norwich Police, over a mile and a quarter. The police crew won after a very close contest.[245]

---

241 Timothy Shakesheff, *Rural Conflict, Crime and Protest: Herefordshire, 1800-1860* (Woodbridge: Boydell Press, 2003), p. 71.

242 *The Bury and Norwich Post*, 13 January, 1857.

243 *The Norfolk Chronicle*, 7 May, 1898.

244 *Ibid.*, 19 January, 1897.

245 *Ibid.*, 2 October, 1878.

Hostility to the New Police

Initially, hostility to the new police in Norfolk was widespread, as it was elsewhere in England, even if it was found only amongst a minority of the political nation. It was not just the rural force that attracted antipathy. In May 1838 John Nixon, a Thetford police officer, wrote to a regional paper decrying what he thought had been a biased but anonymous report in a previous edition as to how the new borough police in the town had dealt with a primitive Methodist preacher. The clergyman had been arrested and fined 5 shillings by magistrates for obstructing traffic. Nixon noted that there had been problems with the "groans and loud vociferations" of members of this sect, which apparently disturbed their neighbours.[246] However, because the introduction of borough forces in 1836 represented less of a change in what had already been relatively highly policed environments, and there were considerable continuities when it came to policing and personnel, they attracted less initial hostility than did their rural counterparts a few years later.

At first antipathy to the new county force transcended social class. For example, in early 1840 four Norfolk gentlemen who had ridden in a steeplechase held near Fakenham dined at an inn there. They became intoxicated and created a disturbance. The new rural police attended, threatening to take the quartet into custody. They were then the victims of what was termed a "genteel assault" during which four officers were seriously injured. The case came before the quarter sessions held at Walsingham, where the four gentlemen pleaded guilty to assault. The chairman, Lord James Townshend, noted that nobody had opposed the introduction of the new police more strongly than he. However, now that they were on duty, they would have his full protection. Each man was fined £50 (a modest punishment for wealthy individuals) and required to enter sureties of £300 to keep the peace in future.[247]

At the other end of the social scale, some indication of the resistance faced by the new county force in 'rough' rural areas can be seen in a cluster of petty sessions cases that were heard at Downham Market in June 1849. For some time prior to this a "portion of the labourers belonging to West Dereham, Wereham, and Hilgay, and the surrounding parishes, have taken a dislike to the police and sought every means to obstruct them in the execution of their duty." So strong had this been that, until shortly beforehand, no county police officer had been regularly stationed in West Dereham, although (and significantly) a traditional parish constable continued to be appointed there.[248]

Nevertheless, due to persistent misconduct by young men in the area who allegedly obtained their living by poaching and other dishonest practices, it was decided to station a rural police officer in the parish. This then precipitated a conspiracy to drive him away. During large-scale drunken disturbances in late May and early June

[246] *The Bury and Norwich Post*, 16 May, 1838.

[247] *The Champion*, 12 April, 1840.

[248] *The Norwich Mercury*, 16 June, 1849.

1849, police officers were assaulted while on duty, often being pelted with volleys of stones and told to leave. About a dozen men and one woman were convicted at lengthy petty sessions in mid-June, during which the police struggled to maintain order among an attending crowd of fellow labourers. The two JPs who made up the bench imposed large fines of up to £10, with up to two months' imprisonment in lieu of payment. Most of those found guilty could not pay the sums involved and were taken into custody.[249]

A modest degree of official hostility also survived for some time after the new rural police went on duty. At a meeting of the county magistrates held at the Norwich Shirehall, at the start of 1842, the Earl of Orford noted that some parts of the county had asked to be exempted from having to fund and be policed by the new force. He also presented a petition with numerous signatures asking for "considerable change, if not a total abrogation, of the police force, as the introduction of the force had not decreased either the number of robberies or cases of vagrancy." However, by then this was clearly a minority view. Indeed, the Reverend J.C. Collyer presented a counter-petition from the clergy, landowners, and inhabitants of Reepham asking that there be no alteration in the county police, who they said had been highly effective. A resolution was unanimously adopted affirming their approval, and thanking Colonel Oakes, the chief constable, for his work in forming the new force.[250]

As elsewhere in England, the middle and upper classes, including those who had initially opposed their introduction, were most swiftly reconciled to the new police, something that meant that most JPs and other officials also became enthusiastic supporters. In early 1844 official communications from Norfolk and Essex actively encouraged those parts of Suffolk that had not acquired their own rural police force to follow suit.[251] In June 1849 the magistrates at the Downham petty sessions dealing with alleged attacks on the county police (see above) declared that they did not have the slightest reason to doubt the police evidence, notwithstanding the witnesses who had been called for the defence, and "expressed their determination, in every case, to protect the police who had the most onerous duty to perform."[252]

Hostility from workingmen was much longer lasting, although the animosity often seen immediately following the introduction of the new police eventually abated into tacit, if frequently uneasy, acceptance. As George Sturt, the late-Victorian writer on rural life in Surrey, a police officer was often mentioned with the same "grudging caution which the villagers use in speaking of unfriendly property-owners, as though he belonged to that alien caste." Constables, largely drawn from the working-class, had to police their social counterparts, so that officiousness and heavy-handedness were quickly resented.

[249] *Ibid.*

[250] *The Norfolk Chronicle,* 7 January, 1842.

[251] *The Essex Standard*, 22 March, 1844.

[252] *The Norwich Mercury*, 16 June, 1849.

Illustrative of this, at the Norfolk Assizes in April 1877 William Duffell was indicted for criminal libel against two police officers. The defendant owned a sweet shop in Yarmouth and had often traded on a Sunday. The local police had repeatedly prosecuted him for this offence, which attracted a small fine under a town byelaw. On one occasion, a constable had asked children for some of their sweets, after they had made a Sabbath purchase, presumably to make sure that he could confirm that confectionery had been traded when giving evidence in court. This finally prompted Duffell to action. He had handbills printed and distributed accusing the local chief constable or "head bluebottle" (a widespread term of abuse for policemen) and the constable who had asked for the sweets (identified by number) of misconduct. This led to ridicule from townsmen, with people hooting at the constable and offering him sweets in the street. As a result, he claimed it was "horrible to him to go about." Duffell was convicted and sentenced to one month's imprisonment.[253]

There were more general reasons for working-class antipathy towards the police. For example, officers acquired a reputation for "hard swearing" (perjury), so that members of the judiciary were sometimes nervous about encouraging convictions on their uncorroborated evidence, even when it was provided by several constables.[254] This reputation extended to Norfolk, especially in the early days of the new force. At the Swaffham sessions in January 1842, counsel for a man accused of animal-maiming, and facing a largely circumstantial case, launched a fierce attack on the new county force in his closing speech to the jury, claiming that they "made up cases to gain applause and popularity, and that their evidence was too often such as could not be relied upon."[255]

The new police also sometimes had recourse to summary punishment of working-class children, something that could cause popular resentment. Nevertheless, there were limits as to how far this could go. For example, in July 1859 PC George Grimsey was charged before Suffolk magistrates with assaulting seven-year-old Alfred Boggish in Great Whelnetham. Boggis said that he had been chasing bullocks in a field and pulling their tails when the constable came along, broke a small stick from a hedge and beat him with it until he cried and ran away. After examining the boy's back in private, the magistrates told the defendant that he should be more careful about taking the law into his own hands and fined him 6d with 9s costs. (They also stated that the boy had richly deserved his treatment).[256]

Even so, at times, popular reaction to the police could be actively supportive, particularly as they became an accepted fact of life. Working people often had recourse to their assistance, and this frequently displaced informal, customary forms of dispute settlement. Inevitably, the level of such support was influenced by the

---

253 *The Bury and Norwich Post*, 3 April, 1877.

254 Thomas Wemyss Reid, *Briefs and Papers: Sketches of the Bar and the Press* (London: Henry S. King, 1872), p. 99.

255 *The Bury and Norwich Post*, 19 January, 1842.

256 *Ibid*. 26 July, 1859.

character of individual officers. In 1875 John Paget, a police-court observer, noted that where an officer did his duty without excessive harshness, even those pitted against him would treat him as an honourable enemy, to be feared and avoided, "to be defeated by stratagem, or if need by force; but he excites no feeling of hatred or malignity." When faced by decent officers, some suspects even gave themselves up without a struggle.[257]

Physical Dangers of Policing

Norfolk, especially its rural parts, was a relatively benign environment for policemen, and became more so after the early years of the new police, as initial hostility towards their more intrusive form of policing waned. This was a national phenomenon. Thus, Hampshire saw a major fall in assaults on the county police between their introduction in 1840 and 1850.[258] In 1872, within Norfolk's border, there were just 107 formally recorded assaults on police in the execution of their duty, and in 1873 there were only 75, most of them in Norwich and Yarmouth.[259] Little changed during the latter years of the period. In 1899 only 81 people in Norfolk were accused of assault on a constable in the execution of his duty and tried summarily.[260] Typical of such cases, at the Swaffham petty sessions in August 1865, a local labourer, Thomas Yull, was convicted of assaulting PC William Noy during a riot over an election for the western division of the county. Yull was fined £10, with 16s 6d in costs, and two months' imprisonment being specified in lieu of payment.

Doubtless, many minor assaults on policemen went entirely unrecorded, especially where there were more serious charges against their perpetrators, and they could be dealt with as an aggravating factor in these offences. In July 1845 William Spragg was convicted at quarter sessions for stealing five bushels of wheat from Sarah Bloomfield in Mattishall. The chairman, when passing sentence of seven years' Transportation, noted that Spragg, as well as having a bad criminal record, had "used great violence in resisting the police."[261] JPs could also be quite relaxed about technical assaults on police that did not result in tangible injury. At the Thetford borough sessions in July 1850, Mary Ann Woods was merely "severely reprimanded" by the recorder for abusing and assaulting local officers.[262] This might also occur where JPs thought that, in the words of a parliamentary report of 1875, police "indiscretion" had encouraged such attacks.[263]

---

257 Wood, "Self-Policing," pp. 109-128.

258 Shakesheff, *Rural Conflict*, p. 71.

259 *The Ipswich Journal*, 19 December, 1874.

260 Anon, *Statistics Relating to Criminal Proceedings, Police, Coroners, Prisons, Reformatory And Industrial Schools, And Criminal Lunatics For The Year 1899* (London: HMSO, 1901), p. 122.

261 *The Norfolk Chronicle*, 5 July 1845.

262 *The Bury and Norwich Post*, 24 July, 1850.

263 Wood, "Self-Policing," pp. 109-128.

In 1873 there were 13,463 assaults on policemen recorded in England and Wales, so that Norfolk's figure of 75 cases was well below the national average when considered on a per capita basis. This is partly explained by the disproportionate number of cases in major cities such as London and Manchester.[264] Nevertheless, extra-metropolitan Kent, which was more directly comparable, saw an annual average of 214 cases of assaulting the police between 1859 and 1880, a significantly higher rate than in Norfolk.[265]

Even so, there were periodic instances of very serious attacks on policemen in the county. Only one professional (rather than parish) police officer in Norfolk was killed by hostile action in the line of duty during the Victorian era (two more were murdered in the Edwardian period). PC William Callow of the Norwich City Police died in 1848. Callow, a 52-year-old officer, had enlisted shortly before reaching the (unusually high) 50-year age limit for the force and had been in poor health for 18 months before his death. During a major crowd disturbance caused by the introduction of new workhouse rules, local police were pelted with stones, although there were questions about their own degree of restraint. One rock struck the middle-aged officer on the head; he died from the effects of the blow a week later. At the inquest into his death, the jury returned a verdict of murder by a person or persons unknown.[266] So many stones had been lobbed, by so many people, that the perpetrator was never identified.

Several other Norfolk officers had very narrow escapes from fatal injury. The isolation and remoteness of much rural policing, the lack of ready assistance, and the solitary operations of many constables all made for potential danger. In October 1867, PC Henry Brooks was patrolling next to a field near Swafield during the small hours when he confronted two men who were armed with loaded coshes and carrying a sack. A vicious fight broke out, and the officer was knocked to the ground and beaten. Eventually he feigned death and the men left. He managed to crawl to a nearby cottage and received help from John Wortley and his wife, who summoned medical assistance and nursed the wounded constable for 15 weeks. Fragments of bone came from his skull and his life was in danger for several days, while it was feared that he would never be fit to return to duty. The two defendants, a miller and a labourer, were convicted at assizes of wounding with intent to do grievous bodily harm and sentenced to 20 years' penal servitude.[267] The county police force subsequently presented a silver gilt cup to Mr and Mrs Wortley in recognition of their assistance.[268]

---

264 *The Ipswich Journal*, 19 December, 1874.

265 Conley, *Unwritten Law*, p. 33.

266 *The Ipswich Journal*, 1 July, 1848.

267 *The Illustrated Police News*, 4 April, 1868.

268 *The Bury and Norwich Post*, 3 March, 1868,

Several more officers were shot, albeit not killed, while on duty. In February 1889, an apparent (if deranged) attempt was made to murder PC Southgate of the Norwich Police. Joseph Betts, a commission agent who had a history of sending threatening letters to the Bishop of Norwich, allegedly fired at Southgate with a small revolver, after speaking to him as he was returning from night duty.[269] The bullet narrowly missed, after which Betts ran off and barricaded himself in his home. Some 20 officers summoned from the central police station then went to his house to arrest him. While Inspector Gulett was preparing to climb a ladder to the bedroom window Betts fired again, the bullet hitting the peak of the inspector's cap, and inflicting a minor wound to his head. Betts was eventually seized without further injury and tried at the Norwich assizes on a charge of firing a pistol with intent to murder. He was convicted of the lesser offence of firing with intent to do grievous bodily harm and sentenced to 15 years' penal servitude.[270] As with all English forces, no police officers in Norfolk routinely carried firearms; the Home Secretary, the Marquess of Normanby, had expressly forbidden even superintendents in the new rural force to carry pistols as part of their normal duty.[271]

Effectiveness of the New Police

The new police presence probably made a major contribution to the decline in crime rates that appears to have occurred in England during the nineteenth century. Unsurprisingly, the chief constable for Norfolk gave a very reassuring picture of the performance of his force at a meeting of the county magistrates in October 1853. He claimed that, over the previous four months, three-quarters of reported crimes had been solved (to the extent of producing a prosecution), although the environs of Norwich provided something of an exception to the general situation (and allowed some responsibility to be attributed to the city police force). The chief constable also argued that much of the unsolved crime was relatively minor.[272] A few years later, at the county quarter sessions in January 1861, Colonel Black went even further and claimed that only 20 percent of all reported crimes had failed to produce a suspect and so gone undetected over the previous three months.[273] At the end of the period, in 1900, the Norfolk County Police still had an exceptionally high ratio of prosecutions to reported crimes. On one analysis, it was bettered only by that for Monmouthshire – it had 248 reported indictable crimes, but 264 people were prosecuted (some cases had multiple defendants and some had none). This produced a ratio of 106 people indicted for each 100 crimes reported.[274]

---

[269] *John Bull*, 30 June, 1883. *Norfolk Chronicle,* 21 February, 1889. *The Star,* 23 February, 1889.

[270] *The Norfolk Chronicle,* 21 February, 1889; *The Star,* 23 February, 1889.

[271] *The Champion*, 19 January, 1840.

[272] *The Bury and Norwich Post*, 26 October, 1853.

[273] *Ibid.*, 8 January, 1861.

[274] *Judicial Statistics 1900* (London: HMSO, 1901), p. 16.

In the Norfolk boroughs, the official picture was more mixed. In 1900 the Yarmouth force was ostensibly even better than its surrounding county. The borough saw 74 crimes reported and 88 people prosecuted, producing a ratio of 119 defendants per 100 reported crimes. By contrast, Norwich had one of the lowest ratios in the country, at 50 people prosecuted for each 100 reported crimes. (The City of London, at 36 people prosecuted, may have had the worst ratio.)[275]

Unfortunately, the variables in reporting and recording offences, along with the suspicious differences between neighbouring counties and cities (East Suffolk had one of the worst clear-up rates in the country, with a ratio of 60 people prosecuted for every 100 crimes reported), make these figures of very limited, if any, value. [276] Even so, the historian Victor Gatrell has argued that the emergence of a "policeman-state" was responsible for much of the apparent decline in crime in late-Victorian England. According to this analysis, many criminals of the era were devoid of sophistication and so vulnerable to even basic forms of policing. For example, well into the Victorian period, criminals often had recourse to various charms, rituals, and superstitions to avoid detection and capture, such as carrying a black pebble when burgling premises.[277] When James Fisk, a notorious Norfolk housebreaker, was apprehended at Surlingham in 1843, it was found that to avoid arrest he had sewed into the waistband of his trousers a copy of the Lord's Prayer "written backwards, which he carried about with him as a fancied protection against the power of human law."[278] According to Gatrell, such men made easy targets for the police, so that the Victorian era saw a historically rare success for policing when it came to fighting crime.[279]

It is certainly the case that the new police were readily able to tackle what had previously been ignored, or at least unprosecuted, crimes involving low-level street disorder, drunkenness, and vagrancy.[280] Typical of such cases, at the start of 1851, two police constables arrested three women in Downham Market and charged them with being prostitutes and behaving in a "riotous and disorderly manner" in the small town's streets. At the local petty sessions, they each received one month's imprisonment in the Wymondham Bridewell. One of the women, Sarah Souter, had been incarcerated for similar offences on five previous occasions. In a separate case, involving different police officers, conducted at the same sessions, two men who had been arrested for playing pitch-halfpenny on the public highway of Stoke Ferry were discharged after paying costs of 4s 6d. [281] Similarly, in some parts of

[275] *Ibid.*

[276] *Ibid.*

[277] *The Graphic*, 17 June, 1876.

[278] *The Bury and Norwich Post, and East Anglian*, 19 April, 1843.

[279] Victor Gatrell, "Crime, authority and the policeman-state" in F.M.L. Thompson (ed.), *The Cambridge Social History of Britain, 1750–1950,* vol. 3 (Cambridge: CUP, 1990), pp. 243-310.

[280] Koyama, "The law & economics," pp. 277–298.

[281] *The Norfolk Chronicle*, 4 January, 1851.

England, over a third of police arrests during the late 1840s were for alcohol-related offences, and numerous such cases can be seen in Norfolk throughout the era.[282] For a standard example, from late in the period, in 1888, at the Great Yarmouth police court (effectively petty sessions), Charles Whitmarsh was fined 5 shillings for being drunk and incapable in King Street in the same town (with five days' imprisonment in lieu of payment).[283]

Vagrancy, which was another major concern at the start of the Victorian era, because it was thought to lead to more serious crimes, was particularly susceptible to police intervention. Thus, in December 1842, PC Richard Barham prosecuted William Humphreys and William Davis at the North Erpingham petty sessions for being "idle and disorderly." They were convicted and sentenced to ten days and two weeks' imprisonment (with hard labour), respectively.[284] By 1853 an MP for the county even claimed that in Norfolk, the police were "useful and efficient, and had completely succeeded in putting down vagrancy."[285]

This focus continued to the end of the Victorian period. Numerous summary convictions for vagrancy were still being returned at the North Erpingham petty sessions in 1894. Almost without fail, the allegation was premised on begging, the prosecutor was a police officer, and the accused man (all were men) was convicted. Defendants came from throughout Britain. Some, such as James Willis from Liverpool, were expressly identified as "tramps." He received seven days' imprisonment with hard labour in Norwich Castle gaol after being caught begging at Cromer. Others, such as Edward Meare, a London saddler given an identical punishment for the same crime, had an occupation.[286] In 1896 243 allegations of begging were prosecuted summarily in Norfolk.[287]

Chief Police Officers

The Norfolk "rural" police force was headed by a chief constable, as were most other county forces. (Initial suggestions that such men might be termed "commander of forces" were swiftly rejected after eliciting hostility.)[288] Nationally these men were often drawn from former military officers and were usually of a socially superior background; this was the case in Norfolk. For example, Lieutenant Colonel Oakes had served in the First Life Guards, although a successor, Captain (later Volunteer Colonel) Black, had been in a less prestigious regiment. By the late-Victorian period,

282 Wood, "Drinking, Fighting," pp. 1-10.

283 *The Ipswich Journal*, 31 January,1888.

284 Hundred of North Erpingham Norfolk Special and Petty Sessions Record Commencing 3 July, 1841 NRO PS 24/1/1.

285 Hansard HC Deb 26 April, 1853 vol. 126 col. 545.

286 NRO 24/4/1 North Erpingham Petty Sessions, Minute Book B, p. 11.

287 *Judicial Statistics of England and Wales, 1896, Part I: Police; Criminal Proceedings; Prisons* (London: HMSO, 1898), p. 81.

288 *John Bull*, vol. xx, no. 995, 5 January, 1840, p. 9.

such positions were actively sought-after. In 1880, when Colonel Black resigned due to failing health and increasing age, there were 300 applications for the £700-a-year office.[289]

By contrast, the senior officers in the new borough forces of the country were commonly appointed at the rank of superintendent. In late 1856, in an action for defamation heard in the Court of Common Pleas, Stephen English, the "Chief Constable" of Norwich, sued Captain Black, the Chief Constable of Norfolk, in a dispute that originated over titles. It was alleged that Black had resented English styling himself as Chief Constable and wrote to the Norwich Watch Committee stating that his proper title was "superintendent of police". When his letters were ignored, Captain Black published handbills making malign comments about English's character and history.[290]

Such superintendents were often career policemen. Frequently, they were of comparatively modest social origins. Many moved around the country as opportunities for promotion presented themselves and, in the early years of the new borough forces, advancement could be rapid. Superintendent John Dunne, appointed to head the Norwich police in 1851, had first joined the Manchester police as a constable in 1840, served there for just a year, and then moved to Essex, where he spent eight years in the county constabulary, and was appointed to the rank of inspector in 1846. He had subsequently served in the Bath police force for 13 months before being appointed to the Kent force as a superintendent. Norwich was his first appointment as a chief officer.[291] He appears to have experienced a tempestuous period in command of the city's force, working to improve what he thought was its defective discipline. In the early summer of 1853, he left his position on the ground that he had been "obstructed by those who ought to have assisted him in the discharge of his duties." (He went on to become chief constable of Cumberland and Westmorland, serving for over 40 years in total). A few weeks later, Stephen English, a policeman from Pontefract, was chosen as his replacement.[292]

In early 1878, when Great Yarmouth needed a new superintendent of police, the position was advertised nationally. Fifty applicants applied and were eventually whittled down to five men, who were called for interview by the town watch committee, whose members then voted on their preferred candidate. Two men stood out, an inspector in the Hanley (Staffordshire) borough force and a superintendent from the Banbury (Oxfordshire) borough force. (The other three applicants were also career policemen, including one from the Great Eastern Railway Police). The

---

289 *The Ipswich Journal*, 13 April, 1880.

290 *Norfolk Chronicle,* 28 January, 1857.

291 Juliet Esme Leigh, *Early county chief constables in the north of England 1880-1905*. Open University PhD thesis, 2013, p. 49.

292 *The Norfolk Chronicle,* 18 June, 1853.

Banbury man won 13 ballots, while the one from Hanley, Joseph Ogden, had 19, and so secured the position.[293]

However, William Brogden, Ogden's successor three years later, was not elected, and the position was not publicly advertised. Brogden had been educated at Fulneck Moravian School in Leeds before being apprenticed to his leather-cutter father. In 1868, at age 30, he changed career and joined the Scarborough borough police force. Thereafter his promotion was rapid; eleven months after entering the service he was appointed detective, and, about two years after that, detective inspector. In April 1874 he joined the Yarmouth borough force as a detective inspector (a sideways move) and was commended on several occasions for his diligence. In 1881, on the resignation of Ogden, the watch committee felt that Brogden would ably discharge the duties of the £230-per-annum position (plus house and coal) and did not consider it worth advertising the vacancy. He served until 1894.[294]

Police Accountability

The new police had unprecedented power, especially in rural areas. It was quickly recognized that this could be abused. As a result, many observers felt that there was a need for a "more vigilant and efficient control for this new and more powerful agency."[295] However, unlike the Metropolitan Police (who answered to the Home Secretary), provincial police, whether borough or county forces, were accountable to local government, something that had helped to ease their introduction.

Borough Force Accountability

Borough constables were supervised by their watch committees, which met regularly, sometimes on a weekly basis. Typically, in 1835 the Norwich Council appointed a committee of 12 men, with the mayor as chairman, to fulfil this task for their new force. Most borough police forces were relatively small, so their watch committees often exercised a great deal of day-to-day control. Their head constables (usually appointed as superintendents) tended to have much less independence from these committees than did county chief constables. Watch committees had, and often employed, the power to appoint, promote, and dismiss police officers. In 1853 Captain Dunne, then superintendent of the Norwich force, complained that the committee would often ignore his recommendations as to suitable recruits and appoint other, perhaps less able, men.

Members of the watch committee could also go much further in micro-managing officers' duties, something that could occasion problems and even bring them into conflict with borough magistrates. For example, several of those on the Norwich watch committee in the early 1850s were brewers, with a vested interest in how

---

[293] *The Ipswich Journal,* 2 March, 1878.

[294] *Ibid.*, 10 November, 1894.

[295] *The Spectator,* 26 March, 1842, p. 11.

taverns and alehouses in the city were policed.[296] In many towns the new police continued to be regarded as municipal servants who could be tasked with carrying out a variety of routine administrative functions, until well into the twentieth century. These might include tasks such as collecting market tolls and acting as municipal mace bearers.[297]

County Force Accountability

County forces were managed by a police committee of JPs who met at quarter sessions until the Local Government Act of 1888 came into force in early 1889, and by a standing joint committee of magistrates and county councillors thereafter. These committees did not have (or at least did not exercise) the same day-to-day powers over appointment and dismissal of officers as their borough equivalents, such matters usually being left to the chief constable, who also tended to have much greater operational independence.[298] As George Black observed, "In all that relates to authority and command, the chief constable [of a county] occupies the same position as that held by the Watch Committee of a borough." However, although the senior officer of a county was not appointed by the Home Secretary (unlike the Metropolitan force), this politician did have some involvement in their appointment and operations, even in 1856. He had to confirm the officer's appointment and could issue regulations affecting the position. His consent was required for an adjustment in size in the force while copies of all the chief constable's reports to quarter sessions and all resolutions made by the magistrates on those reports had to be forwarded to him.[299]

Although less likely to be used as general public servants, even rural police officers became involved in functions that were on the fringes of policing, such as combatting fires and returning stray animals. In 1842 Isaac Jermy, a county JP and the recorder of Norwich, deprecated their use in some of these tasks.[300] However, this appears to have been an inherent part of service. Thus, in 1870 the Norfolk Police were reporting the weekly incidence of foot-and-mouth disease and sheep scab in the county.[301] In January 1888 there was a debate at the Norfolk quarter sessions as to whether the police should become involved in enforcing the recent Agricultural Children Act, regulating juvenile work on farms. Although it was thought desirable that the government appoint specialist inspectors for this task, some JPs argued that, in their absence, and to prevent the statute becoming a "dead letter," it was necessary that police officers become involved.[302]

296 *The Bury and Norwich Post*, 13 July, 1853.

297 Emsley, "A typology," pp. 29-44.

298 *Ibid*.

299 Black, *The police*, p. 28.

300 *The Bury and Norwich Post, and East Anglian*, 6 July, 1842.

301 *The Times*, 19 February, 1870, p. 9.

302 *The Ipswich Journal*, 17 January, 1888.

Policing Techniques

Victorian policing techniques, over and above simple patrolling, were not usually very sophisticated anywhere in the country during the Victorian era. Only a very small number of the cases in Victorian Ipswich, for example, were solved by the police through the exercise of any sort of expertise.[303] A cluster of cases from Norfolk is indicative of provincial policing methods. For example, in August 1855 William Holland, a labourer, was accused of stealing a chicken worth two shillings from a Mr Gowing in Mattishall. Gowing had several such birds. His wife saw one with its neck broken and informed the police. As a result, a constable kept Gowing's premises under surveillance, and eventually saw Holland put his hand into a shed, take out a chicken, and put it into his pocket. The constable pursued and apprehended him. Holland was convicted and sentenced to ten days' imprisonment with hard labour.[304]

Even more simply, in 1888 Earnest Dean, a deaf-and-dumb man, was seen by a sergeant of the Yarmouth police wandering around the town with a clearly marked pewter tankard from the Crown Tavern in his hand, one that was also inscribed with the owner's initials. Dean was stopped by the sergeant, arrested, and produced before the town police court, where he elected trial at assizes. (By then, given the mug's value of just 2s 6d, he could have asked for a summary hearing.)[305] In the same year, Moses Webb, a middle-aged labourer with numerous convictions, was found guilty at the Thetford borough sessions of stealing a chicken from a stable in the town and going equipped for housebreaking. The owner of the chicken had lost poultry on a regular basis over previous weeks and, eventually, two police constables hid in the darkened stable during the late evening and seized Webb as he attempted to leave the building with the near-dead bird. He was searched and found to be in possession of 13 keys, the basis for the second count. (He was sentenced to a year's imprisonment with hard labour.)[306]

Patrolling officers were expected to be observant and to exercise a degree of common sense. Ideally, they would develop an instinct for spotting both crime and criminals. For example, at the Norfolk assizes in April 1847, two young men, George Docking and James Shears, were indicted for having broken into Robert Land's grocer-cum-draper's shop at Stoke Ferry during the small hours and stolen a shawl handkerchief and 6 or 7 shillings in cash. Shears' cap was found near the crime scene. When he returned to his lodgings, shortly before 3 am, he was seen by PC William Carter, a local officer on nocturnal duty, without his customary headwear. On a hunch, Carter "apprehended him and found a knife and nine shillings in his pocket." Shears was convicted and sentenced to a year's imprisonment.[307]

---

303 Wim Mellaerts, "Criminal Justice in Provincial England, France and Netherlands, c. 1880-1905: Some Comparative Perspectives," *Crime, History & Societies*, vol. 4, no. 2 (2000), pp. 26-29.

304 *The Norfolk Chronicle*, 20 October, 1855.

305 *The Ipswich Journal*, 31 January, 1888.

306 *The Bury and Norwich Post*, 24 April, 1888.

307 *The Norfolk Chronicle*, 3 April,1847.

Similarly, in 1875 (Detective) Inspector Brogden of the Yarmouth Police noticed a stranger in the town. His "keen sense of thieves" quickly led him to suspect that the man was there for nefarious purposes, and he stalked his suspect for the rest of the day. Eventually, he arrested him in a tavern, albeit on rather vague grounds. The man was searched at the police station and confessed that he was James Hardacre, a former convict, and that he had committed a recent burglary at Burlingham in Norfolk in which £24 in gold and cash had been taken. Hardacre was brought up before the Yarmouth magistrates, who complimented Brogden on his diligence and skill, and ordered that the prisoner be handed over to the county police to be dealt with for the burglary. Fortunately, Hardacre had retained a distinctive handkerchief from the break-in, which allowed a positive identification to be made, corroborating his admissions.[308]

Such instinct might even be exercised off duty. In early 1889 a Norfolk police officer travelling in plain clothes by train from Norwich to Cromer fell into conversation with a boy who had a new silver watch. His intuition, based on the boy's account and the value of the timepiece, correctly told him that it had been stolen (from the youth's London employer, as it turned out). He arrested the lad.[309]

Nevertheless, rather than relying on a sixth sense for identifying criminals, instinct often seems to have entailed keeping an eye on the "usual suspects" – men and women who were known to local officers to be on the margins of the law – and rounding them up for investigation when necessary. For example, after a major burglary in the city in early 1843, local police swiftly detained "three of the most notorious housebreakers in Norwich." These men were held for a week, until committal proceedings, when they were produced before magistrates, along with victims of the burglary who identified two of them (albeit in less-than-ideal circumstances). They were sent for trial, while the third man was remanded for further investigation.[310]

Similarly, at the Thetford borough quarter sessions in July 1880, Moses Webb, an "old offender," was accused of being in possession of housebreaking implements in the form of two skeleton keys. He had been arrested one night by two police officers who "knew" him and had been keeping him under covert surveillance as he entered a yard in the town. Although he claimed that the police had planted the keys on him, he was found guilty and sentenced to five years' penal servitude (he had six previous convictions). The town recorder also advised the police to be more professional when searching prisoners.[311]

The police became better at securing convictions after the early years of the Victorian era, largely because they became better at gathering evidence and preparing cases

---

308 *The Ipswich Journal*, 1 May, 1875.

309 *The Bury and Norwich Post*, 26 February, 1889.

310 *Ibid.*, 19 April, 1843.

311 *Ibid.*, 6 July, 1880.

for trial. For example, although 40 percent of those brought before metropolitan magistrates were discharged in 1858, this had fallen to 30 percent in 1865.[312] Certainly, the new police were a vast improvement on traditional parish constables in this regard, something that can be observed in Norfolk as much as in the capital. However, it took time to master these skills. After the Rush case in 1848, there were allegations of lost evidence, and it could be noted that "the efficiency of the Norfolk police is questioned".[313]

By contrast, in 1896, after John Cubitt, a Norfolk gamekeeper, was shot and injured while intercepting nocturnal poachers, two of them were captured and charged with wounding. A police officer from the county force subsequently identified the tree where most of the poachers' shot had ended up, cut out the relevant part of the trunk, and extracted the shot, which he then matched to similar shot found in one of the defendants' guns and pockets. He produced this evidence at committal, and the pair were sent for trial at the assizes.[314]

Officers became especially adept at footprint recognition, in an era in which surfaces were often soft (due to a lack of tarmac and concrete), and shoes and boots, usually individually made, had distinctive nail patterns on their soles. In late 1846 a workbox containing gold and silver coins, along with a chisel, were stolen from the room of Robert Gunton, who lodged in a house in Mattishall. He traced footmarks from the house to that of a suspect (who had recently been in Gunton's house), and from there to a pond a quarter-of-a-mile away. When the pond was dragged, the box was recovered. A PC Willis duplicated this tracking by following the same footprints. He then took the suspect's shoe print and found it to correspond in every respect with the footprints. The man was convicted.[315] In an arson case of November 1892, the Norfolk police even covered up with tiles footmarks that had been seen in a field to prolong their life in inclement weather and so allow more time for consideration.[316]

Searching Premises

A considerable part of police work involved searching premises, usually when it was thought that stolen goods or fugitives were being concealed within them. This normally required a warrant authorized by a JP. For example, in 1838 the magistrate James Bulwer signed warrants authorizing the constables of Wood Dalling and Heydon to search the house of Edward Strike for stolen ducks.[317] In 1874, after a pair of juvenile telegraphic clerks were suspected of stealing from parcels sent through the mail, the manager of the King's Lynn post office, who had kept his employees

312 John Walliss, "Lies, Damned Lies and Statistics? Nineteenth Century Crime Statistics for England and Wales as a Historical Source," *History Compass*, vol. 10, no. 8 (2012), pp. 573-584.

313 *John Bull*, 2 July, 1849, p. 412.

314 *The Ipswich Journal*, 18 January, 1896.

315 *The Norfolk News*, 9 January, 1847.

316 *The Bury and Norwich Post*, 6 December, 1892.

317 NRO BUL 4/206, 614X1.

under close observation for several weeks, accompanied a police superintendent to their parents' homes with a warrant. The boys were arrested, searches made, and stolen items found in their possession. (They quickly made admissions when questioned.) [318]

Securing such warrants was not very problematic in Norwich or the three corporate towns of Norfolk, where borough magistrates could normally be located very swiftly. However, it was more difficult in remote parts of the county, which might be far from a JP, especially when a warrant was needed urgently. In some situations, it seems that officers conducted searches without such authority. Sometimes the subjects of their investigations may have invited them in when requested, unaware that they could refuse admittance. On other occasions, the situation may have fallen into the category of limited and urgent circumstances in which such authority was not needed. However, in some cases, simple ignorance of police powers may have allowed officers to get away with what would technically have been illegal searches.

Police Questioning of Suspects

Given that active questioning by JPs during the committal hearing had waned rapidly and then disappeared during the first half of the nineteenth century, even as the new professional police forces became established, it is not surprising that the latter should attempt to step into the investigative void, and assume the role vacated by the former. This then raised questions as to the status and validity of police interviews, and any information secured by them, the role of a formal caution in such questioning, and whether a suspect had a right to silence. These issues remained in a state of considerable flux throughout the Victorian era, and until well into the twentieth century.[319]

During the two decades prior to the new Queen's accession, judicial attitudes towards police interrogation varied significantly. In the 1820s courts had evinced nervousness about police officers' (usually parish constables) usurping the function of investigating magistrates and questioning suspects in an attempt to secure confessions. Of course, judges insisted that officers should not pressure or bribe suspects into making incriminating statements that could be used against them at trial (neither a novel nor controversial idea), but a few went further and suggested that such conversations were improper per se. However, there had not been a firm rule of law barring the admission of material at trial that had been secured in this fashion. Thus, in *R* v. *Thornton* of 1824, a 14-year-old-boy had been arrested, possibly without due cause, and questioned by a Liverpool officer. He had been examined robustly, but without threats or promises, and eventually provided a confession that was largely the basis for his subsequent conviction for arson. The trial judge had some concerns about this and referred the issue to the Court for Crown Cases

---

[318] *The Ipswich Journal*, 5 December, 1874; *The Bury and Norwich Post*, 8 December, 1874.

[319] Pat McInerney, "The Privilege against Self-Incrimination from Early Origins to Judges' Rules: Challenging the 'Orthodox View,'" *The International Journal of Evidence & Proof*, vol. 18, no. 2 (2014), pp. 131-134.

Reserved, which considered questions of law or procedure that arose during a trial. It decided that in the absence of threats or inducements, the confession had been properly received into evidence.[320] Most legal observers did not feel that there was any formal bar to police questioning, if properly conducted, or that its fruits, in the form of confessions, were *necessarily* inadmissible.[321]

However, by the time the new Queen came to the throne, judicial attitudes were starting to change. Early Victorian legal observers sometimes argued that such questioning impinged on the JPs' (rapidly waning) investigative role and thought that police officers should not actively question suspects given the danger of inaccurate recollection or even deliberate twisting of evidence.[322] Unsurprisingly, much of the jurisprudence on this issue arose from the Metropolitan area, with its powerful police force and readily scrutinised Old Bailey court. However, assizes and quarter sessions were not immune to the debate, even in Norfolk.

In April 1844 Mr Justice Patterson took the opportunity to discuss police questioning of suspects when addressing the Norfolk grand jury. He claimed that bad habits had developed amongst the relatively new rural force, whose officers seemed to "wholly misunderstand their duty." Many of them thought that it was their role to question suspects with a view to establishing their guilt by, for example, asking them to account for their movements at a particular time. This was "utterly illegal." The judge acknowledged that some observers thought that such a practice was desirable (he did not agree with them) but was adamant that, as the law then stood, it was forbidden: "It cannot be tolerated that persons should be entrapped by those who apprehend them." Subsequently, the judge told the trial jury to entirely ignore the evidence of a police officer who had vigorously questioned an 11-year-old boy accused of arson, even though the lad appeared to have repeated his admissions when questioned by magistrates. The boy was acquitted. The judge did the same thing with another arson case, involving a 13-year-old boy, who was alleged to have made a confession to an officer, and again, he "reprobated the conduct of the police." This boy was acquitted as well.[323]

Four months later, in August 1844, Edward Standing, a 57-year-old man, and James Taylor, who was 21, were indicted at the Suffolk assizes for sodomy. Among the prosecution witnesses was a policeman who stated that the older man had made a statement admitting to the offence after he was arrested, which was taken down in writing by another officer. Again, the trial judge publicly censured the police for recording such statements and questioned their reliability. The jury duly acquitted.[324]

---

320 Edward Ryan, *Crown Cases Reserved for Consideration; And Decided by the Twelve Judges of England from the year 1824 to the year 1837* (London: Saunders and Benning, 1837), p. 28.

321 Bentley, *English Criminal Justice*, pp. 229-230.

322 *Ibid.*, pp. 229-230.

323 *The Bury and Norwich Post and East Anglian*, 3 April, 1844.

324 *The Liverpool Mail*, 24 August, 1844.

Even so, some early Victorian judges still felt that active questioning of suspects by officers was acceptable, if preceded by a caution and conducted properly. When in 1841 Charlotte Yaxley murdered her husband's infant daughter in Norfolk, it was claimed that a police officer had questioned her under a "new system" allowing such interrogation. Perhaps unsurprisingly, her lawyer likened it to the Spanish Inquisition, as she had made admissions.[325]

By about 1850 the judiciary had largely turned its face against the active police interrogation of suspects. At the Norfolk assizes in 1853, Superintendent Dunne was strongly criticized by the trial judge for conducting a formal, recorded (in writing) interview with a female infanticide suspect.[326] The judge was adamant that this was not a police duty: "This is the first time that I ever saw such a laborious investigation of a case, very premature in my opinion, on the part of a superintendent of police." In response, and indicative of the uncertainty surrounding the subject, Dunne asserted that Lord Denman had approved such a practice at the Essex assizes. The judge thought that this was highly unlikely and gave a direction encouraging acquittal which the jury immediately followed.[327] His analysis was broadly accepted until the end of the Victorian era. Thus, in 1852 Lord Chief Justice Campbell stressed that no police interrogation should normally take place, while in 1898 another judge observed: "No one, either policeman or anyone also has a right to put questions to the prisoner for the purpose of entrapping him into making admissions."[328]

This still raised the problem of prisoners who voluntarily, without any prompting, made a confession, and what to do about apparently reliable admissions that had been obtained by measured police questioning, even if it should not have been conducted. In the former case, Mr Justice Sir John Patteson opined that if a prisoner voluntarily made a confession in front of police officers, there was no obligation on the officers to prevent him from doing so.[329] For example, in 1852 a police constable who apprehended a man on a charge of murder, having told him the nature of the allegation, informed him that "he need not say anything to criminate himself–what he did say would be taken down, and used as evidence against him." The prisoner then made a confession. It was held that this was rightly admitted.[330] Some, such as Lord Denman, thought it was not even a police officer's duty to stop entirely unprompted admissions to issue a caution.[331]

More specific to Norfolk, at the borough sessions for Thetford in 1846, a woman was accused of stealing a watch. When informed that she was being arrested, she

325 *The Bury and Norwich Post and East Anglian*, 14 April, 1841.

326 *Ibid.*, 23 March, 1853.

327 *The Bury and Norwich Post and Suffolk Herald*, 23 March, 1853.

328 *R* v. *Baldry* (1852) 2 Den CC Res 430; *R v Histed* (1898) 19 Cox CC 16.

329 *The Bury and Norwich Post and East Anglian,* 3 April, 1844.

330 *R* v. *Baldry* (1852) 2 Den CC Res 430.

331 *R* v. *Watts* 1844 and *R v Priest* 1847. *Examiner*, 2 August, 1845.

immediately claimed, without questioning, that she had found the timepiece lying on the ground. When adducing this evidence, PC Tyler stressed: "I said nothing to induce her to confess".[332] Similarly, in 1853, after William Thompson was arrested in connection with a vicious murder in Norfolk, he was handcuffed to a county officer. At some point, and without any prompting, he allegedly made admissions to the constable, although he later denied this. The officer subsequently gave evidence of the alleged confession.[333]

Attitudes to mistakenly conducted but fruitful questioning varied, depending on the nature of the examination; in a case from 1888, the court excluded a statement made to a constable who questioned his prisoner in a way that amounted to cross-examination.[334] By contrast, in another case, eight years later, the court did admit a statement made by a prisoner to a constable who had questioned him in a more anodyne manner.[335]

Detectives

For much of the nineteenth century, detective work was relatively marginal to many English police forces, especially those found outside the great cities. As a result, the Bow Street Runners were occasionally employed for this purpose in the provinces until 1839, when they were disbanded.[336] In 1836 it was claimed that, whenever a serious robbery or murder was committed that could not be readily solved, rural magistrates would send to London for an experienced officer to investigate it.[337] Additionally, there might still be a role for private detectives, instructed by members of the public or organizations, especially when very serious crimes were committed against wealthy victims, particularly early in the Victorian period. For example, in June 1843 William Sangar, a 21-year-old clerk, stole £4,000 from the East of England Bank at King's Lynn, in the absence of the manager, and then absconded.[338] The bank's solicitors instructed private detectives to track him down, while also offering a reward of £100 for his apprehension. He was eventually arrested near Pooley Bridge, at Ullswater in Cumberland, in early July, with all but £20 of the money still in his possession.[339]

Nevertheless, provision was quickly made for plain-clothes work by normally uniformed officers in the new provincial forces, while formally appointed detectives

---

332 *The Ipswich Journal*, 17 January, 1846.

333 *Bell's Life in London and Sporting Chronicle*, 27 November, 1853.

334 *R* v. *Gavin* (1888) 15 Cox 656.

335 *R* v. *Goddard* (1896) 60 JP 491.

336 See generally David J. Cox, *A Certain Share of Low Cunning: A History of the Bow Street Runners, 1792-1839* (Cullompton, Devon: Willan Publishing, 2010).

337 *The Spectator*, 19 November, 1836, p. 13.

338 *The Age*, 25 June, 1843.

339 *John Bull*, 8 July, 1843.

emerged after the early Victorian period.[340] Many, but not all, extra-London forces, especially those for the counties and larger boroughs, had such officers by the 1890s. In Norfolk the county, Norwich, Great Yarmouth, and (eventually) even the King's Lynn police forces all introduced their own detectives, the short-lived and diminutive Thetford force being the only exception. Thus in 1860 the Norfolk county police had two specially appointed "detective officers," as did the Norwich force; the Great Yarmouth borough force made do with just one. (The King's Lynn force still lacked such officers at this time.)[341] Their numbers subsequently increased, and one commander of the Great Yarmouth police, William Brogden, had previously served as a detective inspector in the same force.

The Metropolitan Police Criminal Investigation Department (CID) often set the standard for provincial police detection.[342] Even so, although it was considered the most advanced force in the country in this regard, the media periodically questioned the quality of their detective abilities and methods and their willingness to embrace new techniques, as occurred following the unsolved murder of Arabella Tyler at Blackheath in 1898.[343] Some observers thought that detectives, both in the capital and the provinces, constituted a weak link in the police system, being inadequate for the work given to them, and often not marked by any higher intelligence and education than those of ordinary uniformed officers. It was claimed that they were prone to frequenting taverns in their search for information, while drinking to excess. As a result, it was sometimes suggested that, "The ordinary detective is [merely] of service in watching the movements of ticket-of-leave men [the Victorian version of the parolee], or persons under the surveillance of the Police. In short, he is [only] a match for the stupid, small-brained criminal."[344] This may have been a little harsh, but it is true that provincial detective techniques were not necessarily very sophisticated.

A case from late 1887, in which James Wright was accused of stealing a pair of boots from a lugger that was moored in Yarmouth, is probably typical of their day-to-day operation. Detective Constable Lingwood from the town force discovered that the boots had, at some point, been pledged with a local pawnbroker, and from this identified and apprehended the man responsible when he returned form a fishing trip. He was still wearing the boots, which had been redeemed on his behalf by a woman.[345] Of course, it was very difficult for detectives in borough forces to avoid

---

340 Rachael Jones, *Crime, Courts and Community in Mid-Victorian Wales: Montgomeryshire, People and Places* (Cardiff: University of Wales, 2018), p. 72.

341 *Judicial Statistics 1860,* p. 2.

342 Haia Shpayer-Makov, *The Ascent of the Detective: Police Sleuths in Victorian and Edwardian England* (Oxford: OUP, 2011), p. 61.

343 *The Daily Mail*, 17 August, 1898.

344 *The Spectator,* 18 August, 1877, p. 8.

345 *The Ipswich Journal*, 31 January, 1888.

being recognized by local people, even when out of uniform, making undercover work exceptionally challenging.

A practice gradually developed whereby provincial forces could call in the assistance of detectives from the Metropolitan Police if needed, just as they had the earlier Bow Street Runners. Sometimes other force detectives were requested as well, even in anticipation of potential problems. Thus in 1848, fearing that the crowds that would come to watch James Rush's execution might attract criminals from around the country, especially the capital, Superintendent Yarrington of the Norwich city police called in the assistance of Michael Haydon and three more of the "most energetic and successful members of the London detective police."[346] Haydon himself was drawn from the City of London (rather than Metropolitan) force and had a high reputation as a detective.[347]

Similarly, in 1869, when the new Alexandra Dock was opened by the Prince of Wales at King's Lynn, another huge crowd was anticipated. The small police force of the town was strengthened by detective officers from Norwich, but also London, Birmingham, and York. The men selected were known for their "sagacity" and, it was hoped, might identify offenders from their own cities who had joined the throng looking for criminal opportunities. Inspector Shiels, a detective from the York force, had considerable success in this regard, identifying several career criminals from the cover of a wagon, and chasing them down, when they were forced to disgorge stolen items and skeleton keys.[348]

Occasionally, demands for the detective expertise of outside forces went further. In 1846, after Jonathan Balls' poisoning spree on the Norfolk coast came to light, the Home Secretary asked for an investigation to be conducted into why there had not been inquests into the deaths of his apparent victims, especially when rumours were widely circulating about the man. This was headed by Mr Smith "of the London detective force," aided by Superintendent Smith from the local county police.[349]

The various Norfolk forces also used contacts within Scotland Yard to assist with detecting offenders who had crossed county lines. For example, in August 1887 three members of a highly mobile gang of horse thieves that was operating in Norfolk were confronted by PC Davis near New Buckenham. They beat and shot at the officer, before escaping. The Norfolk police sought the cooperation of the Metropolitan force to secure the arrest of the gang. A few weeks later, two Scotland Yard detectives went into a public house on the Holloway Road in London and seized an ex-convict named John Raith, who had already served two lengthy terms of imprisonment for horse theft, and who was suspected of involvement in the incident. He was found to be carrying a loaded revolver and was subsequently handed over

---

346 Anon., *The Stanfield Hall Assassinations!* (London: Cleave, 1849), pp. 1-10.

347 Shpayer-Makov, *Ascent of the Detective,* p. 361.

348 *The York Herald*, 24 July, 1869.

349 *The Derby Mercury*, 3 June, 1846.

to the Norfolk Police.[350] At trial, he admitted horse theft, but denied the shooting, blaming it on a companion. Nevertheless, he was swiftly convicted and sentenced to 22 years' penal servitude. (The judge also ordered that a reward of £5 be paid to PC Davis out of county funds.)[351] Such cooperation between detectives could extend further. In August 1874 it was noted that a detective named Williamson from the Norwich police had gone with a counterpart from Scotland Yard to Spain to accompany the Norfolk fraudster Josiah Buttifant back to England.[352]

In subsequent decades, Metropolitan detectives were called in to investigate some serious provincial crimes. A famous instance was the Road Hill House murder in 1860, when the chief constable of Wiltshire called in detective inspector Jonathan Whicher to investigate the murder of a three-year old. (There is some debate as to whether he was the first Scotland Yard detective to be employed in this fashion). The Metropolitan Police did not have to accommodate such requests, but it became customary for them to do so, although it could cause tensions with the local force, who had to deal with possibly grandstanding outsiders coming onto their territory. In 1903 these arrangements were put on a formal basis. By the end of the Victorian period the Home Office had also started to issue circulars to provincial forces outlining detective methods, such as how to take a cast of footprints from mud, with a view to improving investigative standards.[353]

---

[350] *The Morning Post*, 10 September, 1887.

[351] *The Ipswich Journal*, 18 November, 1887.

[352] *The Essex Standard*, 14 August ,1874.

[353] G.R. Rubin, "Calling in the Met: Serious crime investigation involving Scotland Yard and provincial police forces in England and Wales, 1906–1939," *Legal Studies*, vol. 31, no. 3 (2011), p. 412.

Chapter 4: The Magistracy

Introduction

In the 1830s, part-time, unpaid, untrained, justices of the peace or 'JPs' were central to both the administration of criminal justice and wider civil governance in provincial England. (For the purposes of this book, "magistrate" will be used synonymously with "JP.") The latter role had expanded rapidly as the financial responsibilities of the counties grew during the early decades of the nineteenth century. As a result, quarter sessions appointed committees of diligent magistrates to deal with county expenditure and the fixing of a county rate, as well as, *inter alia*, to oversee the new rural police (when introduced), county prisons, lunatic asylums, bridges, and roads. These committees would report regularly to quarter sessions.[354] For example, and typically, in July 1844 the committee for the county prison in Norwich Castle gave details of the average number of inmates being held in the gaol, its physical condition, any structural work necessary on the building, recruitment of staff, etc.[355]

In their criminal-justice function, JPs presided over both petty sessions and quarter sessions (the latter with a jury) and processed indictable cases (for both quarter sessions and assizes) out of sessions, during the pre-trial phase of criminal litigation, by dealing with first appearances and committal hearings. They also issued search and arrest warrants and swore in parish constables. In consequence, they were the pivotal figures in the entire criminal-justice system.

By the start of the Victorian era, the JPs' role in both civil and criminal fields was coming under increasing attack. In England their administrative role in the boroughs was largely abolished in 1835. In the counties it survived until the Local Government Act of 1888 created elected county councils, although by then a series of statutes passed over the previous 50 years had significantly eroded their civic power by transferring responsibility for various matters elsewhere. For example, the Prisons Act of 1877 removed from quarter sessions (and therefore JPs) responsibility for the county prisons and vested it in national prison commissioners. In Norfolk, as in many other places, elections for a county council finally took place in January 1889, and the new body assembled in April that year, largely ending JPs' administrative functions other than for licensing. After the passage of the 1888 Act, some members of the Norfolk gentry apparently retired from the bench and public life.[356]

However, and more important from the perspective of this book, the JPs' significance within the criminal-justice system lasted to the end of the Victorian period and beyond, still being vital in the present-day. Even so, well before the end of the eighteenth century the challenges attendant on enforcing the criminal law and preserving order in a growing, industrializing, and urbanizing country, with

---

354 Philips, "A 'Weak' State?" pp. 873-891.

355 *The Bury and Norwich Post*, 10 July, 1844.

356 H. Rider Haggard, *The Days Of My Life* (London: Longmans, Green, 1926), pp. 26-27.

new expectations of social discipline, had led to criticism of their competence. Unsurprisingly, the huge Metropolitan area had been the first to break ranks with the traditional system, appointing 27 stipendiary magistrates in 1792, eventually being followed by some other large towns and boroughs (see below). In Ireland, albeit for different reasons, the system of unpaid JPs had also started to change by the end of the 1700s, increasingly being supplemented by salaried, barrister-qualified, assistant magistrates (officially called "resident magistrates" from 1853), because of concern about the former's effectiveness when dealing with rural unrest.

Although the Anglo-Irish gentry – who provided most of the country's JPs – disliked losing their legal powers, they were a smaller and more vulnerable elite than their English counterparts, and their failure to keep order effectively in the face of endemic agrarian disturbances undermined arguments for retaining them. English JPs, too, were weakened by their apparent failure to deal effectively with the Swing Riots in the early 1830s. Indeed, shortly afterwards a deputy lieutenant for Berkshire had advocated the introduction of a "resident, paid & responsible Magistrate" on the Irish model in rural parts.[357] However, outside the large cities, proposals for reform in this direction were successfully resisted throughout the era.

Appointment and Numbers

Despite their importance to the wider system, and as their critics regularly pointed out during the nineteenth century, county JPs were normally selected by virtue of their social status, and untrained in the duties that they undertook; they would learn 'on the job' by sitting with more experienced magistrates. The Lord Chancellor appointed them, usually on the advice of the lord lieutenant of the county, who consulted senior JPs, especially the chairmen of quarter sessions, and various other sources, very occasionally (albeit extremely discreetly) even consulting clerks of the peace.[358]

County JPs needed no special qualifications, apart from ownership of land worth at least £100 a year, not a very onerous requirement for gentlemen. (Qualified barristers were exempt from even this prerequisite.) In 1875 Conservative peers in the House of Lords thwarted attempts to remove it. This meant that, by the end of the Victorian era, it was almost the only office for which it was necessary to own land in order to serve.[359] The qualification was finally abolished by the Justices of the Peace Act 1906. Those selected as JPs would be formally sworn in at quarter sessions. Thus, at the quarter sessions for Norfolk held at Norwich in January 1857, four magistrates, including Major General Angerstein, "qualified as magistrates for the county."[360]

---

357 Philips, "A 'Weak' State?" pp. 884-888.

358 William Cornish et al., *The Oxford History of the Laws of England* (Oxford: OUP, 2010), p. 919.

359 Edward Porritt, "At Petty Sessions," *Green Bag*, vol. 11, no. 10 (1899), p. 473.

360 *The Bury and Norwich Post*, 13 January, 1857.

Seven years before the accession of the new Queen, in 1830, Norfolk had 395 JPs in its commission of the peace, which had grown steadily over the previous decade. It would continue to do so over the immediately ensuing years. By 1852 the county had a nominal bench of 526 JPs. However, this figure included purely honorary magistrates, such as Prince Albert, several members of the Privy Council, and other nationally important officials. More significantly, and as in previous centuries, many prominent local men appointed to the bench, especially during the first half of the 1800s, did not actively serve as magistrates, merely being interested in the status that it conferred on them. In the early nineteenth century, less than half of those who were named to a commission countrywide even bothered to take out their *dedimus potestatem*, which authorized them to act as magistrates (it did not guarantee that they would do so), although there was considerable regional variation in this regard.[361] In 1830, only 31 percent of Norfolk's Commission had taken out this document.[362] (According to the Attorney General, the writ was no longer needed after the Promissory Oaths Acts of 1868 and 1871).[363] Some magistrates were also JPs for more than one county at the same time, further limiting their ability to actively serve in any one of them. For example, Robert Seaman, who died in 1874, was a magistrate for both Norfolk and Suffolk.[364]

As a result, it has been suggested that, in the mid-1800s, only about half of all English JPs were even qualified to act as such, and only about a third were active.[365] Such a pattern can also be seen in Wales, where large numbers of the county bench did not sit at petty or quarter sessions in mid-Victorian Montgomeryshire.[366]

On one assessment, Norfolk had only 154 active magistrates in 1825.[367] This may have increased to 176 in 1830.[368] On another assessment, in 1852, the county had about 250 "acting" JPs – that is, magistrates who were actively involved in its work – while two years later, the figure was 256. This figure constituted about half of the nominal bench. Unsurprisingly, the great majority, some 236 of them, were qualified by estate rather than by legal professional status (barristers). Of course, not all active JPs were equally committed: some were very occasional participants. As in previous eras, an examination of quarter sessions for almost all English counties during the first four decades of the nineteenth century clearly shows the existence of a sub-group of especially diligent JPs who carried out a quite disproportionate amount

361 Philips, "A 'Weak' State?" pp. 883-884.

362 Rose Madeleine Wallis, *The Relationship Between Magistrates and their Communities in the Age of Crisis: social protest c. 1790-1834,* University of the West of England PhD dissertation, 2016, p. 67.

363 Hansard HC Deb 22 July 1872 vol 212 c1513

364 *The Norfolk Chronicle*, 19 April, 1874

365 Cornish, *Oxford History,* p. 908.

366 R. Jones, *Crime, Courts,* p. 39.

367 John Powell, *Statistical Illustrations of the Territorial Extent and Population; Commerce, Taxation, Consumption, Insolvency, Pauperism, and Crime, of the British Empire* (London: J. Miller, 1825), p. 14.

368 Rose Madeleine Wallis, *The Relationship Between Magistrates and their* Communities, p.70

of legal and administrative work, both in and out of sessions.[369] For example, in Gloucestershire, during the early nineteenth century, some 17 magistrates were named more than 100 times where petty sessions convictions are recorded. By contrast, 47 men were named just once. The great majority of active JPs in the county fell between these extremes.[370] More locally, by the 1850s, although most Norfolk petty sessional divisions had at least half a dozen JPs, and some, such as South Erpingham, had far more magistrates on their books, many petty sessions saw just two or three JPs present, and few more than four.[371]

The number of inactive JPs fell during the Victorian period, although there were still complaints in the early 1900s that large numbers of magistrates did not act at all.[372] Nevertheless, in some respects, it is at least arguable that never sitting was better than doing so on a very occasional basis. The clerical JP Harry Farr Yeatman stressed that it took years to acquire even a basic command of the intricacies of English criminal law.[373] The presence of a dilettante might occasion more trouble than he was worth. At best he might be a puppet in the hands of the court clerk.

Background of the County JPs

At the start of the Victorian era, most county JPs were landed Anglican gentry. In 1838 the Duke of Wellington observed, "Magistrates must be gentlemen of wealth, worth, consideration, and education; that they should have been educated for the bar, if possible; and that, above all, they should be associated with, and be respected by the gentry of the country." These criteria, and the modest property qualification, meant that a squire's younger sons and brothers could often be recruited to the early Victorian magistracy, even if they had made careers in the church, army, or navy.[374]

In practice, it was still normal for adult males from a county's more prominent gentry families to receive an appointment to the bench unless there were very good reasons against this. As the *Spectator* observed in 1842, most country gentlemen were made JPs not because they were supposed to be fit for the office, but because they were of consequence in elections or because their standing in their county would render it an "act of indecorum" to pass them over. In return they viewed the office

---

369 Philips, "A 'Weak' State?" pp. 873–891.

370 Irene Wyatt, *Calendar of Summary Convictions at Petty Sessions 1781-1837* (Bristol: Bristol and Gloucestershire Archaeological Society, 2008), p. xviii.

371 *Return of Number of Justices of Peace for each County in England and Wales, 1852-54*, 1856, House of Commons Papers, vol. 50, pp. 171-172.

372 George Glover Alexander, *The administration of justice in criminal matters (in England and Wales)* (Cambridge: CUP, 1911), p. 70.

373 Yeatman, *A Letter*, p. 6.

374 Carl H.E. Zangerl, "The Social Composition of the County Magistracy in England and Wales, 1831-1887", *Journal of British Studies*, vol. 11, no. 1 (1971), p. 117.

as a public feather in their caps.[375] However, assessment of potential merit seems to have become slightly more important as the century advanced.

A consideration of the backgrounds of a selection of prominent JPs is indicative. For example, Sir William ffolkes, a chairman of Norfolk quarter sessions in the early Victorian period, had been educated at Harrow and Cambridge and was an MP, high sheriff, and deputy lieutenant for the county. Jacob Astley, the 23rd Baron Hastings, one of the largest landowners in the county, was educated at Eton and Oxford, and served in the Life Guards for several years before taking up permanent residence at the family seat in Melton Constable. There he "devoted himself to the duties and pursuits of country life." Fox hunting made up much of the latter, and service as a JP the former.[376]

In like manner, Sir Willoughby Jones, who was born in 1820, and resident at Cranmer Hall, had been educated at Eton and Cambridge and was a major landowner, briefly an MP, and a deputy lieutenant and high sheriff for the county. He was a JP and eventually a chairman of Norfolk quarter sessions from 1856 until his death in 1884.[377] Sir Thomas Leigh Hare, who died at Stow Hall, Downham Market, in 1880, had been a captain in both the Life Guards and West Norfolk Militia, as well as being a JP, deputy lieutenant, and high sheriff for the county.[378] The Right Honourable Thomas de Grey, the sixth Lord Walsingham, was educated at Eton and Cambridge, and was a sometime MP and world traveller, a scientific farmer, and a very keen sportsman, who had once shot 442 grouse in a single day, as well as being a JP and chairman of the Norfolk quarter sessions in the 1880s.[379]

Of course, these men were at the social peak of a very much larger pyramid of Norfolk JPs, helping to explain why they were often also chairmen of quarter sessions, high sheriffs, and lord/deputy lieutenants for the county. Perhaps significantly, most of this group had attended one of the two historic universities, especially Cambridge. Rank-and-file JPs, and there were many of them, would often be gentlemen of much more modest means and education. They might include individuals such as George Francis of Martham, who died in 1842 at the age of 51, and was both a JP for the county and captain in the East Norfolk Militia. He had lodgings in Norwich, but his 'seat' was a large farm, some of it rented.[380] Such men were more likely to have been required to demonstrate personal qualities, such as diligence and aptitude, and to have actively 'networked', before being selected. By the end of the eighteenth century, a high proportion of the busiest JPs (excluding chairmen),

---

375 *The Spectator,* 26 March, 1842.

376 *Baily's Monthly Magazine of Sports and Pastimes*, 1 February, 1871.

377 *The Times*, 22 August, 1884, p. 7.

378 *The Norfolk Chronicle,* 14 November, 1880.

379 *The County Gentleman: A Sporting Gazette and Agricultural Journal*, 14 May, 1887.

380 *The Bury and Norwich Post*, 7 December, 1842.

although certainly genteel, were not drawn from the very highest ranks of the gentry, while many others were clergymen (see below).[381]

Furthermore, not quite all county JPs fit the genteel template, although this was rarely the case in Victorian Norfolk. Even in the 1830s, those counties with large industrial areas, such as Lancashire, often added a significant number of commercial magnates to their benches. The modest property qualification meant that, in theory, even prosperous tradesmen might qualify. Nationally, poorer areas sometimes had recourse to ordinary businessmen. In Merioneth, a group of Welsh JPs temporarily refused to serve after a man who had kept a draper's shop, and who was also a dissenter, was appointed.[382] (The extreme reluctance to appoint anyone involved in retail would survive to the end of the century.)[383] Similarly, in 1859 Kent JPs were horrified when a Rochester innkeeper was appointed to their ranks.[384] At this time, even Whigs like Lord Melbourne favoured barring middle-class men from the county magistracy. On one (national) assessment, in 1842, the English counties had almost no openly middle-class JPs, still actively pursuing their commercial or manufacturing careers, after appointment. This changed to a modest degree over ensuing decades, and such men made up about 15 percent of magistrates in 1887. Middle-class JPs tended to be more active magistrates than many of their elite counterparts.[385]

Of course, even money made in industry or commerce was soon reflected in land, blurring the distinction between gentlemen and commercial men. Sir Edmund Knowles Lacon of Ormesby House in Norfolk, who died in 1839 at the age of 59, was an active JP in the hundreds around Great Yarmouth when the new Queen came to the throne. The Lacon family money had come from beer, Edmund's grandfather establishing a modest brewery and his father expanding it, as well as investing in other commercial ventures, such as whaling. However, whatever his antecedents, Sir Edmund had been educated at Eton, Cambridge, and Lincoln's Inn (where he briefly studied law). He had served as mayor of Yarmouth in 1807, sheriff of Norfolk in 1823, and had been a local MP as well as a major in the East Norfolk Militia.

Although change was apparent by the 1890s, a clear majority of provincial county JPs were still drawn from the gentry, even at the end of the century, especially in counties like Norfolk. A few, well under 10 percent, were aristocrats, though this group still provided most of a shire's lord lieutenants.[386] Major reform in this regard and the advent of large numbers of middle-class magistrates to the county commission would wait until the Edwardian period.

---

381 H.G. Cocks, "Safeguarding Civility: Sodomy, Class and Moral Reform in Early Nineteenth-Century England," *Past & Present*, vol. 190, no. 1 (2006), p. 134.

382 Cornish, *Oxford History,* p. 804.

383 Porritt, "At Petty Sessions," p. 473.

384 Conley, *The Unwritten Law,* p. 17.

385 Zangerl, "Social Composition," p. 115.

386 *Ibid.,* p. 115 and p. 124.

County JPs were also largely Tory during the Victorian era, although there were always individual and regional exceptions. For example, when the septuagenarian Sir William ffolkes died at Hillington Hall in 1860, it was noted that he had been a supporter of Liberal principles as an MP from 1830, through the Reform era, until losing his seat in 1837. He had also been chairman of the (adjourned) Norfolk quarter sessions when they were held at Swaffham.[387] George Danby Palmer was a wealthy Norfolk JP whose politics had, apparently, moved from Tory to Liberal to Radical before his death in 1866.[388] Nevertheless, the political complexion of provincial benches would change significantly only after 1906, when Lord Loreburn, the Lord Chancellor from 1905 to 1912, appointed thousands of politically liberal JPs to reduce Conservative dominance.

Lawyer JPs

Some Norfolk JPs – often about a dozen at any one time – were legally qualified (as barristers), something that, significantly, even the Duke of Wellington had encouraged. For example, when the elderly Sir Edward Stracey died in 1851, it was noted that, after attending Norwich Grammar School and Oxford, he had been called to the bar and served for a time as clerk of the House of Commons as well as being a JP for his native Norfolk (and for several years a chairman of quarter sessions in Cheshire).[389] Barrister JPs were exempt from the £100 property qualification (most could have met it). Although they made up only a small proportion of JPs in Norfolk, they were disproportionately active and influential and very much more likely than others to be made chairmen of quarter sessions.

Indicative of this, at the Norfolk quarter sessions held at the Norwich Shirehall in July 1855, two courts were in operation simultaneously, both with legally qualified chairmen. One was presided over by Edward Howes, a barrister, the other by T.J. Birch, a barrister and local county court judge.[390] Indeed, when the barrister Thomas Blofeld resigned as chairman of quarter sessions in 1908, due to failing health, another JP noted that Norfolk was fortunate in having had chairmen for most of the previous 80 years who had been "practicing barristers in their time."[391] Perhaps this was why, in 1882, Mr Justice Kay, having noted that opposition to extending the jurisdiction of quarter sessions was often based on the alleged legal ignorance of their chairmen, observed that this did not accord with his own experience of the Norfolk bench, where chairmen were normally very competent individuals.[392] (See also Chapter 9.)

---

387 *The Bury and Norwich Post*, 24 July, 1860.

388 *The Norfolk Chronicle,* 4 April, 1865.

389 Charles Mackie, *Norfolk Annals: A Chronological Record of Remarkable Events in the Nineteeth Century*, vol. 2 (Norwich: Norfolk Chronicle, 1901), p. 6.

390 *The Bury and Norwich Post*, 11 July, 1855.

391 *The Times*, 26 October, 1908, p. 2.

392 *Ibid.*, 20 October, 1882, p. 8.

Clerical JPs

During the latter decades of the eighteenth century, the need to recruit educated, permanently resident, genteel, relatively well-behaved, and conscientious men to serve as active JPs meant that the more prosperous and well-born elements of the clergy became a vital segment of the county bench, both in Norfolk and the wider country (although one or two counties, such as Sussex and Derbyshire, resisted this trend). Some 11 percent of English clergymen were JPs in 1761, but this had increased to about 25 percent in the early decades of the nineteenth century.[393] Although by the 1830s the glory days of the clerical magistracy were slowly coming to an end, on one assessment, one in four of the 5,300 active JPs nationally in 1832 were clergymen, and they remained a significant component of most benches until late in the nineteenth century.

Clerical JPs were particularly important in Norfolk, especially in areas without resident gentry. The county had a higher-than-average number of them, as the Earl of Albemarle complained in the House of Lords. (He thought that Suffolk, Essex, Lincolnshire, and Herefordshire shared this characteristic.)[394] Similarly, in 1842 it was noted in the House of Commons that Norfolk possessed a "great abundance of what are called clerical justices." It was claimed, perhaps with a little exaggeration, that there were then 102 of them in the county.[395] More reliably, it seems that in 1837 there were 78 clergymen on the Norfolk Commission, some 19.5 percent of all the county's active magistrates. By 1854 this had fallen to 68, but a general decline in numbers on the bench meant that they had increased as a proportion of the total to 23.7 percent. Their numbers had declined to 57 (19.5 percent) in 1868, and to 47 (17.2 percent) in 1883. Only in the final decades of the Victorian period was there a marked fall, something that accelerated during the Edwardian era, so that the number was just 17, or 5.3 percent of the total, in 1908. [396]

Clerical JPs were usually drawn from the wealthier elements of the clergy, so that more than half of those in Norfolk had a gentry background, even in 1883. The existence of "squarsons" was not entirely a myth. Most important, such men tended to be highly committed, when it came to attendance levels, until late in the century. For example, of the 2,403 petty sessions held in the Blofield and Walsham Division between 1839 and 1878, 1,243 (48.3 percent) had at least one clerical JP present.[397] In some divisions, it was not uncommon for two of the JPs sitting at petty sessions to be men of the cloth. Thus, two of the three JPs on the bench were clergymen at the petty sessions held at the Assembly Room in East Dereham in early November 1855, while an identical bench presided at the same forum at the start of December

[393] Boyd Hilton, *A Mad, Bad, and Dangerous People?: England 1783-1846* (Oxford: OUP, 2008), p. 20.

[394] Zangerl, "Social Composition," p. 119.

[395] Hansard HC Deb 22 March 1842 vol. 61 cols. 1078-84.

[396] Robert Lee, *Rural Society and the Anglican Clergy, 1815–1914: Encountering and Managing the Poor* (Woodbridge: Boydell Press, 2006), pp. 105-107.

[397] *Ibid.*

that year.[398] This was a normal pattern at East Dereham. A year later, in November 1856, two of the three JPs on the bench were clergymen.[399] Occasionally, all three members of the bench were in holy orders, as was the case at the East Dereham petty sessions in June 1853.[400] The Division was no means unusual, if on the high end of clerical involvement. For example, at the Attleborough petty sessions in the second week of May 1858, two of the three magistrates present were clergymen.[401]

At a time when many gentlemen were increasingly reluctant to serve actively as magistrates or had slightly irregular private lives (considered much less acceptable than in previous ages), the attractions of clerical JPs were obvious. They were well educated, locally grounded, and (usually) respectable and sober men who understood their areas.

Of course, their presence also raised pastoral problems, not least in the collection of tithes, although this was much less of an issue after reform in 1836. Nevertheless, and for example, in Diss in January 1865, a house painter named Ambrose Cob came before the Reverend C.R. Manning, rector of the same parish, accused of threatening to force a red-hot poker down his own wife's throat during a domestic disturbance in the small hours of the night. His spouse had fled to the protection of a local police station. The clerical JP bound Cob over in his own recognizance to keep the peace for £50, and required two other sureties from third parties, for £25 each, all for three months.[402] Although quite a lenient disposal, Cob was, at least potentially, one of Manning's congregation.

An awareness of the dangers of this conflict, a wider feeling that it should not be part of a clergyman's mission to engage in such work, along with a growing secularization in the wider society, influenced the withdrawal of clerical JPs towards the end of the nineteenth century, with the 1870s seeing an especially large fall in numbers nationally, although they survived until well into the twentieth century. Just as important, there was a decline in the willingness of such clerical magistrates as there were to sit actively as JPs during the 1880s, unlike the situation found in earlier decades, with increasing numbers viewing it as an honorary appointment or, as they got older, reducing their active involvement.[403]

Thus, the Reverend Benjamin Armstrong, the long-serving vicar of East Dereham in Norfolk, and a prolific diarist between 1850 and 1888, did not approve of clerical magistrates, even though he was otherwise very active in civic society – he helped establish the local rifle volunteers – feeling that the position was not consistent with

---

398 *The Norwich Mercury,* 14 November and 12 December, 1855.

399 *The Norfolk News,* 15 November, 1856.

400 *The Norfolk Chronicle,* 11 June, 1853.

401 *The Bury and Norwich Post*, 18 May, 1858.

402 *The Bury and Norwich Post and Suffolk Herald*, 10 January, 1865.

403 J.W.B. Tomlinson, "The Decline of the Clerical Magistracy in the Nineteenth-Century English Midlands," *Studies in Church History,* vol. 56 (2020), pp. 421-422.

being a friend to the poor.[404] Similarly, in the 1890s, when Canon Hinds Howell, a Norfolk clergyman, was elected chairman of his district council, and was, as a result, required to become a JP, he made it clear that this would be a formality: "It was not his intention to sit as a Magistrate. He was firmly of the opinion that Magistrates' work was not the work for clergymen to do. It would be a most painful thing for him to commit anybody to prison, whatever the offence might be." Nevertheless, even in this final decade of the Victorian era, there were still observers who felt that clergymen were well fitted for the bench, if only because a vicar was often the most educated man in his district, knew the local people and their temptations well, and tended to "possess the impartiality and serenity which are the first essentials of the judicial character".[405]

Removal from Office

By the nineteenth century, it was rare for JPs to be removed from the bench unless they did something very wrong, such as committing a serious crime. (Visiting judges of the assizes might rebuke erring magistrates for lesser transgressions in office.)[406] As a result, they were almost lifetime appointments, unless a magistrate voluntarily retired for reasons of convenience, old age, or health, as not infrequently occurred. In an extreme case, from a decade or so before the start of the Victorian era, when William Manning died at his house in Norwich in 1825, at the age of 93, it was noted that he was the "Father of the Magistracy of Norfolk, and had been 65 years on the commission."[407]

Unfortunately, even high social status did not entirely preclude serious misconduct that warranted removal from office. Two years before the Queen took the throne, Robert Orris, a Norfolk JP and chairman of the quarter sessions that sat at Walsingham, became mired in scandal and fled the country. It was alleged that he had forged documents that had defrauded various people, including some of his relatives, of £25,000. Orris appears to have escaped to America, leaving his motherless 12 children behind.[408] Ironically, he had been admired for his knowledge of the law and willingness to temper justice with mercy prior to his fall from grace.[409]

More commonly, JPs might indulge in excessive drinking and low-level violence. However, during the Victorian period, official tolerance for such high jinks declined. Towards the end of the Queen's reign, in July 1895, at Smallburgh petty sessions, Lord John Wodehouse, another Old Etonian Norfolk JP, was fined for assaulting John Gaymer while the latter was presiding at a Conservative meeting held at North

404 See generally, Susannah Wade Martins, *A Vicar in Victorian Norfolk: The Life and Times of Benjamin Armstrong (1817-1890)* (Woodbridge: Boydell Press, 2018).

405 *The Spectator*, 19 January, 1895, p. 12.

406 Philips, "A 'Weak' State?" pp. 883-884.

407 *The Norfolk Chronicle*, 30 June, 1825.

408 *John Bull*, 4 May, 1835.

409 *The Bury and Norwich Post*, 24 April, 1833.

Walsham. Lord Wodehouse had seized Gaymer by the coat, dragged him from the chair while using foul language, and offered to fight him for £50. Sir Henry Preston, the chairman of the bench, noted that the violence had not occasioned injury, and so fined Wodehouse just £3 7s 6d with costs of £1 12s 6d, for a total of £5.[410] Even so, the Lord Chancellor subsequently removed Wodehouse from the Norfolk commission of the peace.[411] (He was reinstated five years later.)[412] Less seriously, at the county quarter sessions at Swaffham in 1890, Charles Fountaine, a JP and deputy lieutenant for Norfolk (and also a master of fox hounds there), was fined £25 for forcing a Great Eastern Railway train to make an unscheduled stop.[413]

Borough Justices

Norwich, Thetford, King's Lynn, and Great Yarmouth all had their own borough magistrates during the Victorian era, with exclusive jurisdiction over their towns, their selection having been reformed by the Municipal Corporations Act 1835. In theory, under this statute, boroughs could also apply to the Crown for the appointment of a stipendiary magistrate, like those found in the Metropolis, who was required to be a barrister of seven years' standing, provided they were willing to pay his salary. In 1863 all towns of over 25,000 people were empowered to do this, even if they were not covered by the 1835 Act. There were potential benefits in doing so. Stipendiary magistrates were experienced lawyers, authorized to decide on their own what would otherwise require the agreement of a bench of at least two JPs. They were usually reliable, fast, efficient, and not dependent on their clerks for legal advice.[414] In 1845 the barrister J. Stone thought that they should be universal, while in the early 1860s the noted barrister Thomas William Saunders unavailingly urged their general introduction in England, thinking that there was no obvious reason that only large urban environments would benefit from them.[415]

In the late 1840s and early 1850s, some observers in Norfolk itself suggested that there would be benefits to introducing stipendiary magistrates in Norwich.[416] In 1853 Captain Dunne, the superintendent of its police force, went further and claimed that many of its inhabitants thought that the appointment of a stipendiary

---

410 *The Essex County Standard West Suffolk Gazette and Eastern Counties Advertiser*, 3 August, 1895.

411 *The Norfolk Chronicle*, 30 July, 1895.

412 *The York Herald*, 12 September, 1900.

413 *The Bury and Norwich Post*, 15 July, 1890.

414 Alexander, *The administration*, p. 12.

415 *Eighth Report of Her Majesty's Commissioners on Criminal Law* (London: HMSO, 1845), p. 301. Thomas William Saunders, *Quarter and Petty Sessions: A Letter to ... Sir George Grey upon the Present Defective System of Administering Justice in Our Courts of Quarter Sessions and Petty Sessions, with Suggestions for Improvement* (London, 1863), p. 11.

416 "First Report from the Select Committee on Police; with Minutes of Evidence" in *Parliamentary Papers*, volume 36 (London: HMSO, 1853), p. 121.

would be a "very great advantage" to the city.[417] Even so, it did not happen. Indeed, comparatively few boroughs nationally adopted this course, not least because of the expense involved. Only 20 English and Welsh cities, suburbs, and towns had professional magistrates in 1900, none of them in Norfolk.[418] (Three were in and around Manchester and two in Leeds.)[419]

Instead, borough justices remained part-time, unpaid amateurs, like their county counterparts. Nevertheless, their appointment had changed by the Victorian era. The Municipal Corporations Act 1835 provided for them to be nominated by the Lord Chancellor (like those for the county) after consultation with local advisers, something that made them slightly less partisan and exclusive than previously. In practice, the Home Secretary also became heavily involved in this process. However, unlike the situation in the county, the lord lieutenant did not play an important role in borough appointments.[420]

The social provenance of borough magistrates often differed from that of their rural counterparts. They were exempt from the £100 property requirement. Nationally, in 1841, more than 43 percent of them were, in some way, "middle class," and this figure would be over 71 percent by 1885.[421] Although change was slower in older towns and cities, such as Lincoln and Norwich, than in the new industrial centres like Wolverhampton, even the former had very strong middle-class representation on their benches by the mid-1880s.[422] Such JPs tended to be merchants, prominent tradesmen, and successful professional men. For example, George Firth, who died in 1878, had been senior surgeon to the Norfolk and Norwich Hospital and a magistrate in that city.[423] Nevertheless, they were not necessarily homogenous. There could be social tensions between the different groups found or urban benches. In one case from 1853, a Norwich justice disparaged a colleague who was engaged in retail by telling him that he should go home and ticket the items for sale in his shop window.[424]

Boroughs, in Norfolk as elsewhere, did not normally have clerical magistrates, unlike their surrounding counties. On one assessment, clergymen made up well under one percent of the national total in 1841, but considerably more than 13 percent in the counties in 1842 (and far more in Norfolk).[425] In practice, many borough

---

417 *The Bury and Norwich Post*, 13 July, 1853.

418 Bentley, *English Criminal Justice*, p. 22.

419 Alexander, *The administration,* p. 15.

420 Porritt, "At Petty Sessions," p. 473.

421 Zangerl, "Social Composition," p. 115.

422 Cornish, *Oxford History,* p. 911.

423 *The Norfolk Chronicle,* 14 October, 1878.

424 *The Bury and Norwich Post*, 13 July, 1853

425 Zangerl, "Social Composition," p. 115.

magistrates were still drawn from those who were, or had once been, active in corporation politics, such as the mayor and senior aldermen. For example, in 1844 the small and very quiet borough of Thetford had four municipal magistrates, one of whom, Leonard Shelford Bidwell, was also the mayor and an alderman. Another, the fertilizer merchant James Fison, had been mayor in 1840, while a third, Richard Munn, had served as mayor in 1837.[426]

Nevertheless, the two breeds of magistrate, county and borough, were not hermetically sealed from each other. It was not uncommon for individuals to be members of both benches, whether at the same or different times in their lives. In the early nineteenth century, some 19 percent of borough magistrates were also county JPs although very few of them served actively outside their boroughs.[427] For a specific example, George Danby Palmer, who died at the age of 77 in 1865, was the oldest member of the Yarmouth borough bench as well as being a JP for Norfolk.[428] As this suggests, and like their county counterparts, borough magistrates could also be quite elderly and long serving. In January 1876 Abel Towler, one of the most senior magistrates in Norwich, died at the age of 83.[429]

Questions of political allegiance influenced appointment to the borough bench, just as they did with their county equivalents, even if framed in a slightly more parochial context, and with a greater radical (and nonconformist) element. At a meeting of the Norwich City Council in January 1858, Jacob Henry Tillett asked that an inquiry be held into the way in which the city magistrates were selected, and their business conducted. His motion was adopted, and a committee of inquiry appointed, which reported the following month. Its members considered that the selection process in cities and boroughs generally (not just Norwich) was highly objectionable, the appointments often being the result of party influence. It also recommended that the city magistracy be drawn from those who had already served as mayor "to the satisfaction of the Council." Furthermore, it found that there had been well-grounded complaints that some Norwich magistrates, due to excitement or bad temper, made use of inappropriate language "tending to lower the respect of the Bench."[430] Later that same year, Lord Sondes presented the House of Lords with a petition from borough magistrates in Great Yarmouth, asking for an inquiry into the recent appointment of justices in the coastal town. It was claimed that the existing complement of magistrates were conscientious in carrying out their duties and sufficiently numerous, but that all of those recently appointed had owed their allegiance to just one political party.[431]

---

[426] William Creasy Ewing, *Norfolk Lists, from the Reformation to the Present Time* (Norwich: Matchett, Stevenson & Matchett, 1837), p. 119.

[427] Rose Madeleine Wallis, *The Relationship Between Magistrates and their Communities*, p. 84.

[428] *The Norfolk Chronicle,* 4 April, 1865.

[429] *Ibid.* , 29 January, 1876.

[430] Mackie, *Norfolk Annals,* vol. 2, p. 70.

[431] *The Norfolk Chronicle,* 22 March, 1858.

As with their county counterparts, some borough magistrates did not attend court, whether petty or borough quarter sessions, on a regular basis, particularly if they no longer held local political office. In March 1858 the Norwich Council requested that the mayor write to absentee magistrates, requiring them to discharge their duties, and that a rota of attendance be established.[432] Similarly, although the borough of Great Yarmouth had 31 magistrates who were qualified to sit at petty and borough sessions in the late 1850s (about one for every 1,000 inhabitants), many of them did not do so, especially in the non-jury forum.[433] This absenteeism was evidenced by an incident at the town "police court" (petty sessions) in 1862. The editor of a local newspaper had applied to the court to have two men, who he alleged had been abusive towards him, summonsed with a view to having them bound over to keep the peace. On the day that they were due to appear, far more than the usual complement of magistrates turned up. Along with six regular attenders, another 11 "strange magistrates" joined the bench and ensured that, when the decision on binding the two men over was taken, a majority voted against requiring them to keep the peace. The backwoodsmen were all Conservatives, the regular attenders mainly Liberals.[434]

Popular Reputation of JPs

At the start of the Victorian era, the English magistracy did not enjoy a very high reputation amongst many ordinary people. This was largely a result of their involvement in the social conflicts of the 1820s and 1830s. In Norfolk the Reverend Charles Brereton thought that many JPs, having been allowed to exercise discretionary powers during these times, were now so self-satisfied as "to think juries are a great inconvenience, subordinate officers dolts, and law and course of law perfect nonsense."[435] Perhaps indicative of this, in 1833 it was alleged that four Norfolk men had been committed to prison for up to 18 months with hard labour for little more than vigorously encouraging other agricultural workers to participate in a strike. Some observers thought that a verbal reprimand from the bench would have been sufficient, and that the sentence was indicative of the attitudes of many JPs. It was alleged that they made law whatever they thought it should be, and "the peasantry are treated by them as so many asses".[436]

---

432 Mackie, *Norfolk Annals*, vol. 2, p. 72.

433 *The Norfolk Chronicle*, 22 March, 1858.

434 *The Bury and Norwich Post and Suffolk Herald*, 21 October, 1862.

435 C.D. Brereton, *The Subordinate Magistracy and Parish System Considered in their Connexion with the Causes and Remedies of Modern Pauperism* (Norwich: Hatchard, n.d. [c. 1827]), p. 36.

436 *The Examiner*, 3 November, 1833.

Bias

A long-standing criticism of the magistracy during the first half of the nineteenth century was that they sometimes acted as JPs in cases in which they had a personal interest. For example, and notoriously, in 1822 a farmer was accused of an offence under the Game Acts, summonsed by one of the Duke of Buckingham's keepers, and tried and convicted by the duke himself, in the nobleman's own home, on the evidence of yet another of his keepers.[437] In Norfolk, in October 1838, John Robinson, a former seaman, was summarily committed by JPs to two months' imprisonment with hard labour to the House of Correction at Little Walsingham as a rogue and a vagabond, for begging at the door of James Buck in Stiffkey and abusing Buck's servants a few days earlier. The following month, Colonel Fox, a visiting magistrate, reported to the Home Office that the sentence was very severe (it was an archaic power and usually produced sentences of a week or two), and expressed concern that the committing magistrate was also named Buck, suggesting that he was connected to the "victim."[438]

Nevertheless, this was rare by the start of the Victorian period, and subject to official (as well as popular) disapproval. More typically, JPs would recuse themselves from such cases. For example, at the Norfolk quarter sessions held at Walsingham in January 1842, at which Lord James Townshend was the chairman, Nicholas Gould was sentenced to a month's imprisonment for stealing wood and turnips from the same nobleman. However, it was reported that another JP, F.W. Keppel, had passed sentence (although this was normally the chairman's responsibility), suggesting that steps were taken to prevent the latter judging his own case. Even so, Keppel was suitably scathing about Gould's ingratitude, noting that he had been taken on as an employee by Townshend when in the workhouse and given good wages.[439]

By the latter part of the Victorian period, the potential for personal bias was viewed as clearly improper. It was generally felt that, where there was the slightest suggestion of self-interest, JPs should not only not act in the case, but ought to retire from the bench while the matter was heard.[440] For example, in 1887 in Suffolk, when three men were accused at petty sessions of trespassing in pursuit of game on the land of John Chevallier, a county JP, it was noted that "Mr Chevallier retired from the Bench during the hearing of this case."[441]

Of course, it was very much harder to prevent more general (rather than personal) forms of social or occupational bias. Thus, in 1860, the Reverend Edward Neale, the vicar of the isolated parish of Horsey in the Norfolk Broads, was unable to conduct a funeral for the recently born child of two poor (and newly arrived) residents in

---

437 Bentley, *English Criminal Justice,* p. 23.

438 TNA HO 17/38/192.

439 *The Bury and Norwich Post*, 19 January, 1842.

440 Alexander, *The administration,* p. 11.

441 *The Ipswich Journal*, 23 December, 1887.

the hamlet, because the infant had not been baptized. However, he agreed that the body should be interred in the churchyard, after receiving an assurance that there would be no hymn-singing over the grave. Even so, after the small corpse had been buried, the parents broke into song, despite repeated requests to cease. Neale subsequently (and very unusually) preferred a charge of "indecent behavior in a churchyard" at petty sessions. The trial took place in front of a relatively large five-man bench, chaired by Sir Jacob Preston, one that also included two clerics, although they might be considered likely to be inherently unsympathetic to the accused. Both defendants were convicted, and each fined a shilling and costs, with three days' imprisonment in lieu of payment. (One of them indicated an intention to appeal the matter to quarter sessions).[442]

Wider class-bias amongst JPs was also, perhaps, inevitable, and this was often acknowledged at the time. It was not found solely in those dwelling in remote rural areas. In a telling comment from 1880, the *Spectator* observed that those in the neighbourhood of large towns were: "often more tempted to class-justice than even the country justices, at least if game-law cases be excluded." It cited a case from the Edmonton petty sessions, just to the north of London, in which three "gentlemen" were brought up accused of disorder and violently resisting the police. They had caused one of the officers serious injuries and broken a stick over another and bitten his hand. Even so, the defendants were merely fined £4 each and costs, the magistrates noting that they had also suffered the indignity of walking handcuffed to the police station, as if they were felons, so that the Bench had decided to deal with the case lightly. As the journal noted, if the defendants had been workingmen, no allowance would have been made for their public humiliation, yet such conduct was more discreditable in those who were well born.[443]

In rural areas, there was an especially widespread feeling that upper-class JPs were not impartial when determining poaching cases but did their own "game preserving".[444] Admittedly, the most blatant examples of this were usually avoided by the early Victorian period. For example, in 1846 Sir Edwyn Stanhope retired from the Herefordshire bench that was hearing a case of poaching on his own estate.[445] Nevertheless, in 1848 the radical MP John Bright observed in Parliament that the great body of the people, including the tenantry and peasantry in agricultural districts, had "no confidence whatever in the administration of the game laws by county magistrates." He was convinced that, whether intentionally or not, such cases saw a great departure from the legal principles and safeguards that governed other criminal laws.[446] There was considerable support for his view. It seems that in many rural areas between 1844 and 1845 "so much irregularity" had been found in

442 *The Royal Cornwall Gazette*, 19 October, 1860.

443 *The Spectator,* 21 August, 1880, p. 2.

444 *Pall Mall Gazette*, 26 March, 1892.

445 Shakesheff, *Rural Conflict,* p. 142.

446 Hansard HC Deb 23 March 1848 vol 97 cols. 918-64, 931.

the trial of game-law offences that a significant number of pardons and mitigations of sentence had to be issued.[447]

Of course, social bias can be exaggerated. Even in game cases some JPs were very reluctant to strictly enforce the poaching laws, especially in areas where shooting was not a major industry. Captain W.J. Williams, an inspector of prisons in Norfolk, observed that in some places one magistrate would uphold certain laws to their extreme while another would "scarcely have anything to do with them."[448] Many magistrates, whatever their personal interests, tried to be fair, according to their lights. For example, the JPs at the West Riding petty sessions who tried employees accused of workplace appropriations of material frequently included worsted manufacturers in their ranks, and in just over a fifth of cases they made up the entire bench. Even so, cases of this type in which both the magistrates on a two-man bench were textile masters produced average conviction rates.[449] In 1848, when sentencing the well-to-do thief George Thurtell, the chairman of the Norfolk quarter sessions, stressed that the country did not have "one law for the poor, and another for the rich."[450]

Decision Making on the Bench

As with jurors, when it came to communal decisions made by a bench at petty sessions or committal it would be naïve to imagine that all JPs had the same influence. The views of those with experience, ability, high social status, or a combination thereof, might carry more heft than those of more marginal men. In 1875 a correspondent to the *Times* cited a case from several years earlier, in which two young JPs in Norfolk had met to take petty sessions on their own, the older members of the bench, who normally attended, being absent. They were shocked at the large number of weights-and-measures prosecutions that came before them, but found that this was normal, because those convicted were never fined more than 5 shillings a time "so they did not care". On this occasion, the JPs imposed £3 fines when the cases were proved and warned that in future it would be the £5 maximum allowed. It was claimed that this prompted a sharp decline in the number of such cases in the local area.[451]

---

447 Tracey Elizabeth Young, *Popular Attitudes towards Rural Customs and Rights in Late Nineteenth and Early Twentieth Century England*, University of Hertfordshire PhD thesis, 2008, p. 175.

448 *Ibid*.

449 Barry Godfrey, "Judicial Impartiality and the Use of Criminal Law against Labour: The Sentencing of Workplace Appropriators in Northern England, 1840-1880," *Crime, History & Societies*, vol. 3, no. 2 (1999), p. 70.

450 *The Ipswich Journal*, 8 January, 1848.

451 *The Times*, 25 May, 1875, p. 10.

Chapter 5: The Pre-Trial

Introduction

Having been arrested for an indictable offence, suspects would have to be processed through the criminal-justice system to trial, or discharged before getting to a hearing, this phase of proceedings constituting what is sometimes termed, especially in North America, the "pre-trial." This would entail initial detention, production before a magistrate, remand to a committal hearing, a decision about whether to send a matter for trial, and, if so, for what charges and to what court, along with attendant decisions on bail and associated matters such as witness orders.

Initial Detention

In practice, as an observer noted towards the end of the Victorian era, a detained man would normally be marched (often in handcuffs) by a police or parish constable to a magistrate, within 24 hours of his arrest.[452] (Under the Summary Jurisdiction Act 1879 he would usually be released on police bail if this had not occurred within that time.) However, if arrested late in the evening, or a long way from a magistrate or prison, a suspect might have to be secured overnight. At the start of the Victorian era this was often in the cellar of an inn, a cell attached to a constable's house, or a village lockup. The last were normally maintained by traditional local parish constables and were also used for drunkards. Typically, they consisted of a single chamber built from brick or stone with a reinforced door and a small window protected by a grating. (Surviving examples in Norfolk remain at Docking, Stalham, Thetford, and Watton.) They were still used during the early years of the new post-1840 rural police force, when each division had only, at best, access to a pony and trap to move its prisoners.[453]

Occasionally even these expedients were not readily available. In 1842 this led to a major outcry, with questions asked in Parliament, after an incident from the previous year came to notice. Superintendent Smith of the Norfolk rural police was found to be temporarily securing suspects by chaining them to a cattle manger in a barn.[454] In the case that brought this practice to light, a man had been arrested on the minor charge of vagrancy after selling tracts without a hawker's licence. However, the superintendent had to go to Yarmouth to execute a warrant and, in the meantime, left the vagrant chained to the manger, instructing another officer's wife to feed him at a set hour. Someone later freed the prisoner, and he was subsequently found wandering through the streets of Norwich, still wearing two pairs of handcuffs, while shoeless and only partially dressed. Although Colonel Oakes, the chief constable of the Norfolk Constabulary, noted that the barn provided better and more spacious

452 Porritt, "At Petty Sessions," p. 473.

453 Neil R. Storey, *Norfolk Villains: Rogues, Rascals and Reprobates* (Cheltenham: The History Press, 2012), p. 10.

454 *The Bury and Norwich Post*, 4 May, 1842.

accommodation than most village lockups, and that it had not been used to hold anything other than clean straw for a long time, many were shocked by what had occurred.[455]

Another case, from about the same time, involved a Norfolk policeman who had arrested a prisoner for burglary. He handcuffed him to his bedpost on a Saturday night and kept him secured in this fashion during the following day. He eventually took pity on the man and allowed him to get into bed with him on the Sunday night, albeit handcuffed to the officer's arm. The suspect was then produced before a JP on the Monday. (JPs did not normally sit on the Sabbath.)[456] Of course, such cases were not unique to Norfolk, and had their roots in earlier forms of policing. Thus in 1845 there was another scandal after it transpired that some traditional parish constables in Shropshire were in the habit of securing suspects (including women) overnight by handcuffing or chaining them to a chimney support in a local beer house.[457]

The situation in Norfolk (and elsewhere in the country) eased as the century advanced. In late 1840 the JPs of the Norfolk Police Committee recommended building more station houses with cells, on the basis that many lockups were insecure, while the practice of holding prisoners overnight in inns before they were examined was also felt to be unsatisfactory.[458] Most lockups, let alone informal alternatives, became redundant during the mid-1800s, as police stations with their own holding facilities were constructed, and transport improved with the growth of railways. For example, in 1848 part of Wymondham prison was converted into a police station, with three cells for men and women who were under arrest.[459]

First Appearance before a JP

Those detained for a serious indictable offence would normally be produced in front of one or (much less commonly) more magistrates for an initial examination, often held in a public house or similar building, along with the complainant and any potential prosecution witnesses. This JP might then remand them to a formal committal hearing, whether individual or, more frequently for run-of-the-mill crimes, one conducted at petty sessions. At this initial appearance, the magistrate would usually only hear sufficient evidence to justify a remand in custody.[460] Occasionally, a first appearance might be before petty sessions, if someone was held just before they sat. Thus, in April 1875, when a publican named William Wilkinson was charged

---

455 Hansard HC Deb 26 April 1842 vol 62 cols. 1171-5.

456 Hansard HC Deb 22 March 1842 vol 61 cols. 1078-84.

457 Cox, "Habitual Eccentricities," p. 110.

458 *The Bury and Norwich Post*, 28 October, 1840.

459 *Ibid.*, 11 November, 1873.

460 Porritt, "At Petty Sessions," p. 473.

with attempting to murder his brother-in-law, he initially appeared at the Terrington petty sessions near King's Lynn, where he was remanded to a committal hearing.[461]

At this first stage, cases that were extremely weak or unfounded and which were not very serious might be dismissed. For example, one evening in March 1865, when Albert Pell and his brother crossed fields at Caister, together with a dog, the landowner alleged that they were poaching, and gave them into the custody of a policeman. This officer, after detaining them at his cottage overnight, took them before a JP at Thrigby who swiftly dismissed the charge, so that the men were released.[462]

A selection of Norfolk examples is indicative of normal practice. In December 1851, when six poachers were seized by the rural police, after dark, they were produced before a JP the same night and, after a short examination, temporarily committed to the county prison in Norwich to await formal examination and committal.[463] In May 1869, William George Davey, a baker from Swaffham, and his wife, Susannah, were produced before a JP for their initial appearance, after being accused of trying to poison the former's brother. There they were remanded in custody for further examination and committal.[464] In March 1878, after Fuller Williamson attempted to murder his wife, he was produced before a single JP sitting on a Monday at Reepham, where he was remanded to Norwich Castle prison until a committal hearing, to be held on the following Saturday.[465]

In exceptionally serious cases, especially murder, more than one JP might make the effort to take part in the initial hearing, although this was not necessary. For example, in 1853, when William Thompson was arrested for murder and robbery on the highway, he was held overnight in the Griffin tavern because the nearest police station was too far away, and then produced before two county JPs sitting at the Bull Inn in Litcham. These magistrates carried out a preliminary examination of the suspect and other potential witnesses before remanding him in custody to another hearing, where more evidence could be adduced.[466]

In theory, albeit rarely in practice, this first appearance might also constitute the committal hearing or (more commonly) part of such a hearing, especially if two JPs were present, so that bail could be considered. (A single JP could not grant bail until 1848, although he might commit for trial in limited circumstances.) Thus, in December 1875, the notorious triple murderer Robert Edwards first appeared in front of a bench of four Norwich magistrates at the city Guildhall. The town clerk

---

461 *The Manchester Times*, 10 April, 1875.

462 Pell subsequently sued for assault, false imprisonment, and malicious prosecution, albeit with mixed results: *The Norfolk Chronicle*, 28 March, 1865.

463 *The Morning Post*, 15 December, 1851.

464 *The Bury and Norwich Post*, 1 June, 1869.

465 *The Ipswich Journal*, 9 March, 1878.

466 *Ibid.*, 26 November, 1853. *The Morning Chronicle*, 21 November, 1853.

(instructed by the chief constable) prosecuted while the prisoner was unrepresented. When opening the case, the clerk intimated that he only proposed to call sufficient evidence to justify a remand in custody, to allow more time for the case to be prepared properly. A limited number of witnesses were then called, but their formal depositions were taken and read over to them, so that they became part of the committal process. The prisoner was remanded until the following Thursday, when the rest of the committal hearing was held, and he was formally sent for trial at the next assizes.[467]

Very occasionally a suspect who had initially been detained in custody by a magistrate did not subsequently go before examining JPs at a committal hearing. For example, in 1852 John Clerk was arrested in connection with arson (rick burning) committed against his master's premises at Shropham. However, after a couple of nights in Norwich Castle gaol (possibly a Saturday and Sunday), "no bill was preferred, for lack of evidence, and the prisoner was discharged."[468] (He was not so fortunate when accused of a similar crime a year later.)[469]

At the start of the Victorian era, large numbers of people might still be subjected to an initial magistrates' examination, on a rather speculative basis, after a serious crime had been committed, even if they were swiftly discharged. This was a legacy of the JPs' traditional investigative role. For example, more than 30 people were examined before different magistrates, on suspicion of having been concerned in the murder of a Mr Richardson in Surrey in 1834, nearly all being swiftly discharged for want of "sufficient evidence to warrant their detention."[470] This type of old-fashioned quasi-police work was very much less common during the early Victorian era, when magisterial questioning was frowned upon, and disappeared altogether after 1848, when it was banned by statute.

Committal Proceedings

Many routine committals were heard at petty sessions. In these situations, the JPs would take a break from hearing summary trials or dealing with local administrative matters to consider whether a case should be sent for trial on indictment. Thus, at the East Harling petty sessions in December 1876, at which three JPs were in attendance, two matters were committed for trial at quarter sessions, one involving the theft of a guineafowl and the other that of a coat. There were also summary trials for being drunk and disorderly, using abusive language to a vaccination officer, and trespassing in pursuit of rabbits.[471] Similarly, at the petty sessions for North Erpingham held in March 1843, Edmund Fennel was committed for trial at quarter

---

467 *The Norfolk Chronicle*, 18 December, 1875.

468 *The Bury and Norwich Post*, 2 August, 1854.

469 *The Ipswich Journal*, 29 July, 1854.

470 *The Spectator*, 12 April, 1834, p. 4.

471 *The Bury and Norwich Post*, 26 December, 1876.

sessions for shop-breaking and theft.[472] Thirty years later, at the Diss petty sessions of March 1873, George Ward and Mower Gray, were accused of stealing a shilling from a baker in the town. They "reserved their defence" for their trial (see below) and were remanded to the following quarter sessions for a hearing.[473]

Occasionally, even the committal hearing for a serious crime might be heard at petty sessions, as was the case in July 1840, when John Randlesome was accused of murdering his wife. His committal was held along with other business at the Loddon petty sessions (five JPs were on the bench).[474] Many years later, at the start of 1898, the committal of Mark Cross for attempting to murder a former lover was also held at the North Walsham petty sessions. The evidence establishing a prima facie case was straightforward, as he had been recognised and made admissions when arrested, so that he was swiftly sent for trial at assizes.[475]

However, frequently, when a very serious or complex crime, such as murder or fraud, was involved, a bespoke committal hearing might be convened, outside petty sessions, to determine whether the matter should be sent for jury trial, and to draw up the various depositions required. At other times, it was simply more convenient to schedule a special hearing for a particular case.

Bespoke Committal Hearings

Special committals might be conducted in prisons, bridewells, town halls, inns, or, later in the nineteenth century, the same purpose-built magistrates' courts used for petty sessions (where they existed), and would sometimes attract a substantial bench, especially if they involved homicide.[476] Thus a murder committal held in the justice room of the town hall in Yarmouth in October 1852 was dealt with by six borough magistrates.[477] Such hearings might also attract crowds, if open to the public. In 1881, when the child-murderer Henry Stebbing was held for killing Hannah Brett, he was produced before county JPs sitting at Wayland Hall, an events venue in Watton, where petty sessions were held once a fortnight. Hundreds of people were waiting to abuse him as he left under heavy police escort after being committed to the Norfolk assizes for trial.[478]

Such committal hearings might be adjourned and resumed over several days; if the evidence was not initially clear, the court would take time to consider as much material as was available, or to allow further prosecution witnesses to be identified

---

472 PS 24/1/1 Hundred of North Erpingham Norfolk Special and Petty Sessions Record Commencing 3rd July 1841 NRO PS 24/1/1.

473 *The Bury and Norwich Post*, 11 March, 1873.

474 *The Ipswich Journal*, 18 July, 1840.

475 *The Bury and Norwich Post*, 4 January, 1898.

476 *The Norfolk Chronicle*, 18 December, 1875.

477 *The Times*, 21 October, 1852, p. 5.

478 *The Sheffield Independent*, 1 November, 1881.

and brought to court. James Rush's notorious double murder of Isaac Jermy, the recorder of Norwich, and his son at Stanfield Hall near Wymondham in 1848, can be considered an extreme case in this regard. The Norwich city police arrested Rush at his home on the night of the crime and took him to Wymondham bridewell. Shortly afterwards, the first examination of the prisoner took place in the prison before three county JPs. Rush was subsequently taken under guard to Stanfield Hall, where Mrs Jermy (who had been seriously wounded in the attack) identified him as her assailant. At about the same time, he was examined again by JPs at the bridewell. He was then committed to Norwich Castle prison, where a third hearing was conducted a few days later. The fourth and final examination took place at the castle just over a week afterwards, when the prisoner was formally committed to trial on two charges of murder.[479]

Similarly, in October 1877 an intoxicated Henry March committed a double murder, was swiftly arrested, and brought before magistrates who then remanded him in custody to the petty sessions at Wymondham on the following Monday, where he was examined further, but again remanded (while the inquest into the deaths was completed); he appeared before magistrates again on the Thursday and on this occasion was committed for trial at the Norfolk assizes.[480]

Sometimes, in serious and complex cases, JPs might hold preliminary hearings simply to sift the evidence from which depositions grew. The suspect could be absent for these, provided he was present when the depositions were formally taken.[481] Suspects would be held in custody between examinations.

Statutory Regulation of Committal Proceedings

The requirement for a JP's examination in felony cases (it was later extended on a de facto basis to many misdemeanours) dated back to the reign of Queen Mary and was originally governed by a statute from 1554 (2 & 3 P & M c.10). The Criminal Law Act 1826 replaced this legislation, but reiterated many of its provisions, including the requirement that JPs take the examination of those suspected of felony, along with the sworn information of those who knew details of the case (potential prosecution witnesses), and put them in writing. Thus, in July 1840, at the committal hearing that followed a murder at Thwaite, it was noted that a witness who had given a deposition "swore to the contents and signed them."[482] The 1826 Act also reiterated their power to bind over potential prosecutors and prosecution witnesses by recognizance to appear at ensuing quarter sessions or assizes to prosecute or give evidence against the accused person. The depositions and recognisances taken would be sent up to the trial court, whether quarter sessions or assizes, before the

---

479 *The Norfolk Chronicle,* 28 November, 1848.

480 *The Huddersfield Chronicle*, 27 October, 1877.

481 W. Wesley Pue, "The Criminal Twilight Zone: Pre-Trial Procedures in the 1840's," *Alberta Law Review*, vol. 21, no. 2 (1983), p. 337.

482 *The Ipswich Journal*, 18 July, 1840.

relevant hearing, where they would, among other things, be read by the judge or chairman before trial.

By the start of the Victorian era, there was a general belief that such preliminary hearings had two main purposes: to prepare prosecution evidence properly for trial so that the guilty did not escape conviction due to oversight or technicality, and to stop frivolous, vexatious, or misguided prosecutions before they could harm or embarrass the innocent. In the words of Robert Sowler QC (1813-1871): "The preliminary inquiry before the magistrates on criminal charges appears to be well adapted to the purpose for which it was originally instituted – viz., to prevent the incarceration of the innocent as far as possible, and to sift and arrange the evidence against the guilty."[483]

Indicative of the second of these considerations, in 1841 Jemima Stimson, a 15-year-old girl, was murdered while weeding alone in a turnip field near Wymondham Common. Subsequently, her mangled corpse was found hidden in a nearby cornfield. John Self, a 20-year-old labourer, was seen nearby, and immediately suspected. After being arrested, he was taken before two JPs for examination, where he claimed that blood found on his clothes had been caused by binding up another man's wounds. This person was then promptly located and called to testify on the issue, when he denied that any such incident had occurred. (Self was also found in possession of a knife belonging to the victim.) The JPs committed him for trial to the forthcoming assizes, where he was convicted.[484] Furthermore, once a complaint for a crime had been lodged with a magistrate, there was less room for manipulating the criminal process. In theory, if not always in practice, once this had been done, magistrates could not consent to a withdrawal from prosecution.[485]

The character of JPs' examinations had changed by the early nineteenth century. They were more searching and "judicial," less part of a police process, than they had been. Although some early-modern commentators had referred to examining JPs wringing out confessions from suspects, such pressure was no longer viewed as acceptable, and magistrates would usually caution suspects before asking questions. This development was greatly reinforced by Jervis's Indictable Offences Act of 1848, which was aimed at facilitating JPs' "out of sessions" work with respect to those charged with indictable crimes. It re-enacted and consolidated much existing law, both statutory and common law, and what was then considered best practice, without effecting huge changes, even though it was aimed at ensuring both fairness to the accused and the effective repression of crime.[486] However, the 1848 Act did outlaw magisterial questioning of suspects (they could still cross-examine the prosecution's witnesses). Thenceforth magistrates merely asked whether the suspect wished to make a statement or call any witnesses (see below) after hearing

483 Pue, "Twilight Zone," p. 342.

484 *Essex Standard*, 30 July, 1841.

485 Mellaerts, "Criminal Justice," pp. 26-29.

486 Pue, "Twilight Zone," p. 335.

the prosecution case. By then, the hearing afforded as much an opportunity for the suspect to clear, as to incriminate, himself.[487]

More generally, Victorian JPs were increasingly willing to dismiss weak cases rather than commit them for trial, this being the continuation of a trend that can be identified well before 1837. In February 1851, at the Aylsham petty sessions, four men were charged with disturbing the Wesleyan congregation at Cawston the previous month, but only three were committed to quarter sessions.[488] Similarly, at the Diss Petty Sessions in January 1886, four labourers came before the court for a committal hearing after being accused of nocturnal poaching. They were legally represented by an Ipswich solicitor who manged to secure the discharge of one of them, Thomas Harper, but the others were sent for trial at assizes. The solicitor had argued that the case against Harper was based on little more than a set of footprints that had been traced from near where the poachers had been disturbed to his home, and that his boots were damp, something that was not surprising, given that it was a wet night.[489]

In theory, dismissal of a charge by JPs at the committal stage did not constitute an acquittal, any more than a "not found" decision returned by a grand jury at court. Thus, albeit somewhat unusually, in 1866, an allegation of rape made against Judd Towler was thrown out by magistrates at petty sessions who did not think the complainant's testimony sufficient to commit for trial. Several local observers thought that the case had not been properly prepared by the legally unrepresented complainant, a workhouse inmate named Anne Moore, while Towler, a Weeting farmer, had had the sense to bring a King's Lynn solicitor to the hearing. They engaged a Mr Chittock, a Norwich solicitor, on Moore's behalf to pursue the matter on a more thorough basis. On his advice, a fresh summons was served, and the matter reconsidered, with both prosecution and defence at committal being conducted by solicitors. On this occasion, and after a lengthy investigation, the defendant was committed to trial at Norwich Assizes.[490] At the hearing, both sides were represented by counsel, and Towler was convicted.[491]

Most committal proceedings were carried out in public. However, some were conducted in private, whether because they involved indecency, because they were carried out in prisons or some other non-accessible place, or for some other reason. For example, during the mid-1840s, the mayor of Yarmouth seemed to have a penchant for private examinations. Thus, the three men originally implicated in a murder by Samuel Yarham, in 1845, were all examined in the absence of both the press and the public, although what transpired at the hearings was swiftly repeated

---

487 Bentley, *English Criminal Justice*, pp. 29-31.

488 *The Norfolk Chronicle*, 20 January, 1851.

489 *The Ipswich Journal*, 30 January, 1886.

490 *The Norwich Post*, 24 July, 1866.

491 *Ibid.*, 14 August, 1866.

in the newspapers.[492] Two years later, George Thurtell's examination on serious theft charges by county JPs sitting in a room at Norwich Castle prison was "strictly private." Not even the press was admitted. It lasted the whole of an afternoon, after which he was committed for trial.[493]

Section 19 of the Indictable Offences act 1848 reiterated that the room or building where examinations were conducted was not to be deemed open court for such a purpose, and that magistrates could exclude the public at their discretion. Nevertheless, the number of private hearings declined as the era advanced, and increasingly prompted a degree of hostility when they still occurred. For example, when Yarham was questioned in private in 1846, it was the subject of "very general censure".[494] Less extreme measures were taken in 1848, when James Rush underwent his initial examination for murder in the Wymondham bridewell. Reporters were present, but for "obvious reasons" asked not to take notes of the evidence. Presumably, it was thought that this might compromise any subsequent trial.[495] Several of Rush's later examinations, held in Norwich Castle, where he was imprisoned, were "strictly private." However, when the statements taken during the numerous pre-trial hearings in this notorious murder were complete, representatives of the press were admitted "to hear the [32 prosecution witnesses'] depositions read." At the end of this process, Rush was committed for trial on the two murders.[496] Perhaps more understandably, a private committal hearing, for what appear to have been reasons of public decency, was held by the Norwich magistrates at the city Guildhall in September 1885, when two men were accused of committing an "abominable crime" (sodomy).[497]

Legal Representation at Committal

In theory, as the 1845 Law Commissioners noted, it was a matter for the JPs' discretion as to whether a felony suspect had legal representation at his committal hearing. In practice, it appears that it was usually allowed.[498] In Norfolk only a small minority of cases saw any form of defence representation at this stage, but this normally reflected cost and awareness rather than prohibition by the magistrates. As some of the cases discussed above suggest, because it was a magistrates' forum, both attorneys/solicitors and counsel could appear at committal hearings, for both the prosecutor and defendant. For example, in July 1840 John Randlesome, accused

---

[492] *The Morning Post*, 8 January, 1845.

[493] *Bell's Life in London and Sporting Chronicle*, 21 November, 1847.

[494] *The Times*, 7 January, 1846, p. 3.

[495] *Ibid.*, 1 December, 1848, p. 5.

[496] A.D. Bayne, *The Stanfield Tragedy: A Complete Narrative* (London: Jarrold, 1849), pp. 17-19.

[497] *The Eastern Evening News,* 11 September, 1885.

[498] Pue, "Twilight Zone," p. 339.

of murdering his spouse, was legally represented at his committal in Loddon and "frequently stooped down to whisper to his attorney."[499]

In May 1869, when Mary Langford came before the King's Lynn magistrates for her committal, after being accused of fatally poisoning both her infant daughter and her husband, she went further and was legally represented by counsel, something that helps explain the length of the hearing. It lasted two days, being adjourned overnight late on a Friday evening and resuming at 10 am on the Saturday, with the court sitting another six hours that day. Langford's barrister appears to have tested the prosecution evidence, and made extensive, albeit unavailing, submissions to the bench opposing a committal.[500] In like manner, at his committal hearing in 1874, the Diss watchmaker William Andrews was represented by the experienced barrister Thomas Blofeld when accused of stealing two ducks. (The prosecutor was represented by a local solicitor.)[501]

In 1888 John Nunn's lawyer had more success than Langford's when his client was accused of rape. When the matter came before the JPs at petty sessions for committal, the lawyer "submitted the woman to a severe cross-examination, and the evidence was so contradictory that the magistrates dismissed the case."[502] Thomas Blofeld was also successful the same year when he represented a former King's Lynn grammar-school headmaster and clergyman accused of concealing assets when declared bankrupt (a criminal offence). He addressed the bench on the basis that the defendant had had no fraudulent intention, and the magistrates decided that there was not sufficient evidence to commit him for trial.[503]

Unrepresented defendants would have to defend themselves as best they could at committal proceedings. For example, when potential prosecution witnesses were being examined by JPs considering the committal of James Rush, it was noted that, during their examination, he frequently interrupted the magistrate who was asking questions, and took notes of the evidence. Rush also personally cross-examined the prosecution witnesses.[504]

Procedure at Committal

Typically, the victim/prosecutor, his legal representative (where present), or the police, would present evidence at a committal hearing to make out a prima facie case against (and in the presence of) the accused. Quite frequently, they would be assisted by the court clerk (who might also be the town clerk in urban areas), especially if the victim had no lawyer, or the crime was a victimless one. For example, in 1885, after

499 *The Ipswich Journal*, 18 July, 1840.

500 *The Morning Post*, 17 May, 1869.

501 *The Bury and Norwich Post*, 15 September, 1874.

502 *The Ipswich Journal*, 10 January, 1888.

503 *The Bury and Norwich Post*, 22 May, 1888.

504 Bayne, *Stanfield Tragedy*, pp. 17-19.

a man and a youth were accused of sodomy and had several preliminary hearings at the Norwich Guildhall, it was noted that the town clerk, H. B. Miller, "appeared to prosecute on behalf of the police." At a second sitting for the same case, it was recorded that, again, "The Town Clerk prosecuted."[505]

The prosecution evidence would usually consist of witness testimony, whether from victims, bystanders, or police officers. In 1896, after John Cubitt, a Norfolk gamekeeper, was shot in the head and wounded while intercepting nocturnal poachers, the committal hearing for two of the latter was slightly delayed so that he could recover from his injuries and testify, which he was also allowed to do while seated.[506] The accused could cross-examine such witnesses personally or through a lawyer. The justice's clerk would record the testimony given in the form of depositions that were read back to, and signed by, the witnesses and the magistrate(s) at the conclusion of the process. At the close of the prosecution case, and as the Rush case suggests, all the prosecution depositions would be read back again to the accused.[507] Nevertheless, such evidence was not necessarily recorded verbatim as it was given. Occasionally, it seems, depositions were rather sketchy notes of the gist of the evidence given. Furthermore, the cross-examination of a witness was not always recorded, especially early in the Victorian period. Some observers thought that this could be problematic, for both prosecution and defence, as it made showing (in)consistency at trial difficult.[508]

Defence Testimony at Committal

After the prosecution case was completed, the presiding magistrate would ask the suspect whether he wished to say anything or call any witnesses; comparatively few availed themselves of this opportunity (see below). Nevertheless, at his committal hearing for wounding a man with a pocketknife in a Great Bircham tavern in 1875, the defendant testified and unavailingly tried to argue that the injury was the result of an accident.[509] When defence, rather than prosecution, witnesses were tendered at a committal hearing, there was no requirement that their evidence be taken down as a formal deposition until the Criminal Law Amendment Act, also known as Russell Gurney's Act, of 1867.[510]

---

505 *The Eastern Evening News,* 11 September, 1885.

506 *The Ipswich Journal,* 18 January, 1896.

507 J.F. Archbold, *Jervis's Acts, 11 & 12 Victoria, cc. 42, 43, & 44: relating to the duties of justices of the peace out of sessions as to indictable offences, convictions, and orders: and to the protection of justices in the execution of their duties* (London: Shaw & Sons,1851), p. 51.

508 *Eighth Report,* p. 227.

509 *The Bury and Norwich Post*, 9 November, 1875.

510 Bentley, *English Criminal Justice,* p. 220.

Subsequent Use of Committal Depositions

If a suspect made any type of admissible confession during his examination, it might be adduced as evidence against him at trial, like any other informal admissions that had not been obtained by inducements or threats. For example, at the notorious trial of the 14-year-old John Bell for murder, held at the Kent assizes in 1831, it was noted that Mr Farrell, clerk to the magistrates of Rochester, read out a copy of what had been stated by the prisoner and his brother during their examinations. It constituted a full confession, including an unfortunate description of the victim's death: "The boy 'squeaked' when his throat was cut, as a rabbit squeaks." Perhaps unsurprisingly, the jury found the prisoner guilty "without hesitation."[511] At the Middlesex sessions in 1864, the Reverend James Rowton, convicted of indecently assaulting a 14-year-old boy, made the mistake of voluntarily making admissions to both the arresting police constable and the examining magistrates, something that made his not-guilty plea at trial fairly difficult to sustain.[512] (He eventually escaped on a legal technicality identified by the Court of Crown Cases Reserved.)

In Norfolk, at the quarter sessions held at Walsingham in July 1843, William Girdlestone was the only one of a group of three men to plead not guilty to several (separate) sheep thefts. Unfortunately, his case was rather compromised by the lengthy admissions he had made at the committal stage: "William Girdlestone's examination before the magistrates was put in; it revealed such a series of robberies as we could not have conceived it was now possible, with a rural police, to perpetrate". Why he should make such an extensive confession is not known, but it was generally thought that he had mistakenly hoped that he would be permitted to turn Queen's evidence. He was swiftly convicted at trial.[513]

Similarly, at Sarah Snowling's committal hearing held in 1874, after she had attempted to poison one of her illegitimate children, her father announced that she could not afford the nurse's fees for the infant, something that had, apparently, driven her mad. The prisoner herself declared, while sobbing, that her young man had told her he would never have her as a wife while she had such commitments. (A chain of witnesses proving the purchase and administration of the poison was also called.) Snowling was convicted at the Norfolk assizes for administering a noxious substance.[514]

As a result of such dangers, many suspects, especially if legally represented, did not exercise their right to speak after the prosecution evidence had been heard. Typically, in 1900 Herbert Bennett, accused of murder at the Great Yarmouth police court (sitting in the borough's quarter sessions court), declined to make a statement or call any defence witnesses after the prosecution case had been presented to the

---

511 *The Spectator*, 30 July, 1831, p. 10.

512 *Reynolds's Newspaper*, 2 October, 1864.

513 *The Bury and Norwich Post*, 12 July, 1843.

514 *The Ipswich Journal*, 31 March, 1874.

bench, and the magistrates had been invited to commit the case for trial at assizes, noting, "I reserve my defence, Sir." This was reiterated by his counsel.[515]

Of course, there could be a few practical risks in not testifying at committal. At the Norfolk assizes in February 1880, when a labourer named Walker was accused of arson, he raised a specific defence for the first time, some two weeks after his committal hearing. The jury foreman subsequently volunteered their reasons for convicting him. One of them was that the prisoner "did not make the statement [raising the defence] when first brought before the magistrate."[516] It could show consistency and explain aspects of a case. At the Norfolk assizes in 1867, when Susan Grief was accused of poisoning some of her illegitimate grandchildren with arsenic, defence counsel referred to the deposition she had made in front of examining magistrates to account for her possession of the poison.[517]

What of prosecution witnesses' depositions, or those for the defendant after the passing of Gurney's Act of 1867 (which gave them the same status as those for the Crown)?[518] In the case of *R* v. *Dingler* in 1791 it had been held that such depositions – whether taken at a committal hearing or a coroner's inquest – might become admissible, either for or against the accused, if the maker of the statement died before trial or subsequently became too ill to attend court; however, they would have to have been taken in the presence of the accused person in circumstances where he or his lawyer had had a full opportunity to question the witness. These requirements were reiterated in s.17 of the Indictable Offences (Jervis's) Act of 1848 and s.6 of Gurney's Act of 1867. This explains why, a few days after being committed to trial for murder, James Rush was taken back to Stanfield Hall, where the very seriously injured maid, Elizabeth Chastney, gave crucial identification (and other) evidence in his (and the JPs') presence, something that would allow its adduction if she died or was too ill to attend trial.[519]

A similar procedure was followed in 1850, in neighbouring Suffolk, when Charles Piper was stabbed and severely wounded. A few days later, doctors saw that necrosis had set in, and that he would probably be dead within a few hours. Local JPs then directed the police to convey the three suspects to the bedroom of the dying man, where he identified one as his assailant. Piper's deposition was then taken in the presence of this man, who was remanded in custody, and the other prisoners were discharged.[520] (In homicide cases, a potential way of circumventing the requirement for the defendant to be present when a statement was made by a mortally wounded

---

515 *The Times*, 26 November, 1900, p. 15.

516 *The Bury and Norwich Post*, 17 February, 1880.

517 *The Bury and Norwich Post*, 2 April, 1867.

518 Bentley, *English Criminal Justice*, p. 220.

519 *The Norfolk Chronicle*, 28 November, 1848.

520 *The Norwich Post*, 10 April, 1850.

person, who was aware of their imminent demise, was to adduce it as a 'dying declaration', as discussed below).[521]

However, there was often a degree of reluctance about basing prosecutions solely or even primarily on deposition evidence, in part because of the strictness with which the hearsay rule (to which it was an exception) was viewed in the nineteenth century, and because it violated the wider principle of orality. Although Elizabeth Chastney's statement could probably have been admitted (see above), the prosecution preferred to have her taken to Norwich on a litter and then carried into court, with several doctors in attendance, so that she could testify in person at the hearing.[522]

In October 1883, at the Norfolk and Suffolk assizes held at Norwich, Arthur Smith was indicted for sexually assaulting Patience Leggett at Rickinghall Superior in Suffolk. The case had been approved by a grand jury at the previous summer assizes for Suffolk but had then been adjourned because the victim (and main prosecution witness) had been unable to give evidence. She was mentally ill and had been admitted to a private asylum. However, she was still in the asylum, and so unable to give evidence in October, and her prognosis (provided by a doctor from the institution) was not good, suggesting that any further adjournments might be in vain. Nevertheless, the court was reluctant to see the trial proceed purely on the depositions that she had earlier made in front of examining magistrates, although they may well have been legally admissible. In part, this reluctance was founded on their contents, and the nature of her disability, but in part it reflected a nervousness of what would (effectively) have been trial by deposition, unsupported by significant oral testimony in court. The prosecution eventually offered no evidence, and an acquittal was returned.[523]

Such situations apart, although the prosecution could not normally ask for its pre-trial witness depositions to go before the jury, as of right, the defendant could ask that they be read out, although this might be unwise. At his trial in 1848 James Rush insisted that all the prosecution depositions made in front of committing JPs be read publicly, hoping to expose inconsistencies between the witnesses' testimony at committal and trial, although it did him little good, and possibly some harm, as damaging "facts were stated in the depositions, which were not stated in the evidence at the trial. [While] the variations were of very little consequence."[524]

More typically, depositions would be used to inform the judge, recorder, or chairman about a case prior to trial (they would normally read through them beforehand); to refresh witness memory before and even during the hearing; and as the basis for cross-examination by counsel and judicial questioning of witnesses.[525] For example,

521 *The King* v *Woodcock* (1789), 1 Leach 500.

522 *The Norfolk Chronicle,* 28 November, 1848.

523 *The Ipswich Journal*, 27 October, 1883.

524 *Ibid.*, 29 October, 1881. Anon., "Local Distribution," pp. 301-305.

525 Reid, *Briefs and Papers,* p. 99.

at the Norfolk assizes in March 1855, a judge noted a clear discrepancy between the depositions made by a key prosecution witness in a theft case and what he had said in court, something that he could not explain when questioned from the bench. The judge pointed out the contradictions between deposition and evidence to the jury when summing up and asked them "whether they could rely upon such evidence." They acquitted.[526]

By the start of the Victorian period, the defendant had a formal right to see copies of the depositions sworn against him at committal under s.4 of the Prisoners' Counsel Act of 1836. This increased their potential value. Prior to this, there had been no guarantee that he would receive them. If he did not, he might be dependent on any notes that he or his attorney had taken, or on his memory, although copies of the depositions would sometimes be given to the accused on a voluntary basis. At the Norwich assizes in April 1834, the footpad Joseph Jones complained that he had been promised, but then refused, the depositions in his case. He alleged that there were significant differences between what had been said in front of magistrates on the earlier occasion and the testimony given in court.[527]

The Decision to Commit for Trial

At the close of committal proceedings, the magistrates would decide whether to discharge (and release) the prisoner or commit him for trial. The latter decision would require that they could identify a prima facie case, in which the evidence, taken at its highest, supported the charge. Thus, in 1850, when a Wretton horse-dealer named Henry Riches was accused of stealing a pair of donkeys, the two JPs who presided over his committal hearing were not satisfied in this regard, and he was "discharged for want of evidence". (The donkeys were formally returned to their legitimate owner).[528] Inevitably there were disputes as to whether the test for committal had, or should have, been satisfied. For example, at the Norwich city sessions at the start of April 1839, Daniel Archer was accused of the violent robbery of an attorney, allegedly committed with three other men. All four had been arrested separately. Archer was the only one to come for trial. At his hearing, his defence counsel indicated that one of the other suspects had been discharged by committing magistrates. He suggested that there was no case to answer, and that the prosecution had taken advantage of the absence on circuit of an experienced and legally qualified magistrate (the barrister Nathaniel Palmer) from the city, to get Archer sent for trial by a less able and unqualified presiding JP. He claimed that, had Palmer been present, with his (allegedly) superior ability to weigh evidence, Archer would have been discharged. The trial jury acquitted.[529]

---

526 *The Bury and Norwich Post*, 28 March, 1855.

527 *Ibid.*, 9 April, 1834.

528 *The Norfolk News,* 7 December, 1850.

529 *The Ipswich Journal*, 13 April, 1839.

In April 1844 Sir John Patteson, presiding at the Norfolk assizes, complained that some examining magistrates were committing suspects accused of arson for trial too lightly, acting on "very slight evidence," much of it hearsay and surmise.[530] Three years later, when the home of the prolific thief George Thurtell was searched by Norwich police, a large amount of apparently stolen property was found on the premises, some of it hidden in a flower bed. Although some of the police were doubtful about its forensic value, they eventually "considered that sufficient was discovered to take him before the Magistrates. They did so, and he was remanded to Norwich Gaol, from whence he was removed to the Castle [prison]." A private examination, lasting all afternoon, was subsequently held and, contrary to public expectations, ended in Thurtell being committed for trial.[531]

If a matter was of any complexity, and more than one magistrate was sitting (almost invariably the case in such situations), JPs would normally retire to make their decision on whether to send it for trial on indictment. For example, in 1885, after Richard Frary and Mark Knights were accused of sodomy in Norwich, their committal hearing was conducted before the mayor for that year, John Hotblack, and two other magistrates. After the prosecution had finished adducing the evidence (the defendants presumably not doing so), the "Magistrates having deliberated in private, the Mayor [presiding] committed [the] prisoners for trial."[532]

JPs were equally important when reaching a decision on committal, which they could do by simple majority (provided more than two were present). A heated debate as to their personal powers of committal occurred at the Yarmouth police court in September 1859, after three men were accused of stealing wood from their former employer. The town mayor and five other magistrates heard the committal. The prosecutor, a builder named Fox, complained that he had lost more than £500 of material over time, while cuts of wood worth £15, which he positively identified as his property, had been found in the defendants' possession. However, one of the three accused, a man named Angell, exercised his right to call evidence at committal, in the form of testimony suggesting that he regularly purchased similar timber from other sources. Having retired to consider the matter, the mayor, who was also the presiding magistrate, indicated that he intended to commit all three for trial, although the rest of the bench was against this, and one of them said (in court) that he did not feel there was a tittle of evidence against Angell. Angell's lawyer then advised his client to leave the court, which he promptly did, those police officers who were present proving reluctant to intervene when the mayor told them to arrest him. The defence lawyer subsequently cited Jervis's Act of 1848 to support his position. When the mayor reappeared a few days later, he claimed that the clerk had advised him that he had the power to commit without reference to any other

530 *The Bury and Norwich Post and East Anglian,* 3 April, 1844.

531 *The Ipswich Journal*, 20 November, 1847.

532 *The Lowestoft Journal,* 19 September, 1885.

magistrates, but acknowledged that, having involved others on the bench, he had ceded them the right to take part in the decision.[533]

Diversion of the Mentally Ill

It should be noted that, in a few non-homicide cases, examining JPs removed apparently insane or mentally ill suspects from the criminal process at the committal stage, even if some of the alleged crimes were quite serious, irrespective of the strength of the evidence against them. For example, in early 1857 George Gunn, a 64-year-old Norfolk labourer, came before magistrates, accused of having committed an "abominable crime" (probably bestiality) at Mattishall, the previous September. A surgeon informed the JPs that he considered the prisoner to be in an unsound state of mind. As a result, the criminal process was not pursued, and it was ordered that Gunn be taken care of as a lunatic. The matter did not go for trial.[534]

At the Wymondham petty sessions in April 1869, 17-year-old Robert Matthews was accused of stealing three pistols from the shop of Arthur West, an ironmonger in the town, while buying another firearm. Matthews was also charged with stealing two scent bottles from a nearby chemist's shop. He had been apprehended in Norwich by one PC Hook, who had been sent after him in pursuit. By then Matthews had bought yet another firearm and had sold one of the initial three pistols he had acquired. His father attended court with a doctor's certificate explaining his condition, and Matthews was also examined by a Wymondham surgeon. He was found to be of "unsound mind" and discharged, his father promising to keep him under supervision. (Apparently, the youth had also recently stolen £10 10s from his parents' house.)[535]

Such an approach towards the diversion of mentally ill offenders from the justice system had a degree of official support nationwide, if only to prevent them from being convicted and then creating problems in the country's gaols before being transferred to an asylum. Thus, a Home Office circular of 1889 expressly advised JPs to dismiss charges and commit apparently insane defendants accused of lesser crimes to the custody of their friends, an asylum, or a workhouse. However, it also stressed that in "cases of serious crime" insanity should be decided by a jury at trial.[536]

This latter proviso may have been prompted by incidents in which diversion had been abused. For example, there was a major controversy in Norfolk in May 1852, when Elizabeth Bunn, the live-in housekeeper to the Reverend Edmund Holmes, returned unexpectedly to find the vicar attempting to rape her twelve-year-old daughter. A

---

533 *The Daily News*, 22 September, 1859.

534 *The Norfolk News,* 4 April, 1857.

535 *The Norfolk Chronicle*, 17 April, 1869.

536 Victor Bailey (ed.), *Policing and Punishment in Nineteenth Century Britain* (Abingdon: Routledge, 1981), p. 235

police constable was informed, made an arrest, and then took the cleric before a local magistrate, who, despite an absence of any medical training or advice, appears to have decided that the vicar was insane. Holmes was sent to Heigham Hall, a private lunatic asylum near Norwich, where he was examined by two doctors and certified to be insane.[537]

However, Holmes was speedily found to have recovered his sanity, and there were subsequent claims that the original diagnosis was not well founded. It was suggested that, in reality, a "country clergyman, a member of a high county family, had committed a rape, that his family wished to make him out to be mad, and that, in order to save him from a criminal prosecution, they [had] desired to get him into a mad-house."[538] An investigation ensued, amidst considerable public anger. Even the magistrate's son, a clerk at petty sessions, said that the vicar had been spirited away to the asylum because of his station in life: "Probably, had he been a poor man, the case would have been different. The usual course would be to prove the offence first, and afterwards to consider a plea of insanity".[539] At a meeting of the city magistrates in December the Home Secretary was asked to conduct a "searching investigation" into the matter, although it appears to have eventually petered out.[540]

Choice of Charge

If the examining JPs decided that a case warranted trial, a choice would have to be made as to the appropriate charge, which might not always be the one for which the prisoner had been arrested. For example, in 1869 magistrates eventually decided to commit Mary Langford for trial at the Norwich assizes on two counts of murder (her daughter and husband). However, Superintendent Ware of the King's Lynn police, one of the officers who had given evidence at the hearing, thought that an allegation of "feloniously attempting" to cause the death of her husband would be more appropriate for the latter, as the available evidence would not sustain the graver charge. (The magistrates appear to have felt that the second allegation should be shaped by the first.)[541] At trial, Mary was acquitted of murdering her daughter, while the prosecution chose not to proceed on the count involving her husband.[542]

---

537 NRO MC 279.

538 Anon., "Heigham Hall Lunatic Asylum, Norwich," *Journal of Psychological Medicine and Mental Pathology*, vol. 8, no. 29 (1855), pp. 168-170.

539 Sarah Wise, "Did the Victorian Asylum Allow the Rich to Evade Justice?" blog entry, 13 May, 2015, *Psychology Today* psychologytoday.com.

540 Anon., "Heigham Hall," pp. 168-170.

541 *The Morning Post*, 17 May, 1869.

542 *Ibid.*, 10 August, 1869.

Choice of Forum

There were, effectively, three choices when it came to deciding forum for a criminal allegation in Norfolk (and the rest of provincial England): petty sessions, quarter sessions (borough or county), or assizes. Of course, only summary matters, or indictable matters that were triable summarily in appropriate (statutory) circumstances that had been met, could be dealt with at petty sessions. However, for trial on indictment, before a jury, one of the latter two forums had to be selected, so that these were the only options open after a committal hearing if a case was not thrown out. The JPs would send the papers in the case, the defendant's examination and the other depositions, to the court chosen.

The JPs' choice in this regard was not entirely unfettered. Most important, under an Act of 1842 (5 and 6 Vict. c. 38) any offence carrying a potential sentence of death or transportation/penal servitude for life for a first conviction had to go to the higher jury forum. As a result, very serious crimes, such as murder, sodomy, robbery, rape, and (until the 1890s) burglary, could be heard only at assizes. It was also a requirement under the 1842 Act and several other statutes or simply general practice that a few less serious but legally difficult matters be referred to the higher jury forum. For example, although perjury was, technically, a misdemeanour, its legal complexity meant that it was normally indicted at assizes.[543]

Nevertheless, most indictable crimes could be (and were) tried at either of the jury courts during the Victorian era. Thus, many less serious felonies and even a few misdemeanours were still heard at the higher forum, rather than going to quarter sessions, if only for reasons of administrative convenience. This might be because an assizes was imminent, or to flesh out an otherwise thin list. For example, at the Norfolk assizes in July 1846, 18-year-old Robert Fretwell pleaded guilty to having stolen two and a half bushels of beans from a farmer's barn in Stoke Ferry two weeks earlier. He received 14 days' imprisonment.[544] It is likely that the convenience of having the matter dealt with very speedily, especially if a guilty plea seemed likely (perhaps because he had made admissions), accounts for this relatively minor case going to the higher jury forum.

More generally, of the 11 cases tried at the autumn assizes for Norfolk in 1879, only two had to be heard at that forum. Nine were potentially triable at quarter sessions. (This appears to have attracted criticism from the Lord Chief Justice, although, as a local JP noted, the alternative was to hold the prisoners in custody two months longer, until the Epiphany quarter sessions.)[545] The emphasis was a little different at the city of Norwich assizes, where only two of the six cases heard were triable

---

543 Wendie Ellen Schneider, *Engines of Truth: Producing Veracity in the Victorian Courtroom* (New Haven: YUP, 2016), p. 37.

544 *The Norwich Mercury*, 25 July, 1846.

545 *The Times*, 14 November, 1879, p. 11.

at the lower jury forum, while the figures were also more evenly balanced in the neighboring circuit counties of Suffolk and Cambridgeshire.[546]

Conversely, some serious crimes, carrying long sentences of transportation (early in the period) or penal servitude (a little later) were determined at the lower jury court. For example, at the Norfolk quarter sessions held in Swaffham in 1842, two men, aged 17 and 20, were tried for assaulting John Hutson with intent to commit a felony on a highway near Stow Bardolph. (A robbery had not been committed, allowing the court jurisdiction.) Hutson had been viciously struck over the head with a stick from behind and knocked down but had shouted so loudly that a police constable and members of the public had come to his assistance and saved him. One of the youths allegedly later stated that they had planned to murder Hutson after robbing him. Both were convicted and sentenced to 15 years' transportation, the chairman of the quarter sessions noting that the case might easily have been one of capital murder. (It was thought that the pair had been connected to other people in the area who were involved in similar activity.)[547]

Occasionally, decisions as to forum might be changed, for special reasons. In December 1842, the grand jury at the King's Lynn borough quarter sessions found a true bill against Bedford Russell for stealing zinc in the town. Russell had acted as a local sheriff's officer and was a prosperous but generally unpopular individual. His counsel subsequently appears to have got the case transferred from trial at the borough sessions to a hearing at the county assizes, presumably to avoid any prejudice on account of his office.[548] (See also below on county jurisdiction.)

County Jurisdiction

There were territorial limits to the crimes that could be committed to the jury courts of a county. Most important, they usually had to have been committed in the requisite shire or within 500 yards of its borders. A huge legal blunder in this regard occurred in 1899, when a man who was committed for trial at Ipswich in Suffolk was sent to the Norfolk assizes for his hearing, although the latter had "not the slightest jurisdiction to try him." As a result, the judge in Norwich said that any proceedings there would be a nullity.[549] However, some crimes were considered "continuing offences" when they crossed county borders, so that they might be justiciable in either shire.

Very occasionally a serious Norfolk crime would be heard in neither of the county jury forums (or even those of adjacent counties). In 1834, the newly established Central Criminal Court was given jurisdiction beyond London and Middlesex (its normal remit) to cover the whole of England for the major cases in exceptional

546 *Returns of the total number of criminal cases at each assize county at autumn assizes 1879*, House of Commons Sessional Papers, 1880, vol. 59, pp. 1-10.

547 *The Bury and Norwich Post*, 19 January, 1842.

548 *Ibid.*, 28 December, 1842.

549 *The Pall Mall Gazette*, 9 November, 1899.

circumstances. Sometimes this was employed when notorious *causes célèbres* had to be heard, given the frequent lack of effective constraint at the time on media reporting and speculation about specific crimes. In theory publishing prejudicial material about those facing criminal trial might be subject to an action for contempt of court. In practice this does not appear to have been a very effective deterrent, especially early in the Victorian era, when newspapers sometimes produced chilling and inaccurate accounts of serious crimes before trial. As a result, local hostility, sometimes fanned by such reports, might lead the Attorney General to attempt to move a provincial trial to London, especially in the second half of the nineteenth century. Procedural difficulties in this regard eventually led to the passing of "Palmer's Act" in 1856 (19 Vict, c. 16) to facilitate the process.[550]

Such a move was only rarely allowed. Nevertheless, in 1875, when Josiah Buttifant was accused of a huge fraud against his former employer, the Norfolk and Norwich Provident Building Society, which resulted in the liquidation of the society and losses to many local investors, his case was transferred to the Old Bailey after a true bill was found against him at the Norfolk assizes.[551] He pleaded guilty to embezzlement, and was tried and convicted of forgery, receiving a sentence of 15 years' penal servitude (and a prosecution costs order).[552] Similarly, in November 1900, after Herbert Bennett strangled his wife in Yarmouth, he was committed for trial at the Norfolk assizes, but owing to the local prejudice against the prisoner, something that had been encouraged by elements of the regional press, the hearing was removed to the Old Bailey, where he was found guilty and sentenced to death, despite being defended by the celebrated barrister Edward Marshall Hall.[553] Bennett was returned to Norfolk to be executed at Norwich prison in March 1901.[554]

Bail

If examining JPs took the decision to commit a suspect for trial on indictment, they would have to decide whether to bail him or her pending a hearing, although, by the Victorian period, bail was mandatory for most lesser misdemeanours, especially after 1848. Late medieval and Marian statutes had required the presence of at least two JPs for the grant of bail, and this was reiterated in the 1835 Act. It remained the case until 1848, after which s.23 of the Indictable Offences Act of that year allowed a single magistrate to make the decision, provided the suspect could procure and produce such sureties as were deemed sufficient to ensure appearance at trial (see below).

At the start of the nineteenth century, bail might be granted when the evidence given in support of a charge did not raise a strong presumption of the guilt of

550 Bentley, *English Criminal Justice*, p. 47.

551 *The Standard*, 30 March, 1875.

552 OBSP, Trial of Josiah Buttifant, 3 May, 1875, t18750503-368.

553 *The Norfolk Chronicle*, 22 September, 1900. *The Bury and Norwich Post*, 27 November, 1900.

554 *The Penny Illustrated Paper*, 2 March, 1901.

the accused, or when the latter called sufficient evidence to at least cast some doubt on the issue, albeit that there were still deemed to be adequate grounds for committal. Nevertheless, the situation was thought to be confused. In early 1826 Sir Robert Peel, then Home Secretary, opined in the House of Commons that there had long been "very considerable obscurity" about who could be bailed, under various provisions that stretched back to the reign of Edward I.[555] As a result, the rules for bail contained in the Criminal Law Act 1826 and a supplementary statute of 1835 which amended them were aimed at reforming the law, and largely superseded previous legislation on the subject.

Significantly, under the 1835 Act the risk of absconding, rather than the likelihood that the suspect was guilty, became the primary determinant for bail, which could be granted for any offence, so long as it did not endanger the appearance of the accused at trial, even if the "circumstances are such to raise a presumption of guilt."[556] As Lord Chief Justice Coleridge observed on several occasions during the mid-nineteenth century, remand prisoners were committed to gaol "for the purpose of ensuring the certainty of their appearing at trial." The same judge set out three questions that could be considered when determining whether they were likely to appear without being remanded in custody: was the crime grave or trifling; how likely was a conviction (essentially, how strong was the evidence); what was the probable punishment in the event of conviction?[557]

As a result, bail could, in theory, extend both to cases where the suspect had made admissions and to very serious felonies, in appropriate circumstances, although many thought it could not be granted to those against whom a bill for murder had been found by a grand jury.[558] In practice bail was rarely granted in homicide cases, especially those involving murder (rather than manslaughter). Nevertheless, other serious crimes of violence were often bailed. For example, in 1847 a poacher named Richard Mason who, it was alleged, had wounded a gamekeeper with a knife, was granted bail prior to his trial for stabbing with intent to maim at the Norfolk assizes. He answered to his bail, was convicted, and sentenced to ten years' transportation.[559] Similarly, in 1866 Judd Towler was bailed prior to the hearing for rape at which he was convicted at the Norfolk assizes.[560] Even so, in the early Victorian period many observers, such as the recorder of Doncaster, felt that bail was often unnecessarily withheld. Most offenders were from the "humbler classes." Such people often did

---

555 Hansard HC Deb 17 April 1826 vol. 15 col. 284-91

556 A.K. Bottomley, "The Granting of Bail: Principles and Practice," *Modern Law Review*, vol. 31, no. 1 (1968), p. 46.

557 Kurt X. Metzmeier, "Preventive Detention: A Comparison of Bail Refusal Practices in the United States, England, Canada and Other Common Law Nations," *Pace International Law Review*, vol. 8, no. 2 (1996), pp. 413-414.

558 *R* v. *Richard Andrews* (1844) 2 Dow. & Ry. 10.

559 *The Bury and Norwich Post*, 7 April, 1847.

560 *The Norfolk Chronicle*, 23 June, 1866.

not have the means of absconding or moving elsewhere and were easily tracked if they did.[561]

A decision to grant bail also depended on the defendant's ability to provide recognizances or sureties; these were pledged sums that would be estreated if he failed to appear at trial. The Habeas Corpus Act 1679 had provided that a JP should discharge prisoners from custody after taking their recognizance, with one or more other sureties in any sum "according to the Magistrate's discretion." These might be provided by the accused or by relatives, neighbours, and friends on his behalf. The sum would be determined by the "quality" or wealth of the prisoner and the nature and gravity of the offence charged, although the Bill of Rights of 1689 stated that excessive sums for bail should not be stipulated.

In practice, for much of the Victorian era, the bailed party would be required to personally pledge part of the required sum and be supported by one or (more commonly) two others who pledged the remainder. Thus, in December 1842 George Rogers, accused of nocturnal poaching while armed and of assaulting gamekeepers was bailed in a personal recognizance of £40 supported by two local fishermen who entered sureties on his behalf of £10 each.[562] Fairly typically, when it came to men of relatively modest means accused of middle-ranking crimes, a total figure of around £100 was required, at least until late in the era. In 1874, after William Andrews, a Diss watchmaker, was committed for trial at the Norfolk quarter sessions for stealing two ducks, the town petty sessions set bail at £60 personally supported by two sureties of £30 each.[563] Similarly, when Joshua Ruffles was committed for trial at the same forum in 1879, after being accused of receiving one-and-a-half bushels of stolen barley, the Diss petty sessions required him to enter into a surety of £50 personally, and to have two other sureties of £25 each.[564]

However, the sums required could be more modest, even for serious matters, in special circumstances. When Judd Towler (see above) appeared before Norfolk magistrates for committal, accused of rape, the court clerk suggested to the Bench that they should remand the case, as the complainant, who was very ill, was not present. The defendant's lawyer did not oppose this step but asked that the magistrates admit his client to bail in the meantime. The prosecution lawyer objected, but asked that, if the magistrates did grant bail, it should be for a significant amount. Even so, Towler was granted bail on very modest terms: personally for £20, with one other surety for the same amount.[565]

---

561 *Eighth Report,* p. 220.

562 Hundred of North Erpingham Norfolk Special and Petty Sessions Record Commencing 3 July, 1841 NRO PS 24/1/1.

563 *The Bury and Norwich Post*, 15 September, 1874.

564 *Ibid.*, 2 December, 1879.

565 *The Norfolk Chronicle*, 23 June, 1866.

By contrast, if the defendant had substantial means, a higher sum might be demanded, even for a relatively minor crime. In 1857, at the Norwich assizes, the grand jury returned a bill of indictment against Baron Hastings for the misdemeanour of "endeavouring to incite Jacob Henry Tillett to fight a duel." He was not present, so a bench warrant for his arrest was issued. Subsequently a solicitor appeared and applied for bail on his behalf. Hastings was bailed in the sum of £200 (personally), with two sureties of £100 each (these being provided by the Earl of Leicester and Lord Suffield).[566] Similarly, in 1847 the well-bred Norfolk thief George Thurtell was offered bail by committing JPs in the entirely impractical sum of £400. (He remained in custody.)[567] Very occasionally, the bail set could be even more. In 1839 two mechanics accused of Chartist offences (outside Norfolk) were asked to find bail of £1,000 each: £500 personally, with two sureties of £250 each for a criminal libel.[568]

Around the start of the Victorian period, there was concern that sophisticated defendants might "play" the legal system when it came to sureties. In 1835 the Duke of Richmond, speaking in the House of Lords, thought that a rich man who intended to abscond from bail might secure third-party guarantors by undertaking to "pay his sureties for the loss they had incurred."[569] Furthermore, it was feared that some rich people were having their indictments removed by writ of *certiorari* from inferior courts into the court of King's bench. Once there, bail was (legally) necessarily reduced from the substantial amount that had been required by JPs to just £20 or £30. This was an amount rich people could afford to lose. For example, in 1835 it was claimed that a defendant, charged with indecent exposure, had initially been bailed for £500 but then had the case removed into the King's bench, where he was required to give only the "statutable security of 20l., whereupon he fled the country and avoided justice."[570]

The sureties did not normally have to be in cash that was physically produced in advance. However, if the accused failed to attend trial, the sums pledged would be forfeit. For example, in January 1839, when Henry Keane failed to appear at the Norwich quarter sessions to stand trial for conspiracy to defraud, one of his recognizances was in court, and was informed by the recorder that he would have to forfeit the £20 he had guaranteed. He agreed, briefly left the building (with permission), secured the money, returned, and paid it into court. Keane's co-defendant also failed to appear, and the judge ordered that the defendants' personal recognizances, and those provided by other third parties, not then in court, be estreated.[571] Similarly, at the Norwich assizes in March 1851, when Frederick

---

566 *The Norfolk Chronicle*, 31 March, 1857.

567 *Bell's Life in London and Sporting Chronicle*, 21 November, 1847.

568 Hansard HC Deb 02 August 1839 vol. 49 cols. 1188-92

569 Hansard HL Deb 01 July 1835 vol. 29 cols. 128-30.

570 *Ibid.*

571 *The Ipswich Journal*, 5 January, 1839.

Goose failed to appear for trial for conspiring to obtain goods by false pretences from Sarah Tooke, Mr Justice Erle ordered that he forfeit his recognizances.[572]

In an increasingly mobile society, the requirement for sureties could create problems. Some poor suspects, accused of minor crimes, were unable to provide even very modest recognizances, especially if far from home. In recognition of this, by the final decade of the era the sums specified could be quite modest. In July 1895 at the North Erpingham petty sessions, Frederick Thurston, a local labourer, was committed for trial at assizes for breaking into the Primitive Methodist Chapel at Southrepps. He was granted bail in the personal sum of £10 with two sureties of just £5 each.[573] Eventually, in 1898 the Bail Act (61 & 62 Vict c 7) allowed the court to dispense with sureties altogether, in appropriate cases, provided that doing so would not "tend to defeat the ends of justice." In theory, this meant that those who were at no risk of absconding but were poor and friendless were no longer imprisoned for long periods.

Some observers thought that the effect of this statute on the courts' willingness to grant bail was quite modest. Nevertheless, it increased (nationally), from 19.56 percent of those committed for trial on indictment for felony in 1897, to 24.27 percent in 1900.[574] Similarly, in 1904 the Home Secretary, Aretas Akers-Douglas, thought that the percentage of prisoners released on bail pending trial had increased by nearly a quarter between the passing of the 1898 Act and 1902. He felt that this was a satisfactory result, given that the number of prisoners sent for trial who had no respectable friends willing to provide bail for them, but who, even so, could be released on their own recognizance without risk of absconding must necessarily be small.[575]

Appealing Bail Decisions

If committing JPs refused to grant bail, the matter could be argued again before a full bench at the next quarter sessions or referred to a Westminster judge in chambers for consideration, although significant expense would be involved in the latter situation, something that was prohibitive for many defendants. Nevertheless, in his memoirs Sir Henry Hawkins recalled that, around the mid-century, the latter type of bail application was a normal, albeit infrequent, part of the work of the Victorian Bar. He had represented a man who had been committed to trial at Hertford quarter sessions but refused bail, making a successful application before Mr Baron Martin to reverse the JPs' decision.[576]

---

572 *The Norfolk Chronicle*, 29 March, 1851.

573 NRO 24/4/1 North Erpingham Petty Sessions, Minute Book B p. 10.

574 Bentley, *English Criminal Justice,* pp. 32-33.

575 Hansard HC Deb 02 May 1904 vol. 134 cols. 93-493.

576 Henry Hawkins, *The Reminiscences of Sir Henry Hawkins* (London: Edward Arnold, 1904), p. 70.

In Norfolk in 1838, the well-to-do Jonathan Cooper, accused of shooting another man dead in a locally emotive case, was examined by two magistrates, and then committed to the Norwich Castle prison, pending trial for murder, after being refused bail. A further application for bail was then made to the county magistrates at quarter sessions, but again refused. Counsel was then briefed to apply to a Queen's bench judge in chambers for an order requiring the Norfolk JPs to admit Cooper to bail. This was done by the barrister Sydney Tayler in the absence of the accused, but after notifying the attorney for the prosecution, the coroner, the JPs involved in the case, and the next of kin of the dead man. A representative of the prosecution attorney was present, merely to watch proceedings, and notified the judge that the wife of the dead man was too poor to go to the expense of legally opposing it. Having considered the case, Mr Justice Littledale duly granted bail, and the accused was released on his own recognizance of £500 and four sureties of £100 each.[577] The following year he answered to his bail, was found guilty of manslaughter, and sentenced to a year's imprisonment in a local House of Correction.[578] Similarly, four years later, John Utting, accused of perjury at the Norfolk assizes, was eventually bailed by a judge in chambers in the sum of £400.[579]

More drastically, in September 1872, 16-year-old Sarah Minns and her mother, Mary, who were servants in the same private house, were questioned over the death of the former's new-born baby. They were committed for trial at the Norfolk assizes on a charge of murder by JPs and a coroner's inquest. The examining magistrates remanded them in custody in the meantime. However, a bail application was then made to Mr Justice Quain in his chambers in London. The judge, noting that winter assizes were rarely held in Norfolk, so that the two women would stay in custody until the following Lent assizes, and doubtless aware of, and influenced by, the likely verdicts in such cases, granted them bail for £50 with two other sureties of £25 (a total of £100).[580] Both women were acquitted at trial in March 1873.[581]

The Incidence of Bail

By early 1899, three-quarters of those awaiting trial on indictment in Norfolk – some 33 of 44 people – were on bail.[582] However, during the Victorian era, there was considerable variation in the grant of bail, depending on place, time, forum, and, most important, the gravity and legal status of the crime. The proportion of those bailed in felony cases was, of course, very much smaller than it was for misdemeanours (where it was quite normal), while those accused of certain felonies would be particularly unlikely to be released. Thus, even in 1915 (nationally) crimes

---

577 *The Standard*, 2 November, 1837. *Norfolk Chronicle,* 9 September, 1837.

578 *The Norfolk Chronicle,* 4 April, 1838.

579 *The Bury and Norwich Post*, 5 January, 1842.

580 *The Standard*, 28 September, 1872.

581 *The Bury and Norwich Post*, 25 March, 1873.

582 Anon., *Statistics Relating…1899* (1901), p. 192.

against property involving violence, such as robbery, saw just 12.9 percent of defendants being bailed, while for those that did not, the figure was 61.6 percent.[583]

Unsurprisingly, far more of those destined for trial at the higher jury court, with its diet of often serious crimes, were held in custody pending their hearings. In March 1890 16 people came for trial at the Norfolk Assizes, of whom ten were in custody; in July the figures were 17 and eight, respectively. However, at the autumn assizes for the county, held in November, only five of 14 defendants were not on bail. To take these three sessions together, 23 of 47 accused at the higher jury court that year were in custody at the time of their hearings, while a very narrow majority had bail. This produces a slightly higher rate of bailed defendants than was found in some other counties. Even at the Norwich city assizes, heard at about the same time as those for the wider county, 12 of 18 defendants tried at the three sessions that year were in custody, so that only a third were on bail.[584] To the extent that this was not a statistical quirk, it may be explained by the slightly greater willingness of the JPs in Norfolk to send less serious crimes for trial at assizes than was sometimes the case elsewhere.

Nevertheless, the majority of those suspected of a serious felony would be remanded in custody prior to their hearings, so that prisons would usually be most crowded just before sessions, even at the end of the Victorian period. This was less than ideal, both for its physical consequences and because some of those detained would eventually be acquitted. Nationally, nearly 5,000 people had been acquitted at trial in 1853, having undergone at least five weeks' imprisonment, and some of them "much more than the utmost term of the sentence which would have been passed on them had they been convicted."[585] In 1897 it was suggested that (nationally), at the assizes alone, there were 120 cases in which a suspect had been imprisoned before trial for more than 16 weeks. Of these 30 were subsequently acquitted.[586] Nevertheless, in 1899 only one prisoner awaiting trial on indictment in Norfolk was held in custody for more than 12 weeks, and none for more than 16.[587]

Those who were refused bail and subsequently convicted could, at least, have their previous custody taken into consideration in their sentences, and it was common practice to do so. For example, at the Norfolk summer assizes in 1838, William Grand pleaded guilty to stealing a consignment of apples from a storehouse. However, because he had already been in custody for a month, and appeared very penitent, he was sentenced to just a week's imprisonment.[588] Some feared that this risked

583 Bottomley, "The Granting of Bail," p. 41.

584 Anon., *Prisoners (detention before trial). Return for the year 1890, of information concerning the period during which prisoners were detained while awaiting trial at courts of quarter sessions and assizes in England and Wales*, House of Commons Sessional Papers, vol. 64, no. 351, p. 3.

585 Hansard HL Deb 23 March 1855 vol. 137 cols. 952-77, 968.

586 *The Spectator,* 1 July, 1899, p. 16.

587 Anon., *Statistics Relating...1899* (1901), p. 192.

588 *The Bury and Norwich Post*, 8 August, 1838.

producing headline sentences that were too mild to deter crime, asking whether it could be right that the public should frequently be "scandalised by seeing culprit after culprit receiving, on conviction, a sentence wholly disproportioned to the enormity of his offence, because the Judge is told in a whisper by the Clerk of the Crown, 'he has been in prison since August?'"[589] Those who were acquitted would get no compensation for their time in custody awaiting trial.

Ancillary Orders

After committing the accused person to trial, whether in custody or on bail, the examining JPs would usually bind over the victim or other prosecutor (increasingly this would be a police officer) and (sometimes) important prosecution witnesses to appear in court to prosecute and/or give evidence in the case. Thus, the appendix to the Indictable Offences Act 1848 provided three templates for binding over prosecutors and/or witnesses. One named a court (assizes or quarter sessions) and merely required a named individual to prosecute a case there. Another named a court and required a potential witness to attend to give evidence. The third, which would be found very commonly among crime victims, required that someone do both, and "duly prosecute such Indictment, and give evidence thereon." A sum would be specified, and if the person bound over did not appear at court and honour its requirements (to prosecute/give evidence), they would have to forfeit it, just as those would who provided sureties for bailed prisoners who subsequently absconded. For example, in December 1842 the prosecutor of two men accused of armed nocturnal poaching and violence towards gamekeepers entered a recognizance of £40 to pursue the matter; an important prosecution witness was also bound over in the sum of £10.[590]

By the close of the Victorian period, the levels stipulated to ensure prosecution and attendance were often quite modest, perhaps reflecting the greatly increased police involvement in the process; they were much less likely to need such an incentive to do their duty. For instance, in June 1895, at the North Erpingham petty sessions, Inspector Thomas Whitmore prosecuted at the committal of Ada Holmes for attempting to murder her child Gerty. After Ada was committed for trial to the assizes, Whitmore was bound over in the sum of £20 to pursue the matter, while several important prosecution witnesses were bound over in the sum of £10 each to appear at assizes. These were standard sums for the division in the 1890s.[591]

The JPs might also issue witness subpoenas, requiring people to come to court to give evidence. Inevitably, these were not always obeyed, even if this might ultimately lead to punishment. For example, in 1838 Uriah Baldwin's wife refused to comply

---

589 Anon., "Local Distribution of Tribunals," pp. 301-305.

590 NRO PS 24/1/1 Hundred of North Erpingham Norfolk Special and Petty Sessions Record Commencing 3 July, 1841.

591 NRO PS 24/4/1 North Erpingham Petty Sessions, Minute Book B. Ada was also committed for trial for attempting to commit suicide.

with a subpoena to give evidence against her husband at the Norwich assizes, when he was accused of cutting her with intent to murder (one of the rare situations in which a spouse could be compelled to testify). Instead, two men who broke into the house after hearing the victim's shrieks, and saw her flee with injuries to her throat, testified for the prosecution, while two prison surgeons gave evidence that they thought Baldwin was insane, with which verdict the jury agreed.[592]

Journey to Prison

Occasionally, especially before the advent of the railways, prisoners who had been committed for trial in remote parts of Norfolk might have to be escorted on foot for more than a day to the county gaol in Norwich, so that they would spend a night at an inn en route, sharing a bed with the escorting constable while handcuffed to him, as occurred with the alleged East Harling poacher John Hart in May 1842.[593] Hart subsequently died in Norwich Castle prison from the very delayed after-effects of being struck on the head by PC George Dowde, who had been tasked with escorting him to the county gaol. Hart had tried to escape on the way, after having his handcuffs removed so that he could urinate. Dowde had pursued him, striking him with his "staff" as he tried to climb over a gate.[594] The advent of trains and an increased number of horse-drawn wagons meant that this procedure petered out over the century.

Prisoners on Remand

Although no longer constituting the great majority of inmates, as had been the case in earlier centuries, large numbers of prisoners continued to be held on remand, awaiting trial, in local gaols during the Victorian era. For example, at the Norfolk quarter sessions in January 1847, it was noted that the county gaol in Norwich Castle had 11 suspected felons awaiting the assizes, and 40 waiting for trial at quarter sessions.[595] Remand prisoners also made up a significant proportion of those in custody at any one time. The status of the 70 prisoners held at the county gaol in January 1857 is indicative. Of these, 13 were civil debtors, a category that was not fully abolished until 1869 (although long in decline by then); three were prisoners accused of felony awaiting trial at the assizes; and eight were suspected felons awaiting a hearing at quarter sessions. Of the remainder, 19 had been convicted of felony and 27 of misdemeanours and were undergoing punishment. Thus eleven, or almost a fifth, of the (suspected) criminal inmates were on remand.[596] The proportion would have been even higher, but sessions were still far off, while knowledge that they were imminent also encouraged people to pursue offenders

---

592 *The Bury and Norwich Post*, 11 April 1838.

593 *Ibid.,* 18 May 1842 and 3 August 1842.

594 *Ibid.,* 3 August 1842.

595 *Ibid.,* January 13, 1847.

596 *Ibid.* , 13 January, 1857.

through the criminal courts. (In an extreme case, it was claimed that a majority of the 51 defendants at the Norfolk assizes in July 1850 had been committed to trial over the previous month).[597]

Conditions on Remand

Remand prisoners were supposed to be kept separate from other inmates, but this rule was not always followed, especially at the start of the Victorian period. Thus, in 1837 it was noted that Jonathan Cooper had been held in one of Norwich Prison's felons' cells pending his murder hearing.[598] In 1863 the inspector of prisons (southern district) observed that in Great Yarmouth Gaol three convicted and sentenced prisoners were housed in the ward used for those on remand (there was just one such inmate), although technically this was not permitted.[599] Remand prisoners were also entitled to wear their own clothes, and if they wore those provided by the prison, these were supposed to be of a slightly different colour from the uniforms worn by convicts. It was claimed that most English remand prisoners (unlike their Scottish counterparts) preferred their own attire.[600] They could not be required to work, and could, in theory, have their food sent in from outside rather than eating prison meals if they could afford it. James Rush went to great lengths to ensure that he was well fed while in custody prior to his murder trial in 1849, writing to the proprietor of the Bell Inn in Norwich, arranging for hot and cold meals to be sent in, along with covered pint mugs of hot tea. He even suggested that the innkeeper purchase a sucking pig in the local market and roast it for him, garnishing it with plum sauce.[601] Those on remand could also have beer brought in. While incarcerated, prior to trial, they could be visited by solicitors to discuss their legal cases and, where possible, such visits were supposed to be private, subject to the requirements of security.[602]

In practice, many of these benefits were slightly illusory or even totally absent, especially early in the period, and particularly for those without financial resources. In 1839 in the House of Commons, John Leader cited two Chartist remand prisoners, John Lovett and William Collins, who complained of the alleged indignity to which they had been exposed after arrest in Birmingham. This involved having their hair cut by a felon, being washed in a bath with other prisoners, and being restricted to gaol food "unless they paid out of their small wages 2s 6d. each to the turnkey, in order to induce him to cook for them some eggs and bacon." They also complained that they were debarred from the free use of pen and paper, and that everything that they wrote was subject to the inspection of the jailor. Furthermore, they did

---

597 *Ibid.*, 31 July, 1850.

598 *The Norfolk Chronicle,* September 9, 1837.

599 *The Bury and Norwich Post*, 8 September, 1863.

600 Hansard HL Deb 23 March 1855 vol. 137 cols. 952-77, 968.

601 *Jackson's Oxford Journal*, 7 April, 1849.

602 Michelle Higgs, *Prison Life in Victorian England* (Cheltenham: The History Press, 2007), p. 21.

not have liberty to consult with their legal advisers without a turnkey being present. These factors allegedly stymied the preparation of their defence.[603] They were certainly not unique in this. However, the special regime for remand prisoners was considerably improved in 1878, following the previous year's Prison Act, with extra privileges being allowed, albeit that many still required payment.[604]

Direct Approach to a Grand Jury

In theory, and as in previous centuries, a committal hearing might be avoided altogether by presenting a draft indictment and supporting witnesses directly to a grand jury, whether at assizes or quarter sessions. In these situations, if a prima facie case were found against the accused, a bench warrant for the suspect's arrest and production at the following sessions would be issued.[605] This ancient, much criticized, but infrequently exercised power, had been limited by the Vexatious Indictments Act 1859, which provided that certain types of case that were prone to abuse (such as allegations of malicious prosecution, perjury, and indecent assault) could not go directly to a grand jury without first going for a magistrates' committal.[606] Furthermore, in 1867 it was enacted that if a defendant were acquitted, having been indicted without a magistrates' committal, the trial court could order the person prosecuting to pay the defendant's costs, further discouraging recourse to this historic power.[607] Nevertheless, with these restrictions, the ability to commit directly to a grand jury survived to the end of the period and beyond. As the barrister John Mellor noted in 1845, it was sometimes used to put a suspect before a jury where examining magistrates had earlier considered and discharged a case against them.[608] The comparative rarity of this procedure, in Victorian Norfolk as elsewhere in the country, means that it need not be considered further.

---

603 Hansard HC Deb 02 August 1839 vol. 49 cols. 1188-92.

604 *The Bury and Norwich Post*, 5 March, 1878.

605 Anon., *The Law Magazine: or, Quarterly Review of Jurisprudence*, vol. 17 (1864), p. 3.

606 Alexander, *The administration,* p. 97. Matthew Davenport Hill and Sir John Eardley-Wilmot, *Papers on Grand Juries* (London: Longman, Green, 1865), pp. 2-4.

607 Nathan T. Elliff, "Notes on the Abolition of the English Grand Jury," *Journal of Criminal Law and Criminology*, vol. 29, no. 1 (1938), p. 13.

608 *Eighth Report,* p. 227.

Chapter 6: Coroners

Introduction

English coroners have been investigating deaths at proceedings termed inquests since the late twelfth century. Originally, they were men of high social status with broad judicial functions and considerable legal powers. They had gradually yielded most of their responsibilities to itinerant royal judges, county sheriffs, and JPs, largely becoming confined to presiding over inquests by the seventeenth century. This development encouraged a decline in their social standing, so that by the nineteenth century even county coroners were normally professional men (lawyers or doctors), while borough coroners might not always have even this status.[609]

Victorian coroners held inquests where the subject of their enquiry had met a violent, unnatural, sudden, unexpected, or unexplained death. They also investigated all deaths in custody (as they had done for centuries) and those that occurred in certain institutions (such as asylums) and workplaces (such as factories) by dint of several nineteenth-century statutes and the creation of various inspectorates. Thus, after the notorious thief George Thurtell died from longstanding kidney disease while in Norwich Castle prison in 1848, an inquest was held automatically, swiftly concluding that he died from "natural causes."[610] The duties of the coroner and his jury included identifying the deceased person, determining when and where their death occurred, eliciting its immediate medical causes, and establishing its circumstances. They would produce a formal verdict on the general cause of death, such as murder, natural causes, Act of God, or accident etc., or declare their inability to do so.[611]

Incidence of Inquests

For the greater part of the Victorian period the proportion of inquests to total deaths stood at between 5 and (towards the end of the nineteenth century) 7 percent.[612] As this suggests, the number of inquests conducted nationally rose after 1860, and it has been suggested that, by the end of the century, about 60,000 deaths a year, some 10 percent of all deaths in England and Wales, were reported to coroners, with about two-thirds of these reports leading to formal inquests.[613] As a result, some 37,076 inquests were conducted in 1900.

---

609 R.A. Houston, *The Coroners of Northern Britain c. 1300–1700* (London: Palgrave Pivot, 2014), pp. 8-21.

610 *The Cambridge Independent*, 5 August, 1848.

611 Thomas R. Forbes, "Coroners' Inquisitions from the County Of Cheshire, England, 1817-39 and 1877-78," *Bulletin of the History of Medicine*, vol. 59, no. 4 (1985), pp. 481-494.

612 Elizabeth T. Hurren, "Remaking the Medico-Legal Scene: A Social History of the Late-Victorian Coroner in Oxford," *Journal of the History of Medicine and Allied Sciences*, vol. 65, no. 2 (2010), p. 211.

613 Paul Knapman, "The Crowner's Quest," *Journal of the Royal Society of Medicine*, vol. 86 (1993), p. 720.

Most of the cases investigated during the Victorian era involved non-criminal deaths. For example, in 1856, the first year in which verdicts were collated nationally, just under 1 percent of all inquests held in England and Wales returned findings of murder, and another 1.3 per cent produced verdicts of manslaughter or justifiable homicide, so that only 2.2 percent clearly involved deliberate killings (ignoring suicide).[614] More specifically, of 21,801 inquests held that year, some 482 involved cases that produced verdicts of murder, manslaughter, or justifiable homicide. Of these, 265 resulted in criminal trials, 100 produced convictions, and 10 led to hangings.[615]

In 1860, all ten of the coroners' jurisdictions in Norfolk produced just one murder and one manslaughter verdict, both of these being in the liberty of the Duchy of Lancaster.[616] The following year they returned just one manslaughter verdict.[617] Moving to the end of the period, in 1899 the entire county did not produce a single inquest finding of murder, manslaughter, or even justifiable homicide.[618] However, the next year there was one finding of murder and three of manslaughter.[619]

In 1867 Dr William Farr, the registrar general, alluded to these small numbers (nationally) when he suggested that the presence of coroners discouraged homicide even though few inquests led to prosecutions. He referred to Jonathan Balls' poisonings in Norfolk (see below) some years earlier as an example of the dangers of interfering with the coroner's role and work, even if it occasioned some expense: "It is true that of twenty-one thousand inquiries only a few lead to the committal and conviction of criminals; but the utility of the inquest is not to be proved by the number of crimes committed, but by the number of crimes prevented."[620]

Nevertheless, many other inquests produced "open" or narrative verdicts when jurors could not account for a death. For example, in 1856, they made up 16.2 percent of all verdicts nationally. In 1867, one observer claimed that if the truth behind verdicts such as "found drowned" could be established, many would be instances of wilful murder.[621] Similarly, the compiler of the official Judicial Statistics in 1899 candidly admitted that among the 1,981 open verdicts returned that year were

[614] James T. Hammick, "On the Judicial Statistics of England and Wales, with Special Reference to the Recent Returns Relating to Crime," *Journal of the Statistical Society of London*, vol. 30, no. 3 (1867), p. 400.

[615] *The Standard*, 27 December, 1858.

[616] Anon., *Statistics Relating…1860* (1861), p. 40.

[617] Anon, *Statistics Relating…1861* (1862), p. 40.

[618] Anon, *Statistics Relating…1899* (1901), p. 172.

[619] Anon, *Statistics Relating…1900* (1902), p. 123.

[620] Hammick, "Judicial Statistics," p. 403.

[621] *Ibid.*, p. 400.

many homicides. Indeed, it was generally accepted that not a few inquest verdicts of death by accident or from natural causes also involved undetected killings.[622]

An example of a simple narrative conclusion, essentially a form of open verdict, in which foul play could not be excluded, can be seen in a case of 1881. R.A. Wilkie, the deputy coroner for the Duchy of Lancaster in Norfolk, held an inquest at Docking into the death of an eight-year-old boy, Robert Playford, who had been found dying in a local wood. The boy showed signs of both starvation and bruising. The jury gave a narrative verdict noting, "The deceased died from want of the common necessaries of life, accelerated by exposure to the inclemency of the weather; but whether or not death was mainly or partially attributable to the neglect and cruelty of the father and stepmother of the deceased there is not sufficient evidence to show."[623]

Similarly, when a Norfolk county coroner summed up to the inquest jury examining the death by drowning of Thomas Valentine in 1848, he noted that, if they decided that the dead man had fallen into the River Nar by accident, they would return a verdict accordingly, but that the jury "could if they pleased find an open verdict to the effect that he was found drowned, but by what means he got into the water there was no evidence to show." The jury immediately followed this suggestion.[624]

In comparison to the very low number of inquest verdicts identifying homicide, almost 44 percent of investigated deaths were ascribed to accidents and another 32 percent to natural causes.[625] Typical of such cases, in 1879 an inquest was held on the body of 82-year-old Nathan Corble at the Crown and Anchor in Blo' Norton in the Breckland district of Norfolk. The elderly man had been found lying dead in his cottage, where he lived alone. His attending doctor noted that he had shown serious signs of apoplexy and had doubtless died of the condition, not least because "there were no marks of violence on his body." The jury concluded that it was a case of death by natural causes.[626] Changing verdict, in December 1839 an inquest held at the Bell Inn in Stoke Ferry concluded that Thomas Seeker had met an accidental death. He had been driving a wagon and reached forward to whip the forehorse, falling under its wheels as he did so.[627] The same verdict was returned in October 1880, when the Norwich city coroner held an inquest at the Norfolk and Norwich

---

622 Howard Taylor, "Rationing Crime: The Political Economy of Criminal Statistics Since the 1850s," *The Economic History Review*, vol. 51, no. 3 (1998), p. 587.

623 *The Times*, 22 October, 1881, p. 6.

624 *The Lynn Advertiser & West Norfolk Herald*, 11 December, 1858.

625 P. Fisher, "Getting away with murder? The suppression of coroners' inquests in early Victorian England and Wales," *Local Population Studies*, no. 78 (2007), pp. 47-62.

626 *The Ipswich Journal*, 5 April, 1879.

627 *The Norfolk Chronicle*, 4 January, 1840.

hospital into the death of an eight-year-old schoolboy who had been mortally injured by a swing that struck him on the head and fractured his skull.[628]

The balance of cases involved less frequent findings, such as suicide and Act of God (lightning strike, etc.). For example, and very unusually, on a single day in August 1838, the city of Norwich coroner had to determine three suicides – a hanging, a drowning, and a throat-slitting. The first two involved people who were held to have killed themselves while suffering from temporary insanity; the last, a woman with a history of mental illness who had been committed to an asylum in the past, was held to have killed herself while fully insane.[629] More than 30 years later, in 1870, a youth named John Brown, who had been in the service of a clergyman at Fakenham, but been severely rebuked for misconduct in church and neglect of duty, threw himself in front of a train. The inquest jury concluded that he had "destroyed himself while in a fit of temporary insanity."[630]

Types of Coroner

Victorian coroners fell into three main categories, as they had done for centuries: county, borough, and franchise officers. All three types were found in the ten or (depending on time) eleven coroners' districts in early Victorian Norfolk. Thus, two and later three of these were in the main body of the county itself, these being covered by county coroners (at least one of whom would normally be based in each district). Four (later three) more were found in borough jurisdictions. Another four covered the county's liberties or franchises.

County Coroners

Most shires had two or more county coroners, each based in, and primarily responsible for, a specific district within their borders, albeit that there was usually a hierarchy of seniority, and they could, if necessary, exercise their office anywhere within its bounds. As a result, an alternative county coroner could step in if the local man was unavailable. In 1848, after James Rush murdered Isaac Jermy and his son, there were problems finding an officer to preside over the inquest as "Mr. Press, the coroner for the district, had gone to London, and Mr. Pilgrim [the senior Norfolk coroner] was not in the city [Norwich]." Fortunately, Press returned the following day.[631]

County coroners made up almost two-thirds of the well over 300 coroners present in England and Wales in 1837, although precise assessments varied. A parliamentary return in 1832 identified 143 county coroners, but this seems to have omitted many

---

628 *The Bury and Norwich Post*, 12 October, 1880.

629 *Ibid.*, 8 August, 1838.

630 *Ibid.*, 13 December, 1870.

631 *The Times*, 1 December 1848, p. 5.

officers.[632] More reliably, in 1876 it was suggested (in parliament) that in England and Wales their number stood at 233.[633] At the start of the twentieth century it was claimed that there were still about 200 county coroners out of a total of 330 in the country.[634] Their number varied considerably from county to county, ranging from two to a dozen, depending partly on size and population but also on local tradition. Populous Middlesex, for instance, had only five, but Dorset had eleven. In 1876 Lord Francis Hervey, speaking in parliament about the anomalous distribution of coroners, noted that Norfolk had seven such men, but this figure appears to have included its franchise officers. (It also had four borough coroners (see below), producing a total of 11 men for the entire county).[635] The county coroners' jurisdictions in Norfolk were divided into the Norwich district, the King's Lynn district and, in the final years of the century, the Thetford district.

Borough Coroners

Section 62 of the Municipal Corporations Act 1835 obliged each borough with its own quarter sessions to appoint a coroner (already a very long-standing practice), so that after 1835 there were a little under 100 towns nationally that had their own officers.[636] In 1876, it was thought that there were 99 such men.[637] In Norfolk in 1837 there were borough coroners in Norwich, Great Yarmouth, King's Lynn, and Thetford. (By comparison, and for example, Shropshire had five such borough officers.)[638] Under the Local Government Act of 1888, boroughs with fewer than 10,000 inhabitants lost their coroners, becoming part of the county system, as was the case with Thetford, so that there were 76 borough coroners at the end of the Victorian era.[639] Prior to abolition, the Thetford borough coroner had been hearing only a tiny number of cases each year.

Franchise Coroners

Further complicating the situation, there were historic franchise jurisdictions within most counties in which coroners were appointed by special bodies rather than by the county. Thus, a parliamentary return in 1832 identified 62 franchise jurisdictions with coroners in England and Wales, while in 1876, Lord Francis Hervey thought there were 58 of them. It seems that there were still about 54 franchise jurisdictions

---

632 Fisher, "Getting away," p. 60.

633 Hansard, HC Deb 11 July 1876 vol. 230 cols. 1301-14.

634 Alexander, *The Administration,* p. 100.

635 Hansard, HC Deb 11 July 1876 vol. 230 cols. 1301-14.

636 Fisher, "Getting away," p. 60.

637 Hansard, HC Deb 11 July 1876 vol. 230 cols. 1301-14.

638 Pamela Fisher, "Edmund Whitcombe and the detection of homicide in Georgian Shropshire," *Family & Community History*, vol. 14, no. 1 (2011), p. 8.

639 Alexander, *The Administration,* p. 100.

at the beginning of the twentieth century.[640] In an extreme case, Huntingdon was so fully covered by such franchises that it had no need for county coroners.

Norfolk was not like that but was still possessed of four franchises of very different sizes. Most important amongst them was that of the Duchy of Lancaster (the personal property of the monarch), which also had coronial liberties in the counties of Essex, Middlesex, Surrey, Cheshire, and Yorkshire. The coroner for the duchy in Norfolk was based in East Dereham, although his liberty included more than 200 parishes and hamlets scattered around the county, especially its north. The second largest franchise, the liberty of the Duke of Norfolk, was centred on the hundreds of Earsham, Guiltcross, Launditch, and South Greenhoe, and stretched into the neighbouring county, so that in January 1889, when an inquest into the suspected suicide by poisoning of Harriett Watts was held at the King's Head in Bungay, Suffolk, it was conducted by E.E. Garrod, Coroner for the Duke's Liberty, within which franchise jurisdiction the death had occurred.[641] On a smaller scale, the Clackclose Hundred (a former monastic territory that went to the Crown during the reign of Henry VIII) in the southwest of Norfolk, covering 33 parishes, also had its own coroner, though he sometimes had to resist attempts by the county coroners to impinge on his jurisdiction.[642] Even more diminutive, the tiny Clackclose Half-Hundred had parted from the main hundred after the Reformation, and usually had its own officer.[643]

Workloads

Throughout England, the distribution of coroners often bore little relationship to population, so that there was a huge variation in the number of inquests dealt with in different coronial jurisdictions; as a result, the occupation of coroner varied from full-time work to a very sporadically conducted side-line.[644] According to a modern estimate, most county coroners in the period from 1829 to 1831 held fewer than 60 inquests each year, and the overwhelming majority of them earned less than £100 per annum from their position.[645] Thus Edmund Whitcombe, a Shropshire county coroner, averaged just 14 inquests a year in the early 1820s.[646]

---

640 *Ibid.*

641 *Ipswich Journal*, 11 January 1889.

642 Pamela Fisher, *The politics of sudden death: the office and role of the coroner in England and Wales, 1726-1888*, University of Leicester PhD thesis, 2007, p. 70.

643 Anon., *Statistics Relating…1900* (1902), p. 123 and p. 118. William White, *History, Gazetteer, and Directory of Norfolk, and the City and County of the City of Norwich*, fourth ed. (Sheffield: William White, 1883), p. 608.

644 Ian A. Burney, *Bodies of Evidence: Medicine and the Politics of the English Inquest, 1830–1926* (Baltimore: Johns Hopkins University Press, 2000), p. 3.

645 Yvonne King Fisher, *Coroners in London and Middlesex, c. 1820–1888: A Study of Medicalization and Professionalization*, The Open University PhD thesis, 2020, p. 16.

646 Fisher, "Edmund Whitcombe," p. 14.

In 1858, it was estimated that 91 of the 324 coroners in England and Wales presided over fewer than ten inquests a year, and some of these rarely viewed bodies from one year to the next.[647] For example, two of the three coroners for Oxford had jurisdiction only over the bodies of members of the University found dead on academic premises. In general, their workload was very low, perhaps two inquests a year. Typical coroners in cities, on the other hand, might conduct a huge number of hearings. Thus, the city coroner in Oxford had a very time-consuming office, since he had jurisdiction over most of Oxford (the university apart), including an asylum, three hospitals, a prison, and several workhouses.[648]

A similar variation in workloads may be seen within Norfolk. Perhaps unsurprisingly, the county coroner for the Norwich district was very busy. For example, in 1899 he conducted 80 inquests. By contrast, the county coroner allotted to the Thetford district heard just five. When it came to urban areas, the coroner for the city of Norwich considered 113 bodies in 1899, this being the highest number for any jurisdiction in the county. The Great Yarmouth borough coroner sat on 70 in the same year, but his equivalent in King's Lynn heard just 19. Among franchise coroners, the coroner for the large liberty of the Duchy of Lancaster sat on 39 deaths, being by far the busiest of the four.[649] In 1900 the Norwich City coroner again conducted the highest number of inquests, at 124 hearings. As previously, this was followed by those for the Norwich district of Norfolk, at 94, while the number for the Borough of Yarmouth was unchanged at 70. By contrast, the Thetford district saw only six, while the tiny Clackclose Half-Hundred franchise witnessed just two.[650]

Victorian coroners sometimes used deputies, the power to appoint such officers (often their clerks) being given to borough coroners in 1836 and county coroners in 1843. Towards the end of the nineteenth century the appointment of a deputy was made compulsory, so that he could act in the absence of the coroner. As well as increasing the manpower available, the deputies also sometimes served as apprentices for the full position.[651]

Appointment

County coroners were elected by freeholders, if there was more than one candidate for a position, until 1888, after which the new county councils appointed such officers without election. Elections, however, had not been very regular occurrences in the 1700s, or during the first quarter of the following century. In Warwickshire, for example, all four county coroners appointed during the early 1800s were

647 Burney, *Bodies of Evidence,* p. 174.

648 Hurren, "Remaking," pp. 207-52.

649 Anon., *Statistics Relating...1899* (1901), p. 172.

650 Anon., *Statistics Relating...1900* (1902) p. 123, p. 118.

651 Cornish, *Oxford History,* p. 936.

"elected" without opposition.[652] Nevertheless, contested elections were slightly more common in some parts of the country in the 1840s. Since the constituency was very large, such contests could be expensive, and irregularities were common. Inevitably a degree of corruption crept in. In May 1857 polling for the election of a coroner for the King's Lynn district of Norfolk was unusually fiercely contested, given the modest pecuniary value of the office; its fees were, at most, about £30 a year (salaries were not introduced until 1861). The two candidates apparently brought in potential voters from miles around, paying for their railway and coach fares, as well as for breakfasts and dinners.[653]

County coroners were elected for life (or until they resigned). In an extreme case, Edward Press of Hingham was a Norfolk coroner for more than 40 years, having originally been elected by 1,073 votes to the 766 cast for his opponent, Henry Hobart. On his death in 1878 his assistant, R.T. Culley, was elected his replacement.[654]

Franchise coroners were appointed in the manner prescribed by their original charters. Frequently this would be by the lord of the manor or by senior local dignitaries or clerics. For example, the four coroners for the county of Durham were appointed by the Lord Bishop of Durham until 1837, after which, like ordinary county coroners, they were elected by freeholders.[655] In 1876, Lord Francis Hervey claimed that one Derbyshire franchise coroner was appointed by right of the possession of a horn (a hereditary relic), while in Suffolk another was appointed by the dean and chapter of Ely.[656] In Norfolk Martin Coulcher, the Coroner for the Clackclose Hundred in 1840, had been appointed by Sir Thomas Hare, while William Townley, Coroner for the Clackclose Half-Hundred, had been selected by his relative Richard Townley.[657]

In the boroughs the corporation (town council) usually chose the coroner; most were appointed for life, though some were chosen annually, and so were potentially vulnerable to local political changes, although this was rarely an issue in practice. In some boroughs the mayor was the coroner ex officio. How much ability such men could demonstrate is debatable. Lord Francis Hervey claimed that he would not like to die suddenly in some English towns, because the ensuing inquest would probably be of the most imperfect character.[658]

The rather eccentric and archaic manner of appointing coroners of all types was the subject of periodic criticism during the Victorian era, amid claims that it had become

---

652 Gordon H.H. Glasgow, "The Election of County Coroners in England and Wales *circa* 1800–1888," *The Journal of Legal History*, vol. 20, no. 3 (1999), p. 78.

653 *The Norfolk Chronicle,* 18 May, 1857.

654 *The Bury and Norwich Post*, 11 June, 1878.

655 Glasgow, "Election," p. 75.

656 Hansard HC Deb 11 July 1876 vol. 230 col. 1301.

657 *Sessional Papers Printed by Order of the House of Lords, or Presented by Royal Command, in the Session 1840*, 1840, Parliament, London, vol. xx, p. 22.

658 Hansard HC Deb 11 July 1876 vol. 230 col. 1301.

so antiquated and obsolete as to call for urgent reform.[659] Little changed until the following century.

Qualifications

The only formal qualification needed for the office of county coroner was the vague requirement that such an officer hold enough land in the shire that he might "answer to all manner of people." However, as Lord Francis Hervey noted in 1876, no two authorities could agree as to how much land this was, and, in any event, the possession of land was a "ridiculous qualification for a Coroner at the present day."[660] Even so, despite its inherent ambiguity, this requirement was incorporated into the Consolidation Act of 1887. For a borough coroner, the requirement was even more modest: he only had to be deemed to be a "fit person," while no qualification at all was formally specified for most franchise coroners. Most important of all, until 1926 there was no need for coroners to hold a professional qualification.

Nevertheless, by the Victorian period, it was generally accepted that a county coroner should normally be medically or legally qualified.[661] In practice, nearly all county coroners and most franchise officers were either lawyers (usually attorneys or solicitors) or doctors of some description. The latter were much less common, although they had made up a quarter of coroners in some eighteenth-century counties, and several English shires, such as Shropshire, were regularly appointing medical men by the early nineteenth century, as did many Welsh counties.[662]

There was a degree of rivalry between the two professions as to which was better suited for the position. Thomas Wakley, a surgeon, MP, London coroner, and eventual founder of the medical journal *The Lancet*, actively campaigned for the use of medical coroners, and when he died in 1862 there were 59 out of well over 300 of all types nationally, although their numbers did not progress much further.[663] Wakley thought there was a danger of homicides going undetected when coroners were not medically qualified.[664] However, many other observers rejected this argument, claiming that expert medical evidence was readily available at inquests, and that it was "a matter of common-sense that a man who has had the advantage of legal training must, as a general rule, be better able to perform this duty than a mere

---

659 *Ibid.* cols. 1301-14.

660 *Ibid.* col. 1302.

661 Cornish, *Oxford History,* p. 937.

662 Fisher, "Edmund Whitcombe," p. 5.

663 Gordon H.H. Glasgow (2004), "The campaign for medical coroners in nineteenth-century England and its aftermath: a Lancashire focus on failure, Part I," *Mortality*, vol. 9, no. 2 (2004), pp. 150-167. Katherine Watson, *Medicine and Justice: Medico-Legal Practice in England and Wales, 1700–1914* (Abingdon: Routledge, 2021), p. 104.

664 Mary Beth Emmerichs, "Getting away with Murder?: Homicide and the Coroners in Nineteenth-Century London," *Social Science History*, vol. 25, no. 1 (2001), pp. 93-100.

layman."[665] Furthermore, most solicitor-coroners used their own clerks at inquests, something that put medical coroners at a disadvantage when it came to clerical assistance, and helped ensure legal dominance.101

As this suggests, Norfolk coroners were usually attorneys or solicitors (the latter absorbing the former profession during the period), and most remained engaged in normal professional practice. Thus, Edward Press, the son of a clergyman, practised as a solicitor at Hingham for many years but was more widely known as a county coroner, an office he held for 50 years. He died in 1878.[666] Five years later, a disappointed client was committed to the assizes for trial after threatening to kill Joseph Stanley, who was both a Norfolk coroner and a solicitor in the same county. He claimed that Stanley had ruined his business by his poor legal work.[667] Conversely, in 1887 it was noted that Stanley had been fined £2 and costs by the Norwich magistrates for assaulting another former client, Donald Edwards, who had complained about his professional conduct at assizes. (Stanley hit Edwards with his umbrella after the two men met in the street.)[668] Many franchise coroners in the county were also lawyers. For example, in 1845 a Downham attorney, William Townley, was the coroner for the Clackclose Half-Hundred, while Martin Coulcher, another attorney from the same small town, was the coroner for the Clackclose Hundred itself.[669]

The almost de facto requirement that county coroners have a medico-legal background did not necessarily extend to borough coroners, whose ranks might include ironmongers, builders, and other prosperous tradesmen.[670] As Lord Francis Hervey noted in the 1870s, although they had to be fit persons, and (by then) were usually neither aldermen nor councillors, some were "auctioneers, retired tradesmen, and other persons of a similar kind." (Hervey was in favour of the office's being formally limited to barristers or solicitors, though aware that this would occasion extreme annoyance to medical men.)[671] Nevertheless, most Norfolk borough coroners were also lawyers. Thus, the long-serving Thetford coroner Robert Eagle Clarke was a prominent solicitor in the town in the 1850s and 1860s.[672] Similarly, Edward Beloe was both a solicitor and coroner for the borough of King's Lynn during the 1870s and 1880s.[673]

---

665 *The Spectator,* 15 July, 1876, p. 8.

666 *The Norfolk Chronicle,* 15 May, 1878.

667 *The Pall Mall Gazette*, 4 August, 1883.

668 *The Lancaster Gazetteer*, 6 August, 1887.

669 *White, History, Gazetteer*, p. 38.

670 Emmerichs, "Getting away," pp. 93-100.

671 Hansard HC Deb 11 July 1876 vol. 230 col. 1301.

672 *The Morning Chronicle* 13 July, 1861.

673 *The Bury and Norwich Post,* 10 November, 1874.

Removal from Office

The Lord Chancellor had a longstanding but very rarely exercised power to remove county coroners for "inability or misbehaviour." The Coroners Act 1860 placed this on a statutory footing, something that, with minor changes, was reiterated in the 1887 Act. It normally required that someone lodge a formal complaint against a coroner before action could be taken. Even then, removing him could be an onerous task. In 1854, when the Warwickshire quarter sessions ordered the clerk of the peace to remove William Poole as a coroner on the grounds that he had become bankrupt and been struck off the rolls as a solicitor, the Lord Chancellor's secretary informed them that it required a proper statement setting forth his malpractice, supported by affidavits, and would have to be heard in open court.[674] Lesser failings in office by coroners might be the subject of rebuke, whether by visiting judges of assizes or the JPs at quarter sessions. Even so, they enjoyed very considerable discretion in conducting their affairs, and so a large measure of independence.[675]

Criticism and Change in the Victorian Era

In the nineteenth century, the coroner and his inquest were subject to much criticism, and radical reform, or even total abolition, of the office was sometimes proposed. In 1873 the judicature commissioners were prepared to recommend only that the system be allowed to remain "for the present," and a Commons select committee on the issue in 1879 sent for only two witnesses, both to give evidence on the supposedly superior workings of the Scottish system of procurators fiscal. Nevertheless, the coroner and his inquest survived largely intact to the end of the Victorian period, albeit with some statutory and de facto changes.[676]

It is sometimes suggested that, at the start of the nineteenth century, the coronial system was relatively unprofessional, its medieval roots still evident, and its inquest often disorganized, while by the end of the Victorian period, and after much debate, the modern coronership had started to emerge. However, this analysis can be exaggerated.[677] Long before 1837 the coroner's inquest could be extremely thorough, in Norfolk as elsewhere in the country. For example, in 1813 the body of a woman named Gooderham was found in Diss. An inquest was held that lasted six days, during which 41 witnesses were examined; the jury returned a verdict of "wilful murder against some person or persons unknown."[678] This thoroughness was unusual, but hearings of many hours were not uncommon, with medical evidence regularly being adduced. Nevertheless, the mixed provenance, abilities, and energies of coroners across the country meant that some inquests at the start

---

674 Glasgow, "Election," p. 97.

675 Cornish, *Oxford History,* p. 938.

676 *Ibid.*, pp. 934-935, p. 944.

677 Fisher, *Coroners*, p. 13.

678 Mackie, Norfolk Annals, vol. 1, p. 263.

of the era were conducted in a superficial manner, while others were sometimes lacking in suitable expert testimony.

The years immediately before and after the accession of the new Queen saw several changes to the coronial system nationwide, some of them influenced by various campaigns mounted by Thomas Wakley and other prominent (often Metropolitan) coroners. They included the amount paid to county coroners.

Payment and Financing of Coroners

Before 1837 the only inquest expenses that county ratepayers normally had to meet were the coroner's fees and his incidental expenses. The former were quite modest, a statute of 1751 permitting 20 shillings for each inquest conducted, plus a modest travelling allowance. Any other costs fell on the friends and family of the deceased or on the parishes where the deaths had occurred, and the ensuing inquests were conducted. However, in 1837 the sum paid to county coroners for each inquest was increased to £1 6s 8d. By then they would also receive 9 pence a mile travelling expenses for their journey to the scene of the inquest (but nothing for the return leg). If two (or more) inquests were held in the same place on the same day (as would be the case with a murder-suicide), they would not be able to claim expenses twice. Early in the era, if franchise jurisdictions did not pay into county rates, their coroners were not entitled to a fee from the county, and they would have to look elsewhere for remuneration.[679]

The payments made to county coroners had to be authorized by quarter sessions. Even in the late eighteenth century, there had sometimes been tension between coroners and JPs on this matter. For example, in 1791 a Norfolk coroner had gone to the high court to challenge the county JPs' refusal to pay him for holding an inquest on a drowned man whose body showed no marks of violence. Occasionally, even then, such a threat may have influenced coroners' behaviour, making them reluctant to conduct inquests for which they might not be remunerated. This tension continued into the following century but was greatly exacerbated by changes that occurred during the early Victorian period.[680]

The Medical Witness Act of 1836 gave coroners the power to compel qualified medical witnesses to testify at inquests and to conduct autopsies when necessary. It also introduced a statutory payment of one guinea (£1 1s) for giving medical evidence at such forums, or two guineas if the coroner had also ordered a post-mortem examination. The Inquest Expenses Act of 1837 transferred these fees to the county rates, together with other incidental expenses. As a result, most counties allowed payment to be made to the parish constable (for fetching the coroner), to cover any expenses incurred by non-medical witnesses and jurors, and for the hire of

---

679 Richard Clarke Sewell, *A Treatise on the Law of Coroner: With Copious Precedents of Inquisitions ...*, 1843, p. 213.

680 Katherine D. Watson, *Poisoned Lives: English Poisoners and their Victims* (London: Hambledon, 2006), p. 158.

the venue where the inquest was conducted, as well as the fee due to the coroner himself (including his travel expenses) and to any medical men who assisted him (including chemical analysis).10 In consequence, the average cost to the county ratepayer of each inquest increased significantly. For example, in some places, it rose 188 percent between 1836 and 1839, from £1 5s 4d to £3 12s 7d per hearing.[681] The national average by 1856 was £3 1s 7d.[682] These costs were paid from county and borough rates.

Furthermore, payment of parish officers encouraged them to notify the coroner of even vaguely unusual deaths. Additionally, the Births, Deaths, and Marriages Act of 1837 required the registration of all deaths, so that many that were suspicious were investigated in order that a death certificate could be issued.[683] Both factors increased the number of inquests, even as the proceedings became more expensive. This also occurred at a time when the county rate was becoming an increasingly heavy burden, throughout the country, for a variety of reasons, many of them linked to the cost of the new poor-law rate. More, and more expensive, inquests, contributed to this growing financial problem, although the great majority of them did not find anything untoward in a death.

To achieve economies, some county benches established committees of JPs to approve expenditure. Thus, after the Norfolk magistrates received a series of petitions in 1843 from various boards of guardians seeking a reduction in the administrative costs of running their county (a situation that had been exacerbated by the new rural police), they established such a committee to investigate all heads of expenditure. Its attention quickly fell on the coroners, and eventually it reported that "many unnecessary inquests have been held; and that number has been much increased in consequence of their having been held upon the application of parish constables acting on their own opinion only."[684] This was, apparently, particularly common among inquests into natural deaths of, *inter alia*, the elderly and children.

In response Norfolk was one of the first counties to issue local guidelines aimed at reducing the number of inquests, especially where there were no apparent signs of violence and no mystery as to how a death had occurred. In July 1844 its magistrates decided that, before a parish constable informed his local coroner of a death, he had to obtain from a magistrate, minister, churchwarden, or overseer of the poor in the parish where the death had occurred, a certificate that an inquest was necessary; without this, payment would normally be refused. The JPs did not envisage any dangers in doing this; some even feared that the new safeguard might

---

681 Fisher, "Getting away," pp. 47-62.

682 *Judicial Statistics relative to Police and Constabulary, Criminal Proceedings and Prisons, 1856* (London: HMSO, 1857), p. vii.

683 Karyo Magellan, "The Victorian Medico-Legal Autopsy, Part I – Dissection in Pursuit of the Cause of Death," *Ripperologist*, vol. 71 (2006), pp. 23-43.

684 Fisher, "Getting away," pp. 47-62.

still be inadequate. Most thought that it would bring an end to ignorant parish constables running for the nearest coroner "to make a few shillings."[685]

Norfolk was not alone in this, and it was not just an idle threat. For example, in 1846, in the absence of such a request, JPs in Devon declined to pay Adoniah Vallack his fee for conducting an inquest into the death of a man whose body had been found on a common, despite the open verdict reached by the jury (the corpse bore no obvious marks of violence). Later that year, this may have prompted Vallack not to hold an inquest into the suspicious death of an illegitimate baby whose mother had just left the workhouse to seek a position in service.[686]

Unfortunately, this meant that a few homicides that took place in Norfolk during the 1840s may have been missed, simply because such permission was not forthcoming. (It has also been suggested that this might have been the case, for the same reason, with regard to some child poisonings in Manchester during the mid-1840s.)[687] However, the number of any avoidably missed homicides should not be exaggerated; in the four provincial counties – Norfolk, Devon, Carmarthenshire, and Staffordshire – where magistrates made significant cuts before 1848, no obvious reductions in the local murder rate appear to have ensued.[688] (It seems that Shropshire JPs also refused payment in a handful of cases during the 1840s.) Even if they had been reported to a coroner, there is no guarantee that such, less obvious, cases would have been identified as deliberate killings. A study of hundreds of London coroners' inquests during the nineteenth century suggests that, whether the coroner was a doctor, lawyer, or (very unusually) neither, it was rare for him to bring in a verdict of "wilful murder" in cases that were not blatantly suspicious.[689]

Nevertheless, caution about authorizing inquests may have contributed to what occurred at Happisbugh, on the East Norfolk coast, during the 1840s. This became a national *cause célèbre* and helped expose some of the weaknesses of the coronial system. A poor elderly couple, Jonathan and Ann Balls, had eked out a living in the seaside village with the assistance of parish relief. They had three married daughters and several grandchildren. Several of the latter had died unexpectedly, as had other people linked to or associated with Jonathan, who had a bad local reputation as a petty offender.

For example, in 1843 nine-week-old Ann Pestle had expired suddenly and been buried within a few hours without an inquest being held; it seems that the area's coroner may not have had the correct form to justify holding such a procedure and so feared not being paid. Her brother Samuel died in similar circumstances in 1845.

---

685 *The Bury and Norwich Post*, 10 July, 1844.

686 Fisher, "Getting away," p. 51.

687 Emmerichs, "Getting away," pp. 93-100.

688 P. King, "The Impact of Urbanization on Murder Rates and on the Geography of Homicide in England and Wales, 1780–1850," *The Historical Journal*, vol. 53, no. 3 (2010), p. 687.

689 Emmerichs, "Getting away," pp. 93-100.

Jonathan's wife and another of the grandchildren followed a few months later and were buried on the same day that they expired, again without scrutiny. After Balls' own death in May 1846 rumours began to circulate that it was the result of poison, in this case self-administered. He was buried, but the local county coroner, Mr Pilgrim, was eventually informed about popular concerns, and issued a summons to the authorities for the exhumation of Jonathan, Ann, and two others, and the empanelling of an inquest jury to look into their deaths. He then conducted the relevant inquest. A surgeon who examined the bodies claimed to have discovered traces of poison. After the witnesses had been heard, Pilgrim said that the finger of suspicion pointed at Jonathan Balls, but he was now beyond the reach of the law. After half an hour's deliberation, the jury concluded that Jonathan Balls, Elizabeth Balls, Samuel Pestle, and Ann Pestle had all died from the effects of poison "but how administered there was no evidence to show".[690]

This decision prompted a more general enquiry, and within a few weeks further potential murders had been detected and were the subject of their own inquests. On this occasion, the coroner's jury found that Maria Lacey and Maria Green had died from the effects of arsenic but (again) there was no firm evidence to show who had administered it. In three other deaths – those of Martha Green, William Green, and Hannah Pegg – the verdict was left open. It was noted that the supposed murderer, Jonathan Balls, was largely dependent on his married daughters for support during the last 15 or so years of his life, and the supposition was that he poisoned four of his grandchildren so that their parents might be better able to maintain him. It was also thought likely that he had killed his two sons and his father and mother many years earlier.[691]

The Balls case occasioned considerable concern; as the foreman at one of the later inquests commented, "We all naturally wish to keep down the county expenses, but not at a sacrifice of human life".[692] It was eventually discussed in Parliament and reopened the issue of inquest funding. In 1851, during a debate in the House of Lords, Lord Harry Vane urged that coroners be paid fixed salaries rather than fees. He thought that this might put an end to squabbles between such officers and magistrates. He identified Norfolk (along with Cumberland and Staffordshire) as a county where disputes had arisen in consequence of the disallowance of coroners' fees for holding inquests in cases of apparently accidental death.[693] The Coroners' Society also actively campaigned for salaries during the 1850s.

Salaries were finally introduced for county (but not borough) coroners in 1861, their initial level being based on the average earnings of the individual coroner over the previous five years, these being eligible for subsequent review every five years. This meant that variations in salary among coroners (like fees before them) could

690 *The Illustrated London News,* 23 May, 1846.

691 *Ibid.,* 13 June, 1846.

692 Fisher, "Getting away," p. 50.

693 Hansard HC Deb 28 May 1851 vol. 117 col. 101.

be enormous. At one extreme, some big cities such as Birmingham paid four-figure sums to what were effectively full-time coroners; by contrast, rural counties were likely to be served by part-timers earning less than £100 a year.

A meeting of the Norfolk JPs at quarter sessions at the end of 1861 resolved that Mr Press, the coroner for the busy Norwich and Eastern division of the county, should receive £220 per annum, although he threatened to appeal this determination to the Home Secretary. The coroner for Lynn and the Western Division received £45; the Duchy of Lancaster £165; the liberty of the Duke of Norfolk £87; one part of the Clackclose Liberty some £24, while the officer for the other part earned just £10. The coroner for the county and city of Norwich received the modest sum of £2 for those rare inquests conducted in the castle (those who had been hanged or otherwise died there) on top of major payment for his work in the wider city.[694] The total cost to the county was £553 per annum. Nevertheless, even at the end of the Victorian period, borough coroners were still being remunerated with fees for each inquest held.[695] Although significant, the 1861 reforms did not quite end conflict between coroners and JPs, which lasted until 1888, when magistrates lost their last element of control over the coroners' salaries.[696]

694 *The Bury and Norwich Post*, 8 January, 1861.

695 Alexander, *The Administration,* p. 100.

696 Emmerichs, "Getting away," pp. 93-100.

Chapter 7: The Inquest

The Inquest as Indictment

Inquests could not only make express findings of murder or manslaughter but, where appropriate, could name a suspected perpetrator and commit him for trial at the assizes. In these circumstances it was not necessary for magistrates to commit the matter for trial or a grand jury to find a "true bill" for it to go to a hearing, although they usually did so as well.[697] The inquisition was, effectively, the indictment, a power that was formally abandoned only in 1977. Having sent a suspect for trial, the coroner would usually bind over a constable or other police officer to prosecute the matter.[698]

For example, in 1844 a tanner named William Frost went mad and killed his four young children (one just ten weeks old) in his cottage in Whitwell while his wife was out on an errand. The coroner's inquest swiftly returned a finding of murder. As a result, he was "indicted on the coroner's inquisition" at the Norfolk assizes. (At trial, he was found "not guilty, on account of insanity").[699] Similarly, in June 1890 a group of men were drinking in the King's Head at Great Bircham, in the north of the county. One of them, William Osborne, treated one of his fellows to a glass of whisky, but secretly put snuff in it as a prank. The recipient, William Wadlow, drank the "filthy compound" and died. A coroner's inquest sat on the incident and the jury returned a verdict of manslaughter against Osborne, who was committed for trial at the following assizes.[700]

Strictly speaking, a coroner could commit a murder suspect to prison for safe custody, pending an inquest, although this was usually done by JPs.[701] More significantly, after a homicide verdict was returned at an inquest, whether murder or manslaughter, the coroner could remand a named suspect in custody until their trial at assizes, if they were present at the hearing. Thus, in 1844 the coroner issued a warrant committing William Frost to the county gaol, and he was taken to Norwich that evening.[702] Similarly, in October 1877, after Henry Marsh killed two men at Wymondham, an eight-hour coroner's inquest led to a verdict of "wilful murder," and Marsh was committed to Norwich prison to await the assizes.[703] However, not all those implicated in a homicide would be remanded in custody, even if present at court. At the start of 1854, a coroner's jury returned a verdict of manslaughter by gross negligence against Peter Ashcroft and John Latham, two railway superintendents,

697 TNA, HO 45/7989, Power of coroners to commit people for trial, 1867.

698 *Eighth Report,* p. 239.

699 *The Bury and Norwich Post and East Anglian*, 7 August, 1844.

700 *The Bury and Norwich Post*, 17 June, 1890.

701 TNA TS 25/231, Document dated 21 March, 1846.

702 *The Ipswich Journal*, 13 April, 1844.

703 *The Sheffield Independent*, 23 October, 1877.

following a fatal accident, but both men were bailed (never having been in custody) with suitable sureties prior to their trial at the Norfolk assizes (where they were acquitted).[704]

If a named suspect in a homicide case was not present at the inquest, the coroner could issue an arrest warrant to secure their detention pending trial on the inquisition. In April 1828, in a famous case from neighbouring Suffolk, the coroner dispatched the parish constable of Polstead in search of William Corder, who was suspected of murdering his lover Maria Marten the previous year; it had taken considerable time for her corpse to be discovered in the notorious "red barn."[705] More specifically to Norfolk, in 1841, after an inquest jury returned a verdict of "wilful murder" against the absent Sarah Harvey, following the death of her newborn baby, the coroner issued a warrant for her arrest and placed it in the hands of Mr. Andrews, a superintendent of the Norfolk Police.[706]

Of course, a particular perpetrator might not be identified in what was apparently a homicide case, so a verdict of murder by "some person or persons unknown" was returned. Thus, the inquest jury reached such a verdict in 1877 when Fanny Nunn was found drowned in the river at Diss, in circumstances that strongly suggested foul play, but with no indications of a particular suspect.[707]

In the early Victorian period, the first legal proceedings in an alleged homicide case would frequently (though not invariably) be the coroner's inquest rather than the magistrates' examination and committal proceedings.[708] Quite exceptionally, if there had been an unusually thorough inquest, it seems that the magistrates' enquiry might be omitted, and the matter go straight to the petty jury at assizes without a bill of indictment approved by the grand jury.[709] However, far more cases went for trial on both the coroner's inquest and the grand-jury indictment. In such cases it might be reported that the defendant was "indicted" for wilful murder and "charged on the coroner's inquisition with the like murder." Thus, in a domestic homicide case from Leicester in 1864, it was noted that "Timothy Baum was charged upon the coroner's inquisition, and also upon an indictment, with the murder of his wife and daughter."[710]

It was very rare for a homicide prosecutor to rely solely on an inquest finding of murder or manslaughter, and often very ill-advised to do so, not least because some inquisitions lacked clarity, and so were quashed for technical defects. As was

---

704 *The Bury and Norwich Post*, 1 February, 1854. *The Standard*, 25 March, 1854.

705 *The Bury and Suffolk Herald,* 30 April, 1828.

706 *The Bury and Norwich Post*, 13 January, 1841

707 *The Morning Post*, 6 December, 1877.

708 Pue, "Twilight Zone," p. 335.

709 Alexander, *The Administration*, p. 100.

710 *The Times*, 7 December, 1864, p. 11.

noted to the 1845 Commission, many coroners were "imperfectly acquainted" with criminal law, and their drafting was often poor as a result, while the inquest was often conducted hurriedly, in the place where the body was found, and local passions strongest.[711] As a result, even at the start of the Victorian era, nearly all prosecutors would also make sure that a bill of indictment went before a grand jury, following a preliminary inquiry in front of magistrates. If the grand jury rejected this, the defendant could still go for trial solely on the coroner's inquisition, but if the latter failed for technical reasons the defendant might be tried on the indictment.[712]

Occasionally, especially early in the Victorian period, a grand jury would find no case to answer in a homicide allegation, and the suspect would stand trial solely on the coroner's inquisition. For example, at the Norfolk assizes in April 1839, Henry Gathercole was tried for manslaughter on a coroner's inquisition, the grand jury having thrown out the bill of indictment. He had tried to drown himself and, when a youth jumped in to save him, struggled so that his would-be helper drowned. At trial, medical evidence suggested that he was mentally unwell at the time and did not know right from wrong. As a result, the jury found him not guilty by reason of insanity, and it was ordered that he be detained at Her Majesty's pleasure.[713] In like manner, and at the same forum in 1842, Gamaliel Thomson stood trial for manslaughter, solely on a coroner's inquisition, in connection with the death of William Godfrey during a public-house quarrel in Walpole St. Peter, the grand jury having thrown the matter out. The trial judge gave a sympathetic summing-up to the jury, declaring that it was a "very mitigated case," and Thomson was acquitted.[714]

However, long before the end of the nineteenth century, if a bill of indictment in a homicide case was dismissed by the grand jury in such situations, it was common (although not legally necessary) for the prosecution to offer no evidence on the coroner's inquest.[715] As a result, in the early 1870s, Mr Justice Lush thought that a coroner's inquisition led to needless expense: "If the [grand jury] bill is found the trial takes place on the finding of the grand jury, and as a matter of form the prisoner is arraigned on the coroner's inquisition also. If the bill is ignored, it is the practice not to offer any evidence on the inquisition."[716]

This was not an entirely new phenomenon even then. In January 1841 the body of a recently born female child was discovered in the parish of Hackford. A lengthy inquest was held at the Ringers' Inn at Hingham in mid-Norfolk. Two surgeons conducted a post-mortem examination on the diminutive corpse and then testified

---

711 *Eighth Report,* p. 215.

712 Pue, "Twilight Zone," 1983, p. 335.

713 *The Ipswich Journal*, 13 April, 1839.

714 *The Bury and Norwich Post*, 3 August, 1842.

715 Alexander, *The Administration,* p. 100.

716 Cassie Watson, "Prosecuting Homicide on the Coroner's Inquisition," Legal History Miscellany, posted online 26 December, 2018.

that the infant had been born alive but died shortly afterwards from neglect. The mother of the baby was identified as Sarah Ann Harvey. The inquest jury returned a verdict of "wilful murder" against Harvey. Even so, the grand jury at the ensuing assizes refused to commit Harvey, so that she was facing trial solely on the coroner's inquest. The prosecution accepted the grand jury's assessment of the evidence and declined to proceed on the inquest; Harvey was formally acquitted.[717]

Relationship to the JPs' Examination

Although the first legal proceeding in an alleged homicide case might be the coroner's inquest, at others they would occur at much the same time as the JPs' examination. For example, in 1865 the initial magistrates' examination of a Dutch sailor who had murdered a shipmate in a Great Yarmouth tavern took place on the same day (that following the killing) as the first sitting of the coroner's inquest. Both took evidence but then adjourned for a couple of days.[718] Occasionally, the JPs' examination might even precede the inquest.

Inevitably, given that many homicides were subject to two, often (roughly) simultaneous, investigations, one conducted by a coroner and the other by JPs, difficult questions arose as to the relationship between the two, while there was often duplication in the giving of pre-trial evidence. Frequently the same witnesses would have testified twice, before two forums, before a matter even got to trial. In 1848 James Rush alluded to this in his statement to a jury at assizes' when discussing alleged discrepancies in the pre-trial evidence of a prosecution witness: "The Prisoner here read over the evidence of Watson on his first examination....He would now tell the jury what this witness said before the coroner." While JPs were holding committal proceedings for Rush's murder of Isaac Jermy, an inquest had been opened by Mr Press, a county coroner, at the King's Head Inn in Wymondham. It first sat on 30 November, and adjourned sittings were then held on 1, 2, and 5 December. The final sitting was held on 19 December, when the jury returned a verdict of wilful murder against Rush, so that (as was common) he stood trial on both the coroner's inquisition and a grand jury indictment that originated with the magistrates' examination.[719]

There could be logistical problems and tensions between the two forums when it came to sharing witnesses. In mid-July 1841, after Jemima Stimson, a 15-year-old girl, was murdered in a turnip field near Wymondham Common, John Self, a 20-year-old labourer, was immediately suspected. Local JPs examined and committed him for trial to the forthcoming assizes. The death, and Jemima's corpse, then came before the coroner. However, the suspect was in custody, and the gaoler refused to let him attend the inquest unless he first received an order of *habeas corpus*. The coroner

717 *The Bury and Norwich Post*, 13 January, 1841.

718 *The Morning Post*, 16 October, 1865.

719 *The Norfolk Chronicle*, 28 November, 1848.

thought it wrong to attribute death to a suspect who was physically available but not present and adjourned his hearing.[720]

Conversely, sometimes there was cooperation between the two investigations. In June 1865, a committal hearing was held for a Miss Sexton at Thetford petty sessions. She was suspected of concealing a birth, following the discovery of the decayed remains of a baby in a privy in the Anchor tavern at Thetford. At the hearing, the chairman "read the depositions taken before the coroner" during the inquest, which had, eventually, made no finding of homicide. (The inquest, conducted before the borough coroner had, eventually, found that it could not be proved that the baby had been born alive.) Having done so, the chairman concluded that there was no evidence to convict the prisoner of concealment of birth; there was suspicion, but nothing more.[721]

Extenuating Circumstances

Coroners' inquests tended to be cautious about accepting extenuating circumstances for killings, unless they were clearly justified, preferring to leave these to criminal prosecutors and juries at assizes to determine and reflect in their indictments and verdicts. Thus, although coroners' juries might (and often did) commit to trial for manslaughter, if there was any doubt about this issue they would normally do so for murder, even if this was not followed through at trial. Indicative of this, in 1865 inquests identified 227 cases of murder nationally and 282 of manslaughter. However, there were just 60 criminal prosecutions for the former crime, while there were 316 for the latter.[722]

Inquests were especially reluctant to make any finding suggesting insanity, even when this was clearly evidenced. Indeed, most legal observers thought that inquest juries could not do so. In 1875, when an inquest was held into Robert Edwards' triple killing at the Norwich Hospital, the coroner, E.S. Bignold, expressly advised the jury on "the question of the sanity or insanity of the man Edwards. That is a question which this jury cannot go into, and which must be left for decision at the assizes."[723] Very unusually, in December 1822, an opinion was expressed on this matter when an inquest was held on the body of James Dale, who had been killed the preceding day by Thomas Coleman, a patient in a private lunatic asylum at Loddon. The inquest jury decided it was murder but opined that it was by a clearly insane man.[724] More typically can be considered a case from the summer of 1837, in which James Moy, a labourer from Cromer, rocked his infant son to sleep, then cut the child's throat from ear to ear with a pocketknife. He had apparently shown signs of mental illness for some time and had previously spoken about putting his

720 *The Essex Standard*, 30 July, 1841.

721 *The Bury and Norwich Post*, 6 June, 20 June, 1865.

722 Hammick, "Judicial Statistics," p. 385.

723 *The Norfolk Chronicle*, 25 December, 1875.

724 *The Morning Post*, 10 December, 1822.

seven children out of the world. Even so, at the inquest the coroner's jury returned a verdict of wilful murder, and the prisoner was committed to Norwich Castle to await trial.[725] In April 1838 a jury at assizes found that Moy was so insane as to be incapable even of entering a plea.

An inquest verdict did not preclude a suspect's being prosecuted for a crime that was at variance to its findings. For example, evidence might emerge to suggest that what had been deemed an accidental death by a coroner's jury had been occasioned by foul play; if a suspect was identified he could then be indicted by a grand jury for a homicide offence, although a fresh inquest could not normally be held. More commonly, an inquest jury's finding of manslaughter did not preclude an identified suspect's being indicted for murder at assizes and vice versa. In 1852 a Norfolk coroner, sitting at Outwell specifically advised his jury to this effect after it decided that James Pearce, a 12-year-old boy who had shot William Day, a lad of similar age, during a violent quarrel, while they were out scaring crows, and then buried his body in a drain, was only guilty of manslaughter. (Day had first given Pearce a black eye.) The coroner, who had carefully directed them on the distinction between the two forms of homicide, expressed surprise at their decision, saying that it "ought clearly to have been one of wilful murder; and for which offence, notwithstanding the verdict just returned, the boy Pearce would no doubt have to take his trial."[726] The child was subsequently examined before JPs who committed him for trial for murder as well as the less serious homicide.[727] Nevertheless, it seems that a plea to manslaughter was tendered and accepted at the Norfolk assizes in August 1852, the boy being sentenced to ten years' transportation, and the judge expressing the charitable hope that he had "acted on sudden impulse" without appreciating the likely effect of firing the gun. Of course, by the 1850s, it was inconceivable that such a young person would be executed, even if convicted of murder, making this an administratively convenient disposal.[728]

Moving on a few years, an inquest jury into some of the deaths occasioned by the Norwich Thorpe train crash in 1874, spent two hours considering their verdict against a pair of railwaymen, ultimately deciding that just one had committed manslaughter by gross negligence. Even so, both were prosecuted for the lesser form of homicide at assizes (the absolved man being found culpable by another coroner's inquest on a different victim). Ironically, the trial jury at assizes found that the man whom the first inquest jury had not held to be responsible was guilty but acquitted the man they had found against (who, it seems, had antagonised the coroner's jurors with his apparent levity).[729]

---

725 *The Standard*, 21 August, 1837.

726 *Bell's Life in London and Sporting Chronicle*, 18 April, 1852.

727 *Ibid.*, 25 April, 1852.

728 *John Bull*, vol. xxxii, no. 1,652, 7 August, 1852, p. 510. *The Standard*, 16 April, 1852.

729 *The Huddersfield Chronicle*, 30 September, 1874.

Notification of the Coroner

A death had to be brought to a coroner's attention before he could investigate it. There was a longstanding, if rather vague, common-law duty on "respectable" members of the public and representatives of their wider communities to inform the local coroner of deaths that called for such an investigation. Traditionally, a "first–finder" (of the body), or suspicious parish "searcher" (engaged in laying out a corpse), would notify a constable, JP, clergyman, doctor, or overseer of the poor, who would, in turn, inform the coroner. However, by the 1840s, notification was often being done by members of the new police forces, something that increased with their growth over ensuing years, albeit that they sometimes confined themselves to reporting obviously violent deaths and tended to conduct a preliminary investigation before doing so. Nevertheless, a coroner could not go "looking for work." In 1865, when the very high mortality rates among children in the Norfolk village of Emneth was raised in Parliament, it was noted that the local coroner apparently regretted that he could not take formal notice of these deaths unless officially informed, "for unless he (the coroner) was set in motion by a magistrate, minister, or guardian of the parish, he held no inquest."[730]

The death of Hannah Neale's husband provides an illustrative example of a suspicious death coming to notice. The doctor attending the dead man during his final, and rather strange, illness in 1851 asked that he be allowed to conduct a post-mortem on the corpse. This was firmly rejected by Hannah, leading the physician to conclude that all was not right. The death was duly reported to the coroner and an inquest conducted, at which it appeared that Hannah had been administering arsenic to her spouse to free herself to move in with another man. The coroner issued a warrant for Hannah's arrest so that she could go on trial for murder at the following Norfolk assizes.[731] Nevertheless, notification could be a weak link in the process everywhere in the country. In 1846, when carrying out an investigation into one of the possible victims of Jonathan Balls, the Norfolk coroner professed to be shocked that, "although there was talk about this poor woman's death, no inquiry should take place." [732]

Inquest Accommodation

Most Victorian inquests were conducted in the nearest suitable building, which was often a public house, in Norfolk as elsewhere in the country.[733] The use of such establishments only started to wane at the end of the nineteenth century, subsequently being actively discouraged by the 1902 Licensing Act. However, in some places it lingered until well into the twentieth century. (It should be noted that public houses were used for many other matters at this time, even doctor's

730 HC Deb 31 March 1865 vol. 178 cols. 562-3.

731 *The Lady's Newspaper,* 9 August, 1851, p. 72.

732 *Lloyd's Weekly London Newspaper,* 7 June, 1846.

733 Vicky Holmes, "Death of an Infant," *Home Cultures*, vol. 11, no. 3 (2014), p. 305.

appointments.)[734] Inquests were normally open to the public, provided there was room for them. In July 1884, when a hearing was held into the suspicious death of Edna Carter's ten-month-old child, in the Angel Inn at Wrentham in Suffolk, it was noted that so large a crowd attended that it spilled out of the premises.[735]

Nevertheless, in 1829, when an inquest was held at Runhall, on the body of a female infant that had been found buried in a local field, Edward Press, the Norfolk county coroner, signified to a reporter from the *Norwich Mercury* that, although the proceedings were open to observers, and he would not be prevented from attending, he would not be allowed to take notes. As a result, his report was dependent on his memory.[736] This does not appear to have been normal practice in the Victorian era.

Speed of Sitting

Inquests normally took place, or at least held their initial meetings, very rapidly after a death was reported. By the Victorian period, they were usually convened within 48 hours of a body's being found, even in rural parts. Frequently, this was on the day following its discovery.[737] A delay of more than two days was very rare, even for county coroners, who often had much further to travel than their urban counterparts, although inquests could not be held on Sundays, which might slow down proceedings. Such coroners might be alerted to a suspicious death that had occurred or been discovered during night hours at the crack of dawn and respond immediately. Unsurprisingly, inquests could be held especially swiftly in towns that had their own borough coroner(s). For example, in 1841 the inquest into the death of 14-month-old Mary Ann Karrington first met in Yarmouth on the same Tuesday that she had been killed, and was then adjourned until the following Thursday, when it returned a verdict of willful murder against Charlotte Yaxley and committed her for trial at assizes.[738]

Most inquests were determined in a single session, even if they lasted several hours or more. Thus, in 1877 the hearing into the deaths of two men who had been murdered by a "bad tempered" Henry March, at his place of work in Wymondham lasted eight hours.[739] However, and as the Yaxley case suggests, coroners had the power to adjourn proceedings to allow further enquiries to be carried out, or extra evidence secured; sometimes these postponements could draw the inquest out for several weeks. For example, in 1849 a man named Haward was stabbed in the back and mortally wounded by Frederick Prime at Ditchingham, near the Suffolk border. He returned home after the incident, a surgeon was called, and the police informed.

---

734 Burney, *Bodies of Evidence,* p. 81.

735 *The Ipswich Journal*, 19 July, 1884.

736 *The Norwich Mercury,* 30 May, 1829.

737 Holmes, "Death of an Infant," p. 305.

738 *The Bury and Norwich Post*, 31 March, 1841.

739 *The Sheffield Independent*, 23 October, 1877.

Haward lingered for two days before expiring, without explaining why Prime should have "pricked him." An inquest was immediately opened and then adjourned for a week, to allow time to secure more information on what lay behind the violence.[740]

Similarly, in a very unusual case from December 1858, human bones were discovered near King's Lynn. It was popularly rumoured that they were the remains of an old man named Bell who had disappeared in very suspicious circumstances almost a decade earlier. The inquest on the remains sat seven times over a three-month period before the jury concluded that they were of an unknown person, and that it could not be said who the murderer or his victim was.[741] The case was effectively closed.

Assembling the Inquest Jury

After being summoned, the coroner would normally issue a warrant to a local constable, authorizing him to empanel a jury. Inquest juries consisted of 12 to (normally) 24 men, with 14 or 15 jurors being a common number, a figure that had been expressly recommended by several eighteenth-century legal authors. For example, the inquest that sat at Norwich Hospital on the triple-murder perpetrated by Robert Edwards in December 1875 had 15 men on its jury.[742]

Inquest jurors were recruited in the locality where a death occurred, usually being drawn from the same, or its immediately neighbouring, parishes. In 1844, after William Frost murdered his young children in their cottage in Whitwell, one of the county coroners, Mr Pilgrim, on being told of the incident, "instructed the constable to empanel a very respectable jury from different parishes." (Pilgrim arrived the next day to conduct the hearing.)[743] There was no formal property requirement for jurors, other than that they be "lawful" householders. In practice – and as Pilgrim's comment suggests – it was acknowledged that the officer summonsing such a jury "generally gets hold of any respectable male householder he can."[744] As a result, more marginal members of the community were not normally summoned.

In both rural and urban areas inquest jurors would often be craftsmen, while juries in the former would also have a large admixture of farmers and in the latter both tradesmen and shopkeepers. Many were similar in background to the men found on trial juries. For example, in his personal diary, Christopher Parsons, a prosperous Essex farmer, noted that in early 1849 he had considered a possible servant-perpetrated infanticide when he served on a coroner's jury in that county.[745] At times, a few more socially elevated men might also be found in their ranks. Thus, an inquest into the

---

740 *John Bull,* 9 April, 1849.

741 *John Bull and Britannia*, 27 March, 1858.

742 *The Norfolk Chronicle*, 18 December, 1875.

743 *The Times*, 12 April, 1844, p. 5.

744 Alexander, *The Administration,* p. 99.

745 ERO D/DS 67/22.

murder of Benjamin Black at Barton Bendish in Norfolk, in May 1867, had as its jury foreman a local clergyman, the Reverend S.G. Read.[746]

Physical proximity to the death under investigation meant that inquest jurors often had a degree of local knowledge that was not normally found among trial jurors. At the inquest into the two murders perpetrated by James Rush in December 1848, one of the jurors, William Glasspool of Wymondham, contributed evidence to the hearing when he realized that, having served as parish clerk a decade earlier, he could identify Rush's handwriting in some of the disputed documents.[747] In 1858, at the inquest following the discovery of Thomas Valentine's corpse in the River Nar in Norfolk, "The jury stated that the deceased would have to go over the bridge to go home....If he fell in at the bridge, the stream (when the stanches were drawn for the lighters) would be sufficient to carry the body to where it was found."[748] More specifically, in 1890, at an inquest held at the Crown Inn in Pulham into the death of a Mrs Brown, the coroner asked if there was any evidence of ill feeling between victim and alleged killer, Elijah Snelling. One of the jurors immediately pointed out that Brown had given evidence against the latter's son-in-law in a criminal case some years earlier.[749]

Of course, local jurors also brought the risk of local prejudices. For example, in 1839, two young men, being tutored by a clergyman in Middlesex, had a heated argument over a broken watch. One of them attempted to beat the other with a stick, after abusing him verbally, at which point the latter stabbed him in the stomach with a flick-knife. Although, at first, the wound did not appear very serious, it proved mortal a few days later. On his deathbed, having been told that he had little time to live, the victim admitted that he had called his assailant a "liar and a blackguard," that there had been nothing premeditated on his assailant's part, and that he had forgiven him. There was also a question about whether the dead youth had received the best possible medical treatment. As a result, it seemed to be an obvious situation for a manslaughter, rather than murder, verdict to be returned. Even so, there was much ill feeling and prejudice towards the accused in the immediate area, so that a coroner's inquest returned a verdict of "wilful murder." However, when the matter came before a magistrate the committal was for manslaughter only. This meant that the accused was tried simultaneously for murder (on the coroner's inquest) and manslaughter (on the indictment). He was found guilty only of the less serious homicide and sentenced to three years' penal servitude.[750]

Nevertheless, basic steps were taken to avoid excessive personal bias. For example, in Shropshire in 1823, when a possible case of wife-killing was considered, two

---

746 *The Bury and Norwich Post*, 21 May, 1867.

747 *John Bull*, 23 December, 1848.

748 *The Lynn Advertiser & West Norfolk Herald,* 11 December, 1858.

749 *The Ipswich Journal*, 18 January, 1890.

750 Pue, "Twilight Zone," p. 352. OBSP, Trial of Francis Hastings Medhurst, 8 April, 1839, t183908-1290.

men who had been summoned to serve on the woman's inquest jury were released because they had a history of quarrels with her husband.[751] In Norfolk in 1848, James Rush was given the names of the prospective jurors who would sit on the inquest into the deaths of his two victims and asked if he objected to any of them. They were apparently drawn from very respectable members of the local "yeomanry." Rush returned the list with just four names erased; presumably, these men were excluded.[752]

It seems that, in most cases, after his arrival at the place where an inquest would be held, the coroner would hold an informal but very important, albeit little recorded, meeting with local people, especially parish officials, in which he would make enquiries about who could be called to testify as to what had occurred, these individuals then being summoned or requested to do so.

The Need for a Corpse and the Jury View

Coroners had to have a body to work with, even if it was just a set of bones; an inquest could not be held without one. They could order an exhumation to secure it. When one of Jonathan Balls' (see below) suspected poisoning victims, Hannah Peggs, was exhumed at Hingham in June 1846, years after she had been interred, only her skeleton remained. Even so, before an inquest could be held into her death, "it was brought to the village for the purpose of affording the jury a view of it, a ceremony necessary in the inquiry."[753] However, the previous year, Jane Lovett's corpse, interred just six weeks before exhumation, after doctors belatedly expressed concern about her death, was still in good condition, and could be subject to a post-mortem.[754]

In November 1853 the body of William Richmond, an eight-month-old infant, was even less decayed when it was the subject of an inquest held at Mattishall. The child had died about a fortnight earlier and been buried during the night by his parents, his father being the sexton of the parish. The death had not been publicly known for some days. Eventually, the authorities became aware of it and instituted inquiries. It transpired that the mother, Susannah, had had 14 children, nine of whom had died, three of them, it seems, being buried in a similar manner. This had led to suspicions and rumours, so that it was thought wise to hold an inquest. It was established that William had been much neglected by his mother, who frequently left him with two or three other small children while she was attending places of entertainment, as had been the case on the night in question. She had also regularly administered laudanum to the infant. William's body was duly exhumed and subject to a post-mortem examination by a local surgeon, resident in the village, who concluded that death had been caused by inflammation of the right lung. The jury found a narrative

751 Fisher, "Edmund Whitcombe," p. 10.

752 *The Times*, 1 December, 1848, p. 5.

753 *Lloyd's Weekly London Newspaper,* 7 June, 1846.

754 *The Ipswich Journal*, 8 March, 1845.

verdict in accordance with this opinion, and severely reprimanded William's father and mother. (Unsurprisingly, they also suggested that the former was an improper person to be sexton).[755]

As the Peggs case suggests, once a jury had been assembled and sworn in, its members would formally view the body. This could be done where it had been discovered, or the corpse might be moved to a nearby building or outhouse, or even placed on a table in the building where the inquest itself would be held. For example, in 1844, after William Frost murdered his children, the inquest jury viewed the bodies in the cottage where the killings had occurred; the inquest was then held in a nearby public house a day after the deaths.[756] The jurors in the inquest into the double murder of Isaac Jermy and his son in 1848 also surveyed their bodies in the house where they had been shot. Similarly, in November 1867, when an inquest was held on a female infant in neighbouring Suffolk, who was thought to have been accidentally overlain by her mother while sleeping, the jury proceeded to view the girl's body in the cottage bedroom, although it was so small that only a few of them could go in at a time. They then returned to a local inn, where the inquest had been opened.[757]

If a body was found in a remote or inaccessible spot, it would usually be moved somewhere more convenient for the inquest-jury view. Thus, in 1841, after a girl who had been working in the fields near Wymondham was raped and murdered, her corpse was removed from the pond in which it had been found and taken to a nearby barn, where it was viewed before the inquest, which was held in a local public house.[758] Similarly, after William Thompson murdered and robbed Lorenzo Beha on the highway in 1853, a group of young ladies and gentlemen found the victim's corpse near the road, a short distance from Tittleshall, after following a trail of blood through a hedge. They returned to the village to inform the local rector, who arranged for a cart and two shepherds to carry the corpse to the Griffin Inn, where it could be viewed, and an inquest held.[759] However, decay might make using an inn for a view difficult, if only because of the noxious smell it occasioned. In May 1846, when an inquest was opened at Happisburgh by Mr. Pilgrim, one of the county coroners, on the bodies of Jonathan Balls, his wife, and four grandchildren, their bodies were exhumed and placed in a tent specially erected in the churchyard for the view.[760]

Although the jury view of a body was still compulsory during the Victorian era, it was often an unpopular duty and sometimes conducted quite perfunctorily. By the

755 *The Norfolk News,* 19 November, 1853.

756 *The Ipswich Journal,* 13 April, 1844.

757 Holmes, "Death of an Infant," p. 305.

758 *The Examiner*, 24 July, 1841.

759 *The Ipswich Journal*, 26 November, 1853.

760 *The Norfolk Chronicle,* 18 May, 1846.

end of the period, it was thought that squeamish jurors would often file past the corpse with their eyes half closed, while holding their noses.[761] Some questioned value of such a proceeding in an era of increasing medical evidence.

The Conduct of the Inquest

Apart from the view, there were relatively few formal rules regulating inquests and so encouraging a degree of uniformity in proceedings. Some observers, such as the barrister Thomas Jefferson Hogg, thought that their proceedings were often "partial, passionate, violent, and disorderly."[762] This was slightly exaggerated. Nevertheless, there was normally no inquest clerk to advise a newly appointed coroner, and only rare attendance by lawyers to constrain his autonomy. However, the latter were not invariably absent, especially when potential homicide cases were being examined, whether briefed for the suspect or a member of the victim's family.

Unusually, in 1875 the triple murderer Robert Edwards had a solicitor present at the inquest into his victims in Norwich in 1875. The latter's status appeared uncertain but may have been arranged because of the suspect's evident mental illness. When, in 1850, an inquest was conducted at Ballingdon in Suffolk into the killing of Charles Piper during a public-house quarrel, it was noted that a local solicitor had "appeared for the father of the deceased."[763] The Home Office might also provide guidance to coroners on difficult points, if requested, but its opinions had no authority and were not binding; nor where they made widely available.[764] Nevertheless, general patterns in the conduct of such hearings can readily be discerned.

The Coroner's Opening

The coroner would formally open the hearing to the inquest jury at the start of proceedings, explaining in outline the case in front of them, their role in the process, and the issues that they would have to determine. Thus, after Robert Edwards' murderous rampage at the Norfolk and Norwich Hospital in 1875, the City of Norwich Coroner, E.S. Bignold, gave the 18-man jury firm guidance on their task, and what he thought would be their likely decision, making it clear that any issue of insanity (obviously a possibility) should be left to the assizes to determine: "The fact of your finding a verdict of wilful murder will be to send the man for trial at the Assizes, where the case will have every attention. There will be counsel on both sides, and the case will have the benefit of the knowledge of the presiding Judge who will direct the course to be pursued."[765]

---

761 Burney, *Bodies of Evidence*, p. 97.

762 *Eighth Report*, p. 225.

763 *The Norfolk Chronicle*, 3 April, 1850.

764 Cornish, *Oxford History*, p. 950.

765 *The Norfolk Chronicle*, 25 December, 1875.

Next, any witnesses who could give an account of any circumstances relevant to the death being examined, whether neighbour, bystander, police officer, or medical expert, might be called to give evidence. It was for the coroner to decide who would testify at his inquiry. In 1876 the *Spectator* noted: "It is not his business to discover the cause of death; he has only to select the witnesses who can best testify to it, and assist the jury in drawing the right inferences from their evidence."[766] However, jurors could suggest appropriate witnesses for the coroner to summon, and these suggestions were often followed. Thus, when the Reverend John Gunton, who had petitioned for the homicidal Robert Edwards to be admitted to the hospital where the killings occurred, appeared reluctant to give sworn testimony, arguing that he had attended the inquest purely as a mark of respect: "Several of the jury intimated that Mr Gunton should be sworn." This duly occurred.[767]

The Course of the Evidence

The coroner's inquest was unusual in that it adopted a largely inquisitorial, rather than adversarial, procedure, unlike (English) criminal courts. The coroner would summon and then examine the available witnesses. Typically, at the inquest into the killings perpetrated by Robert Edwards in 1875, it was noted that a "Miss Margaret Graham was then called, and having been sworn, was examined by the coroner."[768] However, after this had occurred, coroners' jurors were able to ask their own questions, and sometimes exercised this power very freely, in a way that was no longer normally found in trials on indictment. For example, in July 1884 the inquest held at Wrentham in Suffolk into the killing of a two-year-old infant, a case that would end up being tried at the combined winter assizes in Norwich later that year, had a particularly active jury. At times as many as three questions in a row were asked of witnesses, one after the other, in quick succession, by separate jurors. The jurors were also swift to make interjections about aspects of the case that they found implausible or unconvincing.[769] In practice, it seems that relatives of the deceased were also often allowed to ask questions of the witnesses.[770]

If a coroner suspected that he was dealing with a homicide, he was bound to take depositions of the evidence given, something that was not required with other types of death, although he might still jot down notes in such cases to assist him in addressing the inquest jury on possible verdicts. Sometimes, if a coroner started an inquest believing that the case involved was homicide, but changed his mind during its course, he might stop recording the evidence as it was given, and vice versa. If a potential homicide case appeared complex, a coroner who did not have his own solicitor's clerk to assist him might hire a clerk to help record such testimony,

---

766 *The Spectator,* 15 July, 1876, p. 8.

767 *The Norfolk Chronicle,* 25 December, 1875.

768 *Ibid.*

769 *The Ipswich Journal*, 19 July, 1884.

770 Fisher, "Edmund Whitcombe," p. 4.

allowing him to concentrate on the evidence as it was given.[771] As with the formal statements taken at magistrates' committal hearings, those made by coroners might be adduced at any ensuing trial at assizes.

It should be noted that the evidence adduced at an inquest did not always meet the requirements of criminal courts, in an era in which various exclusionary rules had become increasingly strict. Thus, in 1847 Mr Baron Alderson, while addressing a Norfolk grand jury, pointed out that a coroner's inquisition might receive evidence that would not be legally admissible at a criminal trial.[772] Some legal observers criticized this situation and urged greater observance of these rules at inquests. The Oxford coroner Edward Hussey alluded to this when considering a potential homicide in April 1894. He warned the inquest jury that if they found that a criminal offence (some form of homicide) had been committed, he would have to commit the man to prison, and urged that in such a case, he "must not have any but legal evidence against him [the suspect]. By attending courts and reading newspapers one saw how often judges complained of coroners putting down what is not evidence [i.e., local 'knowledge' that had not been formally adduced] and going beyond the inquiry as to what is the cause of death."[773]

Suspects and their Evidence

In potential homicide cases, suspects, if available, would be present at the inquest, and called to testify about their involvement in the deaths of their (putative) victims, although they would first be warned as to the dangers of doing so. Well before the Victorian era, in 1829, when Rose Nelson was called to testify at the Norfolk inquest into the death of her new-born illegitimate baby, "she was cautioned by the Coroner not to say anything which might criminate herself – [and] she merely named the person whom she considered to be the father of the child."[774] Similarly, when, in 1844, the (detained) murderer William Frost was called before the inquest into his victims (also his children), he was cautioned prior to testifying that anything he said would be recorded and could be used against him at trial.[775] Many said little or nothing as a result. Nevertheless, at the Norfolk assizes in August 1835, Frances Billing and Catherine Frarey, accused of the murder by poisoning of Mary Taylor, did testify, and the statements they made to the coroner at the inquest were adduced into evidence at their trial.[776] Silence was usually prudent, not least because most suspects were legally unrepresented at the hearing.

---

771 Watson, *Poisoned Lives*, 2006, pp. 149-150.

772 *The Bury and Norwich Post, and East Anglian*, 28 July, 1847.

773 Hurren, "Remaking," pp. 207-252.

774 *The Norwich Mercury,* 30 May, 1829.

775 *The Times*, 12 April, 1844, p. 5.

776 *The Standard*, 10 August, 1835.

Medical Assistance and Testimony

It has sometimes been suggested that, during the early Victorian period, coroners' inquests were often compromised by the lack of high-quality medical evidence. Occasionally, it is claimed, this meant that their decisions on an apparently unmarked body were little more than conjecture.[777] However, this analysis can be exaggerated, as medical testimony was regularly called in the 1830s, even if it was sometimes of mixed quality. For much of the nineteenth century, many coroners who sought a medical opinion would summon the practitioner who had attended the deceased prior to his or her death. For example, in 1850 an inquest was conducted into the death of Charles Piper, in Suffolk. Piper had been stabbed and (as it transpired) mortally wounded in a quarrel after leaving a public house. During his final days he was attended regularly by Maurice Mason, a surgeon, who dressed Piper's wound and applied leeches and poultices. After Piper's death, Mason conducted the post-mortem examination, and concluded that he had died from the stab wound, testifying to this effect at the inquest.[778] In the absence of such a doctor, the nearest medical man was usually selected, irrespective of his qualifications. In the early 1800s this was often the parish surgeon.

The Medical Witnesses Act of 1836 facilitated this process when it formally authorized coroners to summons a medical man, such as a surgeon or (less commonly) an apothecary or physician to attend an inquest and, if necessary, conduct an autopsy or a toxicological analysis. It also gave them the power to pay a maximum fee of 2 guineas for these services. A refusal to answer such a coroner's summons could lead to a fine. This greatly improved the quality and availability of medical assistance to inquests. For example, when in 1857 the skeleton of a long-dead man was found buried near King's Lynn, Thomas Kendall, a surgeon from the same town, was called to give expert evidence at the ensuing inquest. He observed that they were the bones of a man over 40, and that there was nothing "inconsistent" with their coming from a much older individual. (The teeth were in very good condition, but extremely worn.) He also noted that, because the body had not been buried very deep, it had decayed quickly.[779]

Post-Mortems

A coroner could order that a full post-mortem or autopsy be conducted, something that the Medical Witnesses Act 1836 facilitated. Frequently this was done in advance of an inquest, but it could also be ordered after a hearing had begun. For example, in 1865, at an inquest held at the Anchor Inn at Thetford into the apparent drowning of George Mothersole in the local river, evidence was called that he had seemed depressed, shortly before his death, as he was facing trial for stealing eggs from his employer. However, the coroner suggested to the jury that the case be adjourned to

---

777 Forbes, "Coroners' Inquisitions," pp. 481-494.

778 *The Bury and Norwich Post,* 26 March, 1850.

779 *John Bull*, 19 December, 1857.

allow a proper post-mortem to be conducted on the body, and they agreed "after some deliberation." The case was put over for two weeks to permit this.[780]

The advance of science during the nineteenth century made the autopsy procedure an increasingly valuable tool for determining cause of death. To consider one medical field, during the 1830s truly expert toxicologists emerged in England, while the methods used to establish the presence of poisons started to become properly scientific. Thus, in 1836 James Marsh established the first reliable test for arsenic, one that could identify tiny amounts of the poison in both human remains and food. Its use had spread to provincial medical practitioners and chemists by the early 1840s. In 1841 the German chemist Hugo Reinsch invented a simpler and quicker test for the same poison, using water, hydrochloric acid, and copper foil; this largely replaced the Marsh test over ensuing years.[781]

As a result, in 1847, when an inquest was held at Tibenham into the deaths of two local farmers' wives, post-mortem examinations revealed that both deaths were due to arsenic poisoning.[782] In the same year, in the neighbouring county of Suffolk, a coroner ordered a post-mortem after the newly married teenager Catherine Foster poisoned her husband's dumplings. It was conducted by a Mr Jones, the physician who had attended after the man's death, and another "professional gentleman" from the neighbourhood. Jones took the precaution of taking out the dead man's stomach. It was then handed over to William Image in Bury St Edmunds, who subjected it to a thorough chemical examination, which revealed the presence of a large quantity of arsenic.[783] Image was a general practitioner who had developed an expertise in toxicology and forensic medicine, and who provided testimony at several high-profile murder trials involving poison. Essentially, he was one of several local experts in provincial England, whether hospital-based surgeons or GPs, who used their medical training to master the conduct of autopsies and chemical analysis of body parts.[784]

The quality of such examinations was further improved after the position of Home Office analyst was established in 1882, partly under the pressure occasioned by a number of fatal poisonings and the resulting need for toxicologists. Thomas Stevenson was appointed to the new office, a position that he would hold for many years. He was frequently called as an expert witness in difficult murder cases and might also be asked to examine crime scenes and clothing.[785] Some of his cases were from Norfolk. Thus, in June 1890, after William Wadlow drank snuff-impregnated

[780] *The Bury and Norwich Post*, 20 June, 1865.

[781] Katherine D. Watson, "Medical and chemical expertise in English trials for criminal poisoning, 1750-1914," *Medical Hist ory,* vol. 50, no. 3 (2006), p. 383.

[782] *The Norfolk Chronicle,* 30 March, 1847.

[783] *The Bury and Norwich Post*, 27 March, 1847.

[784] Watson, "Medical and chemical," pp. 373-90.

[785] Alison Adam, *A History of Forensic Science: British Beginnings in the Twentieth Century* (Abingdon: Routledge, 2015), pp. 156-157.

whisky, part of his body was sent to Dr Stevenson, for further examination when the initial post-mortem proved inconclusive.[786]

Post-mortems also became more thorough and increasingly professional during the Victorian era. For example, in 1865, after Hendricus Erenshuisen stabbed a fellow Dutch sailor during a quarrel in a Yarmouth tavern, a Dr Stafford cut out the dead man's heart and showed the inquest jury how a stab wound from a stiletto-type dagger, like the one owned by the suspect, had gone straight through it. (This occasioned considerable shock to the jurors.)[787] This improvement was aided by growing awareness of foreign practice, such as the standard method for performing autopsies introduced by Rudolf Virchow in Germany during the 1870s. (An autopsy instrument for exposing the brain, invented by Virchow, is still in use today). In this system, the whole body is examined in a methodical and ordered manner, in a strong light, with all the major bodily cavities being opened (not just those adjacent to the suspected fatal injury), and samples taken for further examination.[788] T.P. Smith's English translation of Virchow's work allowed his techniques to spread in Britain, and the latter was awarded the Copley Medal for his services to pathology by the Royal Society in 1892.

Of course, not every such analysis, especially those held outside major cities, involved state-of-the-art medical practice. For example, in 1849, when Anne Mead, a slow-witted Essex servant girl, was accused of murdering her new-born baby, the county coroner ordered a full post-mortem. As conducted, this included the ancient but by then widely discredited lung float test (babies whose lungs floated in water were deemed to have been alive at birth), as well as the more appropriate opening of the body cavities.[789]

Nevertheless, by the latter years of the nineteenth century, the conduct of post-mortems everywhere in England was usually (if not quite invariably) of a reasonable standard, while a majority of homicide trials were assisted by the results of such an autopsy, the proportion having grown steadily over previous decades. For example, at the Old Bailey, between 1809 and 1818, 40.8 percent of homicide trials had an autopsy report, but by the years from 1869 to 1878 this had risen to 61.7 percent (with only 10 of 251 such trials having no medical evidence at all).[790] Their use was correspondingly widespread in Norfolk.

---

[786] *The Bury and Norwich Post*, 24 June, 1890.

[787] *The Morning Post*, 16 October, 1865.

[788] Edward Walter and Mike Scott, "The life and work of Rudolf Virchow 1821-1902: 'Cell theory, thrombosis and the sausage duel,'" *Journal of the Intensive Care Society*, vol. 18, no. 3 (2017), pp. 234-235.

[789] *The Essex Standard*, 9 February, 1849.

[790] Christopher M. Milroy, "A Brief History of the Expert Witness," *Academic Forensic Pathology*, vol. 7, no. 4 (2017), pp. 516-526.

Directions to the Inquest Jury

When all the available evidence had been heard, the coroner would sum up to the inquest jury on the possible verdicts open to them. For example, in 1842 PC George Dowde dealt with an escaping prisoner by striking him on the head with his truncheon, mortally wounding him. His account was supported by an eyewitness. At the inquest, a doctor testified that the dead man had one of the thinnest skulls he had ever examined.[791] The coroner directed the jury that if the force employed by Dowde was reasonable it would be justifiable; if excessive, it would be manslaughter. After lengthy consideration, the jury decided on the latter verdict, and Dowde was committed to the prison to await trial.[792] (He was subsequently bailed and then acquitted at assizes, the judge giving a sympathetic summing-up to the trial jury.)[793]

The coroner had considerable influence when it came to steering jurors in a specific direction when summing-up. Cases in which infant deaths in Norfolk had resulted from laudanum poisoning provide an example. In the early part of the nineteenth century, children regularly died of overdoses of the sedative, which was used in many pacifying medicines. For example, in 1835 William Sweatman was poisoned by the "incautious administration" of laudanum by his mother. The coroner's inquest decided that the death was accidental. However, in 1865 the coroner for the King's Lynn district told Sir George Grey how he had dealt with the problem of opiate-based child-soothers after noticing that many children had died from the indiscriminate use of Godfrey's Cordial and similar medicines: "I put a stop to its use by recommending verdicts of manslaughter in two or three instances."[794]

More specifically, in 1845 an inquest was held into the death of Jane Lovett shortly after she had given birth at Costessey, to the west of Norwich. It was alleged that she had died due to grossly negligent treatment from Raymond Gaches, an apothecary-cum-midwife (the baby survived). When summing up to the inquest jury, Mr Pilgrim, a county coroner, firmly directed it towards a manslaughter verdict rather than one of accidental death, telling them that, in his opinion, there was "sufficient evidence of gross ignorance and inattention" to warrant it. After briefly considering the issue, the jury returned such a verdict.[795] (Gaches was acquitted at the Norfolk assizes, after another sympathetic summing-up by the presiding judge, the jury accepting that he had simply made an error of professional judgment).[796]

After the coroner's summing-up, the jury could retire to consider their verdict in private, although this may not always have occurred in practice. In a Norfolk

791 *The Bury and Norwich Post*, 3 August, 1842.

792 *Ibid.*, 18 May, 1842.

793 *Ibid.*, 3 August, 1842.

794 *Letter from T.M. Wilkin to Sir George Grey, MP, 25 March, 1865.* House of Commons Parliamentary Papers Online.

795 *The Ipswich Journal*, 8 March, 1845.

796 *Ibid.*, 12 April, 1845.

homicide inquest of 1852, after the coroner had summed up the evidence and possible verdicts open to the jury, the latter body "requested that the room might be cleared, which was accordingly done, and some time elapsed before the coroner was re-admitted." The foreman then said that they had reached a verdict and delivered a finding of manslaughter.[797] As well as returning verdicts, inquest juries might occasionally take the opportunity to make more general observations about what had occurred. In December 1875 a jury considered the deaths of three boys murdered by the mentally disturbed Robert Edwards in the Norfolk and Norwich Hospital; it condemned in very strong terms the surgeon and the clergyman who had arranged for Edwards to be admitted, as they ought to have been aware that he was not remotely suitable for such an institution.[798]

It appears that conflict or active disagreement between jury and coroner was rare. Nevertheless, it was not unheard of. For example, in 1848 an inquest was held at Diss before the deputy coroner for Norfolk into the death of a child, Albert Aldrich, after he suddenly fell ill, along with two other members of his family. It received evidence from a surgeon who had conducted a post-mortem on his body. The doctor testified that, although apparently a healthy boy, Albert had a perforation in his stomach. The surgeon suggested that a corrosive poison was responsible, though he could not identify the toxin involved. The jury asked that the case be adjourned to allow a proper analysis of the boy's stomach. The coroner was unwilling to do this. The jury then asked about the law and, finding that the coroner "had the option of acting as he pleased on the matter," asked that the depositions in the case be referred to the Home Secretary. When the deputy coroner refused to do this, the jury declined to return a verdict. Eventually, the deputy-coroner adjourned the inquest to allow the coroner for the county (his immediate superior) to be consulted. The jury's decision apparently reflected widespread disquiet in the town about the death.[799]

Of course, inquest jury attitudes to certain types of death also changed over time, reflecting different social mores. In turn, this affected verdicts. Eighteenth-century inquests had often judged fatalities resulting from fights as accidental; by the 1830s these were more likely to be viewed as crimes (usually manslaughter).[800]

The Verdict

Inquest jurors did not normally have to be unanimous when reaching a decision, but at least a dozen of them had to be agreed; this meant that if only 12 sat they did have to be as one, helping to explain why many observers recommended that a minimum of 14 or 15 men serve. To consider a *cause célèbre* from outside Norfolk, there were 14 jurors at the inquest held into the death of James Maybrick near Liverpool in 1889. They retired for 35 minutes to consider their verdict before returning to

797 *Bell's Life in London and Sporting Chronicle*, 18 April, 1852.

798 *The Times*, 22 December, 1875, p. 7.

799 *The Examiner*, 23 December, 1848.

800 Wood, "Drinking, Fighting," pp. 1-10.

the room of the hotel employed for the inquest. The coroner had structured their decision-making by giving them three questions to answer: had the deceased died as a result of poison; if so, who had administered it; if the answer to the second question was Mrs Maybrick, had she done so intending to kill her husband? The foreman noted that the answer to the first question was unanimously "yes"; to the second, 13 were persuaded that it was Mrs Maybrick (one dissented); and to the last question, a dozen jurors felt that she had meant to kill her spouse (two dissented). As the coroner noted, "That [still] amounts to a verdict of murder".[801]

In Norfolk in 1846, at an inquest into the death of a train driver and his stoker in a railway crash in the county, three of 15 jurors dissented from the rest. They felt that there had been an element of culpable (and so criminal) neglect by the rail company, something that would warrant forfeiting the train engine as a £500 deodand (deodands were abolished by statute later that year). However, that a dozen jurors were still in agreement allowed the coroner to accept a less serious verdict.[802]

A coroner's decision could not normally be appealed at a rehearing. However, if a jury failed to find a homicide in what had potentially been a killing, for example by returning an open or accidental-death verdict, the matter could still be pursued before a criminal court through the magistrates' process. As a Norfolk coroner noted to an inquest jury considering a drowning in 1848, "At present, he (the coroner) did not see the slightest suspicion of any foul play, but if anything should turn up hereafter the police could take it up."[803] This occurred in Shropshire in 1823, after the death of a married woman produced an open verdict at inquest. The next day a suspicious conversation, that put a different light on the case, was reported to two local JPs who then instigated their own investigation into the husband.[804] Nevertheless, the coroner's court was subject to the supervisory jurisdiction of the Queen's Bench, and its decision might, in certain circumstances, be challenged, usually by way of *certiorari*.

In practice, because so much less turned on an inquest's decision than a verdict at assizes, coroners' courts tended to be far more willing to make findings of homicide than were criminal courts. Frequently, a not-guilty verdict followed an inquest finding of murder or manslaughter, or the lesser form of homicide was returned at trial after the inquest decided that it was a case of murder.

---

801 Bernard Ryan and Sir Michael Havers, *The Poisoned Life of Mrs Maybrick* (New York: Harper Collins, 1977), p. 102.

802 *The Northern Star*, 17 January, 1846.

803 *The Lynn Advertiser & West Norfolk Herald,* 11 December, 1858.

804 Fisher, "Edmund Whitcombe," p. 12.

Controversy over Inquest Verdicts

Occasionally an inquest's decision to return a verdict that was inconsistent with homicide was a source of public controversy. In September 1837, at Catton, Jonathan Cooper, a Norwich attorney, was driving in a gig with his clerk when he was accosted by or encountered Cornelius Moor. Cooper drew a pistol, fired it towards the man, and mortally wounded him. The following day, he was apprehended and committed to the Castle prison, accused of killing Moor. The case caused great excitement. It was alleged that Cooper had held malice towards the dead man arising from a recent Norwich election. However, at the coroner's inquest, this, along with any imputation of premeditation, was negated by the evidence, not least by the dying declaration of Moor, who was, apparently, quite unknown to the prisoner. The inquest jury returned a verdict of manslaughter rather than murder, although this so "excited the indignation of the populace that they were with difficulty prevented from assaulting the jurymen on their leaving the Coroner's court."[805]

Furthermore, not all members of the public invariably accepted the coroner's decision as conclusive, even though a quashed coroner's inquest could not be resurrected, and the matter could then be carried to a public forum only if JPs committed it for trial or (very unusually) a grand jury made a presentment in its own right.[806] For example, in 1873 John Neal was found dead in a Thetford road, and an inquest was duly held. It returned a verdict of "accidental death," the suggestion being that Neal had fallen from his horse and fractured his skull. Some of his friends and family were unsatisfied with this decision, with local gossip suggesting foul play. Although the dead man's injuries were officially attributed to his being dragged along the ground by his stirrups, it was thought strange that his whip and gloves were found apart from his body, while his watch had disappeared.[807] Neal's mother commissioned a barrister to investigate the matter. This lawyer concluded that it was a homicide and placed his report before the Home Secretary.[808]

---

805 *The Norfolk Chronicle*, 9 September, 1837.

806 Pue, "Twilight Zone," p. 335.

807 *The Bury and Norwich Post*, 13 May, 1873.

808 *The Illustrated Police News*, 24 May, 1873.

Chapter 8: Prosecution and Prosecutors

Introduction

By the early 1800s prosecution in both Continental Europe and Scotland (with its system of procurators fiscal) had long been a largely public function, exercised on behalf of the state, which also funded it to a significant degree. As the Scottish Lord Advocate observed in 1855, "The Scotch system acknowledges the right of a private party to prosecute; but the duty of the public prosecutor is altogether irrespective of that."[809] By contrast, in England and Wales the system was essentially private, as it had been for centuries. However, the terminology can be a little misleading. In the words of the legal historian F.W. Maitland, writing in 1885, it was England that had "Public prosecutions, for any one of the public may prosecute; abroad they have State prosecutions or Official prosecutions."[810] At its simplest, the prosecutor in a case was the person who laid charges against a suspect and was then bound over by an examining magistrate to pursue an offence, whether personally or through a solicitor and counsel, to and at trial.

For example, in 1880, when Emily Watkins fraudulently obtained a long period of accommodation and meals at the White Horse Inn at Attleborough, in South Norfolk, it was noted that "the prosecutor was the keeper of the White Horse."[811] Although prosecutions were brought in the name of the Crown, it was traditionally assumed that the prosecutor would take the initiative in reporting the offence to a magistrate, provide relevant evidence to establish it at a committal hearing, draw up and sign an indictment (with the aid of a lawyer or court clerk), and then marshal Q;'the case through the criminal-justice system to the grand jury and then trial. As part of this process, he would also ensure that any prosecution witnesses attended the hearing.[812] As a result, in 1823 a Norfolk case could be described as "The King (on the prosecution of the Rev Frederick Money) against Charles Spragg for an assault committed upon the prosecutor, who is a curate of Mattishall." Money was the 'real' prosecutor.[813] A prosecutor's subsequent failure to pursue a matter could lead to forfeiture of a previously designated sum of money. Thus, in October 1893 James Lovelace was bound over by magistrates in the sum of £20 to prosecute Frederick Smith, a waiter who had stolen a banknote from him, at the Norfolk quarter sessions.[814]

---

809 Paul Rock, "Victims, prosecutors and the State in nineteenth century England and Wales," *Criminology and Criminal Justice*, vol. 4, no. 4 (2004), pp. 331-354.

810 Matthew Dyson, "Overlaps and Undercurrents: The Timing of Tortious and Criminal Actions for the Same Wrong," *The Cambridge Law Journal*, vol. 71, no. 1 (2011), p. 107.

811 *The Bury and Norwich Post*, 26 October, 1880.

812 Shakesheff, *Rural Conflict,* p. 59.

813 *The Norfolk Chronicle,* 18 October, 1823.

814 NRO 24/4/1 North Erpingham Petty Sessions, Minute Book.

Although private prosecution was inherited by the colonies, they usually abandoned the system quite swiftly. For example, the United States of America had dedicated prosecuting attorneys by the Revolution, as did upper Canada in the early 1800s. Similarly, shortly after the establishment of the Western Australia colony, it was thought necessary to appoint a public officer, the Advocate General, to take responsibility for prosecuting criminal cases. (In part, these developments may have reflected the lack of lawyers and sparse populations found in many colonies, something that could make briefing someone in private practice difficult.)[815]

However, this change did not occur in early nineteenth-century England, although many thought that it should. Critics in Parliament, some of them senior judges, attempted to introduce a system of public prosecution in England in the 1830s, 1850s, and 1870s. Evidence was gathered from foreign countries, where public prosecution was well established, to support such campaigns. In 1845 Lord Denman favoured the introduction of a public prosecutor, as did some others, who submitted evidence to the Criminal Law Commission. Francis Rogers QC thought that "private parties, who are usually required as the principal witnesses, ought not also to be charged with the duty of prosecution, and consequently I think no party whose evidence is required should be bound over to prosecute." He felt that this should be left to public prosecutors appointed to each area (or police officers of more than basic rank).[816] In Norfolk in 1857, Mr Gay, a local JP, suggested at the county quarter sessions that a public prosecutor would be "advantageous to the kingdom."[817] Even so, support was not universal. Mr R. Leigh, the Wigan clerk of the peace, was opposed to such an idea, not least because it would impinge on victims' rights.[818] He was not alone. Some lawyers even thought that interested parties, such as victims, were more likely to take the responsibility to prosecute seriously.

In part, as a result, it was only in 1985 that a state agency, the Crown Prosecution Service, was established to conduct most criminal prosecutions in England and Wales, rather than the task normally being entrusted to police solicitors, although private prosecutions by members of the public still occur. More pertinently, it was not until the Prosecution of Offences Act 1879, and after decades of debate, that the position of Director of Public Prosecutions (DPP) was introduced in England, although such an officer had first been recommended by the Criminal Law Commission in 1845. (The County and Borough Police Act 1856 had permitted the Home Office to ask the Treasury Solicitor's department to take on cases of particular significance.) Even when he started work, in 1880, the DPP was only allowed to deal with a very small number of cases of "importance or difficulty."

---

815 Peter Handford, "Criminal Prosecutions in Western Australia:
A View from the Nineteenth Century," *University of Western Australia Law Review,* vol. 43, no. 1 (2018), p. 145.

816 *The Examiner*, 2 August, 1845. *Eighth Report,* p. 302, p. 332.

817 *The Bury and Norwich Post*, 13 January, 1857.

818 *The Examiner*, 2 August, 1845. *Eighth Report*, p. 332.

However, although private prosecution was still dominant at the start of the Victorian era, there were already several important exceptions to the general situation by 1837, and these increased further during the remainder of the century, as did state involvement. Furthermore, and vitally, the period saw the gradual decline of the role of victims in criminal prosecutions. Much of this was the result of a change in practice, rather than in the black-letter law, and, most important, the impact of the new police on the prosecution process.[819]

Exceptions to Private Prosecution

Long before the Victorian era, parish constables had often prosecuted minor, especially "victimless" crimes that occurred in their localities. Several new private bodies and government Inspectorates, such as the Royal Society for the Prevention of Cruelty to Animals (RSPCA), joined (or replaced) them in this function during the nineteenth century. They often prosecuted the new, specialist, statutory offences, many of which were only triable summarily. For example, in 1874 a charge of cruelty to dogs was preferred at the Norwich Police Court against Dr Eugene Magnan and other local medical men by an officer from the RSPCA. (It was alleged that they had injected alcohol into the veins of several dogs for amusement.)[820] Almost two decades later, at the North Erpingham petty sessions in January 1894, an RSPCA Inspector prosecuted William Thistle for cruelly beating a horse with his whip. [821]

The Attorney General, however, would always manage and prosecute cases of treason, those with a heavy political element, and some *causes célèbres* of a conventional type, this last category becoming more important as the period advanced. He was supported in this towards the end of the century by the Treasury Solicitor and the DPP. Thus, when, in March 1870, Robert Hardiment, a tanner, was indicted at the Norwich assizes for bribing voters at the previous general election to vote for Sir Henry Josias Stracey, the Attorney General appeared for the prosecution.[822] Similarly, in 1885, when the captains of three Great Yarmouth smacks were charged with the unusual offence of piracy, after robbing a German vessel that was supplying fishermen near the Dogger Bank with liquor and tobacco (a diplomatically sensitive crime), the prosecution was conducted by the Attorney General supported by two local barristers.[823]

Additionally, some government institutions, such as the Bank of England, the Mint, the Board of Inland Revenue, and the Post Office actively investigated when they were victimised and appointed their own lawyers to prosecute forgery, coining, and duty offences, as well as theft from the mail. In December 1874, when William Dack

---

819 Barry Godfrey, "Changing Prosecution Practices and their Impact on Crime Figures, 1857–1940," *The British Journal of Criminology*, vol. 48, no. 2 (2008), pp. 171-189.

820 Wiener, *Reconstructing,* p. 65. *The Norfolk Chronicle,* 9 December, 1874.

821 NRO 24/4/1 North Erpingham Petty Sessions, Minute Book.

822 *The Norfolk Chronicle,* 31 March, 1870.

823 *The Bury and Norwich Post,* 5 May, 1885.

and Herbert Bocking, 13- and 14-year-old telegraph clerks at the King's Lynn post office, were accused of stealing gold rings and other valuable items from parcels, they were remanded to the Lynn petty sessions for committal, where they were prosecuted by a lawyer instructed by the post office.[824] They were convicted at the following assizes.[825] In late 1856, at the Norwich Police Court (in effect, the city petty sessions) the commissioners of Inland Revenue prosecuted George Holt and Stephen Gilbert for having an illicit still. (Holt was fined £50 and Gilbert £200).[826]

Nevertheless, with these qualifications and caveats, the victim of a crime was the person most frequently identified as its prosecutor during the early Victorian period, homicides obviously apart (helping to explain the importance of the coroner's inquest). On one assessment, in 1836, about 80 percent of cases at the Staffordshire and Worcestershire quarter sessions were brought by victims.[827] However, there was ostensibly no reason that a prosecution should not be brought by any other private individual. Such third-party prosecution was not uncommon, especially when the victim was a child or female and a father or husband became involved. For example, in 1837 a newspaper reporting an attempted rape in Sheffield described the victim as the "prosecutrix." As she was a small child, this must be inaccurate in any meaningful sense. Doubtless a close family member, such as her father, laid charges and was bound over to pursue the case.[828]

Problems Attendant on Private Prosecution

From the eighteenth century onwards many English legislators, officials, and lawyers argued in favour of increased state prosecution on the basis that crime affected the whole of society, not just its immediate victims, and needed to be pursued more consistently if it was to be controlled. By the 1830s and 1840s, aspects of private prosecution that had been viewed as acceptable in the 1700s were occasioning particular concern. As society moved from a penal theory based on selective but draconian example to one stressing milder but uniformly applied sanctions, the lack of consistency in prosecution became increasingly troubling, and the view that this was encouraged by its essentially private nature more prevalent. For example, in 1845, Lord Denman, the then Lord Chief Justice, claimed that potential prosecutors were often ignorant, corrupt, and irresponsible.[829]

Denman's analysis was a little harsh; prosecution was often an unattractive option for very good reasons. As the Criminal Law Commission of 1845 noted, it was "usually irksome, inconvenient and burthensome." It was time-consuming, personally

824 *The Ipswich Journal*, 5 December, 1874. *The Bury and Norwich Post*, 8 December, 1874.

825 *The Bury and Norwich Post*, 6 April, 1875, p. 3.

826 *The Norfolk Chronicle,* 2 December, 1856.

827 Mark Koyama, "Prosecution Associations in Industrial Revolution England: Private Providers of Public Goods?" *The Journal of Legal Studies*, vol. 41, no. 1 (2012), p. 98.

828 Andrew Christopher Williams, *Police and Crime in Sheffield, 1818-1874,* PhD thesis, 1998, p. 267.

829 *The Examiner*, 2 August, 1845. Rock, "Victims, Prosecutors," pp. 331-354.

distressing, and could make prosecutors unpopular with their neighbours, let alone with those they pursued (and their families).[830] There was also the risk of a civil action for malicious prosecution or false imprisonment being brought against the prosecutor by a discharged suspect or acquitted defendant.

An example of such an action, *Doland* v *Farney*, was heard at *nisi prius* at the Norfolk spring assizes before the Lord Chief Baron in March 1862. Both parties had been on holiday in Yarmouth. The defendant had used a bathing machine and left his watch in it. Missing it, he returned to the scene. The owner of the machine remembered that the only previous customer had left in a great hurry before getting properly dressed. The owner's boy then accompanied the defendant and a policeman around Yarmouth, searching for this man (the eventual plaintiff). They finally identified and arrested him. He was taken to a police station, where he and his luggage were searched, but no timepiece was found. However, at this point, the complainant, a solicitor's clerk, insisted on pursuing a criminal charge. The plaintiff spent at least one night in a police cell before being produced before local magistrates on the following Monday morning for examination, where the JPs swiftly dismissed the matter and told the suspect that he left without a stain on his character.[831]

It was not contended at the civil trial that the plaintiff *had* taken the watch, merely that the defendant had reasonable grounds to suspect that he had done so, and so ought not to be liable for damages. In summing up to the jury, the Lord Chief Baron commented that the matter had been pursued by the defendant after the search had revealed nothing and after the suspect's respectability might easily have been ascertained. (He printed overseas stamps for the government.) The jury, following a brief deliberation, awarded the significant, but not enormous, sum of £25 to the plaintiff. It appears that it was the defendant's pursuit of the matter after the initial investigation that made out the tort.[832]

Expense of Prosecution

Most important of all, when it came to factors discouraging private prosecution, was that it could be expensive, even for modest crimes. To be performed properly it normally required the use of an attorney, and possibly counsel, who would often cost more than the court would allow in expenses.[833] To consider a slightly extreme case, in the early 1820s the Eyam Association for the Prosecution of Felons in Derbyshire financed the prosecution of a case involving the theft of cheese. The total cost of the action came to over £46. Some £5 went on lawyers' fees prior to trial, for tasks such as drawing up an indictment, interviewing witnesses, and taking preliminary depositions. Another £5 went on counsel's fee *at* trial. A chaise to bring the cheese to court (as an exhibit) cost a further £6. Yet more was spent keeping witnesses in

830 *Eighth Report*, p. 24.

831 *The Ipswich Journal*, 29 March, 1862.

832 *Ibid*.

833 *Eighth Report*, p. 24.

Derby. Ultimately, a technical flaw in the indictment led to an acquittal at trial. The county eventually reimbursed just £14 of the £46.[834] (However, the situation for prosecutors seeking reimbursement improved, to some extent, shortly afterwards, as discussed below).

Unsurprisingly, in these circumstances, and as the Criminal Law Commission of 1845 noted "the injured party would often rather forgo the prosecution than incur expense of time, labour and money." Alternatively, they might put the matter into the hands of an inferior attorney, offering a cut-price prosecution service, whose aim was to secure the modest amounts likely to be allowed by the courts. As a result, in many cases, prosecutions were conducted in a loose and unsatisfactory manner.[835]

Other victims would settle a matter privately with the perpetrator, whether by compounding (accepting payment for not prosecuting) or simply by requiring restitution of stolen property. For example, at the Norfolk summer assizes in 1837, two brothers named Nixon were convicted of stealing £8 12s from the person of James Watts. The brothers were millers who had purchased wheat from their victim. He subsequently attended their mill and received the cash in payment, signing a docket showing its receipt. As he left the premises the two men forcibly took it back from him, and when Watts's mother later went to the mill and remonstrated with them, they showed her the receipt. The Nixons were subsequently prosecuted for robbery and sentenced to transportation. Had they apologized to the victim's mother and returned the cash, the matter might well not have gone any further.[836]

The compounding of offences, although illegal in the case of felonies, was probably still common, if less so than in the previous century. In 1875, in a tavern at West Tofts, John Ashton, a building labourer, ate one of a colleague's plums. The latter, George Waters, who was eating cheese with a pocketknife, would tolerate "no larking tricks" and stabbed Ashton, inflicting a serious wound. As Ashton left the establishment (with assistance), he noticed Waters holding up half a sovereign, and inferred from this that it was being offered as compensation and in exchange for not prosecuting him. An associate warned him not to take it.[837]

Malicious Prosecutions

Conversely, the reliance on private actions sometimes occasioned problems with malicious prosecutions. In these situations, as the Justices' Clerks' Society noted in 1845, unfounded cases might go to trial "unchecked" before they had been

---

[834] John Cragg, "The Broseley Anti-Felons, Part 1," *Journal of The Wilkinson Society,* vol. 9 (1981), pp. 11-13. John Cragg, "The Broseley Anti-Felons, Part 2," *Journal of The Wilkinson Society*, vol. 11 (1983), pp. 6-10.

[835] *Eighth Report,* p. 24.

[836] *The Bury & Norwich Post, & East Anglian: Or, Suffolk, Norfolk, Essex, Cambridge, and Ely Intelligencer*, 9 August, 1837.

[837] *The Bury and Norwich Post*, 9 November, 1875.

adequately investigated. A few of these cases even produced convictions and condign punishment.[838] For example, in April 1842 John Utting, a parish constable from Filby, and Anna Bunn, a local woman, were indicted at the Norfolk assizes for conspiring against Daniel Durrant, a publican from Winterton, then under sentence of transportation for life (he was still on one of the hulks) after being convicted of rape on their evidence the previous year.[839] Soon after his conviction, Durrant's 27-year-old wife died, allegedly of a broken heart, leaving three small children without a provider.[840] Bunn, apparently feeling remorse, subsequently confessed to the rector of Acle that the testimony that procured Durrant's conviction was false, and motivated by a desire to ruin him.[841] Durrant was released and returned home. Subsequently, Utting was convicted at assizes of perjury and sentenced to twelve months' imprisonment. Bunn was discharged; she appears to have given accomplice evidence for the Crown against Utting.[842]

Encouraging Prosecutions

Various expedients and initiatives, both public and private, were in use by the early 1800s to actively encourage private prosecution, some of which have already been alluded to. Others had been tried and abandoned, in whole or in part, over the previous century.[843] They warrant further consideration.

Public Provision of Prosecution Costs/Prosecuting Counsel

Provision for the public payment of prosecution costs had improved steadily after the middle of the eighteenth century. Section 28 of the Criminal Justice Act 1826 made statutory allowance for the "better remuneration" and reimbursement of both prosecutors' expenses and those of their witnesses, for a range of felonies, such as, inter alia, murder, robbery, rape, poisoning, arson, burglary, and horse theft, as well as some serious misdemeanours. Under s.29 of the statute, any payments ordered by a court would be made by the sheriff of the relevant county, who would, in turn, be able to recover some of the money from the Treasury. Sir Robert Peel justified the change by noting that the lack of costs often denied justice to the poorest. Thus, at the Norfolk quarter sessions in January 1847, Isaac Jermy asked that £12 3s 6d be allowed from public funds for the justices' clerks' fees and expenses incurred in the

---

838 *Eighth Report,* p. 320. D. Hay and F. Snyder (eds.), *Policing and Prosecution In Britain 1750-1850* (Oxford: Clarendon, 1989), pp. 343-395.

839 *The Northern Star*, 16 April, 1842. *The Bury and Norwich Post*, 13 April, 1842.

840 *The Bury and Norwich Post*, 2 March, 1842.

841 *Ibid.*, 5 January, 1842.

842 Mackie, *Norfolk Annals*, vol. 2, p. 417.

843 Gregory J. Durston, *Fields, Fens and Felonies: Crime and Justice in Eighteenth-Century East Anglia* (Hook: Waterside Press, 2016), pp. 203-226.

committal of William Johnson, who had been indicted at the previous July sessions for horse stealing (£11 18s was ultimately permitted by the JPs).[844]

It is likely that the availability of such expenses encouraged an increase in prosecutions, even if conducted by money-seeking "low attornies".[845] Of course, those specially briefed to prosecute major crimes, such as murder, might receive much more substantial fees and would be carefully instructed in advance, as was the case with the murder prosecution of Samuel Yarham at the Norfolk assizes in 1846.[846] This was significant, as the briefing of defence counsel (a Mr Dasent) in this case appears to have been a rushed, last-minute, effort.

By the 1830s concern was being expressed at the impact of prosecution costs on the county rates, despite assistance from central government. (In 1848 the Treasury spent £400,000 helping the counties defray the expense of compensating prosecutors' costs.)[847] Even so, some magistrates periodically called for further increases in the funding available. During the county business carried out at the Norfolk quarter sessions in January 1857, a clerical JP urged that counsel prosecuting at the lower jury forum receive the same amount as those employed at assizes. He noted that, by then, expenses would also normally cover an attorney, if so employed.[848] Nevertheless, at the start of 1862 there was considerable anxiety amongst county magistrates throughout England about a proposed reduction in Treasury allowances for prosecutors and witnesses which, it was feared, would impede the criminal-justice system. At the Norfolk quarter sessions, it was resolved that Sir Willoughby Jones and a local MP would raise the issue at a meeting for chairmen from throughout England.[849]

Furthermore, by the Victorian period, local authorities were often directly funding prosecution counsel at trial on indictment on a modest basis if counsel had not been arranged and financed by the prosecutor. It seems to have become common practice for prosecution briefs at quarter sessions to be prepared by an officer employed by the relevant county or borough, and then distributed to barristers at court without the use of an intermediary solicitor.[850] W.H. Cooke (1843-1921), an English barrister who appears to have been the author of the legal chapters in a slightly whimsical book published by his friend Thomas Reid in 1872, described how this was done.

---

844 *The Bury and Norwich Post, and East Anglian*, 13 January, 1847.

845 Emsley, Storch, "Prosecution," p. 48. *Eighth Report*, p. 239.

846 NRO Y/L 16/26. Brief for the Prosecution, 24 March, 1846.

847 Conor Hanly, "Summary Jurisdiction and the Decline of Criminal Jury Trial in Victorian England," *The Journal of Legal History*, vol. 42, no. 3 (2021), p. 282. Emsley, Storch, "Prosecution," p. 48.

848 *The Bury and Norwich Post*, 13 January, 1857.

849 *The Lancaster Gazette, and General Advertiser for Lancashire, Westmorland, Yorkshire, &c.* 11 January, 1862.

850 Cornish, *Oxford History*, p. 1042.

Quarter and Borough Sessions were often, apparently, referred to by barristers as "soup sessions." The town clerk (for example) would hand out prosecution briefs for all cases that did not already have counsel to those barristers present in court, in order of seniority. Each would be given a single brief. If there were not enough briefs for all, the juniors missed out, and it would be said that the "soup had not gone round." On the rare occasions when there were more briefs than barristers, the process would start again, so that some (relatively) experienced junior barristers would get two cases. (QCs would never attend quarter sessions unless specially briefed in advance.) The fee for a soup sessions' brief would be a guinea, but in some parts of the country two guineas would be allowed if there were more than six witnesses to be examined.[851] Although not very financially rewarding (the fee was normally the same as a defence dock brief), soup sessions provided valuable training for young barristers, and allowed them to gain a professional reputation.

Towards the end of the Victorian period this appears to have been viewed as almost the standard system for prosecuting cases at the lower jury forum, as the recorder of the Southampton quarter sessions noted in a letter to the local council, and one that even extended to some cases at assizes, at least in certain areas.[852] Although there would still have been a few matters, such as lesser assaults, where a local corporation did not think a barrister was necessary, the prevalence of this system helps to explain why it was so rare for the Crown to be legally unrepresented at Victorian trials on indictment, especially after the early years of the Queen's reign.

Nevertheless, the soup system provided a very basic form of prosecution representation, with minimal time for case preparation, while there was no guarantee that privately funded prosecutors, who paid for their own lawyers, would be awarded all their expenses. Indeed, the presiding judge or chairman (at quarter sessions) retained considerable discretion to withhold such an award altogether. For example, men who were victimized by women of bad character with whom they had associated, especially when drunk, might receive reduced payments or none, even if successful in their prosecutions for pickpocketing or other crimes. Thus, although James Johnson, an intoxicated commercial traveller who had been robbed by a prostitute with whom he had consorted in Great Yarmouth, secured the woman's conviction and imprisonment at the Yarmouth Borough quarter sessions in 1839, the town recorder refused him both costs and expenses.[853]

Similarly, in January 1851 Robert Hubbard was the victim of youths who stole two sovereigns and some silver from him while he consorted with a pair of women. Although he secured the thieves' conviction and seven years' transportation at the Norfolk quarter sessions, "the expenses of the prosecutor were disallowed."[854] It was not only salacious cases that might lead to such a refusal. Theft victims who

851 Reid, *Briefs and Papers,* p. 105.

852 *The Southampton Herald*, 17 February, 1900.

853 *The Ipswich Journal*, 20 July, 1839.

854 *The Bury and Norwich Post, and Suffolk Herald*, 8 January, 1851.

had been careless about the security of their property, such as shopkeepers who displayed goods in the public street, might also fail to be reimbursed.

Prosecution Associations

Prior to the Victorian period, the challenges faced by individual prosecutors had encouraged the formation of prosecution associations, which flourished during the late eighteenth and early nineteenth centuries. For example, the Harleston Prosecution Association in Norfolk was involved in an average of seven prosecutions a year between 1805 and 1815.[855] Such associations were still being formed on a regular basis in the 1820s. Thus, in November 1825 the Norwich Association for Assisting in the Detection and Prosecution of Criminal Offenders was founded at a meeting held at the city Guildhall.[856] Although in decline by 1837, as a result of the establishment of borough and county police forces, there were still about 500 such associations in England in 1840.[857] Thus, in June 1843 the Stoke Ferry Association for the Prosecution of Felons elected a treasurer after the death of the incumbent.[858] Some of these associations even outlived the century.

Each member of a prosecution association usually paid a joining fee and an annual subscription, the money being used to provide rewards for information leading to the arrest and successful prosecution of offenders who had victimized members of the society, and to pay for lawyers' fees expended in such prosecutions. For example, in 1839 the North Elmham Association for Prosecution of Felons, which operated (under different names) from 1787 to 1889, funded the prosecution of John Hall and others for stealing a church bell.[859] However, by then, many observers criticized the need for such voluntary bodies, feeling that it was indicative of the "prostrate condition of the penal administration of the country." It was argued that they were doing what should be the business of government.[860]

Rewards

During the eighteenth and early nineteenth centuries the country had encouraged prosecution by providing statutory rewards for securing felony convictions. Unfortunately, these had been the source of several notorious miscarriages of justice, including scandals in which people had been entrapped so that their enticers could secure reward money. As a result, they had been abolished in 1818.[861] Nevertheless, individual rewards were still sometimes offered in specific crimes by both private

855 Koyama, "The law & economics," p. 290.

856 *The Norfolk Chronicle,* 23 November, 1825.

857 G.M. Young, *Portrait of an Age* (Oxford: OUP, 1992), p. 20.

858 *The Bury and Norwich Post*, 14 June, 1843.

859 NRO PD 711/124.

860 *First Report from the Commissioners Appointed to Inquire as to the Best Means of Establishing an Efficient Constabulary Force in the Counties of England and Wales*, 1839, p. 97.

861 Hansard HC Deb 2 March 1818 vol. 37 cols. 690-693.

individuals and (less commonly) the state, especially early in the Victorian period. For example, in 1832 Lord Melbourne offered £100 of government money in addition to an existing private reward of £200 for information leading to the discovery of the perpetrators of an arson attack at Thomas Cloweys' farm near Great Yarmouth (there was also the promise of a pardon to marginally involved accomplices who testified against their colleagues).[862]

More modestly, in October 1839, the Stoke Ferry Association for Prosecuting Felons offered a £5 reward for the apprehension and conviction of burglars who had stolen silverware, boots, and a tea caddy from Samuel Taylor's house in Whittington. A personal reward of a further £5 was also offered by one of the members.[863] The following year, Richard Montague Oakes, the new chief constable for Norfolk, discussed, in correspondence with the Home Office, the possibility of offering a reward for information about the murder of Mary Randalsome.[864] In a letter of 1882, George Waddington, from Brandon, noted that following a fire in a barn two private rewards of £100 and £400 for the arrest of the arsonist had been offered by groups of local people.[865]

Furthermore, in some minor regulatory offences, common informers, who gave evidence for a share of any fines or penalties, continued to operate during the early Victorian period. In 1840, at the Norwich police court, George Seales, well known as a common informer, secured the conviction of a coach proprietor for carrying more than the permitted number of passengers. Such men were usually very unpopular. On leaving the Guildhall, Seales was violently assaulted by a mob, and had to be escorted to his home by 20 police officers.[866]

Prosecution and the New Police

How did the advent of the new police affect prosecution? The answer seems to have been twofold. In some situations, the police or, more particularly, specific officers, became the prosecutors after a crime had been committed, just as the father of a child might be the prosecutor when his offspring was victimized. They would lay charges and be bound over to pursue the case to trial. In these situations, the victim (if available) would simply become a prosecution witness rather than both witness and prosecutor. This process started quite quickly after the new forces came on stream, although the speed at which it occurred varied around the country. For example, it was happening on a regular basis in Bedfordshire during the early 1840s but started slightly later in Nottinghamshire. However, initially, it seems to have occurred only in a minority of cases, perhaps 20 percent nationally by mid-century, although there were counties where it was more (or less) common. Thus,

[862] TNA HO 64/3/57.

[863] *The Norfolk Chronicle*, 26 October, 1839

[864] TNA HO 44/36/51.

[865] TNA HO 64/1/69.

[866] *The Norfolk Chronicle,* 5 October, 1840.

and typically, only about a fifth of matters tried on indictment in Bedfordshire in 1860 were prosecuted by police officers.[867]

Most commonly, during the early Victorian period, police prosecution occurred where an offence was very serious, where patrolling officers witnessed a crime or detained an offender after a hot pursuit, or where the victim, especially a female, was obviously too poor or otherwise indisposed to pursue the matter effectively. Thus, in November 1855, at the East Dereham petty sessions, conducted at the town Assembly Room, a saddler named Robert Johnson was summonsed by one PC Coghlan, the "prosecuting" police constable in the case, for assaulting Elizabeth Webster a few days earlier. He pleaded guilty but could have gone for trial on indictment. (He was fined £2 along with 14s 6d. costs.)[868] In March 1878, after Fuller Williamson allegedly attempted to murder his wife with a knife and poker, and was produced for examination before the Reverend John Fenwick, a JP sitting at the Reepham police court, it was noted that "Mr Chambers, the superintendent of police, attended to prosecute."[869] There was some initial and short-lived official and political resistance to police-initiated prosecutions. In 1849 the Home Office expressed doubts about the police monopolising prosecutions and stated that they should not be bound over to prosecute if the victim was willing to do this.[870]

In theory, police prosecution could allow proceedings to be brought even if the victim was totally set against it, although such cases were unlikely to be successful and so unusual. For example, in April 1859 James Lincoln, a farm labourer, was tried for setting fire to a stack of straw at Great Witchingham the previous September. The stack was owned by his employer, a local farmer. Lincoln, of previous good character, had been seen running from the stack after it caught fire in the middle of the day. He claimed that ashes from his pipe had set fire to it and that he had been running to find help to deal with the conflagration. Very significantly, his master had "refused to prosecute." Despite this, the matter had reached a jury, which acquitted Lincoln.[871]

More commonly in these situations, the police would decide that indicting a matter was not practicable. For example, in 1859 a stoker named Frederick Harvey gave himself up to a detective in the City of London, saying that a fortnight earlier he had stolen £12 10s from a woman in King's Lynn with whom his sister lodged. He had since become concerned that his sibling would be blamed for the theft. The detective then wrote to the King's Lynn police force, asking them to enquire into it. Word came back saying that the victim did not wish to prosecute the matter. The Lord Mayor of London, sitting as a City magistrate, admonished Harvey vigorously,

---

867 Emsley, Storch, "Prosecution," p. 49.

868 *The Norwich Mercury,* 14 November, 1855.

869 *The Ipswich Journal*, 9 March, 1878.

870 Emsley, Storch, "Prosecution," p. 49.

871 *The Bury and Norwich Post*, 5 April, 1859.

but then discharged him "as the lady does not choose to press any charge against you."[872]

Similarly, in September 1861, after a fierce domestic argument, Martin Pearce threatened to murder his mother and fired a shot at her through a locked door before leaving the family home at Toft Monks near Beccles. He was subsequently arrested. The matter came before a local JP. The mother and brother of the suspect suggested that it could be dealt with by binding Martin over to keep the peace. The magistrate rejected this very lenient option, and he was subsequently charged with attempted murder.[873] However, in October Pearce was brought back to court, and the mother reiterated her belief that her son had merely attempted to frighten her; he was bound over to keep the peace in the sum of £200, with two independent sureties of £100 each.[874]

More than 20 years later, in 1888 two men from Great Yarmouth were stabbed by George Edwards, a sailor armed with a clasp knife, during a drunken altercation. The wounds were not very serious and were treated at the local hospital. One of the victims "did not wish to take proceedings," and no further action was taken in his case, the police limiting themselves to pursuing the attack on the other man, finding several eyewitnesses to the incident, and bringing it before the town police court.[875]

Indirect Effect on Prosecution

However, the advent of the new police also had an important secondary or indirect effect on prosecution. It quickly became normal practice to summon officers to a (potential) crime scene. Typically, in late 1877 when 18-year-old Fanny Maria Nunn's screams and cries of "Don't!" disturbed the inhabitants of Diss at midnight, two of them immediately found a policeman before going with him to the source of the noise, a stretch of water known as the Mere.[876] More generally, it seems that some 78 percent of criminal cases that resulted in proceedings in late Victorian Ipswich (Suffolk) were reported to the police by the victim or by someone acting on their behalf, with others being reported by a third party. Few were discovered by the police themselves.[877]

However, once the police were involved they could take control of a case without formally prosecuting it themselves, by ushering reluctant crime victims before an examining magistrate, where they would be bound over to prosecute, without having the chance to think twice about whether to do so.[878] For example, in a

872 *The Daily News*, 1 November, 1859.

873 *Ibid.*, 30 September, 1861.

874 *The Liverpool Mercury etc.*, 14 October, 1861.

875 *The Ipswich Journal*, 9 November, 1888.

876 *The Glasgow Herald*, 6 December, 1877. *The Morning Post*, 6 December, 1877.

877 Mellaerts, "Criminal Justice," pp. 26-29.

878 Emsley, Storch, "Prosecution," p. 50.

Suffolk case, a builder found himself prosecuting a slater for stealing 24 tiles.[879] He freely admitted to the court that he "would not have instituted proceedings had not the constable been with him." Similarly, in 1869, after a tramp stole a pair of trousers from a shop in Newton in Montgomeryshire, the shopkeeper pursued and "thrashed" him. He subsequently admitted to JPs that he intended to let the man go, but a passerby had summoned the police in the meantime.[880] Once this was done, there was much less room for backing out of, or manipulating, the criminal process, as magistrates could not consent to a withdrawal from prosecution, while a failure to attend trial could lead to recognizances being forfeited (even if this did not always occur in practice). For example, in July 1844 50-year-old David Barker was accused of refusing to prefer a bill of indictment against Maria Harvey at the previous Norfolk quarter sessions. He stated that he had "wished to be excused prosecuting" her but did not have the funds to pay the recognizances he had entered to do so, and so attended court. The matter was referred to the assizes.[881]

Although such actions were ostensibly still private prosecutions, with the police merely acting as witnesses, they almost amounted to a form of police prosecution. As a result, the new police greatly amplified private prosecutions.[882] For this reason, in 1856 the chief constable of Norfolk thought that in nine felony cases out of ten a policeman was "virtually the public prosecutor." However, he had to keep this concealed as best he could, or people would think that the case had been "got up" by the officers.[883] This indirect relationship could occasion other problems. Thus, in 1849 a Lancashire woman who wished to prosecute her servant for theft, using her own solicitor, was informed by the magistrates' clerk that at Ulverton the superintendent of police was considered the "public prosecutor" and so had the power to employ a solicitor of his choice to conduct prosecutions. Apparently, this was usually the magistrates' clerk! Both the clerk and the bench refused to give the woman's solicitor the committal depositions. He duly informed his client that the "prosecution has been taken away from us against our will."[884]

Police pressure on victims to prosecute was not applied in all cases, being more likely if the crime was grave, the suspect had a bad criminal record, or if he had been detained after extensive police involvement. For example, in one Suffolk case, a chemist had a 13-year-old paper boy arrested for shoplifting. After the boy had been held overnight, the chemist was willing to let him go, provided he did not enter his shop again. Even so, proceedings still followed, not least because he had previous convictions and, as the chemist claimed during cross-examination, his prosecution was brought at the behest of the police. In another case, the landlord

879 Mellaerts, "Criminal Justice," pp. 19-52.

880 Jones, *Crime, Courts,* p. 63.

881 *The Bury and Norwich Post*, 10 July, 1844.

882 Emsley, Storch, "Prosecution," p. 50.

883 Black, *The police,* p. 35.

884 Emsley, Storch, "Prosecution," p. 53.

of a public house who had caught a 12-year-old boy attempting to steal money from his premises, handed him over to a police constable simply "with the intention of frightening him." Again, he ended up prosecuting the boy for attempted larceny; the youth had a bad criminal record.[885]

Increase in Police Prosecution

In the final decades of the nineteenth century, another change became apparent. The Criminal Law Commission had noted in 1845 that when the "party injured is compelled by the magistrate to act as prosecutor, the duty is frequently performed unwillingly and carelessly." Perhaps as a result, during the 1870s and 1880s the police began to prosecute more minor and routine offences, of a type that they had previously left to private prosecutors, rather than merely pressuring the latter to pursue a matter. (A few crimes, such as common assault, were still often entrusted to complainants).[886] As has been noted, the private prosecutor was turning blue by the end of the 1870s.[887] Victor Gatrell has characterized the years between the 1880s and the 1930s as the era of the "policeman state," and one aspect of the extension of police jurisdiction in the early part of that period was their increasing willingness to act as prosecutors in court.[888] It made prosecution a much more reliable process. Even earlier in the century, only a handful of cases had failed to proceed for non-attendance by a prosecutor once committed for trial, and this number dwindled further as the century advanced. In Norfolk some 203 people were committed for trial on indictment in 1879. All prosecutions went ahead.[889]

---

[885] Mellaerts, "Criminal Justice," pp. 19-52.

[886] Koyama, "Prosecution," p. 98.

[887] Douglas Hay, "Controlling the English Prosecutor," *Osgoode Hall Law Journal*, vol. 21, no. 2 (1983), p. 176.

[888] Gatrell, "Crime, Authority," vol. 3, pp. 243-310.

[889] *Return of Judicial Statistics of England and Wales, 1879* (London: HMSO, 1880), p. 51.

Chapter 9: Norfolk Criminal Courts

Introduction

The criminal courts of Victorian Norfolk can, very loosely, be divided into summary and jury forums. Summary courts, especially petty sessions, were the base of the pyramid of importance, presiding over large, and ever growing, numbers of lesser offences. Moving up the hierarchy, there were two or (depending on definition) three types of jury court. The lower two forums, which were of the same status, and filled the same niche, were the county quarter sessions and the borough (quarter) sessions. The latter were the borough equivalent of the former, and very similar, but employed a legally qualified (barrister) recorder rather than a JP chairman to preside over their hearings. The third, and highest, jury forum were the courts of assizes that sat in Norwich, and which were covered by pairs of visiting Westminster judges at least twice a year. Norfolk criminal courts will be dealt with in ascending order of importance.

Summary Courts

The Victorian era was to see a huge increase in the power of magistrates to dispose of criminal offences summarily, without a jury, while sitting outside quarter sessions. For example, by the end of the century, they could deal with children under 12 years of age charged with any indictable offence, other than murder or manslaughter, when their parents or guardians consented.[890] There were urgent practical reasons for such a change. Until well into the eighteenth century, the jury trial for serious crimes had been largely lawyer-free, judge-dominated, and conducted so rapidly that it could be used for most criminal matters. However, over ensuing decades, the rise of adversarial trial procedure, the advent of lawyers to the criminal process, and the increasing rigidity of the law of evidence introduced considerable complexity into such hearings. The problems this created were hugely compounded by the growth in jury trials. Between 1805 and 1842 the number of prosecutions in courts of assize and quarter sessions in England and Wales rose from 4,600 to 31,300. This was largely the result of a combination of rapid urbanization, population growth (by about half), enhanced policing, increased financial support for prosecutions, and perhaps a genuine, if exaggerated, real increase in crime.[891] This meant that trial on indictment ceased to be viable as a routine dispositive procedure. (In America it eventually contributed to the development of an aggressive form of plea bargaining.)[892]

---

890 *Judicial Statistics 1896*, p. 11.

891 Randall McGowen, "Getting to know the criminal class in nineteenth century England," *Nineteenth-Century Contexts*, vol. 14, no. 1 (1990), p. 44.

892 See generally, John H. Langbein, "Understanding the Short History of Plea Bargaining," *Law and Society Review*, vol. 13, no. 2 (1979), pp. 261–272.

Summary trial freed up the jury forums, especially quarter sessions. As a result of its increase in the early Victorian period, the number of jury trials, which had grown exponentially earlier in the nineteenth century, stopped rising after the early 1840s, and eventually started to fall, with a particularly sharp decline after 1855, despite the growing and increasingly regulated (by criminal law) population. By the close of the era, some 98 percent of criminal cases nationwide, very broadly construed to include all regulatory matters, were being dealt with summarily. Unsurprisingly, in these circumstances, many observers thought that the growth of summary forums amplified crime. Even in the late 1820s, the Norfolk clergyman and pamphleteer the Reverend Charles Brereton, like many other observers (both contemporary and modern), was persuaded that such courts had helped produce large numbers of offenders, who committed crimes that had previously been ignored.[893]

However, summary jurisdiction was not a recent phenomenon in 1837. Its growth had occasioned concern in the eighteenth century. It was purely a creature of statute (it did not exist at common law) and could be exercised in two forms. Some very minor, matters, such as simple drunkenness and vegetable theft, could be determined by a single lay justice sitting alone. In the early nineteenth century this might still be done in the magistrate's own home, some of which even had a "justice's parlour" for this very purpose. The use of such domestic premises for legal work gradually died out after the passing of an Act for the Better Regulation of Divisions in 1828.[894]

Even in the 1820s, trial of most summary offences required the presence of a bench of two or more JPs (stipendiary magistrates could sit alone) sitting together in what had become known as petty sessions (see below), and this was normal after the Summary Jurisdiction Act of 1848 came into force. The extension of trial for indictable offences to summary forums during the nineteenth century always required the use of a bench rather than a single magistrate. These courts could, of course, also determine the small number of matters that required only one JP, if only for the sake of convenience, and this often occurred in practice, so that the great majority of Victorian summary trials were held at petty sessions.

Attractions of Summary Trial

The advantages of summary proceedings were obvious; they made prosecuting minor offenders a relatively local, fast, inexpensive, and straightforward affair. Their procedure was simpler than that found on indictment, while their standards of evidential proof were probably lower in practice than those in the jury courts, whatever the theory may have been. Some modern academic observers have even suggested that, in some summary cases, the burden of proof was effectively reversed, with suspects being required to account for goods found in their possession, so dispensing with the need for private victims to testify to their provenance, and

---

893 Brereton, *Subordinate Magistracy*, pp. 5-6.

894 Cox, "Habitual Eccentricities," pp. 109-127.

permitting police officers to initiate and manage prosecutions.[895] However, the generality of such an interpretation has also been vigorously challenged, especially when considered outside the Metropolitan context, which was, to some extent, *sui generis*, and even had its own "special to area" offences.

Nevertheless, such a reversal in onus of proof did apply to some of the poaching cases that were tried summarily, in Norfolk as elsewhere in the country, under the Poaching Prevention Act in 1862. For example, at the Mundford Petty Sessions in 1862, a man named Fuller, who had been found in possession of a hare, in broad daylight, well away from any game preserves, but who refused to explain how he came into possession of the animal, was convicted of poaching despite there being no positive evidence of this. (He had a previous conviction for the same crime.)[896] Whatever the situation in this regard, summary courts did not experience the uncertainty engendered by use of a jury, while the increasingly complicated rules of evidence nationwide were probably tacitly ignored on many occasions, so that convictions were easier to obtain.

Significantly, their trials were also very much cheaper for the county than those held on indictment. At the Norfolk quarter sessions in January 1857, it was noted that, over the previous six months, there had been 81 cases tried at quarter sessions at a total cost of £577 10s, an average of about £7 2s 6d each. By contrast, under the Summary Jurisdiction Act 1855 there had been 79 trials at a total cost of £173 17s, an average of about £2 3s 6d for each trial. (This figure ignores summary trials for minor matters that had not previously been indictable.)[897] As a result, summary trials were well under a third of the cost of those conducted for the same offences in front of a jury at quarter sessions. The difference between those tried at petty sessions and assizes was even greater. Petty sessions clerks also pared down prosecution costs as much as possible, so that the average amount, if awarded, was just over £1, while those at trials at quarter sessions and assizes averaged over £9 each (those for the latter forum being significantly greater). Fewer lawyers, whether counsel or solicitors, were employed at summary forums. Fewer witnesses were called and the distances they travelled were much smaller, so that incidental expenses were also greatly reduced and general convenience increased.[898] Those in custody awaiting trial were held for much shorter periods of time, saving further expense for the county.

It was hoped that the availability of summary trial might help prevent extremely trivial examples of indictable crimes going for a jury hearing, something that was thought to undermine the reputation of the higher forums as well as leading to disproportionate cost. In April 1847 the JP and MP Robert Palmer opined in

---

[895] Bruce P. Smith, "English Criminal Justice Administration,1650-1850: A Historiographic Essay," *Law and History Review*, vol. 25, no. 3 (2007), p. 620.

[896] *The Era*, 14 December, 1862.

[897] *The Bury and Norwich Post*, 13 January, 1857.

[898] Taylor, "Rationing Crime," p. 575, p. 588.

parliament that, having acted for many years as chairman of quarter sessions, he thought that "not three-fourths of the criminal cases were, if they looked to the value of the article stolen, worth the trouble of being brought into court. If an apple were taken out of a basket, a magistrate must send the case to the quarter-sessions; and many instances occurred in which prosecutions for stealing articles not worth 1s., entailed a charge upon the county-rate of not less than 12l."[899] For a specific, if extreme, example can be considered a case from the Norfolk quarter sessions held at Swaffham in January 1842. A man from Old Buckenham, some 26 miles away, was brought to court to stand trial for stealing cut timber worth just a penny. He was acquitted, as it was impossible to positively identify the wood as stolen, no one being willing to swear to its provenance. The absurdity of this case, and its disproportionately expensive disposal, occasioned surprise, even at the time.[900]

Those accused of very minor or regulatory offences might be summonsed to appear at petty sessions; if they failed to attend, a warrant could then be issued for their arrest. Others, accused of more serious offences, would be arrested, charged, and produced by the police. For some relatively minor crimes a summary trial might even be carried out *ex parte*, in the suspect's absence, if they failed to attend court, this being allowed by statute. For example, in April 1853, in neighbouring Suffolk, two men named Bean and Brewster, accused of an assault, were summonsed to appear at Melford petty sessions. They did not attend, and the bench heard the evidence and convicted them, sentencing the former to four months' and the latter to two months' imprisonment. The same evening, the pair were apprehended in a tavern at Glemsford.[901]

Many petty sessions prosecutions during the Victorian era continued to be for longstanding minor and regulatory offences, matters that had always been dealt with summarily, whether they involved carrying excess numbers in a carriage or evading tolls on private roads. Even at the end of the period, a high proportion still involved highway offences and violations of the poor laws.[902] For example, in 1896 307 cases involving breach of county or borough byelaws were prosecuted summarily in Norfolk, along with 243 allegations of begging.[903] More specifically, in October 1837, at the Thetford petty sessions, a man was fined for persistently leaving his cart in public thoroughfares in the town.[904] In November 1855, at the East Dereham petty sessions, William Daynes, a Mattishall labourer, was summonsed by

---

899 Hansard HC Deb 28 April 1847 vol. 92 cols. 33-47.

900 *The Bury and Norwich Post*, 19 January, 1842

901 *Ibid.*, 27 April, 1853.

902 Porritt, "At Petty Sessions," p. 473.

903 *Judicial Statistics, 1896*, p. 81.

904 *The Bury & Norwich Post, & East Anglian: Or, Suffolk, Norfolk, Essex, Cambridge, and Ely Intelligencer*, 18 October, 1837.

the police for wilfully obstructing free passage on a highway in Hockering, and fined 1 shilling, with 5 shillings costs.[905]

Many other cases involved alcohol related offences. The Licensing Act of 1872, which clarified the law on alcohol-related offences, further encouraged such prosecutions.[906] In 1899 Norfolk saw 705 people accused of drunkenness being tried summarily.[907] For example, in September 1837, at the East Dereham petty sessions, John Billham was fined 14 shillings (including costs) for being drunk and disorderly, while Stephen Stern was fined the same amount for being drunk on a Sunday morning. At the same petty sessions, the owners of four public or beer houses were fined for various licensing offences, such as allowing disorderly conduct on their premises late at night or failing to close at appropriate times.[908] Almost 50 years later, in March 1886, in neighbouring Suffolk, the strangely named Golden Bugg from Flowton appeared before the petty sessions at Needham Market for being drunk on a local highway. He pleaded guilty and was fined 6s and 8s 6d costs (which he immediately paid).[909] Those with previous convictions for similar offences, or who had been disorderly, as well as inebriated when arrested, might pay more, perhaps twice as much in fines and costs. Summary prosecutions for defective weights and measures and game-law offences were common long before the advent of the new Queen and continued to be after 1837.

However, numerous new, minor, offences were created during the Victorian era that could only be determined in front of JPs. In 1867 James Hammick even claimed – with considerable exaggeration – that there were 2,000 offences for which magistrates could impose a fine or imprisonment.[910] For example, the advent of the new railways created numerous minor crimes. Thus at the Diss petty sessions in May 1880 Robert Gayner was fined £1 for travelling on the railway without a ticket, after being prosecuted by an inspector from the Great Eastern Railway police.[911] At the same forum in December 1887, Frederick Rogers, a butcher from Scole, was convicted of the same offence and fined £2 plus costs.[912] In 1899 20 people accused of railway-related offences (mainly fare evasion) were tried summarily in Norfolk.[913]

Some new regulatory offences were of a highly technical nature. Illustrative of such novel "crimes," in April 1890 the Earl of Leicester, who was the lord lieutenant of

---

905 *The Norwich Mercury*, 14 November, 1855.

906 Wood, "Drinking, Fighting," pp. 71-80.

907 Anon., *Statistics Relating…1899* (1901), p. 122.

908 *The Bury and Norwich Post*, 20 September, 1837.

909 *The Ipswich Journal*, 18 March, 1886.

910 Hammick, "Judicial Statistics," p. 387.

911 *The Bury and Norwich Post*, 4 May, 1880.

912 *The Ipswich Journal*, 16 December 1887.

913 Anon., *Statistics Relating…1899* (1901), p. 123.

Norfolk, was summonsed at the Walsingham petty sessions for failing to report that two cows on his estate were suffering from pleuro-pneumonia. The nobleman's agent appeared on his behalf and admitted the charge, offering mitigation, and the earl was fined the full penalty of £20 and costs. (Given his status, this prosecution was itself an indication of an expansion in the rule of law.)[914]

Other new summary offences were indicative of changing social mores and a state that was continuously expanding its involvement in the lives of its subjects. For example, offences protecting animals were first created in 1822, and cases were quickly being brought on a regular basis. Typically, in 1873 the Society for the Prevention of Cruelty to Animals (RSPCA) prosecuted a cattle dealer named James Coker at the Walsingham petty sessions, for failing to provide food and water for a large flock of sheep being sent by rail from Scotland to Norfolk (two of the animals died). He was fined £52 (including costs) but announced that he would appeal the matter to the Court of Queen's Bench.[915] In November 1888, at the Blofield Petty Sessions, a farmer, his steward, and two farm workers were summonsed for dehorning 16 bullocks the previous month, after an information for ill treatment was laid by an inspector of the RSPCA.[916]

The summary courts became particularly involved in enforcing school attendance and the vaccination of children after both became compulsory. The latter would often follow an order from the court requiring that a named child be treated. For example, at the North Erpingham petty sessions in September 1894, Louisa Catherine Thursby, a vaccination officer, secured numerous orders that specified local children who were to be vaccinated within three months. In these cases, the defendants were usually the children's fathers.[917] A failure to comply with such an order could lead to punishment. Thus, in June 1888 James Raspberry, a Gayton farmer, was fined 2s 6d at the Grimston petty sessions for neglecting to have his child vaccinated.[918]

On one assessment, the Elementary Education Act 1870 resulted in 96,601 parents nationally being brought before the courts in its first year of operation for the non-attendance of their offspring. By the late 1870s, a little over one in 1,000 people nationwide were being prosecuted annually, a figure that had risen to just under three by the early 1890s. A total of about 500,000 were prosecuted during the initial 20 years of the legislation.[919] Such actions were well evidenced in Norfolk. Thus, in February 1894, at the North Erpingham petty sessions, Henry Allen, a

914 *The County Gentleman: Sporting Gazette, Agricultural Journal, and "The Man about Town,"* 12 April, 1890, p. 510.

915 *The Ipswich Journal*, 28 October, 1873.

916 *The Norfolk Chronicle,* 26 November, 1888.

917 NRO 24/4/1 North Erpingham Petty Sessions, Minute Book B p. 11.

918 *The Bury and Norwich Post*, 5 June, 1888.

919 Yue-Chim Richard Wong, "An Economic Analysis of the Crime Rate in England and Wales, 1857-92," *Economica*, vol. 62, no. 246 (1995), p. 238. Taylor, *Hooligans, Harlots,* p. 32.

fisherman, was fined just 6d plus costs (much more than the fine) with three days' imprisonment in lieu of payment for failing to ensure that his daughter Florence went to school. A more typical penalty at this forum was a shilling fine with four shillings' costs (with the same three-day imprisonment in lieu of payment).[920] The sums could be greater, with fines of 2s 6d not being uncommon.

The summary courts also continued to exercise the JPs' ancient powers to bind people over to keep the peace, even where a conviction had not been sought or secured. (It could also be used as a minor punishment for those who *had* been convicted, as discussed in Chapter 15.) In these situations, the person bound over would forfeit a designated sum if they troubled the courts again within a specified period. Thus in 1837 at the Thetford petty sessions, Ann Hauxley was bound over for three months for using obscene language in the street and creating a disturbance.[921] More than 40 years later, at the Norwich police court, in May 1879, two prize-fighters, their seconds, the referee, and various others who had been actively involved in organizing a public bout for a ten-guinea cup, were all summonsed and then bound over to keep the peace.[922] This power was also frequently used in domestic cases. For example, a late example of a "wife sale" (a form of de facto divorce) lay behind a case involving Samuel Wilkinson, who appeared before the Norwich magistrates, accused of assaulting his wife. He produced a witnessed receipt for the sale of his spouse for a guinea and was merely bound over to keep the peace.[923]

Indictable Offences Tried Summarily

Very significantly, when it came to their impact on the wider criminal-justice system, a series of nineteenth-century statutes meant that many previously "indictable only" crimes could, in certain circumstances, be determined by magistrates sitting on their own (without a jury) at petty sessions. As a result, in 1875 only 30 percent of indictable crimes in England and Wales were still going for jury trial; by 1889 the figure had fallen to 20 percent. It remained at about this level to the end of the Victorian era (and for some time beyond).[924] Interestingly, the figure was smaller in Norfolk than in many other English counties. In 1901 just over 74 percent of indictable cases in Norfolk were dealt with summarily, giving it one of the lowest rates, if not the lowest, in the country (County Durham, at over 91 percent, may have had the highest).[925] Nevertheless, summary hearings had become the norm for

---

920 NRO 24/4/1 North Erpingham Petty Sessions, Minute Book B p. 11.

921 *The Bury & Norwich Post, & East Anglian: Or, Suffolk, Norfolk, Essex, Cambridge, and Ely Intelligencer*, 18 October, 1837.

922 *The Sheffield Independent*, 27 May, 1879.

923 *The Norfolk Chronicle*, 6 May, 1842.

924 R.M. Jackson, "The Incidence of Jury Trial during the Last Century," *Modern Law Review*, vol. 1, no. 2 (1937), pp. 134-135.

925 Anon., *Statistics Relating...1899* (1901), p. 14.

less serious but indictable offences of violence and dishonesty, even in Norfolk.[926] This process had started before the accession of the new Queen.

Crimes of Violence

In the early nineteenth century, only a small number of very specific assaults, such as those made on collectors of turnpike tolls, had been triable by JPs sitting without a jury.[927] During the 1820s various observers, including some magistrates, suggested that making ordinary assaults triable in a summary forum would be less costly and more convenient, and especially helpful for those of limited means.[928] As a result, it was thought "expedient" under s.27 of the Offences Against the Person Act of 1828 to grant two or more magistrates the power to determine common assaults summarily, allowing them to impose fines of up to £5 (with custodial sentences of up to two months in lieu of payment). Henceforth such crimes could be tried at petty sessions or committed for trial on indictment (as previously), depending on the view taken by the magistrates as to their seriousness.[929] The latter course would be employed where the magistrates were persuaded that the case was a "fit Subject for a Prosecution on Indictment." It was hoped that this development would free up the quarter sessions, limiting them to more serious assaults.[930] Subsequently the Offences Against the Person Act 1861 and the Summary Jurisdiction Act 1879 extended the maximum sentences that magistrates could pass for such crimes in specific situations.

After 1828 comparatively few simple assaults were referred to a jury court for trial; instead they quickly became a mainstay of the offences tried at petty sessions. For example, at those held for Blofield and Walsham in North Norfolk between 1839 and 1878, some 1,425 cases (31.2 percent of the total heard), an average of about 35 a year, were for assault, by far the largest category of crime determined at this forum.[931] By contrast, in 1838 just six cases of simple assault were sent for trial on indictment in Norfolk (of which three produced convictions). There were also five indicted cases of assault on officers in the execution of their duty while a handful of the new, much more serious, statutory assaults also went to jury trial.[932] (Most

---

926 Taylor, "Rationing Crime," p. 576.

927 Wyatt, *Calendar,* p. xvi.

928 Lisa Surridge, "On the Offenses Against the Person Act, 1828." *BRANCH: Britain, Representation and Nineteenth-Century History*. http://www.branchcollective.org Extension of *Romanticism and Victorianism on the Net.* http://www.ronjournal.org. Last accessed 18 March, 2022.

929 David Philips, Crime and Authority in Victorian England: The Black Country 1835–1860 (London: Croom Helm, 1977), p. 40.

930 Surridge, "Offenses," *BRANCH*.

931 Lee, *Rural Society,* p. 248.

932 *Criminal Offenders…1838* (London: HMSO, 1839), p. 50.

of these could not be tried summarily). In 1899 567 people in Norfolk accused of common assault were tried at petty sessions.[933]

For example, in one such summary disposal, in October 1837, at the Thetford petty sessions, held before the town mayor and magistrates, Henry Beets was fined 9 shillings and costs for assaulting another man.[934] At the same forum, in August the following year, Elizabeth Crane, a married woman, was convicted of a violent assault on another female and, when she could not pay the fine, sentenced to 14 days' imprisonment.[935] Some received the maximum sentence. In November 1840, at the Thetford petty sessions, William Fuller received the highest fiscal penalty of £5 for assault, and, when he could not pay this sum, was committed to the borough gaol for the full two months.[936] Similarly, at the East Dereham petty sessions in November 1856, Elijah Goff, a Mattishall labourer, was convicted of assaulting a farmer the previous month, fined £5 plus 12s costs, and in default of payment was committed to Norwich Castle prison for two months' imprisonment with hard labour.[937]

Less typically of such cases, given the social status of the defendants, in August 1866, the Reverend Samuel Homfray of Bintree and his churchwarden were tried, convicted, and fined £5 for assault at the Reepham petty sessions (the bench included a clerical magistrate). The offence occurred when Homfray and the warden attempted to physically evict Thomas Cronshay, formerly the leader of the parish singers, from his customary pew during morning service. An affray ensued, and Cronshay later brought charges against the two men. (Homfray unavailingly brought countercharges against Cronshay over a separate scuffle in the churchyard.)[938]

The use of petty sessions encouraged the prosecution of assaults that might previously have been considered too minor or otherwise inappropriate for court action, fuelling the advance of social regulation. Even in the late 1820s, the Norfolk clergyman and pamphleteer the Reverend Charles Brereton, like many other observers (both contemporary and modern), was persuaded that such courts had helped greatly increased the number of offenders, as they committed crimes that had previously been ignored.[939] In these situations some JPs, dealing with very technical cases of assault, merely required a defendant to pay the cost of the prosecution, as was expressly permitted by the 1828 statute.[940] For example, in May 1859 Christmas

---

933 Anon., *Statistics Relating..1899* (1901), p. 122.

934 *The Bury & Norwich Post, & East Anglian: Or, Suffolk, Norfolk, Essex, Cambridge, and Ely Intelligencer*, 18 October, 1837.

935 *The Bury and Norwich Post*, 15 August, 1838.

936 *Ibid.*, 2 December, 1840.

937 *The Norfolk News,* 15 November, 1856.

938 Lee, *Rural Society,* p. 248.

939 Brereton, *The Subordinate Magistracy,* pp. 5-6.

940 Tim Shakesheff, "Wood and Crop Theft in Rural Herefordshire, 1800–60," *Rural History*, vol. 13, no. 1 (2002), p. 10.

Tofts, a cattle dealer from Mattishall, accused David Catton, a horse dealer from Hingham, of throwing sheep dung at him on the public road. The assault case was dismissed by JPs after Catton paid the 7s 6d costs of the prosecution, albeit with a verbal caution that, if he were brought before the bench again on a similar charge, he would be bound over to keep the peace.[941]

Similarly, at the North Erpingham petty sessions in February 1894, a rural postman, William Fisher, was accused of assaulting his wife, Mahala (who was also the complainant). An order was made by the magistrates dismissing the information on payment by the defendant of costs of 11s 6d (with seven days' hard labour in lieu of payment).[942] The bench went further at the Fakenham petty sessions in 1890, when a clergyman, the Reverend Morris Fuller, was prosecuted for assaulting the assistant overseer of Great Ryburgh. They dismissed the case outright, on the basis that the allegation was of "so trivial a nature that they refused to convict," as was also allowed by the statute. The magistrates blamed the prosecution on ill feeling among the parish officials.[943]

As the Fisher case suggests, jurisdiction over such crimes allowed Victorian petty sessions to expand their role in policing domestic violence, a previously neglected area. Although wives could prosecute their husbands in the jury courts prior to the 1828 Act, they had often been reluctant to do so, if only because of the expense, physical inconvenience, and delay that it entailed. Summary proceedings were a very much more attractive proposition.[944] For example, in 1874, at the King's Lynn petty sessions, a case of wife-beating by a local town councillor came for trial. Both parties were legally represented. The husband admitted the assault but claimed that there was provocation. The wife denied this, said that such violence had gone on for 35 years, and that she could no longer endure it. As was common in marital situations, the case was adjourned to allow the parties to draw up a deed of separation.[945]

Magistrates' powers in this regard were enhanced by the Matrimonial Causes Act of 1878, which gave them the authority to grant quick separation orders to women who had been the victims of aggravated physical assault.[946] Thus, at the Norwich Police Court in 1888, Charles Dover, a clerk, was sentenced to a month's imprisonment for a "brutal assault" on his wife. A judicial separation order was also granted to the woman, and her husband was ordered to pay her 10 shillings

---

941 *The Norwich Mercury,* 11 May, 1859.

942 NRO 24/4/1 North Erpingham Petty Sessions, Minute Book B p. 1

943 *The Bury and Norwich Post,* 8 January, 1889.

944 Clark, Anna. "Humanity or justice? Wifebeating and the law in the eighteenth and nineteenth centuries" in Carol Smart (ed.), *Regulating Womanhood: Historical Essays on Marriage, Motherhood and* Sexuality (Abingdon: Routledge, 1992), p. 198.

945 *The Bury and Norwich Post*, 24 November, 1874.

946 Jo Turner, "'A Shocking State of Domestic Unhappiness': Male Victims of Female Violence and the Courts in Late Nineteenth Century Stafford," *Societies*, vol. 9, no. 2 (2019), p. 40.

a week in maintenance.[947] At the Yarmouth police court, the same year, a Norfolk militiaman was fined £1 and costs for striking a woman who appears to have been his spouse.[948]

However, well into the Victorian period, the longstanding tradition of minor offences, particularly common assaults, being settled without adjudication, with the knowledge and approval of the magistrates, can be identified at summary forums, although some observers, such as the clerk to the Westminster magistrates, had thought it "hazardous" even in the 1840s. Indeed, it was often actively encouraged in domestic cases. This also reflected the reluctance of the new police to become involved in such prosecutions. For example, half the assaults set down for trial before the North Erpingham petty sessions in 1852 received such a disposal. Thus, in May 1852 Mary Hammond accused Charles Peace of common assault, but the matter was "settled out of court." At the same petty sessions James Middleton accused John Bishop of an identical crime, but the matter was settled in the same fashion. By contrast, two other cases of common assault went for trial, were proved before the magistrates, and produced fines of 6d and costs of 8s 6d for each defendant. [949]

Offences Against Property

The process of extending summary trial to indictable crimes did not stop at low-level violence. It eventually extended to many crimes of dishonesty. At the start of the Victorian period, vagrancy provisions had sometimes been used, in a rather elastic fashion, to deal summarily with minor property crimes that might, in theory, have been indicted as theft. Additionally, a few crimes governing the taking of wood from trees and fences, and the theft of fruit and vegetables from orchards, gardens, and fields, had long existed, some of them being restated in the Larceny Act 1827.[950] For example, in May 1838, at the Thetford petty sessions, Sarah Ricketts was committed to the borough gaol for 14 days after being convicted of stealing a quantity of turnip tops that had been planted for seed.[951] However, the Victorian era saw ordinary forms of theft and related crimes of dishonesty coming within the summary courts' jurisdiction, in appropriate circumstances.

This was a controversial development and followed the recommendations of various parliamentary committees and politicians, made over several decades, who were attracted by the speed and economy of such a disposal. Nevertheless, there had been considerable resistance to such suggestions. Thus, proposals that juveniles

---

947 *The Bury and Norwich Post,* 19 June, 1888.

948 *Ibid.,* June 12, 1888.

949 NRO PS 24/1/1 Hundred of North Erpingham Norfolk Special and Petty Sessions record commencing 3 July, 1841. Assault cases were not the only ones dealt with in this manner. The following month, in June 1852, at the Erpingham petty sessions, an allegation of malicious (i.e., criminal) damage made by William Ward against Thomas Bell was also "settled out of court."

950 Hanly, "Summary Jurisdiction," pp. 285-286.

951 *The Bury and Norwich Post*, 16 May, 1838.

be denied jury trial in some situations had attracted strong opposition when first mooted in the 1820s. In 1841 the Reverend Harry Farr Yeatman, a Dorset magistrate of 28 years' standing, deplored proposals to make JPs judges of both law and fact. He (rightly) thought that arguments that such cases would be confined to a modest list of offences would prove mistaken, as "the wedge, when once inserted, might be driven deeper and deeper."[952]

Despite such opposition, the Juvenile Offenders Act 1847 allowed certain forms of theft that had been committed by children below the age of 14 to be dealt with summarily, *provided* they consented to such a disposal. Inevitably, this prompted renewed concern. John Roebuck complained in the House of Commons that "these extraordinary powers were to be given, not to a learned Judge, but it might be to a fox-hunting justice."[953] Even so, in 1850 statute raised the jurisdictional age limit for juvenile offenders to 16 years, although the MP Charles Law noted the irony of extending summary jurisdiction so soon after Parliament had passed the 1836 legislation protecting the accused when tried on indictment by allowing them to make a full defence using counsel and to inspect and use prosecution depositions.[954] (Modern historians might see some connection between the two developments.) Additional statutes in 1855, 1879, and 1899 further extended the possibility of summary trial for the young.[955] This had a significant impact on the number of juveniles who fell into the criminal-justice system. Thus, an apparent rise in the number of young offenders between 1848 and 1850 can simply be explained by the 1850 Act's increasing summary jurisdiction for thieves from 14 to 16 years of age. [956]

Even more significantly, the Criminal Justice Act 1855 extended summary trial for theft to adults, in certain situations, despite Charles Law's fears that this would deprive a JP of popular respect and make him the "enemy of the poorer classes of society."[957] The statute allowed magistrates' jurisdiction where the goods appropriated were worth less than 5 shillings, and the defendant agreed to have his case dealt with summarily or, alternatively, where the goods were worth more than 5 shillings, the magistrates were prepared to accept jurisdiction, and the defendant was willing to plead guilty before them (rather than there being a contested trial). The sentences passed in these circumstances were often much more modest than those imposed for the same crimes in the jury courts, while under the 1855 Act a summary conviction for what was technically a felony did not lead to forfeiture, unlike

---

952 Yeatman, *A Letter*, p. 9.

953 Hansard HC Deb 28 April 1847 vol. 92 cols. 33-47.

954 Hansard HC Deb 20 March 1850 vol. 109 cols. 1199-205.

955 Kate Bradley, "Inside the Inner London Juvenile Court, c. 1909-1953," *Crimes and Misdemeanours* vol. 3, no. 2 (2009), p. 37, p. 40.

956 Walliss, "Lies, Damned Lies," pp. 573-584.

957 Hansard HC Deb 20 March 1850 vol. 109 cols. 1199-205.

the (theoretical) situation with trial on indictment until 1870, further increasing its attractions to the accused.[958] (See Chapter 15.)

An early example of the exercise of such rights by adults can be seen in a case tried at the East Dereham petty sessions in December 1855. John Loveday, an elderly Mattishall labourer, was charged with stealing 11 harvested swedes (not taken from the fields), worth just 3d. Loveday consented to the case being heard by the magistrates, pleaded guilty, and was sentenced to prison in Norwich Castle for 21 days, without hard labour ("being an old man").[959]

Similarly, in 1879 two men were accused of involvement in the theft of a bushel-and-a-half of barley from a Diss-based maltster. It was claimed that Charles Bacon stole the grain from his employer and that Joshua Ruffles, a local small farmer and bricklayer, received it from him. At the Diss petty sessions, Bacon accepted summary jurisdiction, pleaded guilty, and was sentenced to six weeks' imprisonment with hard labour. Ruffles pleaded not guilty and was committed for trial at the Norfolk quarter sessions. (He was bailed in the meantime.) At the same sessions, two labourers were accused of stealing wheat, a whip, and a greatcoat from a barn. The property had been found in the possession of another man, Solomon Raynor, who was also charged with stealing the items or alternatively with receiving them. The two labourers pleaded guilty and were sentenced to two months' imprisonment with hard labour in Norwich Castle. Raynor pleaded not guilty and was committed for trial to the quarter sessions (bail also being granted).[960] Presumably, in both cases, the alleged receivers were intending to rely on the prosecution's having difficulty proving that they knew or believed that the items were stolen.

As with juveniles, changes to jurisdiction had a major impact on adult prosecutions. The immediate effect of the Criminal Justice Act 1855 was to reduce committals for trial on indictment by a fifth, as cases were diverted to summary forums.[961] More specifically, there was a fall in the number of adult committals nationally for indictable offences against property from 23,241 in 1853 to 15,928 in 1856. [962]

Ultimately, several previously indictable-only property offences became "either way" crimes for adults, along with simple larceny. They included theft from the person (pickpocketing), theft by servants, receiving stolen goods, embezzlement, and obtaining property by false pretences. The financial value of appropriations that could be dealt with by magistrates was also increased. In 1879 the Summary

---

958 K.J. Kesselring, "Felony Forfeiture in England, c.1170-1870," *The Journal of Legal History*, vol. 30, no. 3 (2009), p. 221.

959 *The Norwich Mercury,* 12 December, 1855.

960 *The Bury and Norwich Post*, 2 December, 1879.

961 Hammick, "Judicial Statistics," p. 404.

962 Walliss, "Lies, Damned Lies," pp. 573-584.

Jurisdiction Act raised the 5 shillings jurisdiction limit (irrespective of plea) for theft or embezzlement to £2, provided that the accused person agreed.[963]

Furthermore, under s.13 of the 1879 Act, an adult charged before a court of summary jurisdiction with any of a range of indictable offences – apart from very serious crimes such as murder, manslaughter, rape, and robbery – might have the opportunity to plead guilty and be dealt with summarily. In these situations, the court would need to be satisfied that, having regard to the nature and circumstances of the alleged offence and the antecedents of the accused, it might be adequately punished by a maximum sentence of six months' imprisonment (with or without hard labour). If he pleaded not guilty (or failed to answer when the matter was put to him), he would be referred to trial on indictment before a jury (at quarter sessions or assizes) in the normal manner.

For example, in a case of June 1888, two locally resident sailors appeared at the Yarmouth police court, accused of stealing a publican's watch. Perhaps conveniently, it was valued at precisely £2, which meant the men could be dealt with by the same forum (with their agreement) even if they pleaded not guilty. They were convicted and sentenced to just a month's imprisonment.[964] At the same petty sessions, Jemima Legatt was sentenced to six weeks' imprisonment for stealing a dress and two jackets together worth £1 3s.[965] On a larger scale, in October the following year, after Wroxham House was destroyed by fire, a large quantity of wine was stolen from its cellars. At the petty sessions held at the Shirehall in Norwich the following month, seven people were convicted of the theft. (It was alleged that one of the accused had taken away wine in a bucket.)[966]

As a result of these developments, by 1860 73 percent of all non-violent larcenies nationally were being tried summarily, and by 1900 this figure had risen to 88 percent.[967] Theft quickly made up the second-largest general category of "conventional" crimes tried at petty sessions, albeit well behind assault. Thus, at those held for Blofield and Walsham between 1839 and 1878, 10.2 percent of cases involved larceny.[968] More generally, in 1899, 256 people in Norfolk accused of simple larceny were tried summarily, along with 12 accused of larceny from the person (pickpocketing), 23 of larceny by a servant, nine of receiving stolen goods, nine of

---

963 Emsley, *Crime and Society,* p. 215.

964 *The Bury and Norwich Post*, 19 June,1888.

965 *Ibid.* , 12 June, 1888.

966 *The Norfolk Chronicle,* 25 October, 1889.

967 V.A.C. Gatrell, "The Decline of Theft and Violence in Victorian and Edwardian England," in *Crime and the Law: The Social History of Crime in Western Europe Since 1500*, Gatrell et al. (eds.), (London: Europe, 1980), pp. 301–2.

968 Lee, *Rural Society,* p. 238.

embezzlement, and four of obtaining property by false pretences (all of which were potentially indictable crimes).[969]

As with assault, for defendants planning to plead guilty, the statutory limitations on maximum sentences found at the summary forum, and the magistrates' frequent reluctance to impose even these, along with the speed and convenience of the hearing, could be very attractive. Quite often, when a defendant elected summary trial for an either-way matter, the decision was closely followed by a guilty plea, as was the case at the Thetford petty sessions in August 1891, after John Thompson unsuccessfully attempted to steal a large piece of lead. He was stopped by another workman before he had got very far and returned the metal. Even so, the matter was reported to the police, and he eventually received three months' imprisonment.[970]

Of course, six months' imprisonment was often not deemed to be an adequate punishment, even for juveniles. Thus, at the Thetford petty sessions of June 1882, 13-year-old George Ward was accused of arson after setting fire to a shed and destroying it. (He had earlier been told off by its owner.) He initially blamed two innocent people before confessing to the crime. After the prosecution evidence had been given, and the magistrates retired, they decided both that there was a case to answer and that, despite the defendant's age, it was too grave for them to determine. They committed the matter to the assizes. (The boy was bailed in consideration of his youth, after his mother was bound in the sum of £10 for his appearance at trial.)[971]

Nevertheless, JPs could sometimes be erratic as to when they would accept summary jurisdiction, agreeing to it or rejecting it in inappropriate circumstances. In March 1871, at the Norwich police court, Richard Hoskins, a National Provincial Bank clerk, was charged with stealing £1,835 from his employers. The magistrates agreed to deal with the case summarily and, on the prisoner's pleading guilty, sentenced him to just six months' imprisonment with hard labour (the maximum punishment available to them), despite the very large amount taken and the gross breach of trust.[972] Seven months later, in October 1871, at Norwich quarter sessions, Henry Brown Woolsey, a former clerk at the Carrow Works, pleaded guilty to feloniously embezzling £558 from his employers. He was sentenced to five years' penal servitude, although the prosecutor had recommended him to mercy.[973] Even at the time, observers could not help noting that there had been a major discrepancy in sentencing between the two cases.

Where present, the legal entitlement to jury trial was taken seriously, the courts being careful to ensure that there had been a genuine consent to summary disposal.

969 Anon., *Statistics Relating...1899* (1901), p. 122.

970 *The Bury and Norwich Post*, 1 September, 1891.

971 *Ibid.*, 13 June, 1882.

972 *The Norfolk Chronicle*, 9 March, 1871.

973 *Ibid.*, 26 October, 1871.

If a defendant had not been informed of his right to trial by jury (for an either-way offence) before he pleaded guilty in the magistrates' court, his plea would be deemed bad. Thus, in a case of 1898 Mr Justice Wright held that the "duty to inform having been imposed upon the Court for the protection of all accused persons, the right to be informed could not be waived."[974]

Even very minor matters continued to go for trial on indictment if the accused so wished. At the combined Norfolk and Suffolk spring assizes held at Ipswich in May 1886, James Barnes, a fisherman, sat on his entitlement when accused of stealing 4d worth of tarts from a Norwich shop after the assistant refused to serve him. As prosecuting counsel observed to the jury in this case, the "reason that the case occupied their time was that the prisoner had claimed his undoubted right of trial before a jury instead of being summarily dealt with before the Norwich Justices." (Barnes was convicted and received 14 days' imprisonment with hard labour).[975]

The Organization of Petty Sessions

Petty Sessions had evolved from the meetings of groups of JPs that took place around the country during the seventeenth and eighteenth centuries. Along with their criminal jurisdiction, they also handled many local administrative issues, such as poor relief, parish public works, licensing of alehouses, bastardy orders, and disputes between employers and employees.36 To some extent, they became minor quarter sessions in this regard, their increased uniformity and professionalism allowing powers that had hitherto been exercised by the lower jury court to be transferred down to them. They also conducted some direct supervision of parish constables, instructing them to perform certain duties, and sometimes even issuing search or arrest warrants for them to serve, although most of these were still issued by JPs sitting out of sessions.

Petty sessions were usually held in divisions that were based on the ancient county hundreds. In 1825 Norfolk had 33 petty sessions divisions, one of the highest totals in the country, and second only to the huge county of Yorkshire (the number subsequently fell slightly). By contrast, and to consider a range of other counties, Somerset, Cornwall, Wiltshire, and Lincolnshire all had 16 each, Kent 14, Surrey 11, Huntingdonshire only three, and tiny Rutland just one.[976] Gloucestershire had 18 petty sessions divisions after 1828.[977]

In 1828 quarter sessions were formally empowered to revise these divisions every ten years, and to create additional divisions where necessary, while after 1836 attempts were sometimes made to link them to the new poor-law unions.[978] (There were 22

974 *Regina* v. *Cockshott and Others* [1898] 1 QB 582.

975 *The Ipswich Journal*, 6 May, 1886.

976 Powell, *Statistical Illustrations,* p. 14.

977 Wyatt, *Calendar,* p. viii.

978 Bentley, *English Criminal Justice,* p. 21.

of these in Norfolk, administered by Boards of Guardians). As a result, at the start of the Victorian period, there were just over 700 petty sessional divisions nationally, 25 of them in Norfolk, still largely based on the boundaries of the historic hundreds. Its four major boroughs – Great Yarmouth, King's Lynn, Norwich, and Thetford – also had their own petty sessions and areas and can be added to the total (making 29).

Each Division would hold petty sessions on a regular basis at set times and places. For example, those for the South Erpingham division were held at Aylsham; the petty sessions for Eynsford were conducted at Reepham; those for Tunstead and Happing were held at North Walsham; and those for Earsham were conducted at Harleston. Occasionally the chosen town or village within a division would be changed. Thus, in 1878, a petition was drawn up for the removal of petty sessions from Mundford to nearby Methwold.[979]

The frequency with which petty sessions were held depended on the level of criminal and administrative work within their bounds, but would be at least monthly, and much more often fortnightly or even weekly. Thus, in 1831 the Greenhoe Division, with 16 parishes and 10,411 inhabitants, held petty sessions on the first and third Mondays of each month.[980] In 1845 the Shropham Hundred, which had 21 parishes and 8,656 inhabitants, held them on the first Thursday of every month; one year these would be conducted at East Harling, and the following year at Larlingford.[981] However, divisions could hold extra or "special" petty sessions outside their designated times when necessary, and this was not uncommon. For example, in 1893 two magistrates (the minimum required for quoracy) were present at a special sitting of the Thetford petty sessions to hear a local blacksmith plead guilty to being drunk in public and using threatening language (as a first offender he was fined just 5 shillings).[982]

In theory, any justice in a county could attend and act at any one of its petty sessions, but custom normally confined the bench to locally resident justices from the surrounding division, although there was some, very limited, overlap in particular divisions, such as that between the benches of Lynn and Swaffham.[983] Typical of rural areas, in the East and West Flegg Hundred there were, in the latter half of the 1830s, four active local magistrates: Sir Edmund Knowles Lacon, his son, and two clerical JPs who held livings in the divisional area.[984] Many hundreds had a somewhat larger complement. Nevertheless, in Norfolk, unlike some other places in England, it was very rare for the number of magistrates attending petty sessions to reach double figures, even at the end of the century, and benches of between two and

---

979 NRO PD 313/92.

980 White, *History, Gazetteer,* p. 599.

981 *Ibid.*, p. 410.

982 *The Bury and Norwich Post*, 26 September, 1893.

983 Rose Madeleine Wallis, *The Relationship Between Magistrates and their Communities*, p. 75.

984 White, *History, Gazetteer,* p. 235.

five men were normally found throughout the era.[985] This is partly explained by the relatively low ratio of JPs in Norfolk to its unusually large number of petty sessions. On one assessment, in 1825 Norfolk had 154 active magistrates for its (then) 33 petty sessions. By contrast, Gloucestershire had 179 active magistrates for fewer than half that number, while Kent had 168 magistrates for just 14 petty sessions.[986]

Under the Summary Jurisdiction Act of 1848, and as had normally been the case before this statute, petty sessions were quorate with two JPs present. Thus, in June 1891 two JPs (one of them a clergyman) sat at the Watton petty sessions to hear a case of trespass in the pursuit of game, during which three partridges had been taken.[987] Such a small bench was not unusual, though not ideal, not least because it could not produce a majority in the (uncommon) case of disagreement between the magistrates. A little more typically, three JPs (including two clergymen) made up the bench at the Dereham petty sessions that sat in early December 1855.[988] Exactly the same bench presided over the forum in early November 1856.[989] Similarly, in 1886 three JPs sitting at petty sessions (two of them clerics) heard a case of illegal fishing with nets, by two men from Rockland St Mary (the third JP had the title "Doctor").[990] However, larger benches were also found in Norfolk. For example, the Swaffham petty sessions in July 1882 were held before five JPs (three of them clerics).[991] The same number of JPs were present at the Diss petty sessions in early August 1891.[992]

The four major Norfolk boroughs had their own petty sessions, served by their town magistrates. Those for urban divisions would be held much more frequently than the petty sessions in mainly rural parts, especially in Norwich and Yarmouth, where they might take place on two or three days each week. For this reason, they were sometimes referred to as police courts, even though this nomenclature was, perhaps, more appropriate for forums serviced by stipendiary magistrates (who were granted the powers of a two-man lay bench when sitting alone), as had been the case in much of urban Middlesex since 1792, and subsequently in other major conurbations, such as Salford and Manchester.[993] Thus, in April 1846 the ill-fated George Thurtell, a horticulturist, was charged with assaulting the Norwich correspondent of the *Daily News*, before what was termed the "Norwich Police Court."[994]

---

985 Porritt, "At Petty Sessions," p. 474.

986 Powell, *Statistical Illustrations,* p. 14.

987 *The Bury and Norwich Post*, 9 June, 1891.

988 *The Norwich Mercury,* 12 December, 1855.

989 *The Norfolk News,* 15 December, 1856.

990 R. Moll, "Illegal Fishing On Rockland Broad," *The Fishing Gazette*, vol. 12, no. 463 (6 March, 1886), p. 136.

991 *The Bury and Norwich Post*, 8 August, 1882.

992 *The Ipswich Journal*, 15 August, 1891.

993 Bentley, *English Criminal Justice,* p. 22.

994 *The Norfolk Chronicle,* 30 April, 1846.

Sometimes, at the start of the Victorian period, rural petty sessions might still be conducted in a private house. However, by then, it was much more common for them to be held in a public place, such as (most commonly) a room in a local inn/tavern/hotel or some other significant public building, such as a nearby bridewell or workhouse. For example, in 1836, in the small (combined) East and West Flegg Hundreds, which surrounded the (jurisdictionally separate) town of Great Yarmouth, petty sessions were held every Saturday at the Feathers Inn in Yarmouth, and every Tuesday at the House of Industry in Rollesby.[995] In 1845 those for the Depwade district were held in the Swan Inn at Long Stratton, while those for Grimshoe were held in the Crown Inn at Mundford. In the 1840s the petty sessions for the Downham district were held at the Crown Hotel in that parish.[996] At some commercial venues, a small rental was paid by the magistrates. At others there was no payment: presumably the landlord received extra custom from thirsty litigants and witnesses.[997] Nationally, almost half of all petty sessions were held in private premises, such as taverns, in 1845, but the figure appears to have been higher in Victorian Norfolk, where petty sessions were twice as likely to be held in licensed premises as in a public building, such as a town hall.[998]

The use of improvised buildings was not an entirely satisfactory situation. The impact of the Petty Sessions Act of 1849 slowly reduced the employment of such expedients (it was a permissive not compulsory statute) by allowing a dedicated courthouse to be used for such forums. While it was going through Parliament, Lord Campbell noted the inconvenience to which magistrates in some of the 730 petty sessions nationally had been put "for the want of proper accommodation." However, the Marquess of Salisbury expressed concern about the potential expense of changing this situation, suggesting that each court would cost at least £500, which would eventually have to be paid out of the county rate. This helps explain why take-up was sometimes slow.[999] Of course, not all new dedicated courts were purpose built. In 1879 the south wing of the Wymondham bridewell was converted to a courtroom, and petty sessions were held there until 1992. Just after the Victorian era, the Licensing Act of 1902 finally forbade the use of public houses or other licensed premises for petty sessions after 1907. As a result, a dedicated Court House was built for the Blofield Division, opening in 1908. Prior to this, the Globe public house had been the site of the petty sessions.

By the Victorian era, magistrates at petty sessions had long imitated quarter sessions in selecting a specific chairman to preside over their hearings. The JPs present would usually sit in a row behind a long desk, with the chairman, who spoke for all, in the

---

995 White, *History, Gazetteer,* p. 235.

996 *The Norwich Mercury,* 16 June, 1849.

997 Anon., *Petty sessions. Return of the description of building in which the justices of the petty sessions district hold their usual sittings. House of Commons Papers*, 1845, vol. 36, paper number 606, p. 24.

998 Hanly, "Summary Jurisdiction," p. 291. Taylor, *Hooligans, Harlots,* p. 108.

999 Hansard HL Deb 27 March 1849 vol. 103 cols. 1364-6

middle. In a purpose-built courtroom the bench would normally be set above the floor level, but this was often not practical in a public house.[1000] As today JPs would decide by a simple majority if they could not agree. If they were evenly divided, a matter would normally have to go for a rehearing in front of a separate bench or be abandoned. However, and perhaps surprisingly, in 1911, it was reported that, in these situations, where there were four or a larger even number of magistrates present, the most junior JP might sometimes withdraw, so that the bench could reach a decision without the need for a fresh hearing.[1001] Nevertheless, and as today, a failure to agree was rare. As with other criminal courts, proceedings were usually open to the public (this was sometimes refused at the start of the Victorian era), so that in 1874 the King's Lynn petty sessions were "crowded to excess" when a case of wife-beating by a local town councillor came for trial.[1002] Petty sessions would usually convene at about 10 am. In a well-populated division, the court would often remain in session until 2 or 3 pm or even later.[1003]

Reputation

In the late 1820s, the Norfolk clergyman and pamphleteer the Reverend Charles Brereton was scathing about the petty sessions (an "upstart court") that had boomed in Norfolk over the previous 30 years, and its system of summary justice. He thought – presumably after personal observation – that they often heard only one side of the evidence, acted without legal precedent and even "without course of law," operated without their witnesses' being under oath when testifying, and did not keep a proper record of their transactions. Frequently, a copy of Richard Burns' *Justice of the Peace and Parish Officer* or an equivalent authority was the only source of legal information available to the bench. (The thirtieth and last edition of Burns' *vade mecum* came out in 1869.)[1004]

Although the cleric's analysis was slightly extreme, it is certainly true that, in the first years of the Victorian era, procedure at summary trial was relatively informal, sometimes extra-legal, and often left entirely to the court to determine. Some hearings were closed to the public or excluded the press. At a much more legally elevated level than Brereton, Henry Brougham, Lord Chancellor from 1830 to 1834, was also a strong critic of petty sessions, feeling that "costly justice is much better than cheap [magistrates'] injustice."[1005] More specifically, S.M. Phillips, the Undersecretary of State at the Home Office, informed the Select Committee on Game Laws that, of the 1,849 committals to prison for poaching from May 1844 to March 1845 a "great many have been illegal." Most of these had been made by

[1000] Porritt, "At Petty Sessions," p. 474.

[1001] Alexander, *The administration,* p. 12.

[1002] *The Bury and Norwich Post*, 24 November, 1874.

[1003] Porritt, "At Petty Sessions," p. 474.

[1004] Brereton, *The Subordinate Magistracy,* pp. 5-6.

[1005] Hansard HC Deb 07 February 1828 vol. 18 cols. 127-258.

magistrates, sitting summarily, who were not well informed about the law, so that there was a "very great deal of irregularity and injustice."[1006]

As late as 1847, John Roebuck claimed in the House of Commons that a suspected offender might be brought to the back parlour of a local squire's house, where he would be tried by men not "knowing the least of the law, but both having strong prejudices in the case." There would be no lawyer or newspaper representative present. He thought that a trial under such circumstances was a perversion and denial of justice to the poor. However, by then Roebuck's analysis was exaggerated, or at least anachronistic, as several other MPs pointed out to him at the time, not least because the use of justices' parlours was extremely rare by the 1840s (unlike holding petty sessions in public houses).[1007]

Even at the start of the Victorian period, summary hearings sometimes mimicked aspects of trial on indictment. This would become very much more common as a result of the various statutes introduced by the Attorney General, Sir John Jervis, towards the end of the 1840s. Taken together, the Summary Jurisdiction Act, Indictable Offences Act, Protection of Justices Act (all of 1848) and the Petty Sessions Act 1849, overhauled summary jurisdiction, along with other aspects of the magistrates' work, although they did not quite amount to the transformation Sir John had originally intended.[1008] The Petty Sessions Act, in particular, attempted to bring a degree of statutory regulation and a set procedure to summary forums.[1009]

Unsurprisingly, in what was an amateur-dominated system, there were still periodic and glaring failures to the end of the Victorian era and beyond. Notoriously, in 1875 the Reverend Edward Moore, the vicar of Spalding in Lincolnshire (to the north of Norfolk) and chairman of the local petty sessions, sitting with several other magistrates, sentenced a girl of 13 years of age to 14 days' imprisonment and four years in a reformatory, for plucking a geranium from the garden of the Spalding alms-houses. Richard Cross, the Home Secretary, immediately remitted the sentence, and it was thought that the Lord Chancellor would dismiss the clergyman from the bench. Nevertheless, Moore had been a magistrate for 15 years, and passed, it was claimed, hundreds of judgments a year during this period. He had apparently read various private reports on the girl and decided that she was of a "peculiar temperament" and so would benefit from a few years in a reformatory. He had then persuaded his fellow magistrates to his way of thinking.[1010]

Even so, Moore was not typical. By the close of the Victorian era, one observer thought, albeit with some exaggeration, that there was nearly as much law and decorum in a petty sessional court as there was at quarter sessions or assizes, even

[1006] David Roberts, *Paternalism in Early Victorian England* (London: Croom Helm, 1979), pp. 143-145.

[1007] Hansard HC Deb 18 April 1850 vol. 110 col. 506.

[1008] Cornish, *Oxford History*, p. 926.

[1009] Hansard HL Deb 27 March 1849 vol. 103 cols. 1364-6.

[1010] *The Spectator,* 17 July, 1875, p. 2.

if it was still sometimes held in the assembly room of a country hotel. Police officers would be stationed by the doors and in the aisles of the courtroom and would quickly check any levity of behaviour. More important, rules of procedure were, apparently "much the same as in the higher criminal courts, as regards evidence and cross-examination; and generally the whole proceeding has an impressiveness which is not lost, either on the delinquents who are appearing before the magistrates, or on the spectators". He felt that it was necessary only to sit through petty sessions to realize how much of the good order and respect for law which characterized English rural life was due to the work of the county magistracy in such forums (along with that of the police).[1011] Their increased professionalism was probably one of the factors behind the spread of previously indictable-only offences to summary forums.

Assisting this process, after the Act for the Better Regulation of Divisions 1828 came into force, it became normal for JPs' clerks at petty sessions to be qualified lawyers (although this was not normally mandatory until the Justices' Clerks Act 1877).[1012] Significantly, the Prosecution Expenses (Amendment) Act 1851 allowed benches to pay them salaries, increasing the attractions of the position; prior to this date, they had taken a cut of any fees due to their JPs. (The statute also encouraged the creation of court records and minute books.) Such men were usually local solicitors or (early in the period) attorneys. For example, in 1836 Haddon Adcock, an attorney from Little Walsingham, was clerk to the JPs in the hundred of Greenhoe.[1013] Similarly, in 1845 William Clarke, the clerk for the magistrates in the Shropham Hundred, was a solicitor from Thetford.[1014] Most worked part time for the justices rather than drawing all their remuneration from the position, although a few might work for more than one division.[1015]

The low level of legal knowledge among many of the JPs sitting at summary forums meant that the petty sessions clerk became an important and influential figure. As was noted in 1899, "immediately below the chairman sits the magistrates' clerk, who is constantly in communication with the bench, and who retires to the magistrates' room with the bench when any legal point has to be determined." Some observers felt that it was not necessary that either county or borough magistrates be learned in the law because each petty sessional division and each borough bench had a clerk who was always a lawyer of "high standing; almost invariably of the solicitor's branch of the profession."[1016] However, this carried dangers.

[1011] Porritt, "At Petty Sessions," p. 476.

[1012] Cox, "Habitual Eccentricities," pp. 109-127.

[1013] White, *History, Gazetteer... 1836,* p. 599.

[1014] *Ibid....1845,* p. 410.

[1015] Sarah Flynn and Mark Stevens, "Petty criminals, publicans and sinners: Petty sessions records in the Berkshire Record Office," *Journal of the Society of Archivists*, vol. 16, no. 1 (1995), pp. 41-53.

[1016] Porritt, "At Petty Sessions," p. 474.

In the early 1860s Thomas William Saunders thought that because JPs were often manifestly unqualified for their duties, the clerk was the real judge of proceedings, and so the "life and soul" of petty sessions. His legal expertise and experience meant that he decided nearly all questions of evidence, interpreted all Acts of Parliament, informed the JPs of their duties, and advised them of the judgments they could pronounce. If legal issues were raised, magistrates deferred to his view, and adopted his opinions, so that their presence was almost a sham.[1017] This analysis was not entirely fair; as another observer noted almost 50 years later, not all JPs were legally ignorant, even those who were not barristers. Nevertheless, he also felt that it was obvious that, where a bench was weak, and its clerk was strong-minded, the latter might control the JPs, although most were sound individuals.[1018] Sir Henry Hawkins (1817-1907) recalled petty sessions he had seen in Hertfordshire as a young man in which the chairman was a slightly pompous but very diligent clergyman. He was apparently strict in his application of the law when he knew it, "but it was fortunate for some delinquents, although unfortunate for others, that he did not always possess sufficient knowledge to act independently of his clerk's opinion."[1019] Much must have turned on the experience and ability of the JPs in attendance, especially the chairman, and on the self-restraint of the clerk.

Defence legal representation "by counsel or attorney" was allowed at petty sessions, something that was expressly guaranteed by s.2 of the Prisoners' Counsel Act of 1836. Although relatively unusual for the accused – it had to be privately paid for and was prohibitively expensive for many poor defendants – it was certainly not rare in Victorian Norfolk. It could be, and frequently was, provided by local solicitors, who had full rights of audience in such forums. According to Captain Dunne, in the early 1850s, one of the Norwich city magistrates was a practising barrister who had two sons who were local solicitors and who (somewhat irregularly to modern eyes) frequently appeared before benches on which he was sitting in criminal matters.[1020] A few such men even specialized in summary advocacy. When Samuel Linay, a 57-year-old solicitor, died at Norwich in 1894, it was noted that he had been a "well known practitioner in petty sessional courts throughout East Anglia."[1021] More specifically, when, at the East Dereham petty sessions in February 1866, George Squire, a Lincolnshire merchant, was charged with assaulting Charles Howard, the keeper of the town Corn Hall, Mr J.C. Chittock, a Norwich solicitor, represented him. The bench dismissed the case.[1022]

A few defendants and prosecutors employed counsel. In November 1888, at the Blofield petty sessions, when a farmer and several of his workers were summonsed

[1017] Saunders, *Quarter and Petty Sessions,* p. 11.

[1018] Alexander, *The administration,* p. 19.

[1019] Hawkins, *Reminiscences,* p. 3.

[1020] *The Bury and Norwich Post*, 13 July, 1853.

[1021] Mackie, *Norfolk Annals*, vol. 2, p. 449.

[1022] *The Norfolk Chronicle,* 16 February, 1866.

by an RSPCA inspector for ill-treating bullocks, both prosecutor and defendants had legal representation, in the form of a barrister and local solicitor respectively.[1023] Even the occasional QC might be briefed by wealthy defendants, as was the case when a prosperous shopkeeper was accused of selling laudanum in a solution of methylated spirits, rather than properly licensed spirits, at the King's Lynn petty sessions in 1882. His silk secured an acquittal.[1024]

Conviction Rates at Petty Sessions

When mainstream offences were tried at petty sessions, conviction was not a certainty, even if most defendants were found guilty. Unfortunately, many Norfolk petty sessions records from the Victorian era have not survived, making a precise assessment of verdicts difficult. (The records improve slightly after 1848, when many documents had to be passed on to quarter sessions.) Nevertheless, even at the start of the Victorian period, at the Thetford petty sessions in October 1837, when Ann Hauxley accused a man of assaulting her, the magistrates decided that she was the aggressor in the case, acquitted the defendant, and ordered her to pay costs.[1025] Similarly, when, at the North Erpingham petty sessions held in April 1843, John Neave prosecuted Thomas Bright for assault, the case was "dismissed with costs 10s paid by the complainant."[1026] Towards the end of the period, at the North Erpingham petty sessions in January 1894, Obadiah Gray was accused of larceny, after allegedly stealing a pair of reins, but was discharged by the JPs.[1027] Even poaching offences, which had one of the highest summary conviction rates in the country, saw 16 per cent (1,300 of 8,267) of those prosecuted (nationally) being acquitted.[1028] More specifically to Norfolk, of the 290 poaching cases tried in the county in 1863, 53 produced acquittals.[1029]

Acquittal rates depended in large part on the nature of the crime being tried summarily. Theft was much less likely to produce a conviction than was common assault. On average, only 8 percent of the minor property offenders tried by Ipswich (Suffolk) magistrates were discharged, although it must be remembered that many of those accused of indictable crimes accepted summary jurisdiction with the intention of pleading guilty (and benefitting from a lighter sentence in the inferior court). The relatively lower acquittal figure for common assault probably also reflects the

---

[1023] *Ibid.*, 26 November, 1888.

[1024] *The Bury and Norwich Post*, 31 January, 1882.

[1025] *The Bury & Norwich Post, & East Anglian: Or, Suffolk, Norfolk, Essex, Cambridge, and Ely Intelligencer*, 18 October, 1837.

[1026] PS 24/1/1 Hundred of North Erpingham Norfolk Special and Petty Sessions Record Commencing 3 July, 1841 NRO PS 24/1/1.

[1027] NRO 24/4/1 North Erpingham Petty Sessions, Minute Book B p. 10.

[1028] *Pall Mall Gazette*, 26 March, 1892.

[1029] Michael J. Carter, *Peasants and Poachers in Norfolk: A Study in Rural Disorder*, (Woodbridge: Boydell Press, 1980), p. 122.

much greater willingness of the new police to take charge of it, and make sure that only well-supported cases went to petty sessions; they continued to be reluctant to become involved in theft, which was still frequently left for private complainants to pursue.[1030]

More specifically, a pair of cases heard at the Thetford petty sessions in 1887, with the same defendant, show a careful attempt to weigh the evidence against him. In February James Overton, a porter at the town railway station, was accused of stealing lace and a book from a bag that had been left in the station for safekeeping. The case against him appeared strong. The box in which the lace had been contained was found in his locker, and other items had previously gone missing while he was on duty. Perhaps for this reason, he "elected to be dealt with summarily, but pleaded not guilty." He called no witnesses in his own support, and after the bench – made up of the mayor and other borough magistrates – retired to consider their verdict, it was decided that the case had been proved. Overton was sentenced to a month's imprisonment in Norwich Castle prison. However, barely a month later, following his release, he was tried again, before the same forum, for stealing a silver watch from a drunken woman, shortly before his conviction. On this occasion, the evidence was not deemed sufficient to secure a guilty finding, and he was discharged with an informal verbal caution.[1031]

Juveniles

At the beginning of the nineteenth century few legal distinctions were drawn between the trial of children and adults. Children coming before the courts were usually regarded as "little adults" and tried in the same forums and manner as their fully grown peers, in open court before a judge and jury. Of course, below the age of seven years, a child could have no criminal responsibility at common law. However, the doctrine of *doli incapax* provided some, if modest, protection for those between seven and 14 years of age. This had been developed by centuries of judicial precedent and was enunciated by William Blackstone in 1796, when he noted that, in this age range, the "capacity of doing ill, or contracting guilt, is not so much measured by years and days, as by the strength of the delinquent's understanding and judgement." Criminal liability was contingent on the child's being proved to have sufficient knowledge and discernment of right and wrong in addition to forming the appropriate mental state or *mens rea* for the crime. To establish this, the prosecution had to show "malice" or a "mischievous discretion," along with all the other elements of the offence. This would rebut the presumption that such a child would otherwise be deemed incapable of forming the necessary intent. A judge at the Norfolk Assizes in 1842, charging the grand jury, discussed how this might be done in the context of a youth named George Barker, who was accused of murder. The judge suggested that before deciding whether to find a true

---

[1030] Mellaerts, "Criminal Justice," pp. 19-52.

[1031] *The Bury and Norwich Post*, 22 March, 1887.

bill in the case they might look at any attempts at concealing the crime or denying personal involvement, which might indicate the presence of such discernment.[1032]

A later illustration of its working can be seen at the same forum in August 1862, when nine-year-old John Aldborough was accused of stealing a gelding from a farmer at Fritton in the southeast of the county (the farmer employed his father as a labourer). The boy had seen the horse in a stable, removed the animal, and ridden off on it, offering to sell it to another farmer, in a neighbouring parish. Unsurprisingly, given the age of the vendor, this man immediately became suspicious. Eventually, the gelding was returned to its rightful owner, who (perhaps surprisingly) prosecuted young John. There was little dispute about the facts of the case, so that the trial judge directed the jury in his summing up that the key issue was "whether the child knew very well what he was about." In particular, did he intend to steal the horse and appropriate the money to his own use? The jury retired but acquitted after just five minutes, and John was discharged, but with a sharp judicial caution to his father that he should "look sharp after him".[1033]

However, by the early 1800s, the general lack of formal differentiation between children and adults was starting to cause concern, for a variety of reasons. The pomp and ceremony of trial by jury seemed inappropriate for juveniles who were too young to appreciate its significance and the solemnity it conferred, as well as being needlessly expensive.[1034] It also encouraged them to associate with adult criminals at court, risking their corruption. In the 1820s a Warwickshire JP, John Eardley-Wilmot, suggested that minor offences by children should be classed as misdemeanours, not felonies, and dealt with summarily. Magistrates in petty sessions would follow "the domestic regulation of families" and provide punishments appropriate to children to avoid the stigma of public trial and imprisonment. His proposals were attacked because such differentiation between child and adult would deprive the former of the right of all freeborn Englishmen to trial by jury. Even so, by the close of the century, almost the only juvenile perpetrated offence that could never be tried summarily involved homicide. Nevertheless, a designated juvenile court was not established until the Children Act 1908, which statute also covered the legal procedures to be followed when children were arrested by the police and outlined the options available to magistrates.[1035]

[1032] *Ibid.,* 6 April, 1842.

[1033] *Ibid.,* 5 August, 1862.

[1034] Margaret May, "Innocence and Experience: The Evolution of the Concept of Juvenile Delinquency in the Mid-Nineteenth Century," *Victorian Studies*, vol. 17, no. 1 (1973), p. 7.

[1035] Bradley, "Juvenile Court," p. 37, p. 40.

The Jury Courts

All serious, and many less serious, crimes, were determined by trial on indictment in front of a jury, the traditional common-law method of adjudication. Almost all such trials, especially those held in Norfolk, were heard by common, rather than special, juries. The latter were comprised of men of higher than usual social standing, profession, and education, and were largely used in commercial cases or crimes of a political nature, although a special jury had been used to try a clergyman accused of sodomy at the Norfolk assizes in August 1812.[1036] However, this was exceptionally rare when it came to criminal trials held in the county during the Victorian era.

In the early 1800s the law regulating juries was contained in a plethora of statutes, common-law rules, and accepted practices stretching back far into the past. Reform was thought necessary, so that the law was subject to major consolidation under the auspices of the Home Secretary, Sir Robert Peel, in the 1825 Jury Act (which came into force the following year). This statute, as amended by the Juries Act 1870, set out the circumstances under which Victorian trial juries, whether at assizes or quarter sessions, were selected, summoned, and sworn in, and under which they operated. It transferred the registration of suitable jurors from parish constables to churchwardens and poor-law overseers and required that juries be summoned to court by the sheriff's officers rather than constables, as had been the case. It was hoped that this would reduce the incidence of petty bribery aimed at avoiding being called for service, although this does not necessarily appear to have happened.[1037]

Men qualified for jury service on the basis of nationality, residence, age, and the value of their property, though some argued that their general characters should be considered as well. (The accrual of serious criminal convictions did preclude service). For half the Victorian era, service on a jury was normally restricted to British subjects, although s.47 of the 1825 Act reiterated the ancient right of foreigners to have one-half of the jury judging them made up of their own countrymen or other foreign nationals, a privilege that was abolished only in 1870, when, under s.8 of the Juries Act of that year, aliens of ten years' residence became liable to serve as normal jurors, if otherwise suitably qualified, being treated "as if they had been natural-born subjects of the Queen."

Under section 1 of the 1825 Act, to be qualified for county jury service (a distinction was not drawn between criminal and civil juries), whether at assizes or quarter sessions, a man had to be a householder between 21 and 60 years of age and satisfy a property qualification. This could be met by owning land worth at least £10 a year if rented; holding a lease of at least 21 years on land with an annual rental value of £20 or more; or being a householder in a property that had 15 or more windows and an annual rental value of at least £20. The minimum limits were raised to £30

[1036] *The Morning Post*, 5 August, 1812.

[1037] Niamh Howlin, "English and Irish Jury Laws: A Growing Divergence 1825-1833" in Seán Patrick Donlan and Michael Brown (eds.), *The Laws and Other Legalities of Ireland,* 1689-1850 (Abingdon: Routledge, 2011), pp. 117-132.

in 1870. However, several of the ten towns and cities (such as Norwich and Exeter) that had their own assizes summoned jurors according to custom, rather than the terms of the Juries Act 1825, until shortly after the Great War.[1038] Similarly, boroughs set the property requirements for their own quarter sessions, so that these varied around the country, but were not normally greater than those for the surrounding county.

Significantly, and problematically, various groups and professions were exempt from jury service even though otherwise amply qualified. These included, inter alia: peers, judges, Church of England clergy, Catholic priests, Protestant preachers, practising lawyers, constables, officers of the court, military and naval officers, coroners, jailers, apothecaries, and physicians. Consequently, many influential professional men lacked personal experience of jury service, and so were ill-informed about its operation. These exemptions also had the effect of reducing the average educational level and social status of trial jurors.[1039]

Because of the formal qualifications required for service, the number of potential jurymen varied in each county, depending on its wealth and population. Under the (fairly similar) pre-1825 requirement for jury service of the early 1820s, some observers thought that, in Yorkshire, the largest county in England, there were about 10,000 men eligible for service, not including those in boroughs with their own jury courts, while in Lancashire there were about 8,000.[1040] In mid-Victorian Kent and Sussex the figures were about 12,000 and 7,500 respectively. On this basis, Norfolk would have had several thousand such men at the start of the era, and many more at its close.

The common jurors who determined the verdicts in nearly all the criminal trials in the country, whether at assizes or county quarter sessions, were, because of the property requirement, not quite typical Englishmen. For example, it appears that only two of 47 Chartists tried nationally on indictment in 1839 and 1840, about whom firm details as to income and wealth can be established, would have qualified as jurors (these being a smith and a miner).[1041] However, because the qualification was relatively modest, and because so many well-to-do and professional people were exempt or otherwise able to avoid service, they were not necessarily high-status individuals. The qualification was low enough for men with very little formal education to be able to serve, something that became a subject of regular complaint during the Victorian era (see below).

[1038] K. Crosby, "Restricting the Juror Franchise in 1920s England and Wales," *Law and History Review*, vol. 37, no. 1 (2019), pp. 163-207.

[1039] Roland Quinault, "Victorian Juries," *History Today*, vol. 59, no. 5 (2009), pp. 47-53.

[1040] M. [*sic*] Cottu, *On the Administration of Criminal Justice in England; and the Spirit of the English Government* (London: Richard Stevens, 1822), p. 57.

[1041] Jacqueline Fellague Ariouat, "Rethinking Partisanship in the Conduct of the Chartist Trials, 1839-1848," *Albion: A Quarterly Journal Concerned with British Studies*, vol. 29, no. 4 (1997), pp. 596-621.

In 1860 it was claimed that Victorian trial jurors were often farmers (in the countryside) and shopkeepers (in towns).[1042] The 1863 Jurors' Book for Buckinghamshire suggests that this assessment of petty jurors was realistic. In the rural areas of that county, they were mostly tenant and freehold farmers, along with manufacturers and craftsmen (such as wheelwrights and millers), as well as a small number of minor gentlemen. By contrast, most of the jurors for the borough of Aylesbury were tradesmen, with numerous shopkeepers, publicans, and small manufacturers among their ranks.[1043] According to Peter King, in late eighteenth- and early nineteenth-century Essex, only 0.3 percent of jurors at quarter sessions and 2.7 percent of those at assize were of the gentlemanly classes.[1044] However, in Kent, between 1859 and 1880, some 15 percent of the county trial jurors at assizes were gentlemen; just 2 percent were labourers, with most being skilled artisans, merchants, or farmers.[1045] Of course, much depends on the definition of "gentleman," which could be interpreted very loosely.

Although the selection of a trial jury was, in theory, the responsibility of the sheriff, his functions were usually exercised on his behalf by a salaried, often long-serving under-sheriff. The process began with the issue of a writ from the relevant court, asking the sheriff to draw up a jury panel from which trial jurors could be selected. According to Charles Cottu, a French judge who observed the English system in the early 1820s, the general jury lists were made out each year, based on the register of taxes. A list of potential jurors would be posted on the walls of the parish church by the local constable for 20 days so that everyone would have an opportunity to inspect it and challenge their in-/exclusion.[1046]

However, after 1825 the jury panel was taken from the names in county jurors' books that were drawn up from eligible local men by churchwardens and overseers rather than constables. The sheriff or under-sheriff summoned a selection of these individuals. They had considerable discretion as to who was called from the lists, although service normally resulted in immunity from selection for two years (the sheriff and the clerk of the peace maintained a list of those who had previously served). The jury summons was served in person until 1862, when statute allowed it to be sent by post as an alternative. Under the 1825 Act, ten days' notice of service had to be provided, but this was reduced to just six days by the Juries Act 1870. Trial juries would be selected from those of the panel (the great majority) who responded to the summons by attending court.[1047]

[1042] *The Spectator*, 11 February, 1860, p. 14.

[1043] Quinault, "Victorian Juries," pp. 47-53.

[1044] Peter King, *Crime and Law in England, 1750–1840: Remaking Justice from the Margins* (Cambridge: CUP, 2006), p. 245.

[1045] Conley, *Unwritten Law,* p. 17.

[1046] Cottu, *Administration,* p. 63.

[1047] Conor Hanly, "Jury Selection in Victorian England," *American Journal of Legal History*, vol. 61, no. 1 (March 2021), p. 41.

A failure to respond to a jury summons or to attend court on time without a judicially approved excuse could lead to punishment. Even if an excuse was presented, if it was for medical reasons, and there were any suspicions as to its truth, the courts might send for the physician who had signed the relevant certificate and make him swear to its veracity in person. A fine of between 40 shillings and £5 could be imposed on absentees, the former being by far the most common penalty, although the sum due could be increased by listing the absent juror more than once during sessions. According to Cottu, these fines were strictly levied in the 1820s, and could lead to arrest if not paid.[1048] In 1861, the Treasury decided that jurors who were ineligible to serve due to old age should still be fined for not attending, as it was their own fault if they had not been removed from the lists. In 1866, when the Treasury Solicitor was asked whether he would exercise his discretion to remit such fines, he explained that he would do so only in unusual circumstances.[1049] Nevertheless, the determination with which fines for juror non-attendance were imposed and enforced varied around the country during the Victorian period. It seems that, in practice, not a few of those summonsed who failed to appear, without justification, escaped punishment.

Under the 1825 Act, jurors at assizes and quarter sessions were supposed to be drawn from the "body of the county" rather than from specific areas. (Obviously, this did not apply to borough courts.) In practice, in most large counties, the sheriff was reluctant to summon too many men from distant parts, because travelling to court was difficult. Instead, they often concentrated on drawing their jurors from parishes or hundreds that were not too far from the forums where they would serve, even if this was (legally) slightly irregular. Thus, in Hertfordshire juries were often taken from as few as four parishes, while in Lancashire, they were sometimes drawn only from specific hundreds.[1050] In 1861 it was decided that jurors for the county quarter sessions in Norwich might be taken from, *inter alia*, the Holt, Gallow, North Erpingham, North Greenhoe, and Brothercross divisions, while those for the adjourned sitting at Swaffham would be taken from the Launditch division.[1051]

The Merits of Jury Trial

Ostensibly, most Victorians, like their predecessors, were very proud of the English common-law system of trial by jury. Writing in 1823, Lord John Russell, a Whig reformer and future prime minister, suggested that the jury was more effective than the electoral system of his day in convincing the masses that they had a share in the government of their country, and encouraging an attachment to its laws. It was also regarded as distinctly English and ancient in character. There was a widespread

---

[1048] Cottu, *Administration,* p. 51.

[1049] K. Crosby, "Before the Criminal Justice and Courts Act 2015: Juror punishment in nineteenth- and twentieth-century England," *Legal Studies,* vol. 36, no. 2 (2016), pp. 202-204.

[1050] Hanly, "Summary Jurisdiction," pp. 278-303.

[1051] *The Bury and Norwich Post*, 8 January, 1861.

belief, transcending political party and class, that jury trial had been instrumental in ensuring justice and preserving civil liberties. For example, in 1840 one observer discussing the MP Sir John Eardley-Wilmot's proposal for trying many lesser offenders under 16 without a jury, noted that it would excite intense opposition throughout England because "the reverence for jury trials amounts to a superstition ... people regard juries as safeguards against the oppression of country gentlemen [the JPs]."[1052] The Conservative politician William Forsyth even claimed in his *History of Trial by Jury* of 1852 that it had influenced the national character by inculcating a love of fair play and an abhorrence of injustice.[1053]

Whether the practical reality of Victorian trial by jury was worthy of so much esteem, and whether confidence in the institution was as widespread as is sometimes suggested, and always genuinely held even when expressed, is much more debatable. As many legal observers appreciated, jury service was often acutely unpopular with those selected to serve, many of whom sought to avoid it. There were good reasons for this. Frequently, it was, in the words of an 1857 article in the *Westminster Review*, "painfully disagreeable." Service on common trial juries, which included almost all criminal juries, was unpaid. (There was an unavailing attempt to remedy this in 1870.) Moreover, jurors who had been summoned to court were frequently kept waiting for long periods without being called for service (still a problem today), in badly ventilated buildings that lacked a proper place to sit, devoid of any means to occupy their time, without prospect of being released early, and liable to be called upon at any moment. While waiting, it was claimed, a juror might be "hustled about in a crowded court and may [even] have his pockets picked." During the trial, the jury sat on hard benches in the jury box. Sometimes this was located where it was difficult to hear proceedings, particularly the evidence of witnesses (rather than the judge). The Juries Act of 1870 sought in part to reduce the number of jurors summoned, to give longer intervals between their times of service, and to ensure greater care in the making of jury lists, specifically to reduce the impact of such an experience.[1054]

Additionally, throughout the nineteenth century, doubts were openly expressed by many observers, including the leading constitutional lawyer of the late Victorian period, Albert Venn Dicey, about the abilities of many trial jurors. Some of these doubts may have been misplaced, perhaps derived in part from social prejudice.[1055] Nevertheless, they were reiterated so regularly that they must have had some foundation.

For example, shortly before the Victorian era, in 1834, it was claimed that a jury sitting at the Derby assizes and considering a case of pickpocketing in which two men and a woman were defendants, had produced a bizarre verdict that was indicative

[1052] *The Spectator*, 29 February, 1840, p. 14.

[1053] Quinault, "Victorian Juries," pp. 47-53.

[1054] *The Spectator,* 23 July, 1870.

[1055] Hanly, "Summary Jurisdiction," p. 279.

of profound ignorance. When asked by the court clerk whether the prisoners were guilty, the foreman allegedly replied, "We find the woman not guilty, and the men guilty; but we recommend them to mercy, because there is not evidence enough to convict them." An acquittal was eventually entered for all three. Considering this case, one observer opined that it was almost as if there was a deliberate selection of the "ignorant and stupid" to try men for their lives. He expressed the hope, albeit without any confidence, that in future generations 12 such "blockheads" would not be found on a jury.[1056] Sir Henry Hawkins recalled an equally ridiculous verdict from a criminal trial jury in the early Victorian period.[1057]

In 1860 it was claimed that occasional mistakes in verdict by trial juries were unsurprising, given that the position demanded a certain degree of intelligence and discrimination while the country persisted in filling its jury boxes with men who manifested a "want of education and acuteness."[1058] Towards the end of the Victorian era, a national commentator could still note that jurors were often men of limited abilities, albeit very rarely bribed: "They are often stupid, still oftener prejudiced and sentimental, but almost never influenced in their verdicts by unworthy motives."[1059]

An awareness of the problems occasioned by juries, even if not always publicly acknowledged, combined with concern at the delay they caused, in what was often a very pressured system, helps explain why the civil trial jury was in constant retreat in Victorian England. For example, the trials held at the new county courts, introduced in 1846, were juryless, while the Common Law Procedure Act 1854 gave civil litigants in the Westminster courts the choice of bench or jury trial, and during the remainder of the century the proportion of litigants choosing the latter steadily declined.[1060] Suspicion and dislike of juries also helps explain why, despite the supposed merits of the institution, the trial of a huge number of lesser, and even some middle-ranking, crimes, fell out of the jury system during the Victorian era and were instead dealt with by JPs sitting alone at petty sessions.

The County Quarter Sessions

Quarter sessions were the lower of the two main provincial jury courts, whether held for county or borough (see below for a discussion of the latter). They were conducted with rather less pomp and, in practice, were rather less legalistic than assizes. Traditionally, as their name states, they sat at least four times a year, under a medieval statute, at Epiphany (January), Easter (April), Midsummer (July), and Michaelmas (October). This was changed slightly in 1830 by specifying that sessions would be held in the first week after 28 December, 31 March, 24 June, and 11

1056 *The Spectator*, 5 April, 1834, p. 9.

1057 Hawkins, *Reminiscences,* p. 84.

1058 *The Spectator*, 11 February, 1860, p. 14.

1059 *Ibid.*, 15 May 1897, p. 10.

1060 Conor Hanly, "The decline of civil jury trial in nineteenth-century England," *The Journal of Legal History*, vol. 26, no. 3 (2005), pp. 253-278.

October respectively, instead of tying them to the church feasts (Easter, of course, being moveable.) Subsequently, JPs were given a limited power to fix their quarter sessions so as not to clash with the assizes.

However, the statutes did not limit JPs to holding four sessions a year or confine them to a single location: they could sit by adjournment to another time or place and hold additional sessions if necessary. By the nineteenth century, increased levels of work meant that extra sessions were sometimes being scheduled outside the four traditional times, while the existing sittings might last slightly longer than in earlier centuries. After the early 1800s the concurrent use of two courts at the same sessions at busy forums also allowed them to cover many more cases (see below).

Quarter sessions conducted a majority of the trials on indictment in the country, not least because the Victorian era saw a major move away from sending cases to the assize courts in favour of the lower forum.[1061] In 1900 about three-quarters of all jury trials were held at county quarter sessions and at borough sessions, and of these, two-thirds were held at the former.[1062] Nevertheless, the size of the majority varied around the country and over time. No counties matched Lancashire, where, in 1832, more than 20 times as many cases were tried at quarter sessions as at assizes. However, there were also a few counties where the order was, for very short periods, reversed, as was the case in Hampshire that same year.[1063] Much more typically when it came to forum division, in 1841, the Reverend Harry Farr Yeatman, a JP in both Somerset and Dorset of some 28 years' service, noted that the 20 previous Dorset quarter sessions had tried a total 901 prisoners (an average of 18 each sessions), and just 358 at the county assizes over the same period.[1064] If borough (quarter) sessions trials (see below) were added to the total, the proportion would have been even higher. Much the same distribution was found in Norfolk. In 1832 95 people were tried at the county assizes. By contrast, some 244 people were tried at county quarter sessions (it seems that this figure does not include borough sessions).[1065]

As well as being more frequent and sometimes more conveniently situated, quarter sessions trials were much cheaper for the county than those conducted at assizes, not least because the relevant bills were taxed (assessed) by the magistrates through their own officer, unlike the situation at the higher jury forum.[1066] For example, in 1832 each criminal case determined at the Norfolk assizes was estimated at a per capita cost of £20 7s 9d. By contrast, per capita costs of trial at county quarter

1061 Taylor, "Rationing Crime," p. 576.

1062 Cornish, *Oxford History*, pp. 917-919.

1063 Mullins, *On the Magistracy,* p. 20.

1064 Yeatman, *A Letter*, p. 5.

1065 Mullins, *On the Magistracy,* p. 20.

1066 *The Spectator* 6 June 1840, p. 13

sessions averaged just £6 15s 4d.[1067] This added greatly to the attractions of the latter.

Jurisdiction

Historically there had been no legal limit on the matters that could be heard at quarter sessions, other than a prohibition on hearing cases of treason, which also meant that certain coining offences (considered a form of treason) were deemed to be outside their remit. Nevertheless, from the late sixteenth century onwards, quarter sessions had gradually abandoned hearing serious and middle-ranking felonies. In the late eighteenth century, they concerned themselves largely with the trial of misdemeanours and petty larceny (theft under a shilling in value), the latter being the only felony that had never carried a potential death sentence. They might also hear low-level cases of clergyable grand larceny (over a shilling in value), although the distinction between the two forms of theft was largely abolished in 1827. Most cases determined at this forum were of a less serious or quasi-regulatory nature. For example, at the Norwich quarter sessions in 1799, Thomas Dack was sentenced to six months' hard labour in a house of correction for leaving his family chargeable to the parish.[1068] Assaults might also go to this forum when indicted.

The Quarter Sessions Act 1842 recognised what was already very longstanding practice, and formally prevented the lower jury forum from hearing felonies that carried a potential death penalty or sentence of transportation for life for a first offence, all of which were required to go to the Westminster judges sitting at assizes.[1069] Ironically, however, even as the powers of quarter sessions became more limited in theory, they started to try more serious crimes in practice. As a result, by the Victorian period, many middle-ranking felonies that they had previously avoided were heard before them. Indicative of the new trend, in October 1839 John Morris, a 33-year-old man, was convicted of cattle theft at the Norfolk quarter sessions at Swaffham.[1070] However, these courts continued to deal with their traditional diet of minor thefts and indictable misdemeanours, although many of these were gradually mopped up by the increasingly powerful summary courts. Thus, at the January 1849 quarter sessions in Swaffham, a man received a month in prison for stealing a rabbit.[1071]

By the start of the 1840s the expansion of the de facto jurisdiction of quarter sessions, something that may even have been assisted by the 1842 statute, was occasioning concern amongst some observers. They noted that, although such prosecutions were cheaper than those brought at assizes, they deprived prisoners facing the threat of transportation of trial presided over by professional judges (rather than lay

[1067] Mullins, *On the Magistracy,* p. 20.

[1068] *The True Briton*, 22 January, 1799.

[1069] Bentley, *English Criminal Justice,* p. 58.

[1070] TNA HO 18/30/52. He was sentenced to transportation for 15 years.

[1071] *The Bury and Norwich Post, and East Anglian*, 17 January, 1849.

chairmen) and of the ability to select advocates from the whole bar of the circuit (who would attend assizes but not quarter sessions); they also exposed defendants to the local prejudices of the JPs who were on the bench at the lower (county) jury court. It was one thing for minor cases to be heard there, another to submit prisoners accused of serious offences "to the tender mercies of the great unpaid of their own immediate neighbourhood."[1072]

The risks were real: in most years, more Victorian convicts who were transported to Australia from Norfolk had been sentenced at quarter sessions (whether borough or county) than at the higher jury court. Thus, at the county quarter sessions at Swaffham, in October 1842, Johnson Hemnell was sentenced to transportation for stealing promissory notes, gold, and silver to the amount of £150. (After his conviction, Hemnell accompanied two of his prison warders to a garden in Seething where £108 of the money was concealed).[1073] In January 1843, at the Norfolk quarter sessions held at Walsingham, another man received 15 years' transportation for theft (he had a previous conviction).[1074] Four years later, in January 1849, at the county quarter sessions held in Swaffham, the offences tried included an allegation of horse theft, in which Robert Buck (who "pleaded his own case") was found guilty and sentenced to the maximum term allowed by law, 15 years' transportation. In part this was because there had been other allegations against him that were not pursued following the conviction, but which led the chairman (Lord Walsingham), who had read the depositions on which they were based, to believe that Buck "was an old hand at such practices." A woman at these same sessions received seven years' transportation for stealing 22 sovereigns from an old man. Additionally, two men who were separately convicted of stealing a sheep, and killing a sheep with intent to steal it, were sentenced to a year's imprisonment.[1075] Horse theft would almost never have been heard at this forum in the eighteenth century, and there would have been considerable reluctance to hear cattle and sheep theft after they became (technically) capital felonies during the 1700s.

This development, combined with the effects of population growth, a modest growth in crime and, most important, increasingly assertive policing, meant that the amount of criminal work determined at quarter sessions, even in rural counties, soared in the decades immediately prior to 1837. For example, committals for trial in Oxfordshire rose from 38 in 1805 to 271 in 1835, most cases going to the lower jury court.[1076] More specifically to Norfolk, a total of 417 offenders were indicted in the county during the years from 1805 to 1807. By the period from 1834 to 1838, this figure had risen to 3,362. Although double the timescale of 1805-7, it was eight times its annual rate. Again, most of these cases went to quarter sessions.

[1072] *The Spectator*, 6 June, 1840, p. 13.

[1073] *The Norfolk Chronicle*, 19 October, 1842.

[1074] *The Bury and Norwich Post*, 18 January, 1843.

[1075] *The Bury and Norwich Post, and East Anglian*, January 17, 1849.

[1076] Cornish, *Oxford History*, p. 919.

However, by the years from 1843 to 1847, the rate of increase had fallen to a very modest level, especially allowing for population growth, with a total of 3,683 offenders indicted in the county over the same four-year period.[1077]

From the late 1840s onwards, this process of expansion came to an end, and then went into reverse, as the number of criminal cases determined at quarter sessions started a steady decline. Although about three-quarters of jury trials were still held at the lower jury court – two thirds of them at county rather than borough quarter sessions – in some rural counties, the encroachment of petty sessions and (apparently) falling levels of acquisitive crime gradually robbed them of much of their jury work.108 For example, at the Norfolk quarter sessions held by adjournment at Walsingham in April 1841 there were 38 prisoners awaiting their hearings (nearly all for larceny, obtaining property by false pretences, or receiving stolen goods). By contrast, at the normally busier main sitting of the same court at Norwich in January 1883, there were only seven prisoners for trial.[1078] Perhaps more typically of that decade, Norfolk saw just 11 prosecutions conducted at its Epiphany quarter sessions in 1880. This was one of the lowest totals in the country that year, albeit the same number as for Oxfordshire, and one more than the number tried in Berkshire that January, while tiny Rutland saw just one case and sparsely populated Westmorland only four. (At the other extreme, populous, and very heavily industrialized Lancashire saw 205 people tried at quarter sessions, by far the largest number in the country.)[1079]

Quarter sessions did not merely operate as a criminal jury court. Prior to 1889 it dealt with a great deal of county administration and heard appeals from both summary convictions and administrative decisions made at petty sessions, where allowed (see below). Occasionally, by the close of the Victorian era, this appellate role was almost as time-consuming as their criminal jury jurisdiction.[1080] Quarter sessions also had power to punish summarily instances of contempt of court, such as insults to its JPs.

Illustrative of this range of work, the Norfolk quarter sessions conducted at Norwich in early July 1834 commenced on a Wednesday and ran into Friday, with John Weyland initially presiding as chairman over the trials on indictment, while Henry Dover sat as chairman in what was termed the "appeal court," hearing appeals from summary convictions and decisions, with a bench of magistrates (but without a jury). Friday was given over to "county business," i.e., local-government issues and administration, with Weyland again in the chair, although there was, by then, a "very thin attendance of magistrates." (Some JPs had presumably gone home early.)[1081] This general pattern continued during the Victorian period. For example, in January 1857 the Norfolk quarter sessions in Norwich saw the criminal cases being

[1077] King, *Crime and Law,* pp. 231-233.

[1078] *The Ipswich Journal*, 6 January, 1883.

[1079] *Criminal cases…1879*, 1880, House of Commons Papers, vol. 59, no. 153, p. 9.

[1080] Cornish, *Oxford History*, p. 919.

[1081] *The Bury & Norwich Post, & East Anglian: Or, Suffolk, Norfolk, Essex, Cambridge, and Ely Intelligencer*, 9 July, 1834.

dealt with on a Wednesday, the unusually light load meaning that few if any were left for Thursday, and the "county business" then being considered by JPs on the Friday.[1082]

The quarter sessions for each county were presided over by a bench of at least two (at which they were quorate), but usually far more, justices of the peace, one of whom sat in a presiding role as chairman (acting as a de facto judge). Frequently there were at least six magistrates present, and sometimes considerably more. They did not wear special dress, although in theory it seems that they were allowed to keep their hats on, unlike others in the court. Thomas William Saunders thought that JPs sitting in their ordinary clothes were unlikely to impress people with the majesty and importance of the law, unlike the robed and bewigged judges found at assizes or even the recorders who sat at borough sessions.[1083] The bench sat with both a grand and trial (petty) jury, the latter body deciding all questions of innocence and guilt, apart from those relating to appeals from the summary decisions of JPs sitting in local Petty Sessions.

Appeals from Summary Courts

Appeals from summary convictions and administrative decisions (on illegitimate child maintenance etc.) could normally be made to quarter sessions only where expressly allowed by statute, whether that which created the offence for which the appellant had been convicted or a more general Act. Section 6 of the Poaching Prevention Act 1862 provides an example of the former, allowing anyone found guilty under the statute to appeal to the next quarter sessions (whether county or borough), held not less than 12 days after the date of the conviction. Not all summary findings of guilt were covered by such provisions. This, combined with expense and legal ignorance, meant that appeals were often quite unusual early in the period. Thus, just three summary convictions were appealed to Norfolk quarter sessions in 1844, and this modest total was not uncommon, although Kent saw 25 (easily the largest total in England).[1084] Their number remained low for many years thereafter. In 1879 all of England and Wales saw just 152 appeals, compared to 154 the previous year and 172 in 1877. During these three years, just over half of appealed convictions and findings were upheld, the remainder being quashed. However, a third of these matters involved bastardy, so that in 1879, and ignoring such cases, there was just one appeal for every 5,237 summary criminal convictions, and one reversal of verdict for every 12,571 cases.[1085]

The appellate jurisdiction of quarter sessions was considerably expanded by s.19 of the Summary Jurisdiction Act 1879, which allowed an appeal (with a few exceptions)

[1082] *The Bury and Norwich Post*, 13 January, 1857.

[1083] Saunders, *Quarter and Petty Sessions*, p. 7.

[1084] *Abstract of a return of the number of appeals to the quarter sessions against convictions by justices of the peace, in England and Wales, in 1844*, 1846, House of Commons papers, vol. 33, no. 8, p. 153.

[1085] *Return of Judicial Statistics of England and Wales, 1879* (London: HMSO, 1880), p. xxi.

from every conviction or order of a court of summary jurisdiction that inflicted imprisonment without the option of paying a fine as an alternative punishment. As a result, when, at the Walsingham Petty Sessions in 1890, Reeve Adcock was convicted of "gross cruelty" to a pig and sentenced to 14 days' imprisonment, his counsel immediately evinced an intention to appeal to the higher forum.[1086] Despite this, the number of 'criminal' cases referred to quarter sessions remained quite modest. In 1899 just two summary convictions were appealed from Norfolk petty sessions; neither conviction was quashed, although one sentence was reduced. These numbers were fairly typical of English counties outside Lancashire (where 14 cases were appealed) and those containing major cities.[1087] However, two years later, in 1901, eight appeals were entered from Norfolk summary courts, albeit only three were determined before the end of the year. In one of the three, the original decision was affirmed; in the other two it was reversed.[1088]

Cases appealed to quarter sessions would be reheard in front of a bench of magistrates (sitting without a jury). For example, in 1852 an appeal against conviction in the case of *Colman* v. *Clarke* was heard at the County of Norwich (not Norfolk) Quarter Sessions. Both the appellants and respondents were legally represented. In May the previous year, Colman had established a business to manufacture cake from rice waste. It was alleged that this quickly produced offensive smells. The firm was summonsed before the magistrates for permitting a nuisance and fined. The appeal was based on the informality of the original proceedings and an alleged want of jurisdiction on the part of the JPs. This seems to have found favour with the magistrates and recorder at quarter sessions, as the conviction was quashed.[1089]

Administration

Every court of quarter sessions had a clerk of the peace, who was responsible for its administration. Normally, a qualified solicitor held, or at least discharged, this position, although there was no statutory requirement that this be so before passage of the Justices' Clerks Act 1877. This finally provided that a clerk to the justices had to either be a lawyer or to have served as an assistant clerk. The clerk of the peace recorded the court's proceedings, called on and swore in its juries, drew up a significant number of its indictments, received the bills returned by the grand jury, arraigned prisoners, advised JPs on the law where necessary, and even taxed costs.

For county quarter sessions, this person was often formally appointed by the *custos rotulorum*. At the start of the Victorian era, the position attracted a large fee income, so that the man appointed did not always discharge the duties of the office in person (and was not always even legally qualified), but sometimes selected a solicitor to act as his deputy in return for a share of the fees. The Prosecution

---

1086 *The Bury and Norwich Post*, 15 April, 1890.

1087 *Judicial Statistics, 1899,* p. 129.

1088 *Judicial Statistics, 1901,* p. 177.

1089 Mackie, *Norfolk Annals,* vol. 2, p. 20.

Expenses (Amendment) Act 1851 allowed the benches to pay a salary to a clerk to the bench, and, with payment by salary gradually introduced around the country after 1852, this practice came to an end. In July 1855, when payment of the Norfolk clerk of the peace changed from fees to a salary, the relevant committee at quarter sessions recommended a figure of £1,200 per annum, to be paid from the following January.[1090] Some clerks of the peace served for many years, and a combination of long experience in office and close acquaintance with criminal procedure gave them considerable practical power.

Adjourned Sessions

At the start of the Victorian era, some counties held their quarter sessions at four different locations over the course of the year, while a few, like tiny Rutland, employed just one (on four occasions). Others preferred to meet at one main town four times a year, but then adjourned to other locations a few days later, with an understanding that major administrative decisions would normally only be made at the central sessions, which also usually had the heaviest case load. This was the procedure in Norfolk, where county quarter sessions were always first held at the city's Shirehall in Norwich and then, within a few days of the Norwich sitting, were conducted in one or two of the other boroughs, in what were often termed "adjourned sessions." As a result, there might (effectively) be three sittings, four times a year, producing at least a dozen "separate" sessions annually.[1091]

The sessions held at Norwich, which heard more criminal cases and dealt with almost all county business, were longer than those at the adjourned locations, which normally lasted just a day or, at most, two, so that Norwich was sometimes referred to as the "great division" for the county.[1092] Even so, the county quarter sessions held at Swaffham in January 1839, before Sir William ffolkes, saw 22 prisoners listed for trial.[1093] Those held at the same small town in July 1849 were also quite lengthy, being conducted over two days..[1094]

Different chairmen and JPs from those at Norwich would usually preside over adjourned hearings, although there might be some overlap in personnel, while clerical support and the clerk of the peace would normally be the same. For example, in 1842 the Epiphany quarter sessions for Norfolk held at Norwich took place a few days into the new year, while the adjournment to Swaffham opened on 12 January, followed two days later by that at Walsingham. None of the five "prominent" magistrates present at Swaffham were among those at the latter forum, although, it seems, one or two had been at the initial Norwich hearings. (Both saw numerous

---

1090 *The Bury and Norwich Post*, 11 July, 1855.

1091 *The Ipswich Journal*, 5 July, 1873.

1092 *Ibid.*, 6 January, 1883.

1093 *The Norfolk Chronicle*, 12 January, 1839.

1094 *Ibid.*, 21 July, 1849.

other magistrates present.)[1095] The following year, the same quarter sessions, having been conducted in Norwich at the start of January, were held by adjournment at Swaffham on 11 January, when 36 prisoners came for trial, and Sir William ffolkes presided as chairman. Two days later, they were held at Walsingham, where another 22 prisoners were tried, with Lord Hastings then chairman of the bench.[1096] Crimes would normally be tried at the designated forum for the place where they had been committed.

The boroughs outside Norwich hosting such (adjourned) county sessions varied slightly over the course of the Victorian period but were normally drawn from one of the following: Walsingham, King's Lynn, Swaffham, Holt, Aylsham, Attleborough, and Thetford. Some of these were employed for only short periods or on an occasional basis. Attleborough, for example, was mainly (though not solely) used in the 1870s, while others, such as King's Lynn, were employed much more regularly during the century.[1097] By the final years of the era, Lynn was the only town holding adjourned county sessions outside Norwich.[1098] (For the avoidance of confusion, it should be noted that King's Lynn and Thetford also hosted their own, entirely separate, borough quarter sessions, as did Norwich).

As the above suggests, the towns used for adjourned county quarter sessions changed periodically, usually for reasons of administrative or practical convenience. Thus, at the Norfolk quarter sessions in Norwich in March 1838, Colonel Mason proposed that the sittings at King's Lynn be moved to Swaffham. It was not an easy choice. Some thought that if this were to occur Swaffham would need a new courthouse adjacent to their prison which would cost up to £1,200 to build, while Lynn needed a new prison if it were to continue in use. Even so, the proposal was eventually carried.[1099] As a result, in October 1847 the Swaffham adjournment of the Norfolk quarter sessions were held in the town Shirehall before Colonel Mason (the chairman) and a bench of magistrates.[1100] Quarter sessions continued to be heard at Swaffham in the 1850s and 1860s. However, at the Norfolk quarter sessions at Norwich in October 1874, one JP, Major Hare, tried to reverse the move when he proposed "that at all future sessions the court be adjourned to King's Lynn, and not to Swaffham." His motion lost by just one vote, at 28 to 27, and he intimated that he would bring it forward again at the next sessions.[1101] Even so, sessions remained at Swaffham for some time longer.

1095 *The Bury and Norwich Post*, 19 January, 1842.

1096 *Ibid.*, 18 January, 1843.

1097 *Ibid.*, 30 March, 1875.

1098 Anon., *Statistics Relating…1896* (1898), p. 67.

1099 *The Bury and Norwich Post*, 21 March, 1838.

1100 *The Norfolk News*, 6 November, 1847.

1101 *The Bury and Norwich Post*, 27 October, 1874.

Similarly, adjourned county quarter sessions were regularly held at Walsingham during the early Victorian period. They sat there for the last time in January 1861. On this occasion Sir Willoughby Jones, who presided as chairman, informed the grand jury that the cases previously dealt with at this forum would be moved to Swaffham and Norwich "on account of the expenses being so great in proportion to the number of prisoners for trial."[1102]

Unsurprisingly, by far the busiest county quarter sessions were those conducted in Norwich. Frequently two courts would run concurrently, for more than a day, to deal with the heavy caseload.[1103] Nationally, such simultaneous hearings had occurred from early in the nineteenth century and were expressly authorized by statute in 1819.[1104] The quarter sessions would use the same rooms in the Shirehall building that were employed by the assizes. Thus, in July 1849 one of the two courts was run in the "crown court" used to try criminal matters at assizes, and the other was conducted in the "*nisi prius* court" room, normally employed to hear civil matters. (The grand-jury room in the same complex was later used by the JPs to conduct county administrative business).[1105] This arrangement would require two chairmen and benches of JPs to be present. Thus, at the Norfolk county quarter sessions held at Norwich in March 1838, the bench divided, with John Weyland acting as chairman of one court and Henry Dover the other.[1106] Similarly, at the quarter sessions held in Norwich in July 1844, two courts were presided over simultaneously by Henry Partridge and Henry Dover.[1107]

Reputation

It has been suggested that the reputation of county quarter sessions was consistently bad throughout the nineteenth century; many chairmen on the bench were said to lack legal qualifications, to fail to take proper notes of the evidence, to periodically display bias against the accused, and to frequently hand down sentences far more severe than those imposed for similar crimes at assizes.[1108] There is some truth to such an analysis, although it can also be exaggerated.

A case from Suffolk in 1837 is indicative of what could sometimes be a decidedly rough-and-ready system, especially early in the era. Thirty-four-year-old Rebecca Watling was convicted at the Suffolk quarter sessions in January that year for stealing three quarts of sherry from her master, the Reverend Edward Butts of Hartest, and

---

1102 *The Norfolk Chronicle,* 11 January, 1861.

1103 *The Ipswich Journal*, 5 July, 1873.

1104 Cornish, *Oxford History*, p. 920.

1105 *The Bury and Norwich Post*, 11 July, 1849.

1106 *Ibid.,* 21 March, 1838.

1107 *Ibid.,* 10 July, 1844.

1108 Bentley, *English Criminal Justice,* p. 78.

sentenced to seven years' transportation.[1109] In itself, this was slightly unusual. Many clerical employers in this situation would simply have dismissed such a maid without a reference. However, there were other features to the case. The following month, a petition was presented to the Home Secretary, asking for mitigation of Watling's sentence, signed by the churchwardens, overseers of the poor, and principal inhabitants of Hartest. It claimed that the prisoner had been committed to gaol by examining JPs on 9 January, arriving at the prison at 5 pm, before being tried and convicted the next day. She was 50 miles from her friends and relations, who had no time to attend and speak for her character. The Reverend Edward Barlee, the rector of Southwold, stated that he had known the prisoner for some years, and that she was very respectable, and far above the crime she was alleged to have committed.[1110] It was also claimed that she did not have time to arrange defence counsel, as might otherwise have been the case.[1111] Even so, eight months later, and despite such entreaties, Watling was transferred to the *Alwick*, lying off Woolwich, to begin her voyage to seven years in New South Wales.[1112]

One contemporary observer also thought that the "heavy sentences" meted out to those convicted at the 'adjourned' Norfolk quarter sessions held at Swaffham in January 1879 smacked of the eighteenth rather than the late nineteenth century. For example, 60-year-old James Rolfe received seven years' penal servitude for stealing a pocketknife. Another man received ten years for stealing a horse rug, a halter, three chaff bags, and three manure bags. (Both men had previous convictions.) The same observer thought that the JPs who could impose such draconian and disproportionate sentences must be totally uninformed and ignorant of their effect and opined that the sooner their powers were placed in "competent hands" the better it would be for everyone.[1113]

Nevertheless, such cases were not necessarily typical, and some observers thought that whatever its limitations, the "court of quarter sessions – especially the larger county sessions, where the lay element is strongly represented upon the bench – is a court wherein an innocent man desiring an honest verdict may take his trial with a real sense of security." [1114] Clearly, much turned on the ability of the presiding chairman.

1109 *The Bury and Norwich Post,* 18 January, 1837.

1110 *Ibid.,* 15 February, 1837.

1111 TNA HO 17/43/24

1112 *The Bury & Norwich Post, & East Anglian: Or, Suffolk, Norfolk, Essex, Cambridge, and Ely Intelligencer,* 20 September, 1837.

1113 *The Sporting Gazette and Agricultural Journal*, 11 January, 1879, p. 34.

1114 Parry, *What the Judge Saw,* p. 103.

The Chairmen

As some of the instances cited above suggest, Norfolk usually appointed several chairmen, if only to preside over the different sittings of the court held by adjournment around the county, although they were usually distinguished by seniority. Thus, in 1880, it was noted that Lord Walsingham had been elected "second chairman" of Swaffham quarter sessions, in place of the recently deceased Sir William Bagge.[1115] However, as the barrister John de Grey noted at the end of the Victorian period, if a formally appointed chairman was unavailable to preside over quarter sessions, any JP could take the role: "In his [the Chairman's] not infrequent absence, any other magistrate may be called upon to sit."[1116] Nevertheless, whatever may have been the situation elsewhere in the country, it seems that this did not occur very often in Norfolk.

Ostensibly, chairmen were no different from other JPs, albeit usually being representative of the more socially elevated members of the county magistracy. Many (but far from all) were legally unqualified. This could sometimes occasion problems. The MP Edmund Denison, himself a JP, thought: "There had always been great difficulty in procuring competent chairmen at sessions; and even the most competent of that class often found themselves exceedingly embarrassed without the aid of skilful and learned counsel." Writing in the early 1860s, Thomas William Saunders thought it absurd that chairmen were often drawn from private gentlemen, clergymen, and former naval or military officers. Certainly, some such men could be found in Norfolk. For example, Marsham Elwin (1784-1831) of Thurning, one of the chairmen of the county quarter sessions in the 1820s, was simply a very prosperous country gentleman.[1117] Similarly, Sir Willoughby Jones (1820-1884), a chairman of quarter sessions for almost 30 years (as well as chairman of the Fakenham division petty sessions), was a baronet, son of a major general, and product of Eton and Cambridge, but he, too, was merely a Norfolk landowner, resident at Cranmer Hall near Fakenham.[1118]

Thomas William Saunders thought that this situation was particularly strange as, after the passing of the Municipal Corporations Act of 1835, borough quarter sessions *had* to be presided over by a recorder who was a barrister of at least five years' standing, even though he often dealt with less serious offences than his county equivalent (see below).[1119] Thus, in February 1839, Yarmouth borough sessions were held before the town recorder, the experienced local circuit barrister Nathaniel Palmer.[1120] In the absence of such lawyers, the borough sessions could not

---

[1115] *The Norfolk Chronicle,* 14 April, 1880.

[1116] De Grey, "Is It Expedient," p. 386.

[1117] *The Norfolk Chronicle,* 1 June, 1831.

[1118] *The Bury and Norwich Post*, 26 August, 1884.

[1119] Saunders, *Quarter and Petty Sessions,* p. 5.

[1120] *The Ipswich Journal*, 9 February, 1839.

be held, as was the case in March 1868, when neither the recorder, or a suitably qualified deputy to act on his behalf, appeared on the day fixed for holding the court.[1121]

By contrast, it was sometimes claimed that chairmen of county quarter sessions would often not give public reasons for their forensic decisions, for fear of exposing their ignorance of the law. Instead of being a man of legal ability, the chairman was "more likely to be a worthy squire, a zealous agriculturist, an admirable silent member, and a perfect gentleman." The neutrality of some was also suspect; it was asked: "Why should the offenders of a county be judged by their own landlords, while a small county town pays some 40 1. [£40] to a barrister [its recorder] to come down and make a gaol delivery?" [1122]

Even so, from the 1830s, at least, it seems that nationally there was a greatly increased likelihood that appointment as chairmen of county quarter sessions would not be based purely on social status, but also require some form of legal qualification or at least considerable earlier experience as a JP, as well as a degree of native ability and a willingness to spend a significant amount of time in the role.[1123] Thus, at a meeting of the Cheshire quarter sessions held at Knutsford in the 1870s, it was even claimed that it was always the case that those magistrates who had "worked hardest and done best, at least if they have conjoined with the longest experience of a magistrate's duties a regular legal training, are elected to fill these offices." Inevitably, there were limits on how far this process went. The best-qualified individuals might still be rejected for reasons of political allegiance or inferior social status in favour of somewhat less qualified magistrates with the "correct" views and background.[1124] Nevertheless, the general pattern is fairly clear.

The de facto requirement that chairmen normally be men of some ability and energy can clearly be identified in nineteenth-century Norfolk. The demands of the position meant that chairmen would regularly resign for ill health or the pressure of their other obligations. For example, at the Norfolk quarter sessions in July 1855, the resignations of two such chairmen were announced: Henry Dover for poor health and T.J. Birch for a combination of ill health and increasing work commitments.[1125]

Even more important, many Norfolk chairmen *were* legally qualified. For example, Henry Dover had been elected in 1831 as a chairman in place of Sir Edward Hall Alderson. The former was a barrister while the latter not only had the same status but was an outstanding commercial lawyer who had been appointed as a Justice of the Common Pleas.[1126] Similarly, William Frere, who had been a chairman of Norfolk

[1121] Palmer, *Yarmouth Notes,* p. 319.

[1122] *The Spectator,* 7 September ,1867, p. 7.

[1123] Scollan, *Parish constables,* p. 68.

[1124] *The Spectator,* 30 October, 1875, p. 9.

[1125] *The Bury and Norwich Post*, 11 July, 1855.

[1126] *Norfolk Chronicle,* 8 April, 1831.

quarter sessions before his death at the age of 60 in 1836, had been called to the bar in 1802 and become a serjeant-at-law in 1809. For many years he was also recorder of Bury in Suffolk.[1127] In 1840 Isaac Jermy and Henry Champion Partridge were elected as chairmen of the Norfolk quarter sessions at a meeting of the county magistrates in the Shirehall. Partridge was a barrister with chambers in Inner Temple. Jermy was both a practising barrister and the recorder of Norwich.[1128] This could lead to a full diary. For example, in one week in July 1838 Jermy presided over the city quarter sessions in his capacity as recorder on the Tuesday, and then over the Norfolk quarter sessions on the Wednesday and Thursday in his capacity as chairman.[1129]

Moving on a few years, Sir William Meybohm Rider Haggard (1817-1893), father of the celebrated adventure writer, was Lord of the Manor of Bradenham and the product of several generations of Norfolk squires. However, he had also been called to the bar in 1842 and, although he did not need an income, had conducted a modest practice, including criminal matters, for some time thereafter. He became one of the most active magistrates in the county, and for some 36 years was chairman of the quarter sessions held by adjournment at Swaffham and later at King's Lynn. (He was also a member of the Committee of Visitors to Norwich Castle gaol.)[1130] Even Sir Willoughby Jones (see above) had started training for the bar after leaving university, until the murder of his older brother in Turkey obliged him to take over the family estates. He was considered an able man, becoming high sheriff for Norfolk in 1851 and, briefly, an MP.[1131]

Furthermore, even in the latter decades of the Victorian period, some senior Westminster-based judges and other very prominent lawyers still served as chairmen of their county quarter sessions. Thus, in late 1901 the chairmen of 69 such courts in England and Wales included one Law Lord, four county court judges, two King's Counsel (not including two of the latter rank who acted as assistant chairmen in Devonshire), and eight barristers.[1132] Norfolk had several chairmen of particularly high legal status. For example, in early 1880 Edward Ebenezer Kay QC, who lived at Brockdish, in South Norfolk, was appointed third chairman of the Norfolk quarter sessions.[1133] He became a judge in the Chancery Division of the High Court the following year. Similarly, in January 1883 James Redford Bulwer QC was elected as a chairman of the Norfolk quarter sessions, replacing the retired Sir Willoughby Jones.[1134] He had been called to the bar in 1847, taken silk in 1865, become one of

1127 *The Gentleman's Magazine*, vols. 160-161, p. 235.

1128 *The Norfolk Chronicle,* 20 March, 1840.

1129 *The Bury and Norwich Post*, 11 July, 1838.

1130 Haggard, *The Days*, pp. 26-27.

1131 *The Bury and Norwich Post*, 26 August, 1884.

1132 De Grey, "Is It Expedient," p. 394.

1133 *The Norfolk Chronicle,* 8 April, 1880.

1134 *The Ipswich Journal*, 6 January, 1883.

the Masters in Lunacy and been recorder of Ipswich and then Cambridge for several decades. He served as chairman until the end of 1898 (and died the following year).[1135]

Borough (Quarter) Sessions

Independent of the county quarter sessions, Norwich, King's Lynn, Yarmouth, and Thetford all conducted their own borough or city (in the case of Norwich) quarter sessions during the Victorian period. By comparison, some 15 towns in early Victorian Kent could hold such sessions, while some shires had just two or three.[1136] As with their county equivalent, these forums employed both a grand and petty jury and were both a trial court of first instance and (less important) an appeal forum for decisions from borough petty sessions (which they would rehear without a jury). For an example of the latter, in 1860 the borough quarter sessions, presided over by its recorder, quashed on appeal the sentence of a woman named Cooper. She had been committed by the mayor of Yarmouth (a magistrate for the town) to three months' imprisonment under the Vagrancy Act, having been found in suspicious circumstances in the town marketplace. (She was refused her costs, because she had failed to give the police her address in Norwich when arrested, helping to bring about the conviction)[1137]

The amount of criminal work dealt with by the Norfolk borough sessions varied very significantly from town to town and over time. (Unlike their county cousins, they had lost most of their administrative work in 1835.) Unsurprisingly, Norwich was normally the busiest of the four, followed by Great Yarmouth, and then King's Lynn, while Thetford (small and without a port) was by far the quietest. In February 1839 there were at least eight defendants at the borough sessions held in the Yarmouth tollhouse, in as many cases, set down over two days.[1138] Three months later, there were 23 prisoners for trial at the same forum, although in March 1847 only one prisoner was awaiting his hearing there, an old man charged with stealing a cask of pickled herrings (for which he was sentenced to one month's imprisonment).[1139]

By contrast, in Thetford, only two prisoners went for trial in January 1846, and just one case, which produced a directed acquittal, was tried when they were held three months later. There were five cases in July 1850, although one was thrown out by the grand jury. Perhaps more typically, in July 1880 just one man was set down for trial in the town hall.[1140] However, in June 1865 the Thetford recorder, Thomas Birch, informed the assembled juries (grand and petty) that there was no business

---

[1135] *The Norfolk Chronicle,* 4 March, 1899.

[1136] Conley, *The Unwritten Law,* p. 11.

[1137] *The Bury and Norwich Post*, 3 January, 1860.

[1138] *The Ipswich Journal*, 9 February, 1839.

[1139] Palmer, *Yarmouth Notes,* p. 69, p. 120.

[1140] *The Bury and Norwich Post*, 6 July, 1880.

at all to be heard. He also told them that this was the seventeenth or eighteenth time that he had attended sessions in the town over the years without there being any prisoners to be tried. As a result, he thought that Thetford was "one of the best-behaved towns in the country."[1141] The same situation occurred again in March the following year, while Carlos Cooper, who succeeded Birch, had an identical experience five years later.[1142] In April 1890, when there were (again) no prisoners for trial, the recorder did not even attend, the mayor opening the Thetford Sessions, thanking the grand jury for their presence, and then dismissing them.[1143] The Assizes and Quarter Sessions Act 1908 finally allowed quarter sessions to be dispensed with altogether if there was no business to transact.

This proportionate difference in caseloads among the county borough sessions continued to the end of the century, although the total number of jury matters heard on indictment declined significantly in all of them (the result of a general fall in criminal prosecutions and an expansion in summary jurisdiction.) Thus, during the whole of 1899, Thetford borough sessions saw just one case come for trial on indictment, those for King's Lynn witnessed two, at Great Yarmouth borough sessions 14 matters were tried, and at the Norwich city sessions 31 cases went for a hearing.[1144]

As already noted, Victorian borough (quarter) sessions were presided over by a legally qualified and experienced recorder (frequently a barrister from the local circuit) rather than a (normally) lay chairman (unlike county quarter sessions). He often took the position as much for the prestige as for the modest remuneration. The 1835 statute (see above) had certainly been effective in improving the standard of such part-time judges. In the early 1830s the *Times* had been very dismissive of their quality, thinking that most were not very learned and had obtained their positions through family connections.[1145] This is, perhaps, not entirely surprising, as fewer than half the towns with such officers even formally required their recorder to be legally qualified (even if they usually were). This was outlawed by the 1835 Act.[1146]

Some of the men subsequently appointed as recorders were of a very high calibre, having been appointed as Queen's Counsel ("taken silk"). For example, the Norwich quarter sessions in the early 1860s were conducted before the city recorder, Peter Frederic O'Malley QC.[1147] In the following decade David Brown QC held the same

---

1141 *The Bury and Norwich Post, and Suffolk Herald*, 20 June, 1865.

1142 *The Bury and Norwich Post*, 27 March, 1866. *Ibid.*, 1 August, 1871.

1143 *The Bury and Norwich Post, and Suffolk Standard*, 22 April, 1890.

1144 *Statistics Relating…1899*, p. 109.

1145 *The Times*, 15 June, 1832, p. 3.

1146 Bentley, *English Criminal Justice*, p. 77.

1147 *The Norfolk Chronicle*, 1 July, 1862.

position for King's Lynn.[1148] The recorder of the Thetford borough quarter sessions from 1865 to 1885, Carlos Cooper (1815-1897), a Lincoln's Inn barrister who had been called to the bar in early 1839, was a hugely experienced member of the local circuit mess, one who had cut his teeth as an advocate at county quarter sessions, and also had a home in Norwich. In 1885 he exchanged his recordership in Thetford for that of King's Lynn, a position he held until his death.[1149] When William Metcalfe, the recorder of Norwich, died in 1892 at the age of 74, it was noted that he had been made Queen's Counsel in 1873. He was succeeded as recorder of Norwich by Thomas Richardson Kemp, another 'silk'.[1150]

The recorders, like judges at assizes, would wear wigs and gowns, unlike chairmen at county quarter sessions. Rather inauspiciously, at the borough quarter sessions for Great Yarmouth in June 1847, the "Recorder sat without his wig, that appendage having been stolen."[1151] Recorders usually took all important legal decisions but would be flanked on the bench by other borough magistrates, including the town mayor, and supported by a borough clerk of the peace, who looked after the administration of the sessions on behalf of the mayor and aldermen of the town. For example, the Epiphany Borough Sessions for Thetford in 1846 were conducted in front of its recorder, J.T. Birch, its mayor, H.W. Bailey, and another magistrate, L.S. Bidwell, who had himself been mayor a couple of years earlier (as was often the case with borough magistrates).[1152] At the same forum, more than 40 years later, in April 1888, the recorder was joined on the bench by the mayor and three other borough JPs.[1153] Similarly, when the Yarmouth borough quarter sessions for January 1888 were held before the town's recorder, Simms Reeve, who had been appointed to the position in 1872 (he practised on the South Eastern Circuit), seven magistrates, including the mayor, were also on the bench.[1154]

Most legal representation at borough sessions would be provided by junior barristers earning relatively small fees. However, it was not always confined to such lawyers. In January 1846 at the Thetford Borough Sessions there were just two prisoners, in one case, for trial (not unusual for the town). Elizabeth Fife was charged with stealing a silver watch worth £3, and William Cooper was indicted for receiving it. As it was a traditionally a very quiet borough sessions, solicitors had full rights of audience in the court, and Robert Eagle Clarke appeared for both the defendants. He cross-examined the prosecution witnesses, challenging their identification of the watch, addressed the jury on behalf of the accused, and called a character witness

---

1148 *The Belfast News-Letter*, 10 July, 1876.

1149 *The Times*, 2 November, 1897, p. 8.

1150 *The Norfolk Chronicle,* 8 December, 1892.

1151 Palmer, *Yarmouth Notes,* p. 120.

1152 *The Ipswich Journal*, 17 January, 1846.

1153 *The Bury and Norwich Post,* 24 April, 1888.

1154 *The Ipswich Journal*, 3 January, 1888.

for Fife. The recorder then summed up the case for the jury. Both defendants were found guilty, although the jury recommended Fife to mercy. As a result, the young woman received six months' imprisonment while Cooper was given a year (both with hard labour).[1155]

Thetford borough (and petty) sessions were usually held at the town Guildhall. Its recorder was paid £40 a year (a common sum for such positions), while its clerk of the peace was paid by the fees he received. Money for the former, and some of the latter, was drawn from the borough fund. Under the 1888 Act, small boroughs of less than 10,000 inhabitants (as determined by the 1881 census), with their own quarter sessions and commissions of the peace, were allowed to ask for their abolition and their incorporation into the county system. Although Thetford fell into this category, it preserved its independence and even at one point (unavailingly) asked the county to fund the recorder's salary pursuant to the same 1888 statute.[1156]

The Assizes

Assizes were temporary courts, traditionally sitting twice a year in the counties outside London and Middlesex. One was normally held in late February and March, the other in July and early August (Lent and Summer Assizes respectively). They had a joint civil and criminal jurisdiction, usually discharged simultaneously, in two separate courts, by the pair of judges assigned to cover each sessions. The former, the *nisi prius* jurisdiction, heard civil cases that would otherwise have been determined at one of the Westminster courts (Common Pleas, Queen's Bench, etc.). Thus in August 1840 three cases involving breach of warranty in the sale of a horse were heard at the Norfolk assizes.[1157] In July 1848 a libel action was tried at *nisi prius* before Mr Baron Parke; the plaintiff, a Fakenham solicitor, sued for damages on the basis that the defendants, the proprietors of the *Norwich Mercury*, had claimed in their journal that he deserved to be struck off the rolls for misconduct. (The jury agreed that this was libellous but awarded him only 40s).[1158] In a negligence case of July 1860, before Chief Baron Pollock and a special jury, the plaintiff was a carpenter from Yarmouth, and the defendant the proprietor of a travelling menagerie. One of the attractions of his show was a Zulu, styled a "lion king," who fired pistols in a cage containing several of the animals. While dealing with an aggressive lion, the Zulu fired a wad that hit the carpenter in the face and rendered him blind in one eye. (The jury awarded the plaintiff £150 in damages.)[1159] However, the criminal jurisdiction of assizes was far more important than its civil work.

Prior to the late eighteenth century, most assizes (unlike Old Bailey hearings) were held in improvised courtrooms, frequently set up in a county shirehall, with simple

[1155] *Ibid.*, 17 January, 1846.

[1156] *The Times*, 26 July, 1898, p. 3.

[1157] *The Bury and Norwich Post*, 5 August, 1840.

[1158] *The Norfolk Chronicle*, 28 July, 1848.

[1159] *Ibid.*, 27 July, 1860.

furniture, stored from sessions to sessions, being brought out to create a basic court structure. This gradually changed during the 1800s. For example, some courts, such as that opened in Carlisle in 1808, were purpose-built. In others, a more permanently and formally arranged court was introduced to the building in which they were already being held.[1160]

Traditionally, the Guildhall and Shirehall in Norwich provided the forums for the Norwich and Norfolk assizes respectively. They were (and are) about 400 metres apart. When in 1822 a new Shirehall, designed by the distinguished Norwich-born architect William Wilkins, was built just to the east of the castle mound, it housed purpose-built courtrooms which remained in service throughout the Victorian era (closing only in 1988). Until 1883, when the county and city gaol was moved from the castle to Mousehold Heath, prisoners would be brought from their cells in the adjacent prison, down a spiral staircase and along a tunnel, to a holding cell next to the courtroom door to await their hearings. (The court building was also used for the county quarter sessions.) The Norwich Guildhall, which was the centre of the city government as well as the forum for its own assizes, was (and is) an imposing late-medieval building of chequerboard flint and stone, standing on the north side of the marketplace. By the Victorian era it had a permanently arranged courtroom. It was also home to the Norwich quarter sessions and the city petty sessions.[1161]

Jurisdiction

As the highest provincial jury court, the assizes dealt with the gravest crimes, such as murder, manslaughter, robbery, and rape. These offences could not be heard at the lower jury forum by dint of the Quarter Sessions Act 1842 (5 & 6 Vict. c. 38) because they were punishable on a first conviction by death or penal servitude for life. Burglary (not housebreaking) also fell into this category until 1896, when statute allowed less serious examples of the crime to be dealt with at quarter sessions, a power that was quickly exercised. However, although there had been periodic suggestions after the mid-century that an increased number of serious offences should be tried at quarter sessions instead of assizes, this was the only significant formal devolution of power during the Victorian era, not least because many Westminster judges had doubts about the ability of most quarter-sessions chairmen to preside over serious matters in a satisfactory manner.[1162]

For example, at the Lent assizes for Norfolk in 1837, among the 62 prisoners set down for trial, there were four for murder, three for manslaughter, two for rape, three for arson, and five for highway robbery.[1163] Assizes also normally dealt with certain crimes that were considered legally difficult, even if not always very grave on

[1160] Jonathan Simon, *Architecture and Justice: Judicial Meanings in the Public Realm* (Abingdon: Routledge, 2016), p. 73.

[1161] In 1861 a police station was added to the west end of the building.

[1162] Cornish, *Oxford History*, p. 919.

[1163] *The Ipswich Journal*, 8 April, 1837.

their facts, such as perjury, forgery, bigamy, and praemunire, either because specific statute required it or by convention. Furthermore, the assizes might sometimes be expected to deal with exceptionally serious examples of ordinary crimes, such as simple larceny and housebreaking, that could theoretically have been dealt with at quarter sessions.

However, the assizes also dealt with numerous run-of-the-mill indictable matters, many of them quite trivial, including some misdemeanours. For example, at the autumn assizes in 1879, just two of 11 cases from Norfolk could be tried only at the higher jury forum, although the figure was four from six for the city of Norwich.[1164] Similarly, in 1885, even at the combined Suffolk, Norfolk, and Norwich spring assizes that made up County No. 7 (see below), which forums were expressly encouraged to take serious cases, it was noted that some of the nine prisoners from Norwich were being prosecuted for "minor offences." (The others were tried for burglary and perjury.)[1165]

On a more general basis, at the Lent assizes held for both Norfolk and the city of Norwich in March 1848, the Crown Side caseload was particularly heavy, with 62 prisoners in the calendar. Of these, six were accused of arson, 14 of burglary, two of rape, three of highway robbery, eight of night poaching, three of assault and robbery, one of shooting with intent to murder, three of felonious assaults on constables, one of forgery, one of forging a will, and two of uttering a forged will. Of the remainder, one was accused of horse-theft, one of concealing a birth, three of stabbing, one of administering laudanum, and one of bigamy, while some 13 prisoners, were merely accused of various forms of larceny (all of which could have been tried at the lower jury forum).[1166] At the assizes for Norfolk and Norwich in August 1870, there was a lighter load, and just 16 prisoners for trial, but much the same spread of offences: one accused was charged with murder, two with rape, and two with arson. However, the remainder – one case of unlawful wounding, one of concealment of birth, one of bigamy, two of embezzlement, and six of ordinary larceny – could have been dealt with at the lower jury forum.[1167]

Furthermore, many of the larcenies sent for trial at assizes were not even very serious examples of such crimes. At the Norfolk assizes in July 1887, 45-year-old Henry Woods, was convicted of stealing a coat from another man at Carleton Rode and sentenced to 12 months' imprisonment with hard labour.[1168] There was absolutely no need for this sort of case to go to the higher jury court, but such proceedings were a nationwide phenomenon and certainly not confined to East Anglia. For example, at the assizes held at Reading and Oxford (for Berkshire and Oxfordshire

---

1164 *Criminal cases... 1879*, p. 2.

1165 *The Bury and Norwich Post*, 28 April, 1885.

1166 *The Morning Chronicle*, 31 March, 1848.

1167 *The Bury and Norwich Post*, 8 August, 1876.

1168 *Ibid.*, 26 July, 1887.

respectively) in 1883, 1884, and 1885, 23 of the 89 people who went for trial (more than a quarter) could have been tried at quarter sessions. Additionally, many of the sentences imposed for "assizes only" offences were of a level that was regularly passed for crimes at the lower jury forum. An experienced JP thought it was obvious from this that most business transacted at assizes was no more serious than that heard at quarter sessions.[1169]

The extreme triviality of some of the crimes sent to the higher jury court sometimes angered the judges who presided over them, everywhere in England. In 1840 it was noted that Sir Herbert Jenner, a Kentish JP, had sent a man for trial at the higher forum for stealing a pennyworth of twigs. The suspect had been kept in custody in Maidstone Gaol prior to his hearing, where the case was speedily dismissed, to widespread ridicule.[1170] Shortly afterwards, a journal reminded its readers that, a few years earlier, judges giving their charges to grand juries at assizes had observed that they often found gaols filled with prisoners accused of offences of so light a character that any sentence of imprisonment passed in the event of conviction would, in many instances, be less than the punishment they had undergone before trial. As a result, they urged that such cases be dealt with at quarter sessions.[1171]

At the combined Norfolk/Norwich/Suffolk assizes held at Ipswich in May 1882, Chief Baron Pollock took the opportunity to criticize examining JPs for sending less serious matters, such as poultry theft, to the higher jury court rather than quarter sessions. Although he accepted that there might have been rational reasons for JPs making this choice, such as the proximity of assizes to crimes that had been committed shortly before a circuit started, he opined that it was a "great pity that the Assizes should be made a court of relief to Quarter Sessions."[1172]

Nevertheless, although grand juries (like members of the judiciary) might argue that many cases that might have been sent to quarter sessions went to the assizes, some "barristers complain[ed] that difficult points of law are too often referred to country gentlemen [chairmen] and Recorders [in boroughs] who have no [criminal] practice."[1173] Even low-value cases could be legally difficult.

Norfolk and the Assizes

At the start of the nineteenth century, the Lent Assizes for Norfolk had been held in Thetford, while the Summer Assizes for the county were conducted at Norwich. However, there had been a campaign for centuries to abandon Thetford, a modest town of about 4,000 in the early 1830s, and hold both sittings in Norwich, which had a growing population of more than 60,000 and was much better connected to

---

[1169] C. E. Thornhill, "Spring and Autumn Assizes," *Law Quarterly Review*, vol. 2, no. 4 (1886), p. 466.

[1170] *The Spectator,* 14 March, 1840, p. 13.

[1171] *Ibid.,* 6 June, 1840, p. 13.

[1172] *The Bury and Norwich Post, and Suffolk Herald*, 9 May, 1882.

[1173] *The Spectator,* 7 September, 1867, p. 7

other parts of both the county and circuit. Just as they had done in the eighteenth century, Thetford's inhabitants and political representatives resisted this idea vigorously, valuing the prestige and commerce that the assizes brought to their small town. Perhaps because of this, although many observers thought that the judges had the power to order such a change on a unilateral basis, the judiciary appeared reluctant to exercise it, leaving it to Parliament to make the decision.

MPs clashed in the Commons on this issue, and petitions were presented for and against the suggestion, often being prominently signed by various county JPs. However, the great majority were in favour of confining both assizes sessions to Norwich. Typically, in April 1832, in the House of Commons, Robert Grant stressed that the city was a superior venue for many reasons, not least because it contained the county gaol. The expense of sending prisoners, attorneys, and witnesses to Thetford was substantial. Thetford also lacked suitable accommodation for barristers and judges, while at Norwich it was abundant.[1174] Similarly, Sir John Sebright opined that "to have justice administered in the centre of a county would save time, trouble, and expense."[1175]

The change was eventually made in 1832, something that meant that the assizes for the city and county of Norwich (see below), which had previously been held only once a year (being conducted at the same time as those for the wider county), could be held twice a year if there was the demand. As Robert Grant noted in the Commons, this would avoid the situation in which Norwich city "prisoners were frequently confined eleven months before they were brought to trial."[1176]

As this suggests, Norfolk had two assizes jurisdictions within its bounds: the county itself and the "urban county" of the city of Norwich, the existence of the latter stretching back to the late medieval period. The sessions for both were held within the city, usually in the Shirehall and Guildhall respectively. Frequently, the judges would deal with the city of Norwich assizes first, before repairing to the Shirehall to preside over those for the county, although this was not invariably the case, and the order was sometimes reversed. For example, in the summer of 1838 Mr Justice Park was met outside Norwich on a Saturday and escorted into the city. He then opened the assizes commissions, first at the Shirehall (for the county) and then at the Guildhall (for the city of Norwich). The following morning, he attended divine service. On the Monday morning the judge went first to the Guildhall, where the prosecutors in the only cases listed failed to appear, so that proceedings were over very swiftly, and then moved on to the Shirehall, where the much lengthier county

[1174] Hansard HC Deb 23 May 1832 vol. 12 cols. 1411-4.

[1175] Hansard HC Deb 03 April 1832 vol. 11 cols. 1267-9.

[1176] Ibid.

assizes began.[1177] More than 30 years later, both the Norfolk assizes (in the Shirehall) and the city assizes (in the Guildhall) were scheduled to open on 24 March 1869.[1178]

Norfolk and Norwich were certainly not unique in this bifurcated arrangement. For example, Exeter hosted both its own assizes, as an urban county (like Norwich), and was the home of the Devonshire assizes. Similarly, the borough of Leicester had its own assizes, independent of those for surrounding Leicestershire, which also sat in the town.

Unsurprisingly, and as Mr Justice Park's experiences suggest, the city of Norwich assizes was almost always much less busy than those held for the (far larger) surrounding county. In August 1836 no cases were even listed for trial, Mr Justice Bosanquet congratulating the city's grand jury (it had still assembled) on the absence of serious crime, and then proceeding on to the county assizes.[1179] More typically, a handful of hearings would be held at this forum.

Before their departure from London, the Westminster judges would fix the dates for the opening of the assizes in each town that would host them on the circuit, being guided as best they could by information about the number and complexity of cases, civil and criminal, to be tried in each forum.[1180] Short variations of timing might be accommodated for special reasons. Thus, in January 1849, Edward Postle wrote asking the Home Office to delay the Norfolk assizes as late as possible because of the confinement of Emily Sandford (the killer James Rush's mistress), who was an important prosecution witness in the Stanfield murders.[1181]

Typically, in 1837 the Norfolk circuit's Lent assizes started at Aylesbury (for Buckinghamshire) on 4 March, sat at Bedford (for Bedfordshire) on 9 March, Huntingdon (for Huntingdonshire) on 14 March, Cambridge (for Cambridgeshire) on 18 March, Bury St Edmunds (for Suffolk) on 25 March, and Norwich (for Norfolk and Norwich) on 1 April. A few days later, the sessions being complete, the judges would begin their journey back to London.[1182] The arrangements for the summer assizes for the circuit were broadly similar. For example, in 1839, the sessions for Buckinghamshire opened at Buckingham on 15 July, those for Bedfordshire at Bedford on the 18 July, those for Huntingdonshire at Huntingdon on 22 July, those for Cambridgeshire at Cambridge on the 24 July, while those for both Norfolk and

---

[1177] *The Bury and Norwich Post*, 8 August, 1838.

[1178] *The Morning Post*, 10 February, 1869.

[1179] *The Bury & Norwich Post, & East Anglian: Or, Suffolk, Norfolk, Essex, Cambridge, and Ely Intelligencer*, 10 August, 1836.

[1180] Cottu, *Administration,* p. 41.

[1181] TNA HO 45/2718

[1182] *The Bury & Norwich Post, & East Anglian: Or, Suffolk, Norfolk, Essex, Cambridge, and Ely Intelligencer*, 1 March, 1837.

the city of Norwich opened at Norwich on 29 July before moving to Suffolk, the final venue of the circuit on this occasion, where they opened in Ipswich on 3 August.[1183]

The clerk of assizes was responsible for the administration of each circuit. This was a respected, well-remunerated, and secure position, albeit rarely a steppingstone to higher legal office, so that the most able and well-connected barristers might not seek it. Nevertheless, and indicative of its desirability, when the position fell vacant on the western circuit in 1836, the senior judge at the summer assizes, Baron Gurney, immediately appointed his son, Sidney Gurney, as the new clerk. Sidney was an undistinguished member of an otherwise talented legal family.

The clerks would normally reside in London or a major town on the relevant circuit outside sessions. Thus, at the start of the Victorian period, Harry Edgell held the position for the Norfolk circuit, and was normally resident in Chelsea. When he was not engaged on work for the assizes, he might be employed in other legal offices, such as being clerk of the errors in the Court of Exchequer. In 1841 he was supported by a deputy, John Oliver Jones, who was a London solicitor, and an associate, Harry's third son, Alexander Edgell. There was also a clerk of indictments, Samuel Robert Goodman.[1184] Alexander, who was also a Gray's Inn barrister, would subsequently become deputy, but would die at the age of 47, a year before his father, in 1862. Shortly before his own death in 1863, Harry replaced his son by promoting a London solicitor, Thomas Collisson, from the position of associate to deputy.[1185] Many of the official papers pertaining to the clerk of assize and his associates and colleagues on the Norfolk circuit survive, including correspondence relating to costs, witness expenses, jurors' excuses for non-attendance, estreated recognizances, gaol calendars, certificates of conviction, and conditional pardons.[1186]

At the start of the Victorian period, most judges were still travelling in horse-drawn carriages, employing the same means of transportation as they had for centuries. When doing so, they would be met by a small party at each county border, and a much larger and more formal reception party outside each town where assizes were held. They would then be escorted, with considerable ceremony, and with bells ringing and trumpets playing, to their lodgings or directly to the court.[1187]

In August 1825, in one of the grandest receptions for the circulating judiciary seen for a century, Lord Chief Justice Abbott and Lord Chief Baron Alexander were met at Harford Bridge, near Norwich, by the high sheriff of Norfolk, then entered the city accompanied by liveried riders, the city magistrates and aldermen, the Norwich

1183 *Standard*, 17 June, 1839.

1184 James Whishaw, *A Synopsis of the Members of the English Bar : Containing Their Academical Degrees, Inns of Court, Dates of Call, Courts in which They Practise, Official Appointments, Circuits, Chambers, &c.* (London: Stevens & Sons, 1835), pp. 273-274. *The Gentleman's Magazine, and Historical Chronicle*, vol. 215, p. 241.

1185 *The Solicitors' Journal and Reporter*, vol. 7, 1862/3, p. 347.

1186 TNA ASSI 39/19.

1187 Cottu, *Administration*, p. 43.

under-sheriff and his officers, the sheriffs for both Norfolk and the county of Norwich, two mace bearers on horseback, the under-chamberlain, the mayor, town clerk and sword bearer, the high sheriff's trumpeters and marshal men, 24 javelin men in dark blue liveries with orange cockades, and various other figures.[1188]

This procedure continued, albeit more modestly, during the early years of the new Queen's reign. Thus, at the Lent sessions in 1837, it was noted that one of the judges, Mr Justice Park, had arrived in Norwich at 4 pm on a Saturday afternoon, having been met "at the usual place" by both sheriffs (Norfolk and Norwich) and their retinues.[1189] As late as 1848, the high sheriff of Norfolk, Colonel Mason, rode out in his carriage, accompanied by his chaplain, the Reverend Henry Knatchbull, and what was described as the "usual *cortège*," to meet Mr Baron Rolfe on the Heigham Road. This may have been because this judge had been visiting Henry Dover, a prominent Norfolk JP, at Caston. (His co-adjutor, Chief Baron Sir Frederick Pollock, did not arrive until the Monday evening.) On this occasion, the high sheriff's horses were ornamented with blue and white ribbons. The javelin men were dressed in blue, and wore blue and white rosettes in their hats, their spearheads ornamented with similarly coloured tassels. They proceeded to the Shirehall, where the county assizes were formally opened, and then moved on to the Guildhall, where the judge opened the city of Norwich assizes and, at 2 pm, attended divine service at the cathedral, where the Reverend Knatchbull preached the sermon.[1190] Further ceremony might ensue in the city. In 1835 Lord Chief Baron Abinger, who had arrived for the assizes, was waited upon at the judges' lodgings, in Bethel Street, by the mayor and corporation of Norwich, this being his first visit to the city in a judicial capacity.[1191] During the early Victorian period, trumpeters and javelin men would escort judges every day to the assize hall, and back again to their lodgings.[1192]

However, such ceremony declined in later decades, due to changing modes of travel and the prevailing spirit of the age, the latter of which seems to have affected the judges themselves, despite their supposed reverence for tradition. By the 1840s railways, which were much faster, more comfortable, and more reliable than horse-drawn carriages, were often being used by the judiciary, something that became increasingly common as the national rail network expanded over ensuing years. This meant that the judges might have to be received and escorted from the train stations to their lodgings and the courts, rather than being met outside the town. Typically, in May 1881, the combined spring assizes for Suffolk, Norfolk, and the city of Norwich were held at the Shirehall in Ipswich before Sir Henry Hawkins, who had arrived in the town by the 11.33 am train from Cambridge, being met at

---

1188 *The Norfolk Chronicle,* 1 August, 1825.

1189 *The Ipswich Journal,* 8 April, 1837.

1190 Anon, *Stanfield Hall,* pp. 1-10.

1191 *The Norfolk Chronicle,* 3 April,1835.

1192 Cottu, *Administration,* p. 43.

the station by the high sheriff and his chaplain.[1193] The following year Chief Baron Pollock arrived at 4.16 pm on the same Cambridge train, and was met by the same dignitaries and a police escort.[1194]

In the early years of the Victorian era, the judges' reception, even at a train station, was still carried out by the county high sheriff and javelin men, as well as other local dignitaries. However, over time, some of these ceremonial features became attenuated or were abandoned. This was a nationwide phenomenon, albeit happening at different times around the country. In Bristol mounted police replaced the javelin men at the summer assizes as early as 1836. However, although pageantry had been in marked decline since the early 1840s, it seems that nationally the mid-1850s marked something of a turning point in this regard. For example, at Winchester, the judges were first escorted into the city in 1855 by the Hampshire constabulary "instead of the old retinue of javelin men."[1195]

By 1859 statute meant that it was no longer necessary for the high sheriff even to (notionally) maintain javelin men, if quarter sessions required the chief constable to provide police officers to cover their tasks instead. At the Michaelmas quarter sessions for Norfolk that year, the county Police Committee called attention to this Act and urged that its powers be exercised.[1196] At the start of January 1860, at the quarter sessions in Norwich, the committee formally recommended that the chief constable be allowed to supply police constables for keeping order in the assize courts, in place of javelin men, the high sheriff engaging to pay any additional expense. The chairman, Sir Willoughby Jones, remarked that, although in theory, the javelin men kept order in the courts, in practice they frequented the neighbouring public houses.[1197] This phenomenon was certainly not confined to Norfolk: in July 1851, when Judge Thomas Talfourd presided over his first assize in Carmarthen in Wales, he was met by javelin men who had apparently fortified themselves by partaking of a "handsome dessert and wine" at the local Ivy Bush tavern.[1198] The committee's recommendation for Norfolk was followed. As a result, in March 1860 the high sheriff for Norfolk and a band of police officers greeted Mr Justice Williams when he arrived at Victoria Station in Norwich. Even so, his subsequent arrival at the Shirehall and Guildhall still attracted the customary fanfare, albeit from a "couple of inharmonious trumpets."[1199]

[1193] *The Bury and Norwich Post, and Suffolk Herald*, 10 May, 1881.

[1194] *Ibid.*, 9 May, 1882.

[1195] David Pugsley, "Exeter and the Western Circuit in the nineteenth century", *Bracton Law Journal*, vol. 38 (2006), p. 57.

[1196] *The Norfolk Chronicle*, 21 October, 1859.

[1197] *Ibid.*, 5 January, 1860.

[1198] Richard Ireland, "Putting Oneself on whose Country? Carmarthenshire Juries in the Mid-Nineteenth Century" *Legal Wales: its past, its future: essays dedicated to Professor Dafydd Jenkins on his ninetieth birthday*, Cardiff 2001, pp. 63-87.

[1199] *The Norfolk Chronicle,* 5 January, 1860.

There was occasional resistance to this increased informality. For example, in 1856, active steps were taken in Suffolk to reduce some of the expense pertaining to the high sheriff's office. As a result, in March that year this officer met the circuit judges at the railway station without either javelin men or trumpeters. The presiding judge, Lord Chief Justice Jervis, was not impressed, and fined the sheriff £100 (presumably hoping that it would be paid by the county). The previous week Mr Justice Vaughan Williams had imposed an identical fine on the high sheriff of Carmarthen for a similar faux pas. (There being no work for the court, the high sheriff had sent the under-sheriff to meet the judge informally, without javelin men or police in attendance.) The fines were widely discussed in the press. The *Times* accepted that to some it might appear absurd to have a procession, when a hackney cab would "equally answer the purpose of conveying an elderly gentleman from the railway station to his place of work."[1200]

More locally, in Norfolk one morning in August 1872, the high sheriff was late in sending his carriage to Mr Justice Keating's Norwich lodgings to take him to court. The judge eventually took a cab to the Shirehall and on arrival immediately fined the high sheriff £50 for his lapse. However, later that morning, the sheriff made an abject apology, blaming his failure to provide a carriage on an "unfortunate inadvertence," and stressing that he wished to treat the Queen's representative with all due courtesy. The judge was mollified and remitted the fine.[1201]

The Judges

By the start of the Victorian period, the system of assizes, under which the highest provincial jury courts were served by pairs of circulating Westminster judges who had been temporarily released from their normal duties in the capital, was centuries old. In 1837 the judges were usually drawn from the Courts of Common Pleas, Queen's Bench, and Exchequer. After the Judicature Acts of 1873 to 1875, they would normally be drawn from the newly created High Court. However, in earlier centuries the Westminster judges had been heavily supplemented by temporarily commissioned serjeants-at-law (senior practising lawyers). This had become much less common by the Victorian period, albeit that the Norfolk circuit had been later than some others in reducing the contribution of the sergeants. In 1831 it was noted in the House of Lords that, for many years, it had often fielded just one Westminster judge and a serjeant-at-law or other makeshift part-time appointment to support him. It was hoped that a modest expansion in the size of the Westminster judiciary would bring this practice to an end. Nevertheless, at the Lent Assizes for Norfolk in 1842 Mr Serjeant Atcherley was one of the judges, and this was still not unusual.[1202] Even so, this gradually ceased to be a very common occurrence, except where a full-time judge was taken ill or otherwise suddenly indisposed. For example, the

[1200] David Pugsley, "Exeter and the Western Circuit in the nineteenth century", *Bracton Law Journal*, 2006, vol. 38, p. 58.

[1201] *The Times*, 6 August 1872, p. 12.

[1202] *The Bury and Norwich Post*, 6 April, 1842.

Norfolk assizes in July 1851 were held before Mr Serjeant Adams, who was sitting as commissioner in place of the unavailable Mr Justice Crompton. As the serjeants' profession waned (the last practising serjeant was appointed in 1865), part-time judges, where needed, were increasingly drawn from the ranks of the country's QCs.

Judicial Accommodation

When the judges arrived in Norwich, they would be accommodated in designated lodgings. Nationally, these could be private houses, whether rented or volunteered by local dignitaries, the better sort of inn, or purpose-built residences. In 1827 the London architect Thomas Nicholls had made plans for the erection of grand neo-classical judges' lodgings in Norwich, matching those for proposed new courts in the city, but both projects had been abandoned.[1203] Instead, in April 1833, the county JPs hired the house of Robert Hawkes (a former sheriff and mayor) in Bethel Street, as official lodgings for judges of assizes.[1204] This was still being used at the time of Hawkes's death early in 1836. This sudden event prompted the Very Reverend Dr. George Pellew to invite the judges to stay at his deanery, for which he was duly thanked at the Norfolk quarter sessions in April that year.[1205] However, when Sir James Parke and Sir Edward Alderson arrived at the city in March 1840, they were lodged at St Catherine's Hill.[1206] This was a large, late-eighteenth-century house, possibly built for the recorder of Norwich in 1779. Thereafter, it was regularly used as judicial lodgings until about 1860.

At the start of 1886 the county magistrates decided to rent Eaton Hall in Norwich to use as lodgings, at a yearly cost of £250. Initially the mansion was not universally popular with the judiciary. Mr Justice Hawkins, after delivering his charge to the Lent assizes grand jury, said he could not thank the magistrates for their decision, and suggested that they thought that he and his marshal had the tastes of a polar bear and an arctic fox. Eaton Hall was, apparently, a bleak and freezing house, with men still working on it, even as it was first used, while the rooms were poorly furnished. (It seems that things had improved by the end of the year).[1207] The judge's comments became the subject of a satirical poem in a popular journal.[1208]

[1203] Carole Rawcliffe, *Norwich Since 1550* (London: Hambledon Continuum, 2004), p. 329.

[1204] *The Norfolk Chronicle,* 27 April, 1833.

[1205] *Ibid.,* 24 March, 1836.

[1206] *Ibid.,* 31 March, 1840.

[1207] *Ibid.,* 7 January, 1886.

[1208] *Funny Folks: A Weekly Budget of Funny Pictures, Funny Notes, Funny Jokes, Funny Stories*, vol. 12, no. 584, 30 January 1886, p. 34.

The Bar

Each circuit had its own bar, with an attendant mess, and various arcane rules and practices. For example, barristers might be excluded from taking refreshments in public houses and restaurants and required to take (often overpriced) lodgings, rather than staying at hotels, if only to prevent them from touting for business from local solicitors.[1209] In 1827 the bar mess for the Norfolk circuit passed a resolution stating that it was "unprofessional in any member of the circuit to travel to any circuit town in any public conveyance."[1210] Many barristers on the Norfolk circuit, especially those of any standing, spent much of their time in London, and appeared within its boundaries only during assizes. Those who were more junior, or who lacked work, might spend longer in one or more of the circuit counties, and attend quarter sessions.[1211]

It is sometimes suggested that counsel practising on specific circuits in the nineteenth century travelled to all counties visited by their pairs of judges, carrying their robes, wigs, and legal books with them. Nevertheless, whatever had been the case in earlier centuries, the attendance of barristers on the Norfolk circuit in the 1800s shows that this was no longer necessarily the case. During the 1820s the practising membership of this circuit varied from 19 men in 1822, to 38 in 1827. However, not all of them attended all assizes. In the first half of this decade most towns on the circuit were visited by about 15 barristers, while during the second half the number had increased to about 20 men. At times, especially during the summer circuit, fewer than half the barristers attended all or even most of its locations. Those who visited only a few towns usually confined themselves to one area of the circuit, and attended sessions in adjacent counties, so that the same men might, for example, be seen in Norfolk and Suffolk, but not in Buckinghamshire and Bedfordshire.[1212]

The Norfolk circuit bar subsequently expanded. In 1835 it had 37 men, including one King's Counsel and one serjeant-at-law, as well as 35 junior barristers.[1213] However, by the early 1870s, the number had increased to between 50 and 60 barristers; nevertheless, because the circuit was so much larger after 1863, the number of lawyers in attendance at any single town had increased only to an average of about 28. As before, only a minority of the membership of the circuit attended all its towns, although the advent of railways meant that there was less need for their attendance to be geographically restricted.[1214]

[1209] Reid, *Briefs and Papers,* pp. 46-50.

[1210] Cairns, *Advocacy,* p. 37.

[1211] Cottu, *Administration,* p. 42.

[1212] R.C.J. Cocks, "The Bar at Assizes: Barristers on Three Nineteenth-Century Circuits", *Kingston Law Review*, vol. 6 (1976), p. 38.

[1213] Whishaw, *A Synopsis,* pp. 273-274.

[1214] Cocks, "The Bar at Assizes," p. 38.

The Occasion

Traditionally, the biannual assizes had been major county occasions, with many people, especially members of the local gentry, attending and participating in various meetings and social gatherings. This tradition lingered into the Victorian era, in Norfolk as elsewhere. In 1845 it could still be noted that assizes' week, due to the "great attendance of company, is the gayest period known to the inhabitants of Norwich."[1215] In the same decade, the Norwich Theatre had special performances during the week to entertain visitors and residents. They attracted some of the stars of the era, such as Miss Montague of Drury Lane, and Clara and Sybella Novello.[1216] This significance started to fade shortly after the advent of the new Queen, a phenomenon that can be seen in other parts of the country. For example, early in the century the ball at the Clarence Hotel during the Exeter Lent Assizes was always fashionably attended. However, this declined during the early Victorian period, and the last such ball took place there in July 1845.[1217]

Problems with the Assizes

Some contemporary observers, such as Thomas William Saunders, felt that the quality of justice administered by the assizes, with their professional and often highly accomplished judges, meant that it was the least problematic of the three main criminal forums (the others being the quarter and petty sessions).[1218] Other commentators were much less impressed. Even Saunders accepted that the system of assizes had two major flaws. One was the infrequency of its sessions, which could mean that someone who was arrested for a felony at the end of August might spend seven months in custody prior to trial. In the mid-1870s, one observer claimed that this delay was the "worst scandal" found in the criminal- justice system. He cited a gaoler who had a girl in his custody, accused of arson, who had been confined under the "separate system" since August, and would probably wait until April for the assizes to determine her case.[1219]

On one estimate, in 1897, there were 120 cases nationally in which those awaiting trial at assizes had been in custody for more than 16 weeks. Thirty of the prisoners, a quarter, were ultimately acquitted.[1220] The following year, according to the report of the Bar Council, 27 untried prisoners were in gaol for more than 16 weeks on the South-Eastern and Home Circuits alone, and of these 19 had been held for more than 18 weeks, and one of them for 24 weeks.[1221] Conversely, and perhaps almost

1215 White, *History, Gazetteer,* p. 91.

1216 *The Bury and Norwich Post, and East Anglian,* 29 July, 1843.

1217 David Pugsley, "Exeter and the Western Circuit in the nineteenth century," *Bracton Law Journal*, vol. 38 (2006), pp. 55-76.

1218 Saunders, *Quarter and Petty Sessions,* p. 4.

1219 *The Spectator,* 22 January 1876, p. 3.

1220 *Ibid.,* 1 July 1899, p. 16.

1221 *Ibid.*

equally undesirably, the process could be very swift if a crime was committed just before sessions. John Self, who murdered Jemima Stimpson in mid-July 1841, was arrested, examined by JPs, committed to prison, tried at the Norfolk summer assizes, convicted, and executed, all in the space of about four weeks.[1222]

The other major problem with the assizes identified by Saunders was that changes in the population of the country and its distribution, in particular the growth in industrial towns and cities, especially in the North and Midlands, meant that the centuries-old arrangement of circuit counties and assizes towns no longer reflected English society; this could create difficulties with workloads.[1223] Steps were eventually taken to remedy both these problems with varying degrees of success.

The Incidence of Sessions

The (in)frequency with which sessions were conducted was a perennial issue during the nineteenth century. One observer in the 1850s could note that three assizes a year had been held in the time of Edward III, yet early Victorian England made do with just two, despite the huge increase in population, and in contrast to the situation found in the Metropolis, where the Old Bailey (the capital's equivalent forum) sat once a month. He felt that it was obvious that the assizes should be held at least three times annually, and more often if need be.[1224] Even then, this was a long-repeated suggestion, and it was to be regularly reiterated over ensuing years. Thus, in early 1876 another observer argued that assizes should be held "at least three or four times a year, and [he felt] even that rule would admit of a frightful amount of legalised injustice."[1225]

Nevertheless, such comments were also slightly misleading. During the early and mid-Victorian period, the situation was sometimes ameliorated by ad hoc assizes commissions and sittings, to hear purely criminal matters, outside the traditional twice-yearly times. This was usually done late in the year, often in early December, in counties with high levels of criminal work situated on the busier circuits, such as the Home and Norfolk. For example, additional assizes were held in Bury St Edmunds (Suffolk) and Norwich in December 1844, but in none of the other counties on the Norfolk circuit.[1226] Usually, only a single judge would be involved in such "special" assizes, which would not hold civil cases at *nisi prius*. If held late in the year, as was normally the case, these extra sessions would often be termed "winter assizes," as was the situation in December 1859, when Blackburn J from the Court of Queen's Bench presided over such sessions for Norfolk in the Norwich Shirehall.[1227]

[1222] *The Norfolk Chronicle*, 28 July, 1841.

[1223] Saunders, *Quarter and Petty Sessions,* p. 4.

[1224] Anon., "Local Distribution of Tribunals," pp. 301-305.

[1225] *The Spectator,* 22 January, 1876, p. 3.

[1226] *The Bury and Norwich Post*, 20 November, 1844.

[1227] *Ibid.,* 6 December, 1859.

However, such ad hoc assizes were not particularly common. In the 1850s Norwich was the only town on the entire Norfolk circuit to hold a winter assizes (albeit for both city and county), and it was not a regular event, even there. The sessions held at the end of 1859 were the first conducted since 1855. Furthermore, their use was often confined to grave or difficult crimes. The grand jury at the winter assizes in Norwich in December 1844 even passed a resolution stating that there had been no need to hold the sessions at all, as all the modest number of cases determined could have been heard within two weeks at the forthcoming Epiphany Quarter Sessions for the county.[1228] As this suggests, those accused of lesser offences would normally remain in gaol waiting for January Quarter Sessions or the Lent Assizes, their crimes not being deemed sufficiently grave to warrant the "privilege of the speedy trial to which more serious offenders, for whose special benefit these winter assizes are held, are considered entitled." This is confirmed by the trial calendar for the winter assizes held at Norwich in 1859. The only case for the city involved an allegation of rape. The 13 prisoners for the county were variously accused of murder (one person), shooting with intent to commit murder (two), arson (four), burglary (one), forgery (one), passing counterfeit coin (one), stealing letters from the post office (two), and, in a late addition, bigamy (one).[1229]

A few more informal winter assizes were held in Norwich over ensuing years, as was the case in December 1867, when Jane Jarron was tried for the murder of her new-born child the previous October.[1230] Nevertheless, they were still fairly rare events, and in 1872 a judge could even note, albeit with some lack of historical awareness, that "It seemed that a winter assizes was very seldom held at Norfolk."[1231]

Reform

The need for more assizes' sessions was formally recognized in the second half of the 1870s, when what were, essentially, late-autumn assizes, for purely criminal business, were introduced by the Winter Assizes Acts of 1876 and 1877 and attendant orders in council (made under the former statute), where there was sufficient demand.[1232] It seems that a de facto rule was often applied as to when this would occur. According to the Lord Chancellor, "In any Assize towns where there were six persons committed for trial after the Summer Assizes, Winter Assizes were held." Thus, on one occasion, in Hertford, there were only two people for trial when the lists were made up, and consequently no winter assizes were held, although this meant that the pair were detained in prison until the Spring Assizes, several months later, when one was acquitted. Even so, this rule was not always followed. At the combined Norfolk and Suffolk winter assizes in late October 1881,

[1228] *Jackson's Oxford Journal*, 28 December, 1844.

[1229] *The Times*, 6 December, 1859, p. 9.

[1230] *Ibid.*, 9 December,1867, p. 12.

[1231] *The Standard*, 28 September, 1872.

[1232] Alexander, *The administration,* p. 86.

only two cases were initially set down for trial, and one of them was a case of petty theft (the other involved concealment of a birth), although some 60 potential jurors had been summonsed. The trial judge thought that holding winter assizes in these circumstances was questionable (other cases may subsequently have been added to the list).[1233]

As some of the above reports suggest, for the purpose of the winter assizes most counties were paired or grouped with others, using a shared location for the extra sessions, rather than having an assize of their own. For example, on the Northern Circuit, Westmorland was usually joined with Cumberland. The number of such combined "Winter Assize Counties" varied over time. There were 17 in 1885, and 18 the following year. Rather prosaically, they were given numbers not names. Thus in 1886 Winter Assize County No. 13 was made up of Shropshire and Staffordshire, the assizes being held at Stafford.[1234] Normally, and as with their ad hoc predecessors, they would involve a single judge coming from London to deal solely with criminal matters.

Unsurprisingly, for these purposes, Norfolk and the city of Norwich assizes were often joined with Suffolk, their fellow circuit county to the south. As elsewhere, the numbers given to such groupings changed with time. For the three jurisdictions whose communal assizes was held at Ipswich in 1881, it was Winter Assizes County No. 7.[1235] Although their combined hearings were often held in the Suffolk town, Norwich was an equally popular choice. For example, in November 1886 the combined assizes for Norfolk and Suffolk were held at the Shirehall in Norwich before Mr Justice Field, with 13 Suffolk and 15 Norfolk prisoners going for trial.[1236]

Occasionally the county groupings were even larger. In November 1876 Winter Assizes County No. 6 was made up of Norfolk, Suffolk, Cambridgeshire, and Huntingdon, and sat in Norwich. For some reason, and rather strangely, the city of Norwich itself had not been included in this group but was subsequently made the subject of a special commission, so that several local cases could be heard in the city Guildhall before the same trial judge moved on to its Shirehall to hear matters from the other four counties. Several observers expressed surprise that Norwich was used to host these assizes, when only two defendants came from that county (ignoring those from the city), while seven were from Suffolk. However, it was noted that when the order in council had been made, this could not have been anticipated.[1237] The following year, the assizes were held at Ipswich, and involved a major logistical

---

1233 *The Ipswich Journal*, 29 October, 1881.

1234 *The Norfolk Chronicle*, 10 May, 1886.

1235 *The Bury and Norwich Post*, 28 March, 1882.

1236 *Ibid.*, 16 November, 1886.

1237 *Ibid.*, 28 November, 1876.

exercise, with prisoners arriving by train from Norwich, the Norfolk female prison at Wymondham, Ipswich, Bury, Ely, and Cambridge.[1238]

The situation was still not entirely satisfactory. In June 1877 Hugh Childers, the Liberal Chancellor of the Dutchy of Lancaster, proposed the creation of centres outside London at which criminal sittings would be nearly as frequent as at the Old Bailey, to which prisoners might be sent who had been committed in counties where assizes could be held only two or three times a year. He thought it absurd that prisoners were still normally required to be tried in the counties in which they had offended and suggested that, without interfering with the normal assizes, a special criminal jury court could sit every two months, in prominent cities, to clear backlogs. Thus, one might sit in London for the Norfolk and Home Circuits, so that no one need be incarcerated and untried for more than two months.[1239]

Childers' suggestion did not come to fruition. Nevertheless, the Spring Assizes Act 1879 allowed the introduction of a fourth, Spring, Assizes, often held at the end of April or beginning of May, for a combination of counties. As a result, in early May 1881 the combined assizes for Norfolk, the city of Norwich, and Suffolk were held at the Shirehall in Ipswich before Sir Henry Hawkins. On arrival at Ipswich station, the Suffolk high sheriff and his chaplain, the county's under-sheriff, and an escort of policemen, greeted the judge, who was then escorted to his lodgings and on to the Shirehall. The commission having been formally opened with the same ancient ceremony used at ordinary assizes, Sir Henry attended divine service at the Church of St Mary Tower, with the business of the assizes starting shortly afterwards at 1.15 pm. Thirteen prisoners were to be tried, seven from Suffolk, and three each from Norfolk and the city of Norwich. A single 21-man grand jury was sworn in to consider these cases.[1240] Four years later, in late April 1885, the joint assizes for Norfolk, Norwich, and Suffolk, again held at the Shirehall in Ipswich, were given the title Spring Assize County No. 7. On this occasion, there were 23 prisoners to be tried from Norfolk, nine from Norwich, and just five from Suffolk. The crimes from Norfolk included murder, manslaughter, piracy, perjury, arson, bigamy, and burglary. Again, most of the same formalities were observed as at the ordinary assizes.[1241]

The following year the Norfolk and Suffolk assizes were held at Ipswich at the beginning of May 1886. These sessions included some unusual hearings. George Edward Ray, aged 31, a solicitor from Norwich, was sentenced to seven years' penal servitude for forging the conveyance of real estate with intent to defraud.[1242] At the same sessions, Charles Edward Wigger, a shoemaker, was convicted of receiving a

---

[1238] *Ibid.*, 6 November, 1877.

[1239] Hansard, HC Deb 12 June 1877 vol. 234 col. 1661.

[1240] *The Bury and Norwich Post, and Suffolk Herald*, 10 May, 1881.

[1241] *The Bury and Norwich Post*, 28 April, 1885, p. 8.

[1242] *The Norfolk Chronicle*, 10 May, 1886.

bribe for voting, or agreeing to vote, for Harry Bullard at the Norwich election in November 1885, and sentenced to three months' imprisonment with hard labour.[1243]

Holding extra assizes solved some problems but created others. Any funds saved by having fewer prisoners in custody had to be set against the not inconsiderable cost of the winter/spring assizes themselves.[1244] Some observers were concerned that it took the senior judiciary away from London during legal term time. Metropolitan lawyers and litigants sometimes even claimed that it was an "outrage that the Common Law Judges should be engaged in trying prisoners in distant parts of the country, while the Courts of the Queen's Bench Division are an echoing desert."[1245] The extra assizes were unpopular with many judges, who disliked having to go away from the capital so often, although indulging judicial preferences in this regard also occasioned public hostility; one observer deplored the "absurd" situation whereby society was governed for the convenience of its "shepherds."[1246] Furthermore, many assizes struggled to find enough work of a suitable gravity to justify a fourth sessions, as by then the great majority of middle-rank cases were being dealt with by quarter sessions. As a result, after 1888 most counties reverted to a maximum of three sessions a year, with that in May often being abandoned.[1247]

The Circuits

The other major problem with Victorian assizes was that population growth and urbanization, especially in the Midlands and North, along with the incorporation of Wales and the palatinate counties into the national system in the 1830s, had made the traditional circuits increasingly incompatible with the judges' workloads. Contemporary observers were aware of this. In 1855 Lord Brougham suggested in Parliament that circuits should be arranged differently as (he observed) had frequently been proposed in the past. He noted that by then the Norfolk circuit lasted only half the time of the Northern circuit and thought that it was eminently "possible by combining it with the other short circuit, the Midland, to relieve two of the judges." He thought that this would be especially workable if, for example, Warwickshire was detached from the latter and added to the Oxford circuit.[1248]

As a result of such sentiments, various attempts were made to amend the system during ensuing decades. Unfortunately, this was to produce what has been referred to as a system of musical chairs, as counties were added to and withdrawn from various circuits during the second half of the century.[1249] The first change affecting Norfolk

---

1243 *Ibid.*, 7 May, 1886.

1244 *The Bury and Norwich Post*, 28 November, 1876.

1245 *The Spectator*, 1 December, 1888, p. 12.

1246 Anon., "Local Distribution," pp. 301-305.

1247 Emsley, *Crime and Society*, p. 217.

1248 Hansard HL Deb 23 March 1855 vol. 137 cols. 952-77, col. 952.

1249 Cornish, *Oxford History*, p. 640.

saw three Midland circuit counties – Rutland, Leicestershire, and Northamptonshire – being added to the five traditional Norfolk circuit counties by an order in council made in November 1863. (In compensation, Yorkshire was transferred from the Northern circuit to the Midland circuit). As a result, in 1870 the Summer sessions for the enlarged Norfolk circuit began with those held for Rutland at Oakham on 11 July, followed by those for both Leicestershire and the borough of Leicester (a borough assizes), which were opened at Leicester on 12 July. Those for Northamptonshire were opened at Northampton on 16 July, for Buckinghamshire at Aylesbury on 20 July, for Bedfordshire at Bedford on 25 July, for Huntingdonshire at Huntingdon on 28 July, for Cambridgeshire at Cambridge on 30 July, for Suffolk at Bury St Edmunds on 3 August, and for Norfolk and the city and county of Norwich on 6 August.[1250] This made for a total circuit of almost a month. Similarly, the summer assizes for the Norfolk circuit in 1873, presided over by Baron Bramwell and Mr Justice Keating, followed the same order, starting at Oakham on 8 July and finishing at Norwich, where they sat on 2 August.[1251]

Nevertheless, this arrangement was still felt to be unsatisfactory. As a result, Section 23 of the Judicature Act 1875 allowed the Crown to make regulations respecting the composition of circuits by order in council. Under this power, in February 1876 the circuit system was again drastically remodelled. Rutland, Leicestershire, and Northamptonshire, which had belonged to the Norfolk circuit for 13 years, were returned to the Midland circuit. (Yorkshire was transferred from the latter to the newly created North-Eastern circuit). However, the remainder of the Norfolk circuit and the Home circuit were combined into a new and very large South-Eastern circuit, but with Kent and Surrey (formerly part of the Home circuit) being left out, and the assizes for these two counties being held by judges travelling from London. (In 1899 Kent and Surrey were added to the South-Eastern circuit.) As a result, the Lent assizes for the South Eastern circuit in 1876 opened at Lewes in Sussex on 8 March, Maidstone in Kent on 11 March, Chelmsford in Essex on 17 March, Hertford in Hertfordshire on 22 March, Huntingdon in Huntingdonshire on 25 March, Cambridge in Cambridgeshire on 27 March, Ipswich in Suffolk on 1 April, and the final venue, for Norfolk and the county and city of Norwich, in Norwich on 7 April.[1252]

This rearrangement produced a huge circuit, even allowing for the availability of trains to move around it. It radically altered the character of assizes, with barristers increasingly journeying from London by train to the various venues and then returning to the capital rather than moving around the circuit, taking lodgings, and associating with their colleagues while they did so, as had been the practice at the start of the Victorian era. It aided a process whereby barristers who lived in London became more interested in the matrimonial home than in the company of

1250 *The Bury and Norwich Post, and Suffolk Herald*, 21 June, 1870.

1251 *Ibid.*, 17 June, 1873.

1252 *The Times*, 19 February 1876, p. 12.

their colleagues, something that pained the Norfolk circuit stalwart Thomas Blofeld in the latter decades of the century. (The circuit mess continued to be important in disciplinary and professional matters).[1253]

The debate was not over, even then. Many contemporary observers thought that the situation could not last very long. In the 1880s rumours circulated that several centres might be amalgamated – for example, the Suffolk, Norfolk, and Cambridgeshire assizes might be concentrated in Cambridge – although these reports do not seem to have been very well-founded.[1254] Nevertheless, as was noted in 1888, the judges of the Queen's Bench Division regularly met in the "vain hope" of reforming the circuit system, although many observers thought that a reduction in inconvenience was all that could ever be achieved.[1255]

Preparing for the Assizes

A common early- and mid-Victorian scenario would involve the judges' arriving at the town where the assizes were to be held, with considerable (albeit declining) ceremony, and formally opening proceedings that same evening (at both forums in Norwich), in what was an ancient ceremony, before dining with local notables. The following morning, they would attend divine service at a nearby church or (as was usually the case in Norwich) cathedral, where the chaplain to the high sheriff or a prominent local clergyman would preach a special sermon. The two judges would then proceed to court, one normally taking the civil *nisi prius* cases (at least initially) and the other the criminal trials being held on the Crown side.[1256] The county high sheriff would usually sit beside the judge in the latter court.[1257]

Typically, in August 1836 the judges arrived in Norwich on a Tuesday evening and attended divine service at the cathedral the following morning, where they heard an "excellent sermon" preached by the Reverend George Coldham, the chaplain to the sheriff. At about 12.30 pm they moved on to the court to preside over their lists.[1258] However, if the day following the judges' arrival was a Sunday, legal proceedings would wait until the Monday. For example, at the Lent Sessions in 1837, it was noted that Mr Justice Park had arrived in Norwich at 4 pm on a Saturday afternoon and immediately opened both the city and the county assizes. The following day, Park attended a service in the cathedral. The hearings commenced on the Monday

---

1253 R.C.J. Cocks, "Dignity and Emoluments: Thomas Blofeld's Life as a Victorian Barrister," *Kingston Law Review*, vol. 8, no. 1 (1978), pp. 37-48.

1254 *The Bury and Norwich Post*, 13 May, 1884, p. 7.

1255 *The Spectator*, 1 December, 1888, p. 12.

1256 White, *History, Gazetteer,* p. 91.

1257 Cottu, *Administration,* p. 43.

1258 *The Bury & Norwich Post, & East Anglian: Or, Suffolk, Norfolk, Essex, Cambridge, and Ely Intelligencer*, 10 August, 1836.

morning, by which time Mr Justice Coltman had arrived to join Park. On this occasion, Coltman presided over the Crown side, with Park hearing the *nisi prius* cases.[1259]

The sermon preached before assizes would usually have a legal and/or moral theme, frequently based on a passage from Scripture. In 1885 one legal observer thought that such sermons were often merely a "string of platitudes."[1260] Others could be more impressed. On a famous occasion in 1831, John Keble's delivery of a sermon (later entitled National Apostasy) prior to the Oxford assizes discussed the prophet Samuel's exhortation to the Jews after acceding to their demands for a king. More prosaically, in July 1851, when Thomas Talfourd presided over his first assize in Carmarthen, the sermon was delivered by Archdeacon Bevan at St Peter's church, and took as its text "If thine eye offend thee, pluck it out."[1261] At the Lent assizes for Norfolk in April 1842, the sermon was preached by the chaplain (and brother) of the high sheriff on 1 Kings 3:9: "Give therefore unto thy servant an understanding heart, that he may judge thy people, and discern between good and evil."[1262] In the final years of the Victorian era the service (and its attendant sermon) may have been quietly abandoned in a few places, though that they were still taking place in Norwich shortly before the First World War.

If the judge dealing with *nisi prius* cases finished early, he might assist the judge on the Crown side and vice versa. For example, at the Norfolk assizes in July 1853, both the Lord Chief Justice and Baron Parke ended up simultaneously hearing criminal matters on the Crown side.[1263] The need to clear the county gaol, if possible, meant that criminal matters normally had precedence. (Towards the end of the century, unheard *nisi prius* cases were sometimes adjourned to the final assizes town on the circuit, where they might be tried together.)[1264] As a result, at the Norfolk summer assizes in 1843 the Crown side cases were initially heard by Lord Chief Justice Denman, as his co-adjutor, Mr Baron Alderson, had been late arriving due to the return of a longstanding medical condition at Huntingdon, earlier in the circuit. On his arrival, Alderson took over the trial of the prisoners from Denman, who then presided over the *nisi prius* cases. (The former looked drawn but "bore the fatigues of the day without apparent pain.")[1265]

One of the benefits of having two judges was their ability to consult each other. It was normal practice for judges to temporarily adjourn their hearings and discuss difficult or unusual questions of law with their colleagues. For example, at the Norwich city assizes in 1838, Edward Holmes was accused of assaulting a porter

[1259] *The Ipswich Journal,* 8 April, 1837.

[1260] "At Assizes," *Central Law Journal*, vol. 21, August 7, 1885, pp. 106-108.

[1261] Ireland, "Whose Country?" p. 65.

[1262] *The Bury and Norwich Post*, 6 April, 1842.

[1263] *The Ipswich Journal*, 30 July, 1853.

[1264] "At Assizes," *Central Law Journal*, no. 21, 7 August, 1885, pp. 106-108.

[1265] *The Ipswich Journal*, 5 August, 1843.

at the city workhouse with intent to maim him. Holmes had earlier brandished a knife, after a violent quarrel broke out over whether he could have a new pair of trousers from the institution. However, the blow appears to have been struck with his fist, albeit that it produced a serious facial cut. After representations on the law from Holmes's counsel (it would be interesting to know how this was paid for), who argued that it could not be a transportable felony within the appropriate statute, the "judges, having conferred together, were of the same opinion." Holmes was merely convicted of assault and sentenced to a year's imprisonment.[1266]

Court of Queen's Bench

At the highest level – and uniquely amongst the courts found at Westminster – the Crown side of the Court of Queen's Bench heard a relatively small number of "serious misdemeanour" cases that were brought upon criminal information, rather than indictment, as it had in previous centuries. The number of all such cases heard every year was very small, and those from Norfolk tiny.

However, the court also had the power to review convictions in lower forums. After the unification of the Westminster courts into the new High Court, the Queen's Bench Divisional court took over this function, and reviewed magistrates' findings on points of law. Thus, after the Blofield petty sessions dismissed (with some reluctance) an allegation of animal cruelty occasioned by the dishorning of cattle (a common practice in Norfolk), the prosecutor in the case appealed the matter to the Divisional Court, where the JPs' finding was overturned by the judges, who decided that it was illegal under the relevant statutes. Both sides were represented by a QC and a junior barrister.[1267] Similarly, in 1890 the Queen's Bench Divisional Court upheld the conviction and 14 days' imprisonment imposed by JPs on a Norfolk "gentleman" called Adcock for another case of animal cruelty. He had slaughtered a pig, chasing the animal around a stable while striking blows with a carpenter's axe, which was deemed an inappropriate implement for such purposes. His barrister's submission that his intention to kill the pig precluded there being cruelty in its treatment was rejected.[1268]

1266 *The Bury and Norwich Post*, 11 April, 1838.

1267 *Ibid.*, 23 April, 1889.

1268 *The York Herald*, 28 June, 1890.

Chapter 10: Trial on Indictment: Preliminary Matters

Introduction

The essential structure of trial on indictment was the same at borough or county quarter sessions and assizes, both in Norfolk and the wider country. This was necessarily the case, given that all but the most serious indictable crimes could be tried at either forum. A significant divergence would have occasioned inconsistencies. Furthermore, by 1800 basic jury trial procedure was *fairly* similar to that found today.[1269] Nevertheless, there was still significant change during the ensuing century. Indeed, in the early 1900s, one observer could even opine that progress in the reform of criminal procedure over the past 100 years had been remarkable: "We have at last allowed the prisoner to give his evidence of the matter he is charged with if he desires to do so. We have, under certain restricted conditions, supplied him with legal assistance, and, best of all, there is at length a Court of Criminal Appeal."[1270] However, two of the three changes listed narrowly missed the Victorian era, while the third, the general right to give sworn evidence, arrived only towards its close, in 1898. Some other important nineteenth-century changes, such as those brought about by the 1836 Prisoners' Counsel Act, narrowly preceded the Queen, or occurred in the first decade of her reign. The process by which the common-law rules of evidence became rigid had also largely concluded by the 1840s, something that the increased presence of defence lawyers, prepared to challenge judicial rulings on legal admissibility, encouraged.[1271]

As a result, during the half-century from the late 1840s to the late 1890s, there was a modicum of stability in trial procedure; such change as occurred was often brought about by a developing legal culture rather than reform to the substantive law. For example, the second half of the nineteenth century saw a slow working-out of the extent to which barristers could ethically and professionally advance their clients' cases.[1272]

More generally, it has been observed that, during the first half of the nineteenth century, criminal justice moved from being a series of "expressive, semi-personal confrontations, personally directed by an involved judge and with highly variable results, to a more restrained, rule-governed, predictable, depersonalised process."[1273] This change was well advanced before the Queen came to the throne but developed further during the early years of her reign.

[1269] Bentley, *English Criminal Justice*, p. xiii.

[1270] Edward Abbott Parry, *The Law and the Poor* (London: Smith, Elder & Co., 1914), p. 189.

[1271] Martin J. Wiener, "Judges v. Jurors: Courtroom Tensions in Murder Trials and the Law of Criminal Responsibility in Nineteenth-Century England," *Law and History Review*, vol. 17, no. 3 (1999), p. 474.

[1272] Schneider, *Engines of Truth*, pp. 49-50.

[1273] Wiener, *Reconstructing*, p. 65.

Public Access

Public access to "day-in-court" hearings, in which all the evidence in a case was adduced at a single sitting, even on the rare occasions that it lasted more than a day, was a distinguishing feature of the English criminal-justice system and in marked contrast to those of many Roman law countries, with their numerous private interrogations and formal investigations conducted prior to a final determination. All trial proceedings were open to the public, although provision for spectators, and proper control of their numbers, was often poor, especially early in the era. Murders and notorious or salacious crimes always proved popular, as could other offences if unusually serious. In April 1835, the courtroom at the Norfolk assizes for the trial of Johnstone Wardell, a bank clerk accused of a huge theft, was "crowded almost to suffocation."[1274] Similarly, when, in April 1847, Edmund Saul Dixon was charged at the same forum with having committed an indecent assault on a policeman, the case excited great interest, so that the court was very crowded throughout the trial.[1275] Two years later, Norfolk gentlemen offered large sums of money to secure a seat in court at James Rush's murder hearing.[1276]

Scheduling

At both forums, sessions would start with prisoners being produced from gaol, or answering to their bail at court, before waiting, usually in a cell, for their cases to be called on. In 1887 the Howard Association complained that many English court cells were subterranean and almost devoid of natural light. Those for Norwich, although not in the "bad" category (the worst of four), were deemed "unsatisfactory" (the third) in this regard. It was felt that this was particularly unfortunate as defendants needed their wits about them when they came for trial, something that was not helped by poor pre-hearing accommodation.[1277] Specifically, there was concern that the two rooms (one for up to ten men, the other for six women) used for holding prisoners awaiting trial at the Shirehall (whether county assizes or quarter sessions) were not properly heated, and therefore cold and damp in the winter.[1278]

Prisoners would normally be tried in the order decided by the presiding judge or (at quarter sessions) chairman. Scheduling was poor at most provincial jury courts, with defendants, prosecutors, and witnesses having to be present at the start of proceedings and then needing to be available at very short notice until called on, sometimes several days later, because trials were dispatched with such rapidity that it was "impossible to foresee the day on which any particular prisoner [would] be

---

1274 *The Bury & Norwich Post, & East Anglian*, 8 April, 1835.

1275 *The Norfolk Chronicle*, 10 April, 1847.

1276 *The Bury and Norwich Post*, 21 March, 1849.

1277 Anon., *Unconvicted Prisoners, and Their Officers and Witnesses: England and Wales, 1887* (London: The Howard Association, 1887), pp. 1-2.

1278 *The Bury and Norwich Post*, 12 April, 1887.

tried."[1279] By the 1850s, provincial courts did not follow what was already national best practice in scheduling, leading one informed observer to urge that the assizes, like the Old Bailey, ought to list the causes likely to come on in a publicly released list for each day's sitting, and on no account start a new trial after 6 pm or 7 pm without the consent of all the parties.[1280]

Poor scheduling also meant that being a witness at assizes and quarter sessions could be very inconvenient and financially damaging, especially to those who were on low incomes, causing them to lose their situations or neglect their businesses. (In some courts, bound-over witnesses might receive a small daily subsistence allowance, at the clerk's discretion.)[1281] A Home Office committee in the 1880s cited cases in which poor witnesses, far from home whilst waiting for their trials, were reduced to desperate straits to maintain themselves, and "obliged to sell or pawn every article of clothing not absolutely necessary for actual decency before being released from attendance."[1282]

It was not just the poor who were affected. In the 1870s Frederic Manby, a medical man from East Rudham in North Norfolk, complained about the sheer inconvenience occasioned to professional witnesses by the random scheduling at assizes, which might entail their waiting from hour to hour for a case to be called on, and being summoned on just a few minutes' notice. He had had the experience of being subpoenaed to attend the Norwich assizes and having to be present from before the start to almost the end of sessions, a period (on that occasion) of almost seven days. He had received £8 17s for this, or about 25s a day. This was not nearly enough to cover his lost professional work and the cost of travelling to the sessions. Manby suggested increased use of the telegraph and messengers to avoid this.[1283]

Producing an Indictment

On arrival at court, the victim/prosecutor at a jury forum would produce, create, or receive a draft indictment containing the specific crimes alleged against the accused, this being drawn up by a solicitor or magistrates' clerk in advance, or by or with the assistance of the clerk of quarter sessions or (less commonly) assizes at court. This might be done using one of the model indictments found in the practitioner handbooks of the era or a printed indictment with blank spaces left to be filled in by hand, at least in simple cases. For example, at the start of the Lent assizes for Norfolk in 1842, all the indictments were already prepared. As a result, John Wright voluntarily agreed to retire from the grand jury, to be replaced by another man, because he was a Quaker, and the documents would otherwise have had to be amended to reflect this. This would probably mean adjourning proceedings until the

[1279] Cottu, *Administration,* p. 70.

[1280] Anon., "Local Distribution," pp. 301-305.

[1281] Cottu, *Administration,* p. 70.

[1282] Anon., *Unconvicted Prisoners,* pp. 1-2.

[1283] Anon., "Medical Witnesses at the Assizes," *The British Medical Journal*, vol. 1, no. 751 (1875), p. 682.

following morning.[1284] As this also suggests, at quarter and borough sessions and at assizes such draft bills would first go in front of a grand jury for approval.

Grand-jury scrutiny required that prosecutors and their witnesses had, at the least, attended court. If they failed to do so, without explanation or excuse, those who had been committed for trial on their evidence would usually be discharged by proclamation, in the same way as those who had their cases formally rejected by the grand jury. For example, at the City of Norwich summer assizes in August 1838 just two cases were set down for trial, but in neither was a bill sent to the grand jury, as nobody appeared to prosecute. The grand jury was then released from service. Three men, one of them accused of stealing a corpse (a late example of body snatching), were subsequently discharged by proclamation. They were the defendants whose cases had not gone to the grand jury.[1285] Of course, if prosecutors had been bound over to pursue matters, as was usually the case, and then failed to appear, they would risk having their recognizances estreated.

Prosecutors who attended trial did not have the right to unilaterally abandon matters when they arrived at court. For example, in August 1883 Joseph Betts was indicted at the Norwich assizes for sending threatening letters to the Bishop of Norwich, in which he said he would murder the cleric and destroy his cathedral. By the time the case came to court, the bishop did not wish to pursue the matter further. He sought to withdraw the prosecution, after speaking to counsel for the Crown, believing that the threats were not seriously intended. The trial judge was reluctant to allow this, feeling that "society must be protected as well as the Bishop." Nevertheless, he left his decision on the matter for a day, and eventually the cleric was allowed to abandon the prosecution, so that Betts was released on his own recognizances for future good behaviour.[1286]

The Grand Jury

The grand jury's task was to ascertain whether there was a prima facie case against the accused that warranted a public trial. If they decided that there was such a case, the indictment would be returned into court marked "true bill" or "bill found." This turned it into an operative indictment. If they did not find a prima facie case, it would be marked "no bill" and, in theory, would eventually be torn up. In this situation, no trial could ensue, and the subject of the draft indictment would be discharged and released by proclamation. However, rejection by a grand jury did not constitute *res judicata*, and so was not an acquittal that would preclude future prosecution if, for example, further evidence became available. It was for this reason that a judge directing a Norfolk assizes grand jury in a (not very strong) sodomy case in 1885 reminded its members that "should the Jury not find a true bill this would

[1284] *The Bury and Norwich Post*, 6 April, 1842.

[1285] *Ibid.*, 8 August, 1838.

[1286] *The Ipswich Journal*, 11 August, 1883.

not stop proceedings should evidence at any time be adducible to bring the offence home to the men."[1287]

For example, at the Lent assizes for Norfolk in 1833, Robert Empson was indicted for manslaughter, but the bill was "ignored" by the grand jury because a material witness was allegedly kept out of the way. However, Empson was bailed to appear at the following assizes so that a fresh indictment for the same crime could be brought with the witness present.[1288] Similarly, after an assault bill against Henry Cornell was thrown out by the grand jury at the Thetford borough sessions in July 1850, the town's magistrates appear to have held *ex tempore* committal proceedings on the same man to send him to the Norfolk assizes on a more serious charge of wounding with intent.[1289] Nevertheless, such cases were rare.

Grand jurors also retained a small residual role, independent of scrutinising draft bills of indictment, to act as representatives of their county or borough when raising specific security or policing concerns. They could do this by making a "presentment" through their foreman to the chairman, recorder, or Westminster judge (depending on forum).[1290] Thus, and at a very parochial level, at the borough sessions for Yarmouth in 1841, the grand jury presented the disorderly state of the town's marketplace every evening after 8 pm.[1291] Similarly, in March 1854, at the county quarter sessions held by adjournment in Walsingham, the grand jury, when making their presentment, called the attention of the court to the prevailing nuisance caused by dog-drawn carts, which afforded opportunities for the commission of crimes. They recommended that some decisive legislative steps be taken to deal with them.[1292]

Grand-Jury Composition

Traditionally the grand jury was made up of between 12 (at least 13 was usual) and 23 men, the latter being the most common number at assizes, *if* all those summoned attended (not always the case).[1293] For example, there were 23 grand jurors at the summer assizes for Norfolk in 1838.[1294] In practice, grand juries for the lower jury court (whether county or borough) tended to be slightly smaller, although there was considerable variation, and 23 were often summoned. Thus, and typically, at the Yarmouth borough (quarter) sessions in January 1888, an 18-man grand jury

---

1287 *The Norwich Mercury,* 11 November, 1885.

1288 *The Bury and Norwich Post,* 27 March, 1833.

1289 *Ibid.*, 24 July, 1850.

1290 Alexander, *The administration*, p. 93.

1291 Palmer, *Yarmouth Notes,* p. 82.

1292 *The Norfolk Chronicle,* 25 March, 1854.

1293 Cottu, *Administration,* p. 62

1294 *The Bury and Norwich Post*, 8 August, 1838.

was present.[1295] Failure to attend following a grand-jury summons might prompt a fine of £5, which was rather higher than the 40s often given to non-attending trial jurors.

Grand jurors were often drawn from men of a different social background to that of the trial jurors found at the same forum, especially at assizes. At the higher jury court they would frequently have a smattering of titled men, one of whom would often be its foreman.[1296] For example, at the city of Norwich summer assizes held in August in 1838, Lord Townshend fulfilled this role in a grand jury of 23 men.[1297] Similarly, at the summer assizes for Norfolk in July 1841, the foreman of the grand jury (of the same size) was the Honourable Francis Baring, while there were five baronets amongst the other grand jurors.[1298] Much later in the Victorian period, the Honourable Harbord Harbord (1836-1894) acted as grand-jury foreman at the Norfolk assizes for many years. Resident at Burlingham House, he was the youngest son of Lord Suffield, and a deputy lieutenant for the county.[1299] Other marks of distinction can be identified among assizes grand jurors, including the attainment of high military office. For example, the combined Norfolk, Norwich, and Suffolk spring assizes held at Ipswich in May 1881 had a 23-man grand jury whose foreman was Admiral Horton and which included Major General William Hessey and at least four other former naval or army officers of senior rank.[1300] Much more important, the grand jury at assizes did not just have enhanced social status. By the early Victorian period JPs dominated its ranks, so that a lawyer could note that at this forum "Grand Juries are very much composed of Magistrates."[1301] This continued to the end of the era and beyond and ensured a (small) degree of legal knowledge amongst its members.[1302]

It was because of this socially elite status that, in the 1820s, Charles Cottu thought that everyone deemed it an honour to be invited to join a grand jury at assizes.[1303] Even so, during the latter decades of the Victorian era, enthusiasm for the office waned, in part because some doubted its value (see below), and not everyone summoned attended. At the combined Norfolk and Suffolk winter assizes, held at the end of October 1881, only 17 grand jurors turned up out of the 24 summoned,

1295 *The Ipswich Journal*, 3 January, 1888.

1296 Cottu, *Administration,* p. 44.

1297 *The Bury and Norwich Post*, 8 August, 1838.

1298 *Ibid.*, 28 July, 1841.

1299 *The Norfolk Chronicle,* 11 January, 1894.

1300 *The Ipswich Journal*, 10 May, 1881.

1301 Hill, Eardley-Wilmot, *Papers on Grand Juries,* p. 19.

1302 Alexander, *The administration,* p. 91.

1303 Cottu, *Administration,* p. 49.

although this may also have reflected an awareness of the very small number of cases listed for trial.[1304]

Although the quarter sessions grand jury was very much more modest in social complexion than its assizes counterpart it was still made up of the "better class of ordinary jurors" so that it drew on the more prosperous elements to be found in a county or borough, such as farmers, professional men, and merchants, and was usually superior in profile to the typical quarter sessions petty jury.[1305] Indicative of this, Thomas Kelly, the clerk to the magistrates in Modbury (Devon), when making proposals to the 1845 Commission, suggested that the kind of men then found on the quarter sessions grand jury would be better used as ordinary trial jurors at both jury forums (assizes and quarter sessions), where (he felt) the men selected were often deficient in education and intellect (see below).[1306] This higher status also meant that, as with the assizes, the quarter sessions grand jury was often drawn from a slightly wider geographic area than the trial jury, making its members more likely to be unable to attend due to inclement weather.[1307] (This was not, of course, the case with borough sessions.)

The grand jury would be addressed by the presiding judge or chairman before retiring to consider the tendered indictments.

Charge to the Grand Jury

Immediately after he arrived at court, on the first day of proceedings, the judge hearing criminal matters on the Crown side (rather than his *nisi prius* counterpart) would deliver a charge to the grand jury, while the recorder or chairman would do the same thing to the equivalent body at borough and county quarter sessions respectively. They would discuss the cases set down in the calendar in general terms, and briefly consider the law pertaining to individual bills that would come before the grand jury, especially those that might pose difficulties. For example, at the winter assizes held at Norwich in November 1885, the judge "in his charge to the Grand Jury, said there were ten prisoners whose cases would come before them, and he had some observations to make on most of them."[1308] More specifically, in August 1850 Mr Justice Erle reminded the grand jury at the Norwich assizes that, where an illegal prizefight had resulted in a death, all the seconds could be accused of manslaughter as principals. Indeed, he thought that even the spectators might be accused as accessories: "It cannot be too extensively known, that all parties there

---

[1304] *The Ipswich Journal*, 29 October, 1881.

[1305] Alexander, *The administration,* p. 91.

[1306] *Eighth Report,* p. 328.

[1307] *The Bury and Norwich Post*, 6 January, 1863.

[1308] *The Norwich Mercury,* 11 November, 1885.

inciting the parties to do such an act, or encouraging them, are equally guilty of the felony." [1309]

Sometimes a judge, recorder, or (less commonly) county quarter sessions chairman, would make his opinion clear as to whether or not a particular case should be committed for trial, and this was usually (but not invariably) respected. Thus, when addressing the grand jury at the Norfolk assizes in 1847, the judge specifically commented on a case of child murder in their list "which he thought was a doubtful one." The grand jury took this blatant hint and threw out the tendered bill.[1310] In a similar example from a lower jury forum, at the Yarmouth borough sessions in 1851, the town recorder advised the grand jury that he did not think that there was much of a case against a man accused of theft, and that "it would be too much to find a true bill against him." He, too, was discharged.[1311]

Conversely, in May 1881, at the combined spring assizes for Suffolk, Norfolk, and the city of Norwich held at the Shirehall in Ipswich, Sir Henry Hawkins addressed the 21-man grand jury, which would consider indictments from all three jurisdictions. He discussed a case of actual bodily harm arising from a pub dispute in some detail, and suggested that it warranted further enquiry, so that it should go before a trial jury. Similarly, he warned them that they would have no alternative to committing an 11-year-old arsonist to trial, while making it clear that the issue was ultimately for them to decide. Thus, he advised the jurors that there was extensive evidence against the boy, and that he had made admissions when questioned, so that "whatever may be your desire to save the trial of a lad of that age, that the case is too clear to permit of such a course being taken. However, that is a matter for you."[1312] Such guidance might be particularly influential when it came to highly technical crimes. For example, in March 1879 Mr Justice Blackburn, when charging the Norfolk assizes grand jury, suggested to them that there would be "no difficulty" in finding true bills against those accused of bribery in a municipal election.[1313]

In his charge, the judge, chairman, or recorder might also take the opportunity to comment on the general level and nature of crime and morality found in the county or borough, as revealed by the calendar of offences. For example, at the Norfolk assizes in December 1863, Baron Martin (from the Exchequer Court) informed the grand jury that the number and gravity of the offences before them were more serious than when he had last been on circuit in Norwich, some two years earlier. He also observed that he had not previously appreciated how prevalent and serious a

---

1309 *T he Bury and Norwich Post, and Suffolk Herald*, 7 August, 1850.

1310 *The Bury and Norwich Post, and East Anglian*, 28 July, 1847.

1311 *The Ipswich Journal*, 4 January, 1851.

1312 *The Bury and Norwich Post, and Suffolk Herald*, 10 May, 1881.

1313 *The Sheffield Independent*, 30 March, 1870.

crime arson was in that part of the world, and so had been excessively lenient when punishing it on that occasion.[1314]

Having finished his charge, the judge or chairman would dismiss the grand jury to their duties, usually urging them to be expeditious so that the Crown side of the court could start work as soon as possible. The clerk of assizes would sometimes make sure that particularly strong cases were sent to them first, so that true bills would be returned swiftly, and the court would not have to sit idle for more than half an hour. During this hiatus, the judge might spend the time "reading the informations [depositions], the counsel their briefs, and the public in forming conjectures on the business of the session."[1315] If they did decide that there was a case to answer, the grand jury would endorse the bills of indictment appropriately, and then return them to court, allowing the trials to begin.

Operation of the Grand Jury

Grand jurors were required to take a special oath. In October 1841 at the Norwich city quarter sessions, Jacob Macro, a woollen draper, refused to do so, citing a scriptural prohibition. The recorder fined him £50, to be paid to the use of the Crown. (It was subsequently reduced to £20.)[1316] Once sworn, jurors would elect a foreman. This was often something of a formality at assizes, as it was frequently given to the same high-status men from sessions to sessions (see above). Having received their charge, they would retire to a private room to review the draft bills of indictment laid before them and hear supporting evidence from prosecution witnesses. In the 1820s, in Charles Cottu's words, the prosecutor with his witnesses would then enter the room, where "the former states his case with the circumstances of the crime of which he has been the victim; the others make their depositions [statements]; the jury then deliberate on the presumptive proofs against the accused."[1317] However, by the Victorian period, the victim's duty to organise this evidence had often been replaced by the presence of a prosecuting solicitor and/or the police officer in the case, and these men would usually marshal the prosecution witnesses before the grand jury.

Grand jurors did not hear lawyers for the defence, or evidence from the accused person or his witnesses. They were not normally concerned with the nature of the accused's case, or the defence that he would run at trial. They were not usually allowed to have access to the depositions that prosecution witnesses had made in front of the examining magistrates, whether to reach their decisions or even to compare with the testimony given in front of them (something that made it easier

[1314] *The Bury and Norwich Post, and Suffolk Herald*, 22 December, 1863.

[1315] Cottu, *Administration,* p. 66. *Norfolk Chronicle,* 19 October, 1841.

[1316] *Ibid.*

[1317] Cottu, *Administration,* p. 66.

for witnesses to renege on their earlier evidence).[1318] However, there may sometimes have been departures from this rule, at least in special circumstances, especially at the lower jury forum, where a degree of informality sometimes prevailed.

The grand jury had only to find that a prima facie case had been made out against the accused. Sir John Patteson alluded to what this might entail in his charge to the grand jury at the Norfolk assizes in April 1844. On this occasion the Queen's Bench judge stressed that, although incendiarism was an abhorrent crime, grand juries should not send suspected arsonists for trial on mere suspicion, as he felt had been happening all too frequently in this type of case (which usually depended heavily on circumstantial evidence). In these situations, the ensuing trials almost always led to an acquittal, which also meant that the allegation could never be re-prosecuted. As a result, he felt that grand jurors should exercise great caution and only allow "clear" cases to go before a judge and jury.[1319]

Sometimes, especially at quarter sessions, grand-jury hearings could be a rough and ready process. They were often very hurried, with decisions made in a matter of a few minutes.[1320] Grand jurors were apparently sometimes lax about finding true bills or, conversely, too ready to dismiss charges. For example, although Robert Bailey withdrew his allegations of theft against John Huggins in front of the Norfolk quarter sessions grand jury in March 1847, saying that he had misidentified him, they still committed Huggins for trial, where he was (unsurprisingly) swiftly acquitted. When Huggins unsuccessfully sued his accuser for malicious prosecution at *nisi prius* in the summer of 1847, the judge agreed that the grand jury's willingness to find a true bill, in the absence of admissible evidence, was strange, indeed "stupid." However, he also thought it was not astonishing given that it was a quarter sessions' grand jury.[1321] By contrast, in the early nineteenth century, grand juries at the Old Bailey were sometimes termed the "hope of London thieves" because of their alleged willingness to throw out apparently strong cases. As a result, from 1838 a clerk attended meetings with them, to offer advice, leading to fewer cases being dismissed.[1322]

Grand jurors would listen to no more evidence than was necessary to establish a prima facie case against the accused. However, they were supposed to hear all available witnesses before dismissing a charge. At the adjourned Norfolk quarter sessions held at Walsingham in January 1842, the chairman, Lord James Townshend, addressing its grand jury, complained that their counterpart in Norwich, sitting a few days earlier, had been rather too free about rejecting tendered bills. He reminded them that it was their duty to hear the evidence of all witnesses whose names were

1318 Peter Laurie, *An Inquiry Into the Use and Abuse of Grand Juries* (London: Smith, Elder, 1832), p. 21. *Eighth Report*, p. 239.

1319 *The Bury and Norwich Post, and East Anglian,* 3 April, 1844.

1320 Laurie, *An Inquiry,* p. 13.

1321 *The Bury and Norwich Post*, 28 July, 1847.

1322 Bentley, *English Criminal Justice,* p. 132.

recorded on the back of the indictment before they threw a case out and suggested that they tick them off as they did so to make sure that this happened. He also reminded them that dismissing cases too freely meant that they were likely to come back for consideration before another sessions, although this was, perhaps, a slight exaggeration.[1323]

In practice, grand jurors did not normally follow strict rules of evidence when deciding whether there was a prima facie case against the accused, although this was sometimes the subject of judicial criticism. Thus, they do not normally appear to have considered the admissibility of disputed confessions, leaving this to the trial judge to determine. For example, in 1842 the youthful George Barber made informal admissions to a murder that had, apparently, been "extorted" in extreme circumstances by a local parish constable. At trial at the Norfolk assizes, the judge stopped the prosecution on the basis that no confession made in these circumstances could be received, and the case depended almost entirely on the boy's admissions.[1324] By then it had survived both a magistrates' examination and grand-jury scrutiny.

In practice, it was claimed, the grand jury foreman would often simply ask a "few pertinent leading questions" of the witnesses to secure the required material to justify a true bill.[1325] If a such a bill was found, the witnesses who had given evidence before the grand jury would be required to testify again at the trial, sometimes very soon afterwards, so that "upon quitting the grand jury room, [they] proceed forthwith to give their evidence before the petty jury."[1326]

Although unanimity was not required, at least 12 grand jurors had to concur on any decision to indict a matter before it could go for trial, so that if there were only 13 men present, just two of them could prevent a true bill being returned. As in previous centuries, the defendant did not have to be at court for his bill of indictment to be considered, although this was unusual. Nevertheless, in 1859 the Norfolk assizes grand jury threw out a bill against Charles Mallett, who was alleged to have forged his father's signature on a cheque, even though he had failed to appear at the hearing, having been released on bail and absconded.[1327]

Criticism of Grand Juries

During the Victorian period, the grand jury was subject to persistent and growing attacks from informed observers, including some grand-jury members themselves. They often viewed it as an expensive, time-consuming, and pointless relic of the past, something that was long overdue for abolition. In large part this was because

---

1323 *The Bury and Norwich Post*, 19 January, 1842.

1324 *The Times*, 8 April, 1842, p. 15. *The Standard*, 13 November, 1841. *The Ipswich Journal*, 9 April, 1842.

1325 Alexander, *The administration,* p. 92.

1326 Cottu, *Administration,* p. 72.

1327 *The Bury and Norwich Post*, 2 August, 1859.

of the increased professionalism and thoroughness of the pre-trial examination and committal process, and its ever more judicial character, which, it was claimed, had rendered the grand jury redundant. Men such as W.C. Humphrey, the author of *Observations on the Inutility of Grand Juries* in 1842, argued that all that was necessary in the way of preliminary inquiry was already done by examining magistrates. Indeed, many argued that the grand-jury hearing was inferior to that conducted by JPs. For example, it was thought that the secrecy of their deliberations encouraged witnesses to lie, especially if they wished to renege on the testimony that they had earlier given to magistrates. Furthermore, most quarter and borough sessions' grand jurors were legally ignorant (many grand jurors at assizes were JPs) but, it was claimed, nervous about consulting the time-pressured judiciary or chairmen on technical issues. It was also argued that, if they rejected a bill, it did not clear an accused man's name in the way that acquittal following public trial did.[1328] More generally, Woodforde ffooks' tract of 1849, *Remarks on the Subject of Grand Juries*, concluded that they were a source of expense, inconvenience, and even corruption.

Unsurprisingly, in these circumstances, by the 1850s many observers were arguing for the abolition of the grand jury, especially in the Metropolitan and other urban areas. In 1873 a Birmingham grand jury resolved that the system was "superfluous and unsatisfactory, relating as it does to a state of society long since vanished and gone." Numerous newspaper editorials and many members of the judiciary supported such an analysis, and in 1879 an unsuccessful attempt was made to abolish grand-jury hearings in cases that were not punishable by death or penal servitude.

However, the grand jury was not without its champions, albeit that even some of them thought it needed reform. Thus in 1850 Graham Willmore wrote an influential treatise in its defence, and such support, along with an attachment to tradition, helps explain why the institution managed to limp into the twentieth century, although suspended during the Great War and finally abolished in 1933.[1329] Various suggestions were made in Parliament for reforms that would justify its preservation – for example, that it be limited to hearing appeals from a failure by examining magistrates to commit a matter for trial.[1330]

Norfolk was not immune to this debate and the influence that it might have on potential grand jurors from the county. In 1879 the recorder of Thetford, addressing the borough quarter sessions grand jury, noted approvingly that all 23 men summoned had attended to carry out the duty, even though very few criminal cases went to trial in the generally quiet town. By contrast, in other places, it had often "been his experience of late that Grand Juries did not attend in the numbers in

1328 Hill, Eardley-Wilmot, *Papers on Grand Juries,* pp. 2-4.

1329 Nathan T. Elliff, "Notes on the Abolition of the English Grand Jury," *Journal of Criminal Law and Criminology*, vol. 29, no. 1 (1938), pp. 10-18.

1330 *The Spectator*, 19 March, 1859.

which they ought to attend." At the previous grand jury of assizes for Suffolk, apparently only 13 men appeared, almost the smallest number allowed, and the smallest that was deemed acceptable, although many more had been summoned. The recorder stressed that it was vital that men attend to serve on the body as long as it existed.[1331]

Unsurprisingly, the proportion of cases thrown out by nineteenth-century grand juries was smaller than that rejected by their eighteenth-century predecessors, if only because the increased thoroughness of the magistrates' pre-trial committal process meant that far fewer weak cases survived to go before them. Between 1805 and 1817, about 17 percent of all indictments in England and Wales were returned as not found.[1332] By the start of the Victorian period this had fallen to about 10 percent. According to a Report to the House of Commons, made in 1835, 20,731 people nationally were committed for trial on indictment. Of these, 1,943 cases, were either thrown out by the grand jury, or (much less commonly) not proceeded with by prosecutors.[1333] The proportion was set to fall further. By 1883 the figure for grand-jury rejection was about 3.65 percent nationally, and in 1912 it was just 1.6 percent.[1334] By the middle of the nineteenth century, a recorder in the Midlands could note that at his three previous borough sessions 298 cases had been committed for trial, and just 23 thrown out by its grand jury.[1335] In Sheffield, between 1844 and 1855, only one in 28 (less than 4 percent) bills were thrown out by the grand jury.[1336]

Norfolk broadly matched the national pattern. According to the Reverend Charles Brereton, writing in 1839, over the previous two years the calendars of assizes and quarter sessions in Norfolk, taken together, suggested that only 37 out of 431 indictments (a little more than 8 percent) had been rejected as not found.[1337] As elsewhere, the proportion of cases thrown out by grand juries fell as the century advanced. Some 203 people were committed for trial on indictment at all forums in Norfolk in 1879. Of these, no bill was found by the grand jury in just 11 cases, or about 5 percent of the total.[1338]

Of course, the figures varied considerably between courts and over time. For example, the grand jury at the Norfolk quarter sessions in Norwich in July 1838 threw out only two of 48 cases. (It rejected some but not all allegations in several others.)[1339]

[1331] *The Bury and Norwich Post, and Suffolk Herald*, 22 July, 1879.

[1332] Hanly, "Summary Jurisdiction," p. 279.

[1333] Anon., *The Law Magazine,* p. 5.

[1334] Alexander, *The administration,* p. 94.

[1335] Hill, Eardley-Wilmot, *Papers on Grand Juries,* p. 19.

[1336] Chris A. Williams, "Counting Crimes or Counting People: Some Implications of Mid-Nineteenth-Century British Police Returns," *Crime, History & Societies*, vol. 4, no. 2 (2000), p. 81.

[1337] Brereton, *A Letter,* p. 23.

[1338] *Judicial Statistics, 1879*, p. 51.

[1339] *The Bury and Norwich Post*, 11 July, 1838.

At the Norfolk quarter sessions in Attleborough in 1875, just one man, a labourer named James Houchen, obtained such a result. He was accused of stealing two bottles of British wine, but "no true bill was found by the Grand Jury."[1340] Similarly, at the Norfolk assizes in late July 1887, seven defendants, in as many cases, went before the grand jury on charges ranging from stealing a greatcoat to indecent assault, but the grand jury found no true bill in just one case.[1341] Nevertheless, very occasionally, larger numbers were discharged by the grand jury, including nine out of 54 prisoners at the Norfolk quarter sessions held in July 1844.[1342]

Furthermore, it was widely thought that some of the cases rejected by the grand jury did not reflect a genuine failing in the magistrates' committal process, but were a result of witnesses' resiling from the evidence they had given at committal proceedings so that the prosecution case was "mutilated."[1343] This may have been done to avoid having recognizances to give evidence estreated by simply failing to attend court, an offence having been compounded, or the prosecutor's changing his mind about the merits of pursuing a matter.

Occasionally, a grand jury's decision not to commit a matter for trial may have reflected their personal views on the merits of a prosecution or on the wider criminal law rather than purely legal considerations. For example, in November 1887 the grand jury at the Norfolk assizes returned a finding of "no true bill" against Anna Oxer, a 24-year-old woman who had tried to "kill and murder herself" at Kenninghall. By then, such "crimes" often attracted sympathy rather than a desire to see punishment inflicted.[1344] The grand jurors may have wished to avoid an already fragile woman's sharing the experiences of those like George Robinson, found guilty of attempted suicide the following year at the Yarmouth quarter sessions, and sentenced to a month's imprisonment. (It was not his first such attempt.)[1345]

Of course, grand jurors could discriminate between defendants where there were more than one of them. For example, in March 1854 four men were named in a bill of indictment accusing them of a major burglary at a watchmaker's house at Leighton Buzzard the previous November. One of the allegations, that against George Parker, was thrown out by the grand jury at the Norfolk assizes. The other three men went for trial, were convicted, and were sentenced to long periods of transportation.[1346] It was also open to a grand jury to commit for trial on just some of the counts contained in a bill of indictment (if there was more than one) against an accused, or for a lesser offence than that charged, provided it was legally

[1340] *Ibid.*, 30 March, 1875.

[1341] *Ibid.*, 26 July, 1887.

[1342] *Ibid.*, 10 July, 1844

[1343] Hill, Eardley-Wilmot, *Papers on Grand Juries,* p. 19.

[1344] *The Bury and Norwich Post, and Suffolk Standard*, 15 November, 1887.

[1345] *The Ipswich Journal*, 3 January, 1888.

[1346] *John Bull*, 18 March, 1854.

encompassed in the original count. Thus, if the prisoner was accused of burglary, and the grand jury considered that a forcible entry had not been made out, they might commit for simple theft, and write on the bill, "true bill for felony." Similarly, in a murder bill, where they thought that a prima facie case for premeditation had not been properly established, they might write "true bill for manslaughter."[1347]

The Working Day at Court

Working days at court were often lengthy, especially at assizes. If the criminal list was not too long, proceedings might begin at 10 am, but a significant amount of work could mean an earlier start. For example, at James Rush's trial for murder, held over several days at the Norfolk assizes in March 1849, the court usually sat at 9 a.m. and adjourned at 7 or 7.30 p.m.[1348] Similarly, at the Norfolk assizes in July 1851, Mr Justice Cresswell took his seat at 9 am for what would be almost a day-long murder trial.[1349] Occasionally – much less often than in the previous century – the working day began at 8 am. By contrast, in 1885, the court for the combined Norfolk, Suffolk, and Norwich spring assizes did not sit at the Shirehall at Ipswich until 11 am.[1350] Whatever time was selected, the grand jury might begin hearing matters a little earlier than the main court so that true bills could be returned, ready for trial, as soon as the latter convened.

Although, as the Rush case suggests, a close of about 7 pm or earlier would be favoured, where possible, courts might sit until very late in the evening if necessary. This was typical of the wider country, especially in the early decades of the era, and Norfolk was by no means the worst county or circuit in this regard. For example, on several occasions in March 1838, Mr Justice Bosanquet sat for 14 hours or more at the Exeter assizes, and at one he finished at 2 am. On another occasion, at the same forum, in March 1840, Baron Rolfe finished at an equally late hour. Remarkably, in March 1845, Mr Justice Coleridge went on until 4 am. (After a nap he headed for Bodmin and Cornwall, where Mr Justice Erle had opened the commission of assizes for the county the previous day.) The *Western Times* complained about such working hours, noting with approval that Mr Justice Wightman had decided, where possible, not to keep juries in their box for more than ten hours, on the basis that that was quite long enough for men to maintain their concentration.[1351]

The prisoner would not be manacled during his trial unless he posed a security threat. However, he would usually remain standing throughout the hearing, especially in the early Victorian period. However, if the trial was of any length, or the defendant elderly or unwell, the judge might give him permission to sit on a chair. For example,

---

1347 Cottu, *Administration,* p. 70.

1348 *The Norfolk Chronicle,* 29 March, 1849.

1349 *The Daily News*, 29 July, 1851.

1350 *The Bury and Norwich Post*, 28 April, 1885.

1351 David Pugsley, "Exeter and the Western Circuit in the nineteenth century," *Bracton Law Journal,* vol. 38 (2006), pp. 55-76.

in 1841 Charlotte Yaxley was tried for murdering her husband's infant daughter at the Norfolk assizes. She was in a fainting condition on the day of trial, sobbing continuously, so the judge allowed her to sit down throughout the proceedings, which lasted from the morning until 8.30 pm.[1352] This indulgence became more common as the era advanced.

Brevity of Trial

Like their early-nineteenth-century predecessors, most Victorian criminal trials were very brief by modern standards, particularly early in the period, especially when the accused was not legally represented. Some felony hearings in the 1830s lasted less than half an hour.[1353] Notoriously, in December 1838 Thomas Sanders, a youth of 16, was indicted at the Old Bailey for stealing a pair of trousers from a clothes dealer in Poplar. His hearing, which resulted in a conviction and sentence of transportation for seven years, lasted just six minutes, including jury deliberation and sentencing. During the course of this extremely brief trial, up to six witnesses were examined, and the presiding judge, the common serjeant of London, also found time to make several quips about the young defendant.[1354] Although this case was certainly extreme, Sir Henry Hawkins (1817-1907) claimed, albeit many decades later, that he had timed a pickpocketing trial at the Old Bailey, early in his career, at just two minutes 54 seconds, and claimed that many "after-dinner" trials at that court lasted less than four minutes.[1355] Another observer in 1834 thought that the average time for Old Bailey sessions was just over 22 minutes.[1356]

Provincial assizes and quarter sessions hearings were fairly similar, if slightly less hurried, especially at the latter forum. However, there had always been exceptions to the general brevity, with trials lasting several hours or more, and their number gradually increased as the Victorian period advanced, as did the average length of all criminal trials. In part, this reflected the increased involvement of defence counsel and the growth in technicality at trial, as well as an increased stress on due process. For example, at the Norfolk summer assizes in 1869, George Woodrow's rape trial took most of a day to hear.[1357]

Prior to the late eighteenth century, it had not been possible to adjourn criminal trials overnight. This changed in the 1790s. As a result, Dr William Palmer's trial for murder by poisoning lasted 12 days at the Old Bailey in May 1856, making it one of

[1352] *The Bury and Norwich Post, and East Anglian*, 14 April, 1841.

[1353] Quinault, "Victorian Juries," pp. 47-53.

[1354] *The Times*, 25 December, 1838, p. 5.

[1355] Hawkins, *Reminiscences*, p. 22.

[1356] *The Westminster Review*, vol. 20 (1834), p. 147.

[1357] *The Times*, 10 August, 1869, p. 9. *The Bury and Norwich Post*, 10 August, 1869.

the longest criminal hearings of the Victorian period.[1358] In 1886 Adelaide Bartlett's trial for poisoning her husband lasted over a week at the same forum.[1359] However, these cases were very unusual (poisoning cases often required extensive expert evidence and so took a long time), albeit dwarfed by the notorious misdemeanour trial of the Tichborne Claimant in 1874.

The gravest trials would still normally be concluded on the day that they began, if this were at all possible, leading to very lengthy sittings, if cases were of any complexity, even if it meant starting early and sitting very late. This occurred in the great majority of even serious criminal cases. For example, at the murder trial of John Smith, George Timms, and John Varnham held at the Norfolk assizes in April 1837, the hearing commenced at 10.20 am, and concluded shortly after midnight, when the jury returned verdicts of guilty and the three men were sentenced to death.[1360] This of course meant that fatigued jurors were making their decision in less than ideal circumstances.

One reason for such prolonged sittings was the serious inconvenience caused by an overnight adjournment. Jurors in felony cases had to be kept under the control of a jury bailiff when outside court. This requirement was taken very seriously. In 1892 James Asplin served as a petty juror in a murder trial at the Northampton assizes. During an adjournment he left the court to post a letter. The trial judge considered this a "gross contempt of Court," one that had exposed all the jurors to the danger of external influence. He fined Asplin £50 and discharged the whole jury.[1361] For most of the period, this also meant that jurors were not allowed home during an adjournment. At best they would go to a hotel. At worst they might be required to bed down in the precincts of the court. This did not apply to the trial of misdemeanours, where jurors were, and always had been, allowed to return home at the end of the day, even if a case was adjourned, explaining why the Tichborne claimant was charged with this 'lesser' form of crime, rather than a felony; it would have been impossible to keep a jury "secluded" from their business and homes for 50 days. [1362]

To consider an example from Norfolk, James Rush's murder trial at the Norwich assizes in 1849 started on Thursday, 29 March, and finished on 4 April, lasting six days (there was no sitting on Sunday), and requiring as many overnight adjournments. The jury were conveyed each night to the Maids Head Hotel in the city, where the assembly room was fitted up as a dormitory. On Sunday, 1 April, they attended morning and afternoon service at the cathedral under the constant escort of county

---

[1358] Ian A. Burney, "A Poisoning of No Substance: The Trials of Medico-Legal Proof in Mid-Victorian England," *Journal of British Studies*, vol. 38, no. 1 (1999), p. 59.

[1359] *John Bull*, 17 April, 1886. *Bell's Life in London*, 19 April, 1886.

[1360] *The Norfolk Chronicle,* 6 April, 1837.

[1361] Crosby, "Criminal Justice," pp. 179-208.

[1362] *The Spectator,* 15 May, 1897, p. 10.

officials.[1363] The Maids Head appears to have been a regular venue in such cases; it was used when the jury in the murder trial of Hubbard Lingley had to adjourn overnight in August 1867.[1364] (It is still in business today).

This situation was ended only by the Juries Detention Act 1897, which brought felony trials into alignment with those for misdemeanours and allowed jurors to return home at the end of a day in court when a case had been only partly heard.[1365] Although the distinction between the two types of crime before this date might appear strange, some observers thought that it was justified. It was likely that only the most serious offences, nearly all of which were classified as felonies, would attract concerted attempts at "nobbling" individual jurors during a hearing, warranting the extra precaution: weak men, it was thought, might otherwise "fall an easy prey to the 'jury-fixer.'" However, the latter needed both time and opportunity (largely denied them prior to 1897) to get at the jurymen, who could not be identified before a hearing.[1366]

[1363] *The Norfolk Chronicle*, 29 March, 1849.

[1364] *The Times*, 10 August, 1867, p. 11.

[1365] Alexander, *The administration*, p. 115.

[1366] *The Spectator*, 15 May, 1897, p. 10.

Chapter 11: Trial on Indictment: The Hearing

Fitness to Plead

Defendants had to be fit to plead before they could be arraigned. This entailed more than just the physical ability to enter a plea. Well before the Victorian era, it had been accepted that, if someone were suffering from such severe mental illness or cognitive impairment that they could not follow the evidence adduced at trial, they might be found to be unfit to plead. As with muteness (see below), this was a matter for a specially sworn-in jury to determine, after a hearing on the issue. (A positive conclusion could lead to indefinite detention for the defendant.) Thus in 1830 Esther Dyson, a deaf woman, was charged with murdering her child. Her trial judge instructed the jury to consider whether they were satisfied that she had "from the defect of her faculties, intelligence enough to understand the nature of the proceedings against her." She was found to be "insane" and so spared trial. Further judicial consideration was given (nationally) to the issue when a deaf man named Pritchard was indicted for bestiality in 1836. On this occasion, the trial judge, Baron Alderson, suggested that simply being physically able to plead did not equate to being fit to plead. He asked the jury to decide whether Pritchard was of sufficient sanity and intellect to comprehend proceedings so that he could make a proper defence. In 1853, in *Davies*, the ability to properly instruct defence counsel, by then an increasingly common aspect of the criminal trial, was incorporated into the *Pritchard* test, which rapidly became the legal standard for fitness to plead.[1367]

Findings of unfitness to plead increased throughout the country in the latter years of the Victorian period. They were not uncommon in Norfolk, especially, but not solely, in murder cases. Thus, when Harriet Kettle was arraigned for arson at the Norfolk assizes in 1859, she was found to be unfit to plead. She had been in an asylum, and a surgeon deposed that she was "perfectly crazy." She apparently made the courtroom resound with shrieks and execrations.[1368]

In December 1875, after three boys were killed by Robert Edwards, a mentally disturbed fellow patient in the Norfolk and Norwich Hospital who set about them with a pair of tongs, the coroner's inquest into the deaths returned a finding of "wilful murder" against him.[1369] Even so, at the following assizes, Edwards was found to be so insane as to be incapable of entering a plea; he was committed to Broadmoor Criminal Lunatic Asylum.[1370] In like manner, in November 1884, the wife-killer Richard Hunt Brown was prosecuted at the Norfolk winter assizes, but

---

1367 Penelope Brown, "Unfitness to plead in England and Wales: Historical development and contemporary dilemmas," *Medical Science Law*, 2019, vol. 59, no. 3 (2019), p. 189.

1368 *The Bury and Norwich Post*, 2 August, 1859.

1369 *The Times*, 22 December, 1875, p. 7.

1370 Frank Meeres, *Norwich Murders & Misdemeanours* (Stroud: Amberley, 2009), p. 103.

"certificated to be insane, and was not put on his trial."[1371] The following year, William Everett, a Norfolk labourer form Wormegay, was indicted for the murder of his mother. Significantly, the prosecution stated that there was evidence that he was unfit to plead and asked that this be put to the jury. Defence counsel agreed, and the jury heard from the prison surgeon, after which they agreed with the prosecutor. As in all such cases, the judge then ordered that Everett be confined during Her Majesty's pleasure.[1372]

Nevertheless, trial of a serious criminal allegation was not withheld lightly, and such a course was unpopular with some judges. At the combined Norfolk and Suffolk autumn assizes held at Norwich in November 1887, the Reverend Arthur Cooper, the curate of Cretingham in Suffolk, was indicted for the murder of his rector, the Reverend William Meymott Farley. Just before he was arraigned, his QC applied to the judge for a jury to be empanelled to determine whether he was fit to plead. This was done, and defence counsel then called physicians from the Suffolk County lunatic asylum and the Ipswich prison to testify to the prisoner's "present insanity, and inability to instruct counsel." Even so, the presiding judge, Mr Justice Field, was dismissive, directing the jury that the situation had not yet been reached in English law when a man accused of a criminal offence should escape trial because of the "opinion of an expert, however eminent." He also opined that it was better that a matter be dealt with in open court rather than left to a politician (the Home Secretary) to deal with in secrecy. Perhaps unsurprisingly, given this direction, the jury decided that the defendant was fit to stand trial. Nevertheless, the (different) jury that then tried the issue, decided that he truly was insane at the time that he killed his clerical superior, so that the judge ordered that Cooper be detained during Her Majesty's pleasure.[1373]

Arraignment and Plea

Once the grand jury had returned a true bill to court, and assuming he was fit, the defendant would be arraigned and given an opportunity to plead guilty or not guilty to the indictment. Sometimes, especially at the start of the period, if several true bills were returned together, a small group of defendants might be arraigned at the same time. Thus, in April 1847, at the Norfolk Quarter Sessions, it was noted that: "After a number of prisoners had been arraigned, and their pleas taken, the trials were proceeded".[1374]

After 1827 a deliberate failure to enter a plea at trial on indictment, standing "mute of malice," would be treated as the equivalent of a not-guilty plea, and lead to a full trial. For example, at the Norfolk assizes in 1900, held before Mr Justice Bigham, William Jimby was indicted for setting fire to a straw stack at Surlingham. The judge

1371 *The Bury and Norwich Post*, 11 November, 1884.

1372 *Ibid.*, 5 May, 1885.

1373 *The Morning Post*, 16 November, 1887. *The York Herald*, 19 November, 1887.

1374 *The Norfolk Chronicle,* 3 April, 1847.

was informed that the prisoner was, or pretended to be, both completely deaf and unable to read or write. A jury was then sworn in specifically to decide whether Jimby was "mute of malice or by the visitation of God." They found him to be mute of malice, the judge ordered a plea of not guilty to be entered on his behalf, and the case proceeded, the (different) trial jury ultimately convicting. (The judge observed that he had no doubt the prisoner was pretending to be deaf.)[1375]

As today, a guilty plea had to be unequivocal. When an ambivalent plea was tendered to a count of attempted murder tried at the combined assizes for Norfolk and Suffolk held at Ipswich in early May 1881, it was altered to not guilty after the trial judge asked the prisoner whether he understood the charge. The latter responded by saying, "I had no intention of doing it. I was under the influence of drink."[1376] Similarly, at the spring assizes for Norfolk and Suffolk in May 1885, several English sailors were indicted for piracy after stealing rum from a German boat. When the prisoners were arraigned, "one or two of them said they were drunk, and only took spirits and a few cigars, &c., and they denied stealing. The learned judge told them they had better plead 'Not guilty', which they accordingly did".[1377] In like manner, in 1898, George Watt, a Norwich labourer accused of murdering his wife, had a not guilty plea entered when he was arraigned and replied, "I am guilty of murder, but not guilty of wilful murder".[1378]

Guilty Pleas

During the eighteenth century, guilty pleas in felony (unlike misdemeanour) cases had been very rare, and often actively discouraged by the courts, especially where a matter was likely to be capital. In part this may have been because it was thought that unrepresented defendants might not be aware of potential avenues of defence or that important prosecution evidence might be inadmissible. Furthermore, a contested trial in a capital case might reveal grounds for a reprieve, even if there was a conviction. Judges remained hostile to guilty pleas during the early decades of the nineteenth century, even for offences where commutation of any death sentence was highly likely. Thus, in the early 1820s Charles Cottu noted that a judge would usually caution the accused that the crime alleged was capital, and that it was in "his interest to defend himself; [while] the clerk, the gaoler, almost all the counsel, even the prosecutors, persuade him to take the chance of an acquittal."[1379] In 1826 Sir James Scarlett observed in Parliament that judges "had uniformly evinced the greatest unwillingness to admit a party to plead guilty."[1380] Illustrative of this, in 1825, when Mary Durrant, a 23-year-old woman, petitioned for a free pardon from

[1375] *The Norfolk Chronicle*, 11 June, 1900.

[1376] *The Ipswich Journal*, 10 May, 1881.

[1377] *The Times*, 1 May, 1885, p. 10.

[1378] *The Ipswich Journal*, 1 July, 1898.

[1379] Cottu, *Administration*, p. 73.

[1380] Hansard HC Deb 17 April 1826 vol. 15 cols. 284-91.

her sentence for highway robbery at the Norfolk assizes two years earlier, it was noted that she had insisted on pleading guilty at trial against the advice of Baron Garrow, the presiding judge.[1381] Of course, occasionally in these situations, and as in previous centuries, a not-guilty plea was followed by little attempt to challenge the prosecution case. As late as February 1882, Henry Stebbings, a repeat sex offender, accused of raping and murdering a girl, pleaded not guilty at the Norfolk assizes but offered no evidence or statement in his defence after the prosecution case was made out.[1382]

A reluctance to accept guilty pleas can still be identified at the start of the Victorian era. For example, in 1842, at the Norfolk assizes, George Barber, a ten-year-old, was accused of murdering another boy by throwing him into a river, where he drowned. At his hearing, the defendant was so small that he could not see over the dock and had to be let out. He initially pleaded guilty and asked for mercy. However, the presiding judge would not accept the plea, because of the boy's apparent lack of understanding, and suggested that Barber change it to not guilty, which he did. The judge eventually stopped the case on the basis that the boy's confession was inadmissible, and the case depended almost entirely on his admissions.[1383] Of course, this case involved a child, and so was likely to attract extra care from the trial judge (in any era), but such attitudes also affected adult defendants. At the Norfolk assizes in March 1853, 24-year-old Sarah Hooks of Wells was indicted for murdering her infant son. At trial, she pleaded guilty. Even so, the judge immediately recommended that she change her plea to not guilty, as there was no legally admissible evidence against her: "She did so, and no evidence being offered against her, she was discharged."[1384]

Despite this, even in the late 1830s, some felony arraignments produced guilty pleas in the jury courts. Estimates as to the precise figure vary, although it has been suggested that it might have been as low as 6 percent nationally in 1835.[1385] Doubtless the number differed between courts and regions. More pertinently, it seems that judicial reluctance to accept guilty pleas had declined markedly by the mid-century, presumably because, by then, only murder was (effectively) still capital, more defendants had legal advice, and there was increased pressure of work due to more and longer hearings. (Interestingly, such a change can also be seen in New York at this time.)[1386] Indeed, guilty pleas increasingly produced a modest reduction in sentence, as can be seen in multi-handed trials where defendants entered differing

---

1381 TNA HO 17/97/83.

1382 *Berrow's Worcester Journal,* 11 February, 1882.

1383 *The Times*, 8 April, 1842. *The Standard*, 13 November, 1841. *The Ipswich Journal*, 9 April, 1842.

1384 *The Bury and Norwich Post*, 23 March, 1853.

1385 John H. Langbein et al., *History of the Common Law: The Development of Anglo-American Legal Institutions* (Frederick, Md.: Aspen, 2009), p. 708.

1386 Mike McConville and Chester Mirsky, "The Rise of Guilty Pleas: New York, 1800-1865," *Journal of Law and Society*, vol. 22, no. 4 (1995), pp. 443-474.

pleas, providing some incentive for admitting guilt. Certainly, they became very much more common, even in serious matters, on one estimate making up about 40 percent of all pleas tendered at the end of the Victorian period. By the early years of the twentieth century, this had increased to half of all defendants nationally at quarter sessions and assizes combined.[1387]

The change occurred at different rates, depending on forum and location. For example, those accused of larceny at mid-Victorian quarter sessions in Montgomeryshire were still notable for their reluctance to plead guilty, even when the prosecution evidence appeared strong. However, this was not necessarily the case in Norfolk. A selection of cases from the county is indicative of the new pattern. At the assizes in August 1840 all three women separately accused of theft-related crimes pleaded guilty, as did two male thieves.[1388] At the Lent assizes for Norfolk in 1855, 13 defendants came for trial in as many hearings. Six of them pleaded guilty to a variety of crimes, namely sodomy (death was "recorded"), felonious assault, concealment of birth, commercial burglary, residential burglary, and uttering a forged cheque.[1389] Similarly, in March 1862, 18 prisoners were indicted at the Norfolk assizes, with several others being prosecuted at those held for the city of Norwich. However, and unusually, all the criminal business was concluded in a single day; in part, this was apparently because there had been so many guilty pleas, for offences including manslaughter, rape, and larceny.[1390] At the Norfolk assizes in July 1887, six cases, and as many defendants, went for trial (another was thrown out by the grand jury). Of these, three elicited guilty pleas, one of them involved a breaking and entering, another a theft, and one obtaining money by false pretences.[1391] At the same forum, a year later, an even higher proportion, six out of ten defendants, pleaded guilty.[1392]

A modest expansion in what might be termed ad hoc plea bargaining can also be identified in tandem with the growth in both guilty pleas and legal representation and was probably linked to it. In these situations, defendants would be indicted for a serious and, in the alternative, less serious crime, such as infanticide and concealing a birth, or a substantive offence and an attempt. A plea of guilty to the less serious charge would be offered and accepted by the prosecution, and no evidence presented on the more serious count. For example, in April 1844 James Haydon, a schoolmaster from Woodbridge in Suffolk, was indicted at the assizes in that county on counts of sodomy and assault with criminal intent (essentially, attempted sodomy). He offered a guilty plea on the lesser count, and the prosecution barrister said that, as the case had been left in his hands, and as there was some doubt as to proof of the capital offence, he preferred not to offer any evidence on

[1387] Alexander, *The administration,* p. 11.

[1388] *The Bury and Norwich Post*, 5 August, 1840.

[1389] *Ibid.,* 4 April, 1855.

[1390] *The Ipswich Journal*, 29 March, 1862.

[1391] *The Bury and Norwich Post*, 26 July, 1887.

[1392] *Ibid.*, 24 July, 1888.

it, especially as the prisoner had pleaded guilty to the sexual assault. The trial judge directed the jury to acquit on the capital charge and sentenced Haydon to two years' imprisonment with hard labour.[1393]

Change of Plea

Occasionally, as today, a defendant might change his plea from not guilty to guilty during a trial. In August 1827 two young "respectable" men came before the Norfolk assizes, accused of taking part in disturbances the previous June. They were represented by Serjeant Storks. Storks politely interrupted prosecuting counsel's opening and offered what appears to have been a deal, possibly canvassed on an earlier occasion, which was then discussed with the trial judge, Baron Garrow, in open court. As a result, the two accused changed their pleas from not guilty to guilty, were bound over in the sum of £100 to keep the peace in future, admonished from the bench, and released.[1394] Over half a century later, Robert Turner, a 39-year-old farmer, was accused of sending threatening letters, including threats to murder, to Joseph Stanley, a Norwich solicitor (and newly elected coroner), who had had dealings with him in a professional capacity. In August 1883, after the prosecution opened the case, and read out the letters, Turner changed his plea to guilty, and apologized, which satisfied the solicitor. Turner was merely bound over to keep the peace.[1395]

However, once a matter came to trial, the judge could veto any negotiations between the prosecution and defence. In a case from 1839 involving three poachers alleged to have shot at a group of Norfolk gamekeepers with intent to kill or maim – several of them had been hit with pellets – both prosecution and defendants were legally represented. Having heard the prosecution evidence, counsel for both sides were willing to bargain and accept a guilty plea to a less serious crime of violence. Nevertheless, the judge "refused to allow the compromise." Ultimately, the defendants offered a plea to the full offence charged but did not receive a death sentence (theoretically possible).[1396]

Where a defendant did plead guilty, the judge or chairman would usually ask for a brief statement of the facts of the case, make any enquiries he thought necessary as to his criminal history, and listen to any mitigation (see below) before proceeding to sentencing.[1397] By contrast, after a defendant had pleaded not guilty, his trial jury would be sworn in, the clerk would read out the indictment in front of them, the prosecutor would open his case, and a contested trial would begin.

[1393] *The Suffolk Chronicle,* 13 April, 1844.

[1394] *The Standard*, 9 August, 1827.

[1395] *The Bury and Norwich Post*, 14 August, 1883.

[1396] *Ibid.,* 17 April, 1839.

[1397] Alexander, *The administration,* p. 106.

The Trial Jury

Far more men would be summoned than were needed to make up the initial 12-man petty (trial) jury. This would allow for failures to attend (often up to 10 percent of the total), challenges, attendees proving to be ineligible or physically unfit to serve (some would send in certificates of ill-health; others, such as the deaf, made the claim in person at court); and any need for extra juries to be assembled during the sessions. (In 1845 a few observers proposed reducing the size of the trial jury for lesser indictable matters to seven or even five men.)[1398]

Before the nineteenth century, the jury panel had sometimes been as few as 24 men. However, to avoid the need to call talesmen (from *tales de circumstantibus*, jurors drawn at random from men in the environs of the court) with a reduced property requirement, it had become normal for a panel of at least 48 potential jurors to be summoned.[1399] Thus, when disgruntled jurors raised concerns with Chief Baron Pollock over the enforcement of jury service at the combined Norfolk and Suffolk spring assizes held at the Shirehall in Ipswich in May 1886, it seems that 48 men had been called. Their de facto spokesman complained that no register had been taken to ensure that they all attended, so that some might have absented themselves without risk or cost. (He also felt that the refreshment the jury had been served during the luncheon adjournment had been "unfit for human consumption.")[1400] However, the panel could be larger than 48, sometimes up to a maximum of 72 in total after the 1825 Act became law, although recourse to so many men was slightly unusual in East Anglia. Nevertheless, at the combined Norfolk and Suffolk winter assizes, held at the end of October 1881, 60 potential trial jurors were summoned.[1401]

In theory the drawing of the trial jury from this panel should have been made by ballot, with the names of all those called to service being written on slips of paper and dropped into a box, from which the chosen 12 would be drawn at random. During the 1820s it seems that the court clerk was sometimes satisfied with taking the first 12 names on the list or (less problematically) any 12 names called "at hazard."[1402] Nevertheless, random selection from the panel was considered important during the Victorian period, as it reduced any possibility of jury nobbling, and this was the usual practice.

A defendant could challenge the entire jury array if they believed that the sheriff's official who was responsible for selecting the panel had packed the jury pool with individuals who would find against him (he was entitled to a view of the panel prior to the hearing). However, the decline of such challenges in England during the early nineteenth century made this more of a theoretical rather than a

---

[1398] *Eighth Report,* p. 332.

[1399] Cottu, *Administration,* pp. 84-85.

[1400] *The Ipswich Journal*, 11 May, 1886.

[1401] *Ibid.*, 29 October, 1881.

[1402] Cottu, *Administration,* p. 75.

practical right.[1403] Even so, occasionally informal pre-trial jury screening seems to have occurred, precluding the need for it to be conducted in court, with counsel, whether for prosecution or defence, making the unsuitability of certain men known to the court officer, who would refrain from calling them.[1404] In the 1820s, Charles Cottu thought that this was possible because the jury panel list was produced some days before the session, communicated to the attorneys of those parties with legal representation, and then shown to prisoners, who could point out objectionable jurors. The clerk then "skip[ped] them over" when calling jurors, so that a challenge was very rarely necessary.[1405] How common this was, and the degree to which such a practice survived during the early Victorian era, is uncertain, but it was potentially important in misdemeanour cases, which did not have peremptory challenge.

Once identified, the chosen jurors would be sworn in in court, individually in the case of felony indictments, often in groups of four for misdemeanours. At this point, individual jurors could be challenged.

Challenging Individual Jurors

The Crown could ask any number of potential jurors to "stand aside" (this ultimately became "stand by for the Crown") as their names were called, if they were thought unsuitable, with the understanding that any objections would be explained if the panel was exhausted (rarely the case).[1406] Although potentially very significant, this power was normally exercised sparingly in England. (Ireland was a different matter.) More important, defendants could challenge 20 jurors peremptorily (as of right) without showing cause in felony (but not misdemeanour) trials, and any number for cause (essentially potential personal bias against the accused) in all criminal trials, although these had to be justified by extrinsic evidence. For example, at the Norwich quarter sessions in January 1842, Thomas Hewett was accused of involvement in a serious Chartist disturbance in the city. At trial, he "objected to Mr Nurse being sworn on the jury, alleging that he was prejudiced against the Chartists."[1407] According to a nineteenth-century English criminal-practice guide, this might be done or initiated by counsel simply calling out "Challenge!" as a juror was called to the box, although courts could require legally represented defendants to make their challenges personally.[1408]

[1403] R. Blake Brown, "'A Delusion, a Mockery, and a Snare': Array Challenges and Jury Selection in England and Ireland, 1800-1850," *Canadian Journal of History*, vol. 39, no. 1 (2004), pp. 1-26.

[1404] April J. Anderson, "Peremptory Challenges At the Turn of the Nineteenth Century: Development of Modern Jury Selection Strategies as Seen in Practitioners' Trial Manuals," *Stanford Journal of Civil Rights & Civil Liberties*, vol. 16, no. 1 (2020), pp. 13-17.

[1405] Cottu, *Administration,* p. 72.

[1406] Anderson, "Peremptory Challenges," pp. 13-17.

[1407] *The Northern Star*, 15 January, 1842.

[1408] Anderson, "Peremptory Challenges," pp. 13-17.

However, defendant challenge of either type was not very common in England (unlike Ireland) during the nineteenth century. Sir James Fitzjames Stephen could recall only two cases from his career in which there was "any considerable number of challenges."[1409] In part this may have been due to ignorance. Unrepresented defendants (the majority) may not have properly understood their right to challenge, even if quickly alerted to it by the court clerk. Just as important, they had no power to question prospective jurors to identify reasons for objecting. For example, in a case in 1848, a defendant was not allowed to ask whether a prospective juror was a special constable. There may also have been a fear that exercising the right might risk annoying those called in as replacements.[1410]

Unsurprisingly, challenging jurors seems to have been more common when a defendant was legally represented and so properly aware of the right rather than dependant on a rushed statement from the court clerk. For example, in 1902 Ernest Wild QC removed four jurors prior to William Gardiner's murder trial at the Suffolk assizes, using peremptory challenge, something that may have been responsible for the prosecution failure to secure a conviction (the case produced a 'hung' jury).[1411] It also seems that counsel were sometimes able to get information about jurors just prior to a hearing, using their personal contacts at court.

Unusually, in a Norfolk context, at the trial at assizes of Charles Daines in 1839, for attempting to murder his wife with poison, both the Crown and the legally represented defendant freely exercised their rights in this regard: "Several of the jury were challenged both by the Counsel for the Crown, and by the Counsel for the prisoner, and the panel became exhausted." This led to a debate as to when the Crown would be required to give explanations for exercising its power to "stand aside." However, the matter appears to have been resolved, fresh jurors being found or accepted, as the trial eventually proceeded.[1412] Similarly, at the trial of two men for publishing a criminal libel held at the Norfolk assizes in August 1883, it was noted, "Many of the jurors were challenged by both the prosecution and defence."[1413]

Jury Knowledge

Unlike their medieval predecessors, or their contemporaries on inquest juries, nineteenth-century trial jurors normally had no personal knowledge of a case before it came to court. It was, of course, accepted that jurors should not have a relationship that might suggest bias towards the accused person. Thus, when William Butcher was tried for receiving stolen property at the Thetford borough sessions in July 1879,

---

[1409] R. Blake Brown, "Challenges for Cause, Stand-Asides, and Peremptory Challenges in the Nineteenth Century," *Osgoode Hall Law Journal*, vol. 38, no. 3 (2000), p. 468. Alexander, *The administration,* p. 107. Howlin, "English and Irish," p. 117

[1410] Anderson, "Peremptory Challenges," pp. 13-17.

[1411] *The Times*, 18 November, 1902.

[1412] *The Bury and Norwich Post*, 17 April, 1839.

[1413] *The Ipswich Journal*, 11 August, 1883.

one of the summoned jurors announced that he was a relative of the defendant and so should retire. The recorder agreed, commending him for revealing the fact, and another juror was sworn in his place.[1414] However, a juror might possess more general awareness of the details of a case or defendant by chance, if only very rarely. For example, in April 1851, at the Norfolk assizes, Jeremy Wilkinson, one of the jurors at the trial of a 16-year-old accused of poaching, gave the defendant a good character for "orderly behaviour" but admitted that he knew that the youth had accrued two previous convictions for the same crime. The defendant's mother gave him an alibi for the night in question, as did his brother, both being grilled by prosecution counsel and the trial judge, and not proving entirely satisfactory witnesses. Even so, the young man was acquitted. Subsequently, it was noted that "Wilkinson was then ordered to leave the jury box, and another juror was sworn in his place".[1415] Was this a reprimand for not disclosing that he was familiar with the accused before being sworn in?

Legal Representation

At the start of the Victorian era the final limits on legal representation in trial on indictment for felony had only recently been abandoned, although the restrictions placed on defence lawyers had been subject to sustained criticism during the early 1800s, and between 1821 and 1836 ten attempts had been made to pass legislation granting suspected felons full representation. The 1836 Prisoner's Counsel Act had formally recognised the right of those accused of felony to "make full Answer and Defence thereto, by Counsel learned in the law." As a result, felony defendants could fully delegate the right to present their cases to their barristers, as they had always been able to do in misdemeanour cases.[1416] The defence counsel's role expanded from the simple cross-examination of prosecution witnesses and arguing points of law to formally addressing the jury. This allowed him to offer observations and opinions to the jury, with a view to swaying their decision.[1417] He was aided in this by the liberal code of conduct for barristers that was prevalent in the early Victorian period, one that, according to Henry Brougham, required that they protect their client's interests "by all means and expedients."

All lawyer-conducted advocacy at assizes, and the great majority at quarter sessions, would be carried out by barristers or serjeants-at-law, the latter legal profession gradually disappearing during the second half of the century. Solicitors regularly appeared at petty sessions for both prosecution and defence but might also appear at some of the more remote county quarter sessions, albeit that none of them were in Norfolk. More pertinently, they could appear to conduct jury trials at quite a

[1414] *The Bury and Norwich Post*, 22 July, 1879.

[1415] *Ibid.*, 2 April, 1851.

[1416] Cerian Charlotte Griffiths, "The Prisoners' Counsel Act 1836: Doctrine, Advocacy and the Criminal Trial", *Law, Crime and History*, vol. 4, no. 2 (2014), p. 29.

[1417] Tom Smith, "Zealous Advocates: The Historical Foundations of the Adversarial Criminal Defence Lawyer," *Law, Crime and History*, vol. 2, no. 1 (2012), p. 12.

few of the smaller borough sessions, including those held for Thetford, where, for example, a local solicitor, Robert Eagle Clarke, sometimes acted as counsel in the 1840s.[1418]

Counsel

Each circuit had its own "mess" of barristers, including a handful of QCs and, at the start of the era, one or two serjeants-at-law. They would cover all the work of the higher jury courts, and in the 1830s some of these lawyers would make very similar journeys to those of the judges at assizes, circulating around all the circuit's constituent counties to conduct trials at most of its venues. However, other barristers would concentrate on a smaller number of forums, perhaps those situated near their homes.[1419] Circuit barristers (usually juniors rather than QCs) would also cover work at the lower jury forum on a more ad hoc basis, often concentrating on certain areas or counties. As a result, a significant part of the criminal work at the Norfolk assizes and quarter sessions, both for the prosecution and defence, was undertaken by a very small group of barristers, many of whom had a local connection, and most of whom were intimately familiar with one another.

Prominent amongst these lawyers were men like Carlos Cooper, who had been called to the bar in January 1839, just before his twenty-fourth birthday. He subsequently became recorder of Thetford in 1865, a judge of the (civil) Guildhall Court at Norwich in 1872, and recorder of King's Lynn in March 1885 (all these were part-time judicial positions).[1420] More than two decades after Cooper, Thomas Blofeld was another stalwart of the local circuit. His family had been landowners near Norwich for centuries. He was called to the bar in 1862, and survived the early years of practice, when his remuneration was very modest. In 1865 he made just £14 during the Lent assizes, despite being forced to spend £19 on transport and other outgoings while travelling around the circuit. His earnings gradually increased, and he supplemented his income by conducting arbitrations and sitting as a part-time county court judge in civil matters. More significantly, he became the recorder of Ipswich and finally, in 1881, he was appointed to the chancellorship of the diocese of Norwich, a prestigious, if very poorly paid, position. He usually earned considerably more than £l,000 per annum by the final years of the Victorian era.[1421] (He was also an active JP and chairman of Norfolk quarter sessions).

Obviously, much legal work at assizes, and most of the more lucrative briefs at this forum, was found on the *nisi prius* side. At the peak of his career, Thomas Blofeld would regularly appear in most of the civil cases tried at both the Norfolk and Suffolk assizes. However, by the start of the Victorian period, the use of counsel in serious criminal trials was well established, for both prosecution and defence, and

1418 *The Ipswich Journal*, 17 January, 1846.

1419 R.C.J. Cocks, *Sir Henry Maine: A Study in Victorian Jurisprudence* (Cambridge: CUP, 2008), pp. 42-43.

1420 *The Standard*, 26 March, 1885.

1421 Cocks, "Dignity and Emoluments," pp. 37-48.

set to expand further due to the impact of the Prisoner's Counsel Act of 1836. A few of these would be very well funded cases involving comparatively expensive lawyers, whether because they were prosecuting on behalf of an institution such as the Royal Mint or the Bank of England, or because they were defending a client of means.

To consider an example from a neighbouring county, at the Suffolk assizes in August 1833, the 70-year-old Reverend Charles Holden, vicar of Great Cornard, and his much younger curate, were indicted for a "nameless offence" (sodomy). In this case, the highly regarded barrister and future judge Sir James Scarlett represented the defendants for the enormous sum of 600 guineas (£630). It may have been a good investment, as the pair were acquitted.[1422] More locally, at the Norwich assizes in 1835 Johnstone Wardell, a 23-year-old Bank of England clerk was accused of stealing £1,431 from his employer. He retained the barrister Fitzroy Kelly to conduct his defence, at the substantial fee of 100 guineas (£105), along with two other supporting lawyers. Again, it seems to have been money well spent, as, after a trial lasting ten hours, the jury speedily acquitted him. (The accused claimed, rather implausibly, that he had been knocked down and robbed of the money by two men on the Norwich Castle ditches.)[1423]

However, such lucrative cases were extremely unusual, and many barristers were willing to work for much more modest fees, perhaps as little as a guinea or two.[1424] (In theory, no barrister could accept a brief fee of less than a guinea). Sir Henry Hawkins remembered that, when dealing with a low-level crime being tried at the Hertford quarter sessions in the mid-century, his instructing solicitors had expressly noted in the brief that, as the client was "a poor man, we can't mark much of a fee." This was apparently a regular complaint against solicitors at this forum.[1425]

Defendants of even modest means clearly thought legal representation worthwhile. In 1877, at the insurance fraudster William Dowman's committal hearing, his counsel asked that the gold watch, chain, and ring found on Dowman when he was arrested be returned to him, to help fund his defence. (The magistrates allowed this.)[1426] Poorer people might club together to support a friend seeking the money to pay for lawyers, while strangers might contribute to public collections for defendants charged with serious and well-publicized offences with whom they sympathised. When George Hall was facing a murder indictment at the Warwick assizes, after killing his wife in allegedly extenuating circumstances, collections were

---

[1422] *The Spectator,* 10 August, 1833.

[1423] *The Norfolk Chronicle,* 4 April, 1835.*The Bury & Norwich Post, & East Anglian: Or, Suffolk, Norfolk, Essex, Cambridge, and Ely Intelligencer*, 8 April, 1835.

[1424] Bentley, *English Criminal Justice,* p. 98.

[1425] Hawkins, *Reminiscences,* p. 70.

[1426] *The Ipswich Journal*, 15 September, 1877.

even taken round factories and workshops. As a result, he was able to employ two highly regarded barristers.[1427]

Disparity in Representation

Nevertheless, disparity in legal representation, where present, was nearly always in favour of the prosecution, with undefended prisoners facing professional lawyers, and sometimes even a QC supported by a junior barrister. By the start of the Victorian period, crimes of any gravity, and many that were not, especially those conducted at assizes, were normally prosecuted by counsel, and long before its close this applied to nearly all cases heard on indictment.[1428] So much was this the case that, at the Norfolk assizes in April 1842, William Palmer prosecuted two legally represented burglars on behalf of an elderly female victim, who did not have counsel, at the request of the judge.[1429] (Presumably, as with defendants in homicide cases who were assigned counsel by the judiciary from barristers who were in court, this was not paid for.)

Having a professional lawyer presenting the Crown's case probably made life easier for the judiciary. In March 1853 Mr Justice Coleridge hinted at this, and at the ubiquity of prosecuting counsel in most serious cases, when presiding over the Surrey assizes. The judge, faced by a rare case in which such counsel had not been briefed in advance, handed the magistrates' committal depositions to one of the barristers present in court "to enable him to conduct a prosecution in a case of a serious character, [and] took occasion to observe upon the inconvenience that was created by counsel not being instructed to prosecute in such cases." He thought it was disgraceful if this had been done to save a few pounds, as the administration of criminal justice was too serious a matter for such false economies, especially as a human life might sometimes be at stake. He expressed the hope that he would never see such a case again.[1430]

Prosecution legal representation at the lower jury courts was also encouraged in many locations by the "soup" system, under which prosecution briefs at quarter and borough sessions were prepared by an employee of the county or borough and distributed by him amongst all junior counsel attending quarter sessions, along with a very modest brief fee, but without a solicitor's involvement.[1431] (See Chapter 8).

The situation for poor defendants was very much worse. As Lord Abinger noted in 1836, irrespective of the enhanced rights given to those with legal representation that year, "Many prisoners would still remain without counsel to defend them, for

[1427] Martin J. Wiener, "The Sad Story of George Hall: Adultery, Murder and the Politics of Mercy in Mid-Victorian England," *Social History*, vol. 24, no. 2 (1999), p. 178.

[1428] Bentley, *English Criminal Justice*, p. 71.

[1429] *The Times*, 8 April, 1842. *The Ipswich Journal*, 9 April, 1842.

[1430] *Ibid.*, 21 March, 1853, p. 7.

[1431] Cornish, *Oxford History*, p. 1042.

they would not have funds to procure such assistance."[1432] It was not until the advent of the Poor Prisoner's Defence Act of 1903 that some defendants were able to obtain any form of legal aid, although the Old Bailey had its own scheme, independent of national government, somewhat earlier. However, occasional, local provision for defence representation was being made by the late Victorian period, even in the provinces. For example, in 1888, after the unrepresented Moses Webb was tried and convicted at the Thetford borough sessions for stealing a chicken and going equipped for housebreaking, the town recorder expressed a hope that the authorities would ensure that at future quarter sessions prisoners would be properly represented "so as to relieve himself of the duties of advocate for the prisoner". (This was one of a trial judge's historic, if sometimes neglected, roles.)[1433] Presumably this would be paid for by the town, although that solicitors could appear as counsel at borough sessions in Thetford might reduce the cost. More pertinently, during the Victorian era judges became increasingly willing to cajole barristers to represent poor defendants in very serious cases on a *pro bono* basis via assignment, while other barristers were instructed for a relatively modest sum through the dock brief system.

Assignment

When it came to assignment, the judge would ask a barrister who was present in court to provide his services free of charge. This was not an ideal solution to the lack of legal representation, not least because it was usually limited to murder cases. Thus, at the Norfolk assizes in 1842, George Barber, a ten-year-old boy, was accused of murdering a young associate. The Crown was legally represented. At the judge's request, William Palmer, a barrister who was in court, "watched the case for the prosecution" and kept an eye on the young defendant's interests.[1434] However, occasionally it was extended to other grave or legally difficult crimes, especially if juveniles were involved. For example, in 1861 Mr Justice Wightman asked a barrister who was present in court at the Norfolk assizes to represent Walter Thrower, a 12-year-old labourer, who was accused of setting fire to a stook. He was acquitted. (By contrast, James Davis, an unrepresented adult accused of a similar crime at the same sessions, did not receive this courtesy, and was found guilty and sentenced to ten years' penal servitude.)[1435]

Similarly, at the spring assizes for Norfolk and Suffolk in May 1885, several English sailors, arrested in Yarmouth, were tried for piracy (technically still a capital offence) after stealing alcohol from a small German vessel while at sea. The Attorney General and two circuit barristers appeared for the prosecution (which had diplomatic implications). Perhaps unsurprisingly in these circumstances: "At the suggestion of

---

[1432] Hansard HL Deb 14 July 1836 vol. 35 cols. 171-86.

[1433] *The Bury and Norwich Post*, 24 April, 1888.

[1434] *The Times*, 8 April, 1842, p. 15. *The Standard*, 13 November, 1841. *The Ipswich Journal*, 9 April, 1842.

[1435] *The Bury and Norwich Post*, 30 July, 1861.

the learned Judge, Mr. Simms Reeve [a barrister on circuit] undertook the defence of this case."[1436] Moving county, in a case from the Kent assizes in March 1846, a man and a youth were accused of sodomy, and the prosecution was legally represented. Another barrister in court reported that "Mr. Russell, by the direction of his lordship, undertook the defence of the prisoners."[1437]

Moving to the lower jury courts, at the Yarmouth borough quarter sessions in January 1888, Alfred Denn, a deaf man, was accused of stealing a guernsey from a local shop. The prosecution was legally represented, and at the request of the court a lawyer represented the defendant, while a local solicitor "translated" for him. He was acquitted.[1438] Much turned on the individual judge. Nevertheless, assignment was not normally employed for lesser-ranking felonies.

Even where it was employed, assignment had many limitations. It meant that an unrepresented defendant, indicted for murder, but with (for example) a viable but complicated defence, would be dependent on the judge's ability to find him competent counsel. In practice, once the judge indicated to the courtroom that he was seeking such a lawyer, senior and experienced barristers would often edge away or try to appear busy, to avoid being picked, sometimes leaving "some old man of the law" who was no longer a very competent lawyer to cover the matter. The judge would then be forced to ask this barrister to undertake the case "at a moment's notice, without any previous knowledge of the facts." In these situations, there was no time for a conference between lawyer and client, or even proper consultation, with instructions being taken in the courtroom.[1439]

Dock Briefs

In the case of the dock brief, a defendant in any trial on indictment, when arraigned, could select any barrister who was present in court, and not otherwise engaged, for a guinea. Although a relatively modest sum during the Victorian era, this was not the nominal amount that it became in the twentieth century; it was still more than a week's wages for many workingmen. The prisoner would often make the application for representation from the dock, surveying the available barristers, and pointing out his choice. Again, once it was known that such an application was in the offing, experienced barristers might slip away, although briefless juniors would often come into court in the hope of acquiring such work, and with it experience and even a reputation. James Fitzjames Stephen's early years at the criminal bar were apparently assisted by his friendship with the deputy clerk of the Midland Circuit, who helped him secure numerous dock briefs.[1440] Payment for dock briefs was supposed to be made in advance, and was the same for each case, regardless

[1436] *The Times*, 4 February, 1885, p. 12.

[1437] *The South Eastern Gazette,* 17 March, 1846.

[1438] *The Ipswich Journal*, 3 January, 1888.

[1439] Anon., *The Westminster Review*, "English Courts of Law," vol. 68 (July 1857), pp. 28-29.

[1440] Wiener, "Sad Story," p. 178.

of plea or length of trial. As with assignment, instructions were given in court, and there was no need for a solicitor.

It has been suggested that the presence of counsel for the defendant was almost universal in murder cases after the Prisoner's Counsel Act of 1836.[1441] This is a slight exaggeration, particularly outside London. Even so, nationally, assignment in murder cases had become routine by about 1860, although it seems, on the evidence of the *Times*, that rare instances of alleged murderers appearing at trial without counsel continued until 1879.[1442] Of course, an accused person might reject (free) assigned counsel, which often explains the lack of representation. For example, James Rush, tried in March 1849 for the murder of the recorder of Norwich the previous year, turned down the offer of counsel and defended himself, although he had earlier had recourse to a solicitor. The prosecution was represented by Serjeant Byles and two junior barristers. Rush made a disastrous job of the task, speaking at great length in a rambling and incoherent manner.[1443]

Nevertheless, it seems that a few murder defendants were involuntarily unrepresented in Norfolk until the middle of the nineteenth century. For example, at the summer assizes in 1851, Henry Groom was unassisted by counsel, although two barristers prosecuted his case.[1444] This was especially likely in infanticide cases, where the imposition of capital punishment was unlikely. At the Norfolk assizes in March 1853, 24-year-old Sarah Hooks from Wells was indicted for murdering her infant son without, it seems, being legally represented; fortunately, the trial judge actively assisted her.[1445] However, and more typically by the mid-century, a lawyer would normally be found for the accused in such cases. Thus, in March 1854 at the Norfolk assizes, when William Thompson was tried for the murder of Lorenzi Beha the previous November, he was defended by Carlos Cooper, who was at least the equal of the Crown's legal representative.[1446]

Unrepresented defendants remained extremely common throughout the era when middle- and lesser-ranking crimes (including felonies) were tried. For example, in 1857 it was observed that at the forthcoming Liverpool assizes, only about a third of the 150 or so prisoners drawn from various parts of South Lancashire would have legal representation.[1447] A broadly similar situation was found in Norfolk. This could be slightly unedifying. In January 1874 two young men, one of them just 16 and the other only 22 years of age, were accused of stealing seven hares that had been bagged by a shooting party in Weeting, and temporarily left lying near a covert.

[1441] Wiener, "Judges v. Jurors," p. 473.

[1442] Bentley, *English Criminal Justice*, p. 113.

[1443] *The Norfolk Chronicle*, 29 March, 1849.

[1444] *T he Bury and Norwich Post, and Suffolk Herald*, 30 July, 1851

[1445] *The Bury and Norwich Post*, 23 March, 1853.

[1446] *The Norfolk Chronicle*, 23 March, 1854.

[1447] Anon., "English Courts of Law," p. 28.

When the case came up for trial at the Norfolk quarter sessions, Carlos Cooper and Thomas Blofeld prosecuted, but both the accused were legally undefended, making for a rather uneven contest. The pair were convicted; the youth received just one day's imprisonment, but the adult, who had numerous previous convictions, was given two years' imprisonment with hard labour.[1448]

Some defendants in extremely serious matters, just short of homicide when it came to punishment, were still unrepresented, even late in the period. In July 1887 at the Norfolk assizes, George Frederick Gaymer, a 43-year-old butler, was indicted for sodomy, committed three months earlier at Kenninghall. Again, Carlos Cooper conducted the prosecution, but Gaymer was legally undefended. Although he pleaded not guilty, he made a poor fist of his defence: "The facts, which were of a filthy description, were not disputed by the prisoner, but he made rambling statements, and put questions quite foreign to the issue the Jury had to decide." He was convicted and sentenced to 15 years' penal servitude.[1449]

Very occasionally, other ad hoc expedients to improve defence forensic performance might be used, especially if children were involved. At the Norwich quarter sessions in 1886, when ten-year-old, legally unrepresented Albert Greaves was accused of breaking and entering a shop in the city with another boy, his mother was allowed to conduct the cross-examination of a prosecution witness on his behalf. Although Mrs Greaves had been sobbing when she arrived at court she did not do too badly: "The mother of the prisoner Greaves was then allowed to cross-examine [the] witness, who, in reply, said that he did not see Greaves there."[1450]

There is no doubt that high-quality defence representation could be effective at both jury forums. One observer felt that, although many prosecution lawyers sought to be fair, there "cannot be a doubt that the case is not so strictly conducted in undefended cases as in defended cases."[1451] Occasionally even the judiciary commented on this. In January 1897 John George Foster, a 37-year-old man, was indicted at the Norwich assizes for the murder by stabbing of Alice Maria Newby in a house in Norwich. He had personally informed the police of the killing, immediately regretted it, but said that he had done it because Alice had "tempted" him. He also had numerous self-inflicted injuries on his throat (suggesting a post-killing attempt at suicide). A well-known circuit barrister, Mr Wild, represented Foster, who was merely convicted of manslaughter, and sentenced to penal servitude for life. According to the trial judge, the jury's benign verdict was "largely due to the address of prisoner's counsel."[1452]

Less seriously, at the Norwich quarter sessions in July 1862, a grocer named Edward Durrant was indicted for fraudulently playing cards to win 14 shillings in the Star Inn

---

1448 *The Bury and Norwich Post, and Suffolk Herald*, 20 January, 1874.

1449 *The Norwich Mercury*, 27 July, 1887.

1450 *The Bury and Norwich Post*, 14 September, 1886.

1451 Anon., "English Courts of Law," p. 29.

1452 *Lloyd's Weekly Newspaper*, 31 January, 1897.

in the city. There were several other similar counts against him. Durrant had been able to instruct Serjeant William Ballantine (1812-1887), a well-known advocate, who succeeded in securing an acquittal. The city recorder clearly thought the decision was against the evidence, observing: "Well, prisoner, you have had a most merciful jury; that is all I can say."[1453]

The problems attendant on legal representation were never fully solved in Victorian England. The lack of a level playing field between prosecution and defence was a perennial problem, while a shortage of resources often affected the quality of prosecution work, even where counsel was briefed for the Crown. In 1863 James Fitzjames Stephen claimed that criminal litigation in England worked extremely well when wealthy people, who could afford the best lawyers, and seek out witnesses and put them up at assizes, were involved. Unfortunately, this was not the situation in many cases. Many workingmen accused of a crime could not afford to have relevant defence witnesses conveyed to, and then supported at, court, while waiting for their case to come on, let alone pay for quality defence representation. Even prosecutions were sometimes substandard, to save money. As a result, "The prosecutor is often careless, the prisoner generally poor and ignorant, and a consequence is that the case goes to the jury in an imperfect and unsatisfactory form."[1454]

Role of the Judiciary

In the 1820s the visiting French judge Charles Cottu was struck by the judicial passivity he found in England, and noted that, during the questioning of witnesses at the higher jury forum, the presiding judge would be making notes of their answers, both during examination and cross-examination, and limiting his own questions to seeking clarification of their responses: "Each witness gives his evidence deliberately, pausing at the end of each sentence, to give the judge time to take his notes: the judge himself sometimes puts questions, the object of which is more to obtain an explanation of the witness's depositions, than to establish any additional circumstances against the prisoner."[1455] This is the modern situation and was markedly at variance to that found in England during the early-modern era, in which the trial judge would dominate proceedings (lawyers were very rarely present). In 1836 Lord Wharncliffe thought that, ideally, "The duties of a judge in criminal cases, should be confined to his keeping the evidence within legal bounds, and giving his direction to the jury."[1456]

However, Cottu was exaggerating the situation, especially at provincial assizes, doubtless influenced by the comparative activism of the Roman law judiciary in his native country. Judges still manifested a relatively high level of interventionism by

---

[1453] *The Norfolk Chronicle,* 1 July, 1862.

[1454] K.J.M. Smith, *James Fitzjames Stephen: Portrait of a Victorian Rationalist* (Cambridge: CUP, 2002), p. 94.

[1455] Cottu, *Administration,* pp. 101-102, p. 88.

[1456] HL Deb 14 July 1836 vol. 35 cols. 171-86.

modern standards, particularly early in the Victorian era. Even Cottu appreciated that the trial judge would usually conduct cross-examination for the prisoner "when he has not the means of procuring counsel," as was normally the case for lesser felonies, and as had historically been seen as part of his duties.

Some judges went further, and became quite actively involved in proceedings generally, taking care to protect the interests of unrepresented defendants in some cases, and advancing prosecutions in others, as they saw fit. For example, in October 1881, at the Norfolk and Suffolk assizes, Matilda Annison was called to give evidence against her husband, Alfred, after he was accused of stabbing her with intent to murder. She was evasive, and initially said as "little as possible prejudicial to the interests of the prisoner." She also stressed that she had been very intoxicated at the time of the incident. Although both prosecution and defence were well represented by extremely experienced counsel, the judge took a vigorous part in cross-examining the victim and chief prosecution witness. He reminded her that she had previously made a statement to the examining magistrates implicating her spouse and pressed her on the issue until she eventually admitted that she thought her husband had stabbed her. He was duly convicted.[1457]

There were also cases in which what might be considered questionable acquittals were secured at the behest of an interventionist judge. For example, in 1889 Barnell Joplin, a corn dealer from King's Lynn, was accused of murdering his erstwhile sweetheart, Frances Louisa ("Lizzie") Green, an 18-year-old student teacher at a local infant school, by pushing her into the water from the town quay, before jumping in himself. He made contradictory statements afterwards, and an attempted murder/suicide, with only the first part proving successful after Joplin was pulled from the water, seems a possible scenario (Frances was tiring of his attentions). At trial the presiding judge, William Ventris Field, brought extreme pressure on prosecuting counsel to abandon the case, due to the alleged lack of firm evidence (from an autopsy) as to precisely how Frances had died, in what was a capital matter. A surgeon who had seen (but not opened) her body was not willing to state firmly that drowning was the cause of death. At this point, Edward Beloe, the Lynn borough coroner, repeatedly attempted to interrupt, presumably intending to say that he *had* overseen a thorough examination and could supply such information but was ordered from the court. Prosecuting counsel eventually succumbed to Field's pressure, although he put the responsibility for doing so on the judge (who was trying to place it on counsel), by noting, "I bow to your Lordship's decision that there is no proper evidence of death to go to the jury." Joplin was discharged.[1458] Although Field was well regarded as a lawyer in civil cases, it may be that crime was not his forte.

1457 *The Ipswich Journal*, 29 October, 1881.

1458 *Ibid.*, 22 February, 1889.

Prosecution Opening

Once the petty jury was sworn in, and the court clerk had read out the indictment and the defendants' pleas, prosecuting counsel, if present (as was usually the situation by the Victorian era), would formally open the case against the accused by outlining to the jury its essential facts, issues, and the evidence he proposed to call. Sometimes, this speech might be quite short. Thus, in 1844, in an indecent assault allegation tried at the Norfolk assizes, it was noted that, "The facts of the case having been very briefly stated by the Counsel ... He then called Lydia Cullyer [the victim, to give evidence]."[1459] If a case was straightforward, or the court was trying to clear a backlog of prisoners, he might even omit this stage altogether, especially if this was encouraged by the presiding judge or chairman.[1460] (In 1836 Lord Abinger noted that omission was common practice on some circuits.)[1461] A prosecutor who was not legally represented could not make such a speech in person.

By the early part of the nineteenth century the notion that prosecuting counsel (where employed) should not be striving to secure a conviction at all costs was already established, although they sometimes failed to live up to this convention. It was particularly evidenced in the opening speech, although some barristers might, sometimes, breach the duty of restraint, and give a "hanging speech" in a capital case. Such conviction friendly speeches may have been a little more common in misdemeanour cases. Nevertheless, it was generally thought that an opening should not go beyond a narrative of facts that would allow the jury to follow the evidence and refrain from mentioning doubtful evidence which might be challenged at the hearing.[1462]

In the 1820s Charles Cottu was impressed by the generally restrained nature of such openings, thinking that they were often merely a summary of the case, and a more detailed repetition of the indictment, in which the lawyer would avoid any sort of invective against the prisoner, and refrain from dwelling on his alleged depravity: "We do not hear the prosecutor's counsel paint the prisoner as a monster of whom the earth ought to be that instant rid, and compare him to all the villains who have astonished the world by their enormities." This situation largely survived the forensic changes effected by statute in 1836. Thus, in 1841, when 22-year-old Charlotte Yaxley was tried for murdering her husband's illegitimate infant daughter, it was noted that prosecuting counsel at the Norfolk assizes opened the case by outlining the evidence he proposed to call in a "very temperate" manner.[1463]

Once the opening was finished, prosecution witnesses would be called, being examined in chief, without employing leading questions (Sir Henry Hawkins thought

---

[1459] *The Norwich Mercury*, 10 August, 1844.

[1460] Reid, *Briefs and Papers,* p. 103.

[1461] Hansard HL Deb 14 July 1836 vol. 35 cols. 171-86.

[1462] Cairns, *Advocacy,* p. 39.

[1463] *The Bury and Norwich Post, and East Anglian*, 14 April, 1841.

this restriction was often ignored at the beginning of the period), by prosecuting counsel or a police officer/other prosecutor/the court clerk in the absence of a lawyer. When he had finished, it would be the turn of the defendant's lawyer (if he had one), the defendant himself (if he did not), or even the judge to cross-examine the same witness "with the view of discrediting his testimony by contradictions, or of establishing some circumstances favourable to the defendant."[1464] Leading questions could be employed at this stage.

Witnesses would normally be required to stand when giving evidence, unless they were decrepit or ailing, like the recently poisoned Hannah Daines, who was permitted a chair at the Norfolk assizes in 1839.[1465] Inevitably a few proved woefully deficient on the day. In 1858 a public-house brawl at Earsham in South Norfolk led to a shoemaker named Charles Stone being indicted at assizes for maliciously stabbing and wounding William Hunt with the intention of doing him grievous bodily harm. However, at trial the alleged victim and chief prosecution witness was so drunk, and conducted himself so disgracefully in the witness box, that the judge committed him for contempt of court while the jury acquitted the defendant.[1466]

Witness Testimony and the Oath

Oral evidence, delivered in open court, dominated Victorian criminal trials. Testimony was necessarily given on oath. (The Oaths Act of 1888 (51 & 52 Vict. c.46) eventually allowed solemn affirmation as an alternative to taking a sworn oath.) As a result, by the Victorian period, very small children and the mentally deficient were normally excluded from giving evidence; however, the Criminal Law (Amendment) Act 1885 allowed children to give unsworn testimony in cases involving certain types of sexual offence if they were deemed to be of sufficient intelligence to justify its reception. Taking the oath required some understanding of the religious sanction placed on perjury, although in 1885 Lord Brett MR observed that there was no necessity that the person sworn believe that he would be liable to be punished in a future state: "If there be any belief in a religion according to which it is supposed that a Supreme Being would punish a man in this world for doing wrong, that is enough."[1467]

An understanding of this religious sanction was normally assumed in adults, unless they were obviously in some way mentally defective. The latter was the situation at the Norfolk quarter sessions in July 1844, when William Scott, a 22-year-old man, was convicted of stealing stockings from Rebecca Brundle. Brundle was an "idiot," as persons of very low IQ were then termed, and so unable to give evidence. The chairman thought that Scott was fortunate in this regard, as he suspected that he had also sexually assaulted the handicapped woman.[1468]

[1464] Cottu, *Administration,* p. 88.

[1465] *The Bury and Norwich Post*, 17 April, 1839.

[1466] *The Bury and Norwich Post, and Suffolk Herald,* 30 March, 1858.

[1467] *Attorney-General* v. *Bradlaugh* (1885) 14 Q.B.D. 667.

[1468] *The Bury and Norwich Post*, 10 July, 1844.

However, children under 12 or 13 years old might be questioned to ensure that they were competent to give evidence, and by the Victorian era those under the age of seven very rarely proved satisfactory in this regard. Occasionally, a case might be adjourned to allow a child to receive religious instruction so that they could satisfy the test. In 1888 James Picton, an MP, noted that when children went before the courts as potential witnesses, they were often asked, "'Do you know what the Almighty will do to those who tell lies?' and if the answer was that the child would in that case go to hell, that was regarded as perfectly satisfactory."[1469] Sir Henry Hawkins recalled a spirited debate with a trial judge as to whether a particular seven- or eight-year-old was able to be sworn, with the child being asked what would happen on his death if he lied. He repeatedly replied, "Hellfire," and was eventually sworn.[1470]

With young children, much might turn on their intellectual maturity. For example, at the Thetford borough sessions in July 1850, a gypsy girl named Adelaide Rix was accused of pickpocketing nine pennies from Jane Kent. It appears that Jane's brother had been expected to give important evidence, but, by the time of trial – and presumably being quite young—he had forgotten what had occurred. However, fortunately for the prosecution, an "intelligent little boy" named Wright had also seen Rix remove the money from Kent's pocket and gave telling evidence for the Crown. (Furthermore, two of the coins were physically distinctive, making the evidence "so clear as to leave no doubt.")[1471]

Perjury

Traditionally the oath, and the attendant risk of indictment for perjury, had been considered the primary tool in promoting forensic truth-telling and ensuring witness veracity. However, perjury was a difficult crime to prosecute, reducing its deterrent value. In some years, such as 1846, there were no prosecuted cases at all in Norfolk.[1472] Furthermore, conviction rates for the crime were low when it was indicted, throughout the Victorian era, and punishments were relatively light. It seems that neither judges at assizes nor the post-1879 Director of Public Prosecutions were keen to use the law aggressively in this area.[1473] JPs could show a similar reluctance.

For example, in June 1849 the Downham petty sessions tried several defendants, including Steven Salmon, for assaulting county police officers and committing other public disturbances. One of the defence witnesses, Susan Bushell, testified on oath that Salmon had not been at the Bell public house, the scene of some of the offences, on the relevant night, although Salmon himself subsequently admitted

[1469] HC Deb 09 August 1888 vol. 330 cols. 128-37.

[1470] Hawkins, *Reminiscences,* p. 24.

[1471] *The Bury and Norwich Post*, 24 July, 1850.

[1472] *Criminal Offenders... 1846* (1847), p. 23.

[1473] Michael Lobban, "The Truth, the Whole Truth, and Nothing but the Truth?" *Journal of Victorian Culture,* vol. 22, no. 1 (2017), pp. 128-131.

that he had spoken with the police while at the tavern: "The magistrates threatened to commit her [Bushell] for trial for perjury, but she still persisted in her statement and was locked up for several hours and then discharged."[1474] The following year a newspaper article could suggest that perjury in court was widespread in criminal hearings, and often quite blatant, without normally being prosecuted.[1475]

Even where perjury was prosecuted, it was often difficult to secure a conviction, not least because it was not just the falsity of the statement that had to be established but also its terms and relevance to the trial. For example, in 1858 a labourer named Mark Wicks gave alibi evidence at the Norfolk quarter sessions in Swaffham for two men accused of being involved in a nocturnal poaching expedition who had (initially) escaped capture. Wicks testified that, at the relevant time, they were with him in a public house. Not content with this, he gave similar evidence on behalf of one of the same men in an action for malicious prosecution. At the Norfolk assizes in August 1859, he was prosecuted for perjury. However, he had two lawyers to represent him, and although the magistrates' clerk gave evidence for the prosecution based on the notes that he had taken of Wicks's testimony, the trial judge quickly decided that the case would not be made out, and, following discussion with prosecuting counsel, it was withdrawn from the jury.[1476]

Even if a finding of guilt was returned for perjury, punishments were often quite modest. Thus, at the Norfolk assizes in 1851, Allen Hook, a 21-year-old man, was found guilty of perjury after giving false evidence that led to the conviction of three boys who had been summarily fined 7 shillings each (two had gone to prison in lieu of payment) for destroying some books in Aylsham church. The boys had successfully appealed the matter to quarter sessions. Hook's motivation appears to have been to secure the £5 reward that was offered for information leading to the perpetrators' arrest. (Strangely, the convicting jury recommended that he be treated leniently, in view of the "temptation of the reward.") He received the mild sentence of six months' imprisonment with hard labour.[1477]

Similarly, at the combined Norfolk and Suffolk spring assizes held at Ipswich in May 1885, William Guymer, a brickmaker, pleaded guilty to perjury at the East Dereham petty sessions in the latter county the previous January. Although he had earlier convictions, he, too, was sentenced to just six months' imprisonment with hard labour.[1478] Somewhat more severely, in October 1881 a woman received 18 months' imprisonment for perjury at a hearing at the Norwich police court, at the combined Norfolk and Suffolk assizes. Nevertheless, she apparently left the dock laughing.[1479]

1474 *The Norwich Mercury*, 16 June, 1849.

1475 *The Era*, 7 April, 1850.

1476 *The Bury and Norwich Post*, 2 August, 1859.

1477 *Ibid.*, 6 August, 1851.

1478 *The Ipswich Journal*, 5 May, 1885.

1479 *Ibid.*, 29 October, 1881.

The Hearsay Rule

The primacy of oral testimony in court had been reinforced during the early 1800s by the growing rigidity of the hearsay rule. Very occasionally this could be circumvented by finding a common-law exception to the rule, such as the so-called dying declaration in homicide cases. This required that the person making the out-of-court statement as to the cause of their mortal wounding had, and evinced, a "settled, hopeless expectation of [imminent] death." In 1851, when doctors at the Norwich Hospital concluded that a girl had been mortally wounded by George Baldry, a surgeon warned her that she was going to die and asked if she would like to speak to a magistrate and tell him how she had come to be injured. Significantly, she then acknowledged that she knew she was doomed. A Norwich city magistrate was summoned and arrived with his clerk at 9 am. The surgeon reminded her that she was dying and would likely be insensible within a few hours. She then made a statement implicating the accused which was subsequently adduced at his trial.[1480] Similarly, in March 1878 Fuller Williamson assaulted his long-estranged wife at Foulsham in North Norfolk, using a razor and poker, intending to murder her. So badly was she injured that a magistrate, the Reverend John Fenwick, took her deposition, with his clerk in attendance, but in Fuller's absence, in case she died, and the prosecution needed to admit it at trial.[1481]

Cross-Examination

Cross-examination was increasingly seen as the primary defence against perjury in Victorian England.[1482] It was accepted that some people would lie in certain situations, even on oath, but thought that the best way to address this was through forensic testing of their evidence rather than expecting the threat of punishment for perjury to deter them.[1483] During cross-examination, the opposing party could ask leading questions which suggested the sought-after answer. Witnesses might also be questioned as to credit with a view to undermining their testimony. This was particularly relevant if they had accrued previous convictions, and these were known to the opposing party. For example, at the County quarter sessions at Swaffham in 1859, Cornelius Hyam, a publican, was accused of stealing two larch poles. At trial one William Dyer gave evidence against him. Hyam was legally very well represented, by two experienced barristers, and they appear to have prepared their brief carefully: "In cross examination witness [Dyer] admitted he had been twice convicted of felony.[sic] 33 years ago."[1484] If such previous convictions were put to an opposing witness and denied, they could be proved, this being codified by section 6 of the Criminal Procedure Act 1865.

[1480] *The Bury and Norwich Post*, 2 April, 1851.

[1481] *The Ipswich Journal*, 9 March, 1878.

[1482] Schneider, *Engines of Truth*, pp. 48-100.

[1483] Lobban, "The Truth," pp. 128-131.

[1484] *The Bury and Norwich Post*, 29 March, 1859.

Other discreditable facts might be put to witnesses, even if they had not resulted in convictions. For example, in 1846 George Taylor, a Yarmouth publican and former policeman in the town, gave evidence as to his official duty (when he was still in service) on the night Samuel Yarham murdered his neighbour more than a year earlier. He was forced to admit in cross-examination, "I was discharged from the police for neglect of duty."[1485] Evidence of a notorious reputation for untruthfulness might also be adduced and, if denied, rebutted. At James Rush's murder trial in 1848, Rush called a Mr Waugh, a solicitor, and former employer of an important prosecution witness, Frederick Howe, who stated that he would not believe Howe on his oath if contradicted on reputable testimony.[1486]

However, cross-examination was not confined to attacking integrity; it could be used to elicit material favourable to the opposing party. For example, in March 1841, when Charlotte Yaxley was accused of murdering her stepdaughter, the barrister Sidney Taylor cross-examined, at considerable length, the Yarmouth surgeon who had carried out a post-mortem on the infant, and attributed her death to drowning. His aim was apparently to "render the cause of death doubtful."[1487]

Of course, most defendants were legally unrepresented. In these circumstances they would often have to cross-examine the witness as best they could. Many found this very difficult. In 1847 a vicious fight in the early morning between a poacher named Richard Mason and an under-keeper, William Cook, led to the prosecution of the former for stabbing with attempt to maim at the Lent assizes for Norfolk. After Cook had given his evidence in chief, the trial judge asked the undefended prisoner whether he had any questions for the keeper, who was also the main prosecution witness: "He said he had no questions, but it was quite false what he had been talking about." (His subsequent unsworn statement was, at least, quite thorough).[1488] Many lawyer-less defendants failed to ask any questions. For example, to consider a sample of 17 undefended defendants being tried on indictment at assizes in Mid-Victorian Montgomeryshire, only six cross-examined prosecution witnesses.[1489] However, sometimes in these situations the trial judge or even the court clerk assisted the accused. When, at his trial for murder in 1851, the intellectually somewhat limited, but legally unrepresented, George Baldry was asked to question an important prosecution witness he replied, "I don't recollect what he said. I can't ask him any questions." Fortunately, the judge then reminded him of the salient points of the witness's evidence.[1490]

[1485] *The Standard*, 30 March, 1846.

[1486] Anon., *Stanfield Hall*, pp. 1-10.

[1487] *The Bury and Norwich Post, and East Anglian*, 14 April, 1841.

[1488] *Ibid.*, 7 April, 1847.

[1489] Jones, *Crime, Courts,* p. 131.

[1490] *The Bury and Norwich Post*, 2 April, 1851.

Even those who did question prosecution witnesses in person did not always do so effectively. At James Rush's trial for murder at the Norfolk assizes, in March 1849, the main prosecution witness, Emily Sandford, gave her evidence in chief over two hours, but Rush then personally subjected her to seven and a half hours of cross-examination.[1491] Although he was shown considerable (and surprising) latitude, asking numerous offensive and often irrelevant questions, the presiding judge waited a long time before he intervened and warned Rush: "You are following your own course, without understanding the rules of evidence. I am loath to interfere with what you think is for your interest, but I cannot allow you to wound the feelings of another person; and unless you confine *yourself* within bounds, I shall confine you to the strict part you are bound to pursue, only to ask relevant questions."[1492]

Cross-examination could at times be a robust process. When prosecuting counsel at the Norfolk assizes in 1842 was faced by several people providing an alibi for a defendant accused of robbery, he "cross examined these witnesses severely."[1493] This was not universally admired by laymen. James Fitzjames Stephen thought that cross-examination had been more severely censured by the "unprofessional community" than any other aspect of legal practice. It often excited hostility from members of the public, such as Anthony Trollope, who compared it to the then common practice of skinning eels alive to ensure their freshness.[1494] Early Victorian lawyers were aware of public criticism of excessively aggressive counsel and some endeavoured to make cross-examination a slightly calmer and more clinical process which would uncover the truth without browbeating witnesses. Nevertheless, in 1874 Lord Chief Justice Cockburn still thought that, although he had seen trials around the world, "in no place have I seen witnesses so badgered, brow beaten, and in every way so brutally maltreated as in England." This was particularly bad at the Old Bailey but could also be manifest outside London.[1495] Ultimately, how far a barrister would go in intrusive questioning, especially when cross-examining on collateral issues, depended to a large extent on his judgment and the discretion of the trial judge.[1496]

Jury Activism

By the start of the nineteenth century, and unlike earlier times, it seems that English petty jurors had largely been silenced, and significant interaction between them and other actors in the trial was unusual (a tradition of activist jurors appears to have

[1491] *The Norfolk Chronicle,* 29 March, 1849.

[1492] Anon., *Stanfield Hall,* pp. 1-10.

[1493] *The Norfolk Chronicle,* 16 April, 1842.

[1494] Schneider, *Engines of Truth,* pp. 48-100.

[1495] Andrew Watson, "Victorian Jury Court Advocacy and Signs of Fundamental Change," *Journal on European History of Law*, vol. 7, no. 1 (2016), pp. 36-44.

[1496] Lobban, "The Truth," pp. 128-131.

lasted longer in Ireland).[1497] Nevertheless, although juries were much more passive in asking questions about the evidence than had been the case in previous centuries, they were still not as quiet as their modern counterparts. At a murder trial held at the Norwich assizes in March 1869, Baron Pigott even complimented the jury for its perceptive questions.[1498]

As today, in serious and complicated cases, such as James Rush's six-day murder trial at the Norfolk assizes in March 1849, detailed plans and models of the scene of the crime might be made available to both judge and jury, usually by the prosecution. In Rush's case, they "enabled the jury to understand the different localities better than any oral description could possibly have done."[1499] More commonly, exhibits such as weapons and stolen items might be produced. In an unusual case of early 1844 at the Norfolk quarter sessions, John Lefty was accused of killing a sheep owned by a farmer against whom he had some personal animus. Prosecuting counsel was able to connect the prisoner to the crime by the footmarks and knee marks made by his corduroy clothes: "These marks had been carefully taken up, and were brought to the court in boxes, and shewn to the jury, and were compared with his shoes and clothes."[1500]

After defence cross-examination, the prosecution might re-examine the witness to clear up any ambiguities identified in their testimony. When the prosecution had called all their evidence, they would formally close their case. In the modern era, evidence is not lightly received for the Crown after this point, although this rule was not enforced as strictly during the 1800s. At this point, submissions of "no case to answer" might also be made by defence counsel, leading to a directed acquittal if successful. However, not infrequently, Victorian judges exercised their legal power to terminate prosecutions in favor of the defendant by directing an acquittal on their own initiative, without prompting counsel to make such a submission, something that was important at a time when most defendants were legally unrepresented.[1501]

Directed Acquittals

Judges might direct acquittals when they considered that the prosecution evidence, taken at its highest, was not sufficient to warrant a conviction, and that the defendant should not be required to reply to it. For example, at the Norfolk assizes in April 1838, James Pollard was accused of stealing three hams, two sides of pig, and 20 pounds of bread from his brother William in Stoke Ferry: "The jury acquitted him under his

---

[1497] Niamh Howlin, "Irish Jurors: Passive Observers or Active Participants?" *Journal of Legal History,* vol. 35, no. 2 (2014), p. 145.

[1498] *The Norfolk Chronicle,* 27 March, 1869.

[1499] *The Ipswich Journal*, 29 October, 1881.

[1500] *Ibid.*, 6 January, 1844.

[1501] John H. Langbein, "The English Criminal Trial Jury on the Eve of the French Revolution" in *The Trial Jury in England, France, Germany 1700-1900,* Antonio Padoa Schioppa (ed.), (Berlin: Duncker & Humblot, 1987), p. 34.

Lordship's instructions."[1502] Similarly, at the Norfolk assizes in July 1858, a King's Lynn waterman was prosecuted for stealing half a ton of coal from a consignment of 26 tons that he had been carrying. However, during the hearing, a letter was handed in at court from the recipient of the coal, an engineer at Methwold, stating that he had received the full 26 tons. Unsurprisingly, the judge decided that there "seemed to be some mistake in the case and directed a verdict of 'not guilty.'"[1503] At the Norwich city quarter sessions in October 1871, such a possibility was even raised by prosecution counsel, who had read through his depositions and discovered a lack of legally admissible evidence. The judge quickly agreed. "The jury then returned a formal verdict of not guilty."[1504]

Of course, a directed verdict based on insufficient evidence presupposed some notion of what level of proof was sufficient to be left to a jury for determination.[1505] On this issue, much depended on the individual judge. For example, at the Lent assizes for Norfolk in 1842 newly married Frances Alexander was charged with mixing arsenic into dumplings with intent to poison her husband. Her spouse had ended up retching violently, in great agony. Frances suggested that arsenic might have accidentally impregnated the flour used in the dumplings, possibly after her little brother had played with it. (The two were kept in adjacent shelves.) She had allegedly only eaten one dumpling to his three and was much less seriously sick as a result. Unfortunately, Hannah Stannard, a 14-year-old girl, had earlier overheard her say that she would "poison her husband and have another." Her husband also testified that their three-month marriage had not been a happy one.

Nevertheless, the trial judge, despite thinking that the case had been properly brought, directed the jury to acquit. He thought that there had been considerable carelessness in storing arsenic, facilitating mistakes. Although Frances's comments were very unfortunate, he felt there was not sufficient evidence to justify a conviction, not least because "in all criminal enquiries, especially where the life of the person charged was concerned, it was necessary to act cautiously and vigilantly." He even recommended that the husband take her home with him![1506]

Less controversially, in 1858 Baron Watson, presiding at the summer assizes for the Western Circuit in a case of alleged highway robbery, directed the trial jury that it would be unsafe to convict on the available evidence. This primarily consisted of the assessments of two police constables who had compared the boots of the (legally unrepresented) prisoners with impressions in the soil at the spot where the

---

[1502] *The Bury and Norwich Post*, 4 April, 1838.

[1503] *Ibid.*, 27 July, 1858.

[1504] *The Essex Standard*, 27 October, 1871.

[1505] Langbein, "English Criminal," p. 34.

[1506] *The Ipswich Journal*, 9 April, 1842.

robbery took place and concluded that they matched. A not guilty verdict was duly returned.[1507]

However, assuming that there was no directed acquittal, it would then be for the defence to adduce evidence (if there was any), and the roles would reverse, with the accused person or their lawyer examining witnesses in chief, and cross-examination then being conducted by prosecution counsel. Nevertheless, a judge could still stop a prosecution before it went to the jury, *after* the defence case had started, albeit that this was rare. Even so, at the Norfolk assizes in August 1843, 19-year-old Thomas Taylor was accused of assaulting Mary Ann Bowman with intent (attempted rape). The judge stopped the case during defence counsel's cross-examination of the prosecutrix, and the prisoner was formally acquitted.[1508]

Defendant's Evidence

The defendant's counsel, if present, could make an opening speech (see below) throughout the Victorian period, following which he could call the defendant. However, a defendant could not normally give sworn evidence in his own defence or (if married) call his spouse to do so on his behalf until 1898, although, by then, there were several significant statutory exceptions to the general rule for certain specific offences. The rationale for the wider rule, despite a mounting campaign against it, was founded in a fear that allowing interested parties to testify on oath would encourage perjury, while doing so also raised difficult questions as to the extent to which a defendant should be treated like other witnesses and subject to cross-examination about his previous criminal history (if any). As prosecutions were brought in the name of the Crown, this limitation did not extend to the prosecutor/victim in a criminal trial. However, at the start of the Victorian era, the same rule extended to both plaintiff and defendant in civil matters until abolished in this sphere in 1851.

Ostensibly, an inability to give sworn testimony put the defendant at a disadvantage. At the Norfolk assizes in late 1892, one defendant's counsel, when addressing the jury, and suggesting that there was a reasonable doubt in the case, went so far as to detail what the accused *would* have said had he been allowed to give evidence: "Prisoner was unable to go into the witness box, but if he were he would say that ...."[1509] (This was professionally dubious.)

However, the rule had always been qualified in two important respects. Just months before the law was changed in 1898, while addressing the grand jury at the Norfolk assizes, Mr Justice Grantham referred to both when suggesting that there was considerable misunderstanding of the issue. Although it might seem strange not to allow defendants to give sworn evidence at criminal trial, the law already allowed them an opportunity to put their case before the jury: "Every prisoner before he

[1507] *R* v. *Britton and Others* (1858) 1 F and F 354.

[1508] *The Norfolk Chronicle*, 5 August, 1843.

[1509] *The Bury and Norwich Post*, 6 December, 1892.

was committed for trial was asked if he had anything to say or any witnesses to call, and judges of assize also gave prisoners an opportunity of speaking."[1510] The former was the statement made and recorded at the JPs' committal hearing, although it should be noted that many defendants did not exercise this right and said nothing (see Chapter 5). Much more important, and unlike the situation in civil matters, a defendant in criminal proceedings was always allowed to make an unsworn statement from the dock.

Dock Statements

Dock statements provided the accused with an opportunity to give their version of events or to advance specific defences. This could not be the subject of cross-examination by prosecuting counsel but might lead to comments from the trial judge. The latter could remind the jury that the statement was not on oath and had not been tested by opposing counsel, but, by the Victorian period, judges would often accord some weight to them. The power to make such a statement survived to the end of the Victorian period and long beyond (being abolished only in 1982), even after the accused was allowed to testify on oath, from 1898. Indeed, it was codified by s.1 of the Criminal Evidence Act of that year, which gave the accused the right to give sworn evidence, and which provided that "nothing in this Act shall affect...any right of the person charged to make a statement without being sworn."

Nevertheless, this right was sometimes subject to a restriction during the early Victorian period, because of the initial reaction to the Prisoners Counsel Act of 1836. After this statute came into force, not a few judges decided that legally represented defendants, whose counsel could now give a speech to the jury on their behalf as to the merits of a case, should not be allowed to make an unsworn statement as well. There was little justification for such a decision, as it equated the two functions. In reality, the dock statement allowed the defendant to put information before the court; it was not a simple exercise in advocacy (although this might come into it). Perhaps for this reason, not all judges followed such a practice, even in the 1840s, and it was eventually abandoned throughout the country.

Very few limitations were placed on what the accused could say in his unsworn statement, provided it was, in some way, relevant; even hearsay was normally allowed. Counsel might also refer to such a statement in their closing address. At Hubbard Lingley's murder trial at the Norfolk assizes in 1867, his defence counsel, Sims Reeve, noted: "The law of the country prevented the prisoner or his wife being called; but his statement was that on the morning in question he left his house as usual, and proceeded to his work in the wood."[1511]

[1510] *The Nottinghamshire Guardian*, 29 January, 1898.

[1511] Anon., *Trial, confession, & execution of Hubbard Lingley, at Norwich Castle, this morning, for the wilful murder of Benjamin Black, at Barton and Bendish, near Downham Market, Norfolk, on the 17th of May* (Norwich: Wilson, 1867), p. 1.

How influential or effective was the unsworn dock statement? In theory, it could have provided a very valuable opportunity for defendants to advance their cases, comment on the prosecution evidence, and present helpful information to the court. For example, in July 1849 26-year-old James Fitt was indicted for stealing a mare from an Outwell farmer named Thomas Horton the previous April. The prosecution had legal representation, unlike the accused. Even so, the prisoner, having cross-examined every witness at length, made a lengthy statement, telling the court that he had found the mare when going from Outwell to his home, thought he recognised the animal, and had taken charge of it for the purpose of finding her owner, but had not been able to do so.[1512] (He was still convicted.) Similarly, at the Thetford borough quarter sessions in 1875, held before the town recorder, 23-year-old John Alger was accused of stealing 21 sheep from a field in Thetford. In his defence, he "said that he bought 20 sheep of a person at Lynn Market." He claimed that the other animal had been a gift. (Again, he was convicted.)[1513] A few defendants were even eloquent. It was generally noted that William Jones spoke extremely well, if unavailingly, when making an unsworn statement at his robbery trial at the Norfolk assizes in 1834. His lengthy address was conducted without recourse to notes of any kind.[1514]

However, only a few defendants made good use of this opportunity. Some said nothing at all. For example, although he had made occasional interjections during the prosecution case at the Norfolk assizes in 1851, the legally unrepresented murderer Henry Groom "offered no defence" and was convicted.[1515] Similarly, at the Norfolk assizes in 1853, when George Fayers was accused of stabbing his fiancée with intent to do her bodily harm, "the prisoner declined to say anything in defence."[1516] Other defendants simply asserted their innocence in general terms, or asked for mercy in their statements, perhaps mentioning their family status and dependents in the hope of attracting the sympathy of the jury. For example, when, at the Norfolk assizes in August 1835, Frances Billing and Catherine Frarey were accused of the murder by poisoning of Mary Taylor, they "made a general assertion of their innocence, but offered no substantial defence."[1517]

Some actively damaged their cases. When James Rush made his extremely lengthy unsworn statement to the jury (the indulgence shown by the court was remarkable), he apparently spoke hurriedly, in a rather low tone of voice, so that at times it was impossible to hear what he said, and on two or three occasions the court requested him to speak up. He started shortly after 9 am and had not concluded his statement when the court rose shortly before 8 pm. He resumed at 9 am the following day and

[1512] *The Bury and Norwich Post*, 1 August, 1849.

[1513] *The Ipswich Journal*, 20 July, 1875

[1514] *The Morning Chronicle*, 2 April, 1834.

[1515] *The Daily News*, 29 July, 1851

[1516] *The Bury and Norwich Post*, 23 March, 1853.

[1517] *The Standard*, 10 August, 1835.

concluded at noon, so that over the two days he spoke for nearly 14 hours. Even so, he ran from one evidential point to another, almost at random. His statement "was full of repetitions, and everything material might have been said in a tithe [a tenth] of the time." The end of his rambling and discursive remarks apparently occasioned a sense of relief in court.[1518]

Obviously, it was difficult for many defendants to think on their feet, in what was a very stressful situation. Anticipating this, some would write their statement, or have it written for them (often for a fee), in advance and then read it out, or ask a court official to do this for them. As a result, when, in 1835, at the Norwich assizes, Johnstone Wardell was accused of stealing a large amount of money from the bank that employed him, "the prisoner read a long written statement in his defence, commenting upon the evidence which had been given before the magistrates."[1519] Of course, this risked it not being relevant to the evidence actually adduced at trial, unless the statement was prepared *while* the hearing progressed, which was often inherently very difficult to do.

Sworn Evidence from the Defendant

The defendant's inability to give sworn evidence occasioned mounting concern as the Victorian era advanced. In a notorious case from 1859, the Reverend Henry Hatch, a Cambridge graduate and apparently respectable schoolmaster, was convicted of indecently assaulting a 12-year-old pupil named Eugenia Plummer who was in his charge, at a trial in which he had not been able to testify on oath in his own defence. The following year he successfully prosecuted Eugenia for perjury; he was able to testify on oath against her, as he was no longer a defendant. Plummer was subsequently granted a free pardon. The contradictory convictions fueled widespread popular concern. John Pitt Taylor, a renowned evidence scholar, noted the absurdity of one of the (potentially) best witnesses in a case not being able to give sworn testimony. He was not alone. For decades following the verdict, the Hatch case was cited by reformers.

However, the long-lasting failure to amend the law was not for lack of effort. A bill allowing defendant testimony was introduced in 1858 and was followed by many others over the next 40 years, until success was reached in 1898. (In its final years, delay was partly occasioned by Irish opposition in Parliament.) The content of the bills changed regularly; some gave the accused a special status (as was the situation after 1898), while others made no distinction between the defendant and other witnesses, something that helps to explain the lack of celerity in reform.[1520]

Once defendants were allowed to give sworn evidence in all criminal trials the new right was exercised almost immediately. For example, at the Norwich quarter sessions in October 1898, William Groom, accused of unlawfully wounding John

[1518] Anon., *Stanfield Hall*, pp. 1-10. *Norfolk Chronicle*, 29 March, 1849.

[1519] *The Bury & Norwich Post, & East Anglian*, 8 April, 1835.

[1520] Schneider, *Engines of Truth*, p. 12, p. 181.

Groom, "elected to take advantage of the new Criminal Evidence Act, and, entering the witness-box, denied the statements of the prosecutor." The presiding recorder noted that, if the jury acquitted, their verdict would justify the introduction of the new right. They duly found Groom not guilty.[1521]

Defence Witnesses

Throughout the era, defendants could call witnesses to give sworn evidence on their behalf, although in practice many did not do so, or called them to testify to good character rather than on issues of fact. If called in felony cases, they would testify after the defendant's unsworn statement (or testimony following 1898). For example, in 1835 at the Norwich assizes, Johnstone Wardell, accused of stealing a large amount of money from his employer's bank, called two fellow employees to give evidence.[1522] Nevertheless, getting witnesses to court, if they were available, could occasion problems, even more so than was the case for the prosecution. They could be subpoenaed, but this would normally require legal assistance. In a large county like Norfolk, the journey to court could be lengthy and expensive, and the defendant might have to cover at least some of the cost.

Judges were often very reluctant to grant adjournments in the absence of important witnesses (for both prosecution and defence) and would normally do so only if there was an affidavit before the court, with a very sound reason for their non-appearance. Nevertheless, the local trial of William Denmark for breaking into and stealing from a Yarmouth warehouse in 1838 was deferred to the following borough sessions, because two material witnesses lived in Manchester, and, in the small time between Denmark's arrest and the hearing, it had not been possible to call them.[1523] Similarly, in 1859, when Elizabeth Rose from Yarmouth was accused of murdering her illegitimate child, her trial at Norwich assizes was postponed to the following sessions because her mother, who was "a material witness" in the case, was ill and unable to attend.[1524]

Speeches by Counsel

Speeches to the jury by prosecution and defence counsel, setting out their narrative of a case, had always been allowed in misdemeanour cases. However, prior to the Prisoners' Counsel Act 1836, although prosecuting counsel had an opening speech in felony trials, albeit not always exercised, once the evidence had been adduced, and examined by both parties, the case would normally move straight to the judge's summing up. In the 1820s Charles Cottu commented that "counsel have no right to comment on the evidence, either for or against the defendant; the

[1521] *The Standard*, 13 October, 1898.

[1522] *The Bury & Norwich Post, & East Anglian: Or, Suffolk, Norfolk, Essex, Cambridge, and Ely Intelligencer*, 8 April, 1835.

[1523] *The Bury and Norwich Post*, 7 November 1838.

[1524] *Ibid.*, 2 August, 1859.

jury are left, in this respect, to their own penetration." Cottu thought this meant that the prosecutor's counsel did not try to paint the prisoner as a villain, while the prisoner's counsel did not suggest numerous possibilities to the jury as to how the crime in question might have been committed without their client's being guilty.[1525] Of course, by then competent defence counsel were often adept at advancing their "theory of a case" when questioning witnesses. Nevertheless, until the 1836 Act they could not speak directly to the jury.[1526]

After s.1 of the 1836 Act came into force defence counsel in felony (i.e., most serious criminal) cases could address the jury immediately after the close of the prosecution case prior to calling the prisoner to make an unsworn statement and any defence witnesses to give sworn testimony. If he did call evidence, prosecuting counsel was allowed a closing address to the jury. Thus, at the trial of a man called Fulcher at the Norfolk assizes in 1842, it was noted that defence counsel "addressed the jury nearly an hour, after which he called a number of witnesses to prove an alibi." Prosecuting counsel cross-examined these witnesses, and then addressed the jury for the Crown, after which the judge summed up the case.[1527]

If the accused did not call evidence, defence counsel would address the jury following the close of the prosecution case, after which the judge would sum up. Thus, at Hannah Neale's murder trial at the Norfolk assizes in 1851, a Mr Tozer, of counsel, appeared for the prosecution and called a lengthy list of witnesses. Another barrister, Mr Naylor, defended the prisoner and called no evidence. As a result, at the close of the prosecution case, it was noted that "Mr Naylor then addressed the jury for the defence." Immediately after he had finished, the judge started summing up.[1528]

Initially, there appear to have been a few teething problems over this newly established right. At the Yarmouth borough sessions in November 1838, James Balls was accused of an assault committed during a dispute over a debt. Three prosecution witnesses were called. After they finished, the legally represented defendant did not call any evidence of his own. His counsel, Mr Barker, "was about to address the Jury for the defendant, but before he proceeded far the Jury said they were satisfied, and returned a verdict of guilty against Balls." The defendant was fined £5 with one month's imprisonment in lieu and was committed to gaol in default of payment![1529]

It was not until the advent of s.2 of the Criminal Procedure Act 1865 that defence counsel, like prosecuting counsel, was allowed to make a second speech to the jury after he had called witnesses, summing up the evidence as he did so. The order in which this occurred between the two lawyers, prosecution and defence,

---

[1525] Cottu, *Administration,* p. 89 and pp. 101-102.

[1526] Griffiths, "Prisoners' Counsel," p. 29

[1527] *The Norfolk Chronicle*, 16 April, 1842.

[1528] Transcribed from papers in the collection of the late Dr. Greer and reproduced in, *The Norfolk Ancestor*, "Poisoning at Outwell", vol. 7, no. 2 (2010), pp. 123-125.

[1529] *The Bury and Norwich Post*, 7 November, 1838.

was complicated, depending on several factors. The most important considerations were: was the crime classified as treason, felony, or misdemeanour; was the Attorney General involved in prosecuting it; had the defendant called witnesses; and, of course, was he legally represented? Treason can largely be disregarded in the context of Norfolk. The Attorney General, on the relatively few occasions that he prosecuted a crime in the county, was always entitled to the last word by counsel to the jury. For example, when the Attorney General prosecuted a group of alleged pirates at the Norfolk assizes in 1885 (the case had diplomatic implications), it was noted that defence counsel, the barrister Simms Reeve, spoke before the government lawyer.[1530]

If no evidence was called by the accused, defence counsel, if present, and as was previously the case, would have the final word (before the judge summed up). If he did call a witness, the prosecution would normally go last. (Unlike the situation today). Sir Henry Hawkins deplored situations in which a potential defence witness, who was not of overwhelming significance, was deliberately not called, to ensure that this occurred, as sometimes apparently occurred.[1531] A case in Berkshire in 1877 can be considered in this regard. One Alexander Elliot, who sat on a jury in the assizes court of the county, recalled in his diary trying a case in which a butler had built his own house, which had subsequently collapsed, killing his infant daughter, and who was committed to trial by a coroner for manslaughter by gross negligence. At the hearing, the jury "took the defence's view of the case, and stopped the case, without troubling the counsel to address us a second time, with a verdict of 'Not guilty.'"[1532]

For much of the Victorian period, closing speeches by barristers, especially defence counsel, were not always entirely edifying spectacles, although they may well have been more muted in the provinces than they often were at the Old Bailey. Even so, one observer claimed in 1867 that experienced chairmen, sitting at quarter sessions, were not influenced by them, because they were "aware that the counsel on either side make speeches which are meant to impress the jury, but which, as a rule, may be said studiously to avoid having any reference to the general facts of the case."[1533]

Frequently closing speeches were long and repetitious, replete with blatant appeals to emotion and even prejudice, usually reaching a peak in the peroration. Floral language was regularly employed, in an attempt to awaken jury sympathy, while even the Deity might be invoked. This approach declined towards the end of the Victorian era, although a few barristers, such as Edward Marshall Hall, continued to employ such stratagems well into the twentieth century.[1534] For example, according

---

1530 *The Times*, 1 May, 1885, p. 10.

1531 Hawkins, *Reminiscences,* p. 196.

1532 Berkshire Record Office D/EX902/1.

1533 *The Spectator*, 7 September, 1867, p. 7

1534 Watson, "Victorian Jury," pp. 36-44.

to one account, the speech delivered by Constance Kent's counsel, John Duke Coleridge, at the Wiltshire assizes in 1865, had been "punctuated with sobs." This apparently helped move the jury to their own tears.[1535] In a case at the joint Norfolk and Suffolk winter assizes held at Norwich in December 1876, defence counsel, in his closing address, spoke of passing a sleepless night for fear that an innocent man would be convicted.[1536]

In 1844 the barrister S.R. Bosanquet, considering the benefits of the 1836 Act, thought that both prosecution and defence closing speeches should be abolished. He believed that the latter was of no real benefit to the accused, especially if innocent, and that it encouraged criminals to offend in the belief that retaining a silver-tongued advocate could guarantee an acquittal.[1537] It should be noted that many barristers, far from seeing fresh opportunities for their advocacy, had opposed the change in 1836, sharing Lord Wharncliffe's opinion "that under its operation the verdicts of juries would be more frequently wrong than they were at present."[1538]

Impact of Representation

The presence of full legal representation by counsel speeded up a change by which criminal trials moved from a model that required that the prisoner "speak" (albeit not on oath) to have a realistic chance of acquittal, to one in which the prosecution evidence was vigorously "tested" by the defence lawyer to see if it could establish a case to the appropriate standard. More generally, it encouraged the already ongoing process whereby the criminal conflict became the property, not of the defendant and his accuser, but of their professional representatives. This also meant that, unlike the informal and flexible procedure by which cases were often presented in earlier centuries, parties to a criminal allegation were expected to present their cases in full before being cross-examined.[1539] Defence counsel also gradually, if rather diffidently, began to challenge, or at least question, the legal instructions judges gave juries. As a result, their presence tended to weaken the position of the judge, who could no longer decide these matters on an ad hoc basis.[1540] Of course, extending the role of counsel also increased the prejudice experienced by the many defendants who could not afford legal representation.

More specifically, full representation allowed lawyers to place alternative defences to the jury, even if they were inconsistent, or to advance defences that were speculative, at least in certain situations. For example, at the Norfolk winter assizes in 1863, James Savage was indicted for shooting and wounding a gamekeeper in

1535 Thomas Dixon, "The Tears of Mr Justice Willes," *Journal of Victorian Culture*, vol. 17, no. 1 (2012), p. 9.

1536 *The Essex Standard*, 2 March, 1877.

1537 *Eighth Report*, p. 230.

1538 HL Deb 14 July 1836 vol. 35 cols. 171-86.

1539 Alan Cusack, "From Exculpatory to Inculpatory Justice: A History of Due Process in the Adversarial Trial," *Law, Crime and History*, vol. 2 (2015), pp. 24-27.

1540 Wiener, "Judges v. Jurors," p. 474.

South Acre with intent to murder him. Savage had been out poaching and shot two birds; while picking them up, he was challenged by the keeper. He assaulted and ultimately shot this man with the keeper's own gun. Two barristers prosecuted the case against Savage, but the defendant also had counsel, a Mr Bulwer. The defence case challenged the victim's identification of the accused and, more important, suggested that if he *were* involved, the gun might have gone off accidentally. Such a defence would have been almost impossible without a lawyer. Bulwer elicited an admission from the wounded keeper that the weapon had already been cocked when it went off. The jury convicted of the lesser offence of wounding with intent to do grievous harm.[1541]

In April 1875, at the Norfolk assizes, Matilda Foreman, a 16-year-old, locally born maid, working in the Greyhound public house in Scole, was accused of trying to poison the young son of her employer. It was alleged that she had done this by putting arsenic in his tea. The poison had originally been purchased to kill rats and was taken from a cupboard to which Foreman had access. The child fell ill after drinking it. Foreman immediately admitted putting the arsenic in the teapot in which the tea had been brewed. No motive or explanation for what she had done could be found, or advanced at trial. She had an excellent character. Foreman was legally represented by counsel, and it was suggested on her behalf that she *may* have thought the arsenic was carbonate of soda. The jury were clearly concerned about the case, but "eventually acquitted the prisoner."[1542]

The advent of counsel and their ability to address the jury also appears to have seen a greater emphasis on the standard of proof required to establish a criminal case, and a growth in attempts to place a reasonable doubt in the minds of the jurors by identifying grounds for uncertainty (rather than simply asserting that an accused person must be innocent), while the importance of circumstantial evidence was also stressed. For example, at the Norfolk assizes in March 1841, when 22-year-old Charlotte Yaxley was accused of murdering, while severely intoxicated, her husband's illegitimate infant daughter, her experienced barrister, Sydney Taylor, made a lengthy closing address. He stressed the defendant's apparent lack of motive, the previous good relationship between the infant and Charlotte, and the absence of injuries to the child's body. Taylor suggested that Charlotte's post-mortem statements were delusional and the product of alcohol. (Even so, she was convicted.)[1543]

Similarly, at Hubbard Lingley's trial for murder in 1867, his defence counsel sought to cast doubt on the prosecution case by remarking on the apparent astonishment of the accused man when informed of his uncle's death. Counsel also pointed out that much of the Crown evidence, such as the location of the defendant's gun, had been voluntarily produced by Lingley himself, and dwelt on a second reported shot, fired by an unnamed man, to suggest that this individual was responsible for the

1541 *The Bury and Norwich Post*, 22 December, 1863.

1542 *The Times*, 8 April, 1875, p. 11.

1543 *The Bury and Norwich Post, and East Anglian*, 14 April, 1841.

killing.[1544] Lingley was, however, convicted. More successfully, at the Norfolk assizes in 1847, when Edmund Dixon was accused of indecently assaulting a policeman, his defence counsel, Mr Prendergast, "addressed the jury in defence at great length." He stressed that it was unlikely that an offence of this description would have been committed in such a public place as the one alleged (a meadow), where the parties were so well known to others in the vicinity (and so could be identified) and pointed out the lack of corroborative evidence. The jury acquitted after half an hour's deliberation.[1545]

Prosecution closing speeches were usually a little more measured than those for the defence. In a case from 1865, Mr Justice Crompton directed the jury as to the duty of counsel for the Crown in a criminal trial, and expressed a hope that when "summing up the evidence, they will not cease to remember that counsel for the prosecution in such cases are to regard themselves as ministers of justice, and not to struggle for a conviction, as in a [civil] case at Nisi Prius, nor be betrayed by feelings of professional rivalry, to regard the question at issue as one of professional superiority, and a contest for skill and pre-eminence."[1546] Nevertheless, looking back from 1891, the elderly Lord Coleridge accepted that the 1836 Prisoner's Counsel Act, of which he approved, had encouraged adversarialism, so that prosecuting counsel, in reply to a speech made on behalf of a prisoner, would speak with a "force and energy, and with a partisanship against prisoners which formerly, when there were no speeches by counsel for prisoners, they were not in the habit of doing."[1547]

Judicial Summing-Up

At the close of a jury trial, after counsels' speeches (if made), the presiding judge, or the chairman at county quarter sessions, had the opportunity to summarize and comment on the evidence, perhaps expressing a view on its strengths or defects, while also taking the chance to direct or instruct the jurors on the law pertaining to the case. Historically, judges and chairmen had been very brief when summing up in criminal trials, and such brevity remained widespread in the early Victorian period, especially at the lower jury forum. In a few cases, particularly at quarter sessions, the summing up appears to have been omitted altogether, something that was, perhaps, an indication of the lack of confidence many chairmen had in their legal knowledge and abilities, although such an omission became unusual after the 1830s. More commonly, as was noted of a theft case tried at the county quarter sessions held at Swaffham in 1859, "The Chairman summed up the evidence."[1548]

1544 Anon., *Hubbard Lingley,* p. 1.

1545 *The Norfolk Chronicle,* 10 April, 1847.

1546 *Regina* v. *Puddick* (1865) 4 F and F 497.

1547 Hansard HL Deb 26 May 1891 vol. 353 cols. 1057-72.

1548 *The Bury and Norwich Post*, 29 March, 1859.

However, in 1863, Thomas William Saunders, like many other observers, thought that frequently legally unqualified chairmen did not make a very good job of this task. Unlike the lucid summing-up of the professional judge seen at assizes, or even delivered by the recorder at borough quarter sessions, there would often be, the "illogical, rambling, confused, inconsequential address of the lay Chairman of Quarter Sessions."[1549] Four years later this view was reiterated when it was noted that the aspect of a chairman's duty which was most likely to be neglected was the summing-up: "A Chairman of Quarter Sessions will sometimes content himself with telling the jury that if they believe the prosecutor's story they must convict, if they believe the defence they must acquit, the prisoner."[1550]

Nevertheless, even in the early years of the Victorian period, complicated and serious cases often warranted and received a lengthy summing-up, especially at the higher jury forum, and such cases became more common as the century advanced. Thus in 1839 the attempted poisoning of Hannah Daines produced a summing-up of two hours at the Norfolk assizes.[1551] Two years later, at the same forum, the presiding judge also spent two hours summing up the extremely complicated evidence at Charlotte Yaxley's trial for child murder.[1552] Similarly, at the murder trial of James Rush in 1848, it was observed that, in his summing-up, the judge "went through the direct evidence with great minuteness, and remarked upon it, and on the answers elicited in the course of the cross-examinations, at considerable length."[1553] As is often the case today, in 1852, at Hannah Neale's poisoning trial at the Norfolk assizes, it was noted that, "His Lordship summed up at great length, dividing the evidence very clearly into that which was in favour of and that which was against the prisoner".[1554]

Although judges had been unable to reject (or punish) a jury for its verdict since the late seventeenth century, they were still allowed to comment, in no uncertain terms, as to what they thought should be the appropriate decision, even if they often refrained from doing so. For example, in 1859, at the Lent assizes for Norfolk, during the trial of Charles Butcher and his lover, Maria Gall, for the theft of a sheep, defence counsel suggested to the jury that any animal linked to the pair on the evidence, even if stolen, could not be the one indicted, and so must have come from another theft, something that would warrant an acquittal. The presiding judge was openly dismissive of this possibility when directing the jury, and a conviction ensued.[1555] Similarly, in 1864, when summing up for the jury in the trial of the wife-

[1549] Saunders, *Quarter and Petty Sessions,* p. 7.

[1550] *The Spectator,* 7 September, 1867, p. 7.

[1551] *The Bury and Norwich Post*, 17 April, 1839.

[1552] *The Ipswich Journal*, 10 April, 1841.

[1553] Anon., *Stanfield Hall,* pp. 1-10.

[1554] Transcribed from papers in the collection of the late Dr. Greer and reproduced in, *The Norfolk Ancestor*, "Poisoning at Outwell", vol. 7, no. 2 (2010), pp. 123-125.

[1555] *The Bury and Norwich Post*, 5 April, 1859.

murderer George Hall, at the Warwick assizes, Mr Justice Byles stressed that "there was no evidence to support either of the hypotheses set up [by the defence]." He firmly concluded that "the weight of evidence was on the other side." Hall was duly found guilty of murder (albeit with a jury recommendation to mercy).[1556]

Baron John Huddleston (1815-1890), who had considerable personal experience as a criminal lawyer, was particularly noted for his willingness to exert influence on juries, and, according to Edward Abinger, did so very successfully: "He would leave his seat, and approaching the jury-box, point out most affably perhaps some difficulties in a plan or a document, he would flatter, coax and wheedle them; he became in fact a thirteenth juryman; and it was almost impossible to get a verdict when his views were the other way."[1557] Of course, few judges had this level of ability or the inclination to exercise it.

Such latitude was also found at quarter sessions, and in 1867 a journal noted that chairmen were often tempted to let jurors see what they thought of the issues in a case, albeit that this was sometimes in favour of acquittal. It cited a case in which a chairman had summed up as follows: "If you think the prisoner is not guilty, you will acquit her; if you believe the prosecutor's story, you will convict her; but I can only say I don't believe a word of it." Perhaps unsurprisingly, the jury came to the same conclusion.[1558] However, judicial advice was not always followed. In Norfolk in 1819, when Samuel Wigg was prosecuted by the Yarmouth Corporation at the town quarter sessions for assaulting the deputy clerk to its market in a row over tolls, it was noted that the town recorder, Mr. Alderson, had summed up at length, "urging the conviction of the defendant." Even so, the jury ignored him, and brought in a verdict of not guilty.[1559]

Additionally, Victorian judges might still express displeasure at a jury's verdict, *after* it was returned, sometimes even rebuking them for an acquittal. In 1875 Prime Minister Benjamin Disraeli expressly refused to introduce legislation that would prohibit such judicial reprimands. Some observers thought that they had beneficial effects, encouraging jurors to do their duty, whatever their personal feelings about a case.[1560] Nevertheless, by the latter decades of the Victorian era, there were signs of change, and growing criticism of judges who went too far in urging a certain verdict, or in criticizing jurors who did not return verdicts in accordance with their directions. Increasingly, observers thought, "The judge ought not to express his opinion in such a way as to influence the decision of the twelve men who are to pronounce on the question of fact."[1561]

1556 Wiener, "Sad Story," p. 178.

1557 Edward Abinger, Forty Years at the Bar (London: Hutchinson, 1930), p. 89.

1558 *The Spectator,* 7 September, 1867, p. 7.

1559 *The Times*, 16 September, 1819, p. 2.

1560 Crosby, "Criminal Justice," pp. 179-208.

1561 *The Spectator,* 7 September, 1867, p. 7

In the aftermath of the *cause célèbre* involving Adelaide Bartlett, accused of poisoning her husband in 1886, and the allegedly vigorous judicial summing up at the Old Bailey, some newspapers and journals, with little sense of historical perspective, complained, "Judges are encroaching far too much in these days on the province of juries, and it is high time that they should be taught their proper place."[1562] In 1898 some observers thought that Sir Henry Hawkins, presiding over a murder trial at the Huntingdonshire assizes, had gone to the "limits of a judge's rights" when going through the evidence in what was perceived to be a rather partisan and conviction-minded way.[1563] One barrister, looking back in 1916 on his lengthy career, observed that judges no longer harassed defence counsel or frequently summed up hard against the defence, as had been common in the 1870s.[1564]

However, tension, conflict, and disagreement between judge and jury were not normal in Victorian courts. Many juries happily took their lead from the presiding judge, so that some observers even claimed (or complained) that their verdicts were "generally, the reflex of the judge's charge."[1565] For example, in 1847 a judge at the Cambridge assizes directed a jury that had to determine a serious wounding that it was open to them to convict of the lesser offence of common assault. The jury "took the hint," to use a contemporary observation, and did just that.[1566] According to the *Times*, in 1850, in the vast majority of cases the trial judge, not the jury, decided the outcome of a case by making his views of its merits obvious, sometimes employing a "pantomical expression of disgust or incredulity" when doing so.[1567]

Even so, most judges would attempt to assist the jury to apply the law to the facts in a reasonable manner, with the jurors often being grateful for their help; it should also be stressed that judges were not necessarily conviction minded, even if they expressed firm opinions on the merits of a case, sometimes being less prosecution-focused than their juries. Perhaps significantly, several convicts from Norfolk, like those from elsewhere in England, when petitioning the Home Office for clemency, claimed that they had been convicted despite their trial judge summing up in such a way as to encourage an acquittal, as was the case with John Widdows in 1832.[1568]

More commonly, jurors would follow encouragement to acquit. At the Lent assizes for Norfolk in 1842, William Coe was accused of stealing a shovel that he had found in the road. When challenged by its owner he immediately relinquished it. Even so, he was indicted for theft. However, in his summing up, the judge noted that "there was little evidence of any felonious intention on the part of the prisoner." The jury

1562 *Bell's Life in London*, 20 April, 1886.

1563 Hawkins, *Reminiscences,* p. 194.

1564 Purcell, *Forty Years,* p. 228.

1565 *The Spectator,* 11 February, 1860, p. 14.

1566 *The Morning Chronicle*, 20 July, 1847.

1567 *The Times,* 29 March, 1850, p. 4.

1568 TNA HO 17/119/31.

duly acquitted.[1569] Similarly, at the Norfolk assizes in March 1853, when Jake Brown was accused of having set fire to a wheat and a barley stack at Baconsthorpe, the judge observed to the jury that the principal prosecution evidence in the case was the set of footprints found at the scene of the crime. However, he also pointed out that the prisoner might have produced them innocently, and the jury swiftly returned a not-guilty verdict. In another case from the same sessions, he suggested that the defendant in a case of theft from a church (sacrilege) might have discovered the very small part of the proceeds that were found in his possession, abandoned in the street. Again, an acquittal followed.[1570]

Standard of Proof

Traditionally, English criminal courts had normally required that a high standard of proof be met before a conviction was returned, something that several observers, both foreign and domestic, commented on prior to the Victorian era. In the 1780s the Reverend William Paley railed against jurors who, through excessive scrupulousness or weakness, would "not condemn any man, whilst there exists the minutest possibility of his innocence."[1571] In the 1820s Charles Cottu thought that the courts "dismiss[ed] unpunished those whose guilt is not proved by the most positive testimony." However, this standard had not always been clearly enunciated, limiting its impact.

This started to change in the 1780s, when use of the reasonable-doubt jury instruction emerged. Although the precise reasons for this have been the subject of debate, in 1777 counsel at the Old Bailey argued that an acquittal was necessary if there was "any room upon the evidence to doubt." The first judicial reference to this direction appears to have occurred in July 1784, at Richard Corbett's trial for arson at the Old Bailey. At the end of his summing up of the evidence, the presiding judge directed the jury that "if there is a reasonable doubt, in that case that doubt ought to decide in favour of the prisoner."[1572] This took hold, and the same or similar words were adopted more widely. For example, at the very belated murder trial of Edmund Thrower at the Suffolk assizes in 1819, the judge advised the trial jury that "if a doubt existed in their minds, they would give the prisoner the benefit of that doubt."[1573] At the same forum, in 1847, when Catherine Foster was indicted for murdering her husband with arsenic, even prosecuting counsel, when opening the case, noted to the jury that "if they felt there was any doubt let them for God's sake

---

[1569] *The Bury and Norwich Post*, 13 April, 1842.

[1570] *Ibid.*, 23 March, 1853.

[1571] Steve Sheppard, "The Metamorphoses of Reasonable Doubt: How Changes in the Burden of Proof Have Weakened the Presumption of Innocence," *Notre Dame Law Review,* vol. 78, no. 4 (2003), p. 1175.

[1572] Thomas P Gallanis, "Reasonable Doubt and the History of the Criminal Trial," *The University of Chicago Law Review,* vol. 76, no. 2 (2009), p. 941.

[1573] Anon., *The trial of Edmund Thrower, blacksmith, late of Carbrook, in Norfolk, for the wilful murder of Thomas Carter* (Bury St. Edmunds: Gedge & Barker, 1812), p. 19.

give the prisoner a verdict of acquittal."[1574] In Norfolk, at Hubbard Lingley's murder trial at the county assizes in 1867, the presiding judge finished his summing-up by reminding the jury, "If from this evidence you believe the prisoner guilty your duty to society requires you to say so. If you think there is any reasonable doubt, you will give the prisoner the benefit of that doubt."[1575]

Defence counsel, allowed to speak directly to jurors in felony cases after 1836, increasingly stressed that the key question in the criminal process was whether there was a doubt about guilt, and not whether they thought the accused person was innocent. For example, at the county quarter sessions in July 1874, George Hansey, a hay dealer, was accused of stealing 36 trusses of hay from a field and selling them to another dealer in Norwich. He was legally represented by counsel, Mr Frere, and supported by a local solicitor. Frere stressed to the jury that the "evidence was of a very meagre character." Given that the defendant was of good character, he suggested that "doubt certainly did exist in this case."[1576] He was unsuccessful in this case, but jurors took this point seriously. At the trial of the alleged poisoner Adelaide Bartlett at the Old Bailey in 1886, when the jury delivered their verdict of not guilty, their foreman observed that "although we think grave suspicion is attached to the prisoner, we do not think there is sufficient evidence to show how or by whom the chloroform was administered."[1577]

Late Evidence

In earlier centuries evidence had sometimes been admitted after the jury were charged with a defendant. This was normally viewed as improper by the Victorian era but did sometimes occur (albeit very rarely) in the early years of the period, especially in the lower jury forum. At the Norfolk quarter sessions in March 1838, William Lacey, a farm worker, was convicted of stealing gate hooks valued at 1s 9d and sentenced to three months' imprisonment. At trial he had been represented by a barrister, William Cooper. Among his grounds for clemency, prepared by his lawyer, was that further information or evidence had been introduced by the chairman of the bench after he had summed up.[1578]

Jury Determination

Unlike the modern situation, in routine trials the same jury would often preside over all cases heard in one court session or day, something that the brevity of many nineteenth-century hearings encouraged. Very occasionally, an individual juror might be replaced for fatigue, but a "jury, once chosen, usually goes through the

---

[1574] *The Bury and Norwich Post*, 27 March, 1847.

[1575] *The Times,* 10 August, 1867.

[1576] *The Ipswich Journal*, 4 July 1874.

[1577] Michael Farrell, "Adelaide Bartlett and the Pimlico Mystery," *British Medical Journal*, vol. 309 (1994), pp. 24-31.

[1578] TNA HO 17/66/58.

whole morning's business, without interruption, thus producing a most valuable saving of time."[1579] However, where an unusually long trial was anticipated, it might become the sole work entrusted to a single jury.

Although the judge charged with the Crown side of assizes could preside over only one court at a time (a co-adjutor who had finished his *nisi prius* list could take another), the pressure of work meant that a supplemental jury might be sworn in to take advantage of spaces in the timetable, provided, of course, that the pool of jurors was sufficient and still at court. For example, it was normal practice for a judge to use gaps created by lengthy jury retirements (fairly unusual) to hold trials that looked likely to be short, so that "if, after the lapse of a quarter of an hour, at the farthest, they have not made up their minds, another defendant is put to the bar, a fresh jury chosen, and a new trial commenced." Indeed, in quite exceptional situations, Charles Cottu thought that if this second jury needed time to deliberate, a third jury might be empanelled, so that the business of the court was never stopped.[1580]

In April 1851 this occasioned problems at the Norfolk assizes when a jury retired to consider their verdict in a case of highway robbery. It took them an hour to convict, as the evidence was far from overwhelming. Apparently anticipating this delay, the judge, Sir John Jervis, attempted to empanel another jury with a view to pressing on through his list in the meantime. Strictly speaking, anyone summoned to jury service had to be present from the time the court began its work until it rose for the day, even if not called to serve.[1581] However, Sir John was stymied because the pool of summoned jurors still at court was too small to produce a dozen men, so that the forensic time was lost. He fined all those who were missing without permission £5, and observed that, because of their "absenting themselves, they had probably prevented the assizes for the county terminating that night, and would oblige those who had answered to their names to come again on Monday."[1582] His annoyance can, in part, be explained by their absence resulting in the loss of Sunday (a non-sitting day) for travelling on to the next venue on the circuit.

Jury Deliberations

Trial jurors had to be unanimous before they could reach a decision. Normally the requirement for unanimity appears to have occasioned few problems, although, even in the nineteenth century, there were occasional proposals to allow majority verdicts. Thus, some submissions from practising lawyers to the Royal Commission on Criminal Law of 1845 suggested that one or, most commonly, two dissenters should not preclude a decision's being reached (the situation today), if only to cater for people who liked to be in a minority, while the clerk of the peace of King's Lynn

[1579] Cottu, *Administration,* p. 75.

[1580] *Ibid.,* pp. 101-102.

[1581] Parry, *What the Judge Saw,* p. 97.

[1582] *The Bury and Norwich Post*, 2 April, 1851.

even thought that two-thirds of a jury, eight men, should be enough to return a verdict.[1583] Others strongly supported the status quo.

Sometimes, and as in previous eras, if a case seemed straightforward, jurors merely huddled together in court and chatted for a few moments about the evidence before arriving at a decision rather than retiring. In the early 1820s Charles Cottu thought that this was almost the normal state of affairs: "It is very rare, as I have said, that they request to withdraw to their room to deliberate."[1584] This practice continued during the Victorian period, albeit that a failure to retire became steadily less common, and was eventually slightly unusual, while the average length of deliberations became longer as the century advanced.[1585] Nevertheless, in July 1851 a jury at the Norfolk assizes did not deliberate "for a moment" before convicting the murderer Henry Groom, after a trial that had lasted almost a whole day.[1586] Similarly, at the same forum in March 1854, the jury considering the evidence in William Thompson's murder trial did not bother to leave the court after the judge's summing-up but simply put their heads together and, after a minute-and-a-half of debate, found him guilty. A death sentence immediately followed.[1587] Towards the end of the era, at the trial of Elijah Snelling for murdering his mother-in-law, held at the assizes at Norwich in 1890, the evidence was also apparently very clear, and the jury convicted him "without leaving the box."[1588] The jury in the trial of Henry Potter at the Norfolk assizes in April 1839 went even further, albeit in the other direction, and informed the judge that they did not need to listen to his summing up before acquitting the defendant. Potter, a prosperous farmer, had been accused of stealing barley from an even wealthier neighbour on the word of a disgruntled former employee. He was legally well represented, and his barrister's closing address had drawn repeated applause from those in court.[1589]

Rather more commonly, at least by the later decades of the century, the jury would retire to a private room under the supervision of a bailiff to make their decision. Even so, verdicts were usually reached quite quickly. For example, although Samuel Yarham's murder hearing in April 1846 lasted an entire day, after retiring, his jury deliberated for just 15 minutes before convicting him.[1590] Two years later, despite James Rush's trial's lasting several days, it took his jury just six minutes, after retiring,

---

[1583] *Eighth Report,* p. 327.

[1584] Cottu, *Administration,* p. 101.

[1585] Wiener, "Judges v. Jurors," p. 474.

[1586] *T he Bury and Norwich Post, and Suffolk Herald*, 30 July, 1851.

[1587] *John Bull*, 25 March, 1854.

[1588] *The Bury and Norwich Post*, 25 March, 1890. Mackie, *Norfolk Annals,* vol. 2, p. 406.

[1589] *The Ipswich Journal*, 13 April, 1839.

[1590] *John Bull*, 30 March, 1846. *Ibid.*, 4 April, 1846.
Bell's Life in London and Sporting Chronicle, 5 April, 1846.

to convict him of murder.[1591] However, retirements of several hours were not unknown, even in less serious cases. In March 1843 Henry Watts, who had been acquitted of stealing a sheep at the previous Norfolk quarter sessions when the animal was proved to be a lamb, was re-indicted for stealing the latter. The jury were out for two hours before convicting him. Their nervousness was probably based on the prosecution's reliance on Watts's accomplice in the crime, James Furness, who gave evidence for the Crown.[1592]

Occasionally, both approaches to jury determination were employed, with retirement's being used only after in-court decision making had failed. For example, in a case of criminal libel tried at the Norwich assizes in July 1853, the jury deliberated in court, but after about 20 minutes, being unable to agree, retired in the custody of a bailiff, while the court was adjourned to the Shirehall (where the Norfolk assizes were to be tried), the city list having been completed. Meanwhile, "The jury came to agreement in about an hour, when they repaired to the Shirehall, and returned before Mr. Baron Parke a verdict of *guilty.*"[1593]

Jury deliberations did not involve a meeting of equals; not all jurors' opinions carried the same weight. Sir William Erle, Chief Justice of the Common Pleas until 1880, spoke of one man generally being the "eye of the jury," and of the way in which advocates would address themselves to this man, feeling sure that, if they persuaded him, he would persuade the other 11. [1594] This may have been an exaggeration, but, as a barrister noted, a small group of jurors, perhaps two or three men, probably did dominate most discussions, although they did not necessarily agree.[1595] In the 1820s Charles Cottu thought that jurors who found themselves in a clear minority would often bend to the will of the majority, and his analysis was reiterated by evidence to the 1845 Criminal Law Commission. Specific reports indicate that this continued throughout the nineteenth century. For example, in a case of receiving (a stolen watch) tried at the Norwich quarter sessions in October 1871, the jury initially deliberated in court for several minutes but were divided eight to four in favour of conviction. They then retired to consider their verdict in the jury room, where they reached a unanimous verdict of guilty after just 15 minutes.[1596]

What went on among jurors was, in theory, private, although a few left personal accounts. Some (less than reassuring) hints on the internal working of a trial jury in a serious case at assizes can be seen in an account provided by Joshua Woodcock, from Salhouse in the Norfolk Broads, about the background to the conviction of Charles Prior for his involvement in the notorious Nayland (Suffolk) burglary in February

1591 *The Norfolk Chronicle,* 29 March, 1849.

1592 *The Bury and Norwich Post,* 29 March, 1843.

1593 *The Norfolk News,* 23 July, 1853.

1594 *The Spectator,* 23 July, 1870.

1595 Purcell, *Forty Years,* p. 209.

1596 *The Essex Standard*, 27 October, 1871.

1874. The case was heard at the joint-county winter assizes held at Norwich in December 1876, some two years after others involved in the same matter had been convicted or discharged. Prior was sentenced to a heavy term of imprisonment, but a few weeks later was granted a free pardon, after it transpired that he was the wrong man, and had been confused with another notorious criminal of the same name.[1597]

Woodcock had been one of the jurors involved in Prior's trial. He noted that, after the jury had retired to consider its verdict, he was disconcerted to find that a majority were in favour of conviction. He was also surprised, given the bravura closing speech made by defence counsel, the evidence called on behalf of the accused, and the favourable regard which, earlier in the trial, several of his fellow jurors had shown the prisoner. However, when they retired, just after the judge's forceful summing-up, minds appear to have changed. They were initially divided seven to five in favour of conviction. Four of the latter group changed their vote after an hour of deliberation "rather than be locked up any longer." Woodcock claimed that he had then said to the other jurors that it was pointless for him to continue holding out against the majority but told them that he did not think Prior was guilty. He subsequently claimed that his acquiescence on this issue "smites my conscience to this day," and that he was extremely relieved to learn of the pardon.[1598] This was, of course, a national phenomenon. For example, in 1911, after the Watford doctor Sidney Lightfoot was convicted of carrying out an illegal abortion, despite arguing that it was the unfortunate side effect of a medically necessary procedure, two jurors who had signed a petition for mercy on his behalf claimed that several others had voted guilty simply to avoid missing the last train home.[1599]

Jury riders – statements that accompanied verdicts seeking sentencing clemency – may have been one way of accommodating jurors who had doubts as to the verdict favoured by the majority, so incorporating dissenting opinions into an ostensibly unanimous verdict of guilty, and speeding up agreement (see below).[1600] For example, after John Noden was found guilty of rape at the Shropshire assizes in 1829, a juror, Robert Chilton, came forward to say that he had been firmly against convicting, feeling the evidence inadequate, and had only agreed to join the majority under pressure and in exchange for the jury's providing a very strongly worded recommendation for mercy.[1601]

Jury delay and disagreement was actively discouraged, not least because for much of the Victorian period jurors were kept in bailiff-supervised confinement if they retired and, in theory, denied "meat, drink, and fire [any source of heating]" until they

[1597] *The Bury and Norwich Post*, 13 February, 1877.

[1598] *The Essex Standard*, 2 March, 1877.

[1599] TNA HO 144/1122/204340/29. Crosby, "Criminal Justice," pp. 179-208.

[1600] Mark Coen and Niamh Howlin, "The Jury Speaks: Jury Riders in the Nineteenth and Twentieth Centuries," *American Journal of Legal History*, vol. 58, no. 4 (2018), p. 510.

[1601] Gatrell, *Hanging Tree,* p. 488.

reached a decision. (They might be allowed sustenance in cases of medical necessity certified by a doctor.) Some observers thought this a "barbarous custom" which ought to be abolished, not least because it encouraged poor decision-making.[1602] By contrast, the jurist James FitzJames Stephen thought that telling jurors that they could not have dinner until they had made up their minds was merely a "rough and half-humorous way of mentally jogging them."

How strictly these rules were enforced is a matter of debate. Cottu thought that light refreshment was often permitted in the 1820s, where appropriate, by the judiciary.[1603] Although several nineteenth-century cases have been identified in which jurors were rebuked for having acquired refreshment on their own initiative, in none of them were they actually fined.[1604] Nevertheless, a violation of this rule was used as the basis for an appeal in a civil case from 1832, in which a jury was empanelled to try an action at *nisi prius* at the Lent assizes for Norfolk and retired to consider their verdict at 8 pm. They could not reach a decision, and so were locked up overnight, coming to a verdict at 11 am the following day. Application was subsequently made before the Court of King's Bench for a new trial on the ground that refreshments had been given to one of the jurors during this time.[1605] In any event, the rule was abolished well before the end of the Victorian era. The 1870 Juries Act left the sustenance of jurors to the discretion of the judge.[1606] However, any breach of jury isolation, even to secure refreshment, was still viewed seriously, and might be punished by a heavy fine.

It was unusual for juries to be unable to reach agreement. Even so, this did occur, if only occasionally. In the medieval period jurors who were unable to agree could, in theory, be carted around the circuit with the itinerant judges while continuing to debate their verdict. In 1853, Lord Campbell mentioned this as a joke to a disagreeing *nisi prius* jury at the Norfolk assizes, to considerable public mirth. (He also encouraged the one dissenting juror in this case to accommodate his views to those of the other 11.)[1607] In practice, and as today, a hopelessly "hung" jury would usually be discharged.

For example, at the Norfolk quarter sessions in March 1843, John Isaac was accused of stealing a pair of boots from a woman. The case did not appear very strong, and the accused man called several good character witnesses. The chairman, the legally qualified Henry Dover, summed up in favour of an acquittal, reminding the jury that the accused man was entitled to the benefit of any doubt. Even so, after a lengthy retirement, the jury could not agree because one man "stood out." The chairman

---

1602 *The Spectator,* 23 July, 1870.

1603 Cottu, *Administration,* p. 101.

1604 Crosby, "Criminal Justice," pp. 202-204.

1605 *The Norfolk Chronicle,* 30 March, 1832.

1606 Quinault, "Victorian Juries," pp. 47-53.

1607 *The Bury and Norwich Post*, 23 March, 1853.

ordered that the jurors be "locked up" to continue their discussions, and the case was adjourned for several hours, until 6 pm, and then again until 10 pm, when the single dissenter was still holding out. The chairman made enquiries. Remarkably, it transpired that the dissenter was in favour of conviction, not acquittal. The chairman noted that he had never come across such a case in his 30 years' experience. Whenever such a deadlock had occurred on earlier occasions, the lone dissenter had always been in favour of a not-guilty verdict. The jury and the prisoner were eventually discharged. The chairman was critical of the holdout, opining that he did not show the "mild, calm and Christian spirit" required of jurymen; he expressed a hope that he would not see such a case again. As the jurors left their box, the dissenter, who had clearly been openly identified, was hooted at by members of the public.[1608]

Although it is unlikely that the above matter went for a retrial, most such cases did go for a fresh hearing. Nevertheless, in this regard, much would depend on the facts of the individual case, including, as the case also suggests, how close the jury was to agreement, which might give an indication as to whether unanimity in a future hearing was likely. Thus, at a sodomy trial held at the Nottingham assizes in 1859, one of two defendants turned Queen's evidence, providing the only real evidence against his former lover. The jury retired to consider their verdict at 11 am and did not return until nearly 6 pm, when the foreman said that they were still hopelessly divided, seven to five. The jury was then discharged, and the prosecution formally abandoned, the prisoner being set free.[1609]

Where ordered, a retrial could take place extremely rapidly. At the Norfolk quarter sessions, in October 1894, William Furness was indicted for "unlawfully and riotously assembling" with others to disturb the public peace. He pleaded not guilty, but the jury were unable to reach a verdict. Another jury was then promptly empanelled, the matter immediately reheard, and a verdict of guilty returned.[1610] However, potentially lengthy cases might have to wait for the next sessions for a retrial, particularly at assizes, and especially later in the era (when hearings were often longer). For example, when George Thompson was indicted at the King's Lynn borough sessions in mid-April 1884 for stealing a tablecloth worth 1 shilling, his jury could not agree. In this case, the matter was retried at the combined spring assizes for Suffolk and Norfolk held in early May, just a few weeks later (and almost two months earlier than would have been the case had it been reheard at borough sessions). On this occasion, he was found guilty and, because of an earlier conviction, sentenced to 18 months' imprisonment.[1611]

In Suffolk, the alleged stabbing to death of Rose Harsent, a pregnant servant girl, by William Gardiner, a married Methodist lay preacher and the putative father of the

[1608] *Ibid.*, 29 March, 1843.

[1609] *The Nottinghamshire Guardian,* 22 December, 1859.

[1610] *The Norfolk Chronicle,* 17 October, 1894. *The Ipswich Journal,* 20 October, 1894.

[1611] *Ibid.*, 10 May, 1884.

victim's unborn child, produced two hung juries in 1902 and 1903 when tried at the Ipswich assizes; at each hearing, just one dissenting juror supposedly prevented a verdict. After the second hung jury the prosecution issued a writ of *nolle prosequi* rather than offering no evidence and seeing a formal not-guilty verdict being returned (the normal modern practice after two juries cannot reach a verdict). One correspondent to the *Times* deprecated the stress that was placed on a defendant in these situations, which required that he be remanded back to prison for nine weeks to await a second capital hearing. He urged that such cases always go for an immediate retrial.[1612]

Very occasionally there was confusion as to exactly what the jury had agreed. At the Suffolk assizes in 1892, a jury that retired to consider their verdict in a murder case returned to court after 40 minutes, having apparently reached a verdict, but "disagreed on the way." They retired again and spent another ten minutes making sure that they genuinely were agreed on their decision before going back into court, when yet further debate arose when they were asked to identify the basis on which they were convicting.[1613] In another case in 1853, the court considered the circumstances in which a jury might be allowed to change its verdict. In this case, the jury foreman at quarter sessions delivered a verdict of not guilty. The prisoner was discharged from the dock. Other jurors then interfered and said that the correct verdict was guilty. The prisoner was returned to the dock, and the chairman asked the jury what the true verdict was. All answered that it was guilty, and the foreman suggested that this was what he had said. A verdict of guilty was duly recorded. Subsequently, Chief Baron Pollock approved this decision, accepting that there might come a point at which such a delay was excessive, but observing that in the present case it was not: "Nothing has been done but what daily takes place in the ordinary transactions in life; namely, a mistake is corrected within a reasonable time, and on the very spot on which it was made."[1614]

Jury Equity

The abolition of the "Bloody Code" during the early decades of the nineteenth century, which removed death as even a theoretical possibility for many crimes, encouraged a major decline in the role of jury discretion in the English criminal trial. It was no longer necessary to downgrade charges or to acquit "against the evidence" to avoid burdening jurors' consciences with potentially capital convictions that they viewed as improper. As a result, its use slowly declined, although murder remained something of an exception. In homicide cases, the traditional discretion of the jury to find the lesser non-capital charge of manslaughter to have been established, where murder had been indicted, continued to be an occasional source

---

[1612] *The Times*, 18 November, 1902, p. 12.

[1613] *The Ipswich Journal*, 10 December, 1892.

[1614] *Rex* v. *Vodden* (1853) Dears 229.

of strained relations with the judiciary.[1615] It was for this reason that, in the 1850s, a prosecution-minded barrister, Sir George Stephen, complained that doing away with the Bloody Code had not, as had been promised, stopped juries from bending the law. Indeed, he thought that "nowadays a man cannot get hanged let him try for it ever so anxiously."[1616]

However, discretion (and jury equity) could be exercised in other situations. Alexander Elliot, a Windsor shopkeeper, who sat on a Reading assize court jury in February 1877, noted in his diary that he and his fellow jurors had tried a man accused of attempting to murder his former fiancé with a firearm but convicted him of the lesser offence of firing at her with intent to do her grievous bodily harm. He felt that "there is little doubt he intended to murder her, but we gave him the benefit of the possibility of his intention not being quite so cruel." (The defendant was sentenced to 10 years' penal servitude).[1617] Nevertheless, such cases apart, it seems that the frequent reluctance of Victorian juries to convict (see below) was usually a result of the poor quality of prosecution evidence presented against the accused rather than due to any sympathy for him.

Conviction Rates on Indictment

To some degree, Victorian conviction rates at trial on indictment varied with region, forum, and decade. Nevertheless, general trends can be identified. From early in the nineteenth century, acquittal rates had been in decline, and this continued during the first decades of the new Queen's reign. Thus, in the 1860s it could be noted that, nationally, over the previous quarter-century, the "proportionate number of acquittals has sensibly diminished."[1618]

Even so, it is apparent that, throughout the Victorian era, a significant minority of those indicted who pleaded not guilty were acquitted. To consider an extreme case (and one that may be indicative of gendered attitudes), at the Lent assizes for Norfolk in 1842, Mary Ann White, accused of being an accomplice to robbery, was acquitted of the crime for the fifth time in a row, all of those involved with her on earlier occasions having been found guilty and transported.[1619]

According to a report to the House of Commons, in 1835, 20,731 people nationally were committed to a jury court for trial on indictment. Of these, 14,729, more than two-thirds, were convicted, while some 4,059 were found not guilty. Thus, if a matter went to jury trial there was a 78 percent prospect of a conviction, including those occasioned by guilty pleas, so that it would be significantly lower if confined to contested trials. The remaining 1,943 cases were either thrown out by the grand

---

[1615] Wiener, "Judges v. Jurors," p. 473.

[1616] *Ibid.*, pp. 467-506.

[1617] Berkshire Record Office D/EX902/1.

[1618] Hammick, "Judicial Statistics," p. 404.

[1619] *The Norfolk Chronicle* 16 April, 1842

jury, or not proceeded with by prosecutors. As a result, someone committed for trial to a jury court had a roughly 28 percent chance of escaping conviction through all mechanisms.[1620] In 1858, 25.5 percent of those sent for trial on indictment were acquitted at trial or discharged by the grand jury or for non-prosecution, while the figure was 24.6 percent in 1865.[1621]

This national analysis is broadly reflected in more specific and local figures for the era. Thus, property crimes from Victorian Kent that were tried at the assizes or the Old Bailey (depending on where in the county they had been committed), show conviction rates of 64 percent for the theft of livestock, 74 percent for that of tools, 80 percent for cases of burglary, and 83 percent for stealing clothes, with an overall average of perhaps 74 percent.[1622] At the assizes held for Berkshire and Oxfordshire (taken together) in 1883, 1884, and 1885, 55 out of 89 people who went for trial on indictment (for all crimes) were convicted, making up about 60 percent of the total.[1623] In Sheffield between 1844 and 1855, of an annual average of 27 cases that went to arraignment at trial on indictment, an average of 4.5 (about 20 percent) pleaded not guilty and were acquitted, about 80 percent being convicted after trial or pleading guilty.[1624]

Acquittal was of course a final disposition, regardless of merit, and could not be challenged. However, it might very occasionally be circumvented by indicting a different exemplar crime from a series of offences. Thus, at the Lent assizes for Norfolk in 1831, four men were indicted and acquitted for setting fire to a rick at Swanton Abbott. Prosecuting counsel immediately made clear that he would bring fresh charges in this politically sensitive case, challenged the jury (to secure a fresh tribunal), and then re-prosecuted the four for setting fire to another rick, almost in the same place, on much the same evidence, albeit that this was technically not a breach of *autrefois acquit*. On this occasion, two of the men were convicted.[1625]

It seems that Norfolk was typical of the wider nation when it came to conviction rates. According to the Reverend Charles Brereton, over the two years from 1837 to 1839, the calendars of assizes and quarter sessions in the county, taken together, indicated that there had been 303 convictions (including guilty pleas) and 91 acquittals (less than a quarter of the total) in matters that had gone for trial on indictment. Another 37 cases had been thrown out by grand juries so that 128 of the 431 committed for trial, just under 30 percent, escaped conviction.[1626] In 1879 203 people were

---

[1620] Anon., *The Law Magazine*, p. 5.

[1621] Hammick, "Judicial Statistics," p. 404.

[1622] Conley, *The Unwritten Law*, p. 140.

[1623] Thornhill, "Spring and Autumn Assizes," p. 466.

[1624] Williams, "Counting crimes," p. 81.

[1625] *The Bury and Norwich Post: Or, Suffolk and Norfolk Telegraph, Essex, Cambridge, & Ely Intelligencer*, 30 March, 1831.

[1626] Brereton, *A Letter*, p. 23.

committed for trial on indictment in the county. Of these, no bill was found by the grand jury in 11 cases, so that 192 people were arraigned; of these, 56 were acquitted after pleading not guilty (one more was found to be insane).[1627] Allowing for guilty pleas, this means that more than a third were acquitted if a contested trial ensued.

A selection of figures for individual Norfolk courts and sessions just before and during the Victorian period can also be considered. For example, at the Norfolk quarter sessions in January 1831, 108 people were indicted for taking part in machine-breaking riots the previous November and December. Sixty-seven were found guilty, and 41 were acquitted or otherwise discharged.[1628] More routinely, when on 13 January 1843 the Norfolk quarter sessions were held by adjournment at Walsingham, 22 prisoners came for trial, of whom seven (just over a third) were acquitted.[1629] To consider the higher jury forum, two of the four defendants who went for trial at the Norwich city assizes in April 1835 were acquitted.[1630] Moving on half a century, at the Norfolk assizes in late July 1887, of the three defendants who went to a contested trial, one was acquitted.[1631] Exactly a year later, at the same forum, one of the four defendants who pleaded not guilty was acquitted.[1632] To consider a single offence, in 1846 461 people in Norfolk were committed for trial on indictment for simple larceny, of whom 133 were acquitted.[1633]

As these various figures suggest, a conviction was certainly not a foregone conclusion in contested trials on indictment, at any point during the era. Trial was not a formality, with a significant minority of defendants walking free, at both jury courts. A few others received insanity verdicts, which warrant further consideration.

Insanity Verdicts

For hundreds of years before the nineteenth century, insanity had been a defence against criminal liability, at least in felony cases, and this continued throughout the Victorian period.[1634] By then, claims of insanity were most often seen in cases where a death penalty was a realistic possibility, which meant murder trials. Such a defence was more rarely advanced by lesser offenders, not least because the consequences of a finding of insanity made it unattractive.[1635] Instead, many of those accused of

1627 *Judicial Statistics, 1879*, p. 51.

1628 *The Norfolk Chronicle,* 5 January, 1831.

1629 *The Bury and Norwich Post*, 18 January, 1843.

1630 *Ibid.*, 15 April, 1835.

1631 *Ibid.*, 26 July, 1887.

1632 *Ibid.*, 24 July, 1888.

1633 *Criminal Offenders... 1846* (1847), p. 23.

1634 Joel Peter Eigen, "Lesion of the Will: Medical Resolve and Criminal Responsibility in Victorian Insanity Trials," *Law & Society Review*, vol. 33, no. 2 (1999), p. 427.

1635 Alexander, *The administration,* p. 115.

minor crimes who appeared mentally disordered continued to go for trial and were sentenced to short terms of imprisonment if convicted, on the basis that, if insanity was later certified in prison, they could be transferred to a county asylum, rather than a state asylum for criminal lunatics such as Broadmoor.[1636]

For example, at the Norfolk assizes held in December 1892, Charles Hunt, a middle-aged labourer, was accused of committing arson at Stanford. His behaviour, both when he was arrested and subsequently, was decidedly strange, and it was revealed that, in the past, he had been an inmate in a lunatic asylum. At his trial, Hunt made a series of random remarks and odd comments. The trial judge, when summing up to the jury, admitted that he had entertained doubts about the defendant's mental state, but told them not to worry about this when reaching their verdict, as it could be addressed later, even if they convicted. The jury returned a guilty verdict, but with an appeal for mercy, the foreman opining that they thought the accused "was not quite right in his mind." The judge deferred sentence so that an enquiry into the convict's mental state could be made.[1637]

Even so, lunacy was periodically advanced at trial in non-homicide cases. For example, Uriah Baldwin, a 27-year-old man, had been tried at the Norwich city assizes in March 1838 for cutting his wife with intent to murder her, but acquitted on the basis of insanity, a course that even seems to have been suggested by the prosecution.[1638] At the same forum in April 1839, it was recorded that "John Howard, for cutting his wife's head with a dustpan, was pronounced insane."[1639] Similarly, at the quarter sessions sitting at Swaffham in July 1839, William Wight attempted to advance insanity as a defence when accused of several counts of theft and obtaining property by deception in local towns and villages. He apparently "feigned" madness at trial. However, this was rejected as a ploy to deceive the magistrates and jury, after the court received evidence from the Walsingham prison surgeon and gaoler that he had behaved in a quite sane manner while in custody. He was convicted of stealing a watch and sentenced to a year's imprisonment.[1640]

Procedure in Insanity Verdicts

The procedural law governing claims of criminal insanity had been altered in 1800, following the notorious trial of James Hadfield, who had been acquitted of attempting to assassinate King George III on the grounds of madness. That year the Criminal Lunatics Act provided that if a jury found a defendant unfit to plead (see above), or acquitted him on the grounds of insanity, something that had to be made clear in their verdict, the court would be required to order that the defendant

---

[1636] J.F. Saunders, "Criminal Insanity in 19th Century Asylums," *Journal of the Royal Society of Medicine*, vol. 81, no. 2 (1988), pp. 73-75.

[1637] *The Bury and Norwich Post*, 6 December, 1892.

[1638] TNA HO 17/126/96.

[1639] *The Bury and Norwich Post*, 17 April, 1839.

[1640] *Ibid.*, 24 July, 1839.

be "kept in custody, in such place and in such manner as to the court shall seem fit, until His Majesty's pleasure be known." (As a result, Victorian criminal lunatics were sometimes colloquially known as "pleasure men.") Subsequently, the Crown would give orders for their long-term custody (see Chapter 14).[1641] This was felt to be much safer than relying on dangerous lunatics being committed to an asylum or other carceral institution under the provisions of the 1744 Vagrancy Act, as had previously been the case. In 1883 the Trial of Lunatics Act altered the verdict in such situations again, so that it became "guilty, but insane at the time of committing the crime charged."[1642] The consequences of such a finding remained much the same.

For example, in June 1898, at the Norfolk assizes, Samuel Frederick Steele, a 27-year-old railway carman, was indicted for murdering his former partner, Thurza Ann Bensley, at Yarmouth, earlier the same year. His counsel argued that he had been suffering from "epileptic mania" at the time, and so was not responsible for his actions. Several witnesses supported this assessment. The jury, after a long deliberation, found him to be insane, but expressed (via their foreman) a hope that he would never be allowed out again. The trial judge ordered Steele to be detained in a criminal-lunatic asylum, said that he would add the jury's recommendation to their verdict, and make sure it was made known to the Home Secretary.[1643]

Definition of Insanity

The 1800 Act did not establish a test for what was a legally excusing form of mental illness – for example, that the defendant did not understand that what they were doing was wrong, or at least illegal; was acting under an irresistible impulse; or imagined that they were acting to the public benefit.[1644] This uncertainty as to the definition of exculpatory mental illness moved onto the political agenda in 1843, after a paranoid Daniel McNaughtan (often spelled M'Naghten thereafter) shot and killed Edward Drummond, private secretary to Prime Minister Robert Peel, and was acquitted on the grounds of insanity. This occasioned a degree of public indignation and prompted the House of Lords to ask a panel of senior judges a series of hypothetical questions about the defence. Their answers produced the M'Naghten rules, which governed the issue for the remainder of the era (and to the present day).

The assembled judges concluded that an accused person was to be presumed to be sane, and had the onus of establishing the contrary, albeit only on the balance of probabilities (this was not particularly novel even then). More significantly, they also decided that insanity was as much a legal as a psychiatric concept. Most important – did the defendant know that his act was both illegal and wrong? In Lord Chief

---

[1641] Brown, "Unfitness to plead," pp. 187-196.

[1642] Alexander, *The Administration,* p. 115.

[1643] *The Illustrated Police News etc.*, 2 July, 1898.

[1644] Peter Bartlett, "Legal Madness in the Nineteenth Century," *Social History of Medicine,* vol. 14, no. 1 (2001), p. 107.

Justice Tindal's words, was the accused person labouring under "such a defect of reason, from disease of the mind, as not to know the nature and quality of the act he was doing, or as not to know that what he was doing was wrong." The courts were not willing to entertain suggestions that the defence should be deemed to be established where the accused person had acted under an "irresistible impulse," although this was often used by physicians of the era as a test for mental illness.[1645] As a result, the M'Naghten rules excluded a significant number of offenders who were potentially certifiable as ordinary members of the public but did not qualify for such a finding in the criminal courts. On one estimate, at least half the alleged criminal lunatics in Victorian Warwickshire who had been sentenced to imprisonment, rather than being found insane or unfit to plead at trial, could have been diagnosed as insane in a normal asylum at the time of their committal to prison.[1646]

This produced a tension between the legal and psychiatric definitions of madness. At George Baldry's trial for murder at the Norfolk assizes in 1851, Mr Justice Erle expressly directed the jury that he had little time for the notion that because someone who had previously behaved entirely normally had suddenly committed an appalling and inexplicable crime – in this case fatally battering a child about the head with a hammer without apparent motive – it must, per se, be indicative of madness. The key question for the jury was whether Baldry knew right from wrong. In deciding this question, it might be asked whether the defendant had shown a fear of the consequences of his actions (Baldry had fled afterwards). In this case, a surgeon who had spoken to the defendant expressly opined at trial that the accused was of "feeble intellect, but not incapable of distinguishing right from wrong."[1647] Another observer noted, "Evidence showed that the prisoner was of a weak mind, yet quite cognizant of moral obligations: at the trial he was evidently confused and overwhelmed with a sense of his position."[1648] Perhaps unsurprisingly, given the judge's directions, the jury speedily convicted, and Baldry was sentenced to death.[1649]

Even so, and as occurred quite frequently in these situations, Baldry's sentence was subsequently commuted to transportation for life, the Home Secretary's accommodating doubts about the convict's mental state, and alternative definitions of insanity, with a degree of clemency (see below). Although some Victorian alienists might attack the notions of criminal responsibility generally held during the period, their views were not entirely ignored by the establishment.[1650]

[1645] *Ibid.*, p. 107. Wiener, *Reconstructing,* pp. 88-89.

[1646] Saunders, "Criminal insanity," pp. 73-75.

[1647] *The Bury and Norwich Post*, 2 April, 1851.

[1648] *The Spectator,* 29 March, 1851, p. 10.

[1649] *The Bury and Norwich Post*, 2 April, 1851.

[1650] R. Smith, "The Victorian Controversy about the Insanity Defence," *Journal of the Royal Society of Medicine*, vol. 81, no. 2 (1988), pp. 70-73.

Insanity as a Defence at Trial

In practice insanity provided a defendant with two opportunities to escape (normal) conviction, and those accused of murder with a chance to escape the noose. Some defendants might be considered so mad that they were not fit to stand trial (see above). Others would be found to be insane at trial. Finally, even those who were capitally convicted after a jury had rejected this defence, or if it had not been raised at their hearing, might still be reprieved in light of their mental condition, the Home Secretary effectively second-guessing the trial jury's decision, as with George Baldry.

During the early nineteenth century, the number of forensic claims of insanity remained stable; there was roughly a 50 percent chance of their being successful.[1651] The number of successful claims increased in the late Victorian period, something that was probably facilitated by the growth in what was, effectively, expert psychiatric evidence and increased awareness of mental pathology. Sir Henry Hawkins had a slightly cynical view of insanity as a defence, suggesting that it was often a last resort where better options were not available.

Perhaps because of such attitudes, any pre-crime history of mental disturbance would often be influential with both judge and jury. For example, in 1829 Richard Scott was found to be insane by his trial jury after beating an elderly man to death near Carleton Rode in South Norfolk while claiming that his victim was the devil. He had a history of outbursts of "phrensy," one of them taking place very shortly before the killing, and had even been bled to alleviate pressure on his brain, in the unavailing hope that it would improve his mental state.[1652] In 1887 the Reverend Arthur Cooper (see above) was aided in his claim by his previous incarceration in two private insane asylums and the fact that he had earlier shown signs of homicidal mania. There was also insanity in his family, and he had suffered extreme sunstroke in India earlier in his life, which was thought to have unsettled his brain.[1653]

Generally strange behaviour at the time of committing the crime, or while doing so, was also helpful. In 1881 Charles Monsey, a 57-year-old superannuated excise officer living near North Walsham, quarrelled with his 51-year-old wife and murdered her with a hatchet, "cutting her head to pieces" in the process. Both were apparently "eccentric" individuals. After killing his spouse, Monsey asked a local boy to help move her body into a barn, made no attempt to escape, and was sitting in an easy chair, in bloodstained clothes, when the police arrived.[1654] At the combined spring assizes in May, affidavits were produced as to insanity, and his trial was postponed. He was subsequently detained as a criminal lunatic.

1651 Wiener, *Reconstructing,* p. 84.

1652 *The Bury and Norwich Post*, 12 August, 1829.

1653 *The Morning Post*, 16 November, 1887.

1654 *Berrow's Worcester Journal*, 7 May, 1881, p. 2.

Post-Conviction Claims

As some of the cases cited above suggest, even if a defence of insanity had been rejected by a jury, or for some reason had not been advanced at trial, it was sometimes accepted immediately after conviction, allowing its subject to escape execution in murder cases, even though no jury, whether considering fitness to plead or guilt, had come to such a conclusion. This gave scope for recognising medical definitions of madness that did not satisfy the M'Naghten criteria, such as irresistible impulse, but which might be viewed as strong mitigation. Thus, in 1899 a man and a woman tried at Norfolk courts were found to be insane. One was found to be mad after conviction, the other before arraignment, neither case being decided by a trial jury, although the latter case was, at least, determined by a fitness-to-plead jury.[1655]

Such post-conviction claims might be accepted in even the most emotive cases. For example, in 1881 Henry Stebbings brutally murdered an 11- or 13-year-old girl (reports differ) named Hannah Brett at Saham Toney in South Norfolk. Stebbings had recently been released early from a long sentence, served in Dartmoor, for savagely attacking another adolescent girl in Norfolk a decade earlier. (He had attempted to murder her by cutting her throat.)[1656] He had reported to the Norfolk police just four days before the killing as part of his release arrangements. It was thought that Stebbings had sexually assaulted Brett and stabbed her when she resisted.[1657] At the Norfolk assizes in February 1882, Stebbings was found guilty of murder and sentenced to death.[1658] However, despite this verdict, the heinous nature of his crime, and his previous conviction, two days before he was due to be executed at Norwich Castle prison he was respited on the grounds of homicidal mania.[1659] He eventually died in Broadmoor Criminal Lunatic Asylum in 1911, having been in custody for almost thirty years.[1660]

Similarly, one night in early February 1887, at Kenninghall workhouse, an elderly inmate named Jonas Rivett stabbed Henry Baker, a sick-ward attendant (or "man nurse"), in the neck. He severed Baker's windpipe and jugular vein, so that he died almost immediately. Rivett then ran through the workhouse shouting and attempted to jump from a window before being secured.[1661] At the combined Suffolk, Norfolk and Norwich assizes, held at Ipswich in April the same year, Rivett was indicted for murder and represented by counsel. Despite insanity being advanced at trial,

---

1655 Anon., *Statistics Relating…1899* (1901), p. 212.

1656 *The Bury and Norwich Post*, 4 July, 1871.

1657 *The York Herald*, 29 October, 1881.

1658 *The Standard*, 10 February, 1882.

1659 *The Manchester Times*, 4 March 1882.

1660 *The Reading Mercury*, 16 September 1911.

1661 *The Ipswich Journal*, 15 February, 1887.

he was found guilty of murder and sentenced to death.[1662] Even so, he was swiftly reprieved, and removed to Broadmoor.[1663]

A few years after the Victorian period, in 1909, Thomas Allen, a vermin-destroyer from Gorleston-on-Sea, with several previous convictions, shot and killed PC Charles Alger, who was trying to prevent him from attacking others. He then went looking for another man to kill. At trial at the Norfolk assizes, Allen pleaded not guilty and called one Dr Craig, effectively a psychiatrist, from Guy's Hospital. Craig testified that he was suffering from insane delusions, including a conviction that his wife was having affairs, and that he had no understanding of the seriousness of the charges that he faced. The jury rejected this evidence and found him guilty, and he was sentenced to death. Even so, a reprieve was granted so that Allen, too, spent the remainder of his life in Broadmoor.[1664]

Jury Riders

When returning guilty verdicts, particularly but not solely in capital cases, juries would often add a rider, whether orally via their foreman or, very much less commonly, via a written note handed to the judge (which he might then read out in court). Riders allowed jurors to return a verdict that they felt was in accordance with the evidence while simultaneously calling for the commutation of the death penalty or the moderation of other punishments in deserving cases. On one assessment, in almost a third of Irish murder trials in the years from 1836 to 1914 a jury recommended that the prisoner be treated mercifully. They may not have been quite as common in Victorian Norfolk, but they were by no means rare. In these circumstances, in capital cases, the trial judge generally informed the jurors that their views would be conveyed to the proper quarters. He then donned the black cap and passed sentence of death in appropriate form.[1665] Such riders were frequently, but not invariably, respected by the executive. In non-capital cases the trial judge could immediately reflect the jury's recommendation in his sentence.

For example, in November 1886 Arthur Riches, a 36-year-old fish-hawker, mortally wounded his wife with a razor after what appears to have been a chance meeting in the Haymarket in Norwich (they had been separated for two weeks at the time).[1666] He was tried for murder at the Norwich assizes at the end of that same month and convicted, his motive apparently being his wife's infidelity (she was already living with another man in lodgings in the city).[1667] However, the jury strongly recommended

---

[1662] *The Pall Mall Gazette*, 22 April, 1887.

[1663] *The Morning Post*, 2 May, 1887.

[1664] Neil R. Storey, *Norfolk Murders* (Cheltenham: The History Press, 2006), p. 118.

[1665] Mark Coen and Niamh Howlin, "The Jury Speaks: Jury Riders in the Nineteenth and Twentieth Centuries," *American Journal of Legal History*, vol. 58 (2018), p. 516.

[1666] *The North-Eastern Daily Gazette*, 9 November, 1886.

[1667] *The Dundee Courier & Argus*, 24 November, 1886.

him to mercy on account of the great provocation he had received.[1668] The prisoner was sentenced to death, but within a few days his punishment was commuted to penal servitude for life.[1669] (He appears to have died almost 12 years later, in April 1898, at the age of 48, while still in custody at Parkhurst prison on the Isle of Wight.)

In a similar case, at the Norwich assizes in June 1895, Frederick Miles, a 27-year-old labourer, was indicted for murdering his estranged wife, Mildred, with a bung picker in Norwich some ten days earlier. He had handed himself in to the police after the crime. The jury found him guilty, but strongly recommended him to mercy on the ground that he, too, had received great provocation.[1670] Although the trial judge passed a death sentence on Miles (the only sentence possible for murder), it was subsequently commuted to penal servitude for life, and he died at Parkhurst some eight years later. Nevertheless, by the final years of the Victorian period, increased public concern about wife-killing, even where there had been provocation such as adultery, meant that jury recommendations to mercy on such grounds had become less common, and when made were often ignored, as was the case with the soldier Charles Wooldridge in Berkshire in 1896 (referred to by Oscar Wilde in *The Ballad of Reading Gaol*).[1671]

In a non-capital case, tried at the Norfolk assizes in 1842, Henry Amis, a ratcatcher, was convicted of nocturnal poaching, during which there had been a violent affray with keepers, and a man had been injured. Even so, he was given a very good character by local farmers in the Oxnead area. The jury that convicted him urged leniency for this reason. In light of this, and the character witnesses called, the trial judge, Mr Justice Tindal, sentenced him to just two months' imprisonment with hard labour, but noted that otherwise he would have had to impose transportation.[1672] In August 1883 at the Norfolk assizes, John Rowling, a 48-year-old labourer, was convicted of the manslaughter of his (presumably mentally impaired) wife, by neglectful treatment. The jury recommended him to mercy on the grounds that his daughter, who lived with them, was just as responsible for her mother's maintenance but had not been prosecuted. He was sentenced to just seven years' penal servitude.[1673]

Pleas of Pregnancy as a Bar to Execution

As in previous centuries, a woman who had been convicted of a capital crime could claim that she should not be executed, as she was pregnant. By the Victorian period, this meant that use of the doctrine was limited to women who had been found guilty of murder. Historically an all-female jury of "matrons" would then be

---

1668 *Berrow's Worcester Journal*, 27 November, 1886.

1669 *The North-Eastern Daily Gazette*, 30 November, 1886.

1670 *Norfolk Chronicle*, 11 June, 1895.

1671 Wiener, "Sad Story," p. 178.

1672 *The Times*, 11 April, 1842, p. 6.

1673 *The Ipswich Journal*, 11 August, 1883.

sworn in to determine whether the claim was true. These women had to determine whether the prisoner was "quick with child"; in theory, this meant that the child had started to move in the womb, although any stage of pregnancy appears to have been sufficient by the Victorian era. If found to be pregnant, the convict would be imprisoned until giving birth, or proving not to be pregnant, and then, in theory, her execution could be carried out according to the original sentence.

This rule had been a major source of mitigation for women during the early-modern era. However, employment of the jury of matrons in a criminal context started to decline in the late eighteenth century, a process that was greatly accelerated by the gradual abolition of the death sentence for crimes other than murder during the 1800s. Nevertheless, such juries were employed on a periodic basis until formal abolition of the procedure in 1931. Between 1879 and 1904, at least seven juries of matrons were assembled nationally, while even in the 31 years after 1900, a minimum of 11 such juries were empanelled.[1674]

However, where they were still employed, it became increasingly common for the matrons to receive medical evidence on the issue of pregnancy, rather than being dependent purely on their own examination. For example, in a case from 1838, the prisoner was convicted of the murder of her three-year-old child by drowning. The judge passed sentence of death upon her, but when the clerk of assize asked her if she had anything to say in stay of execution, she replied, "I am with child now." In traditional fashion, the judge then ordered that the sheriff empanel a jury of matrons, and that the doors of the court be shut, so that no married woman present could escape the duty. Twelve suitable women were found and sworn in (with a special oath), and a forewoman identified. The jury of matrons then retired to a private room under supervision of a bailiff, and the prisoner was taken to them. Subsequently, they asked for the assistance of a surgeon; a surgeon-cum-accoucheur, who was present as a witness in another case, was asked to examine the prisoner. He then gave evidence to the matrons in open court, stating that she was not pregnant. The women retired again, and subsequently returned a verdict in court that the prisoner was not quick with child.[1675]

Even so, by the early nineteenth century some judges did not take a negative decision by the matrons as conclusive of the issue, something that was fortunate for Mary Wright shortly before the Victorian period. At the Norfolk assizes, held at Norwich in March 1833, Wright, a 28-year-old woman, was convicted of murdering her husband, William, by poisoning him at their home in Wighton. It had apparently been expected that she would be found to be insane. Even so, the jury convicted her of the capital crime within ten minutes of retiring. When the death sentence was passed, she became hysterical. It was then claimed that she was pregnant, and a jury of matrons was empanelled from the older women who happened to be in or near

---

[1674] K. Crosby, "Abolishing Juries of Matrons," *Oxford Journal of Legal Studies*, vol. 39, no. 2, 2019, pp. 259-284.

[1675] *Regina* v. *Anne Wycherley* (1838) 8 Carrington and Payne 262, 173 E.R. 486.

the court. An hour later, the matrons returned a verdict of "not quick with child." However, by order of the trial judge, three local surgeons then examined Wright, upon whose certificate of pregnancy he respited her sentence.[1676] The following July, the prisoner gave birth to a baby girl while in custody (which was taken from her). Perhaps unsurprisingly, a local doctor thought that the failure of the matrons to detect (fairly advanced) pregnancy in this case demonstrated the need for legal change.[1677]

As a finding of pregnancy postponed execution only until after the birth or the prisoner proving not to be pregnant, Mary Wright, like other women in this situation, was still due to be hanged. As was noted at the time, "Her delivery took place last month, and the law now demands her life." However, several philanthropists attempted to get her sentence changed into one of close custody on the grounds of insanity.[1678] Wright's death sentence was subsequently commuted to transportation for life. (She died while still incarcerated in Norwich Castle at the start of November 1833.)[1679] In reality, this was already longstanding practice in such situations, irrespective of any issue of mental health, although as late as 1902 the Home Office did not feel able to describe it as a de facto rule when asked by the government of Victoria in Australia whether it was "usual to commute the same." The Home Office merely replied that it was exceedingly improbable that a death sentence would not be commuted in these circumstances. The Wright case was sufficiently notorious to still being used as a critique of the jury of matrons almost 40 years later.[1680]

Sentencing

Until the early 1800s convicted prisoners (other than murderers) were still sometimes brought forward in batches at the end of the assizes sessions to be sentenced. However, by the Victorian period, sentences were normally passed immediately after each trial and verdict, as is the modern practice. Inevitably, as the penal repertoire became more sophisticated, sentencing options more complicated, and change more common, mistakes were sometimes made in disposals. In October 1837 12-year-old Francis Henry Coleman was convicted of stealing a horse and cart at the Norwich quarter sessions. He was sentenced to be imprisoned for three months in solitary confinement and to be privately whipped once. However, shortly afterwards, Isaac Preston, the recorder of Norwich, petitioned the Home Office, noting that, when passing sentence, he had failed to consider a recent statute

---

[1676] *The Bury and Norwich Post: Or, Suffolk and Norfolk Telegraph, Essex, Cambridge, & Ely Intelligencer*, 27 March, 1833.

[1677] *The Standard*, 5 August, 1833.

[1678] *The Spectator,* 10 August 1833, p. 9.

[1679] *The Ipswich Journal*, November 2, 1833.

[1680] Anon, "Plea of Pregnancy in Bar of Execution," *The British Medical Journal*, vol. 1, no. 577 (1872), pp. 75–76.

limiting solitary confinement to one month, or three months over the course of a year. A free pardon was prepared, dated 29 November 1837.[1681]

Similarly, at the Norfolk assizes in March 1853, two prisoners were convicted of stealing a 55-gallon cask of brandy in Great Yarmouth. The presiding judge opined that it was one of the most "impudent" crimes he had come across and sentenced the pair to ten years' transportation. This option does not appear to have been open to him, as it was simple larceny, and he swiftly received a communication from one of the barristers in the case, Mr Prendergast, to this effect. The two men were recalled to the dock, where the judge changed his disposal from transportation to two years' imprisonment with hard labour.[1682]

Criminal Antecedents

Once a conviction had been secured, whether by plea or jury verdict, the judge or chairman (at county quarter sessions) would seek to establish the accused person's antecedents. A growing fear of creating prejudice meant that these were not normally adduced during the trial itself, even where highly relevant, the most exceptional cases apart, although many observers thought this ridiculous. For example, the jury convicting a woman at the Middlesex sessions in 1870 and recommending her to mercy were surprised when the judge explained that her six previous (and similar) convictions, of which they had been ignorant, meant that compassion was not appropriate.[1683]

Sometimes antecedent history was legally vital to determining the appropriate sentence; it was nearly always highly influential on disposal. Recidivism was taken very seriously by Victorian courts, and first offenders frequently treated with more leniency than even slightly more hardened criminals. For example, at the Norfolk quarter sessions in March 1857, Samuel Everett and Jonathan Starling were convicted of stealing and receiving, respectively, 400 hundredweights of carrots. The former had a previous conviction for which he had been sentenced to transportation; the latter was of previous good character (although suspected of stealing hay). Starling received three months' imprisonment with hard labour, but Everett was sentenced to four years' penal servitude.[1684] When it transpired that George King, a Yarmouth fisherman convicted at the town borough quarter sessions in January 1888 of stealing a pair of trousers, had 12 previous convictions, the recorder felt that there was no point wasting further time on him. He passed a draconian sentence of five years' penal servitude, despite the minor nature of the crime.[1685]

1681 TNA HO 17/5/79.

1682 *The Bury and Norwich Post*, 23 March, 1853.

1683 Letter to Editor of the *Standard*, 3 September, 1870.

1684 *The Bury and Norwich Post*, 24 March, 1857.

1685 *The Ipswich Journal*, 3 January, 1888.

Of course, in an age of limited bureaucratic capacity, identifying past convictions could pose challenges, especially when they had been imposed by distant courts. The situation was easier if the relevant convictions had been accrued locally. In these cases, the gaoler might be a valuable repository of information about a convict's history, even if records were not readily to hand. For example, in October 1844, when Robert Hunt was found guilty of theft at the Norfolk quarter sessions, the record of a previous conviction almost 20 years earlier for a similar crime was adduced. However, this does not appear to have been his only prior conviction, as the "gaoler here stated that he had been three times tried and convicted,"[1686]

When it came to non-local convictions, the situation was improved by the Habitual Criminals Act 1869, which provided for the maintenance of a single register of those found guilty of significant offences. The Prevention of Crimes Act 1871 provided that the register should extend to all those sent to prison for a month or more. Prison governors were responsible for notifying particulars of their inmates' crimes to the officer in charge of the Criminal Record Office at New Scotland Yard. Eventually, photographs of convicted persons were also added to such details. Indicative of this improvement, when Emily Watkins was convicted of obtaining services by false pretences at the Norfolk quarter sessions, sitting at Attleborough, in October 1880, the Crown was able to adduce a similar conviction two years earlier in Herefordshire.[1687] However, it was not until the advent of fingerprinting just after the Victorian era, in 1902, that identification and adducing convict antecedents would be fully transformed.[1688]

It should be noted that Victorian courts would also sometimes consider antecedent material that would not be considered proper in the modern era, such as earlier proceedings that had ended in not-guilty verdicts. When Robert Hunt was found guilty of theft at the Norfolk quarter sessions in October 1844 a previous conviction was proved. However, the gaoler also stated that he had been tried and acquitted three times in the intervening years. This appears to have influenced the decision to sentence him to transportation.[1689]

Similarly, in 1847, after James Spragg and an accomplice were found guilty at the Norfolk quarter sessions of stealing from a dwelling place, his co-defendant's three previous convictions were adduced, but so were "two indictments against Spragg, upon each of which he was acquitted." The two men received the same sentence.[1690] More generally, when it came to character, at the Yarmouth borough quarter sessions in January 1888, when Thomas Howse pleaded guilty to stealing a tweed coat, not only did the recorder read out a long list of previous convictions,

[1686] *The Bury and Norwich Post*, 23 October, 1844.

[1687] *Ibid.*, 26 October, 1880.

[1688] Terry Thomas, "A Short History of Criminal Records" in *Criminal Records* (London: Palgrave Macmillan, 2007), p. 261.

[1689] *The Bury and Norwich Post*, 23 October, 1844.

[1690] *Norfolk News,* 9 January, 1847.

but the chief constable of the town testified that he knew nothing good of the man, who "was as lazy and drunken as any man in the borough." Howse received six months' imprisonment with hard labour.[1691]

There was a danger that adducing such unproven material could lead to injustice. In 1847 George Thurtell, a well-bred landscape gardener and thief, stole items from his employer, Edmund Farrer, near Swaffham. After his crimes came to light it was found that Farrer had earlier accused a young man of stealing the same chattels. When this individual was convicted of another, unrelated offence, the unproved allegation (of stealing from Farrer) appears to have been adduced, and "from his suspected bad character [he was] sentenced to be transported."[1692]

The Plea in Mitigation

Pleas in mitigation, whether following a trial or, even more important, a guilty plea (which did not afford an opportunity to explore the factual basis of the conviction) are near universal today but were not common during the Victorian period, especially its earlier decades, even where the accused was legally represented. In 1844 the inexperienced Sir Henry Hawkins turned down a defence brief at the Hertford quarter sessions because he did not appreciate that such a plea could be made. (It was picked up by a more experienced colleague.)[1693] However, at the Norwich assizes in 1882, held before Mr Justice Lindley, James Charles Edwards, a 37-year-old solicitor's clerk pleaded guilty to forging certain documents. The prisoner then read out a carefully prepared written statement, in which he said, inter alia, "A love for pictures was my ruin, a craving desire and mania to possess myself of something better than my neighbours gradually developed, until at last it became a madness with me." He was sentenced to ten years' penal servitude.[1694] More formally, at the winter assizes held in Norwich in November 1884, after Henry Green, a mail-cart driver, pleaded guilty to stealing small amounts of cash and postal orders from letters in mailbags that were entrusted to his care, it was noted that "Mr Simms Reeve, on behalf of the prisoner, asked for the court to pass a lenient sentence." (Five years' penal servitude was imposed for what was a gross breach of trust.)[1695]

Mitigating and Aggravating Factors

Various factors might influence the judge, recorder, or chairman (and his fellow magistrates) when passing sentence. For example, a desire for mercy on the part of the victim/complainant/prosecutor (all roles might be combined in the same person) could be important, not least because ignoring it might discourage others from pursuing prosecutions in a system in which private individuals still played a vital role.

[1691] *The Ipswich Journal*, 3 January, 1888.

[1692] *Ibid.*, 20 November, 1847.

[1693] Hawkins, *Reminiscences,* p. 18.

[1694] *The Norfolk Chronicle,* 28 October, 1882.

[1695] *The Bury and Norwich Post*, 11 November, 1884.

Thus, a man convicted at the Norfolk quarter sessions in January 1844 for animal theft was told that he would have been transported had it not been for a plea for clemency from the owner of the beast; as a result, he was sentenced to a year's imprisonment (with hard labour). At the same sessions, the chairman said that he would have transported another convict but, because of the recommendation of mercy by the prosecutor, merely sentenced him to 12 months' hard labour.[1696]

Similarly, in July 1858, when a miller named James Ayton pleaded guilty at the Norfolk quarter sessions to the theft of £15 in gold and silver and two pieces of pork from Edward Summer's house in Northrepps, he was "very strongly recommended to mercy" by the prosecutor. He received the very lenient disposal of three months' imprisonment with hard labour.[1697] More seriously, Richard Roberts, who had tried to murder his fiancée by cutting her throat with his pocketknife, narrowly missing the carotid artery, before turning the blade on himself, received only five years' penal servitude when sentenced at the Norfolk assizes in April 1863. When passing sentence, the judge expressly noted that his intended victim had asked that the court show mercy. (Roberts had also pleaded guilty.)[1698]

Frequently jury recommendations, made in riders to guilty verdicts (see above) were also listened to. In 1878, at the Norfolk assizes, Fuller Williamson of Foulsham was tried for wounding his wife with intent to murder and convicted. However, despite the woman's suffering a quite savage beating, the jury asked for mercy, as they did not feel he had formed the intent to kill her until the attack started. The trial judge thought the case appalling, and the evidence overwhelming, but in deference to their rider noted that he was sentencing Williamson to 20 years' penal servitude, rather than life, as would otherwise have been the case.[1699]

Nevertheless, jury recommendations might be disregarded if considered clearly inappropriate. The chairman of the Norfolk quarter sessions, sitting at Attleborough in October 1880, noted that he was always willing to listen sympathetically to any jury recommendation for mercy when presiding over a case involving the 65-year-old Emily Watkins. She had been convicted of obtaining food, drink, and lodgings worth £1 15s 3d from the White Horse inn by false pretences. The convicting jury asked for clemency in view of her age. However, the chairman told them that if they knew of Watkins' history of similar convictions (normally not disclosed to jurors), they would probably not have made such a recommendation, and gave her nine months' imprisonment.[1700]

Extreme youth as well as old age was also considered a mitigating factor (see Chapter 15). At the Yarmouth quarter sessions in July 1839, two boys, age nine and

[1696] *The Ipswich Journal*, 6 January, 1844.

[1697] *The Bury and Norwich Post*, 6 July, 1858.

[1698] *The Derby Mercury*, 8 April, 1863.

[1699] *The Bury and Norwich Post*, 6 August, 1878.

[1700] *Ibid.*, 26 October, 1880.

11, and a 16-year-old youth, were sentenced to short terms of imprisonment for stealing rope from a lugger. The youngest, Thomas Merryman, received just a week in custody, the last two days of which were to be spent in solitary confinement (in a nod to the separate system). The 11-year-old received a month, and the oldest boy three months', imprisonment.[1701] Similarly, 11-year-old Charles Guyton, a "little lad whose head was barely visibly over the dock," was convicted at the Norfolk assizes in April 1851 of stabbing another boy with a fork after an argument, but sentenced to just one month's imprisonment "on account of his tender age."[1702] In 1875 William Dack and Herbert Bocking, two 13- and 14-year-old telegraph clerks at the King's Lynn post office, were convicted at the assizes of stealing valuable items from parcels sent through the mail, a very grave and specialist form of theft. They were sentenced to six months' imprisonment with hard labour, being shown mercy on account of their youth, despite the gravity of their offence.[1703]

More dramatically, at the Norfolk assizes in June 1895, Frederic Butcher, a 15-year-old carpenter's apprentice, was indicted for feloniously shooting at the Reverend Arthur Hamilton Upcher with intent to do him grievous bodily harm at Baconsthorpe, the previous January. He was convicted but recommended to mercy on account of his youth and sentenced to just nine months' imprisonment.[1704] More generally, in 1861, only 41 children under 12 years of age, and 169 between 12 and 16, were committed to Norfolk prisons, for any length of time (even a few days). Interestingly, almost half the former number were committed to the Yarmouth borough gaol.[1705]

At the other end of the spectrum, at the Norwich assizes in June 1897, John Furness, 64, a solicitor, was indicted for fraudulently appropriating to his own use a deed of mortgage a decade earlier. Although convicted, he was recommended to mercy on account of his age and sentenced to three months' imprisonment without hard labour.[1706]

Previous service to the Crown, especially in the military, particularly if combined with poor health due to such service, would have some, albeit limited, effect. They were both present in a case from the Norfolk quarter sessions in 1875, when an obviously and seriously ill William Allen, a former soldier, pleaded guilty to stealing two calico shirts and three calico nightgowns. Unfortunately, he had a previous conviction. The court was "sorry to see an old soldier, and a man apparently broken down in health, before them on such a charge." However, in the circumstances, they felt that they could not pass a sentence of less than four months' imprisonment.[1707]

1701 *The Ipswich Journal*, 20 July, 1839.

1702 *The Bury and Norwich Post*, 2 April, 1851.

1703 *The Bury and Norwich Post*, 6 April, 1875.

1704 *The Norfolk Chronicle,* 11 June, 1895.

1705 *Judicial Statistics of England and Wales, 1861,* p. 65.

1706 *The Norfolk Chronicle,* 10 June, 1897.

1707 *The Bury and Norwich Post*, 30 March, 1875.

Property crimes that had been encouraged by the carelessness of the victim might attract a degree of leniency in sentencing from judges (as well as from jurors in their verdicts). For example, during the 1840s, Isaac Jermy, the ill-fated recorder presiding over the Norwich quarter sessions, deplored the "shameful practice" of exposing goods for sale by shop doors because, he felt, it encouraged theft. In 1844, when sentencing Harriet Woods for stealing boots and stockings, he noted that, if it were not for these circumstances, she would have been transported; instead, he imposed only three months' hard labour for each of two offences.[1708]

Other forms of lax security might receive similar recognition. In 1879 two men were convicted of stealing cash, wine, tea, spirits, and cutlery from their employer, John Hardy, at the Brandon Railway Hotel. However, the jury expressly recommended them to mercy because of the unusual freedom that they had enjoyed when in Hardy's service, and the consequent "temptations to which they were exposed." The judge agreed and sentenced one of the men to a year's imprisonment, the other to fifteen months' custody.[1709]

As in previous centuries, that a crime was promoted by genuine and immediate need or "want" and was limited to necessaries, could also be a mitigating factor, especially for a first offence. At the Walsingham quarter sessions in January 1842, Caroline Dunham pleaded guilty to stealing half a pound of butter, a piece of ham, a piece of bacon, and two candles from a farmer. She received 14 days' imprisonment.[1710] A convict with numerous dependents of whom he was the sole support could, sometimes, also receive sympathy, not least because they might otherwise become chargeable to the Poor Law.

Previous good character was also a very important factor. Many such offenders were dealt with leniently for a first offence. Conversely, and as the case of Emily Watkins suggests (see above), recidivists might be treated harshly. At the Norfolk quarter sessions held in March 1857 at Attleborough, 19-year-old Benjamin Myfield was convicted of breaking and entering at Catfield, during which just two loaves were taken. This was the precisely the sort of crime that, in a first offender, might attract leniency (see above). Unfortunately, Myfield had a previous felony conviction and received four years' penal servitude.[1711]

Safety of Convictions

Ostensibly, there was considerable public confidence in the safety of the criminal convictions returned at Victorian jury forums. Sir James Fitzjames Stephen thought that most were sound; even if the English system allowed many guilty people to walk free: "No man leaves the dock of our courts under sentence whilst any

---

[1708] *Ibid.*, 17 January, 1844.

[1709] *Ibid.*, 28 October, 1879.

[1710] *Ibid.*, 19 January, 1842.

[1711] *The Bury and Norwich Post*, 24 March, 1857.

rational being can retain the faintest doubt not merely of his being guilty, but of his having been proved to be guilty according to the most elaborate and stringent set of rules that ingenuity ever devised for the purpose of preventing injustice and oppression."[1712] In 1844 the recorder of Doncaster thought that 149 out of 150 jury verdicts were "correct."[1713]

Nevertheless, even Fitzjames Stephen was sometimes less confident in this regard. Many others were consistently less sanguine, not least because periodic miscarriages of justice were clearly and very publicly established during the era (attracting free pardons from the Home Office if their subjects were still alive), so that even those who acknowledged the safeguards present in the legal system readily accepted that "the innocent are at times mistaken for the guilty, and Bar and Bench and Jury are alike deceived."[1714]

For example, in 1844 a newspaper noted that John Clifton of York, who was serving a sentence of 20 years' transportation at Norfolk Island in Australia, had been exonerated a year after his conviction for burglary, when two men committed to prison for another felony confessed to the crime. The paper observed that, had this still been a capital offence, the situation would have been irreversible. This was something that, they felt, provided a strong argument against capital punishment.[1715] Even more worryingly, a couple of early Victorian convictions that had led to the gallows subsequently proved to be unsafe, in one case the true perpetrator making a death-bed confession. Some claimed that, given the prevalent want of "education and acuteness" found in contemporary juries, mistakes in verdict were almost inevitable. [1716]

Around the end of the Victorian period, the manifest blunders established during the various trials of Adolf Beck, an impoverished Norwegian who was wrongly convicted of crimes perpetrated (and eventually admitted to) by another man, and who spent time in prison before being pardoned, would suggest that an excess of confidence was not warranted, even if the English system may have been superior to at least some of those found on the Continent. By then, society was less willing to view mistaken convictions as necessary collateral damage in the war against crime. The Beck case contributed to the eventual establishment of the Court of Criminal Appeal.[1717]

1712 James Fitzjames Stephen, "The Criminal Law and the Detection of Crime," *The Cornhill Magazine,* December 1860, pp. 697-709.

1713 *Eighth Report,* p. 221.

1714 *The Morning Post*, 16 January, 1857.

1715 *The Bradford Observer*, 28 November, 1844.

1716 *The Spectator,* 11 February, 1860, p. 14.

1717 Tim Coates, *The strange story of Adolph* [sic] *Beck* (Tim Coates Books, 1999), p. 234.

Appeals

Despite periodic adjudicatory mistakes by juries, felons convicted at assizes or quarter sessions had no right of appeal during the nineteenth century, other than that provided by the very rarely used, and extremely tightly constrained, writ of error, directed to a superior court – in practice the Court of King's or Queen's Bench – for legal mistakes that appeared on the face of the record. Normally, this involved an error in the wording of the indictment. A conviction might be quashed if such an error could be proved. However, only a handful of these cases were brought each year.[1718]

The general absence of an appeal procedure was unusual in a European context and came as a surprise to many foreigners. In 1859, at the Norwich quarter sessions, the German Meyers Hirsch was convicted of stealing from a commercial traveller and given an exemplary sentence of seven years' penal servitude (he had similar previous convictions). Utterly shocked by this disposal he asked whether there was an appeal against the verdict and sentence but was bluntly told "not in this country."[1719]

Even before the reign of the new Queen, this lack of a proper appeal procedure had occasioned concern. In 1834 one observer thought that it was a "glaring defect" in the country's criminal-justice system and contrasted it unfavourably with the situation found in English civil actions.[1720] Many informed Victorian commentators thought that it was vital that a specialist court of criminal appeal be established.[1721] Thus a barrister giving evidence to the 1845 Criminal Law Commission, thought that not only would it address unsafe convictions, but it would also encourage clear analysis of criminal law by the higher judiciary, something that was then often neglected. When one of many suggestions for a criminal appeal court was rejected in 1860, observers (again) complained that despite having a sophisticated system of civil appeal, "Parliament determines to exclude life and liberty from the same privilege." As a result, the most palpable errors in a criminal case could be remedied only by a royal pardon (see below).[1722]

This lacuna in the system continued to be a source of controversy to the end of the Victorian era, in Norfolk as elsewhere. In 1890, in his charge to the grand jury at the Norwich assizes, Mr Justice Hawkins urged the creation of a Court of Criminal Appeal to deal with "miscarriages of justice." The distinguished lawyer thought that it should also be possible for a retrial to be ordered, at least in some situations, especially if supported by the original trial judge.[1723] Even so, and despite numerous proposals for reform in this regard during the 1800s, and several active attempts

---

[1718] Bentley, *English Criminal Justice*, p. 10.

[1719] *The Bury and Norwich Post, and Suffolk Herald*, 25 October, 1859.

[1720] *The Westminster Review*, vol. 20 (1834), p. 142.

[1721] *The Liverpool Mercury etc.*, 30 March, 1870.

[1722] *The Spectator,* 11 February, 1860, p. 14.

[1723] *The Leicester Chronicle*, 29 November 1890.

to establish such a court, this would wait until 1908, when the Court of Criminal Appeal finally filled this gap by dint of a statute passed the previous year. As a result, two years later, Harry Pope, a Norfolk JP who had been convicted at the Norfolk assizes of misappropriation of a trust under s. 80 of the Larceny Act 1861 and given three years' penal servitude, was able to (unsuccessfully) appeal both his conviction and sentence in the new forum.[1724]

Referral to the 15 Judges

During the early Victorian period it was open to a trial judge to reserve difficult and uncertain questions of law for the informal and private consideration of the 15 Westminster judges sitting together in London, or as many could be assembled, just as they had in earlier centuries, even after conviction. Sometimes they might do this by directing a special verdict in which the jury established essential facts, and the proper verdict on those facts was referred to the judges. At other times, a guilty verdict would be referred with the question that had been identified for consideration. The judges' decision would normally be announced at the next sessions. Despite the informality of the pre-1848 process, the number of judges involved meant that their (majority) collective opinions and decisions carried more authority than those reached in the courtroom. They established very important precedents, although exactly how binding these were, especially at the start of the nineteenth century, has been a matter of some debate.[1725] Nevertheless, the judiciary often used the decisions reached at these sittings to develop legal doctrine.[1726]

For example, at the Norfolk assizes in 1836, held before Mr Justice Gaselee, John Sucker and four other men were convicted of the murder of William Case the previous year, while they were poaching at Methwold, on the edge of the Norfolk Breckland. They were sentenced to death. However, the jury subsequently delivered to the judge a declaration stating, "Our opinion is that the prisoners were guilty of manslaughter, not murder, and it was our intention so to find had we not been called upon to give our opinion as to the facts." The execution was deferred for the collective opinion of the 15 judges (or as many of them as could be gathered together), who assembled in the Court of Exchequer to consider it. On 23 April Lord Denman stated that, after hearing counsel on both sides, they thought that it would be improper to execute the prisoners for murder and the sentences were commuted.[1727]

[1724] *R v Harry Pope* (1910) 4 Cr. App. R. 123.

[1725] Allyson N. May, "The Bench, the Bar, and Crown Cases Reserved," *Law and History Review*, vol. 29, no. 1 (2011), pp. 289-296.

[1726] Phil Handler, "The Court for Crown Cases Reserved, 1848-1908," *Law and History Review*, vol. 29, no. 1 (2011), pp. 259-288.

[1727] *The Norfolk Chronicle,* 1 April, 1836.

Court for Crown Cases Reserved

In 1848 Parliament replaced this informal procedure when it created the Court for Crown Cases Reserved (CCCR). The new court adopted the existing method of reserving cases but formalized it, creating the highest judicial forum in the country for the determination of questions of criminal law. This was a court of record that sat and gave judgment in public. It could quash verdicts and arrest judgments, but it could not order a retrial. Significantly, and unlike its relatively informal predecessor, it could take references from quarter sessions as well as assizes.[1728]

For example, in March 1854 John Eagleton, a Yarmouth baker who had contracted with municipal authorities to supply bread to the poor, was tried at the local borough quarter sessions for fraudulently supplying bread of short weight. He was convicted by the trial jury, but the recorder then reserved the case for the opinion of the CCCR. After a rather convoluted process, the correctness of the conviction was argued before the judges in December 1854, although only ten were present, and again in February 1855, in front of the same ten men. Counsel appeared to argue both in support of and against the legality of the conviction. The judges then took an unusually long time to consider the issues. In July Mr Baron Parke delivered their judgment, affirming the conviction on three counts of defrauding the town's guardians. The defendant was ordered to appear before the recorder at the October sessions for Great Yarmouth to receive sentence.[1729]

However, recourse to the procedure from the lower jury forum, at least for less serious matters, was limited by the potential expense entailed. For example, in 1849 George Wright, who was legally represented by the barrister Carlos Cooper at the Norfolk quarter sessions, was accused of stealing a live rabbit worth 6d from a trap. His counsel argued that this was not, technically, larceny (presumably on the basis that the animal was still wild). The court agreed that it was at least an arguable issue and was willing to "grant a case on that point for adjudication in a superior court, but the expenses were so much that Mr. Cooper declined to do so; and the prisoner was sentenced to one month's imprisonment."[1730]

Moving forum, Frederick Burrell was tried for the unusual crime of "abduction" at the Norfolk assizes in March 1863 after detaining a potentially wealthy relative, Jane Burrell, who was under 21, against the will of her mother, with intent to marry her. Frederick had then wed Jane in London. His brother, Henry Burrell, was indicted for aiding and abetting the alleged crime. The jury returned a verdict of guilty, but sentence was deferred, to allow several legal points to be put before the CCCR. Both the Crown and the accused were represented at this forum, where the latter's barrister argued that there were questions about the indictment and the

[1728] Cornish, *Oxford History*, p. 804.

[1729] *R* v. *Eagleton* (1855) Dears CC 515.

[1730] *The Bury and Norwich Post, and East Anglian*, 17 January, 1849.

mother's degree of control.[1731] The judges in the CCCR were apparently divided in their opinions, not as to the law, but as to its application to the facts of the case. Judgment was delivered according to the majority view, which held that the facts were not sufficient to sustain a prosecution for the crime, and, with "very great regret," they quashed the conviction.[1732]

Some seven years later, in a reference from the Norfolk quarter sessions in November 1870, the CCCR considered a case in which a man named Waters had been convicted of obtaining a mare by false pretences. He had given the prosecutor a cheque for £20 10s but told him not to present it before the following Saturday. The prosecutor ignored this, and presented the cheque, which bounced. Counsel for the appellant argued that the prosecutor had broken the contract by presenting the cheque early, and that if he had followed it Waters might have paid money into the bank to meet the cheque by the Saturday, so that it was honoured. This was accepted by the CCCR, which quashed the conviction.[1733]

It was not just issues pertaining to substantive law that were considered by this forum; evidential matters might also be referred to the court. In February 1898 another conviction from the Norfolk quarter sessions was reviewed at the CCCR. A five-judge court, presided over by the Lord Chief Justice, quashed the conviction at Norfolk quarter sessions of a farm servant, Charles Rose, accused of stealing sheep and poultry from his master because the man had advised him to "make a clean breast of it, as it would be better for him if he did so." His master was not prepared to deny this. The accused man had then made a confession to the farmer, in the presence of a policeman, on the basis of which he was prosecuted for theft. The CCCR held that the confession was inadmissible, having been obtained by an inducement. (They also said that the accused man, who had been sentenced to a two-month term of imprisonment, should have been bailed pending the "appeal"). That the defendant was legally represented at trial was undoubtedly decisive in his ability to refer the matter.[1734] In this case, the CCCR was not prepared to commit itself as to whether the chairman should have directed the jury to ignore the confession, after it had been introduced, or, instead, asked the prisoner if he wished for the jury to be discharged and a fresh one sworn in.[1735]

The CCCR had some effect in encouraging the adoption of more precise legal definitions for a variety of offences and in standardising judicial procedures. However, and ironically, it has also been suggested that there was an increasing judicial reluctance to allow judgments to be reserved for the new CCCR during the second half of the nineteenth century, resulting in fewer references than had

[1731] *The Morning Post*, 2 April, 1863.

[1732] *The Ipswich Journal*, 2 May, 1863.

[1733] *The Times*, 21 November, 1870, p. 11.

[1734] *The Daily Gazette For Middlesbrough*, 5 February, 1898.

[1735] *The Huddersfield Chronicle*, 8 February, 1898.

been made to its informal predecessor. Some 19 cases nationally went to the CCCR in 1860, of which one, the only one from Norfolk, was from the Norwich assizes, involving alleged larceny by a bailee (often a difficult area). (The conviction was upheld.)[1736] By contrast, in 1896, seven cases went to the CCCR, including one from the Norfolk quarter sessions, involving the maiming of a dog.[1737] However, in 1899 just three cases went to the CCCR, none from Norfolk (one was from the Cornwall quarter sessions, one from their equivalent for Huntingdonshire, and one from the Kent assizes).[1738]

Various explanations have been advanced for this reluctance to refer cases. Some judges may have shared Lord Denman's fears that reserving judgments undermined public confidence in the trial, and the exemplary lesson of a verdict delivered in court. This fear may have been exacerbated by the new court's power to quash convictions rather than merely recommending a pardon. This might have inclined the judiciary to think less of the benefits attendant on the potential clarification of a legal issue, and more about the likely outcome in the case at hand. It has also been suggested that the CCCR became increasingly reluctant to articulate general legal principles when given the opportunity to do so. As a result, it has been suggested that what had been an active, innovative, albeit informal process of judicial review for criminal cases between the mid-eighteenth and mid-nineteenth centuries became an almost moribund process during the second half of the 1800s.[1739]

Even ignoring these considerations, the CCCR was still not a "proper" appellate court and would not be replaced by such a body until 1908. It was confined to errors of law. As could be noted in 1857, there was "still no Court of Appeal when they [the accused] are convicted on an error of fact." In the latter situation, convicts would still have to rely on a pardon, and trust to the tender mercies of the Home Office and its attendant "red-tapery."[1740]

Petitions for Pardon and Clemency

Despite the limitations on a formal appeal process, convicts, or those acting on their behalf, could petition the Crown for a pardon, an amelioration of sentence, or both. In practice, these were dealt with by the Home Office during the Victorian era. As a result, and as was noted in 1870 in the context of murder convictions, the Home Secretary – who performed the function on a de facto basis on behalf of the Monarch – had effectively become a one-man final court of criminal appeal, albeit not bound by purely legal considerations, and despite not (usually) having any legal training. He made his decision assisted by his private secretary, the views of the trial

---

1736 *Judicial Statistics 1860,* p. 55.

1737 *Judicial Statistics 1896,* p. 73.

1738 Anon., *Statistics Relating…1899* (1901), p. 115.

1739 May, "The Bench, the Bar," pp. 289-296.

1740 Anon., "English Courts of Law," p. 28.

judge, any opinions given by the petty jury, by public feeling as expressed in the more influential journals, and by any other source that he thought fit to consult.[1741]

The growing power, influence, and availability of newspapers, which increased greatly in number and circulation during the second half of the nineteenth century – something that was assisted by technological breakthroughs such as the steam press and reforms like the abolition of duty on paper – meant that the printed media became particularly important in this regard when notorious cases were concerned, especially those involving murder. This also meant that the process of deciding who was to benefit from clemency became increasingly public. By the close of the Victorian era, newspaper clippings of cases were sent to Whitehall, along with the trial judge's reports and other official documentation. Sir William Harcourt, the Home Secretary in 1882, freely admitted that he sought to gauge popular feeling using this medium: "I always ask to see the local newspaper reports in capital cases."[1742]

Occasionally this could lead to slightly arbitrary results that were motivated as much by emotion as reason. In 1907 William Whiteley, owner of one of the leading London department stores, was murdered by Horace Rayner, his (alleged) illegitimate son, who then attempted to kill himself. There was great sympathy in the press for Rayner, not least because his father had refused to acknowledge him. When he was sentenced to death, a petition for his reprieve was drafted and supported by several newspapers and signed by many thousands. The Home Secretary eventually reprieved Rayner, and he was released after 12 years' penal servitude.[1743]

Whether the process of appealing to the Home Office was entirely satisfactory was debateable, even at the time. As was noted in 1860, to many it was inherently flawed, so that an injustice was done to the prisoner and the public, not least because both were excluded from the Home Secretary's "hearing." Furthermore, any fresh evidence considered was not received on oath. Where a petition was allowed, a jury verdict might be set aside on the opinion of just one man (the Home Secretary) who did not think the evidence adduced at trial sufficient. As a result, the interests of both prisoner and public were sacrificed by the "want of machinery, armed with power, to deal with errors in misdirections, suppressions, or inventions of judges, juries, and witnesses."[1744] In 1865 another observer demanded that if a referral from the decision of a criminal court was necessary, it should be made to a tribunal that was capable of sifting and considering evidence in a rational manner and not (effectively) be left to popular opinion. Furthermore, he noted that such opinion was usually engaged only in death-penalty cases, rather than cases

---

1741 *The Liverpool Mercury etc*, 30 March, 1870.

1742 M.J. Weiner, "Convicted Murderers and the Victorian Press: Condemnation vs. Sympathy," *Crimes and Misdemeanours: Deviance and the Law in Historical Perspective*, vol. 1, no. 2 (2007), p. 110.

1743 *Ibid.*

1744 *The Spectator,* 11 February, 1860, p. 14.

involving severe but non-capital punishment, which might be more deserving.[1745] (Perhaps unsurprisingly, given such problems, many informed Victorian observers thought that it was vital that a specialist court of criminal appeal be established).[1746]

The Home Secretary could make such a pardon free (which would lead to immediate release) or conditional, on, for example, transportation, early in the Victorian period, imprisonment, throughout the era, or penal servitude, after its early years. Alternatively, he could reduce the length of custodial sentences that had already been imposed. A free pardon was most likely to be used where the verdict itself appeared unsafe, and a conditional pardon where a sentence was deemed too draconian, although there was some blurring between the two, whatever should have been the situation in strict legal theory, with doubts about the safety of a conviction sometimes (apparently) ameliorating sentence. Many petitions raised both innocence and the alleged harshness of the sentence imposed.

Claims of innocence were difficult to sustain, and most failed. For example, in 1824 the Norfolk man Robert Gibson unavailingly petitioned for a reprieve from execution on the basis that he could produce alibi witnesses.[1747] There was a similar lack of success after three men were convicted of highway robbery at the Norfolk assizes in Norwich in March 1832. In this case, death had immediately been "recorded" and the sentence commuted to transportation for life. It was alleged that the prosecutor was unable to identify any of them prior to trial; no stolen property was found on them; four other men were subsequently convicted for another, similar, robbery, the investigation of which might suggest that they were the true perpetrators of the crime; the petitioners were too poor to secure potentially exonerating evidence; and the trial judge had summed up encouraging an acquittal but been disregarded.[1748] Similarly, after James Thrower was found guilty at the Norfolk assizes in August 1836 for stealing items from the Locks public house at Ellingham, he unavailingly claimed that three gypsies who had recently been convicted at the Suffolk quarter sessions for stealing fowl had confessed to the same offence.[1749]

Such petitions were not confined to convictions or punishments passed at assizes. For example, in December 1839, Henry Mann was convicted at the Norwich city quarter sessions for stealing a black silk stock and sentenced to six months' imprisonment with hard labour. He unavailingly petitioned the Home Office for a pardon with support from 40 people, including William Wheelhouse (the prosecutor) and (very strangely given their verdict) all members of the trial jury, on the grounds of his previous good character and their belief that the case was not wholly free from

---

[1745] Thomas Beggs, *The Royal Commission and the punishment of death*, 1865, p. 5.

[1746] *The Liverpool Mercury etc.*, 30 March, 1870.

[1747] TNA HO 47/65/16.

[1748] TNA HO 17/119/31.

[1749] TNA HO 17/105/148. James Thrower, was one of 299 convicts transported to Australia on the *Susan*, sailing on 29 July 1837.

doubt. Unfortunately, there was an unfavourable report by the trial judge on the issue.[1750]

Similarly, John Hudson, a 23-year-old labourer who had been found guilty of stealing a pig at the Norfolk quarter sessions held at Walsingham in July 1840, and sentenced to seven years' transportation, attracted a petition supported by 23 people from Dereham and Swanton Morley. They argued that the evidence on which he had been convicted was unsatisfactory (which went to guilt) and claimed that he had dependent family (relevant to punishment). The petition failed after the chairman of the Norfolk quarter sessions sitting at Walsingham, taking the role of the judge at assizes in this regard, responded by claiming that Hudson was a "notorious bad character," noting that his brother Robert had been transported two years earlier, and alleging that they were both members of the "Swanton Gang" of thieves.[1751]

Nevertheless, a few petitioners enjoyed success. In April 1839 23-year-old Thomas Purser, who had been found guilty of horse theft at the Lent assizes for Norfolk, and sentenced to 15 years' transportation, was among them. His conviction had immediately occasioned concern and led to a petition signed by 66 of the inhabitants of Downham Market, along with several new affidavits and witness statements. These suggested that the horse had not been stolen, but legally and fairly sold in a bargain between prisoner and prosecutor, so that Purser was innocent of any crime. This was accepted by the Home Office, and a free pardon granted on 2 April 1840.[1752]

Petitions against sentence tended to be more successful than those against conviction. In these cases, the Home Secretary seems to have been particularly influenced by the presence of special mitigation, such as the petitioner having a peripheral role in a crime. For example, at the Lent assizes for Norfolk in 1837, John Smith, George Timms, and John Varnham were convicted of the murder of Hannah Manfield during a burglary the previous January, and all three were sentenced to death. However, Varnham's sentence was eventually commuted to transportation after the other two made a full confession in which they stressed that he had merely kept watch.[1753] Varnham sailed for Australia in November 1837 on the *Emma Eugenia*.

Less successfully, in 1869, after William Sheward came forward voluntarily, and confessed to and was convicted of the murder and dismemberment of his wife in Norwich some 18 years earlier, efforts were made to obtain a commutation of his death sentence because of the long interval that had elapsed between the murder and the trial and his entirely unprompted confession. These efforts were to no avail, and William Calcraft hanged Sheward in Norwich Castle prison.[1754]

[1750] TNA HO 18/15/32.

[1751] TNA HO 18/35/10.

[1752] TNA HO 17/111/148.

[1753] *John Bull*, 8 May, 1837.

[1754] *The Norfolk Chronicle,* 2 January, 1869.

Equally unavailing was the petition in September 1885 for Robert Goodale, who had denied any involvement in the murder of his wife. However, while awaiting execution after capital conviction, he admitted killing her but said that it was due to extreme provocation after she told him that she was enamoured of other men, and that her death had been, in part, accidental.[1755] Mr Dent, the Norwich Prison governor, took Goodale's statement down and sent it to the Home Secretary. The Reverend Thomas Wheeler, a Baptist minister, then went to London and made representations at the Home Office, asking for a reprieve. This was rejected by the Home Secretary, and Goodale was hanged. (The clergyman thought that had the information been advanced at trial it might have led to a verdict of manslaughter.)

It was not just the sentences in capital cases of murder that attracted petitions for clemency. James Brown, a 25-year-old man, was convicted of burglary at the Lent assizes for Norfolk in March 1836, and initially sentenced to transportation for life. However, a petition was organized, supported by the victim/prosecutor, William Wenham, and 28 other inhabitants of the parishes of Scoulton and Woodrising, including the local vicar. The petitioners observed that they had known Brown for many years as an honest, sober, and industrious man of good character who had never even been charged with an offence. His sentence was commuted to transportation for seven years.[1756]

[1755] *Lloyd's Illustrated Newspaper*, 6 December, 1885.

[1756] TNA HO 17/42/94.

Chapter 12: The Evidence Adduced at Trial

Introduction

Most of the evidence adduced at a criminal trial in Victorian England would be readily recognizable to modern observers, although it was often delivered in a rather more expeditious manner than is the case today. Convictions might be secured on direct testimony from eyewitnesses, evidence from accomplices, confessions or out-of-court admissions made by the accused person, and circumstantial evidence, such as possession of stolen items. Sometimes all were present at the same time. This material might be bolstered by expert testimony, where appropriate. In this chapter, these areas, inter alia, will be considered in slightly more detail.

Identification

The most basic prosecution task was to identify the defendant as the perpetrator of the crime. This was often done by eyewitness testimony. However, despite periodic failures in forensic identification, such as the notorious Adolf Beck case toward the end of the era, the need for this to be reliable was usually taken quite seriously by both judges and juries, and so provided a fruitful line of defence if a perpetrator was not caught red-handed. For example, juries tended to view heavily inebriated victims as inherently unreliable in this regard. Thus, at the Norfolk assizes in 1856, four soldiers were accused of violently robbing James Sharman, a drunken sailor going home on leave, while he was on the highway near Yarmouth. He had flashed the large amount of money and gold he was carrying in various pubs and had had a heated argument with an artilleryman earlier in the evening. In the small hours of the night, as he was "rolling along," the four uniformed suspects allegedly set upon him, beat him on the head with a stone, and left him half dead and covered in blood after emptying his pockets. Sharman recognized one of the men as Richard Daynes, the soldier with whom he had earlier clashed. The four men were based or resident nearby and appeared to have come into money at about the time of the attack (circumstantial evidence). Nevertheless, and doubtless influenced by his intoxicated state, the judge left the issue of "proof of identity" to the jury, and after just ten minutes' deliberation, they returned not-guilty verdicts against all the accused.[1757]

As in previous centuries, alibi defences were regularly run by those who had been identified but not arrested at the scene of a crime, and, as had always been the case, not a few of these were fraudulent. For example, in 1863 John Lemmon shot at and wounded a gamekeeper while poaching in Shottisham. A week later, he was apprehended by a police constable just as he was about to sail from Yarmouth to London on a steamer. At trial he claimed a case of mistaken identity (the victim and another keeper both claimed to have recognised him) and tried to adduce alibi evidence to support this. He called several witnesses to say that he had been drinking in a Norwich public house at the relevant time and had subsequently spent

[1757] *The Bury and Norwich Post*, 9 April, 1856.

the rest of the night there. Unfortunately, his witnesses "did not perfectly agree with each other." A prosecution eyewitness placed him near Shottisham at the relevant time. Lemmon was convicted at the Norfolk winter assizes and sentenced to 18 months' imprisonment.[1758]

Accomplice Evidence

Accomplice testimony had played a major role in law enforcement during the eighteenth century, but by the 1800s several well-publicized scandals had made the authorities more circumspect about receiving it. Even so, it continued to play a significant, if much reduced, role in founding or (more commonly) supporting criminal prosecutions during the Victorian era. For example, in April 1839, at the Norfolk assizes, John Hall and William Palmer were indicted for sacrilege after stealing a bell from North Walsham church. It was claimed that the pair, with the assistance of John Daniels, took it away in a cart, broke it up, and endeavoured to sell the metal in Norwich. At trial, Daniels turned Queen's evidence and testified against the others, so that they were convicted and sentenced to a year's imprisonment.[1759]

Accomplice evidence was particularly valuable when dealing with criminal gangs, whether commercial poachers or professional burglars. There was often little honour among thieves, and even families could break down when immunity or a reduced sentence were on offer. For example, when, at the Norfolk quarter sessions held at Walsingham in April 1841, James Goatson was accused of stealing wool fleeces, his brother Thomas "was admitted evidence" against him. Thomas had been intimately involved in the theft and provided the evidence that convicted his sibling.[1760] Some 16 years later, at a committal hearing, eighteen-year-old Joseph Cole, who had stolen a pocketbook containing a gold sovereign from a druggist, was formally "admitted as evidence against his father for feloniously receiving the same". The latter was sent for trial at the quarter sessions held in Swaffham.[1761]

The evidential status of accomplice testimony had been in a state of flux during the late eighteenth century. At one point, it had required corroboration, and, if this failed to materialize, the trial judge would direct an acquittal. This was subsequently watered down to a mandatory warning to the jury as to the dangers of convicting on such evidence if it was uncorroborated, and the identification of potential corroboration (by the judge), if any was present. This practice was also adopted in Ireland, where a judge noted to a jury in 1825 that, although it was open to a jury to convict on accomplice evidence, it was rare to find a conviction based solely on such "degraded" testimony, not least because jurors appreciated that the witness was himself a criminal and had a huge temptation to save his own skin.[1762]

[1758] *Ibid.*, 22 December, 1863.

[1759] *The Norfolk Chronicle,* 9 April, 1839.

[1760] *The Bury and Norwich Post*, 7 April, 1841.

[1761] *The Norwich Mercury*, 3 January, 1857.

[1762] Declan McGrath, "The Accomplice Corroboration Warning," *The Irish Jurist*, vol. 34 (1999), p. 170.

Nevertheless, it seems that some English judges in the 1830s and 1840s, such as Mr Justice Coleridge, still occasionally directed juries to acquit where accomplice evidence was unsupported, especially if its quality was poor, rather than leaving the decision to them. For example, at the Lent assizes for Norfolk in 1831, members of a gang of poachers who had shot and killed a keeper were tried for murder on the evidence of an erstwhile colleague, Friday Carley. They were acquitted of the killing on the direction of the trial judge (but convicted of nocturnal poaching).[1763]

In 1855 the Court of Crown Cases Reserved reconsidered the issue, reaffirmed that it was not a rule of law that an accomplice's testimony had to be confirmed by other evidence, and stated that juries could convict on such unsupported testimony, although the "usual course is to advise them not to do so."[1764] This meant that although, in strict legal theory, there was no reason that a conviction should not be secured on uncorroborated accomplice evidence, it might be vigorously discouraged by the trial judge, and this was usually the course followed. As a result, in November 1885, a judge giving his charge to the grand jury at the Norwich winter assizes opined, a little ambiguously, in the context of a sodomy trial, "According to law a Jury could not convict a man upon the evidence of an accomplice. He would not say absolutely could not convict, because the Grand Jury and the Petty Jury are supreme in such matters, but it was the duty of the Judge to warn them that they ought not to convict upon the uncorroborated evidence of an accomplice."[1765] Such directions were usually followed by juries.

Ideally, an accomplice would have had a peripheral involvement in the crime for which he gave evidence, and thus less moral culpability than those he incriminated. (Sir Henry Hawkins stressed that this was not always the case in practice during the early Victorian period.) For example, in 1861 Abraham Payne was tried at the Norfolk assizes for night-poaching as part of a gang, during which, it was claimed, he shot a gamekeeper in the forehead using an air gun. (Fortunately, the keeper was merely knocked unconscious for 20 minutes.) The prosecution case was largely established by the evidence of a man named Wade who had initially been charged with the same crime but who stressed that he had told other members of the gang not to shoot at the gamekeepers. He gave "important evidence" for the prosecution which, it was noted (significantly), was corroborated in some respects by other witnesses. Payne was convicted and sentenced to 12 months' imprisonment with hard labour.[1766]

Nevertheless, the use of Samuel Yarham as a prosecution witness in a notorious Norfolk murder case in 1845 was illustrative of the continuing dangers of accomplice testimony and the status it accorded the witness. Yarham was accused of being an

---

1763 *The Bury and Norwich Post*, 30 March, 1831.

1764 *R* v. *Stubbs* (1855) Dears CC 555. Christopher J. W. Allen, *The Law of Evidence in Victorian England* (Cambridge: CUP, 2011), pp. 44-46.

1765 *The Norwich Mercury,* 11 November, 1885

1766 *The Bury and Norwich Post*, 30 July, 1861.

accessory after the fact to the killing of his neighbour, Harriet Candler, in her shop in Yarmouth. When arrested in connection with the crime, he claimed to have spoken to three men, who carried out the murder and robbery, as they left the premises.[1767] He turned Queen's evidence, and, in April 1845, Robert Royal, James Mapes, and James Hall were tried at Norwich assizes for the murder, with Yarham as the chief prosecution witness. However, his bad character was exposed in cross-examination, and all three men were acquitted by the jury in under ten minutes.[1768]

Yarham seems to have thought that, as he had testified against fellow gang members, he could not be accused of the murder, and a few weeks later he made some indiscreet admissions about his own involvement in the crime, to the effect that, in reality, he had been the leader of the gang, and had personally finished Candler off, rather than being peripherally involved. He was then prosecuted on the basis of this evidence and his previous testimony. Given his earlier status, the legality of such a course was slightly uncertain, but the Crown stated, "It will be the object of the present prosecution to prove that Yarham, when admitted approver, did not state the whole truth, which, if they succeed, according to the opinion of the Attorney General, will subject him to a prosecution for murder." They succeeded in this, and Yarham was eventually tried and convicted of murder, and was hanged outside Norwich Castle in April 1846.[1769]

Corroboration of accomplice testimony also became an issue in a Norfolk court in 1847. In December 1846 a gang of men attempted to steal wheat from a barn in Forncett St Peter. At the Norfolk quarter sessions the following March, one of them, Collingwood Browne, turned Queen's evidence, despite out-of-court pressure from his erstwhile colleagues not to do so. He identified Woodhouse Moore, Mark Moore, and Miles Land as his accomplices in the crime. When faced by corroborative evidence from Browne's wife, Land admitted his guilt and was sentenced to ten years' transportation.[1770] In April Mark Moore was tried at the Norfolk assizes, and Browne and his wife again gave evidence against him. However, on this occasion, the judge, Mr Justice Coleridge, warned the jury that in view of Browne's criminal history – he appears to have been a habitual thief targeting grain barns – as well as his accomplice status, they could not safely convict on his evidence or that of his wife. Although the jury were, apparently, "loth" to return a not-guilty verdict, Mark Moore was eventually acquitted and released, albeit being warned by the judge about his future conduct.[1771] Land arrived in Australia in 1849, perhaps ruing his guilty plea. It should be noted that, as was common with many who gave accomplice evidence, Collingwood Browne appears to have returned to crime and continued

[1767] *The Morning Post*, 8 January, 1845.

[1768] *The Bradford Observer*, 17 April, 1845.

[1769] *The Morning Chronicle*, 13 April, 1846.

[1770] *The Bury and Norwich Post*, 24 March, 1847.

[1771] *Ibid.*, 7 April, 1847.

his offending in Norfolk. In 1872 he was convicted for larceny and imprisoned in Norwich for nine months.

Becoming an Accomplice Witness

Occasionally in the years immediately before and after the start of the Victorian era, the historic practice of offering immunity to an accomplice who was still at large, in exchange for their coming forward and incriminating the other perpetrators of a very serious crime, still occurred. For example, in December 1830 Thurlow Dering, a Norfolk JP, wrote to the Home Secretary about a nocturnal poaching by ten armed men in Stow. Gamekeepers and a local parish constable had sought to intervene, and the latter man had been shot dead. Although seven of the poachers had been committed to Swaffham Gaol for examination, it was thought that the killer was not among them. Dering felt that there was no hope of convicting the murderer(s) without accomplice evidence, and asked that a pardon be granted to anyone, apart from those who fired the fatal shots, who would provide information that would lead to the conviction of the latter. Such a pardon was authorized.[1772]

Similarly, in early 1833, in a Norfolk arson case in Mattishall, in which a barley stack had been fired, a reward of £100 and a free pardon from the King was offered to any: "Accomplice who shall give such Information and Evidence against the Principal Perpetrator or Perpetrators of the Crime, as may lead to a conviction."[1773] In like manner, and shortly after the accession of the new Queen, in January 1839, Thomas William Coke, the Earl of Leicester and a celebrated Norfolk agricultural reformer, wrote to the Home Office about a vicious crime in East Barsham: the elderly and frail Joseph Holman and his wife, who kept the White Horse public house there, had been savagely assaulted in their bed by five men armed with bludgeons, and robbed of £55, a watch, and a gun. Coke asked that a reward and free pardon be offered to any accomplice who might give information leading to the conviction of other members of the gang.[1774]

Much more commonly, those who turned Queen's evidence would already be in custody. Although this was often actively encouraged by the authorities, it was also something that detained individuals might suggest themselves. However, the mechanism by which they obtained clemency varied. Sometimes a potential witness who turned Queen's evidence would be identified prior to the committal process and examined before the magistrate on behalf of the Crown, as was the case with Joseph Cole (see above). After this, they would usually be kept in custody pending trial. At the hearing, prosecution counsel would apply to the judge for leave to admit the accomplice's testimony. If this was granted, the witness would be taken before the grand jury to give evidence, and then testify again at trial. Frequently, if the witness gave the evidence expected, duly incriminating his erstwhile colleagues,

---

[1772] TNA HO 64/1/117.

[1773] *The Norwich Mercury,* 16 February, 1833.

[1774] TNA HO 64/9/2.

he would not be prosecuted. If he resiled from his undertakings, a bill could swiftly be laid before the grand jury and a trial ensue, based on his earlier admissions.[1775]

For example, at a private committal hearing held by the Norwich magistrates at the Guildhall in September 1885, two men, one of them a "lad" named Knights and the other an older man named Frary, were accused of committing an "abominable crime" (sodomy).[1776] The town clerk, Mr Miller, appeared to prosecute on behalf of the police. "Upon Mr. Miller's application the prisoner Knights was allowed to leave the dock and give Queen's evidence against Frary."[1777]

However, sometimes, an accomplice might be recruited at the trial itself. In these circumstances, they would normally plead guilty to the crime that had brought them to court, give evidence for the prosecution, and then receive a reduced sentence.[1778] For example, in 1850 John Annison and William Thompson were tried at the Norfolk assizes, accused of stealing eight bushels of bran in Stokesby. At their arraignment, Thompson pleaded guilty, and then gave evidence against his accomplice, who was duly convicted. Subsequently, Thompson received six months' imprisonment, and his erstwhile partner in crime nine months in custody. Given Thompson's guilty plea, which must have been worth something on its own, this was not a very substantial reduction in sentence.[1779] More generously, in 1855, two men were indicted at the Norfolk quarter sessions in Norwich for breaking into a shop at night and stealing £5 worth of hams. At the start of proceedings, one of them, John Baldwin, pleaded guilty. He then testified against his accomplice, John Middleton, who was convicted by the trial jury. Baldwin received just six months' imprisonment, while Middleton was given four years' penal servitude with hard labour.[1780]

An even more generous disposal for an accomplice can be seen at the combined Suffolk and Norfolk assizes in November 1887, when William Wisken was one of two men accused of setting fire to an outbuilding at Occold in Suffolk. Although a labourer, he was legally represented, and pleaded guilty: "...having confessed his fault as soon as charged, he had materially aided in the conviction of the other prisoner". He received a "nominal" sentence of just one day's imprisonment. The other man, William Wright, although merely Wisken's aider and abettor, was convicted (in large part on his evidence) and sentenced to 18 months' imprisonment with hard labour.[1781]

1775 Bentley, *English Criminal Justice,* pp. 253-254.

1776 *The Bury and Norwich Post*, 7 April, 1841.

1777 *The Eastern Evening News,* 11 September, 1885.

1778 Bentley, *English Criminal Justice,* pp. 253-254.

1779 *The Bury and Norwich Post*, 10 April, 1850.

1780 *Ibid.*, 11 July, 1855.

1781 *Ibid.*, 22 November, 1887.

Character Evidence

The calling of character evidence by defendants was widespread, even among the large number who called no witnesses on issues of fact. Such witnesses would testify to the accused person's general good reputation in the community to suggest that it was unlikely that they would have committed a crime; this might encourage a not-guilty verdict. Even if they failed in this, establishing a good reputation during trial might result in a jury recommendation for mercy, or the judge or chairman feeling lenient, and a lesser punishment being imposed than would otherwise have been the case.

For example, in 1847, at the Norfolk assizes, Edmund Dixon, who had been indicted for an indecent assault on George Roberts, called three clergymen and seven other witnesses to give him a good character. "All stated, that they had known him for some years, and could testify to his moral habits." He was acquitted.[1782] Similarly, at the Norfolk quarter sessions in October 1874, a watchmaker from Diss was indicted for stealing live ducks from one Henry Bond. He called extensive evidence to his previous good character. Several gentlemen stated that he was a highly respectable tradesman, one saying that he would be happy to trust him with £1,000. This seems to have been influential. "After a momentary consultation, the Jury returned a verdict of not guilty."[1783]

Of course, even the best character evidence was no guarantee of an acquittal. In April 1843 there was considerable surprise when John Harper, a well-known auctioneer, was convicted at the Norfolk assizes for stealing cloth entrusted to him for sale by a Leeds manufacturer. Three local solicitors, two clergymen, and several other prominent citizens had given evidence of the general honesty and integrity of the prisoner without persuading the jury of his innocence. He was sentenced to seven years' transportation.[1784]

Circumstantial Evidence

Historically, English judges and juries had been nervous about criminal cases that were based solely on circumstantial evidence, especially, but not solely, those involving allegations of homicide. Sir Henry Hawkins thought that this attitude was mistaken, and that such evidence was the most reliable, and often the only, evidence available in serious crimes.[1785] Nevertheless, some of this anxiety appears to have seeped into popular consciousness. At the Norfolk assizes in 1851, the murderer Henry Groom was legally unrepresented. The trial judge thought, from the defendant's occasional interjections during the Crown's evidence, that he had convinced himself that, provided there was no eyewitness to the killing, he could

---

[1782] *The Norfolk Chronicle,* 10 April, 1847.

[1783] *The Bury and Norwich Post, and Suffolk Herald*, 27 October, 1874.

[1784] *The Norfolk Chronicle,* 7 April, 1843.

[1785] Hawkins, *Reminiscences,* p. 194.

not be convicted. This was, apparently, a "fatal delusion" held by many criminals.[1786] As this case shows, throughout the Victorian period, strong circumstantial evidence could found a conviction, even if unsupported by direct testimony, in murder as in other cases.

Similarly, in 1834 a "host of witnesses" gave circumstantial evidence into the murder of Hannah Mansfield in so "connected a chain" that her conviction was thought to have been almost certain.[1787] In like manner, at the Norfolk assizes in January 1886, John Thurston, a 30-year-old labourer, was found guilty of the wilful murder of the elderly Henry Springall at Hingham, the previous December, on purely circumstantial evidence.[1788]

At a more mundane level, at the Norfolk quarter sessions in 1838, George Whiterod and John Tell were convicted of stealing and killing a sheep near Scoulton, largely on circumstantial evidence. The two men were seen going towards the field where the animal was slaughtered, and a comb with the initials G.W. was subsequently found near the place where it had been killed. The clothes of the two men were found to be bloody, and mutton was discovered in their homes.[1789] Similarly, at the Norfolk assizes in February 1879, two youths, newly discharged from Ipswich Gaol, were prosecuted for burgling a police superintendent's house in Pulham St Mary on evidence that was "entirely circumstantial." The jury deliberated for some time, but eventually convicted. Perhaps unfortunately, in this case, 16-year-old Anthony Stewart and 17-year-old Charles Hill were legally unrepresented, although the prosecution was conducted by counsel. They had been released from prison in December, and immediately started to walk to Norwich, where they were arrested. They were apparently penniless when discharged, begging for food and shelter as they went. The following day, after the break-in, in which more than £20 in cash had been stolen, they were flush with a similar amount of money, having taken a carriage for the latter part of their journey. Their footprints "appeared" to be outside the targeted house, and a stolen bottle of sherry (now empty) was found abandoned on the way that they would have taken. A knife that "could" have been used to break open a window was also found in their possession. The youths unavailingly claimed that the money had been sewn inside their jackets, and so was not found when they were searched on admission to Ipswich gaol.[1790]

The increased Victorian willingness to secure convictions solely or primarily on circumstantial evidence probably reflected a more thorough pre-trial investigation and a lengthier trial process. Nevertheless, such evidence could still usually be explained away by advancing an alternative narrative that provided an innocent

[1786] *T he Bury and Norwich Post, and Suffolk Herald*, 30 July, 1851

[1787] *The Royal Cornwall Gazette*, 3 February, 1837.

[1788] *The Dundee Courier & Argus*, 25 January, 1886.

[1789] *The Bury and Norwich Post*, 11 July, 1838.

[1790] *The Ipswich Journal,* 11 February, 1879.

explanation for its presence, making convictions that were purely based on such evidence relatively unusual. As a result, it was more often used to bolster more direct evidence, such as eyewitness testimony or informal admissions.

Possession of Identifiable Stolen Goods

Being found in possession of identifiable stolen items shortly after an offence had been committed, was one of the most common forms of circumstantial evidence used to establish involvement in a property crime. For example, at the Norfolk quarter sessions in October 1843, Robert Childs, age 23, was accused of stealing a silk handkerchief from William Harmer of Mattishall. It appeared that the recently washed handkerchief had been hanging out to dry on a fence, along with other items, when it was missed. A short time later, it was found in the defendant's possession; he was then arrested. The handkerchief was produced and positively identified at trial by the prosecutor (Harmer). The jury convicted, and the court sentenced Childs to a month's imprisonment with hard labour.[1791]

The identical mass-produced goods of the growing industrial era could pose difficulties in this regard, lacking the individual features of their handmade predecessors. Nevertheless, distinctive wear and tear could provide a way around such problems. This extended to stolen coins. For example, one of the cases at the Thetford borough sessions in July 1850 involved the theft of a sixpence that had been put on a counter in a tavern to pay for beer, the suspect picking it up and using the same coin for his own purchase of ale. Fortunately for the prosecutor, a conviction was secured because the sixpence "being a remarkable one, was identified." (The defendant, William Hill, received six weeks' imprisonment with hard labour).[1792] The following year, at the Norfolk assizes, Thomas Stringer was even more unlucky when accused of a burglary at Foulsham during which two purses containing cash had been stolen. A neighbour later saw him burying something in his garden. When his house was searched, money was found, and it was also recovered from the garden, albeit no longer in the purses (presumably thrown away to avoid identification). It was Stringer's bad fortune that the victim could recognize some peculiar marks on three of the 30 farthings that he lost (along with some much more valuable coins). As a result, Stringer was convicted.[1793]

However, defence counsel (if present) would usually challenge such identifications vigorously. For example, in 1846 an ostler in the Green Dragon in Thetford whose watch was stolen by a colleague was grilled at borough sessions as to the accuracy of his identification of the timepiece which had subsequently been found in a Bury pawnbroker's shop. More particularly, he was asked whether he had given the number of the watch to the police before it was recovered, and what distinguishing

---

[1791] *The Norwich Mercury,* 21 October, 1843.

[1792] *The Bury and Norwich Post*, 30 October, 1839. *The Ipswich Journal*, 17 January, 1846. *The Bury and Norwich Post*, 10 April, 1850. *Ibid.*, 24 July, 1850.

[1793] *Ibid.*, 2 April, 1851.

marks it had.[1794] As a result, attempts at identifying stolen property were not necessarily successful. In 1859, when Archibald Brasnett of Mattishall in Norfolk was the victim of a burglary, during which a desk was forced and £2 in silver and copper coins stolen, it was the distinctive appearance of just one of the coins that initially helped make a prosecution viable: "Among the silver was a fourpenny piece, which prosecutor had had eighteen months. It was much flattened, and had on one side a rough appearance, as though it had been scraped. The word 'fourpence', and the date '1838', were distinguishable on the coin." However, doubts about this identification emerged, and the judge directed an acquittal.[1795] The identification of stolen farm animals was also regularly challenged. For example, at the Norfolk quarter sessions in July 1854, Henry Dack was prosecuted for stealing two pigs at Weston, some two months before one of them was, allegedly, found in his garden, near Swaffham. This did not satisfy the court: "the prosecutor spoke to its identity; but the jury acquitted the prisoner."[1796]

Experienced offenders were aware of the danger of stealing distinctive items. As an observer noted when discussing Norfolk shopliftings in 1846: "expert thieves do not allow private marks to remain on once they have gained possession of their booty."[1797] Sometimes they would entirely ignore goods that were unusual or specially marked, even if they were quite valuable. They would also dispose of identifiable stolen assets as quickly as they could. Ideally, this would be as far from the crime scene as possible. Nevertheless, they sometimes failed to do this successfully. For example, in 1892 William Robinson committed a burglary in an occupied house in Banham. He broke in using a mattock and, while the family was sleeping, rifled the ground floor, stealing cash and other items. He then seems to have made off on a pony stolen from the victim, which he galloped hard for several miles and then abandoned. Unfortunately, he had been seen within a mile of the house the previous day, and this, with several other factors, led the police to search his lodgings. There they discovered a distinctive pipe and pencil sharpener that could be identified as belonging to the prosecutor. Robinson was convicted at the Norfolk assizes and sentenced to three years' penal servitude.[1798]

Expert Evidence

Expert witnesses might be called by prosecution and/or defence at trial, although the latter case was comparatively unusual, not least because it was potentially quite expensive. If reluctant to attend a hearing, experts might be subpoenaed to do so. The expenses allowed by the court to professional witnesses summoned in this fashion were quite modest, and for much of the period not available for appearances

[1794] *The Ipswich Journal*, 17 January, 1846.

[1795] *The Norwich Mercury*, 7 December, 1859.

[1796] *The Bury and Norwich Post*, 5 July, 1854.

[1797] *The Ipswich Journal*, 14 March, 1846.

[1798] *The Bury and Norwich Post*, 22 March, 1892.

in the summary courts. In 1875 Dr Frederic Manby spent seven days at the assizes in Norwich after being subpoenaed, waiting to give evidence, and was paid just £8 17s, or about 25 shillings a day.[1799] A huge range of matters could be the subject of expert testimony, provided the courts felt that they were outside the normal realm of jury or magisterial competence and that the tendered witness had special expertise, and so was deemed to be *peritus* in the subject.[1800] For example, at the Norfolk quarter sessions held at Walsingham in November 1851, Thomas Vurley, a silversmith, was called to give evidence in a case involving uttering false half-crowns to the effect that that the coins involved were counterfeit.[1801]

Experts might also be called at summary forums, but this was quite rare. In 1874 the RSPCA called several distinguished experts at the Norwich Police Court to support a charge of cruelty to dogs, allegedly committed during medical experiments. The defendants called their own (less eminent) medical witnesses to prove that their behaviour was justifiable.[1802] Similarly, in November 1888, at the Blofield petty sessions, a farmer and several of his workers were summonsed by an RSPCA inspector for ill-treating bullocks. Both called expert witnesses, not least because it was clearly a test case.[1803]

By far the most common single form of expert evidence was medical testimony about human beings. In the early 1840s three in four Metropolitan homicide trials had a medical witness, whether a surgeon, physician, apothecary, or midwife. By the late 1840s the frequency had grown to nine in ten.[1804] Norfolk was broadly similar, if slightly behind the capital in this regard. For example, in 1833, when Mary Wright was belatedly suspected of murdering her husband and father with arsenic, their bodies were dug up and examined by the physician Charles Buck in the chancel of Wighton church. Their stomachs were then removed and sent to Mr Bell, a chemist at Wells-next-the-sea. He used four tests to "establish" that they contained arsenic. Bell subsequently gave evidence to this effect at Wright's trial at assizes, which resulted in her conviction. The prosecution also called Buck, who described the husband's death (having attended the sick man), and John Crosse, a surgeon from Norwich. The latter gave what appears, in practice, to have been psychiatric evidence and testified that the defendant showed signs of lunacy.[1805]

At the Norwich assizes in March 1869, Francis Clare, a shoemaker, was indicted for murdering his wife, Ann, the previous October. She had been found with her

---

[1799] Anon., "Medical Witnesses," p. 682.

[1800] Per Russell CJ in *R* v. *Silverlock* (1894) 2 QB 766.

[1801] *The Bury and Norwich Post: Or, Suffolk and Norfolk Telegraph, Essex, Cambridge, & Ely Intelligencer*, 2 November, 1831.

[1802] Wiener, *Reconstructing,* p. 65. *The Norfolk Chronicle*, 9 December, 1874.

[1803] *Ibid.,* 26 November, 1888.

[1804] Eigen, "Lesion," p. 430.

[1805] *The Bury and Norwich Post*, 27 March, 1833.

throat cut and a razor by her body. The surgeon called by the prosecution suggested that the dead woman's wound could not have been self-inflicted. Defence counsel argued that the death was a case of suicide, stressing the absence of noise or other evidence of a disturbance at the relevant time (circumstantial evidence), and the jury, eventually, returned a not-guilty verdict.[1806] More successfully for the Crown, at the Norwich assizes in 1886, George Harmer, a plasterer, was convicted of murdering Henry Last by striking him repeatedly on the head with a plasterer's hammer. At trial, an expert medical witness matched the indentations found on the victim's skull to the hammer (which had been recovered).[1807]

Cause of death in homicide cases was an important field for expert medical evidence. For example, in December 1885 Robert Cozens, a King's Lynn porter, gave himself up to the local police after (seemingly) killing his paramour, Mary Chilvers. The parties lived together in the town, and apparently quarrelled, after which Cozens hit Chilvers, following which she died. The police found her dead in bed with a black eye.[1808] The ensuing January, Cozens was indicted for manslaughter at the county assizes. However, a post-mortem had not been able to establish any connection between Chilvers' injuries and her death. The jury acquitted of the homicide offence but convicted Cozens of common assault, for which he was sent to prison for six weeks with hard labour.[1809]

The Victorian period also saw the rapid rise of expert testimony from doctors and the emerging profession of alienists when insanity was in issue at trial, as was the case with Mary Wright. This was not confined to homicide cases. By the 1840s medical witnesses gave testimony in half the trials involving a property offence in which insanity was raised and 90 percent of those that concerned assault.[1810] (Of course, it was only rarely raised in such cases).

However, the partisan nature of expert evidence in the common-law system was already occasioning concern. Baron Bramwell, summing up in a murder trial in 1856, expressed very negative views about psychiatric expert witnesses, believing that the jury were as competent to form a correct opinion on matters of this kind as anybody else.[1811] In the 1870s, Sir George Jessel, the Master of the Rolls, was openly distrustful of experts of all types, seeing them as biased to the side that called them and paid their fees.[1812] This would become a long-lasting complaint.

[1806] *The Norfolk Chronicle,* 27 March, 1869. Meeres, *Norwich Murders,* pp. 50-53.

[1807] *The Dundee Courier*, 23 November, 1886. *The Ipswich Journal*, 14 December, 1886.

[1808] *The Bury and Norwich Post*, 8 December, 1885.

[1809] *The Ipswich Journal*, 23 January, 1886.

[1810] Eigen, "Lesion," p. 430.

[1811] Smith, "Victorian controversy," p. 70.

[1812] Lord *Abinger* v. *Ashton*, (1873) 17 LR Eq 358 and *Thorn* v. *Worthing Skating Rink Co.* (1876) 6 Ch D 415.

Confession Evidence

Out-of-court admissions or confessions of guilt, even if uncorroborated, whether made to laymen, police officers, or JPs could be adduced at trial and found a conviction on their own (unlike the situation in Scotland). In Norfolk this was to become important in a case from 1869. Many years earlier, in June 1851, the dismembered body-parts of an unidentified woman were found scattered around Norwich. The remains were gathered and deposited at the Guildhall, where they were examined by surgeons.[1813] At the start of 1869, William Sheward, by then aged 57, went to the Carter Street Police Station in London and confessed to killing his wife, Martha, in Norwich some 18 years earlier, identifying her as the source of the body parts, and saying that his conscience had plagued him ever since: "I have kept the secret for years, but I can keep it no longer." Liaison with the Norwich police followed, and Sheward was charged on his own confession with murder. He was brought to Norwich and appeared before magistrates. Evidence was called establishing that Sheward's wife had disappeared in 1851. Relatives stated that the prisoner had said that she had left Norwich for a time. At the city assizes in March, defence counsel contended that the defendant was "labouring under delusions when he made the confession." Even so, the jury convicted, after three-quarters of an hour of deliberation. Sheward was duly executed. (He made full admissions again, just prior to being hanged.)[1814]

The absence of many modern forms of forensic evidence encouraged the use of admissions to secure convictions. However, well before the Victorian era, confessions had to be "free and voluntary" to be admissible; those obtained by the hope of advantage or a fear of prejudice had been long excluded, on the basis that they were potentially unreliable, this rule being clearly enunciated by a senior judge in 1783.[1815] (Cases from both the Old Bailey and provincial assizes suggest that the rule was at least a decade old even then.)

Throughout the nineteenth century, threats or inducements could lead to any resulting confessions being rendered inadmissible and this rule was often interpreted very strictly. Indeed, in 1845 the barrister W. Forsyth complained that the "slightest inducement," even if it was of the "most trivial nature," would lead to a statement's being ruled out.[1816] Some courts excluded admissions because a suspect had been told by a JP that it would be "better" for him to confess.[1817] A late Victorian example of such strictness is the decision in *R* v. *Thompson* in 1893, which involved a confession made by the prisoner in an embezzlement case. Prior to his admissions, the prosecutor admitted that he had had an interview with one

---

1813 *The Norfolk Chronicle,* 21 June, 1851.

1814 *Ibid.,* 2 January, 1869. *Ibid.,* 27 March, 1869.

1815 *The King* v. *Warickshall* (1783) 1 Leach 263.

1816 *Eighth Report,* p. 253.

1817 Wesley MacNeil Oliver, "Magistrates' Examinations, Police Interrogations, and Miranda-Like Warnings in the Nineteenth Century," *Tulane Law Review*, vol. 81, no. 3 (2007), p. 777.

of the prisoner's siblings and observed to him, "It will be the right thing for your brother to make a statement". The same witness was also not prepared to swear that he did not go further and say that it would "be better for him to make a clean breast of it." The details of this interview were then communicated to the prisoner, who later made admissions.[1818] It was contended by the prisoner's counsel at the Westmorland quarter sessions that these statements amounted to inducements to confess held out by a person in authority, so that they were inadmissible. This was rejected by the court but upheld by the Court of Crown Cases Reserved. At the latter hearing, Mr Justice Cave was sceptical about the value of informal (out-of-court) admissions generally: "I always suspect these confessions, which are supposed to be the offspring of penitence and remorse, and which nevertheless are repudiated by the prisoner at the trial." He thought it especially remarkable that they were usually provided only when the other prosecution evidence was not very strong.

More specifically to Norfolk, at the county assizes in August 1838, John Bennet was accused of stealing chickens, eggs, and hops at Attlebridge. However, he was acquitted at trial "in consequence of the prisoner's wife having been promised that he should not be prosecuted if he confessed, and there being no other evidence than his confession."[1819]

Four years later, at the same forum, ten-year-old George Barber was accused of murdering an eight- or nine-year-old boy by throwing him into the river Waveney, where he drowned. (Barber had eaten one of the cakes that the younger boy was due to sell, and the latter had threatened to tell his parents.) The coroner's inquisition found it to be murder, and that Barber was responsible, so that he was committed to the county gaol to await trial. The case against the boy was very thin, largely consisting of informal admissions that had been "extorted" by a local parish constable, apparently by threatening to run him through with a hot poker. Unsurprisingly, at trial, these were deemed inadmissible, and an acquittal returned.[1820]

However, at county quarter sessions and petty sessions the absence of professional judges and (often) legal representation may have led to the rule being quietly ignored on some occasions. To consider a case from Suffolk in 1866, Walter Turp, a 17-year-old from Pentlow, was charged with stealing a watch from his father, Samuel (Walter lived with an aunt). When the watch could not be found, the police were involved. One PC Edwards said he looked for the youth on a farm, and took him to his father, who was in an adjoining field. When the constable said to Walter, "If you tell us all about it he [the father] will let you off, the prisoner said, 'I hid it in my Aunt's garden.'" Even so, Walter was subsequently prosecuted and convicted, receiving three months' imprisonment, despite the illegal inducement to confess.[1821]

[1818] *Regina* v. *Thompson* (1893) 2 QB 12.

[1819] *The Bury and Norwich Post*, 8 August, 1838.

[1820] *The Times*, 8 April, 1842. *The Standard,* 13 November, 1841. *The Ipswich Journal,* 9 April, 1842.

[1821] *The Suffolk Free Press,* 15 February, 1866.

However, and as today, even if an out-of-court confession was admitted, it was not conclusive of guilt, and did not preclude a contested trial. At her poisoning hearing at the Norfolk assizes in 1833, Mary Wright pleaded not guilty despite having earlier made a full confession to the crime (she was convicted).[1822]

[1822] *The Bury and Norwich Post: Or, Suffolk and Norfolk Telegraph, Essex, Cambridge, & Ely Intelligencer*, 27 March, 1833.

Chapter 13: Punishment: The Death Penalty

Introduction

At the start of the eighteenth century, the English penal system was focused on execution. By the beginning of the nineteenth century, it was dominated by transportation (though for many their sentence was spent on a hulk moored in English waters) supplemented by the death penalty for graver crimes and imprisonment for less serious matters. By the start of the Victorian period the death penalty had almost slipped out of the equation other than as a punishment for murder, and by the middle of the Victorian period transportation had also disappeared. This left penal imprisonment as the dominant form of punishment for all middle-ranking and serious crimes other than (some cases of) murder, a position that it still holds today. For a few offences this was supplemented, in restrictive circumstances, by corporal punishment, especially when juveniles or some serious adult crimes (often involving violence or immorality) were involved. Lesser offences were punished with fiscal penalties, but, even here, short custodial sentences were usually stipulated in lieu of payment of a fine. Thus, the workhorse of the Victorian penal system was initially transportation, whether served at home or abroad, until this was replaced by custodial sentences, the latter being bifurcated into shorter sentences of ordinary imprisonment and longer sentences of penal servitude. This chapter will consider capital punishment, while transportation, both forms of custodial sentence, and lesser or less significant punishments, such as flogging, fines, and being bound over to keep the peace, will be dealt with in the two following chapters.

Capital Punishment

Traditionally England had had greater recourse to capital punishment than most of its Continental neighbours, and this continued into the nineteenth century, even as the overall number of Englishmen being executed fell. As Sir Robert Peel candidly observed in the House of Commons, "Capital Punishments are more frequent, and the criminal law more severe, on the whole, in this country than in any country in the world." The Committee of the Society for the Diffusion of Information on the Subject of Capital Punishments claimed that in 1831 France, with a population twice that of England and Wales, executed only 25 people, while 52 were hanged in the latter, giving France a quarter of its execution rate. It alleged that the rate in Prussia during the decade ending in 1827 had been even lower, being only an eighth of that found in England.[1823]

In part this recourse to execution reflected English faith in the value of deterrence by draconian example and a fear that, in the words of an Ely judge in 1819, "if we diminish the terror of house-breakers, the terror of the [country's] innocent inhabitants must be increased." It was a rational, if possibly misguided, calculation, not motivated by what Charles Cottu called "indignation against the crime itself."

[1823] *The Sussex Advertiser*, 24 August, 1835.

It was also a relatively cheap disposal, the imposition of which did not require a sophisticated bureaucracy to administer.

Nevertheless, by the early nineteenth century, the great majority of English death sentences were not carried out. From 1800 to 1835, an average of about 60 people (typically 57 males and three females) were hanged each year in England and Wales. This was half the number of executions each year in the eighteenth century, despite the substantial increase in population. As Charles Cottu noted in 1822, were this not the case, the country's gallows would become vast charnel-houses, and the whole nation would be horrified. Instead, with "the exception of murder, and occasionally rape, or forgery, or of uttering forged banknotes, the punishment is always mitigated by the judge." His list of exceptions was too restrictive for the 1820s – men occasionally went to the gallows for other crimes, such as horse theft. However, he was correct about the selectivity of judges when it came to imposing death.[1824]

By the 1830s there was no longer widespread support for the imposition of the death penalty for most crimes, apart from murder. In a House of Commons debate in March 1832, the MP William Ewart noted that in cases involving potential capital penalties for property crimes, it was apparent that "prosecutors trembled at the punishment, that Juries hesitated, that Judges paused, and that guilt escaped unpunished, or [was] rather rewarded with impunity."[1825] For this reason the withdrawal of some offences from the reach of the gallows had comparatively little impact on the rate of execution nationwide.

In 1800 well over 200 criminal offences, many of them extremely arcane, were, at least theoretically, capital under the so-called 'Bloody Code'. Much of this code continued in force for the next quarter of a century. However, in a series of statutes, the first of which was passed as early as 1808, but most of which were enacted between 1825 and 1861, Parliament abolished the death penalty as a punishment for nearly all crimes. By the time that Queen Victoria came to the throne, the fruits of decades of criminal-law reform were already apparent. Most of the Bloody Code had already been abolished, and what was left was living on borrowed time.

In 1808, under Samuel Romilly's guidance, the death penalty had been removed for pickpocketing and some other crimes. In 1827 all clergyable felonies were made non-capital (long the reality in practice), and many non-clergyable crimes (those giving no reprieve for first offenders) joined them in the same decade. Others followed in ensuing years. In 1832 the death penalty was abolished for theft, counterfeiting, and forgery (except of wills and powers of attorney). The death penalty for non-fatal shooting, stabbing, wounding with intent, and abortion was abolished by the Offences Against the Person Act 1837. Housebreaking was no longer a capital offence after 1833, while non-violent burglary ceased to be a capital

---

1824 Cottu, *Administration,* p. 68.

1825 Hansard HC Deb 27 March 1832 vol. 11 col. 948.

crime in 1837.[1826] In 1861, statute (24 & 25 Vict c. 94 to c. 100) reduced the number of potentially capital civilian crimes to just five: murder, treason, espionage, arson in royal dockyards, and piracy with violence. (It was mandatory for treason and murder unless commuted.)[1827]

To a significant (but not total) degree, such legislation was catching up with existing judicial practice. Relatively few executions had been carried out for some capital offences for many years prior to abolition. Death sentences, where passed, had often merely been "recorded" pursuant to the Judgment of Death Act 1823. This statute had accepted the reality that a post-circuit recommendation of pardon by a judge of assizes was always accepted by government, and so saved on bureaucracy.[1828] Trial judges were allowed to enter a verdict of "death recorded" in capital cases, other than murder and treason, where they foresaw that a reprieve would otherwise be forthcoming. This was a death sentence in name only. It could not lead to execution, not least because such a sentence had to be delivered orally in court. Effectively, the Act allowed judges to enter a death sentence on the court record, but automatically commute it to imprisonment or transportation without referring the pardon to higher authority. This sentence became progressively less common as statute reduced the number of potentially capital offences but continued in existence until 1861. Even if a death sentence was not "recorded," but formally passed in court, it could still be (and often was) reprieved following petition prior to execution.

In practice, within a year or so of the accession of the Queen, almost the only people to be executed in England were hanged for murder or, in a tiny number of cases, attempted murder.[1829] For example, in 1855 50 people nationally were sentenced to death: 11 for murder; ten for attempted murder; 20 for sodomy, two for burglary with violence; five for robbery and wounding, and two for arson against dwelling houses. However, only seven of the 50 were hanged, all of them for murder.[1830]

As the above figures also suggest, even those found guilty of murder might be reprieved. Prior to the Victorian era, the likelihood of this occurring, even on condition of transportation for life, had been relatively small. Between 1752 and 1832, about 8 percent of those convicted nationally under the Murder Act 1752 escaped the noose.[1831] It was much more common in Victorian England. On one assessment, by the mid-Victorian period an average of more than 40 percent of

---

[1826] Statement of Capital Crimes in 1830, for which Punishment of Death Had Been Abolished; Commitments and Executions for Burglary, 1832-37.

[1827] Bentley, *English Criminal Justice,* p. 3.

[1828] Simon Devereaux, "Peel, Pardon, and Punishment: The Recorder's Report Revisited" in Simon Devereaux and Paul Griffiths (eds.), *Penal Practice and Culture, 1500–1900* (London: Palgrave Macmillan, 2004), pp. 258-284.

[1829] Bentley, *English Criminal Justice,* p. 12.

[1830] *The Hampshire Telegraph and Sussex Chronicle,* 4 February, 1857.

[1831] Sarah Tarlow and Emma Battell Lowman, *Harnessing the Power of the Criminal Corpse* (London: Palgrave Macmillan, 2018), p. 94.

death sentences imposed for murder were not carried out.[1832] By the end of the century, the proportion had reached almost half.[1833] Thus, of the 17 people convicted of murder in England and Wales in 1860, 12 went to the gallows, but five were reprieved in favour of penal servitude for life (four cases) or ten years (one case). Those executed had killed during the commission of robberies or other property crimes (four instances), as part of domestic and personal murders with little or no provocation and/or considerable premeditation, or had murdered a superior officer in the armed services (always viewed very seriously).[1834] By contrast, women who murdered their new-born illegitimate offspring and murderers of doubtful sanity (even if not found to be insane by a jury) might receive clemency. Reprieves were also sometimes granted because of provocation, such as adultery committed by the spouse of a wife-killer, even if this had not led to a finding of manslaughter at trial. (The incidence of such cases declined towards the end of the era as views about the domestic ideal changed.)[1835]

More specifically to Norfolk, and taking the period from 1805 to 1867, it seems that nine of 27 people convicted of murder in the county, a third, were reprieved from execution.[1836] The percentage had increased to almost half (about the national proportion) by the end of the century. For an example can be considered a case from 1841. After Charlotte Yaxley was convicted of murdering while intoxicated an infant girl by drowning, the trial judge at the Norfolk assizes noted that it was rare that those convicted of such a crime were not executed. However, in the instant case, he decided to make an exception. Instead, she would be transported for life. As a result, it was reported that "sentence of death was recorded" (i.e., it was automatically reprieved), although in reality he may have temporarily reprieved her while recommending such an outcome to the Home Secretary.[1837] Yaxley was one of 180 convicts who left England for Australia on the *Garland Grove* in June 1841.[1838]

Less than a decade later, in 1850, George Baldry, a 35-year-old labourer, attacked the 14-year-old daughter of the family with which he lodged at Thurlton, striking her repeatedly on the head with a hammer, apparently because she refused to get up in the morning. There was no history of antipathy towards this child or evidence of any other motive for the assault. The girl was mortally wounded but able to give a deposition before dying in hospital.[1839] Baldry appeared to be a man of "weak

[1832] Wiener, "Sad Story," p. 178.

[1833] Weiner, "Convicted Murderers," p. 110.

[1834] *Judicial Statistics, 1860,* pp. xix-xx.

[1835] Wiener, "Sad Story," p. 178.

[1836] John Wallis, "Representations of Justice Executed at Norwich Castle: A Comparative Analysis of Execution Reports in the Norfolk Chronicle and Bury and Norwich Post, 1805-1867," *Law, Crime and History*, vol. 3, no. 2 (2013), p. 35.

[1837] *The Ipswich Journal*, 10 April, 1841.

[1838] Meeres, *Yarmouth Murders,* p. 47.

[1839] *The Lady's Newspaper*, 17 August, 1850.

mind" but was deemed capable of knowing right from wrong (the test for sanity), and so was convicted of murder at the Norfolk assizes in March 1851.[1840] Even so, his death sentence was subsequently respited as doubts about his mental state persisted.[1841] It appears that it was eventually commuted to transportation for life.

Similarly, in 1890 Elijah Snelling, a 38-year-old-man, murdered his mother-in-law, Maria Brown, in a lane in Pulham St Mary, near Diss.[1842] He was convicted at trial, and a date set for his execution. Snelling had a reputation as a violent man, and it appears that some years earlier he had been convicted of the attempted murder of his wife and sentenced to 12 months' imprisonment with hard labour. Nevertheless, he was respited shortly before being hanged, and the sentence was subsequently commuted to penal servitude for life, perhaps due to doubts about his state of mind.[1843]

Sometimes, such a commutation was anticipated by the judge. For example, at the Norfolk assizes in July 1893, after Sarah Bligh, a domestic servant, was convicted of the murder of her child, Isaac, at Holme Hale, but strongly recommended to mercy by the jury, Mr Justice Mathew, did not put on the black cap when passing sentence of death, which sentence was subsequently commuted.[1844]

In theory such reprieves could be granted right up until the moment a convict was hanged, although this was exceptionally rare. Nevertheless, in 1846, because of this possibility, and considering low-level attempts to petition for mercy on behalf of Samuel Yarham, on the basis that the evidence adduced against him at trial was insufficient to justify a conviction, the governor of Norwich gaol took the precaution of informing the Home Secretary the time of the last train from London that would arrive in the city before Yarham was hanged.[1845]

The Incidence of Execution

Despite legal change, the number of executions nationally was stable during the first three decades of the nineteenth century, even increasing briefly after the Napoleonic Wars ended in 1815, albeit that population increase meant that the per capita incidence fell slightly. However, the early 1830s saw a small decline in executions, while the year immediately before the start of the new Queen's reign saw a drastic fall. In 1834 there were 35 executions, and in 1835 34. By contrast, in 1836 there were 17, and in 1837 just eight, while 1838 saw the number reduced to six. Some stability then ensued, with 1839 seeing 11 hangings and 1840 eight

---

[1840] *Bell's Life in London and Sporting Chronicle*, 30 March, 1851.

[1841] *John Bull*, 7 April, 1851.

[1842] *The Daily Gazette For Middlesbrough*, 9 January, 1890.

[1843] Anon., *Trial and Sentence of Elijah Snelling for the Wilful Murder of his Mother-In-Law*, (Norwich, 1890), pp. 1-2. *The Bury and Norwich Post*, 25 March, 1890. Mackie, *Norfolk Annals*, vol. 2, p. 406.

[1844] *The Norfolk Chronicle*, 18 July, 1893.

[1845] *The Morning Post*, 13 April, 1846.

executions. Thereafter, there was some variation, with a maximum number of 17 in 1849 and just five in 1854. Numbers would not breach 20 until 1861, and then only barely, and merely for two years. In the period between 1837 and 1861, a total of 350 people (318 men and 32 women) were executed in England and Wales, making an average of about 11 a year. By contrast, there 408 executions in the years from 1828 to 1836 alone, an average of 51 per annum.[1846] This retreat from execution, during the period just before and after the start of the Victorian era, has been termed the most sudden and important development in English penal history.[1847]

In Norfolk, in the first decade of the nineteenth century, 13 people were executed; in the second, some 11 were hanged; 15 met this fate in the third decade, and 12 in the fourth. However, the fifth decade, 1841 to 1851, saw just three people go to the gallows (a figure that was matched in the not dissimilar counties of Suffolk, Warwickshire, Lincolnshire, and Wiltshire).[1848] Victorian Norfolk witnessed just 16 executions (two more took place just weeks before the Queen's accession and one just a month or so after her death), and so averaged about one hanging every four years.

As some of the figures suggest, the change is largely explained by the de facto and de jure end to the use of execution for offences other than murder or (very rarely) attempted murder in the late 1830s. As late as the years from 1828 to 1836, slightly under 29 percent of all 408 executions in England and Wales were for murder (and somewhat under 3 percent for attempted murder), so that just over 68 percent were for non-homicide offences, with 15 percent being for arson, and numerous other crimes, whether highway robbery, burglary, horse theft, rape, and sodomy, *inter alia*, also being represented in the total. By contrast, all but five of the 350 people hanged between 1837 and 1868 were executed for murder, the exceptions being for attempted murder (which remained a capital crime until 1861).

These developments were reflected in Norfolk, though the number of hangings was below the national average, which was boosted by the high incidence of executions found in large urban areas such as London. In the 37 years from 1800 to 1836, 48 people went to the gallows, only six (an eighth) of them for murder, and the final years of this almost four-decade period saw no diminution in the annual average number of executions being carried out in the county. By contrast, between 1837 and 1868, just ten executions were conducted in the county, all for murder or attempted murder. The execution of James Clarke in 1835 for setting fire to wheat stacks proved to be the last non-murder-related hanging in the county.[1849]

[1846] http://www.capitalpunishmentuk.org/1837.html, last accessed 1 June, 2022. *The Hampshire Telegraph and Sussex Chronicle,* 4 February, 1857.

[1847] Gatrell, *Hanging Tree,* pp. 8-10.

[1848] *Criminal Offenders...1850* (1851), p. ix.

[1849] Wallis, "Representations," p. 35.

Capital sentences for offences other than murder would continue to be passed during the first two decades or so of the Victorian era, but they would be commuted. Thus, nationally, of 50 people who were sentenced to hang in 1855, 11 had been convicted of murder, ten of attempted murder, 20 of sodomy, five of robbery and wounding, two of burglary with violence, and two of arson committed against dwelling houses. However, only seven of them went to the gallows, all for murder.[1850] More specifically to Norfolk, in April 1837, at the Lent Assizes in Norwich, Goodyer Long was capitally convicted of bestiality with a female donkey but reprieved a week before he was due to be hanged.[1851] (He was sent to the hulks *Leviathan* and *York* but not, it seems, transported, returning to his native Norfolk after six or so years, and dying there in 1853.) Similarly, at the Norfolk assizes in April 1839 William Allday, aged 70; Samuel Page, aged 22; and William Page, aged 42, were convicted of shooting and wounding a gamekeeper. Although all were initially sentenced to death, this was subsequently commuted to transportation for life.[1852]

Awaiting Execution

While awaiting execution after conviction, usually for a period of up to two weeks, the condemned person would, of course, be held in prison, where he might receive spiritual assistance. Norwich Castle gaol and its successor (after 1887) at nearby Plumstead had its own chaplain, and prior to a hanging outside ministers might be called in as well, as was the case with Henry Groom in 1851.[1853] This was especially common for those who were not Anglicans. Thus, Robert Goodale behaved in an exemplary fashion while awaiting death in 1885 for murdering his wife and received the ministrations of a Baptist minister (his denomination).[1854]

Many, but not all, condemned prisoners availed themselves of the spiritual support available, even if they were initially reluctant to do so. At first, when James Rush was asked whether he would take advantage of the services provided by the Reverend James Brown, the prison chaplain, he replied, "Oh no not at all. I can do without him while I am here." However, even Rush attended divine service in the castle chapel on the Sunday morning prior to his execution. During the delivery of the sermon, which was preached. by Brown, he appeared to be in a deeply meditative mood.[1855] Nevertheless, such behaviour was not universal. Prior to his execution at Norwich in 1875, Henry Webster "paid no particular attention to the ministrations of the chaplain."[1856]

[1850] *The Hampshire Telegraph and Sussex Chronicle,* 4 February, 1857.

[1851] TNA HO 17/75/58. *The Bury and Norwich Post,* 12 April, 1837.

[1852] TNA HO 17/80/100.

[1853] *The Ipswich Journal*, 23 August, 1851.

[1854] *The Singleton Argus* (New South Wales), 27 January, 1886. James Berry, *My Experiences as an Executioner* (London: Percy Lund, 1892), pp. 64-65.

[1855] Anon., *Stanfield Hall,* pp. 1-10.

[1856] *The Nottinghamshire Guardian*, 5 May, 1876.

As in previous centuries, there could be heavy pressure on those awaiting execution to confess to their crimes, if they had not already done so by pleading guilty, so reassuring the public that justice had been served. Outside the county, the alleged murderer Dr. William Palmer, challenged the system in this regard. He went to the scaffold in Stafford declaring that he was innocent of poisoning Cook (the victim) with strychnine. Press reports of the time devoted much space to the efforts made to persuade him to change his mind, one observer noting that from the time of his sentence to the moment he ascended the scaffold Palmer was "entreated, implored day by day, almost hour by hour, to confess his crimes, not to God, but to man." There was considerable public concern when he failed to do so. Some even worried that it might undermine confidence in jury verdicts.[1857] Similarly, newspapers in Norfolk carefully noted the admissions made by those due to hang for murder who had been found guilty after a contested trial, such as John Thurston's post-conviction acknowledgement of the justice of his sentence in 1886.[1858]

The Mechanics of Execution

At the start of the Victorian era, execution of those from the county who had been capitally convicted at the Norfolk assizes normally took place on Castle Hill in Norwich, while those found guilty at the city of Norwich assizes were hanged at the nearby Castle/City Ditches. Both sets of gallows were open to public view. For example, at the Norfolk assizes in March 1854, held before Lord Chief Baron Parke, 21-year-old William Thompson was tried and convicted of the murder of Lorenzi Beha at Tittleshall the previous year. He was sentenced to death and hanged on Castle Hill the following month. In 1822, in the first executions for some years following convictions secured at the city assizes, James Smith and Henry Carter were convicted of burglary (then still a capital offence) and executed at the City Ditches.[1859] Both executions attracted thousands of spectators.

The gallows used for public executions would be set up each time and stored between hangings. Those used to hang James Rush in 1848 were described as a "clumsy and inconvenient structure, as badly arranged and as unsightly in appearance as anyone could conceive. It seemed to be the work of a most unskilful designer."[1860] Sometimes, they were painted black or covered in black cloth. The pinioned convict would ascend a ladder, be attached to the apparatus by a noose, then stood on a trap door which would be released by the removal of a bolt, launching him into eternity.

During the early decades of the Victorian period, the "short-drop" method of hanging inherited from the late eighteenth century was still employed in Norfolk,

---

[1857] Burney, "A Poisoning," p. 59.

[1858] *The Times*, 11 February, 1886, p. 10.

[1859] *The Morning Post*, 29 August, 1822.

[1860] Anon., *A Full Report of the Trial of J.B. Rush for the murder of Mr. Jermy and his son* (London: W. Clark, 1849), p. 98.

as it was in other English counties and at Newgate. Although it was better than the drop-less hanging that had gone before, prisoners executed in this manner often only fell between 12 and 18 inches when the trap door was released, something that meant that a broken neck and immediate death or unconsciousness was by no means certain, or even likely. Most were still strangled, and some lasted several minutes before they expired. In William Thompson's case (see above) a particularly slow strangulation ensued, so that his "struggles continued five minutes."[1861] Charles Daines, hanged at Norwich in April 1839, was only slightly more fortunate, convulsing violently for at least three minutes.[1862] In 1851 Henry Groom's struggles were also "very long and severe." Others were luckier, and either dead or at least unconscious rather faster. Much depended on the skill of the hangman, the quality of the rope used, and the weight and musculature (around the neck) of the person to be executed. One witness to the 1886 Committee on Capital Punishment recalled that when Calcraft had been executioner convicts did not die instantaneously because he used the then normal short drop, of not more than two feet; in one case, "the culprit was strangled, and I saw a twitching for seven or eight minutes". Apparently, this started violently but subsided until just the convict's hands moved.[1863]

More than one person could be hanged at a time by this means, although this was very unusual in Norfolk, as in most other mainly rural counties. Nevertheless, two double executions were conducted in the county shortly before the Victorian era. In August 1835 the middle-aged Frances Billing and Catherine Frarey were hanged on Castle Hill, Norwich, for murder by poisoning. They held hands while on the scaffold and went through the trap door together. Billings had ascended the gallows with the "greatest firmness", but Frarey had to be helped up. In this case, death seems to have occurred swiftly for both women.[1864] Similarly, John Smith and George Timms were hanged together for murder in 1837. Their execution cortège came out of the castle at noon, headed by the high sheriff's javelin men. Smith, who was unwell with consumption, was physically assisted to the scaffold: "After the bolt was drawn and the bodies swung round, a piercing cry of horror rose from the dense mass of people [spectators] of both sexes."[1865]

[1861] *The Norfolk Chronicle*, 23 March, 1854.

[1862] *The Morning Chronicle*, 2 May, 1839.

[1863] Anon., *Minutes of evidence taken before the committee appointed to inquire into the execution of capital sentences. At 8, Richmond Terrace, Whitehall. Tuesday, 16 March, 1886* (London: 1886), p. 3.

[1864] *The Bristol Mercury*, 15 August, 1835.

[1865] *John Bull*, 8 May, 1837.

Crowds

Large crowds might attend public executions. In 1835 Billing and Frarey's deaths attracted between 20,000 and 30,000 spectators, half of them women.[1866] Females seem to have been particularly drawn to such events, even when they did not share the gender of the condemned person. They apparently made up a majority of the more than 10,000 people present to watch Henry Groom hang in 1851, many of them "decked out in holiday attire."[1867] It was not just local people who would attend such events. In April 1837, after John Smith and George Timms were convicted of the murder of Hannah Manfield, large numbers of would-be spectators mistakenly arrived in Norwich from its environs and further afield a week early. An account of the hanging, and of the condemned men's behaviour on the gallows, along with their "last dying words," was already on sale in the streets.[1868] (The capital sentence was carried out at the end of the same month.)[1869] In April 1846, after Samuel Yarham was executed on Castle Hill for the murder of Harriet Candler, up to 30,000 spectators were present. Some 800 people had come from Wymondham alone, in a single train, to view the proceedings, so that it was necessary to use bullock trucks to transport them.[1870]

Such crowds occasioned increasing concern, in Norfolk as elsewhere in England, as the nineteenth century advanced. Some observers claimed that their members usually (and increasingly) came from the lowest classes in the city or wider county and behaved in a disorderly and raucous manner. At John Self's execution in 1841 it was claimed that, as usual at such events, "all sorts of abandoned characters" attended and thoroughly enjoyed the occasion, rather than being overawed by it, although most of the crowd apparently behaved with reasonable decorum.[1871] In 1846 almost all business in the city was suspended on the morning before Samuel Yarham's hanging, and immediately afterwards men with gongs and drums started making an uproar, while street vendors sold their wares, and clowns performed in the roads. Furthermore, the public houses around the hill were very crowded, and hundreds finished the day in a state of "riot and intoxication."[1872] Similarly, at William Thompson's execution at Norwich in 1854, scenes of drunkenness and immorality were apparently widespread.[1873]

Whether there really was any deterioration in crowd behavior, and whether it truly was as poor as was sometimes claimed, is a matter of considerable debate.

[1866] *The Bristol Mercury*, 15 August, 1835.

[1867] *The Ipswich Journal*, 23 August, 1851.

[1868] *John Bull*, May 8, 1837.

[1869] *Ibid.*

[1870] *The Norfolk Chronicle,* 27 March, 1846.

[1871] *The Morning Post*, 18 August, 1841.

[1872] *The Norfolk Chronicle,* 27 March, 1846.

[1873] *Ibid.*, 23 March, 1854.

Nevertheless, it does appear that middle class and "respectable" people became less interested in, or at least more embarrassed about, attending or being seen at such events. In 1849 a railway company had what was described as the "wretched taste" to send a special "gallows' excursion" train from London to Norwich, so that people could watch James Rush's execution there. However, it was only a quarter full.[1874]

Calls for Abolition

There had been various extra-parliamentary campaigns during the early nineteenth century to restrict the death penalty to the most serious crimes, and these had reached Norfolk. In 1830 the Corporation of Norwich petitioned the House of Commons to introduce legislation for remitting the punishment of death "in all cases except murder, arson, burglary, highway robbery, and offences attended with violence."[1875] By the 1840s it seemed possible that the movement away from execution might end in full abolition for all crimes within a few years.[1876] In 1846 the *Daily News* opined that the death penalty was a "bad punishment, at best. Neither remunerative nor reformatory."[1877] The same year, owing to the allegedly scandalous character of the proceedings at Samuel Yarham's execution, a public meeting was held at St Andrew's Hall under the presidency of the mayor, when it was decided to petition Parliament for abolition.[1878] The Society for Promoting the Abolition of Capital Punishment was also established that year, and campaigned strongly against any use of the death penalty.

However, after the mid-century the discourse of reform began to shift again, perhaps under the influence of alarmist press reports about crime.[1879] The ending of public execution in 1868 (see below) further reduced interest in total abolition, and three parliamentary bills to end all capital punishment in the 1870s were heavily defeated.[1880] The death penalty would survive, for murder, until 1965.

The End of Public Executions

Whatever the status of capital punishment, by the start of the Victorian era considerable doubts were being expressed about the value of public execution. In 1841 Henry Rich urged its abolition in Parliament, arguing that it did not have a salutary effect. On the contrary, he felt that the spectacle hardened rather than reformed those who witnessed it. He also thought that in the rest of Europe there

1874 *The Sheffield & Rotherham Independent*, 5 May, 1849.

1875 *The Norfolk Chronicle,* 3 May, 1830.

1876 Christopher A. Casey, "Common Misperceptions: The Press and Victorian Views of Crime," *The Journal of Interdisciplinary History*, vol. 41, no. 3 (2011), p. 367.

1877 *The Daily News*, 15 May, 1846.

1878 *The Norfolk Chronicle,* 27 March, 1846.

1879 Casey, "Common Misperceptions," pp. 367-368.

1880 Taylor, *Hooligans, Harlots,* pp. 157-158.

was a correlation between gruesome executions and a lack of respect for human life amongst the general populace.[1881] By the 1860s change was in the air. A Liberal member of Parliament, John Hibbert, discussing a public execution in 1866, observed that no one anxious to promote civilization could support it.[1882]

Some two weeks after the summer Assizes for Norfolk in 1867, Hubbard Lingley, who had been convicted of the murder of his uncle at Barton Bendish a few months earlier, became the last person in Norfolk to be hanged in public. His execution was conducted by William Calcraft. By then, hangings were so rare that they were usually conducted by one of a tiny number of hangmen, brought in from outside, who served the entire country rather than a particular county or region. Calcraft was the primary English executioner of his era, responsible for over 450 hangings during a lengthy career which began when he was 29 and ended when he was 74.[1883]

Lingley was ministered to by the prison chaplain and, after a fairly sleepless night, received the sacrament, was offered breakfast but took only tea, and was then taken to a small office, where he was met and pinioned by Calcraft. He then proceeded outside the castle to the gallows, led by the under-sheriff carrying a black wand, with the prison governor; the fully robed chaplain, reading part of the service for the dead, and various other officials accompanied him. There he made his last prayers, thanked the prison staff, and was hanged.[1884]

Lingley's execution took place at 8 a.m. on a Monday morning, greatly reducing the number of spectators (12,000) and perhaps helping to explain their sobriety, and what was considered fairly orderly behaviour.[1885] Reflecting changing mores, a local newspaper opined, "The holding of an execution upon Monday instead of on the market-day (Saturday) is a vast improvement, but it is to be hoped the time is not far distant when executions will take place within instead of outside the prison walls."[1886]

They did not have to wait long. The following year, 1868, the law changed, statute requiring that all executions take place privately, and so inside prisons. However, journalists were normally allowed to attend executions over the following 20 years (afterward they were often excluded). Thus, and typically, in 1898 reporters were admitted to the Norwich prison to witness the hanging of George Watt.[1887]

[1881] Hansard HC Deb 16 February 1841 vol. 56 cols. 646-70.

[1882] McGowen, "Civilizing Punishment," p. 261.

[1883] Greg T. Smith. "'I Could Hang Anything You Can Bring Before Me': England's Willing Executioners in 1883," in *Penal Practice*, p. 287.

[1884] *The Times*, 27 August, 1867.

[1885] *Ibid*.

[1886] *The Norfolk Chronicle,* 8 August, 1867.

[1887] *Glasgow Herald*, 13 July 1898.

In April 1869 Calcraft carried out the first private execution in Norfolk when he hanged William Sheward inside the Norwich City Prison (the first city prisoner to be hanged for over 40 years), eight months after Thomas Wells, in Kent, had become the first man in the country executed inside prison walls.[1888] The prison authorities had to borrow the scaffold apparatus from the nearby county prison. Sheward suffered from such severe rheumatism of the ankles that he had been held in the prison infirmary pending his death and had to be carried by warders across the prison to near the place of execution, where he was pinioned.[1889]

In November 1886 George Harmer, who had been convicted of murder at the Norwich assizes, became the last man executed within the walls of Norwich Castle (by this time the county and city prisons had merged).[1890] A new prison on Plumstead Road was completed in July 1887, replacing the castle, and becoming the location for all future Norfolk hangings.[1891]

Once executions were confined to within prisons, a bell might be tolled as the prisoner walked to the scaffold and a black flag would usually be publicly hoisted when they were complete.[1892] Crowds would still attend to witness this, but on a much smaller scale than when the hanging had been visible. Thus, in 1869, when William Sheward was hanged, the raising of a black flag alerted a crowd of about 2,000 people, who had assembled outside the prison, to his death.[1893] Almost 30 years later, the same black flag was raised when George Watt was executed.[1894]

However, the problems that were attendant on using short-drop gallows remained. As late as 1867, Hubbard Lingley had experienced a "convulsive struggle" when the trap door fell at his execution.[1895] (Two years later William Sheward had been more fortunate, and died swiftly when the trap door was released.)[1896] To avoid the risk of a drawn-out strangling, some (national) observers suggested during the 1860s that death by shooting might be substituted for hanging. It was argued that this would also obviate the need for a hangman, who was necessarily something of an outcast from society. Most important, the "possibility of torture," due to the uncertainty attaching to the effect of a short fall upon the human neck would be

---

1888 *The Norfolk Chronicle,* 2 January, 1869.

1889 *The Illustrated Police News*, 24 April, 1869.

1890 *The Norfolk Chronicle,* 14 August, 1886.

1891 *Ibid.,* 16 July, 1887.

1892 Bentley, *English Criminal Justice,* p. 3.

1893 *The Illustrated Police News*, 24 April, 1869.

1894 *The Glasgow Herald*, 13 July, 1898.

1895 *The Times*, 27 August, 1867, p. 9.

1896 *The Illustrated Police News*, 24 April, 1869.

avoided.[1897] These problems were ultimately addressed by the introduction of "long-drop" hangings.

Long-Drop Hangings

Even early in the Victorian period, the potential advantages of the condemned man experiencing a longer fall were well known. For example, John Self benefitted from an "unusually long" drop when hanged at Norwich in 1841 and seemed to die very quickly; certainly, he did not struggle.[1898] Similarly, and whether by accident or design, James Rush benefited from a longer than normal drop in 1848 and appears to have lost consciousness immediately. Nevertheless, the idea of using a drop that was specifically aimed at producing an instantaneously broken neck, and so immediate deep unconsciousness swiftly followed by death, appears to have had its origins in Ireland, especially Dublin, where hangmen were experimenting with much longer drops in the late 1850s and 1860s, being supported in this by surgeons such as the Reverend Dr. Samuel Haughton.

In England William Marwood, who deplored the "very ugly slow process" previously employed, introduced the long drop in 1872, when he became an executioner and hanged the wife-murderer Frederick Horry at Lincoln. From 1872 to 1877, both the short- and long-drop methods were in use, after which time the latter became universal. The growth in the railway system meant that, by then, Marwood, a Horncastle cobbler by trade, could conduct most of the country's executions, so that his views on this issue were decisive. (In 1883 he was paid a flat fee of £10 per hanging, plus travelling expenses, with an additional £5 for each extra person hanged in a multiple execution).[1899]

In the early years of the long drop, assessing the distance that the condemned person should fall was not a precise science, although tables were later produced to allow it to be calculated more accurately, having regard to weight, age, gender, and musculature. However, when Robert Goodale was executed at Norwich in 1885, the hanging went badly wrong. Shortly before 8 am he was pinioned by James Berry (Marwood's successor), and walked to the gallows, which had been erected over a deep pit. Goodale, who weighed 15 stone, fell almost six feet when the trap door opened. Unfortunately, his head was cut off, as cleanly as if removed with a knife. At the subsequent inquest, Berry could only explain what had happened by suggesting that Goodale had very thin vertebrae. He claimed that he had already reduced the planned drop by two feet to allow for the convict's poor musculature and weight, had carefully tested the apparatus, and had hanged a much heavier man in similar circumstances on an earlier occasion without incident. Even so, the gaol surgeon noted that, although unsightly, Goodale's death was instantaneous,

---

[1897] *The Spectator,* 7 March, 1868, p. 3.

[1898] *The Norfolk Chronicle,* 28 July, 1841.

[1899] Smith, "'I Could Hang Anything,'" p. 287, p. 301.

making it much more merciful than the short-drop method. The inquest jury found that no one was to blame for what had occurred.[1900]

John Thurston, who was executed the following year, and who was the first man to be hanged in Norfolk after the Goodale mishap, received special attention to ensure that there was no repetition. The under-sheriff insisted that there were repeated rehearsals and the need for a four-and-a-half-foot drop was carefully calculated. On the day of his death, Thurston was woken at 4.30 am, visited by the prison chaplain at 6 am, taken from his cell at 8 am, and pinioned in the prison bathroom by James Berry. The under-sheriff then led him to the scaffold. As he walked there, he joined in prayers with the chaplain. When the trap door fell, "death was instantaneous, the neck being dislocated." Thurston then hung for the customary hour, and an immediate inquest on his death was held by the city of Norwich coroner; it concluded that "judgement of death was duly executed and carried into effect upon the deceased."[1901] More general lessons were learnt from the Goodale incident. The plump and slightly flabby Amelia Dyer, a "professional" baby killer, executed at Newgate prison in London in June 1896, may have had an even shorter fall than Thurston. Her Prison Commission file noted: "On account of her weight and the softness of the textures, rather a short drop was given. It proved to be quite sufficient."[1902]

There were also very occasional cases of the long drop being underestimated, and death by strangulation resulting. At his execution at Liverpool in December 1883, Henry Dutton, although weighing just nine stone, was given a drop of 7 feet 5 inches using a thick rope. It took eight minutes for his heart to stop beating, and his death appears to have resulted from strangulation.[1903] Similarly, in 1886, when James Berry hanged David Roberts in Cardiff Gaol for murdering a cattle dealer, the latter weighed 13 stone but was allowed an insufficient drop of 3 feet 7 inches. He was seen to struggle for at least three minutes after the trap door opened, at which point, and while he was still alive, attendant journalists were asked to withdraw.[1904] Fortunately, no such cases were reported in Norfolk.

Other aspects of the execution process also became more regulated in the latter decades of the Victorian era. For example, until the late 1870s hangmen normally supplied their own ropes. From 1878 an execution rope of standard pattern with a metal eyelet was available from the Prison Commissioners. County sheriffs could order such ropes from Newgate prison.

[1900] *The Singleton Argus* (New South Wales), 27 January, 1886. Berry, *My Experiences as an Executioner,* pp. 64-65.

[1901] *The Times*, 11 February, 1886, p. 10.

[1902] *The Independent,* 22 February, 2013.

[1903] *The Dundee Courier*, 4 December, 1883.

[1904] *Ibid.*, 3 March, 1886.

Disposal of the Corpse

A corpse was usually left hanging for an hour after death before being cut down for burial, especially in the era of the short drop, as was the case with Charles Daines in 1839.[1905] During the first decade of the Victorian period, there were still periodic instances of people stroking (or seeking to stroke) the hands of hanged men in order to cure swellings, scrofula, skin tumours, and other excrescences, in East Anglia as elsewhere, and such conduct was last mentioned in newspapers as late as 1863.[1906] For example, at a double execution in Horsham, Sussex, in 1835, it was noted that after the pair were dead, the hangman had recourse to "the silly and superstitious custom of passing the hands of the dead men over the necks of two or three females, as a supposed cure for glandular enlargements".[1907]

Traditionally, unless they were convicted of murder, the bodies of executed convicts were released back to friends and family (if present) for interment, usually finishing up in a consecrated cemetery. Thus, in April 1823, after William Bray, a 20-year-old man, was hanged at the foot of the bridge at Castle Hill for a burglary at Shouldham, it was noted, "His parents were too poor to send for his remains, which were interred the same day in St. Michael-at-Thorn churchyard."[1908] Similarly, Richard Nockolds, executed for arson at Norwich in 1831, was returned to his family for burial in St. James's Church in the city. However, after 1832, and throughout the Victorian era, executed felons were buried inside the prison walls.[1909] This was largely because it became the required disposal for murderers after 1832/1834, and the abolition of dissection/public gibbeting, while only murderers normally went to the gallows after 1837. For example, in 1851 Henry Groom was interred in one of the castle passages, next to James Rush's remains, which had been buried there three years earlier.[1910] Rush had found this disposal particularly daunting: "Will they not allow my friends to have my body to be buried in the church yard?"

Cutting down executed convicts provided a brief opportunity to use their corpses for exemplary purposes, at least in the early decades of the century. In April 1830, when 31-year-old John Simmons and 20-year-old William Lovet were convicted at the (soon to be abandoned) Thetford assizes, for several burglaries at Thorpe, they were executed on the Castle Hill by William Calcraft, "After the execution the bodies were laid out in the mill-yard, and the different classes of prisoners were marched

---

[1905] *The Morning Chronicle*, 2 May, 1839.

[1906] Owen Davies and Francesca Matteoni, "'A virtue beyond all medicine': The Hanged Man's Hand, Gallows Tradition and Healing in Eighteenth- and Nineteenth-century England," Social History of Medicine, vol. 28, no. 4 (2015), p. 687.

[1907] *The Sussex Advertiser*, 24 August, 1835.

[1908] *The Norfolk Chronicle*, 5 April, 1823.

[1909] Maurice Morson, *Norfolk Mayhem & Murder: Classic Cases Revisited* (Barnsley: Wharncliffe Books, 2008), p. 37.

[1910] *The Ipswich Journal*, 23 August, 1851.

past."[1911] Seven years later, in April 1837, when John Smith and George Timms were hanged for murder at Norwich, they were carried back inside the prison, when all the other prisoners were brought forward to view their bodies prior to burial.[1912] Presumably, it was hoped that this would deter them from future crime.

1911 *The Norfolk Chronicle,* 10 April, 1830.

1912 *John Bull*, 8 May,1837.

Chapter 14: Punishment: Transportation and Custodial Sentences

Transportation

Transportation was fundamental to the penal system for most of the first two decades of the Victorian era. By then it was the primary form of punishment for most serious offences, given the retreat of the death penalty. Convicts were usually given sentences of seven, ten, fourteen, or fifteen years, or sentenced for the "term of their natural lives." Recipients of the last punishment had often received their disposals as a condition of reprieve from a death sentence.[1913] Many, but far from all, of those so sentenced made the voyage around the world to the Antipodes.

Between 1787 and 1868, 158,702 convicts arrived in Australia from England and Ireland, along with 1,321 from other parts of the Empire, these figures including approximately 25,000 women. Others died *en route*, so that at least 160,000 left the British Isles. In 1833, the peak year for transportation, 16,242 people were convicted of indictable offences in Great Britain, of whom 5,797, more than one-third, set sail for the colonies.[1914] Although the use of transportation gradually declined thereafter, about 51,200 convicts were sent to Australia in the 1840s and another 26,000 in the 1850s.[1915] Allowing for the small number who were sent to West Australia in the 1860s, it seems that a very narrow majority of all those transported to Australia after 1788 went during the years after 1840, and a clearer majority during the reign of Queen Victoria.[1916]

On one assessment, up to 4,000 of those transported to Australia between 1788 and total abolition in 1867 came from Norfolk.[1917] Other estimates might suggest that under 3,000 people from the county made the journey. Whatever the figure, it was sufficiently common that, if a published but very possibly apocryphal broadsheet is to be believed, Ann Webster, a nineteenth-century woman who had been transported to New South Wales for 14 years after picking the pocket of a drunken gentleman in Norwich, was able to socialize with a cluster of felons from her native county. Some of them had apparently flourished in and around Sydney, establishing businesses and becoming respected local people. Others led squalid and depraved lives, engaging in further criminal activity. It was claimed that Webster eventually returned to Norfolk, being treated as "one that had risen from the grave."[1918]

[1913] Bruce Kercher, "Perish or Prosper: The Law and Convict Transportation in the British Empire, 1700-1850," *Law and History Review*, vol. 21, no. 3 (2003), p. 528.

[1914] Taylor, "Rationing Crime," p. 572.

[1915] J.P. Sharpe, *Judicial Punishment in England* (London: Faber & Faber, 1990), p. 52.

[1916] Kercher, "Perish or Prosper," p. 528.

[1917] https://www.archives.norfolk.gov.uk, accessed 1 December, 2022.

[1918] Storey, *Norfolk Villains,* p. 142.

Some 83 of the 5,963 convicts (about 1.4 percent) convicted of simple theft and transported to Australia between 1788 and 1867 had been sentenced in a Norfolk court, while some 40 of the 1,983 convicts (about 2 percent) convicted of burglary and transported to the Antipodes had been found guilty in the county.[1919] A random selection of convict-ship sailings during Victorian times can also be considered. Thus, it seems that some 305 convicts from courts in all parts of Great Britain (but not Ireland) were transported on the *Maitland,* which set sail for Australia on 19 March 1840. Of these, five came from Norfolk criminal courts, four being from the county quarter sessions, and one from the Great Yarmouth borough sessions. (None came from the assizes.) Almost two years later, some 267 convicts were transported on the *Isabella*, which sailed on 15 January 1842 (only a handful of its convicts came from outside Britain). Seven of these came from Norfolk courts; on this occasion, three came from the county assizes. Moving on two more years again, 290 convicts were transported on the *Equestrian*, which sailed on 25 January 1844. Of these, nine came from Norfolk courts, none of them having been convicted at the assizes. Of 300 convicts transported on the *Lady Palmyra*, which set sail on 4 March 1846, four came from Norfolk quarter or borough sessions.[1920] This makes a total of 25 prisoners from the county of the 1,162 convicts on the above four sailings, somewhat under 2 percent of the total.

Norfolk's contribution to the British total of transports was probably typical for a predominantly rural county of its size situated outside the immediate environs of London. As some of the figures above suggest, and perhaps surprisingly, a majority were sent from the lower jury courts rather than the assizes. Most went to New South Wales or Van Diemen's Land (Tasmania). Fairly typically, William Miller (1819-1846), a brickmaker, was amongst 276 convicts sent to the latter colony on the *Asia* in April 1840, arriving there in August. He had been convicted of pickpocketing at the Norfolk quarter sessions and sentenced to ten years' transportation. Similarly, Isaac George Bridges (1827-1890), a plasterer and tiler, was one of 220 convicts transported to Van Diemen's land on the *Theresa*, setting sail in March 1845. He, too, had been convicted of larceny from the person at the Norwich city quarter sessions and sentenced to seven years' transportation.[1921]

It was normal for prisoners under sentence of transportation to return from their convicting court to the gaol where they had been held pending trial, this usually being the county prison in Norwich for those from Norfolk. They usually stayed there until the secretary of state ordered their removal to a convict facility for the initial part of their sentence, which might entail a wait of several months or more. Sometimes this would be a government prison, such as Millbank or Pentonville in

[1919] British Convict transportation register made available by the State Library of Queensland https://convictrecords.com.au/crimes/stealing.

[1920] British Convict transportation register made available by the State Library of Queensland https://convictrecords.com.au/convicts.

[1921] British Convict transportation register made available by the State Library of Queensland https://convictrecords.com.au.

London, or Parkhurst in the Isle of Wight. (They had been built, in part, because of concern about the conditions on the hulks.) Thus, about four weeks after conviction at the Norfolk assizes in the summer of 1843, a group of sheep thieves were sent from Norwich Castle gaol to the newly built Pentonville prison. They stayed there until leaving England for Australia in early November 1844, more than a year later (arriving in Van Diemen's Land in February 1845).[1922]

However, more commonly, at least before 1842, this post-conviction period would be spent in one of the numerous prison hulks. These were former (and now dismasted) warships, anchored along the banks of the River Thames and in or near southern ports. Typically, in February 1837, a dozen convicts under sentence of transportation were removed from Bury gaol in Suffolk to be sent to and put aboard the *Leviathan* hulk moored in Portsmouth harbour.[1923] More locally, in January 1839, after James Moyses, a farmer from West Walton in Norfolk, was convicted at the Ely quarter sessions in Cambridgeshire for stealing pigs and sentenced to seven years' transportation, he was sent to the *Ganymede* hulk.[1924]

Many, but by no means all, of those sent to convict prisons and hulks would subsequently be assigned to a convict ship leaving England for Australia. For example, in March 1834 15-year-old William Swann was convicted of housebreaking at the Lent assizes for Norwich and sentenced to transportation. He went from the city gaol to the *Euryalus* hulk (mainly used for juveniles), where he remained for more than a year. He was eventually put aboard the *Lady Nugent* and, on 22 July 1836, sailed for the Antipodes.[1925]

Arrival In Australia

Convicts were not set free on arrival. As Sir William Molesworth observed, when speaking to the House of Commons in 1840, transportation was a compound punishment, consisting of three elements: banishment from Britain; compulsory labour in a penal colony, whether by working for the government on projects such as building roads through the Blue Mountains in a chain gang, or for a private master, after assignment to a free settler or emancipated former convict; and (thirdly) the various, often severe, punishments by which that compulsory labour was enforced. However, it was not permanent. Although those transported could not return before their period of banishment was over, at the end of four, six, or eight years, depending on the length of their original sentence, convicts would normally obtain a 'ticket of leave'. This allowed them to work on their own account, like other settlers, and as there was a considerable demand for labour in the Australian colonies, they often did so for good wages.[1926]

1922 *The Norfolk Chronicle*, 22 July, 1843.

1923 *The Bury and Norwich Post*, 1 February, 1837.

1924 TNA HO 17/71/91.

1925 TNA HO 17/129/110.

1926 Hansard HC Deb 05 May 1840 vol. 53 cols. 1236-307.

Sometimes, personal freedom would be granted earlier, for special reasons. Frederick Abel, a 21-year-old baker-cum-weaver from Norwich, was convicted at the city quarter sessions in June 1846 for stealing an iron pot. He had a previous conviction for stealing a shawl and so was sentenced to seven years' transportation. He arrived in Van Diemen's Land in November 1848. Abel was immediately assigned to work for one Alfred Bisdee, in Jericho, but received an early ticket of leave in April the following year, a conditional pardon in January 1853, and a certificate of freedom in July that same year. He appears to have died in Australia in 1912.[1927]

Stay-at-Homes

Nevertheless, far more English prisoners were sentenced to transportation than could be (or were deemed appropriate to be) sent to Australia. As a result, and as Charles Cottu observed in the 1820s, many carried out their whole sentences on the hulks or in penal establishments ashore, remaining in England until released (often early), a pattern that continued during the early Victorian period. For example, Edward Chambers, a young labourer, was convicted of robbery with violence at the Norfolk assizes in March 1852 and sentenced to seven years' transportation. In September 1855 he was granted early release while still on the *Defence* hulk.[1928]

Those selected to make the voyage to Australia were chosen for a variety of reasons, such as length of sentence, gender, age, skills, apparent reformability, and physical condition. Thus, healthy young women sentenced to seven years' transportation in the 1830s were more likely, on a per capita basis, to go to the Antipodes than similarly aged men under the same sentence, in part because of a high demand for female convict labour amongst free settlers. By contrast, older and frailer convicts were less able to survive the arduous voyage, and, if they did, would be of limited value. Such men were not usually sent out but would serve their sentences in a hulk or government prison.

In the daytime, convicts on hulks were taken ashore in boats to labour at arduous tasks such as dredging the River Thames. For the rest of the time, they were accommodated aboard ship, being locked below decks overnight. By the start of the Victorian period, conditions on the hulks had improved from their early days in the late eighteenth century, in part because of the work of John Capper, who introduced closer supervision of inmates between 1814 and 1847. Thus, the *Warrior* hulk, moored off Woolwich, had an infirmary, washing room, and chapel. Nevertheless, hulks remained extremely grim and violent places.[1929] Inmates were often crawling with vermin, and largely left to their own devices after dark. In 1841 the *Warrior* housed 638 convicts, of whom 400 were admitted to hospital and 38 died during the year.[1930]

[1927] Australian Joint Copying Project. Microfilm Roll 92, Class and Piece Number HO11/15.

[1928] TNA PCOM 3/37/4017.

[1929] Sharpe, *Judicial Punishment,* p. 52.

[1930] *The Glasgow Herald*, 2 July, 1856.

As a result of the harsh conditions, some prisoners under sentence of transportation could not even be committed to a hulk, at least initially, let alone be sent on to the Antipodes. Some would necessarily be released quite swiftly in consequence. For example, Sophia Tuck was convicted of a felony (probably a serious theft) at the Norfolk quarter sessions held at Swaffham in July 1837 and sentenced to transportation for seven years. However, she suffered from epilepsy, and her fits were getting worse, so that the gaoler at the Walsingham prison for women concluded that she was unfit for transportation. This was supported by a surgeon and visiting JPs, while the prison keeper noted that she had behaved well while incarcerated. After just over two years in custody in Walsingham, she was granted a free pardon in August 1839.[1931]

The septuagenarian Edmund Adcock spent a similar amount of time in custody. He was convicted at the Norfolk quarter sessions at Norwich in June 1837 of stealing corn, sentenced to seven years' transportation, and returned to the county prison. He remained there, his gaoler's report noting that he was "unfit for transportation," being infirm and nearly blind. The prison visitors took a similar view, and, following a petition, Adcock was granted a free pardon in November 1839.[1932]

In like manner, in July 1838 37-year-old Henry Pike was convicted of forgery at the Norfolk assizes and sentenced to transportation for 15 years. His wife, Emma, subsequently petitioned for clemency on his behalf, in part on the basis that he suffered from severe ill health, including scrofula. A medical report of May 1839, drawn up by the surgeon to the county gaol, confirmed that Pike was a cripple. A letter from five JPs who visited the prison in September 1840 recommended that he be released on the grounds of ill health. Pike was granted a free pardon shortly afterwards, without having left Norwich, let alone England.[1933]

Nevertheless, a few convicts in this situation recovered their health, so that their sentences could be carried out. For example, at the Yarmouth borough quarter sessions in March 1840, James Brown, a 22-year-old bricklayer, was convicted of stealing 400 bricks. He had previous convictions and was sentenced to seven years' transportation. He was initially kept in the gaol at Yarmouth, as he was too ill from rheumatism and venereal disease to be sent to a hulk. Instead, he was put in the prison infirmary and monitored by its surgeon, while also being treated with linseed meal and a superior diet. His condition apparently improving, he was transferred to the *Warrior* hulk before going aboard the convict ship *Susan* in March 1842, for the voyage out to Australia. This took four months (it could be as little as 100 days in ideal circumstances), the vessel arriving in Hobart, Tasmania, in late July 1842. Unfortunately, Brown died seven weeks after disembarking from the ship.[1934]

[1931] TNA HO 17/126/160.

[1932] TNA HO 18/8/1.

[1933] TNA HO 17/111/150.

[1934] Helen Rogers, "The Way to Jerusalem: Reading, Writing and Reform in an Early Victorian Gaol," *Past & Present*, vol. 205, no. 1 (2009), p. 78.

Other prisoners could cope with a convict prison but not a hulk, let alone the journey to Australia. In 1839 John Morris, a 33-year-old man convicted of cattle theft at the Norfolk quarter sessions held at Swaffham, had been sentenced to transportation for 15 years. Subsequently he petitioned to be sent to the penitentiary at Millbank in consequence of having broken his back and dislocated his ankle earlier in life, as well as suffering from acute rheumatism. A medical report on the prisoner concluded that he was unfit to be transported. It was recommended that he be sent to Millbank.[1935] Similarly, Luke Grimes, a 50-year-old, was convicted of receiving stolen property at the King's Lynn borough sessions in January 1841 and sentenced to 14 years' transportation. He subsequently petitioned the Home Office, pointing out that he had been afflicted with scrofula for several years and was unable to move without crutches. Two letters sent from the town clerk of King's Lynn advised that Grimes had also been refused admittance to the hulks for the same reasons. It was ordered that he, too, be sent to a penitentiary instead.[1936]

Charles Moore was even more fortunate. His health was very poor, as he suffered from acute asthma. In August 1840 he was convicted of highway robbery at the Norfolk assizes. His sentence of death was immediately commuted to transportation for 10 years, and it was ordered that he be sent to a penitentiary rather than a hulk. However, just over two months later, in late October, he was granted a free pardon. At this point, he was still in Norwich gaol, not having been removed to the government prison because he was so ill. (That the robbery was five years old when indicted probably assisted this disposal.)[1937]

Decline of the Hulks

By the early 1840s, the use of hulks was in decline, and prisons like Millbank were increasingly being used to accommodate those waiting to go to Australia (itself a rapidly declining number) who would previously have spent this time offshore, something that was also assisted by the opening of the new Portsmouth Convict Prison in 1852.[1938] In 1845 an exposé in *The Times* helped make the poor conditions still found on the hulks public, so that their use declined further. By 1850 many of them were in very poor condition, with the *Warrior*, moored off Woolwich, requiring £800 of urgent epair work.[1939] Only two vessels were still employed after 1852.[1940] Although there had been 3,552 people accommodated in hulks off the coast in 1841, the number had fallen to 1,298 by 1854.[1941] Use of the rapidly deteriorating hulks was abandoned altogether in 1857.

1935 TNA HO 18/30/52.

1936 TNA HO 18/43/1.

1937 TNA HO 18/30/17.

1938 *The Newcastle Courant*, 4 October, 1844.

1939 *Report on Discipline and Management of Convict Prisons, 1850* (London: HMSO, 1851), p. 2.

1940 Briggs et al., *Crime and Punishment in England*, p. 163.

1941 *The Glasgow Herald*, 2 July, 1856.

Returning from Transportation

Once their time had expired, or it was shortened by the government, transported convicts could return home. (Those transported for life could not normally come back.) However, many chose to stay on in Australia, especially after the early years of the new colonies' existence, the wages and demand for labour proving attractive. Even so, in May 1851, when the elderly John Rowland died in the King's Lynn workhouse, it was claimed that he had been a blacksmith in the town and had been convicted and transported for stealing iron. At the end of his term of transportation he (allegedly) returned to Lynn and lived there for several years before his death.[1942]

It was a serious crime for convicts to come back early, whether this meant returning from Australia or being at liberty when they should still have been locked up on a hulk. The latter was the situation James Base from Norwich found himself in after (apparently) escaping from a hulk in Woolwich. He was re-sentenced to an increased term of transportation (15 years) at the Norfolk assizes in early 1853.[1943] Nevertheless, it seems that the final convict hanged for returning early went to the gallows in 1814. No prematurely returned transport was hanged after the Napoleonic Wars (something that Charles Dickens, in *Great Expectations,* ignored for dramatic effect) although, in theory, the crime remained a capital offence until 1834.

A strange case involving alleged premature return was heard at the Norfolk quarter sessions in 1840. John Beale, from Ditchingham, had been sentenced to transportation for life after conviction for a felony, but while in Australia had been given an official discharge after he was confused with another convict by the same name (who had, in fact, died). He returned (quite legally) to Norfolk, where he found his wife living in "open adultery" with another man (which was not entirely unsurprising, given his sentence). The lover attempted unsuccessfully to get him prosecuted for returning prematurely. Beale eventually entered his wife's dwelling, where she lived with her new man, while she was out. He was accompanied by a group of other men. At his urging, they consumed six bottles of wine that they found there. Beale was subsequently convicted of theft at quarter sessions and sentenced to a further seven years' transportation. This was considered harsh, as he had been living quietly until the incident that brought him to court, and a petition was started to ask for a reprieve.[1944]

Transportation was at the heart of another unusual case heard at the Norfolk assizes in August 1865, when Cornelius Bradnum, a fruit dealer, was indicted for feloniously being at large at Heckingham that February. Bradnum had been sentenced to transportation for life, after being convicted at the same forum in July 1847 of

---

[1942] *The Bury and Norwich Post*, 7 May, 1851.

[1943] *Ibid.*, 23 March, 1853.

[1944] *The Times*, 30 March, 1840, p. 5.

burglary from a shop. (A previous conviction explained the draconian penalty.)[1945] He claimed that due to giving information and trial testimony on an intended mutiny by convicts at Gibraltar, where he had undergone three years forced labour on the hulk *Euryalus* while en route to the Antipodes, his sentence was reduced 15 years' transportation. (Such lengthy work delays were not uncommon and occurred at Bermuda and Cape Colony as well.) From Gibraltar, he was eventually sent to the Swan River Colony in West Australia. Once he arrived, the governor quickly gave Bradnum his ticket of leave and, after "serving his ticket," he alleged that he had received a free pardon. Brandum then claimed to have gone to Callao, in Peru, where he was press-ganged, put on board an American merchant vessel, and brutally ill-used so that he was left crippled. As he was then useless to the ship, he was eventually put ashore at Hamburg, where, after remaining for some time in hospital, he returned to England with the aid of the local British consul.

Unfortunately, an official who knew his history subsequently identified him in his native county. Even worse, Bradnum alleged that he had left the document granting his free pardon in his trunk at Callao. The prosecution denied that such a pardon had ever been granted. However, the judge decided that it was for the Crown to show that the prisoner's statement was untrue, as they had used it against him as evidence. As it had not been contradicted by the prosecution, he directed the jury in favourable terms: "I must say I don't see why you should not believe it, and why he is not entitled to a verdict of not guilty."[1946] Perhaps unsurprisingly, given this direction, the period that had elapsed since his conviction, and that by then transportation was seen as anachronistic, the jury acquitted. Bradnum was still alive, aged 71, in 1891.[1947]

Decline of Transportation

Transportation to Australia reached its peak in the early 1830s, when some 5,000 people were being sent to the Antipodes each year.[1948] On one occasion in April 1834, 54 Norfolk convicts, sentenced to transportation at the recent assizes and quarter sessions, went on board the *Sarah* while she was moored in the river at Norwich, then sailed for Portsmouth, where they could wait for a place on a ship going to Australia. (Not all would ultimately go.) It was hoped that this would be cheaper to the county than sending them to the port overland.[1949]

However, by the beginning of the Victorian era there was increasing resistance from the colonies to the punishment and to the harm it did to the reputation of the growing number of free settlers in Australia. A committee under the chairmanship of Sir

---

[1945] *The Bury and Norwich Post, and East Anglian*, 28 July, 1847.

[1946] *The Norfolk Chronicle,* 5 August, 1865.

[1947] Mackie, *Norfolk Annals, vol. 2,* p. 147. Reg Reynolds, "*Euryalus*: Trafalgar Flagship to Prison Hulk," *The Gibraltar Magazine*, October 2010, p. 67.

[1948] Briggs et al., *Crime and Punishment in England*, p. 162.

[1949] *The Norfolk Chronicle,* 30 April, 1834.

William Molesworth was established in 1837 to enquire into its continued viability. Sir William was already a strong proponent of a penitentiary system and, perhaps unsurprisingly, produced a negative conclusion on the merits of transportation when he reported the following year. By the early 1840s it was widely accepted that the system could not last for very much longer.[1950]

A few years after the accession of the new Queen, Prime Minister Earl Grey had sent circular letters to all the Australian colonies, as well as New Zealand, Ceylon, and Mauritius, asking if they would accept criminals in a reformed system by which free settlers would accompany offenders; there would also be enhanced management of prisoners sent overseas, and extra investment provided from the mother country. They all rejected this proposal, apart from Western Australia, which had grown out of the Swan River Settlement initiated more than 20 years earlier (see below).[1951] By 1854 it was accepted that it would be hard to find a colony that would not "rebel upon the first hint" of restoring the punishment.[1952] Although the notion of restoring penal transportation to a new destination, such as the Falkland Islands or Vancouver Island, occasionally resurfaced until the end of the 1860s, its having become linked in the popular mind with slavery helped prevent such an experiment.[1953]

Transportation to New South Wales largely ended in 1840 and was officially terminated in 1850. Three years later, it was ended in Tasmania. After the early 1850s, it was no longer a major punishment in the English penal repertoire, and official government policy concentrated on developing a home-based system in which it would be replaced by penal servitude (see below).[1954] Nevertheless, transportation had not been totally abolished, at least for long-term disposals. Uniquely, in 1849 Swan River elected to become a penal settlement, seeking convict labour (healthy adult males) for various building projects. The offer was quickly acted on, and the *Scindian* arrived in June 1850 with 75 male convicts aboard. Some 42 more convict ships followed in the next 18 years, 37 carrying ordinary prisoners from the United Kingdom (one vessel came from Bermuda, and others brought small groups of military prisoners from British troops stationed in India). The *Hougoumont*, the final convict vessel, docked in Fremantle in January 1868, with 229 convicts aboard. By then, the Swan River penal colony had received almost 9,500 male prisoners.

Although such sentences had become rare in Norfolk after the early 1850s, as they were elsewhere in the country, a handful of men from the county still received this disposal, if only as "penal servitude overseas" (see below). As a result, when the Dutch sailor Hendricus Erenshuisen was convicted of a very serious manslaughter at

---

[1950] Judith Rowbotham, "Manipulating The Media: Victorian Lawyers, Transportation, And The Creation Of Panic Over Habitual Criminals," *Law, Crime and History*, vol. 9, no. 1 (2019), p. 67.

[1951] Anon., Special correspondent of the *Melbourne Argus, Transportation: The British Convict in Western Australia*, 1865, p. 9.

[1952] *The Spectator*, 4 October, 1854.

[1953] Rowbotham, "Manipulating The Media," p. 96.

[1954] *Ibid.*, p. 67.

the Norfolk assizes in December 1865 he was sentenced to 20 years' penal servitude. He was subsequently sent to Perth, being one of the last to make the journey, where he was granted conditional release towards the end of 1880.[1955] (He became a boat-builder and died there in 1921). Two men who had been convicted in Norfolk were amongst the 280 prisoners aboard the *Hougoumont*, when she made the very final convict voyage to Western Australia, leaving in October 1867 and arriving the following January. One of them, John Baker, had received ten years' penal servitude at the Norfolk quarter sessions in Norwich while Judd Towler had received the same disposal at the Norfolk assizes.[1956]

Penal Servitude

In the summer of 1847, it was noted that, nationally, about 4,000 people were convicted each year for offences that warranted transportation. If only *faute de mieux*, such convicts would be thrown back on the prison system if the punishment were abolished. Unfortunately, because of "squalid neglect" many of the country's gaols were out of date and required major reform and expansion to accommodate these numbers.[1957] Nevertheless, necessity led to the introduction of the sentence of penal servitude and with it an attendant expansion in the number and size of government-run convict prisons to accommodate those who received such a disposal.

The Penal Servitude Act 1853 (16 & 17 Vict. c. 99) was, to give it its full title, "An Act to substitute, in certain Cases, other Punishment in lieu of Transportation." It largely (but not wholly) replaced transportation with a special form of imprisonment. Under the statute, those convicted of felonies that were subject to transportation for up to 14 years would instead be sentenced to penal servitude with hard labour for a set term, the length of which was referenced to the length of transportation that they would have received. Thus, sentences of up to seven years' transportation were replaced by penal servitude for four years; those of from seven to ten years' transportation with a sentence of four to six years; those of ten to 15 years by six to eight years; those sentenced to 15 years' transportation by eight to ten years, while transportation for life was replaced by penal servitude for life. However, for those who would have been sentenced to transportation for 14 or more years, penal servitude was an option, not a requirement. A sentence of transportation could still be passed instead.

The effect of the new statute was swift. In 1852 4,307 people had been sentenced to transportation, but by 1855 the figure was only 409 (all sentenced to 14 or more years). Of course, many of the latter would still not go to the Antipodes because, whether due to age or health, they were, in Sir George Grey's words, "physically

[1955] *The Police Gazette* (Western Australia), 22 December, 1880.

[1956] Australian Joint Copying Project. Microfilm roll 93, class and piece number HO11/19, p. 248.

[1957] Anon., "What to Do with the 4,000 a Year," *The Spectator,* 19 June, 1847, p. 12.

unfit for transportation."[1958] To help accommodate the extra convicts, especially female prisoners, produced by this change, provision was made in the Convict Prisons Act of 1853 (16 & 17 Vict. c. 121) for creating extra places of confinement.

The Penal Servitude Act 1857 (20 & 21 Vict. c.3), which replaced most of the 1853 statute, ended the formal sentence of transportation and with it the attendant and clumsy system of converting it to penal servitude. Subsequently, by dint of s.2 of the statute, convicts were sentenced directly to penal servitude if found guilty of offences that had formerly warranted transportation for "the same Duration as the Term of Transportation to which such Person would have been liable." Thus, seven years' transportation could become seven years' penal servitude. For example, in 1859, when John Plummer, a Norfolk shoemaker, was convicted of stealing a model of a gold nugget (he thought it was genuine) he was sentenced to seven years' penal servitude.[1959] Of course, early release might well reduce the time that was served and was needed to relieve pressure on the prisons. Thus, in July 1866, when Eleanor Miall was found guilty at the Norfolk quarter sessions in Norwich of stealing 2s 3d from the dwelling house of her aunt, she was sentenced to seven years' penal servitude, but only served half this period before being released on licence at the end of 1870 (see below).[1960]

However, and even more important, the 1857 Act also gave the court a discretion to impose a lesser sentence, provided it was at least three years' penal servitude, in all situations, this being the minimum sentence that could be passed for such a punishment (it was later increased by the 1864 Penal Servitude Act [27 & 28 Vict c.47] to a minimum of five years but reduced again in 1891). Without such a provision, the 1857 Act would often have produced an increase in sentences over those of its predecessor of 1853.

Also significantly, paragraph two of section three of the 1857 Act allowed those who had been sentenced to penal servitude to be conveyed beyond the sea to serve their sentences abroad, and provided that all existing laws regulating their custody and rights to their labour, and punishments for being illegally at large, would continue to apply "as if they were persons under sentence or order of transportation." It was this provision, sometimes referred to as penal servitude overseas, that allowed some convicts sentenced to penal servitude to be sent to Western Australia until 1867.[1961]

[1958] Hansard HC Deb 11 May 1857 vol. 145 cols. 136-81.

[1959] *The Norfolk Chronicle,* 20 October, 1859.

[1960] TNA PCOM 4/44/43.

[1961] David J. Cox, Rights, Responsibilities and Religion in a Mid-Victorian Convict Prison," *Wolverhampton Law Journal,* vol. 4 (2020), p. 32.

Use of Penal Servitude

Penal servitude was used to punish convicts who committed very grave crimes, or those with long criminal histories, even if the latest offence for which they had been found guilty was not especially serious. Thus, after the abolition of transportation, those sentenced for rape and sodomy would always receive a sentence of penal servitude, as would those convicted of serious examples of more common crimes. For example, in August 1877 John L'Estrange, an archaeologist, was indicted for forging the name of Francis Foster, a stamp distributor, with intent to defraud, and with stealing stamps to the value of £1,400. He pleaded guilty at the Norwich assizes in August 1877 and was sentenced to seven years' penal servitude.[1962]

Illustrative of the influence of recidivism on sentencing, in January 1857, Henry Edwards finally exhausted the bench's patience at the Norfolk quarter sessions. He was convicted of stealing a pocket handkerchief from the person of a man at St Faith's fair. However, he had several previous convictions and, as a result, received ten years' penal servitude.[1963] Similarly, at the Yarmouth quarter sessions in January 1888, George Smith, a 26-year-old fisherman with a dozen previous convictions, was found guilty of stealing a pair of trousers. The recorder, his patience with Smith apparently exhausted, declared that he would not waste time on words and sentenced him to five years' penal servitude.[1964] To consider an even more extreme example, in January 1855 Martin Money, another old offender, was found guilty at the Norwich quarter sessions for stealing a muck fork. He was sentenced to 14 years' penal servitude.[1965]

The possibility of such a disposal could also be used as a judicial threat when showing mercy. At the Norfolk quarter sessions in July 1874, Charles Rouse received 18 months' imprisonment for a relatively modest theft but was warned by the court that, if he came before it again, even for a minor crime, he would receive a sentence of penal servitude.[1966] A decade later, the previously convicted George Thompson, found guilty of a minor theft at the Norfolk assizes in May 1884, received the same sentence and a similar warning.[1967]

Convict Prisons

During the Victorian era a "national" system of large, often recently constructed government or "convict" prisons was developed, where inmates served sentences of penal servitude, these existing in tandem with the local prisons. These sentences were usually for a minimum of at least three years (at times the figure was five

---

[1962] *The Ipswich Journal*, 7 July, 1877.

[1963] *The Bury and Norwich Post*, 13 January, 1857.

[1964] *The Ipswich Journal*, 3 January, 1888.

[1965] *The Bury and Norwich Post,* 10 January, 1855.

[1966] *The Ipswich Journal*, 4 July, 1874.

[1967] *Ibid.*, 10 May, 1884.

years) and could be for life. Thus, in 1874, at the Norfolk assizes, Frederick Wales, a 21-year-old labourer, was indicted for murdering Thomas Pettingill but was found guilty of the lesser offence of manslaughter and sentenced to penal servitude for the term of his natural life.[1968] As this suggests, Norfolk fed into these establishments in appropriate situations, although none of them was physically situated inside the county.

Penal servitude would usually start with an initial period of around nine months being served in a prison such as Millbank or Pentonville. These had initially been built before the advent of the punishment, due to concern about the poor conditions found on the hulks. Millbank had opened in 1816, becoming the largest gaol in England, one that could hold 1,200 inmates. The bulk of the convict's sentence would then normally be spent in other national or convict prisons that had been built or expanded after the end of transportation and use of the hulks and the introduction of penal servitude. Many of them were in or near London, among these being Woking, Wormwood Scrubs, and Fulham Refuge (for female convicts). Others included Portland in Dorset and Dartmoor in Devonshire. It was common for prisoners serving long terms of penal servitude to move around the system during their sentence, so that they often spent time in more than one government prison. For example, Patrick Madden, from Wakefield, passed through five of them in the 1880s.[1969] There were still six such convict prisons for those sentenced to penal servitude in 1901, despite a late Victorian decline in inmates.

Government prisons were administered by a Board of Directors of Convict Prisons. Daily life for those incarcerated within their walls was designed to be tough, and even to break the inmates' spirits.[1970] Nevertheless, although penal servitude was deemed a much more draconian sentence than one of simple imprisonment, not least because, by definition, the sentence was longer (at least three, later five, rather than a maximum of two years), it was not necessarily served in less humane circumstances. Conditions in at least some local gaols were harsher than those found in the convict prisons (see below). For example, the treadmill, the crank (pointlessly turning a weighted handle for long periods), and shot drill (carrying a cannonball backward and forwards across a prison yard) were more commonly found in local rather than convict prisons, where initial oakum picking and sewing in the cells, later followed by engagement in outdoor public works, was usually the daily pattern.[1971] Thus, at Millbank many inmates were engaged in tailoring in their cells, employment that was considered "clean," and not viewed as hard or

---

[1968] *The Norfolk Chronicle*, 5 August, 1874

[1969] Barry Godfrey, *Crime in England 1880-1945: The Rough and the Criminal, the Policed and the Incarcerated* (Abingdon: Routledge, 2013), p. 3.

[1970] Cox, "Rights, Responsibilities," p. 33.

[1971] Philip Priestley, *Victorian Prison Lives* (London: Pimlico, 1999), p. 131.

"laborious" work.[1972] Those at Dartmoor might clear moorland for farming or build roads, and so were outdoors for much of the day.

Nevertheless, although convict prisons may have been an improvement on the hulks, they were not necessarily a healthy environment. Woodhouse Moore, sentenced to seven years' transportation at Norwich quarter sessions in January 1847 for stealing corn from a barn at night, was imprisoned at Millbank in March 1847. Moore was in good health when he entered the prison but was transferred to the infirmary within a few weeks, as he was suffering from pleurisy of the chest, and died there in late April 1847, aged just 26. (The inquest into his death found that his lungs had "scrofulous disease.")[1973] John L'Estrange was still in Millbank when he died of natural causes, just two months after he was convicted in Norwich in 1877.[1974]

Government prisoners serving terms of "penal servitude" were usually termed "convicts." Those in local jails who had been sentenced to "imprisonment" (see below) were often referred to simply as "prisoners." The number of convicts was tiny compared to those who received a term of imprisonment. In 1896, for every 516 offenders sentenced to the latter, just 19 received the former disposal.[1975] However, because the average sentence for penal servitude was very much longer than for imprisonment, the proportion of those incarcerated at any one time was vastly greater than their share of committals, so that they usually made up around a third or more of those serving a custodial punishment around the country. As with those in local prisons, the numbers incarcerated in convict prisons fell heavily in the late Victorian period (see below). In Norfolk, as elsewhere in England, those sentenced to penal servitude would normally wait in the local prison where they had been held prior to conviction for a place in a convict establishment to become free. This might take several weeks or more.

Sentences of Imprisonment

In 1837 the direct involvement of the state in imprisonment was limited to the hulks and a handful of centrally funded government prisons, such as Millbank. However, a sentence of simple imprisonment, with or without hard labour, was the most important disposal for indictable crimes by the start of the Victorian period. Such sentences were served in local prisons. It was a relatively new disposal as a mass punishment; historically, custody had been used to secure those awaiting trial or post-conviction punishment. Nevertheless, in 1836, for every 1,000 offenders sentenced throughout the country for indictable offences, 685 were punished by imprisonment in local prisons. Just 33 were executed, 21 were fined, and 245 were

---

[1972] William Hamilton Thomson, *Five Years' Penal Servitude, By One Who has Endured It* (London: R. Bentley, 1878), p. 82.

[1973] *The Era*, 9 January, 1848.

[1974] *The Ipswich Journal*, 7 July, 1877.

[1975] Victor Bailey, "English Prisons, Penal Culture, and the Abatement of Imprisonment, 1895-1922," *Journal of British Studies*, vol. 36, no. 3 (1997), p. 287.

sentenced to transportation. In 1896, towards the end of the era, 516 per thousand convicts found guilty at jury forums received a sentence of simple imprisonment.[1976]

Such sentences involved relatively short periods of custody, from one day to a maximum of two years, with or without hard labour, although most inmates were sentenced to less than three months in prison. The average sentence of local imprisonment was 48 days in 1880, but this had fallen to 34 days in I893.[1977] For an example of one extreme, at the Norfolk quarter sessions sitting at Walsingham in January 1843, 16-year-old George Allcock received just seven days for stealing wood from Lord Townshend in Raynham.[1978] Around the middle of the range, at the Norfolk quarter sessions in Norwich in July 1892, a man who had stolen a magnifying glass received three months' imprisonment.[1979] At the severe end of the spectrum, at the Norfolk assizes in July 1853, after 24-year-old William Curnish pleaded guilty to sending a letter to a farmer, threatening to shoot him if he did not abandon labour-destroying machinery, he received the maximum two years' imprisonment with hard labour.[1980]

Local Prisons

Until control was nationalized in 1877, local prisons were controlled by the county authorities or borough corporations. They were funded from the rates. At the start of the Victorian era, there were about 300 in England and Wales.[1981] As late as 1877 there were still 112 of them, compared to just a dozen convict prisons, and, as already indicated, at any one time they held at least twice as many prisoners as the latter.[1982] Their number had been reduced to just 58 at the end of the Queen's reign.[1983] Their distribution within the country varied greatly. In 1877 Earl Beauchamp observed in Parliament that "Norfolk [ignoring its boroughs] had as many as five prisons, whilst other counties with a greater population had only one." Staffordshire was amongst the latter. Despite a population of 858,000, it had a single county prison.[1984]

As the above figures suggest, during the Victorian era the number of local prisons, both county and borough administered, fell sharply, as smaller or less efficient establishments were closed, and inmates were concentrated in larger gaols.[1985] The

---

[1976] Bailey, "English Prisons," p. 287.

[1977] C. Harding, "'The inevitable end of a discredited system'? The Origins of the Gladstone Committee Report on Prisons, 1895," *The Historical Journal*, vol. 31, no. 3 (1988), p. 594.

[1978] *The Bury and Norwich Post*, 18 January, 1843

[1979] *The Woman's Herald*, 9 July, 1892.

[1980] *The Ipswich Journal*, 30 July, 1853.

[1981] Taylor, *Hooligans, Harlots,* p. 205. Bailey, "English Prisons," p. 286.

[1982] Seán McConville, *English Local Prisons, 1860-1900: Next Only to Death* (Abingdon: Routledge, 1994), p. 5.

[1983] Bentley, *English Criminal Justice,* p. 14.

[1984] Hansard HL Deb 28 June 1877 vol. 235 col. 383.

[1985] Bentley, *English Criminal Justice,* p. 14.

advent of national control of local prisons, as a result of the 1877 legislation, led to a particularly marked decline, with about 50 closing during the immediately ensuing years.[1986] In Norfolk as elsewhere, the county gaol gradually swallowed up most other local prisons (both county and borough) over the course of the Victorian era.

There was also a considerable drop in the number of inmates held in custody (in both convict and local prisons), the total declining by well over a third between the late 1870s and early 1890s despite an increase in national population. During Edmund Du Cane's administration in the late Victorian period, the local prison population fell from a daily average of almost 21,000 in the year 1877-8 to 13,850 in 1893-4. (That for convict prisons fell from just over 10,000 to 4,383 over the same period, producing a combined fall from 31,000 to 18,333 inmates.) Inevitably, these improving figures were used by apologists for the effectiveness of the prison system, although others viewed such trends as being, in part, the result of a change in sentencing practice. Thus, Charles Troup, a senior Home Office clerk, pointed out that the judicial statistics for 1893 showed a decrease of only 35 percent in the number of committals to prison over the previous decade. Not only were fewer offenders being given prison sentences, but they were also receiving shorter terms (a decline of 29 percent in average length of disposal), helping to explain the fall in the prison population.[1987]

The Norfolk County Prisons

The Norfolk County Gaol, situated in Norwich Castle until 1887, was by far the most important county prison, being used to hold prisoners awaiting trial and those who had been sentenced to imprisonment or who were waiting for some other disposal (as well as some debtors until 1867). In the late eighteenth century it had been rebuilt to a design that incorporated the shell of the Norman keep in a manner that reflected the prison standards of the era. However, it was soon thought to be overcrowded and unsuitable, given the increased emphasis on classification and separation of inmates in the early nineteenth century. A new establishment became necessary.

Edward Harbord, in his role as a reformist Norfolk magistrate, took a close interest in the rebuilding of the castle prison and an adjacent House of Correction, to a design by William Wilkins, which took place from 1823 to 1828, at a cost of £50,000. The new institution was larger and more complex than its predecessor, covering the entire top of the castle mound; three three-storey cellblocks, each containing a double row of cells, radiated from a central gaoler's house. There were 240 cells in these wings and 36 in the old keep.[1988] The governor's house was at the centre of the prison so that it could command a view of all its wings, day rooms, and yards.

[1986] Sharpe, *Judicial Punishment,* p. 67.

[1987] Harding, "'Inevitable End,'' p. 594.

[1988] White, *History, Gazetteer,* pp. 90-91.

A variety of statistics, from different years, shed light on its size and operation. Thus some 801 prisoners of all types (remand, debtors, and those undergoing punishment) passed through its doors in 1835, and 813 in 1843, staying for very varying periods of time.[1989] In 1861 it was noted that the gaol could hold up to 225 inmates.[1990] However, in 1876 an average of just 95 prisoners were accommodated there at any one time, at an annual cost per prisoner of £43 2s 10d. At this point, there was a governor (paid a salary of £350 per annum), chaplain (£300), prison surgeon (£120), matron (£40), and 12 prison officers, each of whom received an average of about £56 a year.[1991]

Although the chaplain was paid almost as much as the governor, his remit was not confined to spiritual matters. In October 1856, on the death of the octogenarian Reverend James Brown, it was noted that he had been chaplain to the county prison in Norwich for 20 years, as well as holding other positions and livings. In his prison capacity he had apparently been known for the reports he prepared on inmates; magistrates and prison inspectors considered these "models of what these documents should be – plain statements respecting the spiritual, moral, and educational condition of the prisoners." They were free of the dogmatizing tone that was often seen in such reports.[1992]

Although well received when new, the castle prison buildings proved difficult to adapt to the regular experimentation in carceral regimes over ensuing decades. As a result, it eventually closed in 1887.[1993] In July of that year, a new purpose-built prison on Plumstead Road in Norwich, designed by the surveyor to the Prison Department, was completed. The following month, prisoners from the county gaol were transferred to the new establishment.[1994] It was built to a standard form for the time, involving "one long building with three floors of cells, the upper floors being reached by galleries – so that complete supervision can be exercised." It stood in extensive walled grounds and accommodated both male and female prisoners.[1995]

Other County Prisons

In 1800 the Norfolk quarter sessions had had responsibility for five county bridewells or, as they were more formally termed, houses of correction, as well as of the county gaol in Norwich. The five establishments were located at Acle, Aylsham, Swaffham, Little Walsingham, and Wymondham. By the nineteenth century, they

---

1989 *Ibid.*

1990 *Judicial Statistics, 1861,* p. 40.

1991 *The Ipswich Journal*, 25 August, 1877.

1992 *The Bury and Norwich Post*, 8 October, 1856.

1993 Nicholas Arber, "Presenting Prison History at Norwich Castle," *Prison Service Journal*, no. 210 (2013), pp. 29-33.

1994 Mackie, *Norfolk Annals,* vol. 2, p. 381.

1995 White, *History, Gazetteer,* p. 526.

effectively operated as divisional county prisons, whatever may have been their founding ethos. Each of them had a committee of visiting justices, whose task was to inspect and report to quarter sessions on their condition. County prisoners might be distributed among them according to the division in which they were convicted, available space, their geographical provenance, and any other factors felt to be relevant. Thus, at the start of 1847, James Spragg and James Fitt were convicted at quarter sessions for stealing from a dwelling house and each was sentenced to 12 months' imprisonment with hard labour. Spragg was sent to the county gaol in Norwich Castle, Fitt to Walsingham.[1996]

Acle and Aylsham bridewells had been closed in the late eighteenth and early nineteenth centuries, long before the new Queen's reign. However, the other three survived until well into the Victorian era. For example, in 1834 Little Walsingham bridewell, which been built in 1787, was reported to have 32 cells, but in 1843 it was enlarged, so that it had 53, as well as several day rooms, airing yards, and a well-ventilated infirmary.[1997] In March 1861 the Norfolk quarter sessions having departed from the town, Walsingham ceased to be used, and its male prisoners were moved to the Norwich Castle prison and its female inmates to Wymondham bridewell. (Provision was made to compensate the gaol's officeholders, not least because its chaplain had given up a position to take up the office not long previously and had a young family.)[1998]

The Swaffham bridewell or county prison had been erected in 1787, and considerably enlarged in 1844, at a cost of £1,500. It was a large establishment; in 1861 it could hold 146 prisoners (though it very rarely did).[1999] In 1868 it contained 67 cells and three hospital rooms, as well as a residence for its governor. The prisoners there were employed in mat-making, weaving sacks, tailoring, shoemaking, oakum picking, and pumping water from a 150-foot well.[2000] However, it was closed in 1878 under the Prisons Act of 1877 and pulled down in 1881.[2001]

Although Wymondham bridewell had closed in 1827, with its inmates being relocated to the county gaol in Norwich, it was reopened in 1832 as a county prison for women. Life there was, in some ways, a little easier than for their male equivalents. In 1845 it was noted that the inmates who were "sentenced to hard labour are employed in washing and sewing for the male prisoners at Norwich." The prison held ten women at the start of 1841.[2002] However, an average of 19 were

---

[1996] *The Norfolk News*, 9 January, 1847.

[1997] White, *History, Gazetteer*, p. 680.

[1998] Mackie, *Norfolk Annals, vol. 2*, p. 103. *The Bury and Norwich Post*, 8 January, 1861.

[1999] *Judicial Statistics 1861*, p. 74.

[2000] J.G. Harrod & Co., *Postal & Commercial Directory of Norfolk and Norwich* (London and Norwich: J.G. Harrod & Co., 1868), pp. 610-611.

[2001] White, *History, Gazetteer*, p. 711.

[2002] *The Bury and Norwich Post*, 13 January, 1841.

there at any one time during the following year.[2003] In 1853 the average was, again, 19 inmates. Of these, five were typically under 16 years of age; five were married, and 14 were single (including the juveniles). The women were instructed in reading and writing by the matron and engaged in various tasks, such as matmaking, as well as laundry. Little had changed by 1877, when Wymondham held an average of 18 prisoners. By then its chaplain was paid £125 a year, and the matron fully £90. Its two prison warders each received £82 a year, while part-time surgeon earned £30. There is no mention in the records of a governor, which is unsurprising given its small size.[2004]

Typical of its prisoners, in 1877 Mary Parkinson pleaded guilty to criminal damage at Thetford petty sessions, after breaking six panes of glass in a window in the union workhouse, where she was an inmate, and was sentenced to 14 days in Wymondham (how much worse this would have been than the workhouse is, perhaps, debatable).[2005] The following year, a pregnant Ann Purling (or Purdy) was convicted at the Norfolk Lent assizes for theft and sentenced to three months' imprisonment in the bridewell (where she gave birth shortly afterwards).[2006] Wymondham prison was shut down in March 1878 and its inmates committed to female wings in the Norfolk county prison in Norwich.[2007] Part of the building was subsequently used as a magistrates' court.

The Norfolk Borough Prisons

The second category of local prisons in Norfolk, those controlled by the boroughs, included the city of Norwich common gaol, which fulfilled the same role for prisoners from Norwich that the castle prison did for the wider county. In August 1826 its inmates were moved to a new purpose-built prison outside St Giles Gates in Heigham, designed by Philip Barnes, a local architect, and built at a cost of £30,000. This prison survived for the bulk of the Victorian era.[2008] The Norwich house of correction was located on the same site, and shared its senior management, officially merging with the city's gaol in 1838 to become one institution.

In 1845 the prison was described as a large quadrangular building, with towers on its corners, eight yards, eight dayrooms, and 69 sleeping cells. During 1843 some 859 prisoners passed through its doors (129 were debtors) but there were seldom more than 80 to 100 there at any one time.[2009] By 1877 this had fallen to an average

---

2003 White, *History, Gazetteer,* p. 447.

2004 *The Ipswich Journal*, 25 August, 1877.

2005 *The Bury and Norwich Post*, 11 November, 1873.

2006 TNA HO 18/19/37.

2007 *The Bury and Norwich Post*, 5 March, 1878.

2008 Mackie, *Norfolk Annals,* vol. 1, p. 258.

2009 White, *History, Gazetteer,* p. 88.

of just 40. By then the governor's salary was £200, along with a coal and gas allowance, while the chaplain received just £100. There were nine prison officers.[2010]

The city gaol was closed in May 1878 and its prisoners moved to the county gaol at the castle, which then became a combined prison for both Norfolk and Norwich.[2011] However, the two institutions had some connection, even before merger. For example, during a smallpox outbreak at the castle prison in 1876, in which a dozen inmates became infected (two of them seriously), the county made temporary arrangements with the city authorities to commit its prisoners to the Norwich gaol.[2012]

In 1837 there were also borough gaols at Great Yarmouth, Thetford, and King's Lynn. Yarmouth prison was home to the town gaol, its house of correction, and several debtors' wards. The nineteenth-century gaol had been built in 1818, its floors being divided into galleries, each with several cells; sickrooms and day rooms were also provided for inmates. It was apparently a well-aired and -ventilated prison. Its exercise yards were so divided that different classes of prisoner were kept apart, the debtors being separate from the felons and the convicted from those on remand awaiting trial.[2013] Prisoners were also separated by gender (though men and women still managed to contact one another), but otherwise inmates worked, ate, exercised, and even slept together. At the start of the 1840s, it held about 30 inmates at any one time, most of them men, nearly half under 21 years of age. Many were incarcerated for pilfering, disorderly behaviour, vagrancy, or even absconding from an apprenticeship, and were often drawn from Yarmouth's poorest social stratum. Few served more than six months. They were expected to be quiet and orderly rather than silent, although shouting and loud singing at night were punished.[2014] The prison was eventually closed in 1875.

The King's Lynn borough gaol, which adjoined the Guildhall, had been enlarged and improved in 1831 at a cost of some £2,300. It had four day-use rooms and four small yards for the prisoners. The debtors and felons were kept separate, and other classifications of prisoners (convicted, remand, etc.) in so far as the small size of the prison would allow. It had accommodation for about 50 inmates, but at any one time rarely had more than 30.[2015] It finally closed in 1866. The Thetford gaol had been rebuilt in 1796 and enlarged in 1816. At the start of 1857, it was noted that the Thetford Corporation had asked to accommodate its borough prisoners in the Castle at the same rate, 4s 6d a person a week, as was already sometimes allowed to those from King's Lynn.[2016] The prison closed that same year.

[2010] *The Ipswich Journal*, 25 August, 1877.

[2011] Mackie, *Norfolk Annals,* vol. 2, p. 284.

[2012] *The Essex Standard*, 25 February, 1876.

[2013] White, *History, Gazetteer,* p. 256.

[2014] Rogers, "The Way To Jerusalem," pp. 78-80.

[2015] White, *History, Gazetteer,* p. 526.

[2016] *The Bury and Norwich Post*, 13 January, 1857.

Control of Local Prisons

At the beginning of the Victorian period, local prisons were controlled by county quarter sessions and the boards of visiting JPs that they appointed or by borough corporations and their committees. At this time many observers were expressing concern about the uncoordinated system that localism and the separation of local from government prisons produced and urged the introduction of a more cohesive and uniform prison regime throughout the country. In 1835 the Home Office was authorized by statute (5 & 6 Will IV c.38) to inspect local prisons, appointing paid officers who reported to the Home Secretary, something that encouraged the spread of good practice and so promoted a modicum of consistency.[2017] For example, in February 1841 Aylesbury gaol in Buckinghamshire was the subject of a report detailing breaches of statutory regulations, and describing how the governor was still making money from selling food and drink to inmates and even using prisoners to groom his horses.[2018]

The new post-1835 prison inspectorates could have a major impact on gaol conditions. On his first inspection of the Great Yarmouth gaol in 1836, Captain Williams produced a damning report, portraying an unreformed gaol where the corporation had done little to meet statutory requirements for the standardization of discipline and classification of inmates. Any improvements had been brought about by outsiders, such as the prison visitor Sarah Martin. However, in 1837 a new gaoler, sympathetic to the measures advocated by the inspectorate, prompted a dramatic change in the prison culture. According to Martin, its previous "undisciplined state" was replaced by an environment in which no singing, laughing, bad language, loud talking, gaming, or fighting was permitted. Both inmates and their accommodation were kept clean.[2019]

In 1855 Lord Brougham urged that matters should go further, and argued that the "same prison rules should be universally followed, being prescribed by the executive Government, and only modified under the local authorities according to particular local circumstances."[2020] This would take another 22 years, but uniformity increased after the advent of the Prison Act 1865, which allowed the withholding of central funds from institutions that did not satisfy regulations established by the same statute. In 1877 local control finally came to an end, when Parliament took the drastic step of centralizing the running of all prisons.[2021] As part of this process, the Home Secretary was given extensive statutory powers to administer local prisons,

---

[2017] John A. Stack, "The Juvenile Delinquent and England's 'Revolution in Government,' 1825-1875," *The Historian*, vol. 42, no. 1 (1979), p. 43.

[2018] Eric Stockdale, "A Short History of Prison Inspection in England," *The British Journal of Criminology*, vol. 23, no. 3 (1983), pp. 215-218.

[2019] Rogers, "The Way To Jerusalem," pp. 71-104.

[2020] Hansard, HL Deb 23 March 1855 vol. 137 cols. 952-77, 968.

[2021] Stack, "The Juvenile Delinquent," p. 43.

albeit that this was largely delegated to a new Board of Prison Commissioners, supported by an inspectorate and central staff.[2022]

Local Prison Conditions

Fragmented control prior to the late Victorian period meant that the conditions in local prisons varied greatly around the country and over time. During the nineteenth century, prisons underwent radical change. The rather chaotic, dirty, but often relaxed and even sociable Hanoverian gaol was gradually replaced by the modern prison with its ordered and tightly structured regime.[2023] Nevertheless, life in Victorian prisons, of almost all types, remained very harsh, especially in the early decades of the era, even if better in some ways than in earlier centuries. Judge Bramwell thought that 18 months in many county prisons was as much as most people could tolerate.[2024] Another Victorian judge thought that the maximum penalty of two years' local imprisonment was the most severe punishment known to English law, being "next only to death." However, some local gaols were very much milder than this comment suggests, and still subject to rather relaxed regimes, if only because of their small size and limited resources.

For those who were not in good health when they began their sentence, prison could be particularly dangerous; this was recognized by the authorities, even at the start of the era. A significant number of inmates had at least part of their sentences remitted on the basis that continuing in custody might threaten their lives. For example, in early 1836 James Williamson, who had been convicted of riot at the Norfolk quarter sessions at Walsingham the previous year, avoided the final 19 months of his custodial sentence "on account of [his] state of health." The successful petition on his behalf to the Home Office, made by John Harvey, the chairman of the visiting magistrates to Norwich Castle gaol, was supported by a certificate issued by the surgeon to the prison, opining that Williamson would not survive the remaining part of his sentence without a change of air. (A certificate from the prison chaplain, noting his exemplary conduct while in gaol, also helped his cause.)[2025]

Similarly, some months after Elizabeth Mortar was convicted at the Norfolk quarter sessions for receiving stolen goods in March 1839, and sentenced to 12 months' imprisonment in the Wymondham bridewell, she received clemency. In November that year, it seems that the outstanding part of her sentence was remitted for reasons of ill health, including asthma and lung disease. Again, the prison surgeon produced a report confirming Mortar's poor physical condition, and local JPs supported remitting her sentence.[2026] John Green, convicted of housebreaking at

[2022] Bentley, *English Criminal Justice,* p. 14.

[2023] J.M. Moore, "Behind Victorian Bars," *History Today,* vol. 69, no. 1 (2019), pp. 60-67.

[2024] Carolyn Conley, *The Unwritten Law*, p. 143

[2025] TNA HO 17/38/31.

[2026] TNA HO 18/6/46.

the same forum in October 1839, and sentenced to imprisonment for one year in the county gaol, was discharged more than four months early in May 1840 for the same reason. A certificate from the surgeon of Norwich Castle, Page Nicol Scott, certified that he was dangerously ill with a pulmonary complaint.[2027]

Prison Regimes

Developments in America heavily influenced English prison regimes during the nineteenth century, not least because British officials went across the Atlantic to report on them. Two schools of thought, the separate and the silent systems, emerged in the United States and acquired their own proponents in Britain. The former stressed total separation of inmates. This was extremely expensive, as it required each prisoner to have his own cell, which had to be fit for work, eating, and sleeping. Ideally this necessitated a degree of space, ventilation, heating, and sanitation. In theory, prisoners would emerge from their cells only to perform solitary exercise in airing yards, to power treadwheels, and to go to a partitioned chapel. When they did, some were even required to wear special masks to prevent them from talking to other prisoners. For example, in the government's Pentonville prison, which opened in 1842 and was (initially) an exemplar of the separate system, prisoners were required to wear "beaks" when moving around the establishment.[2028] They were forbidden from communicating with one another and spent almost 23 hours of each day alone in their cells.[2029]

As cruel as this may seem today, the regime was broadly reformist in its ethos. It was hoped that such isolation would encourage inmates to reflect on their lives, and so change their behaviour. As the Pentonville experience suggests, the separate system was introduced in several national (later 'convict') prisons during the 1840s. However, it was also adopted by some local prisons, to varying degrees. For example, JPs and prison governors were still committed to upholding the separate system in the Liverpool borough gaol in the 1850s and 1860s. Although their aims were often thwarted, they went beyond lip service. The system was also introduced to several other local prisons in Lancashire, including Preston and Kirkdale gaols.[2030] A diluted form of the separate system influenced many of the regimes in other county or borough gaols. However, as well as being very expensive, the system often produced acute psychological stress and numerous instances of mental illness.[2031] By 1847 it

---

2027 TNA HO 18/23/9.

2028 Emsley, *Crime and Society,* pp. 285-286.

2029 Catherine Cox & Hilary Marland, "'Unfit for reform or punishment': mental disorder and discipline in Liverpool Borough Prison in the late nineteenth century," *Social History*, vol. 44, no. 2 (2019), p. 178.

2030 *Ibid.*

2031 U.R.Q. Henriques, "The Rise and Decline of the Separate System of Prison Discipline," *Past & Present*, vol. 54, no. 1 (1972), pp. 61-93.

was claimed, albeit very prematurely, that the separate system "never very generally adopted, is abandoned, on account of its shocking morbid effects."[2032]

The silent system was ultimately preferred for most prisons that consciously employed a regime, if only because of the lower incidence of psychiatric illness that it engendered and its smaller cost (always a very important factor). Ironically, it had less emphasis on reform and was more focused on general deterrence.[2033] It was the easier and cheaper of the two systems to introduce since it permitted the use of existing accommodation and allowed for associated outdoor labour. It was aimed at keeping prisoners engaged in hard work, whether individually or communally, something that, it was hoped, would deter reoffending. Even so, by the end of the 1840s it was generally acknowledged that it did not do this, with some noting that "we cannot say that it [the silent system] proves to be very efficacious either in deterring or reforming."[2034]

Nevertheless, despite such scepticism, and accepting that reform was unlikely, the mid-Victorian period saw the triumph of deterrence, which gradually became the major rationale for imprisonment until late in the nineteenth century. This development was reinforced by the Caernarvon Committee and its concern that penal servitude was not sufficiently "dreaded." Its success can be seen most clearly in the Prisons Act 1865 and the promotion of the then Assistant Director of Prisons, Sir Edmund du Cane (1830-1903), to Chairman of Convict Prisons in 1869. Sir Edmund famously promised the public that prisoners would get "Hard Labour, Hard Fare and Hard Board." Under this regime, wooden boards (usually three planks) often replaced hammocks, flogging of inmates for transgressions in prison became more common, and (even more) monotonous low-quality dietary regimes were introduced. The 1865 statute also formally introduced the treadmill, although many were already in use, the first having been established in Bury St Edmunds gaol in 1818, following a plan by a Norfolk designer. Inmates might have to climb the equivalent of 6,000 feet (or more) on a treadmill as part of their daily labour, ascending for 15 minutes and then taking a five-minute break. As late as 1888, when asked in the House of Commons about their use, the Secretary of State for the Home Department, Henry Matthews, noted that the treadmill was still employed, and claimed that he was not aware that this form of hard labour had been condemned as cruel and unprofitable, not least because: "Whenever it is possible [often not the case], the labour is utilized for the purpose of pumping or grinding; so it cannot be called useless, and I do not think it is inhumane".[2035] The treadmill was eventually banned in 1902. The crank and shot drill provided other forms of gruelling, pointless, and repetitive prison labour during the Victorian era.

[2032] Anon., "4,000 a Year," p. 12.

[2033] Taylor, "Rationing Crime," p. 573.

[2034] Anon., "4,000 a Year," p. 12.

[2035] Hansard HC Deb 25 June 1888 vol. 327 col. 1142.

Even so, since most gaols were locally controlled until 1877, even if centrally monitored, there was very considerable variation and modification in the implementation of both the separate and silent systems outside convict prisons. In some gaols, no system at all was employed, with more historic and informal regimes continuing, while many other provincial prisons operated hybrid systems, with elements of older approaches surviving amid selective modern introductions.[2036] For example, the initial period of an inmate's custody might be spent entirely in their cell, chapel apart, in a process that was resonant of the separate system, before they progressed to communal but silent work.

Unsurprisingly, larger local prisons were better placed to enforce regimes based on silence, relative isolation, hard work, and spiritual ministration. Consequently, the two Norwich prisons, by far the largest in Norfolk, were better able to reflect the regimes that came to prominence during the Victorian period than were the county's smaller penal establishments. Both visiting magistrates and the gaols' senior staff influenced how this was done. For example, George Pinson, the long-serving governor of the Norwich Castle prison from 1843 to 1877, appears to have rejected the use of dark cells and the crank, and preferred open seating in chapel rather than the separate-system type of seating found at Lincoln Castle prison. Nevertheless, refurbishment carried out in the year 2000 exposed several previously long-hidden interiors and floor plans in the prison that revealed the attempts made to introduce the separate system into the gaol. It appears that, during the 1850s, communal day rooms had been converted into cells, while previously fixed iron beds had been removed and replaced with hammocks, which could be packed away, creating more space in the cells for working in solitude. (The part of the prison employed for remand prisoners awaiting trial remained unchanged.)[2037]

Frederick Rolfe's experience in the Norwich Castle prison is indicative of local imprisonment in the mid-Victorian era. Rolfe spent a month there in the 1870s for poaching. After leaving court, he was publicly walked under guard through the city streets to the prison gates, admitted to the institution, stripped, given a bath, and issued with prison clothes. His single cell was ten feet by six, with a stone floor, a wooden board as a bed, a stool, and a table. It also contained a Bible, prayer book, and hymnbook. He was periodically visited by the prison chaplain, who usually emphasized the gravity of his offence, and said that he should make sure not to drift into worse crimes. Regular chapel attendance was also part of the regime. Rolfe was required to work up to 12 hours a day, either on the treadwheel or picking oakum, and often at a combination of the two. The former was very hard work, like walking uphill continuously (less breaks) for three hours at a time. Oakum picking was less gruelling, if very dirty and hard on the fingers. Fibres were teased out from old ropes and later mixed with tar for caulking boats. Each prisoner had to do a set amount each day, perhaps three pounds, although some indulgence was often granted for

[2036] Anon., "4,000 a Year," p. 12.

[2037] Arber, "Prison History," pp. 29-33.

failures to achieve the requisite quantity.[2038] After two weeks, Rolfe's initial, largely flour-based, diet improved, with bacon, potatoes and, boiled beef being provided. The prison, like many others, employed a marks system, linking conduct and work performance with reward, with punishment for misconduct or failing to perform set tasks, such as being placed on a bread-and-water diet and/or incarceration in a dark cell.[2039]

Outside the county capital, the situation varied considerably. In 1845 it was noted that the 50 or so inmates of the Little Walsingham bridewell powered four treadwheels, used for grinding corn, while the prison was largely conducted on the silent system; it was claimed that this was very beneficial in "preventing the prisoners from instructing each other in their nefarious arts."[2040] By contrast, in the 1860s there were numerous problems with the King's Lynn borough gaol, which had become very lax and insecure, with neither system being applied. In September 1863, when the inspectors of prisons in the Southern District of England produced their annual report, they concluded that, as a result, it was very unsuited for punishing prisoners. The inmates lived in "idleness," doing no work other than cleaning the prison; discipline was poor; accommodation was unsuitable; and the governor was supported by an insufficient number of turnkeys. Even then, the town council was considering abolishing the prison.[2041] This duly occurred in 1866; prisoners from Lynn were thereafter sent to the county gaol at Norwich.

Change in the Late Victorian Period

By the late Victorian era most observers were aware of the deleterious effects of imprisonment. This prompted limited government action. The Probation of First Offenders Act of 1886, albeit little used, allowed the courts to release first offenders who had been convicted of larceny or a kindred offence, merely binding them over to keep the peace, in certain extenuating circumstances (such as youth, good character, no prior record, or triviality of offence). More generally, the courts became increasingly cautious about having ready recourse to custodial sentences, especially for the young. At the Yarmouth borough quarter sessions in January 1888, two boys, aged 15 and 16, who pleaded guilty to stealing rope worth three shillings from a boat, were dealt with leniently after lengthy discussion between the town recorder and magistrates, the court "not wishing to make gaol birds of them." One was sentenced to five years in a reformatory; the other was released on his own recognizance – provided he did not re-offend, he would not be punished (presumably, this was under the 1886 statute). At the same sessions, Alfred Gibbs a 16-year-old boy, pleaded guilty to stealing £6 10s from his master. He was sentenced

---

2038 Priestley, *Victorian Prison Lives*, pp. 121-122.

2039 Frederick Rolfe, *I Walked by Night: Being the Philosophy of the King of the Norfolk Poachers, Written by Himself* (Machynlleth, Wales: Coch-y-Bonddu Books, 2009), pp. 4-42.

2040 White, *History, Gazetteer*, p. 680.

2041 *The Bury and Norwich Post*, 8 September, 1863.

to just one day's imprisonment, after his employer attended court and indicated that he would give Gibbs another chance and take him back into his service. [2042]

In the final years of the nineteenth century, penal conditions were also reconsidered, as attitudes towards criminals changed. Offending came to be seen less as a rational choice that could be discouraged by severe deterrent punishment (the classical paradigm), and more as a product of social conditions (the positivist analysis). As a result, reform-based notions began to influence penal policy. Even lay observers and inmates noticed this. Looking back, Fred Rolfe thought that the post-1887 combined county and city prison on Plumstead Road was much more humane and comfortable than its predecessor in the castle, its conditions and regime being a great improvement on what had gone before, with inmates even receiving an allowance of cocoa.[2043]

Perhaps indicative of this change was the information adduced in 1888 when an inquest was held on James Sewell, a 44-year-old man convicted at the Norfolk assizes a few weeks earlier who died of consumption in the new prison. He had been sentenced to 18 months' imprisonment with hard labour for a burglary committed at Stanton during which a violin had been stolen. (Sewell had a previous conviction). He was evidently very ill, even when sentenced. This had been privately drawn to the attention of the presiding judge, Mr Justice Field, by the governor of the new prison, where Sewell had also been held on remand prior to trial. However, the judge declined to alter his sentence and suggested that the prison medical officer petition the Home Office for release on health grounds. This had been done immediately, and would almost certainly have been allowed, but the inmate asked to stay in the prison, as he had no place to go to, and did not find the idea of being committed to a workhouse for his final days appealing. Instead, he had spent almost his entire time in the prison infirmary, for which mercy he (apparently) regularly expressed gratitude. According to the governor, considerable care was taken of him; he had been given port, stout, beef tea, milk, and various other digestible foodstuffs.[2044]

This process accelerated in the 1890s, aided by a series of newspaper articles on prison conditions and Oscar Wilde's reports of his experiences as an inmate.[2045] Most important, in 1895, Sir Edmund Du Cane, the chairman of the Prison Commissioners for almost two decades, resigned. Shortly afterwards, the (Herbert) Gladstone Committee on Prisons published its report, confirming a move towards a more liberal penal policy. It has been suggested that England's *fin-de-siècle* reform of its system of punishment was one of the most striking in Europe. To varying degrees, government policymakers, judicial officials, and even the police began to place more emphasis on rehabilitation. Although the Gladstone committee accepted the continuing importance of deterrence, it also stressed the potentially reformative

[2042] *The Ipswich Journal*, 3 January, 1888.

[2043] Rolfe, *I Walked by Night*, pp. 4-42.

[2044] *The Bury and Norwich Post*, 3 January, 1888.

[2045] Bailey, "English Prisons," p. 288.

aspect of the prison system, and the possibility of combining the two. Many of the fruits of this change would be seen just after the Victorian era, being manifest in, for example, the Probation of Offenders Act 1907.[2046] Nevertheless, its influence can also be seen in developments during the final decade of the period, including a milder, more calibrated system of penalties. For example, the Departmental Committee recommended the introduction of individualized treatment in prisons and stressed the importance of separating prisoners by type (first offenders, habitual offenders, etc.).

These principles were reflected in the Prisons Act of 1898, which produced a more enlightened prison regime and, arguably, marked the beginnings of the modern prison system. The treadmill was abolished, and isolation in prison cells was restricted to a month. In 1899 Mr Justice Matthew, addressing the grand jury of the Norfolk assizes, commented on some recent reforms, but noted that plank beds were still part of a sentence of hard labour, albeit looking forward to their abolition as they prevented essential rest: "He was certain that such punishment was not humane."[2047] Later legislation abolished hard labour and recognized that prison work should have a constructive purpose.

In 1901 there was an attempt to identify a sentencing tariff for various offences, the differences in disposal having occasioned concern for some time and been the subject of a memorandum from the Howard Association to the Home Office in 1878, drawing attention to the impact of the "personal opinions of the judges" on the length of sentences.[2048] This was drawn up by judges at assizes, was not binding, and not even the subject of universal agreement. Furthermore, it was not normally released to chairmen and recorders of quarter sessions, although it was at these forums that the greatest disparities in penal disposal could normally be found. Nevertheless, it reflected what most senior judges at the close of the Victorian period thought appropriate, in most situations, and were themselves passing as sentences. Significantly, the *Memorandum on Normal Punishments in Certain Kinds of Crime* usually proposed a range of potential custodial punishment for certain offences and was indicative of the increased penal leniency of late Victorian times. Some thought it excessively weak. For example, it suggested that juvenile offenders under 16 who were convicted of lesser forms of larceny should not normally be sentenced to imprisonment, unless they had a previous conviction. Adults without previous convictions might either be released on their own recognizance or receive a short term of imprisonment.

[2046] S. Auerbach, "'Beyond the Pale of Mercy': Victorian Penal Culture, Police Court Missionaries, and the Origins of Probation in England," *Law and History Review*, vol. 33, no. 3 (2015), pp. 621-663.

[2047] *The Standard*, 15 June, 1899.

[2048] Leon Radzinowicz and Roger Hood, "Judicial Discretion and Sentencing Standards: Victorian Attempts to Solve a Perennial Problem," *University of Pennsylvania Law Review*, vol. 127, no. 5 (1979), p. 1308.

Prison Security

There were periodic attempts to escape from the various prisons found in Norfolk, although most were unsuccessful. For example, in the small hours of a February morning in 1830, William Brooks, held in the Norwich Castle prison while awaiting trial for highway robbery, tried to lower himself from the walls by means of a rope made of blankets. It broke, and he fell, suffering numerous serious fractures. Despite his injuries, he recovered sufficiently to be tried at the summer assizes, being carried into court on the back of a warder. (Although permanently crippled, he was sentenced to transportation for life.)[2049] In 1837 two prisoners, named Smith and Middleton, escaped from the Norwich city gaol: "One lowered himself by a rope of blankets from the cell, and the other leaped down a depth of 25 ft., by which he sprained his ankle, so that they got no further than Dereham, where they were both retaken."[2050] Lynn Henry Pettett, who already had a successful, if short-lived, escape from Norwich Castle under his belt, made another attempt to break out of the gaol in 1838. He removed stones from the floor of his cell, and improvised a rope from his blanket, but injured himself while trying to get out. As a result, and to prevent a re-occurrence, he was heavily shackled and chained to a post.[2051]

The smaller prisons in the county were less secure than those in Norwich. Early in 1861 four prisoners awaiting trial at the borough sessions violently overpowered a turnkey in the Lynn prison and escaped, albeit that they were captured nearby shortly afterwards.[2052] A few were more successful. At the Thetford borough sessions in July 1850, a man who had broken out of the town gaol some 15 years earlier received a month's imprisonment for his escape.[2053] Presumably he had left the area in the meantime.

Detaining the Criminally Insane

Securing the insane posed special problems. This could be the case even if they had not previously offended. Illustrative of this, in December 1822, Thomas Coleman, a long-term patient in a private lunatic asylum at Loddon, killed James Dale, a keeper in the same establishment, after he laid down a carving knife while supervising dinner. Coleman snatched it up and stabbed Dale, the wound proving fatal within four minutes.[2054] Prior to 1863, Norfolk offenders found to be criminally insane were kept in prison with convicts, incarcerated alongside the ordinary mentally ill in a more secure part of a county asylum, or held in a specialist ward of the Royal Bethlehem Hospital ("Bethlem" or "Bedlam") in London or a similar secure asylum elsewhere in England, this option often being used for particularly dangerous prisoners.

[2049] Mackie, *Norfolk Annals,* vol. 2, p. 253.

[2050] *The Norfolk Chronicle,* 20 May, 1837.

[2051] *The Bury and Norwich Post*, 21 March, 1838.

[2052] *The York Herald*, 30 March, 1861. *The Bury and Norwich Post, and Suffolk Herald*, 26 March, 1861.

[2053] *The Bury and Norwich Post*, 24 July, 1850.

[2054] *The Morning Post*, 10 December, 1822.

In the early 1810s, when the governors of Bethlehem were planning the construction of a new hospital building at St George's Fields, the Home Department agreed to fund a new wing (the Criminal Lunatic Asylum), and to help pay for the care of criminal patients from around the country, who would be kept isolated from other inmates. The admission and discharge of such patients was by warrant from the Secretary of State. It was used for several of the criminally insane from Norfolk. For example, in April 1813 James Bullard, the long-term master of the Bethel Hospital for lunatics in Norwich, was stabbed to death with a scythe by Jonathan Morley, an inmate who was engaged in mowing the lawn. Morley was committed for trial at the assizes, where he was ordered to be kept in custody, "being insane at the time he committed the act." In December 1816 an order was received from the Secretary of State for the Home Department for his removal from the Norwich gaol, where he was still detained, to the new Criminal Lunatic Asylum in St. George's Fields.[2055]

Moving into the Victorian period, in 1860, when Anthony Abel died in Bethlehem, it was noted that he had been there for 43 years, since June 1817, after being acquitted at the Norwich assizes for murdering his uncle, on the grounds of insanity. (The killing occurred after the most minor provocation.) Abel had been removed to the Bethlehem hospital from Norwich gaol on the order of the then Home Secretary, Lord Sidmouth. For many years he was considered so dangerous that he was confined in a cell, and, under the regime then in use, was restrained by a strong belt and gloves and put into irons.[2056] Similarly, in March 1828, at the Norfolk assizes, John Kenny, a 22-year-old man, was tried for murdering a boy. He had strangled his victim and then cut his throat before disembowelling him and cutting out a piece of his liver. He, too, was acquitted on the grounds of insanity.[2057] After his conviction, he was initially kept in the Norfolk Lunatic Asylum, but was viewed as a great inconvenience, as it was felt that there was no effective means of treating him.[2058] A letter from the visiting justices to the asylum asked for him to be removed to the Bethlehem hospital, not least because he was upsetting the other inmates by regaling them with gruesome details of his crime. He was sent there in February 1829, and remained until September 1856, when he was sent to the Fisherton Lunatic Asylum near Salisbury in Wiltshire.[2059] Following an arrangement with the government in 1848, and until 1870, this private and relatively secure establishment accepted criminal lunatics from other asylums around England, especially the

[2055] Mackie, Norfolk Annals, vol. 1, p. 104.

[2056] *The Birmingham Daily Post*, 12 October, 1860.

[2057] *Berrow's Worcester Journal*, 3 April, 1828.

[2058] Steven Cherry, *Mental Health Care in Modern England: The Norfolk Lunatic Asylum/St Andrew's Hospital, 1810-1998* (Woodbridge: Boydell Press, 2003).

[2059] TNA HO 17/68/10.

overflow from Bethlehem, albeit usually those criminal lunatics who were deemed to be less dangerous.[2060]

More benignly, when it came to disposal, in 1832 the Reverend Arthur Iveson of South Lynn was murdered by a pistol shot fired by his 34-year-old son, another cleric, who had been behaving increasingly eccentrically. The latter was tried at King's Lynn borough quarter sessions in July that year (the court would lose its special power to hear murder cases in 1835). The jury found that he was insane at the time the crime was committed, and he was ordered to be detained in custody for life. He remained in King's Lynn gaol until 3 September, when he was removed to the lunatic asylum at St Lawrence in Norwich.[2061] At the Lent assizes for Norfolk, in April 1839, William Gathercole, a 33-year-old-man, was acquitted of manslaughter due to insanity. He had attempted to kill himself, and another man had drowned while trying to save him. As a result, it was ordered that Gathercole be kept in custody. He was initially held in the Norwich Castle gaol. However, letters were subsequently sent seeking authority to remove him to the County Lunatic Asylum at Burnham. He was duly moved there, but, at the end of 1841, the establishment's visiting justices forwarded a certificate from its medical officers stating that Gathercole was in a sound state of mind and no longer a fit subject for confinement in the asylum. He was returned to Norwich Castle gaol, prompting a successful campaign to secure his release.[2062] A few years later, in 1847, Eliza Pegg, who had initially been returned to Wymondham bridewell after being found not guilty of child murder by reason of insanity, was moved to the asylum at Thorpe.[2063]

None of these expedients was thought to be entirely satisfactory, as they were lacking in security and had a negative impact on ordinary lunatics in the same establishments. Broadmoor Criminal Lunatic Asylum, which opened in Bedfordshire in 1863, was intended to provide a superior and more secure national alternative, at least for very serious cases.

Broadmoor

After 1863, and as the Baldwin case suggests, Broadmoor took the more dangerous criminal lunatics (and a small majority of the total who were so classified) from all of England.[2064] For example, in March 1838 Uriah Baldwin, a 27-year-old man, was acquitted at the Norwich city assizes as insane after being tried for cutting his wife with intent to murder her. It was immediately ordered that he be kept in strict custody. Initially, he appears to have been the only criminal lunatic held in the gaol at Norwich, where he was considered sullen but not violent. Requests were

[2060] Kathryn Burtinshaw and John Burt, *Madness, Murder and Mayhem: Criminal Insanity in Victorian and Edwardian Britain* (Barnsley: Pen & Sword Books, 2020), pp. 1-30.

[2061] *Norfolk Chronicle*, 28 May, 1832.

[2062] TNA HO 17/126/127.

[2063] *The Bury and Norwich Post*, 7 July, 1847.

[2064] Bartlett, "Legal Madness," pp. 107-108.

then made to move him from the prison, which was not ideally suited to treat the mentally ill. Although the visiting justices of the Norfolk Lunatic Asylum appear to have been reluctant to accommodate him, he seems to have spent time there and in other institutions, until 1871, when there was an application to remove him to Broadmoor.[2065] Four years later, in December 1875, three boys were killed by Robert Edwards, a mentally disturbed fellow inmate in the Norfolk and Norwich Hospital, who attacked them in their beds with a pair of tongs. Two other boys were wounded. At the following assizes, Edwards was found to be so insane as to be incapable of pleading and was immediately committed to Broadmoor.[2066]

Broadmoor housed patients detained at the Queen's pleasure who had been found to be unfit to plead for reasons of insanity prior to trial, as well as those found not guilty by reason of insanity at trial or found to be insane immediately after capital conviction (the Home Office being satisfied that this was the correct decision despite the jury's verdict). It also accommodated prisoners who had become mad while in prison.[2067]

Broadmoor was a controversial initiative, not least because of its expense – it cost two-and-a-half times as much to keep an inmate there as in an ordinary county asylum – and because control ultimately lay with the Home Secretary rather than with local authorities (always a sensitive issue). It was built to house 400 men and 100 women at a time when around 900 people, of whom three-quarters were male, were deemed to be criminal lunatics in England and Wales. (The genders were kept entirely separate except at chapel services.) In 1879 it held 528 inmates.[2068]

The most violent of Broadmoor's inmates (and a quarter of the male and 40 percent of the female detainees were murderers) might be accommodated in its "strong block," where their food was cut before being served, so that they could be limited to using a spoon. As this suggests, the staff were in constant danger of attack, and in its early decades most of Broadmoor's superintendents suffered some form of assault or serious injury.[2069] For example, in 1871 William Douglas, a deputy superintendent, who had been at Broadmoor for just four months, was assaulted so badly by an inmate that he had to be medically discharged from service.[2070] Even so, Broadmoor resembled many other Victorian asylums in stressing purposeful activities such as work, exercise, and games such as cricket, croquet, and chess,

---

2065 TNA HO 17/126/96.

2066 Meeres, *Norwich Murders,* p. 103.

2067 Shepherd, "'I am not very well,'" p. 278.

2068 *Judicial Statistics 1879,* p. 77.

2069 Sarah Wise, "Gaslight Stories: The Early Days of Broadmoor," psychologytoday.com, 26 August, 2013.

2070 Mark Stevens, *Broadmoor Revealed: Victorian Crime and the Lunatic Asylum* (Barnsley: Pen & Sword Books, 2009), p. 20.

while promoting temperance and industriousness. Inmates might be employed at the shoemaker's shop, on the asylum farm, or in the gardens.[2071]

Early reports on the new hospital were generally very positive, something that occasioned fears that prisoners in ordinary gaols might feign madness to gain admission and access to its superior conditions (still sometimes a concern today).[2072] It may have encouraged the already established reluctance of Victorian prison authorities and doctors to accept such claims after conviction. Towards the end of the century Oscar Wilde complained, "When a man grows insane, they treat him as shamming." According to Wilde, the medical Inspectors of prisons did not even appear to properly understand the distinction between lunacy and idiocy.[2073] The Irish nationalist Michael Davitt related how several of his prison companions suffered mental illness in Millbank, although he also talked about prisoners "putting on the barmy stick." Some inmates, known by their fellows to be sane, were apparently adept at behaving in a strange fashion in front of warders.[2074]

However, even after the advent of Broadmoor, many less dangerous but insane criminals were still held in county asylums. For example, minor criminals who became insane in Liverpool borough prison in the late nineteenth century might be admitted to the nearby Rainhill Lunatic Asylum. Similarly, there were seven male and two female criminal lunatics in Norfolk asylums in 1879.[2075] More specifically, in September 1899 a Mrs Altree, a woman of very good family, who had been found unfit to plead at the Norfolk assizes in 1891 after attempting to murder her infant child by throwing it out of a railway carriage, was being held at the Bethel Lunatic Asylum in Norwich when she escaped from the institution on a stolen bicycle.[2076]

Early Release from Custody

By the start of the Victorian period, it had become common to release many of those serving seven-year periods of transportation at home, whether on hulks or in prisons, at about the halfway point in their sentences, especially if they had been well behaved.[2077] For example, William Lawn, a 28-year-old labourer, was convicted of highway robbery at the Norfolk assizes in March 1851 and sentenced to seven years' transportation. The licence for his early release from the *Stirling*

[2071] Jade Shepherd, "'One of the Best Fathers until He Went Out of His Mind': Paternal Child-Murder, 1864–1900," *Journal of Victorian Culture*, vol. 18, no. 1 (2013), pp. 17-35.

[2072] Wise, "Broadmoor."

[2073] Hilary Marland, "'Close confinement tells very much upon a man': Prison Memoirs, Insanity and the Late Nineteenth- and Early Twentieth-Century Prison," Journal of the History of Medicine and Allied Sciences, vol. 74, no. 3 (2019), p. 268, p. 273.

[2074] Priestley, *Victorian Prison Lives*, pp. 179-180.

[2075] *Judicial Statistics, 1879*, p. 77.

[2076] *The Illustrated Police News*, 30 September, 1899.

[2077] Philip Harling, "The Trouble with Convicts: From Transportation to Penal Servitude, 1840-1867," *Journal of British Studies*, vol. 53, no. 1 (2014), p. 1.

Castle hulk was granted in October 1854, on the basis that half his sentence had been served.[2078] At the same time and forum, William Gilloley, a 22-year-old fair-worker, was convicted of stealing a purse containing £2 10s from the person of a Denver labourer (pickpocketing).[2079] He was sentenced to 10 years' transportation, but was in Dartmoor prison in May 1855, when a licence was granted for his early release.[2080] James Roberts, convicted of night-poaching at the Norfolk assizes in March 1851, received seven years' transportation, but a licence for his early release from Portland prison was issued in August 1854.[2081] Henry Edwards, a 27-year-old labourer, did a little better, and served less than half his sentence. At the Norfolk quarter sessions held at Norwich in January 1852, he was convicted of pickpocketing a silk handkerchief and sentenced to 10 years' transportation. (He had previous convictions). He was granted a licence for early release from Portsmouth prison in November 1855.[2082]

The Penal Servitude Act of 1853 expressly allowed individuals serving time in convict prisons to be released part (often about two-thirds) of the way through their sentences on a "conditional licence" much like the already well-established ticket-of-leave system in Australia (the latter phrase was also used colloquially in England).[2083] Thus John Swash was convicted of theft from the person at the assizes at Norwich July 1858 and sentenced to three years' penal servitude. His licence for early release from Portland prison was granted at the end of December 1860.[2084] James Brown, was convicted of three indictments of horse theft and one of stealing a cart and harness at the Norfolk quarter sessions at Norwich in October 1859, and sentenced to four years' penal servitude, but a licence was issued at the end of December 1862 for his early release from Dartmoor prison.[2085]

Such licences were issued on a standard printed form which contained the conditions of release, which normally included reporting to the police and not reoffending. Those who violated their licences, usually by committing a crime during the specified period, might be returned to prison. Thus in 1895 John Sullivan, who had been discharged early from a previous custodial sentence and reoffended, received three years' penal servitude for breaking into a Great Yarmouth jeweller's shop but was also ordered to serve the nine-month balance of his previous sentence.[2086] (This did not always happen if very minor crimes were involved.) Similarly, Charles Cole was

[2078] TNA PCOM 3/19/1879.

[2079] *The Bury and Norwich Post*, 2 April 1851.

[2080] TNA PCOM 3/30/3104.

[2081] TNA PCOM 3/14/1349.

[2082] TNA PCOM 3/40/4338.

[2083] Harling, "The Trouble with Convicts," p. 1.

[2084] TNA PCOM 3/83/8769.

[2085] TNA PCOM 3/118/12259.

[2086] *Berrows Worcester Journal*, 12 January, 1895.

found guilty at the Norfolk quarter sessions at Norwich in July 1850 of stealing potatoes and sentenced to 10 years' transportation (he had previous convictions). In October 1855 he was given a licence for early release from Dartmoor, but this was revoked in June 1857 for reoffending. Robert Howard, who had been convicted of larceny at the Norfolk quarter sessions held at Swaffham in April 1852, and sentenced to seven years' transportation, was granted a licence for early release from Portland prison in July 1855, but this, too, was withdrawn in January 1856 and Howard returned to prison.[2087]

Ticket-of-leave men occasioned periodic outbreaks of public alarm throughout England, as some observers and newspapers became convinced that they were the cause of much of the country's serious crime.[2088] At times, such fears almost amounted to moral panics. This concern was probably greatly exaggerated. In 1856 it was reported that amongst 100 prisoners brought to trial at the York assizes, only three were known (and one was suspected) to have held tickets of leave. The *Daily News* also pointed out that the same objections advanced against the ticket-of-leave system applied to the discharge of all hardened criminals after imprisonment.[2089] Nevertheless, in 1881 Henry Stebbings committed a brutal sexually motivated murder in Norfolk just days after being released on a ticket of leave from penal servitude for another serious sexual offence, and even after reporting to the county police, as required by his licence.[2090]

[2087] PCOM 3/33/3465.

[2088] Harling, "The Trouble with Convicts," pp. 101-102, p. 105.

[2089] *The Spectator*, 20 December, 1856, p. 15.

[2090] *The York Herald*, 29 October, 1881.

Chapter 15: Punishment: Corporal, Fiscal, and Juvenile Penalties

Flogging

At the start of the Victorian era, male offenders could be whipped at common law for a wide range of crimes; such a sentence could also be passed without the number of strokes to be delivered or the implement employed to inflict them having to be specified. However, the public whipping of women had been abolished in 1817, having been in decline since the 1770s, and all female flogging was ended by statute in 1820 (1 Geo. IV. c. 57). The public whipping of men largely petered out in the early 1830s, although it was not formally abolished until 1861. As late as May 1830, William King was whipped in Norwich Market Place for stealing a pewter pot.[2091] All Victorian penal floggings in Norfolk were conducted privately, often in prison.

Flogging was a popular early Victorian punishment for juveniles, frequently being imposed in addition to a short custodial penalty, but its use extended to some adult men, even for comparatively minor crimes. It could be imposed at all forums. For example, at the Norfolk assizes in April 1835 Israel Wright was convicted of stealing a copper boiler and sentenced to serve a year's imprisonment and to be "privately" flogged twice during that period.[2092] At the same forum, in the summer of 1854, nine-year-old Alonzo Mitchley was convicted of setting fire to a haystack with a lucifer match. He was sentenced to serve a week's solitary confinement in gaol and to be "well whipped."[2093] Moving down the court hierarchy, at the Norfolk quarter sessions, in March 1838 two Norwich "boys" were convicted of stealing hempen cloth in Hainford, and sentenced to serve three months' imprisonment and to be privately whipped.[2094]

At the bottom of the pyramid, in 1841 and 1842, two young but adult men were privately whipped in Norfolk gaols on the order of a single magistrate, something that was rare by then, but still legally permitted in certain situations. William Holmes, aged 20, was "corrected as a disorderly apprentice" and also imprisoned for seven days at Norwich county gaol, while Robert Holland, age 22, was imprisoned for a month in Swaffham gaol and whipped for being "drunk, and idle and disorderly."[2095] Over a decade later, before a bench at the Diss petty sessions in June 1854, 12-year-

---

[2091] Mackie, *Norfolk Annals,* vol. 1, p. 255.

[2092] *The Bury and Norwich Post*, 15 April, 1835.

[2093] *Ibid.*, 2 August, 1854.

[2094] *Ibid.,* 21 March, 1838.

[2095] *Flogging*, House of Commons, 9 February, 1842.

old John Leathers was sentenced to serve two months' imprisonment and to be well whipped after being convicted of picking a man's pocket.[2096]

Nevertheless, corporal punishment was in retreat by the early Victorian period.[2097] In 1861 the MP Arthur Kinnaird expressed alarm about the heavy beatings that were still sometimes being inflicted on small children. For example, it was claimed that a child of eight had received 24 lashes at Knutsford in Cheshire. By then, many JPs were apparently reluctant to order the flogging of adults and concerned about the lack of controls on the beatings imposed on juveniles.[2098] Under statutes passed between 1861 and 1863, the use of corporal punishment was both restricted and regulated, but also, to some extent, renewed. Petty sessions lost the common-law right to order the whipping of adults (rather than juveniles), only the higher courts being empowered to mete out corporal punishment to grown men, and then only for a very narrow range of serious offences, such as robbery with violence and living off immoral earnings (the latter being made the subject of corporal punishment as late as 1898).

The flogging of men was imposed very selectively. In 1890 only 29 adults were flogged nationally as a judicial punishment, almost all of them for violent robberies. (Its use in a prison disciplinary context and in the military was much more common.) However, it was employed on male juveniles very much more frequently, so that there were still 4,116 such cases nationally in 1900, the great majority imposed by ordinary magistrates (rather than judges) for a range of offences, most commonly for petty larceny.

After 1863 the courts were required to specify the use of either the birch (for any age) or the cat-o'-nine-tails (confined to those over sixteen) when passing sentence, and to stipulate the number of strokes to be administered. Thus, at the Thetford petty sessions in November 1879, an 11-year-old boy who had been involved in stealing rabbits in the town was sentenced to 12 strokes of the birch, to be administered in the local gaol.[2099] By contrast, at the Norfolk assizes in April 1875, William Sills, a 25-year-old labourer, was convicted of a particularly brutal attempted rape at Great Massingham, and sentenced to 20 strokes with the "cat", along with 18 years' penal servitude.[2100] Prisoners would be secured with straps when beaten; the birch would be delivered to the bare buttocks, while the cat-o'-nine-tails was applied to the flesh of the upper back.

Although subject to growing condemnation, penal flogging continued to have many supporters to the end of the period, in Norfolk as elsewhere in the country. When consulted by Richard Cross, the Home Secretary, in the autumn of 1874, the

---

2096 *The Bury and Norwich Post*, 14 June, 1854.

2097 Casey, "Common Misperceptions," pp. 367-368.

2098 Hansard HC Deb 26 April 1861 vol. 162 cols. 1191-5 on Friday, 26 April.

2099 *The Bury and Norwich Post,* 2 December, 1879.

2100 *Ibid.*, 13 April, 1875.

Norfolk Commission of the Peace was firmly persuaded of its deterrent value and even proposed that its use might be extended.[2101] This was not a local peculiarity. In April 1889, Thomas Shuttleworth, clerk of the assizes on the Northern Circuit, noted that nine of 47 men convicted over the previous year at the Manchester, Liverpool, and Lancaster assizes had been flogged, although judges varied in their willingness to impose such punishment. His own observation apparently persuaded him that criminals had a particular "dread" of corporal punishment.[2102]

Fiscal Penalties

Fines were normally used to punish those convicted of lesser offences and were by far the most common disposals seen at petty sessions, at least as an initial sentence, in some parts of the country amounting to 90 percent of disposals. The sums imposed depended on, inter alia, statute, the nature and gravity of the offence, and the financial means of the offender. A short custodial penalty was usually appended to the fine, to be imposed in lieu of payment. Typically, at the North Erpingham petty sessions in June 1894, George Barham was prosecuted under the Night Poaching Act for taking a rabbit. He was convicted and fined 5 shillings, with an award of 9s 6d costs (14s 6d in total). However, he was also threatened with 14 days' imprisonment with hard labour if he failed to pay the money.[2103]

In theory, fines should have been paid immediately. William Hardwick managed to do this at the petty sessions held at Needham Market in March 1886, when he pleaded guilty to stealing ten eggs, worth 10d, paying his 30s fine right away to avoid a month in prison.[2104] In practice, magistrates would usually give those convicted at least a day, and occasionally several weeks, to find the money.[2105] The East Dereham Petty Sessions that convicted Jonathan Beckett of drunkenness on a Friday in May 1857, and imposed a penalty of 16s in fine and costs, gave him until the following Wednesday (probably their next sitting) to pay, when his failure to do so led to the month's imprisonment imposed in lieu being implemented.[2106] Nevertheless, some of those amerced could not, or would not, pay their fines, and would make this apparent, so that they would begin their custodial sentences at once. In 1909 92,699 people were committed to prison nationally in default of paying fines, about 20 percent of all cases in which a fine had been imposed. [2107]

Fining was rarely used as a punishment for crimes that had been tried on indictment, making up little more than 2 percent of such disposals in 1836. However, it became

---

[2101] *The Graphic*, 31 October, 1874.

[2102] *The Liverpool Mercury*, 20 April, 1889.

[2103] NRO 24/4/1 North Erpingham Petty Sessions, Minute Book B.

[2104] *The Ipswich Journal*, 18 March, 1886.

[2105] Wyatt, *Calendar*, p. xix.

[2106] *Norwich Mercury*, May 27, 1857.

[2107] Edward Moritz, Jr., "Winston Churchill – Prison Reformer," *The Historian*, vol. 20, no. 4 (1958), p. 432.

much more common for lesser indictable offences, when they were tried summarily, after petty sessions jurisdiction was extended in the 1850s. As a result, in 1899 for every 1,000 people sentenced for indictable crimes (whether tried summarily or on indictment) 194 were fined.[2108] It seems that crimes such as minor theft, when determined summarily, might be dealt with by fiscal penalties, while the same offence, if heard at quarter sessions, would normally attract an immediate custodial sentence, helping to explain the attractions of summary disposal.[2109]

However, a few convicts were not even required to pay a fine. In 1896, for every 1,000 offenders sentenced for indictable crimes at higher and summary forums combined, 120 were simply bound over in their own recognizances, only having to pay the specified sums if they came before the courts again.[2110] This disposal was often used for minor assaults. Thus, at the Earsham petty sessions in May 1842, Thomas Howes was bound over to keep the peace towards his wife, Mary, for 12 months in the sum of £80 and two other sureties in £40 each.[2111]

Forfeiture

Traditionally, being convicted of a felony (rather than a misdemeanor) brought about not just the possibility of execution (even if very remote) but also "corruption of blood." This meant that the felon's property was forfeit to the Crown or to any person or corporate body nominated by the Monarch – either in a single instance or permanently – to receive it. For example, in theory, Great Yarmouth claimed rights to the property of felons who had offended within the bounds of the town, even if they had been convicted at the county assizes in Norwich. Thus in August 1857 the Great Yarmouth town council commended the attentiveness of its clerk to the borough's interests when he secured "certain monies and goods" belonging to George and Mary Harris after they had been convicted of felony at the Norfolk assizes some two years previously.[2112] The Corporation of Norwich had the same historical privilege for crimes committed within the city bounds under a royal charter granted during the reign of Henry IV, the Crown having permanently transferred its own rights to the city.

By the eighteenth century, the amount that was seized from convicted felons was relatively modest. Even then, the right was subject to a growing number of legal challenges and was often not enforced. Unsurprisingly, given the poverty of many criminals and the problems attendant on forfeiture, the total sums recovered nationally from convicted felons was relatively modest in the years immediately prior to abolition, ranging from a minimum of £253 in 1849 to a maximum of £1,318 in

2108 Bailey, "English Prisons," p. 285, p. 287.

2109 Jones, *Crime, Courts,* p. 120.

2110 Bailey, "English Prisons," p. 287.

2111 Minutes of the Business transacted at the Petty Sessions for the Hundred of Earsham Commencing 1 April, 1842 NRO PS 21/7/6.

2112 *The Bury and Norwich Post,* 18 August, 1857.

1854.[2113] (Delegated payments to corporations and other bodies are not included in these amounts.) The Norfolk share of this total was very small.

Longstanding complaints that forfeiture unjustly deprived the convict's family and creditors grew during the early nineteenth century, especially as it could, in theory (if not necessarily in practice) extend to very large sums of money that were held in the banks that were rapidly expanding across the country. In 1834 one observer described the procedure as "iniquitous."[2114] Giving evidence to the Criminal Law Commission of 1845, the clerk to the Richmond magistrates described it as "absurd" and noted that, in theory, if a Rothschild or Baring stole a flower, their huge fortune might be forfeit, while the barrister J. Stone thought that where enforced it merely made a convict indigent and so more likely to be driven to commit property crimes from want. Lord Denman suggested to the same body that it might be usefully abolished, although others saw little need for urgent change.[2115]

During the late eighteenth and early nineteenth centuries, the progressive blurring of the vital (for the rule) distinction between felonies and lesser crimes further complicated matters. Indicative of this, in 1852 the father of a recently released convict helped him petition for the return of the hymnbook, knife, and gold chain that had been seized on his arrest. When he was told that they had already been sold at auction, the father angrily claimed that his son had only committed a misdemeanor, for which forfeiture was not allowed. He was forced to back down when this proved not to be the case. By contrast, in September 1863 it was noted that the Corporation of Norwich had jumped the gun in this regard, seizing more than £5 from a suspected felon while he was on remand awaiting trial. The man had sought the return of this money to pay for his legal bills. As a prison inspector noted, seizure may have been appropriate after conviction, but not before.[2116] Nevertheless, and as this case suggests, occasional forfeitures continued to be ordered until 1870, when the Forfeiture Act finally abolished the ancient practice, albeit also providing that a convicting court could order convicts to pay compensation to their victims or to cover the costs of their prosecution.[2117]

Despite its modest level, a fear of felony forfeiture remained widespread until abolition, in Norfolk as elsewhere, whatever may have been the practical reality. In January 1844, when 17-year-old Isaac Bridges was convicted at the Norwich quarter sessions of stealing from the person and sentenced to seven years' transportation (he had a previous conviction), it was noted that he was due to inherit £500 plus

---

[2113] Gatrell, "Crime, Authority," pp. 243-310.

[2114] *The Westminster Review*, vol. 20 (1834), p. 142.

[2115] *The Examiner*, 2 August, 1845. *Eighth Report,* p. 332, p. 301.

[2116] *The Bury and Norwich Post*, 8 September, 1863.

[2117] Kesselring, "Felony Forfeiture," pp. 201-226.

accumulated interest under his late grandfather's will when he gained his majority at 21, but "this now becomes forfeit to the Crown."[2118]

As late as October 1859, Norwich City Council considered the issue at some length. That year, George Valentine was arrested in Norwich, and a large sum of money, some £90, was found in his possession. When Valentine was convicted of a felony at the Norwich quarter sessions, and received three years' penal servitude, the town clerk declared that the city was entitled to the cash. He was supported in this by the council. When the Chief Constable asked how he should dispose of the money, they ordered that it remain in the hands of the city treasurer, and it appears to have stayed with the corporation. The question was considered again in May 1863, when the town clerk reported that since Valentine's conviction it had been found that he had another £60, deposited in a savings bank in London. The town clerk had given notice to the bank directors that the corporation claimed this money as well. However, since Valentine had been released from prison, this official had been pressed to withdraw the notice. He refused to do so without the support of the corporation. Unlike the cash found about Valentine's person, the money was out of the jurisdiction of the city of Norwich, which had no control over it beyond serving the notice. If further steps were taken, the difficult question would arise as to whether it should be forfeited to the corporation or to the Crown, and this would involve a formal hearing, the cost of which would probably be more than the £60. The council decided that, given that Valentine had served his sentence, and needed money to place him in a position to gain an honest livelihood, it would authorize the withdrawal of the notice.[2119]

The Punishment of Juveniles

In the early nineteenth century, young offenders, if convicted, could be sentenced to all forms of punishment, including death, transportation, and imprisonment. In practice, youth (like extreme old age) encouraged compassion from JPs, judges, and the Home Secretary, and this grew during the early 1800s. For example, although 103 children under 14 received capital convictions at the Old Bailey between 1801 and 1836, all sentences were commuted to transportation or imprisonment. The last execution in England of a juvenile under 16 years of age occurred before the Victorian era, being that of 14-year-old John Bell, at Maidstone in Kent, in August 1831. Bell, who had brutally killed a 12-year-old boy for just 9 shillings, in a carefully planned attack, was convicted of murder (partly on the evidence of his younger brother and accomplice) and hanged, his body subsequently being given to surgeons in Rochester for the purpose of dissection (a statutory part of the punishment that was abolished shortly afterwards).[2120] Two years later, in March 1833, 16-year-old Sylvester Wilkes, executed for arson at Dorchester in Dorset, may have been the last

---

[2118] *The Bury and Norwich Post*, 17 January, 1844.

[2119] Mackie, *Norfolk Annals,* vol. 2, pp. 89-90.

[2120] *The Spectator*, 30 July, 1831, p. 10

person under 17 to be hanged in England. Nevertheless, as late as January 1889, 18-year-old William Gower, who was executed at Maidstone for murder despite a jury recommendation for mercy in view of his youth, became the last person who *may* have been 17 years of age when he committed a capital crime to go to the gallows in England.[2121]

Youth Custody

At the start of the Victorian era, juveniles who entered the penal system were usually treated as little adults. Custodial sentences, where imposed, would normally be served in the same prisons, and subject to the same conditions, as those experienced by adults, with whom they often mixed freely. For example, at the Norwich city assizes in April 1835, Michael Clarke, who was 14 years old, was convicted of stealing a handkerchief from John Norgate, and sentenced to three months' imprisonment with solitary confinement in the city gaol.[2122] In 1843, at the county quarter sessions sitting at Swaffham, William Briggs, aged 12, was sentenced to 14 days' imprisonment with hard labour for stealing coal.[2123] In 1847, when ten-year-old George Dunthorn pleaded guilty to having embezzled 10 pence from William Harmer in Mattishall, he received 14 days' imprisonment, again with solitary confinement.[2124]

By the start of the Victorian era, it was increasingly thought that it was wrong for the criminal-justice system to allow juveniles to be exposed to the "contamination and moral ruin consequent on intercourse with other and older criminals."[2125] Change was in the air, both nationally and locally in Norfolk. For example, the hulk *Euryalus* , moored off Chatham, had already been in use for several years as a special place of confinement for juvenile offenders. Thus, when 15-year-old John Presant was convicted at the Great Yarmouth quarter sessions in May 1839 for stealing a pair of women's shoes, and sentenced to seven years' transportation, he was put on board this vessel. (He had several previous convictions, the reason for the draconian disposal.)[2126] However, conditions on the *Euryalus* were heavily criticized by the 1835 House of Lords Select Committee on Gaols, and it was no longer employed for juveniles after 1844.

Although the number of youths under the age of 18 who were sentenced to transportation and then sent to Australia (rather than remaining in England) during the nineteenth century was relatively modest, it was still thought necessary to establish a juvenile penal settlement for their reception at Point Puer, near Port

---

2121 *The Daily Gazette for Middlesbrough*, 2 January, 1889.

2122 *The Bury and Norwich Post*, 15 April, 1835.

2123 *The Norfolk Chronicle*, 8 July, 1843.

2124 *The Norwich Mercury*, 3 July, 1847.

2125 *The Newcastle Courant*, 4 October, 1844.

2126 TNA HO 18/5/11.

Arthur in Van Diemen's Land, in 1834. Most of its inmates were between 15 and 17 years of age, but a few were younger. It closed in 1849.[2127]

More significantly, Parkhurst prison was opened in December 1838 specifically for male juvenile felons, complete with the provision of industrial training (especially tailoring), basic education, and religious instruction. Initially many of its inmates were sent as emigrants to Australia and New Zealand on release. In August 1845 the Queen herself visited the prison, noting in her journal that Parkhurst was "a prison for Juvenile offenders, all boys, to the number of 600, & it is divided into 2 completely separate Wards." One of these held inmates from the ages of 12 to 18, although new arrivals were held in solitary confinement for their first month after arrival. The other ward held younger boys. The juveniles wore grey prison dress and had cropped hair, so that, the Monarch felt, the older boys looked like "real criminals." The prison held about 800 inmates at its peak in the late 1840s, their numbers declining thereafter. Inevitably, some Norfolk youths ended up there. Thus, in January 1840, when 11-year-old William Woodcock was convicted at the Norwich city quarter sessions for stealing two glasses of jelly he was sentenced to seven years' Transportation. (He had been convicted on earlier occasions and twice received a pardon while in prison.) Even so, a petition for clemency resulted in a report from the recorder of Norwich recommending that he be sent to Parkhurst to serve his sentence.[2128] By the mid-1850s, the function of the prison had been broadened to include all boys sentenced to terms exceeding one year's imprisonment. However, it became a focus for reformers campaigning against the use of imprisonment for children, while the rise of reformatory and industrial schools (see below) provided an alternative, and by 1864 all boys had been removed from the establishment.

Reformatories

By the mid-century the notion of introducing a more widely available and constructive form of punishment for children was in the air, explaining the establishment in 1848 of the Norfolk Society for the Reformation of Juvenile Offenders.[2129] In 1846 Lord Houghton unsuccessfully attempted to introduce a parliamentary bill for a national system of reformatory schools for juveniles. However, several local juvenile initiatives did come to fruition. In 1852 a reformatory for Norfolk boys and youths was established by county JPs at Buxton, near Marsham, on a voluntary basis, with a view to accommodating some of the boys who were then being confined in Norwich Castle. It was intended that it would focus on their industrial training and religious education. The project was influenced by the work of John Wright, a

[2127] *The Newcastle Courant*, 4 October, 1844.

[2128] TNA HO 18/12/19.

[2129] *The Ipswich Journal*, 31 January, 1857.

Norfolk Quaker who had employed discharged prisoners on his farms in the early 1850s. The reformatory's initial inmates were transferred from the county prison.[2130]

Eventually, in 1854, a national campaign led by Mary Carpenter, Matthew Davenport Hill, and Joshua Jebb, among others, prompted Parliament to pass the Youthful Offenders Act, also known as the Reformatory Schools Act (17 & 18 Victoria, c. 86). This allowed existing voluntary schools (such as that at Buxton) to be certified as efficient by the Inspector of Prisons, new ones to be created, and such establishments used for juvenile offenders. At the Norfolk assizes in July 1855, Mr Baron Alderson urged that this course be followed in Norfolk, noting that it had worked well in other counties.[2131] Shortly afterwards, the Buxton establishment was duly certified and authorized to accommodate up to 40 boys, making it one of about 20 that had sprung up in England by 1856.[2132] Although children could still be sent to prison, the statute allowed a more rehabilitative option and quickly became popular with judges and JPs dealing with young people.14 In 1856 the Norfolk county police chief constable even thought that some observers "looked upon reformatory schools to be the panacea for all the evils of our social state." [2133]

Under the legislation, convicted juvenile offenders under the age of 16 could be committed to a certified reformatory school for a period of from two to five years, the latter sentence being more common than the former. For example, in the year ending September 1861, of the 12 boys sent to the Buxton facility, two were serving two years, two were there for three years, and eight were sent for the maximum of five years. It was hoped that the long sentences involved would remove the child from "bad influences" in their homes or from their associates.[2134]

However, under the 1854 Act, those entering such reformatories were first required to spend a period of at least two weeks in a prison or other carceral institution, if only to give them a "taste" of custody, until this requirement was abolished in 1893. Thus, of the 1861 cohort, nine had served 14 days of imprisonment and three up to a month.[2135] The statute also provided that the parents of inmates could be required to contribute towards the costs involved by up to five shillings each week. As a result, in 1879 a labourer named James Goddard was summonsed to appear at the Thetford petty sessions to explain why he should not contribute towards the maintenance of his son in the local reformatory. He was ordered to pay a shilling per week.[2136]

[2130] David H. Thomas, "The Home Office Certified Schools in Norfolk, 1855-1933," Norfolk Archaeology, vol. 38, no. 3 (1983), pp. 358-362.

[2131] *The Bury and Norwich Post*, 1 August, 1855.

[2132] *The Morning Chronicle*, 28 August, 1856

[2133] Black, *The police*, p. 2.

[2134] *Judicial Statistics 1861*, p. 90.

[2135] *Ibid.*

[2136] *The Bury and Norwich Post*, 11 March, 1879. *Ibid.*, 18 March, 1879.

Inevitably more provision for this disposal was made (nationally) for males than females, given their greater involvement in crime and disorder. As a result, in 1861 there were 32 reformatories for boys in the country, but only 11 for girls, none of them in Norfolk, so that females given such a sentence in the county would have to be sent elsewhere in England. Nevertheless, this did not prevent Norfolk girls receiving such disposals. Thus, at the winter assizes for Norfolk in 1867, Eliza Sparrow, a 15-year-old domestic servant, was convicted of setting fire to a coal shed and other outbuildings. She was sentenced to a month's imprisonment with hard labour, after which she was to be sent to a reformatory for five years.[2137] At the Norfolk quarter sessions in January 1893, Laura Cushion, a 15-year-old nursemaid, was convicted of feeding pins to the eight-month-old infant she had been babysitting, with intent to endanger his life. The child had only narrowly survived, and Cushion admitted to his mother that she did not like him and hoped he would die. She was sentenced to 14 days' imprisonment, to be followed by five years in a female reformatory.[2138]

Moving gender, between certification and the end of 1857, some 49 boys were admitted to the Buxton establishment, although their numbers declined markedly towards the close of that period, disproving contemporary fears that parents might encourage children to offend to be rid of the cost of providing for them. One founder of the Buxton house (rather optimistically) thought that juvenile crime had declined heavily in Norfolk since its establishment, explaining the fall in numbers.[2139]

All levels of Norfolk criminal court made use of this disposal. For example, of the 12 boys sent to the Buxton facility in 1861, nine had been convicted summarily and three on indictment. More specifically, in late July 1855, at the county assizes, a 13-year-old boy pleaded guilty to setting fire to farm buildings intending to injure others. He was sentenced to 14 days' imprisonment and five years in the Buxton Reformatory.[2140] Moving down the hierarchy, at the Norwich quarter sessions in January 1856, three youths, aged 14, 15, and 16, were sentenced to three years' confinement in the Buxton establishment for committing relatively minor thefts involving whips and overshoes, after first being required to serve a "certain amount of imprisonment."[2141] At the base of the pyramid, at the Thetford petty sessions in November 1879, another three boys, two of them aged 14 and the third 15, pleaded guilty to stealing four rabbits from a shop in the town so that the matter could be dealt with summarily. They were then sentenced to 10 days' imprisonment (perhaps two weeks in reality) in Norwich Castle, and two years in the Buxton Reformatory. The bench observed that they were determined to "spot juvenile

---

[2137] *The Times*, 9 December, 1867, p. 12.

[2138] *The Daily Gazette for Middlesbrough*, 5 January, 1893.

[2139] *Lloyd's Illustrated Newspaper*, 6 December, 1857.

[2140] *The Bury and Norwich Post*, 1 August, 1855.

[2141] *The Bury and Norwich Post*, 9 January, 1856.

crime." (Like many of the boys committed to the reformatory, several of them had previous convictions.)[2142]

In 1857 another reformatory for boys was established at Catton, near Norwich, to relieve accommodation pressure at Buxton. Boys under 16 might be transferred there from Buxton if they showed an aptitude for shoemaking or could be taught another trade. (Its superintendent, John Ellis, was a shoemaker by training.) By April 1858 seven of the 31 boys initially received at Buxton had transferred, while 20 remained at Buxton (one had absconded and the other three had been assisted to emigrate to America).[2143] Part of the grounds at Catton were used to provide each boy with a vegetable plot; there was also a dormitory, schoolroom, and workshop. However, Catton did not last very long. Following an apparent decline in the number of young offenders in the county, it was closed in November 1859, by which time it was down to two inmates. By 1862 the number of inmates at the Buxton establishment had also fallen, to 23 boys, but gradually increased again over the immediately following years.

Industrial Schools

Some observers of reformatories across the country remained concerned at the requirement that those entering first serve a short period of time in prison, as well as disliking the wider penal culture allegedly found in reformatory establishments. There was a growing philanthropic objection to sending children to prison of all types. More important, many felt that there should be provision for vulnerable children *before* they offended. As a result, the Industrial Schools Act 1857 (20 & 21 Victoria, c. 48) empowered magistrates to send children to a special school until they reached the age of 16 without a custodial element being added.

At first, an industrial-school disposal was often employed for juveniles who had appeared before a magistrate for vagrancy, after being found wandering in public. The aim of such a commitment was to prevent them from drifting into mainstream crime. Under the Elementary Education Act 1876, children whose parents neglected to send them to school, or those thought to be at risk from keeping bad company, could also be sent to an industrial school. However, some boys committed to these establishments had accrued convictions for theft and other mainstream offences. Even so, in 1875, the barrister Luke Owen Pike, like other observers, thought that the industrial schools normally incarcerated children who would not otherwise be in custody.[2144] Such schools tended to be employed for somewhat younger children than those sent to reformatories, usually those aged about seven to 15, and to have a slightly more benign regime, although there was a substantial overlap in age between the two establishments. By 1875 there were 82 industrial schools in England and Wales, compared to 54 certified reformatories.

2142 *Ibid.*, 2 December, 1879.

2143 *Ibid.*, 27 April, 1858.

2144 Luke Owen Pike, *History of Crime*, vol. 2 (London: Smith, Elder, 1875), p. 486.

An industrial school for girls, sometimes called the County Industrial School, was opened at Fakenham in Norfolk in around 1858 but not formally certified until 1868. A decade later, it was able accommodate up to 60 female inmates. Initially, until the late 1870s, almost all were either voluntary cases or were placed there by the poor-law authorities. Subsequently, some were placed there by magistrates for reasons such as vagrancy, but it seems that a very small number were conventional offenders. The establishment provided work, education, and religious instruction, and had a good reputation until the end of the century. Thereafter, standards appear to have slipped, and there was a high turnover of staff, with some girls absconding, until the institution closed in May 1903 and its children were transferred to schools outside Norfolk.[2145]

For many years, there was no industrial school for males in Norfolk, and boys given this disposal were sent to establishments outside the county, including some as far away as Manchester and Stockport. However, in June 1894, following a steady decline in reformatory committals in the county, a Home Office order confirmed a change of use for the Buxton Reformatory, converting it to the Red House Industrial School. Thomas Babington and his wife continued as superintendent and matron respectively of the re-certified establishment. Perhaps reflecting its origins, in 1896 the school was described as old-fashioned and cramped. It had a farm and taught tailoring, and there was regular physical drill. In response to criticism, new rooms were built in 1899 and 1900. By then the establishment held about 90 boys. The average detention time of the 12 inmates discharged from the Buxton Industrial School in 1901 – 11 by expiry of sentence and one by order of the Secretary of State – was just under five years. [2146]

Inevitably, there was an overlap between the use of industrial schools and reformatories. In January 1896 13-year-old Albert Ready was summonsed to Wymondham petty sessions after he threatened to kill his schoolteacher and then threw stones at her, inflicting a significant head injury that required medical attention. The chairman of the sessions initially, and quite leniently, thought he should go to some type of industrial school. However, Ready was eventually sentenced to a week in the workhouse followed by three years in a reformatory.[2147]

State recognition of both types of institution in the 1850s marked a radical change in penal policy and an acceptance that juvenile delinquency was a specific social phenomenon, one that required special treatment.[2148] In 1896, for every 1,000 offenders sentenced for indictable crimes at higher and summary forums combined, 34 were sent to a reformatory or industrial school.[2149] Nevertheless, this was almost

---

[2145] Thomas, "Certified Schools," pp. 358-362.

[2146] *Judicial Statistics 1901,* p. 150.

[2147] *The Ipswich Journal,* 11 January, 1896.

[2148] May, "Innocence and Experience," p. 7.

[2149] Bailey, "English Prisons," p. 287.

as far as the state was prepared to go towards treating children differently from adults during the Victorian period. However, attitudes began to change towards the end of the era, and in 1902 an influential experimental school for juvenile and young-adult offenders was set up at Borstal, in Kent, their use for those between 16 and 21 being expanded by the Prevention of Crime Act in 1908. Even so, until the Children Act of 1908, juveniles under the age of 16 could still be sentenced to adult prisons, even if this was not done lightly.[2150]

[2150] Radzinowicz and Hood, "Judicial Discretion," pp. 1288-1349.

Chapter 16: Epilogue

At the start of the nineteenth century, England's historically "robust" approach to law and order, its apparent lack of concern about crime, and its emphasis on self-reliance when it came to dealing with it, were still readily apparent. As late as 1819 Edward Christian, one of the judges in the Isle of Ely, secured his country home with dogs, firearms, lights, and alarm bells, even taking a pair of double-barrelled pistols to bed with him every night.[2151] However, by Queen Victoria's accession, this was no longer viewed as a satisfactory way of providing for security, and by her death, Norfolk, like every other part of England, had been transformed.

Society was much more ordered than it had been in the 1830s. Violence was less widespread, its popular legitimacy had narrowed, and property had become more secure.[2152] Crime had fallen, although how significantly was (and is) a matter of some debate. Constantly rising expectations for public order and security, and lurid newspaper reports, meant that the decline in offending was not always appreciated at the time, although widely acknowledged by thoughtful and informed observers. Nevertheless, as early as 1875, when the county JPs closed the prison in Swaffham, it was claimed that it was "in consequence of the great decrease of crime in Norfolk."[2153] Some crimes that had been quite common in the county in the early Victorian period had become rare. For example, nobody was sent for trial on indictment for killing or maiming cattle or horses in Norfolk in 1896.[2154] Others, such as bicycle theft, were new, if not very serious. Nevertheless, the general downwards trend was clear.

The predisposition of earlier times for settling disputes, including those involving criminal allegations, without recourse to formal legal proceedings had also retreated, even amongst working-class people.[2155] Furthermore, the Hogarthian world that had still been widely evidenced in 1837, with its ready acceptance of cruelty, had substantially (though not entirely) receded, as manners changed, something that the elderly Sir Henry Hawkins stressed when looking back on the widespread "barbarity" evident in his youth, from the start of Edward VII's reign.[2156]

In retrospect, many thought this process to have been inevitable, believing it "certain that, as civilization advances, so will increase the restrictions which civilization demands on any actions or movements of individuals calculated to interfere with

---

[2151] Douglas Hay, "Property, Authority and the Criminal Law" in *Albion's Fatal Tree: Crime and Society in Eighteenth-Century England* (New York: Random House,1975), p. 17.

[2152] Taylor, *Hooligans, Harlots,* p. 36.

[2153] *John Bull*, November 27, 1875.

[2154] *Judicial Statistics,* p. 63.

[2155] Wood, "Self-Policing," pp. 109-128.

[2156] See generally, Hawkins, *Reminiscences*.

the general comfort."[2157] Nevertheless, it had not happened spontaneously. The state had played a major role in the transformation of English society. Its involvement in the daily lives of its subjects had grown relentlessly during the Victorian period, whether directly or indirectly, even in provincial backwaters like Norfolk. The criminal law and its implementation, at all levels, had been a major tool in this process, being consciously used to educate men on where they should set limits on their 'baser' instincts.

Various law-enforcement bodies in Norfolk, especially the new police, like those found in the great cities, had steadily ratcheted up pressure on offending and disorder as the era progressed, with support from the courts, especially the steadily expanding petty sessions. They had gradually reached into spaces and settings, whether aristocratic duels, working-class fights over status, or domestic violence, that had hitherto been largely ignored.[2158] Official tolerance for much casual viciousness, whether manifest in violent pastimes, sexual congress with children, or extreme cruelty to animals had fallen greatly.[2159] More offenders were brought into the criminal law's reach, often for less serious crimes, some of which had not even been offences in earlier ages.[2160]

Of course, the more ordered society of 1901 (compared to that of 1837) cannot be attributed solely to government action and law enforcement. The increased general prosperity of the late Victorian era, the great expansion of elementary education, and a process of political incorporation (something that has often been linked to a decline in crime) undoubtedly played a major part in what occurred. An elderly Essex farm labourer, looking back on the 1840s from the vantage point of the final years of the Victorian era, thought it axiomatic that England was more secure than 50 years earlier, and readily accepted that the police and courts had played a major role in this change: "The parish constable had not [then] been replaced by Sir Robert Peel's well-drilled men in blue, and there was much lawlessness abroad. Incendiary fires and robberies of lonely farmhouses were common." Nevertheless, along with policing deficiencies, he also associated the high crime levels of the 1840s with the harsh economic conditions of the time, with many men being out of work, especially in the winter, very low wages, severe conditions of service for those lucky enough to be in employment, and a poor law that actively discouraged the poor from leaving their parishes to look for work.[2161] Doubtless many of his Norfolk counterparts would have shared this multi-faceted (and eminently reasonable) analysis. Nevertheless, and with this important reservation, the transformation in

---

2157 George Augustus Anson, *The fluctuations of crime* (Stafford, 1895), p. 3.

2158 Martin Wiener, (2004). *Men of Blood: Violence, Manliness, and Criminal Justice in Victorian England* (Cambridge: CUP, 2004) p. 3, p. 15. Wiener, "Judges v. Jurors," p. 474.

2159 Wiener, "Sad Story," p. 178.

2160 Wiener, *Reconstructing,* pp. 49-51.

2161 "Joseph," "Memories of an Essex Farm Worker from the 1840s," *Essex Review*, vol. 9, no. 36, 1900.

the criminal-justice system undoubtedly played a major role in producing a more secure and stable society.

Other changes in the system are also apparent. Foremost amongst them, and unsurprisingly given the above, was greatly increased central control. Sometimes, this came about through direct "nationalization," as with prisons in 1877. At others, it was brought about indirectly, as with the large government subsidies that were provided to "efficient" police forces. Taken together, they meant that the diversity in practice found in England in 1837 had declined markedly by 1901. Legal procedures and institutions throughout the nation were more tightly regulated and uniform, often being shaped by one of the detailed statutes produced by the era and less dependent on custom or tradition for authority, even if the former sometimes merely codified better examples of the latter. More generally, the highly discretionary, particularistic, and heavily personalized justice system of the old regime had given way to a system in which criminal law was seen as a bureaucratic procedure that (ideally) applied uniformly and consistently to all classes of crime and criminals (something that was greatly facilitated by the new police).

The criminal-justice system was also far more professional in 1901 than it had been in 1837. The quality, training, and ability of most of its personnel had improved significantly, whether they were judges, JPs, coroners, prison warders, or police officers, albeit that not all of them had progressed equally, and some were still woefully deficient. It was also a markedly more rational and, to modern eyes, humane system. Many (but far from all) of the glaring abuses of the system present when the new Queen came to the throne had disappeared or at least been ameliorated, as had its more capricious and arbitrary aspects. Executions were rare, carried out in private, and produced a swift death. Transportation had disappeared from the penal canon. Various forms of custody, whether in a local or convict prison, or even in a secure asylum like Broadmoor, dominated punishment. Prison conditions themselves were improving, and the number of gaols (of all types) and their inmates falling, while special provision was increasingly being made for juveniles. Uniformity of prisoner treatment had increased, and the privileges of wealth for those incarcerated greatly reduced or eliminated. Those accused of crimes were more likely to be on bail prior to their hearings in 1901 than had been the case 60 years earlier.

More generally, there had been something of a culture change in favour of allowing defendants due process, however unsavoury or suspicious they might appear, and taking the presumption of innocence and the demanding criminal standard of proof seriously, at least at trial on indictment.[2162] Such hearings were longer and more regulated than they had been at the start of the Queen's reign. Felony defendants could give sworn evidence at their own hearings. Against this, criminal jury trial had become increasingly marginalized, even as it was lionized, by the huge expansion of summary trial, although the latter had, admittedly, improved markedly in quality over the century. William Blackstone's desire that the jury remain inviolate from

---

[2162] Purcell, *Forty Years,* p. 22.

anything that might "sap and undermine it" had proved unavailing. Less significantly, the increase in guilty pleas tendered in higher forums, the latter probably being encouraged by informally discounted sentences, had also reduced the number of contested trials that were considered by jurors. All these developments have been well documented in a Metropolitan context but can also readily be seen at work in Norfolk.

Reform was ongoing, and the Edwardian period would witness a further spate of developments, such as the provision of a basic form of legal aid for many defendants in 1903, the general introduction of the borstal system for youths, and the growth of supervised probation as a substitute for imprisonment under the Probation of Offenders Act 1907, which also initiated the professionalization of the probation service.[2163] The provision for appeal against conviction on indictment would be radically improved in 1908 by the advent of the Court of Criminal Appeal. The Children Act 1908 would create a juvenile court. Winston Churchill's reformist work as an activist Home Secretary in 1910-1911, if not always successful, would see further amelioration in prison conditions.[2164]

Nevertheless, a professional drawn from the modern criminal-justice system in England and Wales, whether judge, lawyer, police officer, or prison warder, would readily recognize the system of 1901, if only because a quarter of prison inmates still live in Victorian-era prison accommodation. However, he might not share the optimism that imbued many of his *fin-de-siècle* predecessors, faced, as they were, by apparently falling levels of crime even as the justice system was reformed. Indeed, he might feel a twinge of sympathy for those involved in the anxious debates on all areas of law and order, from policing to punishment, seen in the troubled 1840s.

[2163] Auerbach, "'Beyond the Pale of Mercy,'" p. 622.

[2164] Moritz, "Winston Churchill," pp. 428-440.

Frequently Used Acronyms

ASSI Assizes

ERO Essex Record Office

HO Home Office

NRO Norfolk Record Office

OBSP Old Bailey Sessions Proceedings

TNA The National Archive

SELECT BIBLIOGRAPHY

Books

Alexander, George Glover, *The administration of justice in criminal matters (in England and Wales),* (Cambridge: CUP, 1911 and 1915).

Anon., *Return of Judicial Statistics of England and Wales,* various dates (London: HMSO).

Anon., *The Stanfield Hall Assassinations!* (London: Cleave, 1849).

Bentley, David, *English Criminal Justice in the Nineteenth Century* (London: Hambledon Press, 1998).

Black, George, *The police of England: as it was, as it is, and as it should be* (London: J. Ridgway, 1856).

Coleman, D.C., *Myth, History and the Industrial Revolution* (London: Hambledon Continuum, 1992).

Conley, Carolyn A., *The Unwritten Law: Criminal Justice in Victorian Kent* (Oxford: OUP, 1991).

Cornish, William et al., *The Oxford History of the Laws of England* (Oxford, OUP, 2010).

Cottu, Charles, *On the Administration of Criminal Justice in England; and the Spirit of the English Government* (London: Richard Stevens, 1822).

Durston, Gregory J., *Fields, Fens and Felonies: Crime and Justice in Eighteenth-Century East Anglia* (Hook: Waterside Press, 2016).

Gatrell, V.A.C., *The Hanging Tree: Execution and the English People 1770-1868* (Oxford: OUP, 1996).

Hawkins, Henry, *The Reminiscences of Sir Henry Hawkins* (London: Edward Arnold, 1904).

Hill, Matthew Davenport and Eardley-Wilmot, Sir John, *Papers on Grand Juries* (London: Longman, Green, 1865).

Jones, Rachael, *Crime, Courts and Community in Mid-Victorian Wales: Montgomeryshire, People and Places* (Cardiff: University of Wales, 2018).

Mackie, Charles, *Norfolk Annals: A Chronological Record of Remarkable Events in the Nineteenth Century* (Norwich: Norfolk Chronicle, 1901).

Saunders, Thomas William, *Quarter and Petty Sessions: A Letter to… Sir George Grey upon the Present Defective System of Administering Justice in Our Courts of Quarter Sessions and Petty Sessions, with Suggestions for Improvement* (London, 1863).

Taylor, David, *Hooligans, Harlots and Hangmen: Crime and Punishment in Victorian Britain* (Santa Barbara: Praeger, 2010).

_______, *The New Police in Nineteenth-Century England: Crime, Conflict and Control* (Manchester: MUP, 1997).

White, William, *History, Gazetteer, and Directory of Norfolk, and the City and County of the City of Norwich,* fourth ed. (Sheffield: William White, 1883).

Wiener, Martin J., *Reconstructing the Criminal: Culture, Law and Policy in England 1830-1914* (Cambridge: CUP, 2008).

Articles

Anon., "What to Do with the 4,000 a Year," *The Spectator,* 19 June, 1847.

Cox, David, "The Habitual Eccentricities of the Solons of Staffordshire: An Investigation of the Circumstances Surrounding the Parliamentary Enquiry into the Ill-treatment of Mrs Eliza Price of Brierly Hill, 1845," *Plymouth Law and Criminal Justice Review,* vol. 3 (2010).

Crosby, K., "Before the Criminal Justice and Courts Act 2015: Juror punishment in nineteenth- and twentieth-century England," *Legal Studies,* vol. 36, no. 2 (2016).

Emsley, Clive and Storch, Robert D., "Prosecution and the Police in England since 1700," *IAHCCJ Bulletin,* no. 18 (1993).

Hanly, Conor, "Summary Jurisdiction and the Decline of Criminal Jury Trial in Victorian England," *The Journal of Legal History,* vol. 42, no. 3 (2021).

Philips, David, "A 'Weak' State? The English State, the Magistracy, and the Reform of Policing in the 1830s," *The English Historical Review,* vol. 119, no. 483 (2004).

Porritt, Edward, "At Petty Sessions," *Green Bag,* vol. 11, no. 10 (1899).

Pue, W. Wesley, "The Criminal Twilight Zone: Pre-Trial Procedures in the 1840s," *Alberta Law Review,* vol. 21, no. 2, 1983.

Wiener, Martin J., "The Sad Story of George Hall: Adultery, Murder and the Politics of Mercy in Mid-Victorian England," *Social History,* vol. 24, no. 2 (1999).

Wood, John Carter, "Drinking, Fighting, and Working-Class Sociability in Nineteenth-Century Britain" in *Drink in the Eighteenth and Nineteenth Centuries: Perspectives in Economic and Social History,* Susanne Schmid and Barbara Schmidt-Haberkamp (eds.) (London: Pickering and Chatto, 2014).

Zangerl, Carl H.E., "The Social Composition of the County Magistracy in England and Wales, 1831-1887," *Journal of British Studies,* vol. 11, no. 1 (1971).

Index

www.ingramcontent.com/pod-product-compliance
Ingram Content Group UK Ltd.
Pitfield, Milton Keynes, MK11 3LW, UK
UKHW051449290926
15471UKWH00008B/1098